ENFRENTANDO EL CAMBIO

Obreros del automóvil y producción esbelta en América del Norte

CONFRONTING CHANGE

Auto Labor and Lean Production in North America

ENFRENTANDO EL CAMBIO

Obreros del automóvil y producción esbelta en América del Norte

CONFRONTING CHANGE

Auto Labor and Lean Production in North America

Huberto Juárez Núñez
Steve Babson
(Coordinadores)

Benemérita Universidad Autónoma de Puebla   Wayne State University

BENEMÉRITA UNIVERSIDAD AUTÓNOMA DE PUEBLA
Dirección General de Fomento Editorial
WAYNE STATE UNIVERSITY
Labor Studies Center

BENEMÉRITA UNIVERSIDAD AUTÓNOMA DE PUEBLA
Enrique Dóger Guerrero
Rector
Guillermo Nares Rodríguez
Secretario General
Rigoberto Benítez Trujillo
Vicerrector de Extensión y Difusión de la Cultura
Víctor Espíndola Cabrera
Director Editorial

WAYNE STATE UNIVERSITY
College of Urban, Labor and Metropolitan Affairs
Sue Marx Smock
Dean
Hal Stack
Director of Labor Studies Center

Fotografías de portada: Rebeca Cook y Wayne Lewchuk

Primera edición, 1998
Segunda edición, 1999
ISBN: 968 863 238 4
ISBN: 968 863 298 8

Dirección General de Fomento Editorial
Juan de Palafox y Mendoza 406
Teléfono y fax 29 55 00 ext. 5763
Puebla, Pue.

Impreso y hecho en México
Printed and made in Mexico

CONTENIDO-CONTENTS

INTRODUCCIÓN - INTRODUCTION
Huberto Juárez Núñez
9

Parte I- Part I
LA PRODUCCIÓN ESBELTA EN AMÉRICA DEL NORTE - LEAN PRODUCTION IN NORTH AMERICA
21

Ambiguous Mandate: Lean Production and Labor Relations in the United States	*Steve Babson*	23
Investment Strategies and "Leaner" Production in the North American Auto Industry	*Ronald S. Blum*	51
Regionalism in the Ford Motor Company's Global Strategies	*Ma. Isabel Studer*	71
Recent Patterns of Production and Investment in the Canadian Auto Industry: Reflections on Management Strategy	*Pradeep Kumar and John Holmes*	95
Trabajadores y Sindicatos ante la Globalización: El Caso del Sector Automotriz Mexicano	*Ma. Cristina Bayón y Graciela Bensusán*	117
Meeting "Lean" Competitors: Ford de México's Industrial Relations Strategy	*P. Roberto Garcia and Stephen Hills*	143

Parte II - Part II
ENSAMBLE – ASSEMBLY
155

The Union Role in Team Concept: A Case Study	*Michelle Kaminski*	157
La Productividad y el Trabajo en el Contexto de la Producción Esbelta en VW de México	*Huberto Juárez Núñez*	173

Cambio Tecnológico y Aprendizaje Laboral en G.M.: Los casos del D.F. y Silao	*Alejandro García G. y Arturo Lara R.*	207
Growing Pains: Lean Production at Mitsubishi Motors.	*Lisa Jordan*	223
The Introduction of Team Programs and Competitive Manufacturing at GM Lordstown: An Historical Perspective.	*John Russo*	237
Chrysler Canada's Windsor Assembly Plant: Lean Production Through Bargained Incremental Change	*John Holmes and Pradeep Kumar*	257

Parte III - Part III

PARTES Y COMPONENTES - PARTS AND COMPONENTS

279

De la Producción Nacional a la Competencia Global: El Caso de la Industria Mexicana de Autopartes	*Carmen Bueno*	281
Lean Production and the Specter of Mexico: A Case Study of a U.S. Auto Parts Plant	*Susan Helper*	303
Then and Now: Observations on New Work Organization at GM Powertrain	*Danny Hoffman*	325
Modernización Empresarial y Organización del Trabajo en GM de México: Complejo Toluca (motores)	*Sergio González y Selene Villa*	341
Maquiladoras en Redes: El caso de Delphi-GM	*Jorge Carrillo y Alfredo Hualde*	369

Parte IV - Part IV

ORGANIZACION DEL TRABAJO - BENCHMARKING WORK ORGANIZATION

387

Work Reorganization and the Quality of Working Life in the Canadian Automotive Industry	*Wayne Lewchuk and David Robertson*	389
Is Lean Enough? Benchmarking Worker Outcomes and Productivity in Small Manufacturers	*Brad Markell*	405

Parte V - Part V
SALUD Y CONDICIONES DE TRABAJO - HEALTH AND WORKING CONDITIONS
427

New Systems of Work Organization: Impacts on Job Characteristics and Health	*Paul A. Landsbergis, Janet Cahill and Peter Schnall*	429
Accidentes de Trabajo en VW de México	*Huberto Juárez Núñez y Cristina González*	441
Lean Production and Workplace Health and Safety	*David Fairris*	463
Worker Health in Two Auto Assembly Plants: A Comparison of Policy in Union vs. Nonunion Environments	*Laurie Graham*	475

Parte VI - Part VI
TLC Y SOLIDARIDAD A TRAVÉS DE LAS FRONTERAS - NAFTA AND CROSS-BORDER SOLIDARITY
485

Building Transnational Coordinative Unionism	*Don Wells*	487
TLC, Legislación y Política Laboral	*Oscar Alzaga*	507
The UE-FAT Strategic Organizing Alliance	*Robin Alexander*	525
El Sindicato en la Reestructuración Industrial y Laboral en Diesel Nacional S.A. Hoy Grupo DINA. Una Semblanza para la Memoria	*Lazaro Osorio*	535
La Autentica Contratación Colectiva y los "Contratos de Protección"	*Luis Fonte, Evaristo Alvarez y Guillermo Rivera*	545

INTRODUCCIÓN

INTRODUCTION

ENFRENTANDO EL CAMBIO:
Obreros del Automóvil y Producción Esbelta en América del Norte

INTRODUCCIÓN

En el ocaso del siglo veinte, se ha vuelto un lugar común hablar en las diversas esferas de la economía de la presencia de *la Producción Esbelta, Flexible o Ajustada.* Constituida en una especie de paradigma productivo, la *Producción Esbelta* ha cambiado jirones completos de la cultura del trabajo y ha establecido nuevos parámetros para la evaluación del desempeño laboral cotidiano, la mayor parte de ellos indexados a las nuevas percepciones patronales acerca de la *productividad del trabajo.*

Como resultado de lo anterior, el interés y la polémica en los mundos académico, empresarial y sindical, se han saturado del saldo que continuamente están arrojando las ponderaciones de los impactos que en diversas tesituras afloran desde las nuevas formas que asumen las relaciones laborales. Como sucede en estos casos, los análisis y las explicaciones se han diversificado y muchas veces polarizado, especialmente, cuando el foco de atención se refiere a los resultados de la *producción esbelta* para el capital y para el trabajo.

En este contexto, es ampliamente conocido que la industria del automóvil representa —dentro del conjunto de industrias manufactureras donde los nuevos sistemas de organización industrial y los nuevos sistemas de trabajo se han desarrollado— además de la parte pionera, la que más ha consolidado y explorado sus experiencias. Esta situación, unida a las posiciones de privilegio que tiene dentro de las estructuras industriales y dentro de las políticas gubernamentales, le han asegurado, en los países del primer y del tercer mundo, una amplia cobertura que entre otras cosas, les ha permitido conservar el lugar de punta en las diversas innovaciones asociadas a la organización del trabajo.

CONFRONTING CHANGE:
AUTO LABOR AND LEAN PRODUCTION IN NORTH AMERICA

INTRODUCTION

As the twentieth century draws to a close, it has become commonplace in diverse sectors of the economy to speak about the presence of *lean* or *flexible production.* Conceived as a type of productive paradigm, *Lean Production* has changed entire aspects of work culture and established new parameters for evaluating everyday work performance, most of them indexed to management's new perceptions of *labor productivity*.

As a result, there has been considerable interest and endless discussion within the academic, business and labor communities evaluating the impact of the new forms of labor relations cropping up in diverse circumstances. As is often true in such cases, analysis and explanation have been varied and frequently polarized, especially when attention is focused on the results of *lean production* for capital and labor.

In this context, it is well known that automaking represents —among those industries where new systems of industrial organization and work have been developed— the pioneering industry that has best consolidated and explored its experiences. This situation, together with the privileged status it has within industrial structures and government policies, has assured the industry, in both first and third-world countries, broad protection for its leadership in the diverse innovations associated with work organization.

We therefore have an auto industry that, after a century of impressive development —rooted in the extraordinary social phenomenon which made owning a car a symbol of social, family and personal well-being and progress— still represents a powerful force in the global complex of large manufacturing corporations.

In recent years, facing a relative stagnation in their rates of growth —and in a social environment that identifies the internal combustion engine as

Tenemos entonces que la industria automotriz, después de un siglo de impresionante desarrollo —fincado en ese extraordinario fenómeno social consistente en que su propiedad se transformó en el signo de bienestar y del progreso, social, familiar e individual— y aún considerando el grado de madurez alcanzado, representa una poderosa fuerza en la estructura del complejo mundial de las grandes corporaciones manufactureras.

En los últimos años, frente a los relativos estancamientos de sus tasas de crecimientos en la esfera de la producción de unidades —y también en un ambiente social que identifica al auto movido por combustión interna, como responsable en buena medida de la fractura del delicado equilibrio ecológico— estas grandes corporaciones automotrices están forzando —en el terreno de la producción y la comercialización— la construcción de mecanismos que han revitalizado aspectos de sus operaciones, tan sensibles e importantes como el incremento de las facturaciones y de las utilidades, al mismo tiempo que han podido desvincularlas de los comportamientos del empleo. La *producción flexible* está detrás de todos los resultados recientes.

Por tanto, hablar de la *producción flexible* en la industria del automóvil es hablar de una especie de *asociación natural* entre un campo específico de las manufacturas y una nueva forma de organización industrial y sistemas de trabajo.

Para las grandes corporaciones del automóvil la *producción ajustada* significa adelgazamiento de costos, sincronía de economías de ámbito de producción y mercado, nuevas relaciones con proveedores, entregas justo a tiempo, desarrollo y mejoramiento de procesos, calidad de productos y por último, un mecanismo global muy eficaz para elevar la rentabilidad de sus operaciones e inversiones.

Por otra parte, para el trabajo, la *producción esbelta* ha significado ingresar al mundo de las tareas polivalentes, a los nuevos ritmos de trabajo, a las nuevas calificaciones, a nuevas asignaciones de materias de trabajo, a nuevos criterios para asignaciones salariales y sobre todo, a una nueva y contradictoria percepción patronal de la función de las organizaciones sindicales.

Dentro del proceso de globalización-regionalización, la constitución *del bloque norteamericano* ha configurado —especialmente para el caso de la industria del automóvil— un escenario muy representativo de las nuevas tendencias en cuanto a las estrategias empresariales referida a los costos laborales. La movilidad del capital hacia zonas con regulaciones blandas, con escasa o nula tradición sindical, es un proceso que ha avanzado desde los

largely responsible for fracturing the tenuous ecological equilibrium— these large automotive corporations have pushed forth mechanisms of production and commercialization that are revitalizing such important aspects of their operations as revenues and profits. At the same time, they have managed to sever the links between such growth and their levels of employment. *Flexible production* is behind all of these recent results.

Therefore, to speak about *flexible production* in the auto industry is akin to speaking of a kind of *natural association* between a specific sector in manufacturing, and a new form of industrial organization and work.

For large automotive corporations, *lean production* means lower costs, synchronization of economies in production and marketing, new supplier relations, just-in-time deliveries, process development and improvement, product quality, and finally, a very efficient global mechanism to upgrade the profitability of their operations and investments.

From labor's standpoint, on the other hand, lean production has meant entering the world of multiple tasks, new rhythms of work, new skills, new work functions, new wage-setting criteria, and, above all, a new and contradictory management perception of the role of unions.

Within the process of globalization/regionalization, and especially in the case of the automobile industry, the establishment of the North American bloc has created a representative setting for these new tendencies, particularly with regard to management strategies concerning labor costs. The movement of capital to areas with weak regulations and little or no union tradition has been taking place since the 1970s, and has defined an increasingly complex geographical map of industrial establishments and dispersion of production. The traditional division between assembly and parts industries has spread into different regions of each of the three countries in the bloc, and the existence of *lean production* is generating processes to equalize productivity at the same time it accentuates sharp differences in wages and in organizing for the defense of labor rights —all within a strategy that promotes competition among workers.

In the case of Mexico, the arrival of work practices inspired by Toyota was not a minor affair. The 106-day strike by GM workers of the Ejercito Nacional plant in 1980 was waged to win back collective bargaining rights for workers in the plants which the company had just built in the northern part of the country. The defeat of that strike signaled the beginning of a long period of darkness for union organizations, still structured around a culture of

años setenta y esto ha determinado un mapa cada día más complejo de asentamientos industriales y dispersión de la producción. Esto significa que la tradicional división entre industria ensambladora e industria de autopartes se ha "espaciado" en diversas regiones de los tres países que componen el bloque y la existencia de la *producción esbelta* está generando procesos de homologación de productividad al mismo tiempo que acentuadas diferencias en los ámbitos salarial y de la organización para la defensa de los derechos, dentro de una estrategia que fomenta la competencia entre los trabajadores.

En el caso mexicano, la entrada de los esquemas de trabajo de inspiración toyotista no fue un asunto menor. En 1980, la huelga de 106 días de los obreros de GM Planta Ejército Nacional, que tenía como propósito recuperar la titularidad del Contrato para las plantas que recién se construían en el norte del país, significó, con su derrota, la apertura de una larga noche para la suerte de las organizaciones sindicales —estructuradas en función de una cultura productiva que muy rápidamente envejecía— y cuyo saldo en su expresión destilada, puede escribirse como: atomización sindical y adelgazamiento de los Contratos Colectivos de Trabajo.

Sin duda, en México, no se trató de hechos asilados, la cobertura gubernamental —la Secretaría del Trabajo más concretamente— propició que las gerencias de las transnacionales obtuvieran derechos a salvo y desregulaciones de *facto* que simplificaron todos los procedimientos orientados a tener mano de obra capacitada para operar dentro de los nuevos sistemas. El esquema toyotista de los años pioneros, es decir de los años cincuenta, pensados para eliminar obstáculos al ejercicio de las prerrogativas patronales, en el escenario productivo mexicano se ha aplicado por las gerencias sin mucho esfuerzo ni mucha imaginación, muchas veces al pie de la letra.

En muchos casos la resistencia sindical del gremio automotriz en este país no nace siquiera como la oposición a los nuevos sistemas de trabajo, no, el asunto es aquí tremendamente elemental porque se refiere a ejercer o no los derechos de asociación y organización instituidos en la regulación laboral nacional. La cronología de las luchas de resistencia sindical se caracteriza por su profundo tono defensivo y se refiere al respeto a los derechos constituidos. Esto puede ser reconocido puntualmente en las luchas obreras que se han dado en los diversos emplazamientos de GM, de Ford, de NISSAN, de DINA y de VW, para hablar sólo de lo más destacado, porque es un asunto que ha estado en todas las plantas automotrices en México en los últimos 15 años.

production that was aging rapidly. The result can be described, in essence, as union fragmentation and weaker collective bargaining contracts.

Without any doubt, what happened in Mexico was not a series of isolated occurrences. The federal government —more specifically the Secretary of Labor— helped management of the transnationals obtain the virtual suspension of laws and *de facto* deregulation, thus simplifying every step taken by the companies to obtain a workforce able to operate within the new systems. The pioneering Toyota system of the 1950s, designed to eliminate any obstacles to the exercise of management prerogatives, has been applied to the Mexican productive setting without too much effort or imagination, often applying it to the letter.

In many instances the resistance of Mexican automobile unions does not stem from labor's opposition to the new work systems. Rather, the issue is the much more basic question of whether or not they can exercise the rights of free association and organization established in the national labor law. Resistance struggles are characterized by a profoundly defensive tone and demands for respect for constitutional rights. This stance is visible in every union struggle against GM, Ford, Nissan, DINA and VW, to speak only of the most important; in fact, it has been part of life in each and every automotive plant in Mexico for the last 15 years.

As the 1980s came to a close, a typical Mexican autoworker had evolved: versatile, flexible, highly productive and competitive. But his labor is priced at Mexican levels, which means as little as one-tenth or one-twentieth of the earnings of his counterparts in the developed countries of the North American bloc.

In Canada and the United States, the existence of large industrial unions has in some ways restrained the most pernicious effects of the new productive systems. However, when we look at the outcome of the restructuring of the early 1980s, we can already identify national differences that, especially with the restructuring and relocation of the parts supplier sector, have followed a logic that reinforces management prerogatives at the expense of union organization.

In the 1990s, in the context of NAFTA, it is "discovered" that factory workers in Hermosillo, Ramos Arizpe, Toluca, Cuautitlan, Aguascalientes, Gomez Palacio, Chihuahua and Puebla are a "competitive advantage" because they can manufacture products to the highest specifications at costs which are a small fraction of those in the United States and Canada. Most

Así tenemos que al cerrar los años ochenta, puede decirse que ya se ha construido la figura del obrero mexicano automotriz polivalente, flexible, altamente productivo y competitivo, pero a precios mexicanos, a un valor que puede representar un décimo, o un vigésimo de las percepciones de sus equivalentes en los países desarrollados del bloque de América del Norte.

En los escenarios canadiense y norteamericano, la existencia de los grandes sindicatos de industria ha contenido de alguna forma los efectos más perniciosos de las nuevos esquemas productivos. Sin embargo, es claro que si se mira el saldo de la reestructuración de principios de los ochenta, encontraremos que ya se acusan diferencias nacionales, y de manera muy especial, tenemos que el segmento de autopartes en su proceso de reestructuración y relocalización, ha seguido una lógica donde las prerrogativas patronales se han reforzado en detrimento de las estructuras sindicales.

En los años noventa, en el contexto de la iniciativa para la firma del Tratado de Libre Comercio, se "descubre" que los trabajadores de las plantas de Hermosillo, de Ramos Arizpe, Toluca, Cuautitlán, Aguascalientes, Gómez Palacio, Chihuahua, Puebla, son "ventajosos competidores" de los trabajadores americanos y canadienses, porque ya pueden elaborar productos con las más altas exigencias de los grandes mercados y a costos que son una pequeña fracción de lo que se paga en los países de origen, y, lo más importante, los costos laborales en México son una muy pequeña fracción de los *costos de producción.*

De acuerdo a diversos análisis, en la industria automotriz mexicana, los costos laborarles respecto de los costos de producción en los años 90 cayeron en promedio al nivel de 6%, casi el cincuenta por ciento del nivel que prevalecía en los años 80. Dentro de este promedio general tenemos empresas filiales que están pagando el 3% de sus costos de producción como costos laborales.

En este plano de homologación productiva y ampliación de la brecha salarial con relación a los trabajadores canadienses y norteamericanos, tenemos que la valía productiva del obrero automotriz mexicano, tan cara a los recientes proyectos de las corporaciones automovilísticas, conlleva una enorme asimetría con su capacidad de organización y de negociación del valor de su capacidad de trabajo.

Sin embargo, la globalización y la modernidad puso a los trabajadores mexicanos en los primeros planos de los flujos de información y con ello se han estado ventilando en las esferas sindicales, académicas, gubernamentales

importantly, Mexican labor costs are a very small fraction of the *costs of production.*

According to a variety of analyses, labor costs as a share of production costs in the Mexican automobile industry fell to an average of 6 percent in the 1990s, slightly below half of the share registered in the 1980s. The average includes data from subsidiaries whose labor costs are just 3 percent of their costs of production.

Against this background of productive parity and a widening wage gap with American and Canadian workers, the productive value of the Mexican autoworker, so dear to the recent projects of the auto companies, bears an enormous asymmetry with his ability to organize into a union and negotiate the value of his labor.

However, globalization and modernization have placed Mexican workers in the foreground of the news and, accordingly, in union, academic, governmental and management circles the issue is now raised of how and when the process of achieving parity of wages and organizing rights will evolve once international productivity standards are reached.

The International Conference on *Working Lean: Labor in the North American Auto Industry,* held in Puebla, Mexico, on April 28 -30, 1997, under the sponsorship of the Benemerita Universidad Autonoma de Puebla and Wayne State University, was convened as a trinational effort of university and union researchers for the examination and understanding of the forms taken by *flexible production* in the auto industry, and their impacts on labor. Most importantly, the conference inaugurated a collective project that will search for ways to articulate *alternatives,* from the perspective of labor, that support solidarity and oppose worker-to-worker competition.

This book is a direct result of the Conference. We regard it as the first phase in a long-term collaboration.

To this end, we have grouped the papers into chapters by themes to allow our readers a comprehensive view of the problem, just as was done at the Conference. We decided to publish the chapters in their original languages in order to maintain the feeling in which we worked, that is to say that we want to represent the actual processes of integration for the readers of whatever country. The necessity to understand our languages, as a means to eliminate barriers, is present in the book and aspires to be an actual presence in our three countries.

y patronales, el tema de cómo y cuándo discurrirá el proceso de homologación, referidos a los salarios y a los derechos de organización, una vez que se han alcanzado los estándares productivos internacionales.

La realización de la Conferencia Internacional *Working Lean: El Trabajo en la Industria del Automóvil en Norteamérica* efectuada en Puebla, México, 28-30 Abril de 1997, bajo los auspicios de la Benemérita Universidad Autónoma de Puebla y de Wayne State University, se inscribe como parte de un esfuerzo trinacional de investigadores universitarios y sindicalistas del ramo, para el análisis y la comprensión de las formas que la *producción flexible* asume en la industria del automóvil, de sus impactos sobre el trabajo y finalmente, como una propuesta de trabajo colectivo que busca hacer contribuciones a una tarea que puede ubicarse en la construcción de *respuestas alternativas,* desde la perspectiva del trabajo, de la solidaridad y en contra de la competencia.

El libro que ahora entregamos, es producto directo de esa conferencia y lo hemos concebido como la primera fase de un trabajo de colaboración de largo aliento.

Para esto, hemos agrupado los trabajos en capítulos temáticos que permitan a nuestros lectores recoger la visión integral del problema, tal y como en la Conferencia pretendimos hacer. Decidimos publicar los capítulos en su idioma original para mantener el sentido en que hemos trabajado, es decir, que tenemos la intención de representar los procesos de integración actuales para los_lectores de un país y de otro. La necesidad de entender nuestros idiomas, como un medio para eliminar las barreras, está presente en el libro y pretende ser un material con presencia en nuestros tres países.

Por otra parte, este libro es la fase inicial de un acuerdo entre investigadores y sindicalistas de los tres países para trabajar en torno a la construcción de una Red de colaboración e intercambios que hemos denominado *Red Trinacional de Investigación: El Trabajo en la Industria Norteamericana del Automóvil* (International Research Network on Autowork in the Americas). La Red —que tendrá su *site* en el *web*— explorará aspectos vinculados a las nuevas integraciones en la industria del automóvil, por ejemplo, la configuración de la industria de autopartes en América del Norte y esperamos estar en la red de internet en el otoño de 1998.

Por último, es importante hacer público nuestro agradecimiento tanto a los directivos de nuestras Universidades que generosamente nos dieron la cobertura para la realización de la Conferencia en Puebla y para la publica-

Moreover, this book is the initial phase of an agreement between researchers and trade unionists in the three countries to build a network of collaboration and exchange that we are calling *International Research Network on Autowork in the Americas*. The Network, which will have a Web site, will explore aspects of the new integration of the automobile industry, for example, the shape of the parts supplier industry in North America. We hope to be on the Internet in the fall of 1998.

Finally, we want to note our gratitude to those officials of our Universities who generously sponsored the Conference in Puebla and the publication of this book, as well as the following people in Mexico and the United States who enthusiastically supported our work: José Cuello, Lydia Fischer, Sue Marx Smock, Judith Chaffee Hopper, Lourdes Trueba, Gabriela Morán Domínguez, Galia Sandoval Jacobo, Patricia Velázquez García, Carlos Cruz Villanueva, Hal Stack, James Burdine, Robert Hullot-Kentor, Geri Hill, Michelle Fecteau, Lorain Alexander, Dave Reynolds and Onzell Patty.

Winter 1997-1998

Huberto Juárez Núñez
Centro de Investigación y Estudios de Posgrado
Facultad de Economía-BUAP

ción de este libro, como a las siguientes personas que en México y/o en los Estados Unidos apoyaron de manera entusiasta nuestro trabajo: José Cuello, Lydia Fischer, Sue Marx Smock, Judith Chaffee Hopper, Lourdes Trueba, Gabriela Morán Domínguez, Galia Sandoval Jacobo, Patricia Velázquez García, Carlos Cruz Villanueva, Hal Stack, James Burdine, Robert Hullot-Kentor, Geri Hill, Michelle Fecteau, Lorain Alexander, Dave Reynolds y Onzell Patty.

Invierno de 1997-1998

Huberto Juárez Núñez
Centro de Investigación y Estudios de Posgrado
Facultad de Economía-BUAP

Parte I
LA PRODUCCIÓN ESBELTA EN AMÉRICA DEL NORTE

Part I
LEAN PRODUCTION IN NORTH AMERICA

AMBIGUOUS MANDATE: LEAN PRODUCTION AND LABOR RELATIONS IN THE UNITED STATES

Steve Babson[*]

INTRODUCTION

General Motors calls it "Synchronous Manufacturing," "Quality Network," and most recently "Competitive Manufacturing." Ford and Chrysler prefer more mundane designations —the "Ford Production System" and the "Chrysler Operating System." All three companies trace the lineage of their new, more "flexible" manufacturing strategies to the same source, the Toyota Production System, or "lean production." Long invoked as the formula for success in global automaking, even as its principles have long eluded precise specification, lean production has only arrived as a detailed prescription for retooling the North American auto industry in the 1990s. The emerging consensus on strategy among the Big Three automakers has not, however, been matched by uniform results, especially in labor relations. The ambiguous nature of lean production's mandate for work and workers has provoked considerable and sometimes bitter controversy. GM, in particular, has experienced a score of local strikes and several system-wide shutdowns while implementing lean production in the United States, while Ford and Chrysler have pursued comparatively tranquil relations with the UAW.

THE MENU

Just as children who see an elephant for the first time only "know" the beast by whichever end, trunk or tail, they first lay eyes on, so have western observers "known" Japanese production management from the 1970s onwards by a succession of parts, each newly discovered and, in turn, deemed to be essential. Driven by the intensifying pressures of global competition and the

[*] Labor Program Specialist, Wayne State University.

spectacular growth of Japanese carmakers, consultants and Big Three managers have successively focused on quality circles, robotics, work teams, and just-in-time inventory systems as *the* core element of the Toyota Production System.

By the mid-1990s, "the beast" had been sufficiently mapped and quartered to permit a reformulation in terms appropriate to a North American context. Certain parts have been deemed unsuitable for direct transfer. Japan's supervisor-led enterprise unions, for one, cannot be legally replicated in the U.S., where federal labor law prohibits management-dominated company unions. The functional equivalent of enterprise unionism is, however, previewed at GM-Saturn, where labor and management leaders intentionally obscure their organizational identities by adopting common titles and overlapping roles. Setting aside this unique and still isolated case, the more common equivalence is found in the growing nonunion sector where supervisor-centered teams approximate Japanese practice. Likewise, the Japanese system of contingent pay, in which a third or more of the autoworker's wage depends upon the supervisor's evaluation and the company's performance bonus, has only a partial equivalent in Big Three profit-sharing plans. The latter rarely generate more than five percent of total compensation, and there is no supervisory assessment of individual workers for so-called "merit pay." In contrast to Japan, where pay varies between companies and from one individual to the next, Big Three wages are standardized by job classification according to industry-wide collective bargaining.[1]

Other elements of Japanese lean production have been found to be very different from the initial, often exaggerated, claims first made on their behalf. Work teams, especially of the "self-directed" variety, have proven to be something of a mirage in a Japanese system that tightly constrains worker initiative and more often "empowers" the supervisor. To the degree that self-directed teams find a place in the North American variant of lean production, they spring from a home-grown lineage of collective bargaining or human-relations theory.[2]

---

[1] On contingent pay systems in Japan, see Takeshi Inagami, "Japanese Workplace Industrial Relations," *Japanese Workplace Industrial Relations Series,* no. 14 (1988), 14-19; John Price, *Japan Works: Power and Paradox in Postwar Industrial Relations* (Ithaca: ILR Press, 1997), 104-107.

[2] On work relations in Japanese auto plants, see Price, *Japan Works,* and Michael Cusumano, *The Japanese Automobile Industry* (Cambridge: Harvard University Press, 1985). For a review of

Incorporating these adjustments to the Toyota model, the lean production "menus" developed by each of the Big Three automakers exhibit considerable uniformity. Figure 1 summarizes the common elements of the new production model across the three companies, and a Glossary at the end of this chapter provides brief definitions of each term.

Figure 1
Lean Production "Menu" in the Big Three

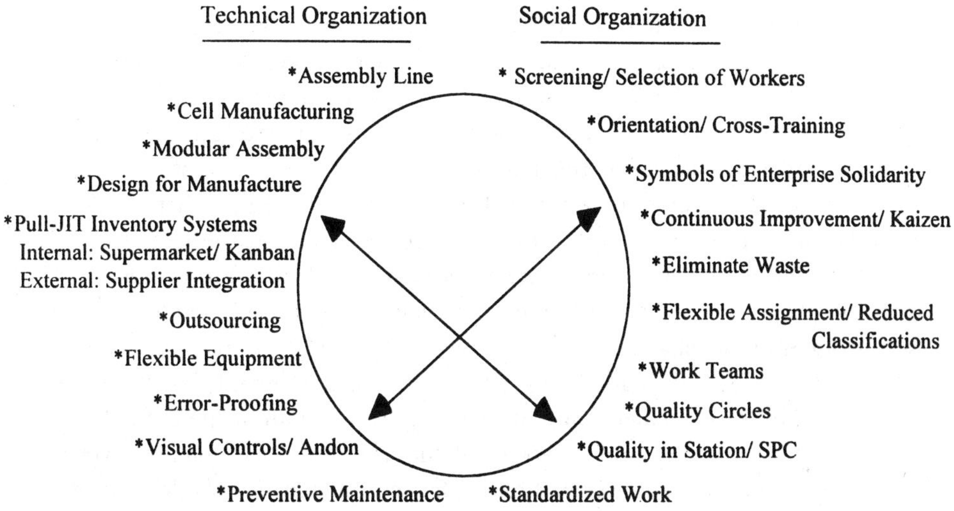

The elements specified in Figure 1 are presented in a circular form rather than separate categories to suggest the overlapping boundaries of a factory's "technical" and "social" organization. The arrows highlight two examples: the common emphasis at GM, Ford, and Chrysler on "building quality in station" (rather than inspecting for quality at the end of the process) is a social mandate of lean production that is strongly enhanced by "design for manufacture," a technical imperative that, in turn, incorporates worker feedback on how to simplify parts for easy fabrication and assembly. Likewise, "symbols of enterprise solidarity" are not only embedded in such social characteristics as common cafeterias and parking lots for hourly and salaried workers, but

U.S. trends, see Eileen Appelbaum and Rosemary Batt, *The New American Workplace: Transforming Work Systems in the United States* (Ithaca: ILR Press, 1994), especially 43-54, 135-142.

also in such technical hardware as the "Andon" Board (see Glossary) and warning lights that elevate a problem at any one work station to a collective concern for the entire work area.

These overlapping technical and social elements of lean production are presented as a menu rather than a blueprint to indicate the potential variation in how the new system is installed (or deferred) site by site. The degree of variation has narrowed over time as more plants are reengineered, usually when new products or technology are brought in with an accompanying package of "lean" methods. Certain elements of change are also tightly linked with others, so that installing one usually entails the rest. Just-in-time (JIT) inventory systems, for example, make the plant's steady and predictable output more vulnerable to disruption, and are therefore usually accompanied by preventive maintenance programs that increase uptime, and by Andon systems and other visual controls that quickly identify trouble spots.

An irreducible variation remains, however, to the degree that different manufacturing processes impose their unique demands on the technical organization of work, and as investment decisions and leadership turnover impact the pace and direction of change. Variation is especially evident in the social organization of lean production, where the particular history of plant- or firm-level collective bargaining, past practices, demographics, and other factors constrain or facilitate implementation. In a nonunion greenfield site, for example, screening and selection of the workforce for certain psychological and performance traits will play a far more determining role than in a Big Three brownfield setting, where "selection" of new workers is constrained by the transfer rights of workers from other plants and the natural preference of incumbent employees (managers and workers) for hiring their relatives and friends.[3]

The menu itself will also continue to change as elements are added, discarded, and amended. Work teams, for example, figured prominently in the initial recipe for workplace change, particularly in the lean production model popularized by MIT's International Motor Vehicle Program. Teams are still a menu item in the 1990s, but they are more often regarded as an option that

---

[3] On the degree of convergence vs. divergence between companies and countries, see John Paul MacDuffie and Frits Pils, "Changes in Auto Industry Employment Practices: An International Overview," in Thomas Kochan, Russell Landsbury, and John Paul MacDuffie, eds., *After Lean Production: Evolving Employment Practices in the World Auto Industry* (Ithaca: ILR Press, 1997), 9-42.

accompanies the entree, one means of securing the commitment of workers and their flexible deployment, but not the only route to this larger goal. Those who regard "team concept" as too radical a departure from the factory's top-down command structures have opposed teams as a disruptive anomaly in the corporate culture. Supervisors long accustomed to these command structures are particularly prone to authoritarian styles that subvert team dynamics and render them meaningless. In such cases, more modest proposals to trim the number of job classifications and cross-train workers for flexible deployment are just as likely to find favor with plant managers who want to loosen work rules regulating the movement of workers, but not at the risk of disrupting workplace hierarchies. The legacy of failure of early team-concept plants —notably, the sudden closing of the Pontiac Fiero plant in 1988— also stigmatizes this approach among many union members who now regard work teams as "just another management fad." As a result, plants which may be similar in their technical organization of lean production may look quite different in their social organization —one plant with teams that manage their work areas without supervision; another with teams that have no clearly defined responsibilities and are little more than job rotation groups; and many more with no teams at all. Indeed, the same variation can even be found within plants, as separate departments (or "profit centers" as some would call them) pilot one or another of these approaches.[4]

ENLISTING WORKERS IN THE WAR ON "WASTE"

What remains at the core of the Big Three's "fixed" menu for lean production is a relentless focus on "continuous improvement" targeted on "elimination of waste" and a corresponding increase in "value-added work." In fact, this imperative flavors the entire lean production menu.

"Workloads are balanced to maximize minutes-per-hour and value-added work content," says GM's *Competitive Manufacturing Planning Guide*, describing the core concept of "Best People Practices" in terms that place the highest priority on eliminating the non-value-added time —"waste"— involved in walking to a parts bin or waiting for the next job to arrive at the workstation. For "Compressed Operations," the *Planning Guide* indicates that work stations should be "compressed within a standard footprint [area]

[4] See Hoffman, this volume, for a case study of the varied outcomes of work reorganization within GM's Powertrain division.

and the idle time created replaced through consolidation of work." GM's definition of "Re-engineering" is pitched in the same terms: "minutes per hour and value-added work are increased." The Chrysler Operating System defines the process in equivalent terms, specifying "Value Added Activities" as a key sub-system of lean production, and highlighting the "Identification and Elimination of Waste" as the key support process.[5]

This unyielding focus on eliminating waste puts those who oppose the management model of lean production in an awkward position, since "waste," as such, is not easily defended. Moreover, there are many workers who appreciate management's new emphasis on coherent planning and a well-organized production process, particularly if workers have input to the redesign and can see a genuine commitment to a safer, cleaner workplace. But it should be equally obvious that much of the "waste" targeted by management also constitutes "rest" for workers: a few seconds here or there waiting for the next job is a welcome breather, but it reduces the "minutes worked per hour" and thereby warrants elimination in a lean production plant. Company documents are straight forward on this score. The training manual for the *Ford Production System 3-Day Plant Awareness Session* quotes the dictum of Taiichi Ohno, chief architect of the Toyota Production System, that "Elimination of Waste" requires management to "reduce the time line by removing non-value added wastes" (sic); the manual then illustrates this concept with an example of a worker who, instead of loading one machine and then waiting to unload it, loads a second machine while the first performs its automated function —thereby "Separating Human and Machine Work" and permitting the plant to "Reduce Manpower."[6]

It can be argued that this focus on time management and continuous-flow production simply restates the original recipe for mass production, as authored by Henry Ford, Frederick Taylor, and others in the opening decades of the twentieth century. This continuity is suggested all the more emphatically by the current emphasis on "standardized work," an apparent echo of Taylor's stress on seeking the "one best way" to perform a task. GM de-

---

[5]General Motors, *Competitive Manufacturing Planning Guide* (1997), 17.0, 19.0, 28.1; "Are We Lean Yet? 2nd Annual Lean Manufacturing Conference," 14-15 May 1996, Dearborn, Michigan, conference binder, Shamel Rushwin, Chrysler Vice President.

[6] John Shook, Mike Rother, Jeffrey Liker, "Lean Manufacturing as a System of Production," in Ford Motor Company, *Ford Production System 3-Day Plant Awareness Session* (1995), loose-leaf binder, 9, 23.

fines "Best People Practices" as "Work functions performed in the same standardized sequence to achieve the highest levels of quality, safety, productivity and ergonomic practice." Ford, like GM, anticipates that the posting of standardized task descriptions at each work station is a critical step in reducing the variation that undermines quality. Each "Standardized Work Chart" in the Ford system therefore details the sequence of tasks, the "footprints" to be followed, the total number of seconds for each task and, within each task, the seconds of "hands-on" work, seconds of machine time, and seconds of walking.[7]

There is, however, a fundamental difference between Frederick Taylor's version of "time study" and the version portrayed in management's current prescription for lean production: while in the former, the stop watch is held by supervisors and plant engineers, who subsequently impose the "one best way" on hourly workers, in the latter the stop watch is to be held by hourly workers as well, and their input is expected to help drive the search for the continuously revised "one best way." Where Taylor's approach was relatively static and certainly top-down, the lean production model calls for "continuous improvement" from the bottom up, as well as the top down.

Workers, in short, are supposed to become active agents in reengineering their own jobs, rather than passive objects of management engineering. This feature of lean production is often celebrated as more humane, participatory, even "democratic." Such commentary misses the point to the same degree that it suggests workers will enjoy more latitude, choice, and initiative on the job. In fact, worker participation in lean production is not intended as an option, certainly not in Japanese practice nor in the model pursued by Big Three managers. Rather, it is an *obligation* of every worker to participate. The Ford Production System training manual calls for "Work Systems that Demand and Support Involvement." In this spirit, "Jidoka", the Japanese term for building quality in station, "not only *provides opportunity* for involvement," according to Ford's manual, "but *demands* involvement" (emphasis in original). Similarly, JIT not only "encourages" but "demands self-management."[8]

It is not difficult to see why the system "demands" participation, particularly with respect to JIT. With only minimal buffers of work-in-process to absorb disruptions, and with jobs already timed to eliminate "waiting" and "waste," a JIT production system is only viable to the degree that workers

---

[7] GM, *Competitive Guide,* 17.0; Shook et al., *Ford 3-Day Session,* 30-34.

[8] Shook et al., *Ford 3-Day Session,* 45.

are willing, and obligated, to immediately address problems and find solutions that re-stabilize the process. Here again, advocates of lean production celebrate the "proactive" role that workers play in maintaining such a fragile production system. The reality is that workers are obligated to be "reactive" rather than proactive, responding to problems forced into the open by a system that is running with the smallest possible buffers and the smallest possible number of workers. Since many companies understaff their teams, and since the inevitable disruptions and downtime make it difficult to meet the production targets mandated for each shift (and prominently displayed on the Andon board), workers in a lean factory are often expected to work overtime, much of it on a mandatory rather than voluntary basis.[9]

In this respect, JIT systems actually limit workers' freedom of initiative, since there are smaller buffers and, therefore, fewer opportunities to vary the work pace or "build ahead" to allow more time for rest— which would be "waste" in any case. GM is straightforward on this score, describing JIT in its *Planning Guide* as "designed and planned to restrict the ability to overproduce." By compelling workers to strictly adhere to a measured pace determined by the carefully metered supply of parts, JIT (a "technical" imperative of lean production) also reinforces the primacy of standardized work (a social imperative). The *Guide* further specifies that "Sub-assembly operations are tied to the line wherever possible," thereby "tying" them to JIT and eliminating the previous opportunity for workers in off-line operations to "bank" extra work at the start of the shift and slow to an easier pace at the end of the day.[10]

AMBIGUOUS MANDATE

What this means for workers is the subject of widening and sometimes acrimonious debate. Advocates of lean production first promoted the system as an unqualified improvement over Fordist-Taylorist mass production, providing workers "the freedom to control one's work." These promotional claims

---

[9] The deliberate "stressing" of the system with virtually no buffers leads some to call lean production "Management by Stress." See Mike Parker and Jane Slaughter, *Working Smart: A Union Guide to Participation Programs and Reengineering* (Detroit: Labor Notes, 1994).

[10] GM, *Competitive Guide*, 18.0, 17.1. See Janice Klein, "The Human Cost of Manufacturing Reform," *Harvard Business Review* (March-April 1989, and "A Reexamination of Autonomy in Light of New Manufacturing Practices," *Human Relations* 44, no. 1 (1991).

have since given way to more qualified assessments, both as research on Japanese practice reveals a tightly regulated system driven primarily by supervision, and as implementation in North America confronts worker responses that range from support, to skepticism, to bitter opposition.[11]

The ambiguous mandate of lean production is evident in many of its featured elements. Standardized work and JIT systems are designed to regiment labor and sharply curtail the in-process buffers that previously gave workers some latitude in the pacing and content of their jobs. But workers can also use standardized work to defend themselves against supervisors who unilaterally push "unprogrammed" tasks on the job; and JIT systems are vulnerable to collective actions that pressure management to address minimal worker needs.

"Worker responsibility" for insuring quality and productivity can likewise generate pride and satisfaction in a job well done, but responsibility without the matching authority to access needed resources —of time, training, tools, and labor power— can just as easily generate psychological and physical stress. "Job rotation" can relieve the tedium of previously specialized factory jobs, and can ease the physical strain of repetitive motion in a single task; but at the same time, rotation can undermine the seniority rights of older workers who feel they have "paid their dues" and now covet the plant's easier duties; rotation might also conceal poorly designed jobs by distributing their physical strain across an entire work team, postponing but ultimately amplifying the long-term harm. "Training" can teach new skills and prepare workers for a wider range of job opportunities; but training can also be restricted to favored recipients, or narrowly focused on socializing workers to the company's agenda for "Elimination of Waste" and increasing "Minutes Worked per Hour."

The ambiguities of "worker empowerment" are especially contentious. For many workers it is taken to mean, at least initially, that they will literally accrue the power to shape the work process, permitting them wide discretion in designing their jobs, solving problems, and deploying resources. This is rarely, however, what managers have in mind, and for this reason Ford explicitly presents the concept of "empowered work teams" in terms of constraints. The company's 1994 "Production System Study Group on Team Concept" puts at the top of its list of "Common Management Concerns" the

---

[11] For the range of worker responses, see in this volume the case studies of Kaminski (Ford), Jordan (Mitsubishi), and Russo (GM).

possibility that team concept will be "Misinterpreted as a Democratic Process." This misconception is countered with the "Management View": "We envision the team *not* as 'independent' but rather as highly '*inter*dependent' with other teams and line supervision" (emphasis in original). Additional constraints include the collective bargaining agreement and public laws, the sum of which make the literal concept of "self-directed" teams a rhetorical extravagance that neither the union nor management can support.[12]

But while labor and management can agree on the general need for constraints, the specific decision boundaries still need to be determined. The Ford Study Group report anticipates three leadership styles under team concept: "Empowered," where management delegates to workers both the analysis of the problem and the decision-making authority to address it; "Participative," where management only delegates analysis to workers and retains decision-making authority; and "Directive," where management conducts the analysis and makes the decision. Under the ground rules for deciding which leadership style will prevail, Directive and Participative styles are likely to predominate, since Empowered decisions are only delegated to workers when a list of seven questions can each be answered with a "yes": does the team have the information needed to make the decision; the training; the time; the team support; the jurisdiction; the standards to guide them; and a common purpose with management?[13] The answers to most of these questions are, of course, pre-determined by whether the necessary resources (information, training, standards, time, and personnel) are made available to the team in the first place, and in plants where the imperative to "Eliminate Waste" is pressuring managers to cut costs quickly and measurably, many teams will find they don't have enough people or time to take on empowered decision making. This potential is underlined whenever sales rise and the company must choose between two options for boosting production: add more people and thereby insure that workers will have the energy and time for off-line meetings, training, and attention to quality, or run flat-out with 50-60 hour weeks and mandatory overtime that leaves no energy or time for such "distractions." In most cases, companies choose the latter strat-

---

[12] Ford Motor Company, "B&AO Production System Study Group on Team Concept" (1994), 1.4, 2.5, 4.2, 5.4-5.7; UAW-Ford, *Continuous Improvement Work Groups Training Manual* (1995), loose-leaf binder, Section 4, 3-5.

[13] Ford, "B&AO Study Group on Team Concept," 5.4-5.7.

egy and reveal their bottom-line commitment to short-term profit performance rather than long-term investment in empowered decision making and shopfloor innovation.[14]

These limits are underlined by the seventh and final question posed by the Ford Study Group for determining whether or not Empowered decision making should prevail: "Is there common interest (no conflict of interest) between management and workforce on this task?"[15] In the factory's contested terrain, where groups of workers and managers make conflicting claims on limited resources of time, tools, and labor power, this is an especially portentous question. If the answer is "no", Empowered decision making is precluded.

How these inevitable conflicts over limited resources are addressed depends on a variety of factors, including overall corporate policy, the company's financial health, the availability of concrete models for emulation, and the surrounding context of public policy and labor law. Of particular importance is the role of the union. Even when there is none, as is the case in most of the Japanese transplant operations that have opened since Honda's 1982 arrival, the threat of union organization forces management to compromise certain features of the Toyota Production System. There is little doubt, for example, that the UAW's efforts to organize Honda (Ohio), Nissan (Tennessee), Toyota (Kentucky), and Subaru-Isuzu (Indiana), though unsuccessful to date, have pressured management to pay higher wages that are less contingent on company performance and supervisory evaluation than is the case in Japan.[16]

In unionized workplaces, collective bargaining can deflect, amend, or incorporate a lean production agenda in ways that confront the system's ambiguous meaning for workers, or succumb to them. The outcome depends in large part on how clearly and forcefully the union defines the interests of workers in a particular plant, and the degree to which it does so independently of its common interest with plant management in the factory's com-

---

[14] See, for example, John Russo's case study of the GM Lordstown assembly plant in this volume. For a similar assessment of the Chrysler North Jefferson plant, see Paul Adler, Thomas Kochan, John Paul MacDuffie, Frits Pil, and Saul Rubenstein, "United States: Variations on a Theme," in Kochan et al., *After Lean Production*, 76-77

[15] Ford, "B&AO Study Group on Team Concept," 5.7.

[16] See Adler et al., "United States: Variations on a Theme," 72, and Kathy Jackson, "Transplant Wages will Rise to Match any Gains at Big 3," *Automotive News*, 2 July 1990, 2, 60.

petitive survival. The balance between these overlapping but distinct imperatives —the survival of the enterprise and the survival of an independent worker voice— is a precarious one. Aggressive defense of production standards and negotiated work rules that limit supervisory discretion can win support from workers beleaguered by the demand to "eliminate waste" and maximize minutes worked per hour; but this same adversarial approach by the union can persuade management that continued investment in such a workforce will pay lower dividends than investment in a more compliant labor force. Conversely, the company's threat to move or discontinue production can so intimidate workers that the union acquiesces to practices that further weaken its capacity to oppose unilateral action.

These contending dynamics are especially critical in negotiating the role of team leaders and the process for selecting them. Team leaders play a pivotal role in many of the "Modern Operating Agreements" (MOA) negotiated in the Big Three, serving as the lead worker in teams of 5-15 people. An hourly worker and union member, the team leader usually has duties that combine the roles of job setter (starting and monitoring equipment), relief (filling for absentees or workers on break), and low-end supervision (trouble shooting, training, and managing rotation schedules). It is a stressful position, but because it entails off-line work, is more varied and challenging, and usually pays a premium of fifty to sixty cents an hour, there are workers who seek the job. Team leaders are not supposed to involve themselves in any dimension of discipline, yet their role may include assigning tasks, or facilitating quality circles, or distributing overtime, or taking attendance, or other matters that have supervisory implications. It is therefore of considerable importance whether team leaders owe their job to the supervisor or to fellow workers. In many nonunion plants, management either picks the team leader and, thereby, defines the role as one of junior foreman, or (as in the nonunion plants GM opened in the South in the 1970s) the supervisor serves directly as team leader. On the other hand, in unionized Big Three plants (as these southern GM plants eventually became), the UAW negotiates a selection process that loosens management's control of the team leader and makes the team, by degrees, less "supervisor centered" and more "worker centered." As indicated in Figure 2, this either entails some form of election process, rotation, seniority progression, or joint labor-management selection.

Figure 2

Team Continuum, Supervisor- to Worker-Centered

Supervisor Centered ◄——► Worker Centered

1) Team Leader Selection

1	2	3	4	5	6	7
Supervisor is team leader	Supervision appoints team leader	Supervision appoints team leader under negotiated guidelines	Joint Appointment of team leader by union-management committee	Senior Worker who volunteers is team leader	Team members elect team leader	Team members rotate position

2) Team Meetings

1	2	3	4	5	6
Supervisor chairs by group*	Supervisor chairs by team	Supervisor chairs by team, union rep is present	Team leader chairs, supervisor monitors	Team leader chairs, supervisor attends only if invited	Team leader °calls meeting as needed

3) Job Assignments

1	2	3	4
Supervisor decides if, when, who, and scope of job rotation	Bargaining determines ergonomic and/or stress-ful jobs to be rotated	Seniority bidding on task assignments within the team, or by job classification	Team decides if, when, who, and scope of job rotation

* "group" indicates supervisor's unit, incorporating two or more teams

A local union that concedes to a supervisor-centered team structure may do so because management has demanded the union's passive cooperation with such an approach as the initial price of reinvesting in the plant. How diligently the union thereafter pushes in the direction of worker-centered teams, redefining cooperation to include the workers' independent voice, depends on how urgently it appraises the long-term danger of team leaders turning into "straw bosses" and "pushers" —a development that would probably undermine the credibility of team concept, and would certainly undermine the credibility of the union.

The importance of role identification and the degree to which a work system is supervisor centered or worker centered is defined by more than just the selection process for team leaders. Much of the management prescription for lean production is driven by a social imperative that defines every relationship in the plant as market driven, with workers encouraged to identify each other as "downstream customers" and "upstream suppliers." The frequently invoked "Teamwork" that links these individual employees in a kind of enterprise solidarity with management is not entirely ideological, since it takes its meaning from the very real competitive struggle that defines the success —or extinction— of the plant. In this context, unions can push for a contending "labor solidarity" that removes human exploitation from the competitive equation, articulating a self-identification as workers that both challenges, and coexists, with "enterprise solidarity." Where this independent identity is lacking, the results can look very much like the enterprise unionism found in Japan. The potential for such an outcome was demonstrated in 1992, when the UAW local at GM's stamping plant in Lordstown, Ohio, went on strike to protest scheduled job cuts. After the strike interrupted parts deliveries to GM's Saturn plant in Spring Hill, Tennessee, the local union president at Saturn —who defined himself as both a union leader and a member of plant management (a circumstance unique to Saturn)— publicly voiced his opposition to the UAW's "adversarial" opposition to outsourcing. "We can't continue to remove wages from competition in the international economy," he was quoted as saying. "That's my position, not the UAW's position." As broadcast by the national media, his comments drew condemnation from union circles and praise from the *Wall Street Journal*.[17]

---

[17] Editorial, "Labor's Days at GM," *Wall Street Journal*, 4 Sept. 1992, A8. The collaborative-enterprise focus of the Saturn local leadership does not go uncontested. The year after this episode, the same president only narrowly won reelection by a 52-48 percent margin over an opponent who criticized the union's lack of independence from management. Local union members in 1994 twice voted down tentative contract settlements, forcing union negotiators to return to bargaining and win restoration of shift rotation and election of team leaders. See Greg Gardner, "Troubles Within: As Saturn's Star Rises, Dissent Divides Workers," *Detroit Free Press*, 23 March 1993, 7D; Harley Shaiken, Steven Lopez, and Isaac Mankita, "Two Routes to Team Production: Saturn and Chrysler Compared," *Industrial Relations* 36 (January 1997): 41-43.

NEGOTIATING THE LEAN PRODUCTION MENU

In negotiating the terms of lean production, both as it impacts workers and is impacted by them, the UAW confronts the daunting fact that much of the lean production menu is beyond the reach of collective bargaining. There are at least two reasons for this.

The first is conveyed in Table 1. Because of plant closings and outsourcing in the Big Three and unionized parts makers, and because the UAW's organizing efforts have not kept pace with the expanding nonunion and transplant sector, the percentage of U.S. auto workers in unions has fallen to little more than 50 percent of the total workforce. Particularly in parts making, management either faces no union at all, or a union harried by nonunion competition.

Table 1
Percentage of U.S. Auto Workforce in Unions

		1978	1988	1995
Assembly		100		94
Parts:	Independent & Big 3	64-82	58	38
	Independent Only	59-62	22-24	18
Overall		69-77		55

Sources: Joel Cutcher-Gershenfeld and Patrick McHugh, "Competition and Divergence: Collective Bargaining in the North American Auto Supply Industry," in Paula Voos, ed., *Contemporary Collective Bargaining in the Private Sector* (Madison, WI: IRRA, 1994), 243-245; *UAW Research Bulletin*, October 1995, 4.

The second reason has to do with the difference between the technical and social organization of lean production. Since the latter tends to have direct implications for the collective bargaining agreement —for example, team concept often impacts job classifications (compressing their range) and seniority rights (limiting their reach)— the Big Three will negotiate these matters with the union, both because it is legally obligated to do so, and because evading that obligation bears a high cost when Big Three union density is still 100 percent in final assembly. However, there is no matching obligation to negotiate the technical organization of lean production, since these matters fall under the management rights clause granting the company the sole right to determine machinery, products, methods, processes, engineering, control of materials, and so on. All of these technical choices have implications for the plant's social organization, and bargaining may address these secondary impacts —training, for example. But in general, the company can take unilateral action on the technical side of the lean production menu.

In many cases, therefore, management is inclined to focus attention on these technical dimensions of lean production and minimize the potentially disruptive consequences of renegotiating the plant's social organization. Work teams are a case in point, as suggested earlier. In the 1980s, GM pushed aggressively for team concept and other far-reaching amendments to the social organization of production, and UAW leaders at GM endorsed most of these initiatives as part of a strategy to save jobs. But continued plant closings and plant-by-plant disputes over how far to proceed with labor-management cooperation provoked a backlash in the late 1980s among workers who saw participation in these initiatives as passive submission to a management-driven process. The opposition movement, "New Directions," that harnessed this backlash found the overwhelming majority of its followers in GM, where the joint labor-management process at the local level had initially proceeded further and faster than at Ford and Chrysler. New Directions failed in its 1989 bid to elect two candidates to the union's national executive board, and the dissident movement thereafter faded. But the political turmoil in GM plants persuaded many in both management and the union that the two sides were better off with joint programs that were more modest in scope and moderate in pace, particularly with respect to team concept. Similar conclusions were drawn at Ford and Chrysler.

The result is that Big Three assembly plants in North America have a lower proportion of workers organized into teams than any other sector of the global auto industry. According to MIT's International Motor Vehicle Program, only 23 percent of all workers in Big Three assembly plants in the U.S. belonged to teams in 1993-1994, compared to 70 percent in Japanese assembly plants (at home and transplanted to the U.S.) and 80 percent in European plants (where unions have advocated worker-centered "groups" long before lean production).[18]

---

[18] MacDuffie and Pils, "Changes in Auto Industry Employment Practices," 17. As indicated by Holmes and Kumar in this volume, the percentage of all workers in teams is even lower in

Joint labor-management programs still promote team organization, but the primary focus of labor-management cooperation in the Big Three is on job security programs designed to absorb the impact of declining market share, new technology, and lean production's relentless elimination of "waste" — "excess" workers included. It is widely recognized that without these employment security provisions, fewer workers would participate in programs to raise productivity and "continuously remove" themselves from their jobs. Consequently, with each triennial round of bargaining, the safety net has become more elaborate: plant-level "job banks" are supposed to hold redundant workers at full pay for retraining and reassignment (since 1984); the company is supposed to replace normal attrition on a one-for-two basis (since 1987) and on a one-for-one basis under certain conditions (since 1996); and management not only has to give the union advance notice of decisions to move work to outside suppliers, it has to consider union alternatives to such outsourcing (since 1990). Advocates of joint labor-management programs argue that these provisions not only protect a workforce confronting lean production, but also provide the union with a forum for discussing —jointly— the technical matters which management otherwise has no obligation to bargain.

At Ford and Chrysler, this strategy has produced relatively stable labor relations, with only a handful of local strikes at Chrysler since 1990. At General Motors, however, labor relations have been marked by bitter confrontation, producing 23 local strikes between 1990 and 1997, as indicated in Table 2.

To a large extent, these contrasting labor relations reflect differences in market performance and timing between the three companies. GM was the least impacted by the market collapse of 1979-1982, and was the only company with the resources for lavish (and often ill-considered) spending on new technology, new assembly plants, and new labor-management programs. GM was especially vigorous in pursuing joint labor-management cooperation in the 1980s, especially at the local level. In contrast, Ford and Chrysler both suffered severe and traumatic crises that winnowed union membership in one fell swoop, generating (especially at Chrysler) a siege mentality that muted dissent and dampened militancy. Since the mid-1980s,

---

Canada, totaling only 4 percent. In those plants that have team concept, roughly 50 percent of the plant workforce in the U.S. is in teams, compared to 25 percent in Canada.

Ford and Chrysler have recovered and even increased their market share, while GM has experienced a disastrous fall from the predominance it had enjoyed since the late 1920s. Burdened with drab and poorly engineered car models, and failing to anticipate the shift to light trucks that brought Ford and especially Chrysler rising sales and profits, GM stumbled downward from 41 percent of the U.S. market in 1986 to 34 percent in 1995. Falling sales exposed an increasingly expensive excess capacity that burdened plant productivity and put GM in a downward spiral of mounting unit costs and bureaucratic floundering.

These trend lines would put any capitalist management at risk of losing investor confidence, but the pressure on GM's corporate leadership has been all the stronger in the unique context of Wall Street's "impatient" capital markets. Unlike Japan, where keiretsu partnerships with allied firms and banks help sustain faltering companies, or Germany, where long-term investments by banks and regional governments can provide patient capital, U.S. capital markets are driven by institutional investors with comparatively short-term horizons. Even GM, once a solid bet for long-term returns, has lost the confidence of many investors after the company's high-tech initiatives and divisional reorganizations of the 1980s fell flat.

With the 1991 recession, as GM's operating losses in North America ballooned towards $5 billion, CEO Robert Stempel tried to answer Wall Street critics of his previous "grow the business" strategy by announcing plans to close 21 plants and eliminate 74,000 jobs, 50,000 of them hourly UAW workers. There was little confidence, however, that Stempel would carry through with these cuts as quickly as investors demanded. In 1992, the outside directors on GM's board therefore engineered a sudden coup that removed Stempel and replaced him with Jack Smith, formerly of GM Europe. Smith's new team included the mercurial and unstable Ignacio Lopez, whose brief career at GM was marked by draconian demands that suppliers put all contracts up for rebidding and that they deliver dramatic productivity increases. After Lopez jumped to VW, GM's new get-tough approach was articulated by board Vice Chairman Harry Pearce, who publicly vowed to play hardball with the UAW. "If at the end of the day a plant can't deliver [world class] competitiveness," Pearce told the union, then "we owe it to our shareholders and our workers to look at outsourcing."[19]

---

[19] These events are summarized through 1992 in "General Motors at a Turning Point," International Metalworkers Federation and UAW Research Department, December 1992; Pearce quote

"The market feels that GM must downsize as quickly as possible," said stock analyst John Casea in 1992, echoing the demands of institutional investors across the board. UAW leaders, however, answer to workers rather than shareholders, and most workers (despite Pearce's claim to the contrary) would rather not be scapegoated by managers seeking a quick fix — outsourcing jobs— for long-term failures in the market place. Worker impatience with GM's inept leadership has mounted with each round of announced plant closings, particularly after 1994, when GM's North American Operations (NAO) were again profitable, and especially after 1995, when NAO profits topped $2.4 billion.[20] After 1990, new UAW leaders have also been more inclined to vent this skepticism in public. Steve Yokich, head of the UAW's GM Department (1989-1995) and, in 1995, President of the union, has contested a growing number of outsourcing initiatives while also moderating the union's previously unqualified support for labor-management cooperation.

This gathering confrontation over how fast and how far to proceed with downsizing has been fought most visibly in local bargaining rather than national negotiations. In 1993, GM did push at the national level for a new agreement that would permit the company to pay lower wages in GM parts plants, where competing nonunion suppliers and importers also pay lower wages. Failing to win the UAW's assent on this score, and seeking to avoid a national strike when the company was just recovering from the 1991-1992 recession, management has since pursued a plant-by-plant strategy of cost-cutting and lean production. In many such cases, the company can use its excess capacity and the threat, implied or otherwise, of plant closings to exert a powerful leverage on factory-level bargaining, playing one local against another in concessionary bidding for the remaining jobs. The union, however, has also been able to exert important leverage at the local level, particularly when an assembly plant makes a high-margin light truck, or a parts plant is the sole source for JIT deliveries. The latter, in particular, has made the union's time-worn strategy of "selective" strikes all the more powerful, since the impact of a work stoppage in a single one of these strategic plants can, with JIT, ripple outwards all the more rapidly.

The issues in each of the UAW's local strikes at GM have been framed in roughly the same way, as indicated in Table 2. From the standpoint of the union, lean production has too often improved productivity at the expense

---

in "'Labor Hawks': How UAW Strike Became Test Ground for GM's Resolve," *Wall Street Journal,* 18 March 1996, A1 and A8.

[20] *UAW Research Bulletin*, February-March 1996, 24.

of fewer jobs, cutting the plant workforce to the bare minimum and beyond, with intensified production standards, mandatory overtime, and more injuries the result. Since the national agreement permits local unions to call mid-contract strikes (subject to the national union's approval) over production standards, health and safety, and subcontracting, the local union can pressure management in these areas and link negotiations to related issues, including the need to hire more workers. The company, for its part, has routinely termed the union's local issues a smoke screen for calling a "strategic strike" that can disrupt operations throughout the company, thereby serving as a de facto "national" strike while only requiring the union to pay strike benefits in the single striking local; those laid off by the strike's ripple effect can qualify in most states for unemployment insurance.

These dynamics have been especially evident in GM parts plants, none more so than the two factories in Dayton, Ohio, that produce brake parts for 90 percent of GM's models. It is a measure of the contrasting circumstances of Ford and Chrysler that neither company makes its own Anti-lock Brake Systems (ABS), while GM produces its own components and sells them to competitors as well. It is this very fact of GM's vertical integration that draws the special concern of Wall Street, since many investors take it as a given that industrial corporations should jettison much of their internal parts capacity, as Ford and Chrysler did in their brush with bankruptcy in the early 1980s. Outsourcing appeals to crisis managers and institutional investors not simply because independent suppliers are likely to be nonunion and therefore pay lower wages, but also because such outsourcing can relieve the company of engineering costs and fixed capital investments if these, too, can be forced upon suppliers.[21]

---

[21] Estimates vary on the degree of vertical integration in Big Three companies. Industry consultant Jim Harbour estimated that GM-owned suppliers produce up to 70 percent of the company's parts, compared to in-house sourcing of 40 percent at Ford and 30 percent at Chrysler. See Glen Burkins, "UAW Strike Hit GM 'Just in Time' to Cripple Firm," *Wall Street Journal*, 14 March 1996, A10. The UAW counters that Harbour's estimates ignore, among other things, the fact that not all GM-produced parts go into GM cars —some are sold to competitors. According Dan Luria of the Industrial Technology Institute in Ann Arbor, in-house parts sourcing at GM, Ford, and Chrysler is, respectively, 43, 38, and 35 percent of the total. *UAW Research Bulletin* (summer 1997), 2.

Indeed, *dis*investment may *precede* outsourcing, and even be used to justify it. According to the union, this was precisely the scenario at Dayton.

Table 2
GM Local Strikes, 1990-1997

Year Plant	Products*	Issues**	Days on Strike: & Idled-Lost***	Strike Settlement
1990				
Flint-AC	Pts: engine/body	OS, PS, HS	6: 6 AP	OS postponed
1991				
Baltimore	Ass: minivans	PS, HS, H	26: 12,000 units	Hiring
Dayton	Pts: brakes/ABS	OS, PS 3: 2 AP		Hiring, new wk
1992				
Lordstown	Pts: stampings	C	9: 9-AP/43,000-w	OS postponed
Lansing	Ass: car bodies	PS, JC	4: $5 mil. profits	Vote tag relief
1994				
Shreveport	Ass: pickup trucks	PS	5: 2,600 units	
Dayton	Pts: brakes/ABS	OS, H	3: 6-AP/17,000-w	Hiring, invest
Tech Center	Engineering	OS, JC	5: New model dev.	Add 136 jobs
Anderson	Pts: lights/bumpers	OS	3: 15-AP	Jobs thru 1997
Flint-Buick	Engines and parts	OS, H	9: 4-AP/11,700-u	Hiring
Flint-AC	Gas tanks		5: 12-AP	
1995				
Flint-Delco	Pts: plugs/pumps	H	3: 9-AP/32,000-w	Hiring
Pontiac East	Ass: pickup trucks	PS, HS, H	6: 5,100 units	Add 3rd shift
1996				
Dayton	Pts: brakes/ABS	OS, HS, H	17: 26-AP/177,000-w	Hiring
Lordstown	Ass: compact cars	F	2: 2 shifts	Court injunction
Janesville	Ass: sport utility	PS, HS, H	8: 7,500 units	Hiring
Indianapolis	Pts: stampings	OS, H	5: 5-AP (trucks)	Hiring
1997				
Moraine	Ass: sport utility	Grievances	3: 6 10 hr. shifts	
Packard	Pts: wire harnesses	JC	1: 2 shifts	Job guarantees
Indiana	Ass: pickup trucks	PS, HS, H	14: 2 weeks prod.	Hiring
Oklahoma	Ass: cars	OS, PS, JC	50: 2 months prod.	No OS, hiring
Pontiac East	Ass: pickup trucks	PS, HS, H	87: 3 months prod.	Hiring
Warren	Transmissions	OS, H	5: 4-AP	No OS, hiring

Note: All strikes are UAW except Packard and Moraine in 1997; latter are International Union of Electrical workers. There were no local strikes in 1993.

* Pts = parts; Ass = assembly
** OS = Outsourcing; PS = Production Standards; HS = Health and Safety; H = Hiring; JC = Job Cuts; F = Firings. *Note:* These are highly simplified descriptions that don't include the many subsidiary issues over work rules, classifications, etc. Many issues are linked, for example, H = Hiring usually indicates excessive overtime and understaffing, which in turn are often related to PS and HS.
*** AP = assembly plants closed; w = workers idled in other plants; u = units lost.

Sources: *Automotive News, The New York Times, Wall Street Journal,* union publications, and interviews.

While GM had an early lead in ABS development, it was slow to invest in the next generation of electronic ABS technology, allowing competitors like Bosch to overtake it. Having surrendered its market lead, GM could argue by 1996 that outsourcing was "necessary" because it could not make certain sophisticated parts. The local union president at Dayton described it differently: "Our members are losing out due to GM's inability to provide new technology for the workers to compete."[22] The union saw "disinvestment" in Dayton as part of GM's plan to justify outsourcing to nonunion suppliers like Bosch that paid wages and benefits less than 40 percent of Big Three levels. By doing so, the company could also discipline a plant that had already struck over outsourcing and understaffing in 1991 and 1994, each time winning promises for future work and hiring that, according to the union, went unfulfilled.

Against this backdrop, the Dayton local went on strike again in 1996 over understaffing and the health-and-safety consequences of working 11-hour days for 6-7 days a week. This time, however, the union's militant actions collided head on with GM's equally militant defense of outsourcing and "lean management," a resolve backed by hefty cash reserves generated in the economic recovery since 1992. Investors rallied to the company's banner once Dayton's 3,200 workers went on strike, driving GM stock higher even as the strike's impact immediately rippled outward. After two weeks, 26 of GM's 29 assembly plants in North America had been starved of brake parts, choking off the entire JIT supply chain and idling nearly 180,000 GM workers in the U.S., Canada, and Mexico.[23]

The settlement that followed the 17-day strike was inconclusive for both sides. As in previous negotiations, the union won yet another promise that the company would hire more workers to ease workloads and retain certain work in house; the company got renewed commitments to continue improving productivity, and avoided further restrictions on outsourcing. At a cost of $500 million in lost sales during the strike, the price seemed high to many. Overall, the four GM local strikes in 1996 (Dayton, Lordstown, Janesville, and Indianapolis) over these and other issues cost the company $1.2 billion, second only (in real terms) to the total strike loses of 1970, when the last national GM strike occurred.[24]

---

[22] Rebecca Blumenstein and Nicole Christian, "Ohio Strike That is Crippling GM Plants Is Tied to Plan to Outsource Brake Work," *Wall Street Journal*, 12 March 1996, A10.

[23] Keith Bradsher, "General Motors and Union Agree to End Walkout," *New York Times*, 22 March 1996, D4.

[24] Keith Bradsher, "GM Says Profits Fell Throughout 1996," *The New York Times*, 29 January 1997, D4.

In the eyes of most analysts, the 1996 national negotiations that followed Dayton did not conclusively settle matters. GM's proposal that new hires be paid at 50 percent of the current rate and spend seven years progressing to full pay was rejected by the union as a potentially divisive wedge between incumbent and future workers, further aggravating morale problems that would rebound on both the company and the union. The company's stated preference for "by-name" job security that would only protect the jobs of incumbent workers was also rejected in favor of further elaboration of existing job security provisions. These now call for the company to maintain a total workforce equal to 95 percent of baseline employment at the start of the three-year agreement, replacing normal attrition below 95 percent on a one-for-one basis if certain conditions apply. Framed as a disincentive for further outsourcing, the agreement permits some flexibility in adjusting the formula to accommodate the future sale of parts plants, market fluctuations that require temporary layoffs, and lower-wage subsidiaries that count towards the 95 percent minimum (if their wages are above average and their products do not compete with GM's core business). While Ford and Chrysler signed equivalent master agreements with the UAW, the terms were seen as largely applying to GM, particularly its at-risk parts plants.[25]

CROSSING THE BORDER

While opinion differs on how the terms of the 1996 master agreement apply to case-by-case scenarios, there is little doubt that these job security provisions will slow the company's downsizing —but not stop it. In fact, declining sales, plant closings, the sale of parts subsidiaries, and early retirements have steadily winnowed GM's hourly workforce throughout the period when such provisions were introduced and strengthened, pushing the number downward from 397,000 workers in 1985 to 215,000 by 1996.[26] Local strikes have forced the company to hire more workers at understaffed plants, but these local battles have detoured, rather than halted, the overall course of GM's war on "waste." Further job cuts are likely as the company sells off more parts plants and promotes the enhanced early retirement incentives it has negotiated with the union.

---

[25] Jim Harbour, for one, termed the 1996 contract "a potential bomb" for GM. "Productivity is the Driver," *Automotive Industries*, November 1996, 16.

[26] 1985 employment figures from UAW Research Department, "Big Three Data From Annual Reports," 15 Aug. 1994 ; 1996 employment figures from Marjorie Sorge, "UAW/GM Bargain a Contract of Faith," *Automotive Industries*, December 1996, 83.

The Big Three that is emerging from these transformations retains a unionized core in final assembly and major components, especially drive trains, where unit labor costs are low and the demands for quality and flexibility are accommodated by well-entrenched collective bargaining regimes. Outside these islands of collective bargaining, however, is a widening sea of nonunion companies, from transplants and first-tier component manufacturers, to medium-scale suppliers of commodity parts or specialized technologies, to nonunion sweat shops that recall the worst conditions of the pre-UAW era.

How —or for that matter, whether— the lean production menu is negotiated in any of these sectors, rather than imposed, depends on thc UAW's capacity to organize these nonunion companies. If nonunion production continues to grow, so will the prospect that "lean production" will be driven by competitive pressures to something more akin to "anorexic production": cutting personnel to the bare minimum and forcing intensified labor on the surviving workforce; defining every second of rest as "idleness" and "waste;" and socializing hard-pressed team members to blame their intensified labor on medically restricted co-workers, absentees, and those who are just plain slower or weaker. Only a large-scale social movement devoted to organizing the unorganized can change these prospects and redefine worker solidarity in terms that give it genuine meaning —that an injury to any one worker driven to the outer limits of physical and psychic stress by "anorexic" production is understood as an injury to all workers who face the same prospect, sooner if not later in a global economy that favors deunionization.[27]

This traditional union imperative to "organize the unorganized" is daunting enough given the many advantages that companies can now exploit against unions in the U.S., from permanent replacement of strikers, to the increasing latitude —legal and illegal— that permits nonunion companies to intimidate, coerce, and fire union activists. It will be all the harder to crack this nonunion sector given the global arena in which multinational corporations now operate. GM is again a case in point. By 1996, the company's parts-making subsidiary, GM-Delphi, employed more workers in Mexico —63,000— than it employed in the United States.[28] While GM pays union wages of $18

[27] On "anorexic production", see Mike Parker and Jane Slaughter, "Unions and Management by Stress," in Steve Babson, ed., *Lean Work: Empowerment and Exploitation in the Global Auto Industry* (Detroit: Wayne State University Press, 1995), 41-53.

[28] Neal Templin, "GM Strike Hits Mexican Output As Talks on Settlement Resume," *Wall Street Journal*, 20 March 1996, A3, A-

an hour in the U.S., its parts workers in Mexico have no independent union and are paid little more than $1 an hour, with real wages declining rapidly since 1994. Pay levels are only marginally higher in the growing number of Mexican assembly plants operated by the Big Three, VW, Nissan, Mercedes Benz, and Honda, where lean production is a unilateral agenda imposed from above.

Because Mexican wages are kept artificially low as a matter of government policy and outright repression, most Mexican workers cannot afford to buy the 1.3 million vehicles assembled annually in Mexico —and so the majority are exported north of the border. Consequently, U.S. and Canadian workers are now "benchmarked" against their Mexican counterparts, with each of the Big Three sourcing the same models from both sides of the border: as of 1996, GM made the Cavalier, Sunbird, Cutlass, Cierra, Suburban, and Chevy/GMC pickup in Mexico and the U.S.; Ford made the Escort, Tracer, Contour, Mystique, and F-Series truck in both countries; and Chrysler did the same with the Neon, Sebring, Cirrus, Stratus, and Dodge Ram trucks.

With auto production now so firmly established on a North American basis, national unions can only raise the standards of work and of living in any single country by raising them in North America as a whole. As Don Wells argues later in this volume, the choice for workers is between a new kind of internationalism that links the labor movements of Mexico, Canada, and the U.S., or a "new feudalism built around workers' loyalty to 'their' firms." It is in this context that worker solidarity needs to cross the very borders which corporate capital already straddles.

GLOSSARY

SOCIAL ORGANIZATION

Continuous Improvement. Rather than accept scripted tasks and perform them without question, workers are expected to identify improvements that *eliminate waste* and enhance *quality in station.* Suggestions are passed upwards to plant engineers and supervisors who decide whether to implement suggestions.

Cross Training. To permit *flexible assignment,* workers are trained to perform related tasks in their particular work area or trade.

Eliminate Waste. "Waste" is defined as any process or activity that does not add value to the product, such as scrap, repair work, downtime, waiting for parts, or walking between tasks. Rest and recovery time are also considered "waste" by many managers.

Flexible Assignment. Many specialized job classifications that limit the availability or willingness of workers to perform tasks outside their designated duties are replaced with generalized classifications. Fewer workers are needed as specialized classifications are eliminated and their tasks distributed to *cross-trained* workers.

Kaizen. The Japanese term for *continuous improvement.*

Orientation. New hires and transfers learn the social and technical organization of the workplace, often with a heavy emphasis on themes and *symbols of enterprise solidarity.*

Quality Circles. "QCs" are off-line groups of workers who volunteer to participate in *continuous improvement* projects focused on quality and productivity.

Quality in Station. Rather than pass defective work along, each worker is expected to fix the problem or stop the process and call for assistance via the *Andon.* Fewer inspectors and repair workers are needed, and problems are identified at their source.

Screening/ Selection of Workers. Workers are tested for skills, aptitudes, and attitudes that are suited to *continuous improvement, flexible assignment, SPC,* and *work teams.* In nonunion plants, they may also be screened for union sentiments.

SPC. "Statistical Process Control" is a quality-control methodology of sampling for variations from a specified standard.

Standardized Work. To minimize variation from quality standards and to maximize "minutes worked per hour," workers are expected to follow detailed task instructions posted near their work stations. These can be amended by *continuous improvement.*

Symbols of Enterprise Solidarity. To promote the idea of a shared commitment to *continuous improvement,* workers and managers use the same parking lots, eat in the same cafeteria, and in some cases (usually nonunion plants) are obligated to wear the same uniform.

Work Teams. Unlike voluntary and off-line *quality circles,* work teams are on-line groups of workers in a particular area who are held responsible for certain day-to-day decisions and tasks. Teams may be, by degrees, "worker centered" or "supervisor centered." (See Figure 2.)

TECHNICAL ORGANIZATION

Andon. The Andon (Japanese for "lamp") is a *visual control* device consisting of a large electronic display board mounted above the work area. As workers responsible for *quality in station* pull a cord signaling a problem, colored lights on the Andon identify the location of the work station. Other indicators may include parts re-supply, equipment status, and a real-time digital readout of units produced.

Assembly Line. As developed by Henry Ford, the assembly line pulls the work past stationary workers who are each responsible for a detailed, repetitive task.

Cell Manufacturing. Rather than group machines by specialized function and move work-in-process from one department to the next, in a cell machines are grouped by process so that the work passes immediately from one machine to the next, reducing inventory and material handling.

Design for Manufacture. To reduce build time, the product is designed to simplify the assembly process, often by reducing the number of parts.

Error Proofing. Designing the work process in such a way that human error is minimized.

Flexible Equipment. Computer-controlled devices —for example, robots— can be programmed for a variety of tasks, replacing the "hard tooling" designed for a single specialized task.

JIT. "Just-in-time" is a *pull system* of production that emphasizes small-lot delivery of parts as they are needed, rather than "just-in-case" stockpiling of parts that ties up working capital and conceals possible quality problems.

Kanban. "Kanban cards" are used in the *JIT / Pull System* developed by Toyota; as one batch of parts is used up, the Kanban (Japanese for "signboard") that identifies the part is posted near the work station as a signal (*visual control*) to material handling that a new batch is needed.

Modular Assembly. To simplify final assembly, whole components can be delivered to the line as pre-assembled "modules" — for example, whole instrument panels. Modular assembly is often linked with *outsourcing.*

Outsourcing. Rather than make components or modules "in-house," some work is sourced to outside suppliers with specialized capabilities and/or lower costs, including wages.

Preventive Maintenance. To reduce downtime, machinery is routinely serviced and upgraded, rather than waiting until there is a breakdown to schedule repairs.

Pull System. Rather than schedule production to meet supply targets, production is scheduled according to customer demand, thereby reducing the amount of working capital devoted to inventory.

Supplier Integration. While *outsourcing* moves more work outside the firm, supplier integration links these suppliers to the customer by requiring them to deliver on *JIT* schedules, to take on design work, and to meet quality and productivity standards.

Supermarket Inventory. Parts are stored in small lots near the assembly area and can be accessed directly as needed, rather than warehousing them in separate departments.

Visual Controls. These include *Andon*, *Kanban*, yellow lights, and other visual (or audio) devices that signal the need for assistance, re-supply, or equipment problems.

INVESTMENT STRATEGIES AND "LEANER" PRODUCTION IN THE NORTH AMERICAN AUTO INDUSTRY

Ronald S. Blum[*]

> *The fact that activities require time is seen as waste. As a consequence, a continuous battle is waged against the constraints of space and time; acceleration is therefore the imperative which rules technological innovation as well as the little gestures of everyday life.*
>
> Wolfgang Sachs
> in *Wasting Time is An Ecological Virtue*

INTRODUCTION

Daily newspapers regularly report announcements of company investments in new plants, along with the number of jobs to be created and the money spent. Behind such announcements are a series of management decisions that flow from some strategy. For example, build the plant on the site of an existing one or go elsewhere? Go to a rural or an urban area? Set up in a traditionally unionized area or in an open-shop state? Build domestically or go over the border?

A company considering such decisions may also want to implement changes in the production system at another of its plants. Workers there are urged to "move forward together and forget the past," and are told of investments to be made if all accept what are to be commonly held objectives. Alternatives are then put on the table —recognized as events that occur if this common understanding is not reached. It's suggested that under the alternative plan, another kind of newspaper report may be printed: of work outsourced, or maybe the whole plant closed.

This kind of scenario is common in the North American auto industry, where the restructuring of the last two decades has occurred in the context of the calamitous early 1980s recession, the large and persistent trade deficits of these years, the entry of foreign transplants, a continued continent-wide integration of production, and a stream of new technologies. Overlaying this vast restructuring has been management's evolving strategy towards workers. Some elements of this strategy —like outsourcing, speed-up, and resisting unions— are as old as the industry itself and are still clearly being exploited today. Others, like just-in-time delivery and modular assembly, are of more recent vintage.

---

[*] Economist, UAW Research Department. Responsibility for content remains solely that of the author.

Whether it be the older or newer strategic elements, management strategies are designed to meet the objective of maximizing return on investment. This has meant a continued drive to cut costs and boost productivity —to drive down unit labor costs. Hourly workers have been the primary target, with the effect for some being leaner wages and/or working conditions, and for others, unemployment.

With the development of "lean production" practices, management has added powerful new strategic elements, related to capital allocation and work organization. Through just-in-time (JIT) inventory systems that keep inventories to a minimum, a scarcity of working capital is purposefully created on an *ongoing and regular* operating basis. To alleviate this intentional shortage, "continuous improvement" essentially stresses saving cash in the form of higher worker productivity and reduced material inputs. When combined with other elements of management strategy, the outcome is definitely "leaner" for workers.

Implementing these strategies often hinges on decisions of where, when and how much capital to invest. Simply put, management can attempt to leverage its investment decisions to extract varied types of concessions from workers, communities and governments. The role that investment decisions play in the drive to lower unit labor costs can take a number of forms. There can be an actual or threatened shift of work to lower-wage producers; or fixed investment in plant and equipment can be withdrawn, withheld, or put into labor-displacing automation. Whichever form, these *periodic* management decisions have long-term impacts that can be targeted at a particular plant, department, or piece of machinery —and at the workers employed there. Such leverage has been used over the last decade to implement "leaner" production, with its intentional scarcity of working capital and other resources.

This paper takes a looks at management strategies with regard to workers in the North American auto industry, and the outcomes of investment decisions. A logical place to start is with the objectives that guide management and the accounting and financial methods required to gauge performance. The next section lays out these objectives and methods, and shows how the logic of lean production has been incorporated into them. Section 3 looks at these relationships over time, and provides some evidence of their outcomes. Finally, if management leverages investment decisions to implement its strategies, we would expect to see this reflected in certain patterns of production and employment. Section 4 looks at these patterns, first in a historic profile of assembly capacity in the U.S., Canada and Mexico, and then by a more detailed mapping of assembly and parts-making activity. The final section draws some conclusions, and points to possible future management strategies regarding workers.

MANAGEMENT OBJECTIVES, MEASUREMENT AND CONTROL

To understand management investment strategies, it is necessary to first look at management objectives, and how performance towards their achievement is measured. Fundamentally, management's objective is centered on maximizing returns on the capital which owners have invested. Various measures of return on investment (ROI) are used to set financial goals, gauge performance, and decide on investments. Additionally, in order for management to effectively control operations, it must also be able to gauge performance down to the point of production on a timely basis. Cost accounting systems serve this role. The choice of ROI measures and cost accounting systems should therefore reflect management's evolving strategy toward workers.

Cost accounting is the part of a company's financial system that provides management with data to cost a plant's product, and monitor and control production. It therefore provides a perspective on how work is organized. Under mass production, standard cost accounting systems in use for decades classify hourly workers as either "direct labor," like assemblers, or "indirect labor," including skilled trades. To calculate the cost of a plant's product, a large pool of overhead or indirect costs (including indirect labor) must be allocated. A key method is to apply a rate of "burden" to direct labor. In the world of high-volume production with dedicated machinery, scale economies are critical, and pushing more product out the door means less overhead per unit. To avoid disruption of production, large buffers of inventories were maintained (until recent years) on a "just-in-case" basis. Organization of production and accounting methods of this type reflect a supply-push logic.

Starting in the mid-1980s, developments in cost accounting and financial controls began to incorporate the logic of lean production. Management adopted new cost accounting methods called activity-based costing (ABC), to supplement the standard methods. Central to this system is the definition of numerous separate and identifiable pools of indirect costs, each associated with an "activity" —say quality testing or machine setup— in place of the large pool of overhead costs under standard cost accounting methods. Each activity, in turn, is viewed as requiring inputs of "resources," meaning labor, material, capital and space. When a customer orders a product, the cost of manufacturing is built up from the costs of specified activities and the resources they require. In this way, ABC mirrors a demand-pull system.

Two differences between standard and ABC accounting methods have particular relevance to management strategies regarding workers. First, under the older standard system, cost reduction activities are almost entirely management driven, and so minimal accounting information is shared with workers. In contrast, under ABC workers are surrounded by accounting data, with trends in performance "metrics" posted at workstations and scoreboards throughout the plant. These metrics quantify "cost drivers", relating the costs of products to activities, and activities to resources. Workers are trained to concentrate on reducing cost drivers by a process called "continuous improvement."

Emphasis is placed throughout the company on minimizing "non-value-added-activity," defined in one training manual as a "designation [that] reflects a belief that the activity can be redesigned, reduced or eliminated without reducing the quantity, responsiveness, or quality of the output required by the customer or the organization."[1] One result of this thinking is the blurring of lines between direct and indirect labor, whereby the former get assigned portions of the latter's work, common to many team-based forms of work organization.

A second difference concerns management's ability to dissect the costs and returns of manufacturing a product. Think of a manufacturing plant as a collection of operations —such as stamping, machining and assembly— in which the workforce adds value to purchased materials. Value-added is equal to a product's sale or transfer price, minus costs of purchased materials used to manufacture it. In this way, a plant —or for that matter, a company or industry— can be seen as a value-added chain, or alternatively, from a management perspective, as a series of make-versus-buy sourcing decisions based on rates of return on investment.

The capacity to analyze and decompose value-added chains is somewhat limited in standard accounting systems because overhead and indirect costs are grouped into large undifferentiated pools that must be allocated. This complicates make-versus-buy analyses. With ABC, separate identifiable cost pools centered around activities allow for a detailed cost matrix to be constructed that can be cut any number of ways —by "cost object" (meaning product or part), activity, and/or resource. Such data are used to establish multiple separate "business units," each of which must compete with outside suppliers to meet specified ROI targets in order to qualify for more resources. Facilitating this process are powerful corporate information systems utilizing network-based hardware and relational database software to gather, analyze, and disseminate accounting data.

What do these differences between costing systems signify for work organization and workers? They signify a shift from strictly top-down management driven processes aimed at lowering unit labor costs, to forms of work organization designed to get workers themselves to participate. Possessing a more fine-tuned

[1] UAW General Motors Department, "Appendix L, Financial Training for Sourcing Decisions: The Cost to Manufacture Versus the True Cost of Acquisition," 1991.

ability to financially map out a company's value-added chain allows management to more easily divvy up the chain to strategically determine those "business units" to receive investment versus those to be spun-off, what work to outsource or in-source, and how to use suppliers to create maximum pressure on in-house workers. This kind of targeting potentially impacts all workers along the company's supply chain, especially given the spread of just-in-time inventory, modularization of vehicle systems, tiering of suppliers, and contract workers.

Ultimately, management judges any cost accounting system by its usefulness in meeting the primary objective of maximizing return on investment. One standard ROI measure is net return on equity (see ratio in Figure 1). This is equal to after-tax profits divided by stockholders' equity (assets minus liabilities), meaning the capital that owners have invested at some point in time. Equity is one source of financing ownership of assets, the other being debt owed creditors. The relative amount of equity and debt determines a company's capital structure. In pursuing the ROI objective, management —and Wall Street— focus on increasing earnings per share, which pushes up the stock price, boosting executive compensation tied to the stock. The nature of this pursuit has changed over recent decades, eventually incorporating lean production logic. What specifically has changed is the way assets are managed, and how they are financed, called capitalization.

For example, in the 1960s and 70s, conglomerates were being formed and capitalized primarily through equity. If a conglomerate could boost its ROI by acquiring a company with a superior ROI, those assets became a target, regardless of size or industry. The conglomerate's rising stock price attracted additional equity which was then used to finance further acquisitions. Then in the early 1980s, leveraged buyouts (LBOs) came on the scene, with capitalization almost entirely in the form of debt. Companies were taken private by highly leveraged financing of assets purchased with junk bonds. Plant-level assets were then sold, closed or consolidated, with the remaining workers squeezed, all to generate cash for tax-deductible interest payments to junk bond holders. Finally, the company went public again though a stock sale, with management and junk bond issuers reaping astronomical returns on their small initial equity investments.

Essential to the LBO strategy is maximizing the cash generated from assets in order to pay interest owed on junk bonds. With only a token amount of equity invested, the need to service a huge debt acts like a giant wringer forcing liquid capital to be squeezed out of assets. In other words, a relative scarcity of equity capital acts as a drive incentive to increase cash flow. In this way, the LBO strategy has a strong parallel with lean production. This should be no surprise given lean production's roots in the Toyota Production System, originally designed to meet the exigencies of capital scarcity in postwar Japan.

ROI measures have been adjusted to capture this logic. One such measure is net return on non-cash assets (see ratio in Figure 2). By excluding cash from this ratio's denominator, and tying management compensation to it, management is rewarded for reducing capital usage as a means of boosting return on investment. This can take the form of converting assets into cash, with inventories a prime example. Rather than maintain a large inventory which is turned less frequently, inventories are cut to a bare minimum and turned more frequently, as is true for just-in-time systems. In effect, working capital to finance daily operations is made more scarce, and the resulting lack of buffers in turn creates pressure on the workforce to eliminate so-called "non-value-added activities." Return on non-cash assets, like ABC, directs attention to squeezing cash out of the production process and moving it to the bottom line.

Management's goal is to repeat the conversion cycle as frequently and as fast as possible: using minimum cash to make the product, collecting maximum cash on its sale, then starting the cycle again. Less cash —meaning less capital and associated costs— is used to generate more profits, which are turned over to shareholders via dividends, stock buyback programs and higher stock prices. Workers, meanwhile, must do more with less. What this boils down to is a drive to increase owners' share of value-added relative to the share going to workers. Value-added for a company or industry as a whole is equal to payments made to all factors of production; that is wages, salaries, profit, interest and rent. One factor's gain often means another's loss, despite ample talk about "win-win" possibilities.

MANAGEMENT STRATEGIES IN PURSUIT OF OBJECTIVES

In the auto industry, the segment of the value-added chain dependent on skilled and production workers runs from the initial vehicle concept to the final delivery of the finished vehicle to the customer. Management aims to pull out as much value as possible from this part of the chain, while minimizing capital use and shifting risk from owners to employees and suppliers.[2] Strategies to increase owners' share of value-added have of course been around from the beginning, but a particular set of strategies intensified in the 1970s.

In the 1960s, all light vehicles built in North America were made by unionized workers. Union density was high throughout the value-added chain; that is, at both the vertically integrated domestic assemblers and their suppliers. However,

---

[2] The ongoing consolidation and restructuring of the dealership network is evidence of an extended effort to pull value out of the distributional part of the value-added chain running from the time of new vehicle purchase, to used vehicle resale, to eventual scrappage.

fissures that management could exploit began to appear. In 1962, for example, U.S. customs regulations established duty-free importation of U.S. components sent abroad for processing or assembly (TSUS items 806.30 and 807.00). In 1965, the Mexican government instituted the Border Industrialization Program that gave rise to the maquiladoras, following the end of the U.S. bracero program the year before. Then the first oil shock hit in 1973, providing market inroads to smaller, fuel-efficient vehicles built overseas.

Figure 1
ROI and Lean Strategies #1*

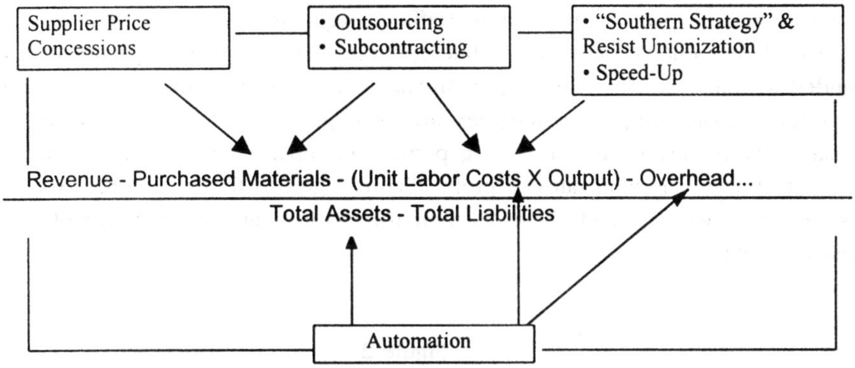

* Figure shows probable direct effects of strategy on ROI.

U.S.-based automakers responded with strategies that weren't necessarily new in their particulars, but which together represented a more concerted threat to North American autoworkers. The strategies included outsourcing and subcontracting work to lower-wage suppliers, marked by shifts to southern open-shop states and to maquiladora plants in northern Mexico; speeding up the pace of assembly lines; demanding price concessions from suppliers; and increasing the rate of automation. From the point of view of workers impacted by these actions, referring to such strategies as "lean" isn't a misnomer. Figure 1 illustrates how these elements— categorized as Lean Strategies #1— contributed to management's objective.

With the second oil shock later in the 1970s, along with double-digit interest rates and continued growth of imports from Japan, the U.S. auto industry was sent reeling. Widespread layoffs, plant closings and bankruptcies swept the industry in the early 1980s. By 1982, U.S. production had fallen a crippling 45 percent from the 1978 level, with a 30 percent drop occurring in 1979-80 alone. With trade tensions running high, the first transplant started up in 1982. Others followed, eventually putting in place a cumulative total of four million units of assembly capacity in North America.

During the subsequent recovery of the industry, North American management began their push to implement elements of demand-pull production systems. In essence, management expanded its set of strategies designed to pull value out of the industry's value-added chain, going well beyond outsourcing of work to lower-wage suppliers. Work pace has been intensified for many workers in the industry by eliminating inventory buffers, moving to just-in-time systems, and reorganizing work to increase management's flexibility at the expense of worker control over the pace of production. Staffing levels are kept at a minimum with heavier dependence on overtime, while operating hours of existing plants are extended to minimize new capital investment. In addition to actively resisting unionization, more supplier companies are willing to invest in outright union-busting, by forcing strikes and using permanent replacement workers in an attempt to boost long-term rates of profit. Figure 2 groups these elements together as Lean Strategies #2, and illustrates their role with regard to management's adjusted objective.

Figure 2
ROI and Lean Strategies #2*

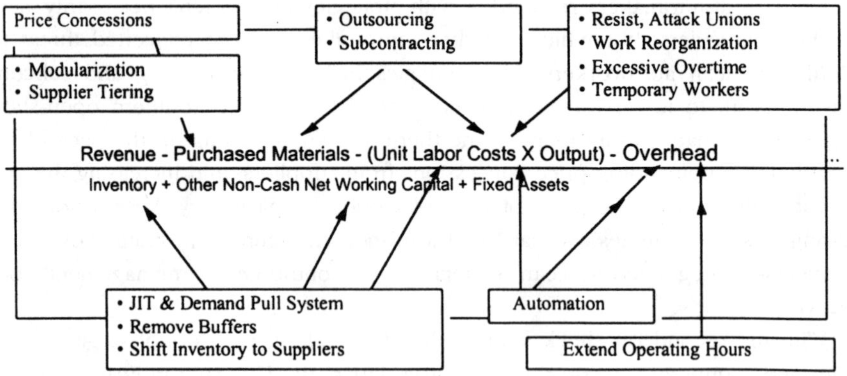

* Figure shows probable direct effects of strategy on ROI..

In recent years, companies all along the value-added chain have tried to implement lean strategies to one extent or another, and this is expected to continue. To boost shareholders' portion of value-added, some have crafted and executed long-term concerted plans utilizing all the elements of Lean Strategies #2, regardless of how great the toll paid by workers and communities. Whatever the extent, it is in general the huge multinational companies that sit atop of the industry's value-added chain —whether they be based in the U.S., Japan or Europe— that disproportionately benefit from such strategies. And as one goes down the chain from OEM assemblers, through the tiers of suppliers, the value-added left to be distributed tends to shrink.

Evidence for this is indicated by sectoral trends in value-added that goes to factors of production other than labor, on a per-hour-worked basis. For the U.S. auto industry (SIC 371), this rate nearly doubled between 1981 and 1994, after adjusting for inflation, from about $18 to almost $34 per hour worked. However, as Figure 3 illustrates, the distribution across sectors varies widely. For vehicle assembly and body operations (SIC 3711), the rate jumped by more than 200 percent, from $19 to $58 per hour worked. For major components (SIC 3714), the rate rose by about 25 percent in real terms, from almost $18 to just over $22 per hour. Meanwhile, the rate for stamping and trim (SIC 3465) adjusted for inflation actually declined by 14 percent, from $14 down to $12 per hour worked.[4]

Figure 3
Value-Added Minus Labor Compensation*
Per Hour Worked, By U.S. Sector

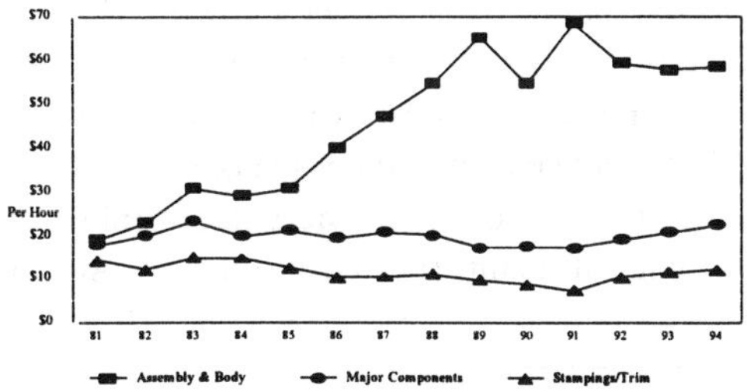

* Adjusted for inflation

[4] Variation in relative capital intensity across sectors can lead to differences in their ratio of value-added minus labor compensation to hours worked. However, it is unlikely that the relative capital intensities of SIC 3711, 3714 and 3465 have diverged enough over the period to explain much of the sharply different trends of the graphed ratio for the three SIC sectors.

INVESTMENT AND EMPLOYMENT OUTCOMES

The current geographic profile of North American auto-related production is the result of a very complex historical process, reflecting the continent's diverse development of economic, political and social structures. At one level, it is the cumulative outcome of a myriad of investment decisions.[4] From this vantage point, the current geographic profile provides some evidence of past and current management efforts to implement lean strategies, in the context of changes in government policies and worker counter-strategies.

Before turning to the current profile, a brief historical overview of final assembly capacity follows. Mapping the regional development of light vehicle final assembly capacity over time is a reasonable starting point since these operations sit atop the production value-added chain. Moreover, the location of assembly plants influences to varying degrees the location of manufacturing operations situated lower on the supply chain. To do this mapping, a time series of currently operating and closed assembly plants in the U.S., Canada and Mexico was constructed. Data for each plant included location, year established, year closed if applicable, and maximum capacity attained. Each country was divided into two or more geographic regions (see Appendix 1 for regional designations).[5]

At the onset of the 1950s, there were already almost 9 million units of assembly capacity in place in the U.S., increasing to 14 million by the mid-1960s with all but about 4.5 million units located in the Midwest, as shown at the top of Figure 4. The balance was evenly disbursed between the South and the coasts. This state of affairs held until the 1970s when General Motors attempted a "southern strategy" with several plants established in open-shop states. Aside from a Volkswagen plant put up in 1978, all the facilities were owned by U.S. companies. Major changes, however, began in the 1980s after the severe drop in domestic production. Construction of Japanese transplant capacity in the South and Midwest accelerated while Big Three midwestern and coastal operations closed.

Canadian capacity stood at just over one million units until the Auto Pact was negotiated in 1965, with all plants located in Ontario. Auto Pact terms, which in-

---

[4] See James M. Rubenstein, *The Changing U.S. Auto Industry -- Geographical Analysis* (New York: Routledge, 1992) for further discussion.

[5] U.S. regions correspond to categories used by the Bureau of Labor Statistics. Canadian and Mexican regions represent groupings of provinces and states that take account of the economic geography of each country's auto industry over time. Capacity additions and closures are accounted for at the maximum capacity attained. In other words, expansions of already operating plants are not shown. The effect is to show some capacity coming on stream earlier than actually occurred.

cluded safeguard requirements on minimum ratios for production to sales, and Canadian value-added to sales, helped draw more than a million additional units of Big Three capacity to Ontario, with a GM plant and a small Volvo assembly operation constructed in the eastern provinces. Another boost in capacity began in the mid-1980s with the arrival of the Japanese transplants and a new Chrysler plant, partially offset by later GM and Chrysler closings.

In Mexico, the government's import substitution strategy of the early 1960s was an early impetus to the build up of assembly capacity. The Auto Industrialization Program triggered construction of a number of assembly operations by the Big Three, VW and Nissan, pushing total capacity up to one million units. Assembly and engine capacity was added after the 1977 Auto Decree strengthened local content and trade balancing requirements. More additions followed the 1989 decree which promoted integration of Mexican production into the continental structure.[6] By the second half of the 1980s, Mexico's export orientation intensified when VW shuttered its U.S. plant, shifting the work to Puebla, and Ford established an export-only small car assembly operation in northern Mexico. The latter plant was one of three constructed in the region after 1980, along with GM's Ramos Arizpe plant in 1981, and the recent Chrysler truck plant in Saltillo built in 1995, after the passage of NAFTA. GM's large truck operation in Silao is another recently built plant coinciding with NAFTA. Meanwhile, GM shuttered the much smaller Mexico City plant in 1996, shifting its work to Silao.[7]

Turning now to the current geographic profile of the industry, there is a clear divergence between the regional distribution of final assembly capacity and parts sector employment, as indicated in Figure 5. Note that this compares assembly capacity measured in vehicle units, with parts sector employment measured in jobs. Use of the former measure emphasizes the geographic aspect of the locational decision. This allows us to ask what impact management's decision on the location of assembly capacity has had on the relative distribution of parts jobs, bearing in mind effects of the variation in relative labor-to-capital ratios across regions.

[6] Limited importation of fully built-up units was permitted, together with provisions that promoted production for export and the regional integration of the national industry.

[7] Wages that GM paid workers at the new Silao plant ranged from 4 to 13 pesos per hour in 1996, with very few workers at the top end of the scale. In comparison, wages at the now closed Mexico City plant ranged from 6 to 12 pesos *ten years ago*. Silao's wages are therefore lower than those paid a decade earlier in Mexico City, even before adjusting for inflation that has significantly reduced workers' purchasing power.

Figure 4
Assembly Capacity by Region

U.S. Assembly Capacity by Region

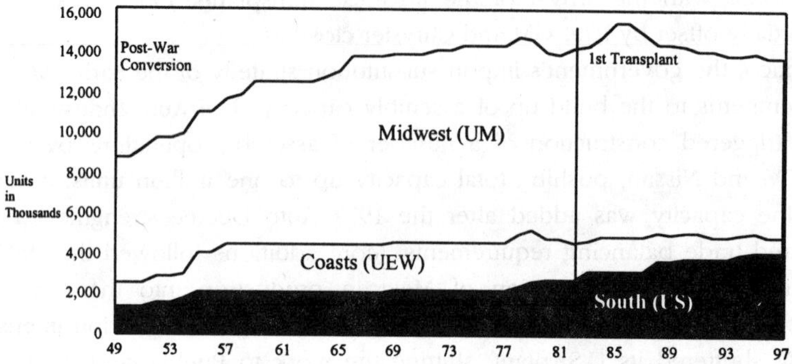

Canadian Assembly Capacity by Region

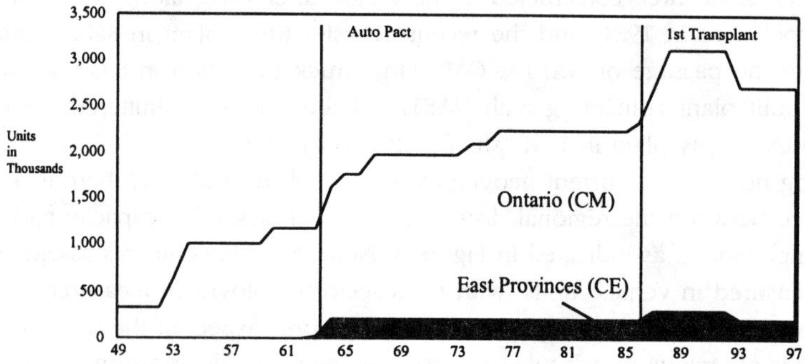

Mexican Assembly Capacity by Region

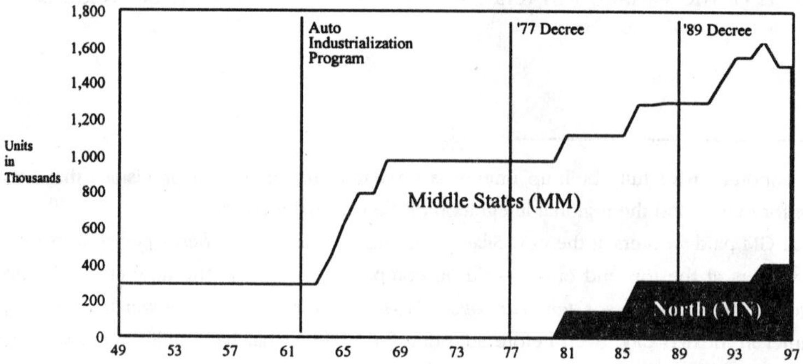

To more fully answer this question, however, it is necessary to disaggregate the data. Therefore, separate regional distributions are shown in Table 1 for Big Three and transplant assembly capacity. For parts, separate regional distributions are provided for jobs at original equipment manufacturing (OEM) parts plants owned by the assemblers (also referred to as captive parts operations), and for independent parts suppliers (IPS). The OEM and IPS distributions are then each further broken down into five separate vehicle component systems (see Appendix 2 for system designations).

The analysis required plant-level data that included location, employment and parts produced. For a continent-wide sample of parts plants, the *Elm Guide* database was used, with checks against other data sources. There were 2,483 plants in the IPS sample with average employment of 339 workers per plant. For the OEM sample, the number of plants totaled 222 with average plant employment of 1,503 workers. The former sample represents primarily first- and second-tier suppliers, and is likely biased toward larger plants. Although this means that the sample does not provide the best estimate of the entire IPS plant population, it does provide a good estimate of those suppliers closest to the assemblers on the value-added chain, and therefore those with the next most leverage after assemblers. Because the OEM sample captures nearly all of the population, it is expected to give an unbiased estimate of the OEM sector.

As shown in Figure 5, the midwestern United States (designated UM) accounts for the largest share of continent-wide assembly capacity with 49 percent, as well as of parts employment, with a 45 percent share. The southern region of the U.S. (denoted US) has the second largest share of each, 23 and 18 percent, respectively. In general, the U.S. distributions reflect both the importance of the Midwest as the historical center of North American auto manufacturing, as well as the later shift of investment towards the open-shop states of the South.

Canada's mid-region (CM) —also part of the industry's historical center— has a continent-wide share of assembly capacity of 14 percent, double its parts employment share of 7 percent. This pattern reflects the outcome of companies' investment strategies that take into account government policies, relative labor costs, market size, as well as other factors. Auto Pact provisions partly explain Canada's skewed distribution toward assembly. Another possible influence is the monetary difference between the social wage paid autoworkers, and labor costs that companies incur. This difference is probably greatest for workers at Canada's assembly operations —due in part to the success of Canada's national health care system.

Figure 5
Regional Shares of North American Assembly Capacity
vs. Parts Employment

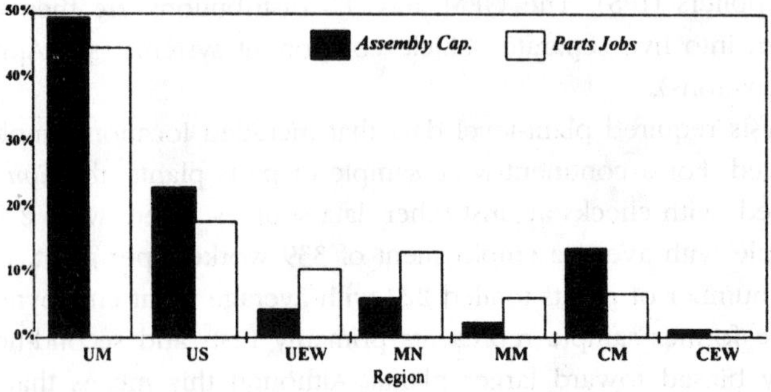

For Mexico's northern region (MN), the opposite of Canada's pattern is seen, as its continent-wide assembly capacity share of 6 percent is less than half its parts employment share of 13 percent. Mexico's skewed distribution towards parts manufacturing mostly reflects the Big Three U.S. automakers' huge investment in the maquiladoras, where autoworkers are paid abysmally low wages and provided minimal, if any benefits. That investment accelerated after the mid-1980s debt crisis which drastically cut the real wages of Mexican workers.

Disaggregated assembly data in Table 1 shows that transplant capacity is skewed towards the southern regions compared to the Big Three. More than half of the combined continent-wide capacity of GM, Ford and Chrysler is located in the mid-U.S. states, a fifth in southern states, and 14 percent in Ontario. In contrast, the transplants have almost equal thirds in the Midwest and southern U.S. states, with 13 percent shares each in Ontario and the mid-region of Mexico. That many foreign automakers have chosen to invest and locate greenfield transplant operations in rural areas and/or southern open-shop states, and have actively resisted North American unions —despite having unionized workforces at home— clearly points to union-avoidance as part of their management strategy.

IPS jobs are also relatively more skewed to the south than the OEM sector. The estimates show that 61 percent of OEM jobs are in the mid-U.S. region versus 38 percent of IPS jobs. However, for the combined southern U.S. and northern Mexico regions, 23 percent of continent-wide OEM jobs are located there, compared to a significantly higher 34 percent for IPS. It is important to bear in mind that the

IPS group includes Japanese, German, British and French-owned suppliers that began to establish component manufacturing operations in North America in the early 1980s. Many took a southern route —as is, of course, true for a number of U.S. and Canadian-owned suppliers.

Regional distributions by component system provide additional detail. Both powertrain and body systems are skewed towards the U.S. Midwest. This reflects the preponderance of OEM engine, transmission and stamping operations serving Big Three assembly operations. Overall, powertrain and body systems have experienced relatively less outsourcing than the other three vehicle system groups. Economies of scale, large fixed investments, a highly skilled workforce, and union leverage, among other factors, underlie this pattern. Some key IPS powertrain suppliers in the sample include Dana, Eaton, and Federal Mogul. For body systems, there's also a significant IPS share in Ontario, reflecting Magna. Budd is prominent both there and in the mid-U.S. region.

The story differs somewhat for the other three component systems. First, outsourcing has been a more significant factor,[8] and second, there is a regional skew to the south. Interior systems most closely mirror the distribution of assembly capacity among the five groups, not surprising since suppliers such as Lear and Johnson Controls have set up nearby plants to deliver seats on a just-in-time basis. However, there is a relatively large share of interior system jobs in northern Mexico. Big Three operations in such towns as Juarez and Matamoros, as well as suppliers such as TRW and Allied Signal produce safety restraint components, with others building seating and other interior trim components.

While OEM chassis system jobs are concentrated in the midwestern U.S. region (including GM Delphi-C operations), the share of IPS jobs in the Midwest and southern U.S. regions are even at 36 percent each. Note that the IPS distribution resembles that of transplant assembly capacity. Some of the main suppliers include Robert Bosch, Lucas-Varity, Dana, Tower and the tire manufacturers.

Finally, for electrical-electronic systems, northern Mexico accounts for the largest percentage of the sector's continent-wide OEM and IPS jobs. The former includes GM Packard Electric and Delphi-E, and the latter includes the independent wiring harness assemblers such as American Yazaki (which owns formerly spun-off Chrysler operations). Investment by the U.S. Big Three automakers and top-tier suppliers in the maquiladoras is the primary factor behind this pattern.

---

[8] Some evidence for this is provided by comparing the ratio of OEM and IPS shares. Caution is necessary in interpreting the results, however, since there is significant variation in sample coverage. Therefore, the relative ranking of the ratios, not their absolute value, is most useful.

Table 1
Regional Distribution of Assembly Capacity and Parts Jobs

		Region						
		UM	**US**	**UEW**	**MN**	**MM**	**CM**	**CEW**
Assembly Capacity	All	49%	23%	4%	6%	2%	14%	1%
	Big 3	54%	21%	3%	3%	4%	14%	1%
	Transpl	31%	33%	10%	0%	13%	13%	0%
Parts Jobs	All	45%	18%	11%	13%	6%	7%	1%
	OEM	61%	8%	7%	15%	5%	4%	0%
	IPS	38%	22%	12%	12%	7%	8%	1%
Powertrain	OEM	66%	7%	6%	7%	7%	8%	0%
	IPS	54%	15%	9%	8%	8%	7%	0%
Body Systems	OEM	82%	3%	5%	2%	8%	0%	0%
	IPS	55%	14%	7%	5%	3%	16%	0%
Interior Sys.	OEM	50%	21%	9%	16%	1%	2%	0%
	IPS	39%	22%	11%	11%	6%	10%	1%
Chassis Sys.	OEM	64%	3%	11%	14%	2%	6%	0%
	IPS	36%	36%	8%	2%	8%	6%	4%
Elect. Sys.	OEM	34%	9%	5%	48%	3%	1%	0%
	IPS	21%	18%	21%	30%	7%	3%	0%

CONCLUDING COMMENTS

Management's ability to implement strategies that are "leaner" for workers depends critically on the degree to which management can leverage investment decisions in pursuit of its objectives. That leverage depends on a complex set of economic, political, legal and historical factors that determine whose interests are promoted and protected. Take NAFTA, which places the protection of investment and capital above that of workers and the environment. Or labor laws that allow permanent replacement workers to take jobs from striking workers. Both shift power towards management and undermine workers' ability to organize and defend against lean strategies.

Labor and community organizations continue to challenge such policies by developing and implementing their own strategies. To successfully do so requires a thorough understanding of the rhetoric versus reality of lean strategies. Take, for example, just-in-time delivery systems with flexible forms of work organization. These can lead to a scarcity of resources —that is, elimination of buffers that result in an unsafe and non-sustainable pace of work. In such cases, "continuous improvement" and eliminating "non-value-added activities" will undermine working conditions, despite management claims to the contrary. For workers, counter strategies begin with putting sufficient buffers in place for training and discretionary downtime, hiring more workers for secure full-time jobs that pay family supporting wages and benefits, improving working conditions, and providing more training. Increasing working capital is necessary, too. Essentially, the answer for workers is a more equitable distribution of resources through a fair apportionment of value-added, continent-wide and across the industry.

One thing that's been learned is that some aspects of lean practices are double edged. This is true of just-in-time inventory systems, as witnessed by UAW strikes in Dayton against GM, and against Johnson Controls to win a solid first contract. Another example —one with a cautionary note— is the fire at a single Aisin Seike brake plant that resulted in Toyota losing production of 70,000 vehicles in Japan over a ten-day period. Afterwards, some argued the fire exposed the vulnerability of just-in-time sourcing from a single plant. Toyota executives, however, responded that just the right mix of efficiency and risk existed, since its suppliers were able to cobble together a temporary alternative source, and also make up for most of the lost production.[9] This highlights the nature of risk and cooperation for just-in-time systems.

---

[9] "Toyota's Fast Rebound After Fire at Supplier Shows Why It Is Tough," *Wall Street Journal*, 8 May 1997.

We already have a view of a possible future as management might envision it. Modularization, supplier tiers, and just-in-time have been combined together to form GM's Plant-X, the NedCar, and VW's new Brazilian truck plant in Resende. These concepts bring outsourcing and subcontracting close to the top of the value-added chain. Whether or not management will be able to spread this kind of model to further increase shareholders' portion of value-added remains to be seen. What it does illustrate is the challenge of management's continued development of even "leaner" strategies.

Appendix 1: Definition of Auto-Related Regions

UNITED STATES

Midwest States (UM)	
Iowa	
Illinois	*
Indiana	*
Kansas	*
Michigan	*
Minnesota	*
Missouri	*
Nebraska	
Ohio	*
South Dakota	
Wisconsin	*
Southern States (US)	
Alabama	*
Arkansas	
Delaware	*
Florida	
Georgia	*
Kentucky	*
Louisiana	*
Maryland	*
Mississippi	
North Carolina	
Oklahoma	*
South Carolina	
Tennessee	*
Texas	*
Virginia	*
West Virginia	
Eastern States (UEW)	
Connecticut	
Massachusetts	
Maine	
New Hampshire	
New Jersey	
New York	*
Pennsylvania	
Rhode Island	
Vermont	
Western States (UEW)	
Alaska	
Arizona	
California	*
Colorado	
New Mexico	
Nevada	
Oregon	
Utah	
Washington	

CANADA

Middle Provinces (CM)	
Manitoba	
Ontario	*
Eastern Provinces (CEW)	
New Brunswick	
Nova Scotia	*
Quebec	*
Western Provinces (CEW)	
Alberta	
British Columbia	

MEXICO

Northern States (MN)	
Baja Calif. Norte	
Chihuahua	
Coahuila	*
Nuevo Leon	
Sonora	*
Tamaulipas	
Middle States (MM)	
Aguascalientes	*
Distrito Federal	*
Durango	
Guanajuato	*
Hidalgo	
Jalisco	*
Mexico State	*
Michoacan	
Morelos	*
Puebla	*
Queretaro	
San Luis Potosi	
Tlaxcala	

* Assembly plant(s) located in State/Province.

Appendix 2: Definition of Components Systems

Powertrain

engine (except electrical)
transmission
axles & drivetrain components

Body Systems

body parts
stampings
exterior trim
bumpers
mirrors

Interior

seats
instrument panels
HVAC
carpeting
door systems
interior trim
windows, glass
seat belts, airbags
headliners

Chassis Systems

steering
suspension
brakes
fuel system
wheels, tires
exhaust/emission system
guages

Electrical/Electronic Systems

engine electrical
chassis electrical
electronics

REGIONALISM IN THE FORD MOTOR COMPANY'S GLOBAL STRATEGIES

*Ma. Isabel Studer**

INTRODUCTION

A popular view in the press and academic circles is that the global integration strategies of Multinational Enterprises (MNEs) are creating a genuine global system of production. These enterprises' level of mobility/flexibility is a matter of concern for actors who are relatively immobile and are dependent on MNE investments. In spite of the prevailing view that through their new global strategies MNEs are creating a truly global system of production, there is a great deal of conceptual ambiguity about the very meaning of the term "global strategy." Empirical analyses that measure the extent to which MNEs have adopted global strategies are not abundant, and those that exist generally demonstrate the regional rather than the global scope of MNE strategy. This chapter shows that Ford Motor Co.'s worldwide operations are regionally, not globally, integrated, specifically in Europe and North America.[1] The paper is divided into eight sections. Following the introduction is a brief review of the debate over the meaning of global strategies and an explanation of why Ford is a relevant case study. The next five sections are devoted to important areas of Ford's strategies during the past two decades, i.e., production; sales, competition, and R&D; trade; strategic alliances; and organization and management. A final section is reserved for some concluding remarks.

WHAT IS A GLOBAL STRATEGY?

As mentioned, a great deal of conceptual ambiguity exists about the very meaning of the term "global strategy." The most basic definitions refer to the standardization of a product to be manufactured and sold the same way

* Departamento de Estudios Internacionales, Instituto Tecnológico Autónomo de México (ITAM).

[1]. For a more thorough analysis of Ford's strategies over the 1960-1993 period, see Studer 1997.

throughout the world (Levitt 1983); or, to the ability of the firm to build a broader product portfolio, with many product varieties, so that investments in technologies and distribution channels can be shared (Hamel and Prahalad 1985). For Kogut (1985), a global strategy requires the flexibility to achieve multiple sourcing, permiting shifts in production to low-cost sites in response to changes in factor costs and exchange rates. By contrast, for Hamel and Prahalad (1985), two key elements of a global strategy are the cross-subsidization of products and markets and the development of a strong distribution system, which may not require flexibility to shift to different production sites.

One popular definition of a global strategy is a complex and efficiency-oriented approach that implies the rationalization or re-organization of the MNEs' value-added activities and the launching of production networks on a global basis (Doz 1986, Bartlett and Ghoshal 1989, Porter 1986). According to this view, global strategies consist of a dispersed geographical location of each or some parts of the value chain or company function, and a more centralized coordination of linked activities that are performed in different countries (Porter 1986, 23). Such strategies entail the division of the production process into discrete functions (assembly, procurement, finance, research and development), and the re-distribution of these functions "wherever they can be carried out most effectively in light of the overall needs of the firm as a whole." As operations become dispersed across different national locations, the fragmented activities of MNEs are integrated into global production and distribution systems, being "subject to one unified strategy that governs the entire corporate system" (UNWIR 1996, 98, 138-40; Gereffi 1996, 64).

This definition is not without problems. One is the difficulty of measuring the extent to which MNEs have adopted these global strategies. For example, MNEs could disperse each or all the activities in the value chain —production, marketing and sales, service, technology, development, procurement (Porter 1986, 23-27). Research may not be integrated at all, while product development may be integrated at a worldwide level and manufacturing at a regional level, with marketing being integrated in certain aspects (pricing) but not in others (advertising). Furthermore, MNEs that choose a global strategy may rationalize their international operations in a number of ways, standardize some products and/or diversify others, and integrate manufacturing vertically or horizontally (Kobrin 1991, 18). For this reason, alternative rankings could be used to assess the level of internationalization or globalization of MNE strategies (for a discussion see Ruigrok and van Tulden 1995, 152-175; UNWIR 1996). Another problem is that some other variables that are critical for developing a global integration strategy are non-measurable. This is the case, for example, with the organizational capability to acquire an integrated network (Stopford and Wells 1972, Hedlund 1986, and Bartlett 1983).

Therefore, MNEs face multiple options for deciding what and where to locate the different value-added activities in the production chain, or for designing a firm's organizational structure. Assessing if a MNE has a "global strategy" thus requires one to select specific aspects of its global activities.

During the 1980s, many academic and newspaper articles pointed to the emergence of the MNEs' global strategies, and this coincided with the Big Three's fundamental restructuring of their U.S. operations. The view is not uncommon that the causes of such change are found in the emergence of new competitors, particularly the Japanese; in new technologies and methods of production —lean production and just-in time— which became the best-practice standards of production; and in spiraling costs of R&D and design. But the U.S. automobile industry's transformation resulted also from a combination of other significant events, which also shaped the Big Three's strategic responses: the two oil shocks of the 1970s; the introduction of new and more stringent U.S. standards on safety, energy, and the environment; the drastic fall in vehicle demand and the protectionist policies introduced in North America and Europe. While Japanese automakers showed the flexibility to adapt to this new context, the U.S. Big Three automakers were struggling to find ways to survive the new competitive challenges. Their U.S. operations were at a competitive cost disadvantage vis-à-vis the Japanese.[2]

The U.S. Big Three automakers reacted in a similar fashion to the new conditions, locating plants overseas and outsourcing[3] products from suppliers in South Korea, Taiwan, Japan or Mexico (this was an attractive strategy for the U.S. automakers because they could "gain some benefits of the integration quickly, at a low cost, while preserving the firm's autonomy, and avoid the administrative and managerial difficulties and uncertainties involved in full-fledged mergers," see Doz 1986, 70). The Big Three's imports of components and cars, particularly small ones, from Europe, Asia, and Mexico came to play an important role in their corporate strategies. They also sought "quasi-integration" projects, or joint-ventures, with Asian vehicle producers both to source low-cost small cars and components, and to spread the cost of new product development; and they undertook the rationalization of production

[2]. The degree to which the Big Three had a cost disadvantage vis-à-vis the Japanese is a matter of debate (see Studer 1997, Chapter VI; and OSAT 1992).

[3]. Outsourcing could take place through arm's-length transactions with large-volume parts suppliers (domestic or foreign) or joint ventures with foreign automakers that could build cars at lower costs.

and increased coordination among subsidiaries at a regional (in Europe and North America) and inter-regional level.

Despite these similarities in the Big Three's strategic responses, Ford seemed to have been better prepared to face the challenge of globalization, given its extensive network of international operations and the company's management experience in handling such operations (Womack et al. 1990, 207). Ford is the second largest vehicle manufacturer in the world, and the most transnational, having operations in more than 200 countries and territories and employing about 350,000 workers. Ford's International Automotive Operations coordinates activities in 26 countries grouped in three principal regions: Europe, Latin America, and Asia Pacific. Its international network of operations has historically given Ford a competitive advantage over GM,[4] and Chrysler.[5] Economies of learning and the ability to create linkages with host governments, local labor groups and suppliers allowed Ford to become a leader in complying with a range of host-country regulations, facilitating its entry or gaining first-mover advantages in foreign markets. This notwithstanding, and even if global integration was a clear strategic goal for Ford, a number of obstacles limited the scope of the changes that were required by Ford to put that strategy fully in place. In order to better understand those obstacles, and in which direction Ford's world-wide strategies really moved, a detailed analysis follows of five important areas of Ford's international operations: vehicle and parts production; competitive strategies, including sales and R&D; trade policies and defensive market strategies; competition through strategic alliances; and inter-subsidiary coordination.

LOCATING VEHICLE PRODUCTION FOR EXPORT MARKETS IN LOW-COST SITES

In the late 1970s, Ford introduced its "world car" program (the Ford Escort, also called the Erica program), which sought to integrate its operations on a global scale. Like similar projects of other automakers, the world car was conceived as a response to the Japanese competitive challenge, and was based on

---

4. In the late 1970s, for instance, one-fourth of GM's vehicles were produced abroad, while Ford's proportion was close to 50 percent. At the time, GM's fixed assets were highly concentrated; almost half of its overseas investments were in Germany, while an additional 35 percent were located in Brazil, Great Britain, and Australia. The company started to diversify in the early 1980s by building plants in Austria, Spain, Egypt, Mexico, and Taiwan (Whitman 1981, 14).

5. Due to its financial problems in the late 1970s, Chrysler sold most of its major Latin American, Western European and Australian interests. "The only important operation outside the United States and Canada is Mexico" (UNCTC 1982, 85).

the idea that only enormous economies of scale and large sales volumes could produce the cost structures which would enable survival in the new competitive environment. The car would be built in production runs of millions of units, with one assembly plant or subsidiary being responsible for developing and engineering the car and other subsidiaries for manufacturing the completed design. Interestingly, developing countries (with the exception of Brazil and much later Mexico) were excluded from this program. Ford's world-car project, like those of the other automakers, failed because of distinct consumer tastes in different national markets, the difficulty in coordinating the production processes taking place in different countries, and the high risk of disruptions in the production process originating in political or economic problems arising in one or more countries.

Indeed, as data in Figure 1 shows, the bulk of Ford's vehicle production has been concentrated in the United States —accounting for about 45 and 50 percent of Ford's total production. Traditionally, Ford kept its vehicle production in the United States or in other industrialized countries (between 25 and 30 percent in Europe, and 15 percent in Canada), with developing countries representing less than 10 percent of the company's worldwide total. Ford, like GM, traditionally sought access to foreign markets, and was generally reluctant to open production operations in developing countries. Before the late 1950s, most manufacturing operations of those companies were located in developed countries, although they had assembly or sales branches in a number of developing countries. Also, their sales and production strategies responded to the particular needs of each national market, largely because their main interest was expanding market access.[6] This started to change in the 1960s, as Ford (and to a lesser extent GM) began integrating production and sales in Europe and North America (excluding Mexico), and opening manufacturing operations in Latin America. Both strategies were related to increasing levels of competition in the world industry and changing levels of economic development and industrialization in foreign countries, but the first strategy was also made possible by the free trade policies adopted in those two regions. The second strategy was explained by both Ford's interest in defending regional markets in the face of heightened competition from European automakers, and the company's perception that Latin American markets had significant growth potential.

[6]. While trade liberalization policies prevailed in Canada and Europe in the 1960s, allowing Ford to rationalize its operations and follow integration strategies there, most Latin American countries imposed restrictions on imports of finished vehicles, vertical integration, and foreign ownership, thus preventing Ford and other vehicle assemblers from seeking cross-border integration.

Figure 1
Ford Production by Region, 1979 - 1993.
(In Units)

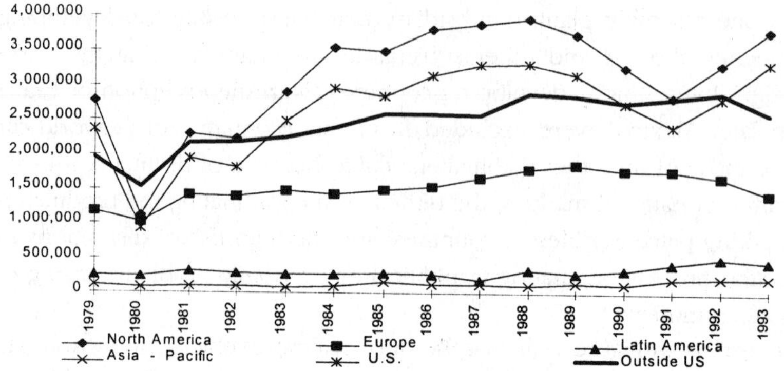

Source: *Ford Motor Co.'s Annual Reports, several years.*

Figure 2
Ford Production to Sales Ratio by Region, 1974 - 1993.
(In Percentages)

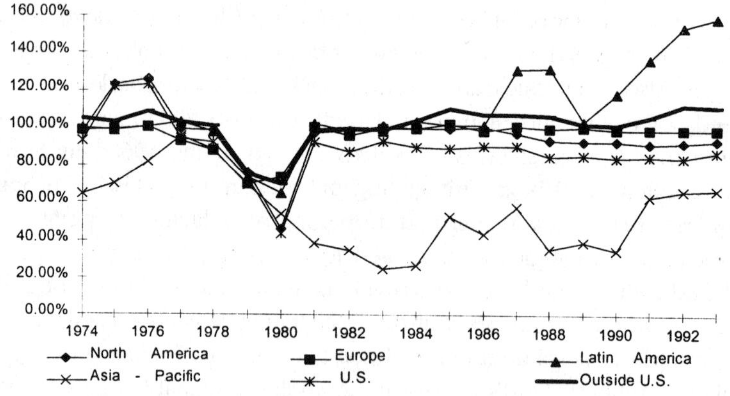

Source: *Ford Motor Co.'s Annual Reports, several years.*

Although the evidence does not support the widely-held belief in the 1970s that major shifts in vehicle production would take place to low-wage production sites in the developing world, it does show changes in the geographical distribution of such production. After 1987, Latin America, and to a lesser extent the Asia-Pacific region,[7] increased in importance as production sites for Ford vehicles, and not just as markets for the company's products (which obviously continue to be important). Figure 2 illustrates this point: Ford's production-to-sales ratios outside of the United States changed from less than 100 percent in 1988 to 112 percent in 1993, with the major relative change taking place in Ford's Latin American operations.[8] Whereas in the 1975-1989 period, the bulk of Ford's vehicles produced in the Latin American region were sold there, after 1987 a growing proportion of vehicles produced there were sold elsewhere in the world, as confirmed by a growing production-to-sales ratio, which reached 1.6 in 1993.[9]

Most importantly, data in Figure 2 shows the regional, rather than the global, character of Ford's production operations. Except for the 1979-1981 period, most Ford vehicles sold in each major regional market —North America, Europe, and Latin America— are produced within each region. As is explained further below, this strategy was accompanied by an important rationalization of operations so as to build/consolidate true systems of regional production. Here the most significant change took place in North America.

Figure 3
Ford Inter-Company Sales to Total Sales Ratio, 1977 - 1993.
(In Percentages)

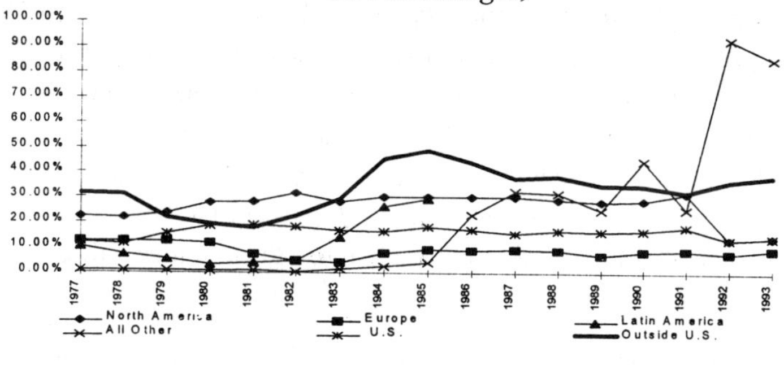

Source: *Ford Motor Co.'s Annual Report, several years.*

[7]. The importance of Ford's production in the Asia-Pacific region also increased, doubling from about 2 to 4 percent of Ford's total production between the mid-1980s and the early 1990s.

[8]. Naturally, the United States continues to be the largest market for, and the largest production site of, Ford's products.

[9]. Although it must be emphasized that the specific impact of that change is minor in Ford's worldwide operations, considering that Ford's operations in that region represent only 10-15 percent of Ford's total overseas production.

The argument could be made, however, that the U.S. Big Three did not shift "vehicle" assembly to other countries as much as they increased their offshore outsourcing operations, and that this shift in auto parts production is, in fact, creating "globally integrated" networks of auotmotive production. In the absence of complete data series for Ford's parts production and trade by region, one proxy to measure the level of integration of Ford's worldwide operations is inter-company sales. Ford's data on inter-company sales, taken from the company's annual reports, are presented in Figure 3. In absolute dollar values, those sales grew significantly, between 1987 and 1994. Measured as a proportion of the company's total worldwide sales, inter-company sales in the U.S. do not show dramatic changes, and represented 20 percent on average.

It is worth mentioning that Ford did not follow an aggressive strategy of outsourcing parts and small cars, as GM and Chrysler did.[10] Ford's long-term strategy stressed maintaining a conservative approach to capital expenditures;[11] revamping the company's in-house component operations as part of its also long-term quality improvement program[12]; and building a cooperative management-labor relationship, manifested in every labor agreement between Ford and the UAW since 1982.[13] All this limited Ford's outsourcing operations. However, by the mid-1980s, Ford faced the risk of losing its competitive ground to other automakers whose delivered cost of small cars in the North American market was substantially lower. Therefore, as Figure 3 shows, in the 1982-1993 period, inter-company sales outside of the United States show a growth trend, although it is somewhat erratic. As a share of total company sales, inter-company sales outside the U.S. shifted from about 20 percent in the early 1980s to record highs of 49 percent in 1985, then fell to 38 percent in 1987, and thereafter remained at an annual average of 36 percent between 1987 and 1993. Most likely, these shifts were due to changes in countries other than

---

[10]. Before 1985, Ford had limited its offshore sourcing to manual transaxles, some automatic transmissions, and front-wheel-drive halfshafts from Mazda, as well as four-cylinder engines from Mexico.

[11]. GM launched an aggressive $40 billion (U.S.) investment program to completely overhaul its world-wide operations. In contrast to GM, Ford invested in modernizing its plants and equipment rather than building anew or investing in extensive automation.

[12]. According to one estimate, by 1985, imports of components made in Japan and Taiwan represented only 5 percent of Ford's total manufacturing costs (Salter et al. 1987, 170).

[13]. In the 1987 agreement the company reiterated it by explicitly specifying that "no worker could be laid off due to a domestically made vehicle or component being replaced by an imported product...." (*Ward's Automotive Yearbook* 1988, 263; Ford Motor Company *Annual Report* 1987, 7).

Europe, as inter-company sales there did not exhibit dramatic changes during the 1980s and early 1990s. Contrawise, major changes are registered in "other countries," particularly after 1986. Although data for Latin America is not published separately from "other countries" in Ford's annual reports after 1985, anecdotal evidence suggests that such changes reflect the integration of Ford's Latin American operations into the company's regional/global strategy.[14]

The changes registered in Ford's production operations in Latin America largely reflect Ford's investments in Mexico during the 1980s for production of engines, parts and small cars. It is important to underscore that these significant changes in Ford's Mexican operations did not result from a previously well-designed corporate strategy, but rather from a fortunate coincidence of factors that allowed foreign automakers to realize Mexico's potential as a competitive production site. Ford's Mexican investments in engine production largely resulted from the company's need to respond to GM's and Chrysler's competitive moves in the late 1970s and early 1980s. While the latter companies were export leaders from 1982 on, Ford's engine exports did not increase significantly until 1984, just after its Chihuahua engine plant came on stream. Similarly, Ford's production in the Mexican *maquiladoras* was not as extensive as GM's: while in 1989 GM had twenty-five *maquiladoras* in Mexico employing more than 25,000 workers, Ford had only ten with 7,000 workers, compared to Chrysler's four plants with 5,000 workers (Rubenstein 1992, 244). Notwithstanding this, Ford established a number of joint-ventures with Mexican firms to produce parts and components,[15] and established a number of operations, such as Altec (Chihuahua) to produce 750,000 raidos annually, and a glass plant in Mexico that came with the purchase of Carplastic, S.A. in 1988 (this had been a joint venture with a Mexican company since 1980).

---

[14]. In the 1970s, Ford had increased its Latin American investments to produce parts for export markets, but the volume and value of this production was insignificant.

[15]. In 1981, Ford joined with Grupo Alfa to open Nemak, which is one of the largest suppliers of aluminum engine heads; in 1982, with Grupo Vitro and Grupo Visa to create Vitroflex and Carplastic which produce glass and plastic boards, respectively (Berry 1992, 17; Arjona 1990, 138-139).

Figure 4
Ford Production to Sales Ratio in North America, 1974 - 1993.
(In Percentages)

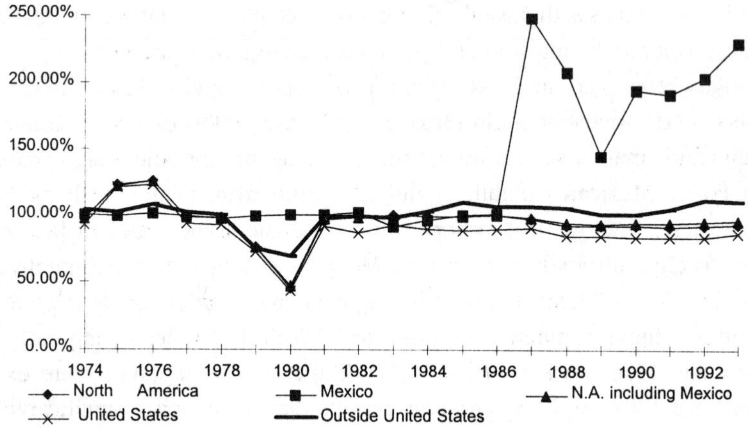

Source: *Author's Own Calculations, based on Ford Motor Co.'s Annual Reports, several years.*

Most significantly, Ford's investments in Mexico during the 1980s were oriented towards strengthening the company's small car strategy. Since 1986, Ford's production in Mexico increased proportionally more than Ford's sales in that country, as it is shown in Ford's production-to-sales ratio of Figure 4. While in 1988 Ford's captive imports, plus imports of Ford's vehicles produced in Mexico, plus Ford's joint production with Asian manufacturers at U.S. plants, accounted for 23 percent of all small cars sold by Ford in the United States, by 1993 that figure had increased to 40 percent (author's calculations based on Ford Motor Co.'s Annual Reports, several years, and *Ward's Automotive Yearbook* 1995). Ford's plant in Hermosillo (Sonora, located in Northern Mexico), which came on stream in 1987 and produces the company's world cars (the Mercury Tracer and the Ford Escort) for the U.S. market, is considered one of the most productive and modern in the world. This plant represents an important breakaway from the traditional practice of establishing plants in Mexico with obsolete technology. The Hermosillo plant was, by the late 1980s, the only facility in North America to combine stamping, manufacturing and assembly. The plant was linked to Detroit's Lincoln Mercury Division and to Mazda's plant in Japan through computers and telecommunications, making it fully integrated with decision-making centers (Morales, 132). The Hermosillo plant also gave Ford the opportunity to experiment with lean production in Mexico.

Some of the factors that contributed to increaing the attractiveness of Mexico as a production site for autos included the Mexican government's gradual liberalization of trade and investment policies, the country's geographical proximity to the U.S. market, which meant reduced costs of transportation, particularly after the 1982 peso devaluation, and the quality of the labor force. Other factors that made Mexico particularly attractive for assembly operations were the flexibility offered by the lack of unionization in some of Mexico's northern states and/or the existence of weak unions in Mexico. These labor considerations were particularly important for the U.S. Big Three automakers because they perceived U.S. labor costs as increasingly fixed and a major cause for their cost differentials vis-à-vis their Japanese competitors.[16] In addition, those labor conditions enabled companies to implement flexible methods of production.

Ford's Hermosillo plant, as with other investments by U.S. automakers, also reflected a new strategy of integrating Mexican operations with the North American system of automotive production. In the early 1990s, Ford appeared as the company that had done "the most to integrate its Mexican operations into its international production system" (ECLAC 1995, 23), moving faster than the other automakers toward a rationalization of its assembly operations on a continental basis. After 1990, the company started a $2 billion (U.S.) upgrading program that included its engine plant in Chihuahua (to produce its modern Zeta engine, which is also produced in Cleveland, Ohio), its Hermosillo assembly plant (for the production of a new Tracer model and the Escort), and its Cuautitlán plant in central Mexico (to start assembly of the new global cars —the Mercury Mystique and the Ford Contour, also produced in Kansas City). With these investments, Ford's Mexican operations became an integral part of Ford's North American system of production. The coming of NAFTA facilitated this move towards a truly regional system of production and a market that is also gradually becoming regional.[17]

---

[16]. For a full discussion of this point, see OSAT 1992.

[17]. Ford's strategy towards specialization of vehicle assembly on a North American basis also became clear when the company announced its decision to stop assembly of such luxury cars as the Cougar and the Thunderbird in Mexico. Ford started to import these cars, as well as the Lincoln Mark VIIIs and Town cars and entry-level cars —such as the Escort— into Mexico as the country's Mexican trade regulations became liberalized. In 1994, Ford became, with GM, the largest importer of finished vehicles into that country.

In sum, Ford's investments in Mexico are unique in that they show that not only labor costs but also other factors are relevant to make a country attractive for investments to produce for export markets or to be part of an automaker's global/regional strategy. They require trade and/or investment liberalization measures that allow for economies of scale; the existence of a basic automotive infrastructure and the accumulation of know-how by local auto-workers, managers, and suppliers; the proximity to both developed markets and other developing countries that enhance the feasibility of achieving economies of scale (UNCTC, 1982, 79); and an overall attractiveness relative to other countries (as happened in the case of Latin America vis-à-vis Asian countries after the 1986 Yen revaluation relative to the U.S. dollar). There were, in fact, few developing countries (most clearly, Mexico and Brazil) that could simultaneously meet all these requirements.

GLOBAL COMPETITION, MANAGING CASH FLOWS

Implementing a global integration strategy implies not only managing the manufacturing cost system worldwide, but also maintaining or strengthening a firm's presence in multiple national markets. What matters is managing cash flows and strategic coordination, "even when global integration across subsidiaries in terms of product flow does not take place" (Doz and Prahalad 1987, 39-40). Maintaining a presence in major markets has become increasingly difficult as competition has intensified on a global scale. That competition has stemmed from an aggressive export strategy by the Japanese, and the protectionist policies adopted in North America and Europe. In the United States, Voluntary Export Restraints (VERs) encouraged the Japanese automakers to move from the small-car to upgraded market segments, to increase the price of their cars, and therefore, to substantial profits.[18] Most importantly, those quotas induced the Japanese to establish production operations in the United States, Canada, and, to a lesser extent, in Europe.[19] In 1994, for instance, vehicles

---

[18]. Although having positive effects in terms of raising substantially the U.S. automakers total profits, which all-together amounted to $9.8 billion in 1984 and $8 billion in 1985, VERs had also negative consequences.

[19]. In 1981, Honda started the construction of a new plant in Ohio to produce 150,000 Accords, with plans for increasing it to 500,000 in 1990. In 1984, Nissan announced plans to start, in 1985, the production of 100,000 Sentras at a new plant in Tennessee. Toyota also started a new joint venture with GM (NUMMI), and then an assembly plant in Tennessee. Mitsubishi and Mazda also established joint ventures with Chrysler and Ford.

produced at Japanese plants located in the United States accounted for nearly 15 percent of total sales in the U.S. market, while Japanese imports accounted for an additional 8 percent—compared to a 15 percent market share for Japanese vehicle imports in 1990. (*Automotive News Market Data Book* 1995). Because of this competition, but also due to reductions in the product-cycle life times and rising costs of R&D, maintaining a presence in major markets has become a key requirement for automakers for their survival.

The United States continues to be, by far, the largest market for the Big Three, in terms of both sales volume and value. In 1993, that market accounted for over 60 percent of Ford's worldwide sales (Figure 5). Historically, Ford and GM have had a presence in major markets, with the bulk of their foreign sales concentrated in Europe (Chrysler, on the other hand, has a minor presence in Europe). During the 1980s, Europe was Ford's second largest market, accounting on average for 30 percent of the company's worldwide sales in dollar value. Ford's sales in Latin America reached record highs of over 10 percent in 1980-1981, and then declined continuously until 1987 (data for 1987-1993 are not available in published form). In the 1990s, Ford's sales in dollar value outside Europe and the United States represented an average of 13 percent of the company's worldwide sales.

Figure 5
Ford Sales by Region, 1979 - 1993.
(In Units)

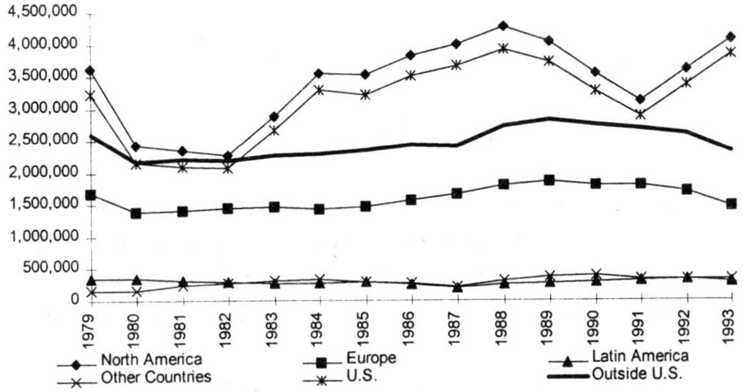

Source: *Ford Motor Co.'s Annual Reports, serveral years.*

During the 1970s recession, Ford's operations outside North America provided the cash flow needed by the parent company to survive, to modernize its operations, and to develop new products. Europe was the most significant source, generating excess cash flow that saved the company from bankruptcy in 1979, and supporting Ford's North American automotive operations through the worst years of the industry's recession. As indicated in Figure 6, while between 1979 and 1982, Ford's operations in North America lost $5 billion, the company earnings outside North America were about $3 billion, accounting for two thirds of Ford's total capital expenditures in that period.[20]

Figure 6
Ford's Net Income by Region, 1975 - 1993.
(In Millions of U.S. Dollars)

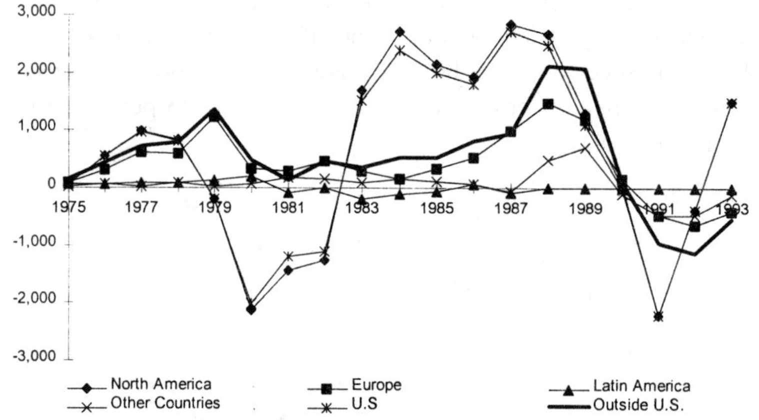

Source: *Ford Motor Co.'s Annual Reports, several years.*

Of the $40 billion spent by Ford in capital expenditures in the 1979-1988 period, the net income of Ford's foreign operations contributed more than 20 percent —European operations accounted for $7.3 billion and operations in other countries (Canada and Mexico excluded) added approximately $1.2 billion. In

[20]. In 1979, alone, Europe earned $1.2 billion and other international operations, about $150 million more. Again in 1988, Ford registered record automotive profits of $4.6 billion, and while North American profits were down 28 percent from the previous year to $2.5 billion, the company's international operations showed earnings that jumped 80 percent to $2.1 billion.

other words, Ford's operations outside North America contributed more than one-fifth of the funds required to cover Ford's worldwide capital expenditures.

TRADE: PROTECTING REGIONAL MARKETS

Contrary to commonly held beliefs, the Big Three have not been unconditional supporters of free trade, bur rather of preferential or managed trade. In order to protect market shares, Ford and Chrysler joined the UAW's lobbying effort in the late 1970s to establish protection against the Japanese. At first, GM opposed these demands. For instance, in the 1980 hearings of the U.S. International Trade Commission about establishing import quotas on Japanese automobiles, GM was the only major domestic automaker that favored free trade, largely because it was less threatened by the Japanese under free trade than under quotas (Perry, 69). Only in the spring of 1981 did GM join Ford and Chrysler in demanding import restraints that resulted in the Voluntary Export Restraints.[21]

The U.S. Big Three, however, opposed the UAW's demands for local content in the United States. "As parts from Mexico and imported vehicles from Japan and South Korea became a more integral part of the Big Three's competitive response to Japanese-based firms, local content threatened to interfere with the U.S. automaker's plants as well as their competitors" (Herzenberg 1991, 257). In contrast, Ford of Europe led industry calls for the establishment of an 80 percent local content rule in the European market. As Hoffman and Kaplinsky (1988) have noted "Ford's position on this matter must be seen as somewhat equivocal given that it had previously berated Western European governments for their protectionist tendencies and also because the local content of the autos it assembled in the United States and the United Kingdom had come under attack" (p. 95). The different position between Ford of Europe and the parent company could be explained by the fact that the former relied mostly on its regional trade, rather than on global sourcing of parts, components, and cars, as did the parent company.

21. The United Kingdom negotiated a VER with the Japanese in 1975, followed by other European nations, France, in 1977, Germany, in 1979, Belgium and Spain, in 1981, and Sweden, in 1983. In April 1981, the U.S. government negotiated a VER limiting Japanese imports to 1.76 million. These limits were maintained until 1983, when the import quota was raised to 1.876 million, and then to 1.94 million for the year beginning in 1984. The quota was raised again in 1987 (Hoffman and Kaplinsky 1988, 86-88).

The Big Three also favored "managed" free trade in the Canada-U.S. Auto Pact of 1965,[22] the Canada U.S. Free Trade Agreement of 1988 which granted them a 50 percent rule of origin, and the North American Free Trade Agreement (NAFTA) that raised that rule to 62.5 percent. NAFTA removed a series of remaining obstacles to achieve a full integration of the production systems and the markets of the three countries. The Canadian duty-remission programs and the Mexican local content and export-performance requirements were eliminated (although the Big Three opposed a complete and immediate liberalization of the Mexican auto industry and sought to protect the domestic market from Japanese competition), and high rules of origin were established.

The impact of these strategies on the power relations of national governments is not the subject of this analysis, but it is interesting to note that the dynamics of what has been called Triangular Diplomacy (State-to-State, firm-to-firm, State-to-firm diplomacy) apply in the case of the North American auto industry. NAFTA formally restricted the Canadian and the Mexican governments margin to use sectoral or trade policies to determine the U.S. automakers' decisions on what, where, and how to produce and to directly shape the future of their "national" automobile industries. Their future actions will be shaped by NAFTA rules or by the bargaining between the three national governments and the firms on how to modify those rules. They may affect the competitive advantage of automotive production —efficiency, costs of production, quality of the labor force— or attract non-regional automotive investments only indirectly, with such non-trade policy measures as exchange rates or education policies. The U.S. government's traditional position of relying on market forces to shape outcomes in the North American automotive industry has prevailed, but so long as the Big Three are protected against offshore producers through the new regulatory framework.

In the case of Ford, political considerations explained the company's decision to maintain production operations in major markets. As long as trade balances are important to governments, firms operating in strategic industries have to consider the trade impact of their production, sales, and trade operations, not only in foreign countries but also in their own home country. It is therefore difficult to offset exports that could balance automotive trade among regions, when one considers that personal consumption in developed economies devoted to the purchase of cars is about $240 billion in North America only. As Womack et al. (1990, p. 204) have argued "the fact remains that in the long run

[22]. The Big Three got preferential market access to the Canadian market.

producers must either locate within the market of sale [...] or cede that portion of the world-vehicle market" (see also UNCTC, 1982, 79 and Whitman, 12).

STRATEGIC ALLIANCES: FORGING THE GLOBAL CHARACTER OF COMPETITION

Like other automakers, Ford's alliances with Asian automakers represented a major change from the company's past strategies against joint ventures with foreign manufacturers. The 100 percent ownership and control of foreign and domestic operations had been a key principle in the U.S. Big Three's strategies, one that in fact was the source of conflict and negotiations with a number of host countries. However, rising costs of R&D has caused a multiplication of these associations (see above). Ford's strategy of offshore sourcing of small cars relied heavily on an alliance with Mazda, of which Ford has owned 25 percent since 1979.[23] By importing fully or partially assembled cars from Mazda, Ford was able to earn a high profit margin on those cars (Mazda could build a sub-compact car with 25 percent fewer labor hours than Ford). With the Yen revaluation vis-à-vis the U.S. dollar after 1986, Ford established alliances with Lio Ho Motors, a Taiwanese automaker, to produce the Mercury Tracer, and with Kia Motors in South Korea, to build the Ford Festiva. Although the company plans were to increase its captive imports to 350,000 a year by 1989 (Dyer et al. 1987, 170), in that year Ford's captive imports amounted to 85,000 cars only, or about half of GM's captive imports and 80 percent of Chrysler's (*Market Data Book of Automotive News* 1994). These figures, however, did not account for imports of small cars that the Big Three built in Mexico and Canada.

International corporate alliances also had the objective of spreading extraordinarily high design and engineering costs. In the mid-1980s, Ford's goal was to create six or seven "common-development programs" with Asian vehicle companies (see Table 1). During its almost 20 year association with Mazda, Ford developed and produced jointly a number of components and at least five vehicles to market in North America and the Pacific Rim: the Probe (based on Mazda's 626 platform), several models of the Mexican-built Ford Escort and Mercury Tracer (Mazda's 323 front-drive platform), and the 1990 Ford Laser, a

---

23. Ford began negotiations to buy 10 percent of Toyo Kogyo (Mazda) in 1972, but did not succeed. This Japanese company was rescued from bankruptcy by Japanese banks and became profitable again in 1979, when Ford purchased a 25 percent interest (Rubenstein 1992, 157).

subcompact built and sold in the Asia-Pacific region. The Australian-built Capri was another international cooperative effort (which, however, was terminated in 1994), with Ford's Ghia studios in Italy in charge of the design and Mazda, of the mechanical engineering. Ford established a similar arrangement with Nissan, which designed and engineered the Villager minivans, supplied the powertrains and all major stampings, provided technical assistance to help Ford develop the assembly process, and even designed and built the plant's new body shop (Ford Motor Company's Annual Report 1991, 3 and 9; Ward's Automotive Yearbook 1992, 17).

Also, as prospects of surplus global capacity in truck and passenger cars for 1990 reached the 20 percent mark, the nature of the Big Three's low-cost supply links with Asian automakers shifted to production-sharing agreements (see Table 1). GM had moved first in establishing those type of operations, with New United Motor Manufacturing Inc. (NUMMI), opened in 1984,[24] followed by Diamond-Star Motors Corp., a joint venture between Mitsubishi and Chrysler,[25] and then by Ford-Mazda's Auto Alliance International Inc. (AAI).[26] Ford also established a limited product-sharing relationship with Nissan for the production of the Quest/Mercury Villager minivan at Ford's Avon Lake, Ohio assembly plant.

Table 1

Ford Motor Company: International Collaborative Projects

Equity Arrangements			*Joint Supplier Arrangements*	
Company	Country	Holdings	Company	Country
AC Cars	U.K.	51%	Fiat	Italy
Aston Martin Lagonda	U.K	75%	Renault	France
Kia Motors Corp.	Korea	10%	Mazda	Japan
Lio-Ho Motor Co. Ltd.	Taiwan	70%	Nissan	Japan
Mazda Motor Corp.	Japan	25%	DeTomaso	Italy
Jaguar plc.	U.K.	100%	Volkswagon	Germany
Associated Motor Ind.	Malasya	30%		
Iveco Ford Truck	U.K.	48%		

24. A 50-50 percent GM-Toyota joint-manufacturing venture, located in Fremont, California.

25. Today, Diamond-Star Motors Corp. is fully owned by Mitsubishi, but produces cars with a Chrysler badge.

26. Initially a wholly owned Mazda plant in Flat Rock, Michigan, in which Ford bought a 50 percent share.

Autolatina	Brazil/ Argentina	49%

Marketing / Distribution Arrangements

Company	Country
Kia	Korea
Suzuki	Japan
Mazda	Japan
Fiat	Italy

Technology Arrangements

Company	Country
Chrysler	U.S.A.
G.M.	U.S.A.
Mazda	Japan
Nissan	Japan

Joint Ventures

Company	Country
Fiat	Italy
Toyota	Japan
Volvo	Sweden
Mazda	Japan
Nissan	Japan
Volkswagon	Germany

Manufacturing Arrangements

Company	Country
B.M.W.	Germany
Fiat	Italy
Kia	Korea
Mercedes Benz	Germany
Suzuki	Japan
Mazda	Japan
Nissan	Japan
Rover	U.K.
Volkswagon	Germany

Source: *The International Automobile Industry in Canada*, April 1992, 49.

Ford's co-production associations were not restricted to the United States, as illustrated by Ford's ventures with Volkswagen, one in South America (Autolatina, opened in 1986, although it was dissolved in 1995), which included production facilities in Brazil and Argentina, and one in Portugal to produce multi-purpose vehicles. Captive imports did start to decrease in the early 1990s, declining from 3.7 percent in 1988 to 0.8 percent of the U.S. market for passenger cars, while production of cars at the Big Three transplants more than doubled, growing from 1.7 percent to over 3.5 percent of the U.S. market for passenger cars (*Ward's Automotive Yearbook* 1995, 119). In that period, Ford accounted on average for about one-fourth of all sales of the Big Three's transplants. Although they were a cornerstone in the company's global integration strategies, Ford's collaborative projects faced problems. Ford canceled its cooperative project with Mazda to jointly-engineer and build Ford's Capri in Australia; and its co-production association with Volkswagen in South America was dissolved in 1995.[27]

27. Autolatina was envisioned under the rationale that both the Argentinean and the Brazilian markets were too small to support either company individually. The project was facilitated by

THE LIMITS TO GLOBALIZATION: MANAGEMENT AND ORGANIZATION

Ford did become the leader in achieving a high level of coordination in design and production facilities on a global basis (Doz 1986, 67; Womack et al. 1990, 213). But this coordination program faced important obstacles, and it became very expensive. Management changes in terms of corporate organization showed a "trial and error" pattern, as illustrated by the failure of Ford's world car project of the 1970s.

After 1985, Ford started to work on a new "world-car" project, the Mondeo line of mid-size cars (launched in the European market in 1992, and the Contour/Mystique models in North America, in 1994). In order to cope with previous difficulties of the world-car projects of the 1970s and with coordination problems with other automakers, the new global cars are jointly designed and produced by Ford's affiliated subsidiaries in Europe and North America, rather than coordinating with outside automakers.[28] These "global cars" have also entailed organizational changes to better respond to different consumer tastes in major markets, as well as national government requirements to produce locally in exchange for market access. In 1989, Ford established Centers of Expertise that were divided by regions and that specialized in designing specific types of products. Through that system, Ford assigned the leading role to Mazda at Hiroshima for small cars; to Ford North America in Dearborn, for mid-size and full-size cars; and to Ford of Europe in Great Britain and Germany, for compact cars. Brazil concentrated on tractors and Australia on specialty cars. In order to facilitate the coordination among its subsidiaries, Ford set up a computerized global communications network, called the Worldwide Engineering Release System (WERS), so that 20,000 Ford people around the world share design and manufacturing information as they develop new prod-

---

government regulations, particularly in Brazil, that encouraged production of small cars, through lower duties and taxes. A declining market share for Ford during the Autolatina's lifespan, a change in the Brazilian government policy (increased duties on imports and raising taxes on popular cars), and expectations about a growing Brazilian market for vehicles that could reach 2 million units annually by year 2000 prompted Ford to dissolve Autolatina, and to build new assembly and component plants in Brazil (*Ward's Automotive Yearbook* 1995, 86).

28. Ford European Automotive Operations were responsible for product design, program management and production engineering, along with the development of the new four-cylinder, multi-valve Zeta engine. North American Automotive Operations provided the distinctive design for the North American version and the development of a new V-6 engine, as well as the transmissions and steering components produced in several U.S. facilities.

ucts (Ford Motor Company's *Annual Report* 1989, 8). Even with the new organization, which focused more on sharing design rather than production (as the earlier world car projects did), Ford was not totally successful in achieving higher levels of coordination. Many differences between Ford Europe and Ford North America remained unsolved.[29]

In April 1994, Ford announced its 2000 program, which represented a further step in re-organizing the coordination of its worldwide operations. The goal was to centralize such key activities as design, engineering, and R&D of subsidiaries established in a handful of developed countries. The program was to maintain some previous re-organizations, such as merging of Ford's seven worldwide design operations (Michigan, California, Turin, England, Germany, Australia and Japan) into one group called Ford Corporate Design (FCD). Since 1995, Ford's North American and European Operations and its Automotive components Group were merged into a single operating unit, dubbed Ford Automotive Operations (FAO). Five Vehicle Program Centers (VPC), four in the Ford Research and Engineering Center in Dearborn and one split between the United States and Germany, were set up under FAO. Each VPC has a worldwide responsibility for the design, development and engineering of the vehicles assigned to it.[30] Interestingly, in North America, the global cars are built at Ford's plants in Kansas City and Cuautitlán, Mexico. Only one other developing country, Brazil, was fully incorporated into Ford's new global organization, becoming a new production site for the Ford Fiesta (*Ward's Automotive Yearbook* 1995, 86).

Ford 2000 also introduced a decentralized management scheme that sliced management layers from 10 to 7, mainly through early retirement (this represents a 15 percent reduction of its top 25,000 executives). The program was

---

[29]. In the late 1980s, for instance, Ford of Europe argued that the new Mazda 323/Escort was too small for Europe, and pushed ahead with its own design. Similarly, Ford of Europe introduced a new Fiesta model in the next smaller size class after rejecting the Mazda 121 design, also considered too small for European markets. Ford Europe also opposed the inclusion of the European large car (the Scorpio) in the Taurus/Sable replacement program arguing that "no single design [could] satisfy both American and European consumers in that class of cars" (Womack, et al. 1990, 212-213). Despite these difficulties, the 1991 Ford Tempo and the Mercury Topaz and the Ford Sierra were jointly designed by Ford of Europe and the parent company.

[30]. The European Center was responsible for small, front-wheel-drive cars, and the Dearborn Center, of large front-drive cars, rear-wheel drive cars, personal-use trucks and commercial trucks. Asia Pacific and Latin American Operations were incorporated into the new global organization in 1996.

expected to save the company about $2 billion to $3 billion annually by the end of the century. However, these organizational changes took "too long to develop" and were extremely expensive. They cost about $6 billion, more than four times what Chrysler spent in its Dodge/Plymouth Neon, and included the coordination of Ford's U.S. and European operations to differentiate them for the two markets and the modernization of nine major plants to produce them. It must be noted that those efforts involved just one line of products. Also, while it expected to sell up to 800,000 of those cars annually in 59 countries by 1995 (Ford Motor Company's Annual Report 1993, 3, 8-9), in that year Ford actually sold 260,000 (*Ward's Automotive Yearbook* 1995, 114).

CONCLUDING REMARKS

In sum, Ford's attempts at creating a global integration strategy were not completely successful. The failure of the Big Three's "world-car" projects of the 1970s also confirms the multiplicity of obstacles to moving towards a fully globalized system of production. Ford's production operations are regionally, not globally, integrated, specifically in Europe and in North America. Here the most important change was the incorporation of Mexico in the North American system of production, as a producer of parts but also as a site for one of Ford's global cars. The fact that Brazil also was included in the company's global production plans confirms that automakers take sunk-costs seriously and try to take advantage of previous investments to increase their world-wide competitiveness. Although one could argue that parts production is more globalized, available information suggests that Ford has relied more on building a regional system of production. Ford's worldwide sales operations reveals that the United States continues to be the most important market and that political considerations as much as different consumer tastes inhibited the company's attempts to seek standardization of products across the Atlantic. The organization of markets and production on a regional basis also explain Ford's and the other U.S. automakers' demands to introduce regional trade policies that protect them from foreign producers through preferential access. R&D and design are the areas which Ford was able to move beyond trans-Atlantic coordination. However, recent failures in maintaining some of those international corporate alliances are questioning the viability of such a task. Finally, changes in the company's worldwide organization have been very expensive and very difficult to implement, pointing to the social character of MNEs, or the social/national embeddedness of these economic, complex organizations.

BIBLIOGRAPHY

Bartlett, Christopher. 1983. "MNCs: Get Off the Reorganization Merry-Go-Round." *Harvard Business Review*, Vol. 61, No. 2, pp. 138-146.

Bartlett, Christopher and Sumantra Ghoshal. 1989. *Managing Across Borders.* Boston: Harvard Business School Press.

Doz, Yves L. 1986. *Strategic Management in Multinational Enterprises.* Oxford: Pergamon Press.

Doz, Yves L. and C.K. Prahalad. 1990. "How MNCs Cope with Host Government Intervention." *Harvard Business Review*, March-April, pp. 149-157.

———. 1987. *The Multinational Mission: Balancing Local Demands and Global Vision.* New York: The Free Press.

Economic Commission for Latin America and the Caribbean (ECLAC). 1995. *Restructuring and International Competitiveness: The Mexican Automobile Industry.* Santiago, Chile: Economic Commission for Latin America and the Caribbean, July, 2.

Ford Motor Company Annual Reports. Washington D.C.: Securities and Exchange Commission, several years.

Gereffi, Gary. 1996. "The Elusive Last Lap in the Quest for Developed-Country Status." In *Globalization: Critical Reflections.* James H. Mittleman (Ed.). Boulder, Co.: Lynne Reinner, pp. 53-82.

Hamel, Gary and C.K. Prahalad 1985. "Do You Really Have a Global Strategy?" *Harvard Business Review*, Vol. 63, No. 4, July-August, pp. 139-148.

Herzenber, Stephen. 1991. "Towards a Cooperative Commonwealth? Labor and Restructuring in the U.S. and Canadian Auto Industries." Ph..D. Dissertation. Massachusetts Institute of Technology.

Hoffman, Kurt and Raphael Kaplinsky. 1988. *Driving Force. The Global Restructuring of Technology, Labour, and Investment in the Automobile and Components Industries.* Boulder Co.: Westview Press.

Kobrin, Stephen J. 1991. "An Empirical Analysis of the Determinants of Global Integration." *Strategic Management Journal*, Summer Special Issue, No. 12, pp. 17-31.

Kogut, Bruce. 1985. "Designing Global Strategies: Comparative and Competitive Value-Added Chains." *Sloan Management Review*, No. 26, Summer, pp. 15-28.

Levitt, T. 1983. "The Globalization of Markets." *Harvard Business Review*, Vol. 61, No. 3, May-June, pp. 92-102.

Morales, Rebecca. 1994. *Flexible Production. Restructuring of the International Automobile Industry.* Cambridge, Mass.: Polity Press.

Perry, Ross. 1982. *The future of Canada' s Auto Industry. The Big Three and the Japanese Challenge.* Canada: Canadian Institute for Economic Policy.

Porter, Michael. 1986. *Competition in Global Industries.* Cambridge, Mass.: Harvard Business School Press.

Rubenstein, James M. 1992. *The Changing U.S. Auto Industry. A Geographical Analysis.* London and New York: Routledge.

Ruigrok, Winfried and Rob van Tulder. 1995. *The Logic of International Restructuring.* London and New York: Routledge.

Stopford, John. M. and Louis. T. Wells Jr. 1972. *Managing the Multinational Enterprise.* New York: Basic Books.

Studer, Ma. Isabel. 1997. "Multinational Global Strategies and Government Policies: the case of Ford Motor Co and the Mexican and Canadian Automobile Industries in the 1960-1993 period," Ph.D. Dissertation, Johns Hopkins University-School of Advanced International Studies.

United Nations Center on Transnational Corporations. (UNCTC). 1983. *Trasnational Corporations in the International Auto-Industry.* New York: United Nations Center of Transnational Corporations.

United Nations World Investment Report. (UNWIR). 1996. *Investment, Trade and International Policy Arrangements.* New York: United Nations.

Ward's Automotive Yearbook. Michigan: Ward's Communications, several years.

Whitman, Marina. 1981. "International Trade and Investment." Essays in International Trade and Finance, Princeton: Princeton University Press. No. 143.

Womack, James P., Daniel T. Jones, and Daniel Roos, 1990. *The Machine that Changed the World.* New York: Basic Books.

World Motor Vehicle Data. Washington D.C.: American Automobile Manufacturer's Association, several issues.

RECENT PATTERNS OF PRODUCTION AND INVESTMENT IN THE CANADIAN AUTO INDUSTRY: REFLECTIONS ON MANAGEMENT STRATEGY

Pradeep Kumar and John Holmes[*]

INTRODUCTION

The Canadian automobile industry has undergone significant restructuring since the early 1980s, the nature and scope of which has been particularly noteworthy at the Big Three (General Motors, Ford and Chrysler). Over the past ten years the Big Three have invested close to $15 billion in modernization and rationalization of their plant facilities and equipment, application of new state-of-the-art technology, and new production and management systems. The restructuring at the Big Three, in particular the increased emphasis on outsourcing and consolidation of supply chain management, has stimulated a similar process of change in the independent auto parts sector. New capital spending on modernization and rationalization in the parts industry has almost tripled over the past five years, averaging $1.5 billion annually since 1993 (see Figure 1).

The restructuring and rationalization of the Canadian automobile industry over the past decade raises questions about management strategy for production and investment in Canada in view of the continued momentum towards continental integration of the industry under NAFTA. When NAFTA is fully phased in by 2004, the North American automobile industry will consist of Canada, the United States and Mexico, and the production of vehicles and component parts will be fully integrated on a continental basis. A number of questions and concerns have arisen as a result. What will be Canada's role in the integrated industry? Will the Canadian industry be able to maintain its current share of North American

---

[*] Pradeep Kumar is a Professor at the School of Industrial Relations, Queen's University. John Holmes is a Professor in the Department of Geography, Queen's University.

production? How and to what extent will the rationalization and integration of the Mexican auto industry affect Canadian assembly and component parts plants? What are the short- and medium-term prospects for the Canadian auto industry in view of the continued restructuring at the Big Three?

This study offers some answers to these questions and some insights into the challenges facing the industry. It attempts to draw inferences about management strategy through an examination of the current structure of the Canadian assembly and parts manufacturing industry, the recent patterns of production, investment and trade, and the key factors shaping Canada's competitive advantage. At present, none of the auto producers appear to have an *explicit* management strategy for production and investment in Canada. All vehicle assemblers and a number of major auto parts producers in the country are foreign multinational firms. The integration and rationalization of their Canadian facilities with their U.S. operations is reflected in the very high levels of trade in vehicles and component parts between the two countries. The product mandates of the Canadian subsidiaries are rarely, if ever, independent of those in the United States, and vary markedly with changes in corporate strategy. While trade and investment policy regimes, exchange rate changes, and differences in unit labour costs continue to be important determinants of plant location, lean production has become the dominant influence on corporate strategies. Thus locational decisions are increasingly governed by considerations of cost, quality, delivery, service and flexibility, and by proximity to suppliers and markets.

Figure 1

New Capital Expenditures in Canadian Automotive Industries, 1980-1997 (millions of dollars)

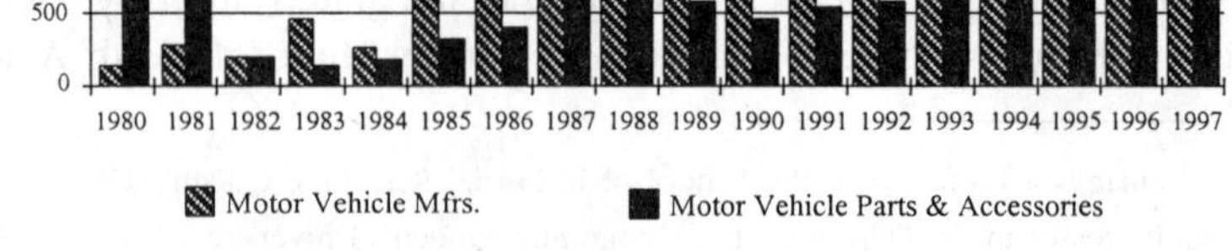

Source: Industry Canada 1997

CURRENT PROFILE OF THE CANADIAN AUTOMOTIVE INDUSTRY: SIZE, STRUCTURE, AND SIGNIFICANCE

The Canadian automobile industry is one of the oldest, most successful, and highly integrated industries in the world. Since its modest beginning in the first decade of the century, vehicle production has grown from an estimated 1,067 units during 1904-1908 to 2.4 million in 1996, accounting for 5 percent of world production and 15 percent of North American production. Canada ranks as the world's fifth largest producer of motor vehicles and has the highest assembly-to-sales ratio of any motor vehicle producing nation in the world (Industry Canada 1996). A unique characteristic of the industry is its very high level of integration with the U.S. industry.[1]

Nationally, the automobile industry plays a vital role in the Canadian economy because of its size, its input-output linkages with other sectors which produce significant multiplier effects, and its substantial contribution to international trade. The industry accounts for 11.5 percent of Canada's manufacturing gross domestic product and over 4 percent of the total GDP, one-third of all retail sales and manufacturing exports, and nearly 5 percent of total employment. The industry's contribution to the economy is much greater when the multiplier effects of its input-output linkages are taken into account. According to one estimate, $1 of automotive output generates over $3 of output in the total economy (Industry Canada 1996).

The automotive industry consists of automobile manufacturers (SIC 323 and 325), automotive dealers (SIC 631), and aftermarket sales, service station and repair shops (SIC 552, 633, 634, and 635). Automobile manufacturing, the focus of this study, is composed of two major industries: motor vehicle assembly (SIC 323), and automotive parts and accessories (SIC 325). The two industries produce a wide array of products: passenger cars and light trucks (vans, minivans, sports/utility vehicles, and pick-up trucks) as well as a wide range of component parts (engines, transmissions and related drive-train

---

[1] The integration dates back to the early 1900s, since the founding of the Ford Motor Company of Canada in 1904 and the formation of General Motor Corporation in 1908 (Chrysler Canada was incorporated in 1925), and was formalized in 1965 with the signing of the Canada-United States Automotive Trade Pact, popularly known as the Auto Pact. The Pact permitted duty-free trade in motor vehicles and original equipment parts while guaranteeing levels of production and employment equivalent to Canadian sales. The free trade regime was reinforced by the 1989 Canada-U.S. Free Trade Agreement and the North American Free Trade Agreement (NAFTA) in 1994.

components, steering and suspension parts, wheels and brakes, stampings, plastic parts, interior and exterior trims, and electrical parts and wiring assemblies). Parts production is primarily geared to the assembly sector. In 1994, the latest year for which information is available, motor vehicle assemblers purchased 80 percent of auto parts shipments.

Motor Vehicle Assembly Industry

The motor vehicle assembly part of the industry, which accounts for nearly 70 percent of total industry shipments, includes 14 major car and light-truck assembly plants, 10 of which are owned by the Big Three. General Motors owns four plants, Ford and Chrysler each have three, and the remaining four are transplants of Toyota, Honda, Volvo and CAMI, the latter a joint venture of General Motors and Suzuki[2] (see the Appendix for a detailed profile of the plants). Twelve of the 14 plants are located in southwestern Ontario, adjacent to the state of Michigan, the heartland of the U.S. auto industry. One plant (GM's Ste. Thérèse plant) is located in Quebec, and the small Volvo plant is in Halifax, Nova Scotia. The Big Three also have 12 parts plants (Ford: 5; General Motors: 4; and Chrysler 3). All three Japanese plants have on-site stamping facilities, and Toyota also has an engine plant on site.

The vehicle assembly industry is totally foreign-owned, highly oligopolistic, and dominated by the Big Three, which account for over four-fifths of total production, three-quarters of Canadian vehicle sales, and nearly sixty percent of total employment. The industry has the highest foreign direct investment concentration in the Canadian economy. The total productive stock of foreign investment was $17 billion in 1994, of which 86 percent was from the United States (Industry Canada 1996).

Both the production and sale of vehicles in Canada are highly integrated with the United States. Of the 2.4 million vehicles produced in 1996, almost

---

[2] The total combined production capacity of the 14 assembly plants is currently 2.7 million and is expected to reach 3.0 million by the year 2000 when plant expansion at Toyota, Honda, and Ford is completed. In 1996, they produced a total of 2.37 million vehicles (1.28 million passenger cars and 1.09 million light duty trucks). Of the 2.37 million vehicles produced, nearly 2.0 million, or 84 percent, were assembled at the Big Three plants. Transplants accounted for 16 percent of the total vehicle production (25 percent of passenger cars and 5 percent of light trucks). General Motors was the largest producer with a total production of 752,371 units in 1996 (493,489 cars and 258,882 trucks) or 32 percent of total vehicles and 38 percent of passenger car output. However, Chrysler, the second largest producer, was the leading assembler of light trucks, especially minivans, accounting for 43 percent of total Canadian truck output.

96 percent were exported to the United States. Similarly, of the 1.2 million vehicles sold in Canada in 1996, nearly two-thirds were imported from the United States. However, although the Big Three operations in Mexico are covered under the Auto Pact and the NAFTA, there is minimal integration with Mexico. Imports from Mexico constitute only 9 percent of total Canadian vehicle sales (15 percent of passenger car sales and 2 percent of truck sales). Canadian exports to Mexico are minuscule, a little over one-fourth of one percent of total vehicle imports into Mexico in 1996.

Canada is a net exporter of motor vehicles, with a net trade surplus in 1996 of $27.5 billion ($31.0 billion with the United States). The total value of vehicle exports was $47.6 billion ($46.8 billion to the U.S.), while imports were valued at $20.1 billion ($15.8 billion from the United States). The United States is Canada's principal trade partner, accounting for 97 percent of the exports and 80 percent of the imports of vehicles. Similarly, exports to Canada constitute nearly three-fifths of total U.S. vehicle exports, and close to one-half of vehicles imported into the U.S. are from Canada. A large part of this trade is intra-firm. Mexico, since 1995, is Canada's second largest automotive trading partner (replacing Japan), although the volume of vehicle trade is small with $64 million of exports (one-eighth of one percent of total exports) and $1.67 billion of imports (8.4 percent of total imports). Nearly 80 percent of the imports from Mexico were under the Auto Pact, as a part of Big Three operations. Unlike the United States, with which Canada enjoys a trade surplus, Canada has a trade deficit with Mexico, amounting to $1.6 billion in 1996 (Industry Canada 1997).

Although relatively labour intensive, the vehicle assembly industry is a high value-added industry, a result of nearly $25 billion in investments in plant modernization, automation and rationalization over the past 15 years. In 1995, the latest year for which data are available, value added by manufacturing per worker in the vehicle assembly industry was $200,289, over 60 percent higher than the manufacturing average. It was the highest value-added manufacturing industry with the highest value of shipments of any manufacturing industry in Canada. Labour costs were 36 percent of the total value added by manufacturing, compared with 29 percent for all manufacturing.

The Canadian vehicle assembly industry is also highly unionized, noted for above-average wages, benefits, and working conditions that set the national pattern for collective bargaining. Overall, union density is around 72 percent, nearly twice the average density for Canada. All assembly plants with the exception of Honda and Toyota are unionized. The Canadian Auto

Workers Union (CAW), the largest private sector union in Canada, is the principal union in the industry.[3]

Hourly earnings in the industry average over $25 (Cdn) an hour, nearly 54 percent above the manufacturing industry average. The industry provides generous benefits in the form of paid time off, cost of living adjustments, supplementary unemployment benefits and other related income security benefits, an indexed pension and extended medical benefits —all totally financed by employers. The industry is also characterized by flexible work scheduling through extended shifts, weekend work, and other forms of alternative work arrangements. Workers also enjoy opportunities for both technical and social training (health and safety, human rights and literacy training). Unionized Japanese-owned assembly plants conform to the same wage and benefits pattern established by collective bargaining between the Big Three and the CAW. In national currencies the average hourly labour costs are similar between Canada and the United States, but when expressed in U.S. dollars the Canadian costs are nearly 26 percent lower. The differential, which is estimated to be about $13.00 (U.S.) an hour in favor of Canada, is attributable to lower health care insurance costs and the exchange rate.

The Canadian vehicle industry is also noted for its high productivity and product quality levels despite the absence of such "high performance work organization" practices as team concept, job rotation, contingent compensation, employee involvement, and "partnership" with management in shopfloor decision-making (Pil and MacDuffie 1996, Kumar and Holmes 1997a). Overall, Canadian plants are ranked higher with regard to productivity, as measured by workers per vehicle (Harbour 1997), and product quality, measured by problems per 100 vehicles in the J.D. Power Initial Quality Survey.

Automotive Parts Industry

The Canadian auto parts industry, unlike the vehicle assembly industry, is highly diverse, both in its product array, ownership structure, and institutional characteristics. There were a total of 567 establishments in 1994

---

[3] The CAW was formed in 1985 following a split in the UAW, the American International union which had represented Canadian autoworkers since 1937. The CAW is a strong and progressive union, noted for its hard and innovative bargaining, and its "social unionism" philosophy with a clearly articulated agenda for workplace change and macro-economic and social reforms (CAW 1993, Kumar and Holmes 1996).

engaged in the manufacturing of auto parts and accessories. Nearly two-fifths were small establishments employing less than 50 workers and accounting for only four percent of total employment and total shipments. On the other hand, there were 36 large establishments with 500 or more employees which accounted for nearly one-third of total employment and one-half of total shipments. Ownership was equally divided between Canadian and foreign-owned firms including the Big Three. Nearly twenty firms, both American multinationals and Canadian companies, dominate the industry as first-tier and second-tier suppliers. Magna International, a Canadian multinational corporation which is ranked 26th in sales among the top 50 global parts producers, is the largest and most diversified systems developer and integrated producer. Nearly three quarters of parts manufacturers are located in Ontario, in proximity to assembly manufacturers and the U.S. midwestern auto industry. The industry employed 92,500 workers in 1996, 58 percent of total automobile manufacturing employment. Total shipments were valued at $22.8 billion, 30 percent of total industry shipments (Industry Canada 1997).

The auto parts industry, like the vehicle assembly industry, is also highly integrated and rationalized with its counterpart in the United States.[4] Nearly 70 percent of the parts produced in Canada are exported, 63 percent to the United States. Similarly, over 80 percent of parts and accessories used in Canada are imported, nearly 74 percent from the United States. Over four-fifths of the imports come duty free under the Auto Pact. Unlike vehicle assembly, Canada is a net importer of component parts products and in 1996 ran a trade deficit of $20.1 billion in parts and accessories, $17.2 billion (86 percent) with the United States and another $1.42 billion (7 percent) with Mexico.

Relative to vehicle assembly manufacturing, the auto parts industry in Canada is much more labour intensive, adds less value, and is only partially unionized. Labour costs in 1995 constituted 43 percent of total value added by manufacturing, nearly 12 percent higher than vehicle assembly. Total value added by manufacturing per production worker was $107,502, only 54 percent of value-added per worker in vehicle assembly. Hourly earnings averaged nearly $18 (Cdn) an hour, nine percent over the manufacturing average, but 30 percent below the average in vehicle assembly.

---

[4] The import and export of parts and accessories, except tires and tubes, for use as original equipment in the manufacturing of vehicles by the Big Three is duty free under the Auto Pact and NAFTA.

Nearly one-half of the auto parts workers are unionized. The unionization rate is over 80 percent in parts facilities operated by the Big Three and CAMI, but only 45 percent in independent parts establishments. Almost all of the large parts producers are unionized in varying degrees. Unionization rates vary between less than one percent at Magna to between 70-85 percent at A.G. Simpson, Siemens, Lear Siegler, Johnson Controls and Budd Canada, firms which typically design complete high-tech products or parts systems (CAW 1997). The CAW is the principal union in the parts industry, with nearly two-thirds of its membership in this sector concentrated in the dozen largest parts companies (CAW 1997).

Wages, benefits and working conditions in the industry vary according to the degree of unionization, size of the plants and the nature of employers. The terms and conditions of employment at the captive parts facilities of the Big Three are identical to their vehicle operations. Workers in these facilities, therefore, enjoy above average wages, benefits and working conditions. Labour conditions, including wages and benefits at other unionized plants, vary considerably (CAW 1996a). Nonunion plants generally pay lower wages and provide few benefits to their workers.

According to a recent publication (APMA 1997, 45), the major strengths of the Canadian parts industry include: 1) a strong materials supply base for high quality steel, powdered metals, non-ferrous metals and plastic feedstock; 2) availability of casting, stamping, and plating operations and heat treatment facilities; 3) a world class tool and die industry; 4) strong second-tier manufacturers that produce components for first-tier suppliers; 5) a highly skilled workforce; 6) an abundant supply of low cost energy; 7) a reputation for quality production; 8) a well developed transportation infrastructure; 9) a supportive public policy environment; 10) an expanding vehicle assembly industry; 11) location of plants close to major customers and in proximity to the large and expanding U.S. market; 12) availability of capital; and, 13) the presence of companies with the expertise and technology to develop systems capabilities. Many of these competitive advantages have been highlighted in a number of comparative studies conducted by consultants (see, for example, KPMG 1996; Industry Canada 1992; and Booz, Allen, Hamilton 1990).

The APMA (1997) publication also highlights the weaknesses of the Canadian parts industry which include: 1) a preponderance of small manufacturers with limited R&D and product development capabilities; 2) a very limited number of true first-tier systems suppliers; 3) a growing shortage of skilled workers; 4) an over reliance on the Big Three sales within Canada;

5) growing competition from parts makers in both low-wage and high-wage countries; and, 6) lack of presence in global markets and a limited commitment to expand globally.

RECENT PATTERNS OF PRODUCTION AND INVESTMENT

As noted at the beginning of the paper, the Canadian automobile industry has been undergoing significant restructuring since the early to mid-1980s, creating both threats and opportunities for labour. The process of restructuring has entailed both the expansion of production and investment in new plants by foreign manufacturers, as well as large-scale rationalization and modernization of plant facilities and equipment by the Big Three and parts producers. The restructuring has been shaped by four dynamics: 1) currency fluctuations, in particular the rise of the Japanese yen against the U.S. dollar in the mid-1980s (leading Japanese manufacturers to set up plants in Canada and the United States), and the decline of the Canadian dollar in relation to the U.S. since 1990 (which has bolstered Canada's competitive position); 2) internationalization of production, due in large part to the competitive pressures from Japanese automakers; 3) changing consumer preferences towards more fuel efficient, high quality vehicles, resulting in a steady decline in the market share of the Big Three and the rising proportion of imports and/or transplant sales; and 4) growing momentum towards continental integration of the industry, spurred by the new trade and investment policy regime under the Canada-U.S. Free Trade Agreement in 1989 and NAFTA in 1993.

The nature and scope of this restructuring of production and management systems, aimed at greater efficiencies and operational flexibilities as well as improvements in product quality, has been particularly significant at the Big Three. The key initiatives pursued by management have included: 1) a significantly altered product mix towards mid-size/intermediate passenger cars, minivans, and pickup trucks to meet the growing demand for these products in the U.S. market; 2) adoption of lean production methods with emphasis on new technology, just-in-time inventory systems, and reduction in sub-assembly processes and indirect labour to increase value added; 3) greater outsourcing of component parts, materials and services, and a new supply-chain management philosophy favoring consolidation of suppliers and their increased involvement in product development to ensure cost efficiencies and better quality; 4) greater capacity utilization through alternative work scheduling; and 5) downsizing of the workforce and a new system of work organization that includes management delayering and reduction in supervisor/worker ratios, increased employee involvement in shopfloor administration, greater information sharing, improved union-management relations, enhanced training and skill formation, and — wherever possible— introduction of performance-based compensation and union involvement in continuous improvement and product quality matters. The restructuring at the Big Three, in particular the emphasis on outsourcing and consolidation of supply-chain management, has stimulated a similar process of change in the independent auto parts sector.

The restructuring of the industry, with both the investment in new plants by foreign manufacturers and the process of modernization and restructuring at the Big Three, has had a significant impact on production, product mix, productivity and product quality. A number of trends and patterns are noteworthy.

First, the volume of production of both vehicles and component parts has gone up substantially since 1985. The total volume of vehicle production (in physical units) during the period 1985-1996 was up 24 percent —truck production by 30 percent and car production by 19 percent. Vehicle production reached an all time high of 2.4 million vehicles in 1995, and the value of shipments (in constant dollars) was over 60 percent higher than the 1985 value. Consequently, the Canadian share of North American production increased from 13.8 percent in 1985 to 15.8 percent in 1995 (the U.S. share over this period declined from 83.3 to 78.3 and Mexico's share went up from 2.8 to 5.9).[5] Canadian automotive components and accessories production also has grown substantially since 1985 in tandem with vehicle production.[6] The total value of parts shipments (in constant dollars) was a record 20.4

---

[5] It is noteworthy that almost all of the increase in vehicle production over the 1985-1995 period has been due to 1) expanded transplant production and 2) rising exports to the United States. Transplant production was one-half of one percent in 1985 (the only foreign plant was Volvo in Halifax) compared with 387,367 units or 16 percent of the total Canadian production in 1995 as a result of the three new Japanese transplants (Honda, Toyota, and CAMI). Canadian vehicle exports to the United States over this period increased 40 percent from 1.5 million in 1985 to over 2.1 million in 1995. The growth in vehicle exports was in sharp contrast to domestic sales which have been depressed and declining steadily since 1985.

[6] The Canadian value-added rules attached to the Auto Pact mean that an expansion of vehicle production in Canada is accompanied almost automatically by an expansion of parts production.

million in 1995, up 55 percent from 1985. Exports were up 25 percent and imports, principally from the United States, increased 54 percent. However, although imports grew faster than the exports, the ratio of imports to domestic consumption declined from 94 percent in 1985 to 85 percent in 1995, suggesting that domestic parts producers have been gaining in market share. The strong performance of the parts sector is related to the new capital spending by parts producers to modernize and restructure their production and management systems. New capital expenditures in the parts industry have more than quadrupled over the past ten years. Since 1992, parts suppliers have invested over $7 billion in upgrading machinery, equipment and new technology (Industry Canada 1997). The healthy state of the Canadian parts industry is reflected in the industry's share of total North American parts production and sales. According to a recent study (APMA 1997, 14-15), Canada's share of OEM parts sales has grown from 12.7 percent in 1986 to 17.6 percent in 1995, although its share of North American parts production has remained steady at around 10 percent.

Second, restructuring has led to a significant change in the product mix, from passenger cars to pick-up trucks and minivans, and within the car segment from compact cars to mid-size/intermediate cars.[7] Production of trucks has more than doubled since 1980, from 527,000 to 1,145,000 and in 1996 constituted 49 percent of the total Canadian vehicle production compared with only 38 percent in 1980. The shift from cars to light trucks started in 1983 with the production of minivans by Chrysler at its Windsor assembly plant (the plant assembled mid-sized passenger cars earlier) and gained momentum in 1994 when Ford switched from compact cars (Tempo and Topaz) to the production of the new Windstar minivans at its Oakville assembly plant.[8] In the car segment, all Big Three manufacturers have

[7] Product mix changes have been more pronounced at the Big Three than the transplants. Among the transplants, CAMI produces sports utility small cars and trucks, and Toyota and Honda assemble small sub-compact cars. In 1997 Honda also started producing the Acura CL in luxury car segment and has announced plans for making new minivans in the near future.

[8] The two companies (Ford and Chrysler) accounted for almost 70 percent of Canadian truck production in 1996. Truck production has increased nine fold at Chrysler, from 54,000 in 1980 to 467,000. In 1996, light trucks (mainly vans and minivans) constituted 63 percent of total vehicle output of Chrysler Canada. Similarly, at Ford the production of light trucks (including Windstar minivan and pick-up trucks) has gone up from 186,000 in 1980 to 311,000 in 1996, largely as a result of minivan production since 1994 (between 1993 and 1996 Ford production of trucks jumped from 136,000 to 311,000). Currently, Ford produces more trucks than cars in Canada (311,000 trucks compared with 226,000 cars).

switched from the production of a variety of compact and intermediate size cars in the early 1980s to the production of a small number of mainly intermediate mid-size cars. For example, General Motors at its Oshawa and Ste. Thérèse plants now assembles the Lumina/Monte Carlo, Regal, Camaro and Firebird, whereas in the early 1980s the company was producing seven makes of cars ranging from the Pontiac 6000 to the Pontiac Grand Prix. Similarly, Ford now has only one car plant in Canada assembling the large-size Crown Victoria/Grand Marquis. In the early 1980s, the company had two car plants and produced eight car models in different car segments from compact the Escort, Tempo and Topaz, to the Ford LTD, Crown Victoria, and Grand Marquis. Chrysler also now has only one car plant, acquired from American Motors in 1987, dedicated to the production of intermediate-size LH cars.

The changes in product mix reflect the growing demand for light trucks (including minivans) and intermediate size cars in the U.S. market, since 90 percent of the cars and trucks assembled by the Big Three in Canada are destined for export to the United States. Retail sales of trucks in the U.S. have more than doubled, from 2,480,000 in 1980 to 6,570,000 in 1996. Similarly, the sales of intermediate size cars has gone up from 1,836 thousand to 4,191 thousand, accounting for close to one-half of the total car sales in 1996 compared to 28 percent of the total in 1980.

Third, there is a growing trend towards sole sourcing particular models of cars and trucks in Canadian plants for the North American market. In 1996, over four-fifths of cars and two-fifths of trucks produced in Canada were sole sourced, compared with only 14 percent in 1985.[9] The increasing emphasis

---

[9] Most products are sole sourced for export to the U.S. market. The exceptions are Honda Civic, Dodge Intrepid, Chrysler minivans and Ford and GM trucks which are made in both U.S. and Canadian plants. For example, General Motors has been sole sourcing such intermediate size cars as the Regal and Lumina at its Oshawa plants since 1989, and the Camaro and Firebird at the Ste. Thérèse plant since 1993. All of the 535,602 cars produced by GM in Canada in the 1996 model year were sole sourced. Similarly, Ford of Canada has been sole sourcing large intermediate cars (Crown Victoria/Grand Marquis) from its St. Thomas plant since 1986, and Windstar minivan since 1994. In 1996, all of the car production and 77 percent of the truck production at Ford of Canada was sole sourced for the North American market. Chrysler, while lagging behind Ford and GM, sole sources intermediate LH cars (LHS, New Yorker and Vision) at its Bramalea plant and large vans at its Windsor Pillet Road operation. In 1996, nearly one-third of car production and one-seventh of truck production of Chrysler Canada was sole sourced. Among the transplants, all of CAMI's car and truck production and Toyota's car production in 1996 was also sole sourced for the North American market.

on sole sourcing is attributed to the growing integration of North American automobile production.

Fourth, the Big Three are increasingly outsourcing and sub-contracting component parts, materials, and services to achieve cost efficiencies. The shift from in-house operations to outsourcing, a part of the lean production strategy with an emphasis on maintaining and developing "core capacities" and reducing non-value added activities, has led to the closure of a number of in-house component parts plants. Over the past ten years Chrysler has closed or sold three parts plants, Ford has sold one plant and consolidated its engine production into two plants, and General Motors has sold three component parts facilities. According to a recent publication by the Parts Manufacturers' Association (APMA 1997, 45), "[increased] outsourcing by the Big Three has resulted in a decrease of parts sales from the captive producers from 46 percent of all parts shipments in 1986 to under 33 percent in 1995." An important consequence of increased outsourcing and the closure of in-house parts production is a marked reduction in the Big Three workforce. The downsizing has been particularly pronounced at General Motors, where total hourly employment has declined from its peak level of over 38,000 to under 25,000, largely on account of the closure of one assembly plant and the sale of three component parts facilities. Chrysler and Ford employment has also declined by nearly 5,000, between 10 percent (in the case of Ford) and 25 percent (Chrysler) of their total employment.

The outsourcing of component parts and subcontracting of services has been particularly threatening to labour in view of the low and declining levels of unionization in the independent parts industry and the large differentials in wages and benefits between unionized and nonunionized workplaces. According to one estimate (APMA 1997), workers in Big Three in-house parts plants are paid nearly $42 per hour in wages and benefits compared with $23-28 per hour paid to workers in the independent parts sector. The importance of this issue to labour was highlighted by the 1996 bargaining round between General Motors and the CAW. The company wanted to sell two of its component parts facilities and contract out several hundred jobs, affecting over 4,000 of the total 26,000 unionized employees, in an effort to reduce costs, "to become competitive," and "to allow GM to focus ... on core components, assembly and new product programs" (GM 1996). The union demanded protection against outsourcing, asking GM to ensure that existing wages and benefits would be maintained in the event that in-house plants were sold to an independent parts supplier. The dispute led to a six-week work stoppage. The union succeeded in getting protection through a successor-rights clause, extending the terms and conditions of employment at GM to the new purchaser, and securing a commitment from the company that "there will be no reduction in community employment levels as a result of outsourcing during the term of the new agreement." The issue, however, continues to be a source of tension in the industry. Independent parts suppliers consider the union commitment to limit outsourcing a threat to their competitiveness. The suppliers are particularly concerned about the Big Three commitment to "responsible labour relations" in developing supplier relationships (APMA 1997). They are afraid that the Big Three will be under pressure to promote the unionization of nonunionized parts plants, leading to the narrowing of labour cost differentials between the independent parts suppliers and assemblers. Indeed, the union publicly states (CAW 1997) that "new organizing to maintain CAW membership at a 'critical mass' in the independent parts sector remains a top challenge."

Finally, all the Big Three, in addition to increased outsourcing, have been developing a new supply management system to further reduce their material costs. The new system emphasizes consolidation of supply sources, fewer direct suppliers, longer contracts to reduce the overhead costs of managing and coordinating the supply system, and shifting more of the responsibility for product design and program management to the suppliers. The new supply chain management has led to a big shakeout in auto parts industry since 1989. The industry has undergone significant restructuring over the past five years, marked by increased capital spending for modernization of plants and facilities, introduction of new technology (especially among parts manufacturers aspiring to become first-tier or second-tier suppliers), a wave of mergers and acquisitions, and a reduction in the number of plants. The consolidation trend is particularly pronounced among firms producing wiring assemblies and plastic parts, and among small plants (Kumar and Holmes 1997b).

The process of modernization and consolidation of plants has had positive effects on the parts industry, resulting in higher output and employment as well as varying degrees of improvement in productivity (Kumar and Holmes 1997b). While overall productivity in the auto parts sector increased nearly 10 percent between 1985 and 1995, some industries, such as wiring assemblies, motor vehicle fabric, engines and plastic parts, have shown growth of 25 percent to 80 percent.

CONCLUSION

In this paper we have examined the automakers' manufacturing strategies in Canada in the context of the growing momentum towards full continental integration of the industry. Through an analysis of the current structure of the industry and the changes in the pattern of production and investment, we have demonstrated that the industry has responded and adapted well to the changes in the competitive environment since the early 1980s, and has recorded impressive gains in output, employment, productivity and product quality. As a result, major manufacturers continue to invest heavily in new and expanded production facilities. The ratio of vehicle production to sales has almost doubled. Net exports of automotive products have quadrupled and both the ratio of domestic parts production to imports and the ratio of exports to domestic shipments are increasing. The restructuring and rationalization of the industry, we argue, has also led to significant regional product specialization, especially in vehicle assembly. Within North America there is a growing intra-industry specialization, with increasing production by the Big Three of compact and subcompact cars and light trucks in Mexico, and mid-size/intermediate passenger cars and minivans in Canada, both aimed at the U.S. market. A similar trend is evident in the component parts industry, with increasing small engine and electrical systems parts production in Mexico, and large/medium-size engines, stamping, and seating production in Canada. We believe that NAFTA will reinforce and probably accelerate the trend towards full continental integration of the industry as Mexican production is rationalized and integrated with production in Canada and the United States.

While there does not appear to an *explicit* management strategy, changes in product mix, sourcing patterns, and supply management at the Big Three suggest that production and investment decisions are being guided by the lean production strategy within the framework of highly integrated vehicle assembly and parts production operations in Canada and the United States (see Womack 1991 and Eden 1994 for the rationale). In the context of lean production, the Canadian industry enjoys a competitive advantage due to its proximity to key suppliers and markets, availability of skilled labour, well developed supplier base, high quality transportation infrastructure, lower labour costs,[10] and a stable labour relations climate. These factors augur well for the successful integration of the Canadian industry into the expanded North American market under NAFTA.

[10] Compensation per hour in Canada was $13 (U.S.) an hour lower than the U.S. at the Big Three in 1995. The wage gap was $3 an hour and non-wage benefits were $10 an hour higher in the U.S. than in Canada (CAW 1996b). Productivity, measured by hours per vehicle, was around fifteen percent higher in Canadian assembly plants (Pil and MacDuffie 1996). The labour cost differential is smaller in auto parts plants due to higher rates of unionization in Canada than in the U.S. However, the labour cost gap between the two countries has been increasing over the past five years due to the declining value of the Canadian dollar, the lower inflation rate in Canada, and the steady improvements in productivity as a result of modernization and upgrading in both the assembly and the component parts

APPENDIX

Table A-1
Profile of Big Three Car Assembly Plants

Location	Bramalea (Ontario)	St. Thomas (Ontario)	Oshawa #1 (Ontario)	Oshawa #2 (Ontario)	St. Therese (Quebec)
Year of Start	1987	1967	1955	1957	1965
Current Product Line	Concord, Intrepid, LHS, Vision, New Yorker	Crown Victoria, Grand Marquis	Lumina, Monte Carlo	Lumina, Regal	Camaro, Firebird
Capacity/Units	252,000	226,000	248,000	248,000	210,000
Line Speed (Units/Hour)	67	60	66	66	56
No. of Shifts	2	2	2	2	1
Production in '000 units (1996)	239.0	226.2	217.6	187.9	88.6
Employees/1996 (hourly)	2,726 (2,506)	2,8888 (2,650)	2,830 (2,629)	3,111 (2,905)	1,588 (1,398)
Productivity (Workers per Vehicle) 1996	2.54	3.01	2.68	2.95	3.54
Quality (1996)*					
-problems per 100 Vehicles	97	85	99	91	141
-ranking	20	10	21	14	39

* Based on ratings of 42 car plants in the U.S., Canada, and Mexico

Source: *The Harbour Report* 1997, and unpublished data from J.D. Power Associates' 1996 North American Rankings.

Table A-2
Profile of Transplant Car Assembly Plants

Location	Alliston (Ontario)	Cambridge (Ontario)	Ingersoll (Ontario)	Halifax (Nova Scotia)
Ownership	Honda	Toyota	GM-Suzuki	Volvo
Year of Start	1986	1988	1989	1963
Current Product Line	Civic Acura EL	Corolla	Metro, Swift Firefly	Volvo 850 Series
Capacity/Units	150,400	97,760	141,752	8,500
Line Speed (Units/Hr)	40	26	38	NA
No. of Shifts	2	2	2	2
Production in '000 units (1996)	144.0	97.3	80.4	7.6
Employees/1996 (hourly)	1,100 (950)	927 (777)	1,144 (964)	200 —
Productivity (Workers per Vehicle) 1996	2.44	2.35	3.51	NA
Quality (1996)*				
-problems per 100 Vehicles	69	63	97	NA
-ranking	2	1	19	NA

* Based on ratings of 42 car plants in the U.S., Canada, and Mexico

Source: *The Harbour Report* 1997, and unpublished data from J.D. Power Associates' 1996 North American Rankings.

Table A-3
Profile of Light Truck Assembly Plants

Location	Windsor (Ontario)	Windsor (Pillette Rd.)	Oakville #1 (Ontario)	Oakville #2 (Ontario)	Oshawa (Ontario)	Ingersoll (Ontario)
Ownership	Chrysler	Chrysler	Ford	Ford	GM	CAMI
Year of Start	1925	1975	1953	1965	1965	1989
Current Product Line	Caravan, Voyager (minivan)	Ram Van, Ram Wagon	Windstar (minivan)	F-Pickup Trucks	Chevrolet K, Sierra	Geo Tracker, Sidekick, Sunrunner
Current Capacity	325,000	120,000	282,000	169,000	229,000	83,472
Line Speed (Units/Hour)	72	30	75	45	61	22
No. of Shifts	3	2	2	1	2.5	2
Production in '000 units (1996)	373.2	93.3	236.5	74.4	258.9	47.9
Employees/1996 (hourly)	4,966 (4,698)	1,625 (1,536)	3,421 (3,110)	1,353 (1,216)	3,608 (3,362)	1,089 (962)
Productivity (Workers per Vehicle) 1996	3.42	3.69	2.85	3.68	3.06	4.61
Quality (1996)* -problems per 100 Vehicles	154	176	111	170	110	107
-ranking	27	32	12	31	11	9

* Based on ratings of 33 light truck plants in the U.S., Canada, and Mexico

Source: *The Harbour Report* 1997, and unpublished data from J.D. Power Associates' 1996 North American Rankings.

BIBLIOGRAPHY

APMA. 1997. *Automotive Components: June 1997 Industry Outlook.* Toronto: Automobile Parts Manufacturers' Association of Canada.

Booz Allen Hamilton Inc. 1990. *A Comparative Study of the Cost Competitiveness of the Automobile Parts Manufacturing Industry in North America.* Toronto: The Automotive Parts Manufacturers' Association of Canada.

CAW. 1997. *Sectoral Profiles: Independent Parts.* North York, ON: Canadian Auto Workers.

CAW. 1996a. *Independent Auto Parts: Report and Summary.* North York, ON: Canadian Auto Workers.

CAW. 1996b. *GM Profits and GM Workers of Canada: Facts and Figures for 1996 Bargaining.* North York, ON: Canadian Auto Workers.

CAW. 1993. *Work Reorganization: Responding to Lean Production.* North York, ON: Canadian Auto Workers.

Eden, Lorraine. 1994. "Who Does What After NAFTA? Location Strategies of U.S. Multinationals." In Lorraine Eden, ed., *Multinationals in North America.* Calgary, AB: University of Calgary Press.

GM. 1996. "Why are General Motors of Canada and Chrysler Canada Different?" (mimeographed). Oshawa, ON: General Motors of Canada.

Harbour. 1997. *The Harbour Report 1997: North America.* Troy MI: Harbour and Associates.

Industry Canada. 1996. *Automotive Industry: Part 1 - Overview and Prospects.* Ottawa, ON.

——. 1997. *Statistical Review of the Canadian Automotive Industry.* Ottawa, ON.

——. 1992. *The Canadian Automobile Industry: Issues and Options. Report of the Automotive Advisory Committee.* Ottawa, ON: Industry Canada.

KPMG. 1996. *A Comparison of Business Costs in Canada and the United States.* Ottawa, ON: Department of Foreign Affairs and International Trade, USA Trade and Investment Division.

Kumar, Pradeep and John Holmes. 1997a. "Continuity and Change: Evolving Human Resource Policies and Practices in the Canadian Automobile Industry." In Thomas Kochan, John Paul MacDuffie and Russell Lansbury, eds., *After Lean Production: Evolving Employment Practices in the World Auto Industry.* Ithaca: Cornell University Press.

——. 1997b. "The Canadian Automobile Industry in the Context of North American Integration" (mimeographed). Kingston, ON: School of Industrial Relations, Queen's University.

——. 1996. "Change, But In What Direction? Divergent Union Responses to Work Restructuring in the Integrated North American Auto Industry." In Frederick C. Deyo, ed., *Social Reconstructions of the World Automobile Industry.* New York: St. Martin's Press.

Pil, Frits K. and John Paul MacDuffie. 1996. "Canada at the Cross-Roads: A Comparative Analysis of the Canadian Auto Industry." A paper presented at the Canadian Workplace Research Network Conference in Vancouver, October 1996. Pittsburgh: University of Pittsburgh.

Womack, James P. 1991. "A Positive Sum Solution: Free Trade in the North American Motor Vehicle Sector." In Delal Baer and Guy F. Erb, eds., *Strategic Sectors in Mexican-U.S. Free Trade*. Washington D.C.: The Center for Strategic and International Studies.

TRABAJADORES Y SINDICATOS ANTE LA GLOBALIZACION: EL CASO DEL SECTOR AUTOMOTRIZ MEXICANO *

Graciela Bensusán **
Ma. Cristina Bayón ***

INTRODUCCIÓN

La globalización de los mercados y la restructuración productiva a lo largo de las últimas dos décadas han obligado a los sindicatos a emprender una transformación profunda de sus estrategias con el propósito de recuperar su capacidad de defensa de los intereses de los asalariados. La revisión de estas experiencias muestra un comportamiento diferenciado en razón de las características de los contextos políticos e institucionales en que actúan. De allí que pueda esperarse que los cambios que se adopten y los resultados que se obtengan presenten importantes variaciones, incluso ante la existencia de claras semejanzas en la direccionalidad de los procesos de reestructuración productiva y en su impacto en las condiciones laborales. En este sentido, resulta clave el análisis de los factores que posibilitan u obstruyen la renovación sindical encaminada a lograr un reparto social más equilibrado de las pérdidas y ganancias generadas por los los retos de la competitividad, a fin de revertir los efectos disgregadores del nuevo modelo de desarrollo.

En México se advierte que mientras el proceso de reconversión productiva en la industria combinó innovaciones tecnológicas y organizativas con el objetivo de aumentar la competitividad, afectando fuertemente las condiciones laborales, el sindicalismo siguió por lo general actuando de manera tradicional. Las empresas tendieron a imponer unilateralmente sus estrategias y el gobierno siguió controlando al movimiento sindical, el cual ha jugado un importante papel como defensor del viejo sistema político y de representación social frente a quienes lo impugnaron, sin por ello detener el creciente deterioro de su capacidad de negociación frente al capital. La situación descrita puede ilustrarse con lo ocurrido en la industria automotriz.

---

* Este trabajo recoge los avances parciales del proyecto de investigación trinacional "Estrategias sindicales frente al TLC: México, Estados Unidos y Canadá", financiado por CONACYT y El Colegio de Mexico.

** Profesora-Investigadora. Universidad Autónoma Metropolitana-Xochimilco.

*** Investigadora. FLACSO-México

Esta industria ocupa un lugar estratégico en la economía mexicana —representando el 12% del PIB manufacturero— y ha constituido un motor fundamental de la integración regional y global del país, por lo que los cambios adoptados en esta rama para aumentar la productividad adquieren un carácter paradigmático. Se trata de un sector con fuerte presencia sindical y tradiciones de combatividad, cuyas organizaciones fueron parte importante de la vanguardia del movimiento obrero y ejercieron una gran influencia sobre el destino de los sindicatos y de los trabajadores del resto de los sectores. Así, puede esperarse que los éxitos o derrotas de las organizaciones sindicales de esta rama estratégica en su intento por defender los intereses de sus agremiados frente a la restructuración y recuperar poder, marquen las pautas de las transformaciones del sistema de relaciones laborales hacia la inclusión o la exclusión, opciones actualmente en disputa.

Ante los profundos procesos de cambio producidos, las respuestas desarrolladas por los sindicatos automotrices mostraron fuertes limitaciones, tanto para desarrollar una estrategia articulada a nivel de sector, capaz de enfrentar la ofensiva empresarial en la industria, como para replantear su presencia y espacios de acción a nivel de cada una de las plantas. A su vez, la recuperación de la hegemonía de la CTM en el sector a partir de los años ochenta -al obtener la titularidad de la mayor parte de los contratos colectivos en las nuevas plantas y mantener los que ya poseía en las más antiguas-, restringió de manera considerable el margen de maniobra y autonomía de cada uno de los sindicatos. Junto al vasto control cetemista, se produjo un marcado debilitamiento del sindicalismo independiente por la represión de que fueron objeto sus organizaciones y los ajustes de personal que se produjeron en las plantas más antiguas donde tenían mayor presencia.

La extensión del "modelo contractual flexible" de las plantas del norte del país al conjunto del sector, condujo a una fuerte pérdida de bilateralidad en el control de los procesos de trabajo y a una creciente precarización en las condiciones de empleo y salariales de los trabajadores de la industria, desdibujándose las diferencias que existían en este aspecto entre las grandes empresas ensambladoras y las de autopartes, en general de menor tamaño.

En el presente trabajo se analizan las principales tendencias del proceso de restructuración productiva del sector automotriz y su impacto en las condiciones laborales. Se examinan también la estructura sindical de la industria y las estrategias seguidas por las organizaciones, identificando los factores que las determinan, tanto en lo que se refiere a las características de los actores y sus recursos de poder, como a los arreglos institucionales en los que se inscriben. Finalmente se incluyen algunas conclusiones orientadas a evaluar las limitaciones de las estrategias sindicales utilizadas hasta el momento, así como sus perspectivas futuras.

TENDENCIAS DE LA REESTRUCTURACIÓN PRODUCTIVA Y SU IMPACTO SOBRE LAS CONDICIONES LABORALES

La industria automotriz mexicana resultó severamente afectada por las recurrentes crisis económicas que la condujeron a la búsqueda de nuevos mercados, lo que supuso esfuerzos previos para mejorar la competitividad, reduciendo sus costos y aumentando la calidad. Para lograr tales objetivos las empresas experimentaron en las dos últimas décadas profundos cambios, tanto a nivel tecnológico como en las formas de organización del trabajo, con su consiguiente impacto en las relaciones laborales, convirtiéndose en un modelo a seguir en los procesos de restructuración de las demás ramas manufactureras, principalmente de aquellas ubicadas en el sector exportador de la economía. La modernización en este sector adquirió un carácter temprano en relación al resto de la industria, precediendo en una década al proceso de integración en el norte del continente, institucionalizado con la entrada en vigor del Tratado de Libre Comercio (TLCAN) en enero de 1994.

Otro elemento distintivo de este proceso, como complemento de la previa desindustrialización y posterior reindustrialización, radica en la relocalización de las plantas automotrices hacia el centro y norte del país, acercando de esta manera la producción a su principal mercado en el exterior (De la Garza, 1990). A su vez, las crisis económicas de los años ochenta indujeron a un crecimiento de la exportación en el sector, estimulando los cambios necesarios para asegurar la calidad internacional requerida. En este contexto crecientemente competitivo, las empresas de autopartes mexicanas se vieron fuertemente impactadas, puesto que los bajos niveles de calidad de sus productos constituyeron uno de los principales problemas resultantes de la política de sustitución de importaciones, en el marco de la cual surgieron dichas empresas .(Arjona, 1990)

Paralelalemente se produjo una fuerte atomización sindical y la destrucción de los altos niveles de protección contractual existentes en las viejas plantas automotrices con el propósito de reducir al máximo los costos laborales y la presencia sindical en las nuevas plantas, reproduciéndose en México la "southern strategy", aplicada durante los setenta en los Estados Unidos con los mismos fines. (Arteaga, 1992 a y b; Katz, 1994)

Un elemento clave de las características asumidas por la restructuración fue la existencia en esta rama de un sindicalismo combativo que debía ser derrotado o por lo menos contrarrestado como premisa fundamental para imponer una salida unilateral a la crisis por la que atravesó la industria desde inicios de los ochenta. La insurgencia sindical de los años setenta había logrado recuperar importantes espacios de acción colectiva independiente, antes controlados por la CTM. El avance del poder sindical en el sector, traducido en prerrogativas contractuales -como las restricciones a los procesos de subcontratación o a la utilización de trabajadores eventuales- así como en prácticas informales que permitían cierto control de las cargas e intensidad del trabajo y, sobre todo, la posibilidad de que ese poder se ejerciera en adelante con una mayor autonomía respecto de las centrales sindicales oficiales y del propio gobierno, se constituyeron en obstáculos a superar a fin de imponer unilateralmente las estrategias empresariales de reconversión. De esta manera, el carácter paradigmático y disciplinador de la derrota sindical en el sector ante los intentos de resistencia -como los conflictos de General Motors, 1980; Ford, 1987-1993; Dina, 1983-1987-1989; Volkswagen, 1992- junto a la recuperación de la hegemonía cetemista, constituyeron una condición previa y esencial para llevar a cabo la modernización unilateral de esta rama. A su vez, la innovación tecnológica fue mayor y siguió un ritmo más acelerado en aquellas plantas donde la conflictividad laboral fue más intensa. (Bayón,1997)

La relativa "paz laboral" instaurada a partir de la recuperación del control cetemista no se tradujo en un mayor poder de negociación sindical ni en el mejoramiento de los niveles de consenso necesarios para posibilitar el éxito en los procesos de reorganización del trabajo, si bien éstos se intensificaron desde mediados de los años ochenta. El aumento de la productividad se logró fundamentalmente a través de la combinación de innovaciones tecnológicas y organizativas aunadas a la mayor intensidad en el trabajo y la disminución de los salarios reales.

En cuanto a su impacto sobre las condiciones laborales, las pérdidas mayores se dieron a nivel de los salarios, dado que el volumen del empleo se vio beneficiado por la apertura de nuevas plantas a partir de los ochenta. Durante este período el ajuste en el empleo afectó fundamentalmente a las viejas plantas ensambladoras y a las pequeñas y medianas empresas de autopartes que producían para el mercado nacional, tanto por despido de personal como por cierres definitivos.[1] El incremento se produjo fundamentalmente en las nuevas plantas del norte, sobre todo en las maquiladoras, con un nuevo perfil de la fuerza de trabajo, caracterizada por su mayor juventud, niveles de escolaridad más altos y escasa o nula experiencia laboral y sindical previa. Este proceso fue acompañado por un profundo deterioro salarial, con salarios más bajos a medida que las plantas se acercan al norte. Sin embargo, en los últimos años, frente a la extensión del modelo flexible de las nuevas plantas, se advierte una mayor homogeneidad salarial en el conjunto de la industria. Las estrategias de competitividad privilegiadas, sustentadas en alta productividad y calidad junto a bajos salarios e intensificación de los ritmos de trabajo se tradujo en un in-

[1] En el caso de la ex para estatal DINA, desde 1982 el empleo se redujo en casi el 90%, pasando de 12,800 trabajadores a menos de 1,400 en la actualidad; Volkswagen pasó de 15,409 trabajadores en 1981 a 9,000 en 1996; Nissan-Civac de 4,800 trabajadores en 1987 a los 1,755 actuales; en Ford-Cuautitlán laboraban 5,515 trabajadores en 1986 y actualmente menos de 3,300. (Bayón, 1997)

cremento de más del 100% de la productividad entre 1988 y 1995, mientras que el empleo se redujo en cerca de un 30% en el mismo período.

Sin que la caída salarial pudiera frenarse, sobre todo frente al estallamiento de una nueva crisis económica en diciembre de 1994, a partir de 1992 la disminución del volumen de empleo en la industria fue muy acentuada. Esto demuestra la profundización de la restructuración para aumentar su competitividad en el contexto de las oportunidades que ofrecía el TLC al establecer la reducción gradual de los aranceles para la industria terminal y de autopartes.

La industria automotriz mexicana jugó un papel clave, junto con la industria maquiladora, al dar los primeros pasos hacia la integración económica en el norte del continente americano. En líneas generales, las estrategias empresariales desplegadas a lo largo de los últimos quince años han priorizado la combinación de una alta productividad y calidad con bajos salarios y precariedad en el empleo, debilitamiento sindical y unilateralidad en la selección e implementación de las nuevas formas de organización del trabajo y la tecnología.[2]

Las variaciones en las estrategias empresariales se centraron en la selección, combinación e intensidad con que adoptaron las siguientes modalidades: relocalización geográfica hacia el centro y norte del país, apertura de nuevas plantas, cierre o refuncionalización de las más antiguas, redistribución del volumen del empleo, descentralización de las relaciones laborales a nivel de las plantas y flexibilización de los contratos colectivos en sus diversas dimensiones -funcional , numérica, salarial y de los tiempos de trabajo-. Este último fue un recurso ampliamente utilizado por la totalidad de las empresas del sector, para lo cual contaron con el apoyo gubernamental a fin de frenar cualquier intento de resistencia obrera (Arteaga, 1992a; Bayón, 1997). Junto a la heterogeneidad tecnológica se advierte una mayor homogeneidad, sobre todo desde mediados de los ochenta, en cuanto a la flexibilización del proceso de trabajo: amplia movilidad de turnos y puestos de trabajo, reducción de categorías de calificación, equipos de trabajo, programas de calidad total y cerro error, etc. (Carrillo, 1990).

Con respecto a las innovaciones introducidas en el sector de autopartes se advierte una fuerte tendencia a la incorporación de tecnología dura privilegiando la inversión en máquinas flexibles y en menor medida la introducción de robots. En relación a la organización de la producción y el trabajo, se destacan como las limitaciones fundamentales en sus formas de implementación el mantenimiento de estructuras organizativas piramidales y la deficiencia en la capacitación de los

[2] Junto a estas tendencias comunes, pueden identificarse estrategias tecnológicas y organizativas diferenciadas en relación al núcleo productivo en el que surgieron las plantas, a su ubicación geográfica, a su orientación hacia el mercado interno y externo y al tipo de organizaciones y respuestas sindicales generadas durante el proceso de reestructuración. (De la Garza, 1993; Arteaga, 1992a)

trabajadores, tanto cuantitativa como cualitativamente (Bueno,1995). En general se carece de programas en donde se incentive y reconozca la capacidad innovadora de los trabajadores y su desempeño laboral, ya que los incentivos se limitan a premiar la puntualidad y la asistencia.

Hasta ahora, las estrategias empresariales han privilegiado la búsqueda de un tipo de consenso obrero basado en una "identificación simbólico-ideológica" con los objetivos de la empresa (Regini, 1992), el cual se centra en una aceptación pasiva de las innovaciones, dada la ausencia tanto de mecanismos institucionalizados capaces de garantizar una participación activa de trabajadores y sindicatos en los procesos de cambio, como de formas de implicación sustantiva -a través de incentivos materiales- que estimulen el efectivo involucramiento de los trabajadores.[3]

Los cambios en la política industrial que regulaba internamente el desempeño del sector automotriz, a través de sucesivos decretos presidenciales emitidos desde fines de los setenta hasta la entrada en vigor del TLC en 1994, muestran el desplazamiento de sus objetivos.[4] La política de sustitución de importaciones, caracterizada por una fuerte protección estatal a fin de impulsar una industria automotriz integrada sobre bases nacionales, fue reemplazada por la gradual liberalización, de acuerdo a un proceso de restructuración en función del mercado mundial y muy particularmente, del de los Estados Unidos. El resultado de este proceso, paralelo a recurrentes crisis que provocaron estancamiento con inflación, ha sido un cambio radical en el destino de la producción automotriz, al punto que actualmente más del 80 % se dirige a la exportación, principalmente a EEUU y Canadá, lo que constituye un indicador de la gran vulnerabilidad de la industria al hacerla depender de la demanda en esos dos países y fundamentalmente de los Estados Unidos. Por el contrario, el mercado interno en México representó en 1995 menos del 20% del destino de la producción total, aunque tiende a recuperarse lentamente de la caída experimentada durante ese año.

Ante esta situación, un documento de la INA (Industria Nacional de Autopartes) de 1995, plantea que si México no logra desarrollar su propio mercado y mercados

---

[3] Sin embargo, en determinados casos- como sucedió en los últimos años en la Ford de Hermosillo- se han tenido que suavizar ciertos aspectos de las radicales flexibilizaciones para reducir los altos índices de rotación de la fuerza de trabajo que se presentaron a fines de los ochenta y su impacto negativo en la productividad. A ello se debe el otorgamiento en dicha planta de prestaciones importantes para los trabajadores -como la construcción de 500 viviendas, pagadas por los trabajadores con créditos de interés social - y la utilización de nuevos criterios de selección -menor escolaridad que la inicialmente requerida, trabajadores casados, experiencia laboral previa, etc.- que permitan retener el personal luego de las importantes inversiones destinadas a la capacitación. (Carrillo, 1996)

[4] Nos referimos al Decreto para el Estímulo al Desarrollo de la Industria Automotriz de 1977, el Decreto para la Racionalización de la Industria Automotriz de 1983 y el Decreto para la Modernización de la Industria Automotriz de 1989. Al respecto ver Carrillo, 1990 y Arteaga 1992a.

alternativos, el sector automotriz quedará ligado al mercado norteamericano como un productor residual y fuertemente dependiente del ciclo de la economía estadounidense, lo que aunado a la centralización de las decisiones en las casas matrices de la industria terminal bajo el concepto de proveeeduría global, apuntan a un esquema de absorción de las plantas mexicanas a la órbita de las empresas ensambladoras estadounidenses. En este sentido se señala que de continuar las tendencias actuales, al terminar la transición del TLC en el 2003, México podría encontrarse con un sector automotriz que represente un lastre para toda la economía por su déficit comercial, por lo que se reclama la necesidad de contar con un mercado interno sólido que proporcione una escala eficiente de manufactura a las ensambladoras y empresas de autopartes instaladas en el país.[5]

Durante la década de los ochenta e inicios de los noventa estallaron diversos conflictos que terminaron invariablemente con una evidente derrota de los trabajadores y dirigencias dispuestos a respaldarlos. Este desenlace mostró hasta dónde eran capaces de llegar las empresas, el gobierno y los sindicatos oficiales a través de su principal central, la CTM, para imponer una flexibilización salvaje de las relaciones laborales en el sector automotriz como factor de atracción de la inversión extranjera.

En la actualidad, predomina en esta industria reconvertida un modelo laboral de incentivos negativos, en el que la docilidad sindical, los bajos salarios y la precariedad en el empleo constituyen sus rasgos distintivos. Si bien es cierto que el Estado mexicano dejó a las empresas en libertad de decidir el rumbo de los procesos de reestructuración, su intervención a través de una política laboral represiva, resultó fundamental para disciplinar a la fuerza de trabajo y garantizar el carácter unilateral de las decisiones que se tomaron.

NUEVO ESCENARIO, VIEJAS PRÁCTICAS

A partir de diciembre de 1987, la dirigencia sindical vinculada al gobierno actuó, junto a los empresarios, como sostén fundamental de la estrategia pactista adoptada a nivel nacional para enfrentar las recurrentes crisis que afectan al país desde el comienzo de esa década. Bajo diversos nombres y con distinta duración se acordaron sucesivos pactos destinados a lograr la estabilidad macroeconómica y el crecimiento, a través del manejo de las principales variables de la economía: tipo de cambio, finanzas públicas, políticas de precios, salarios, etc. (Bensusán, 1993).

La expectativa de lograr la defensa de la planta productiva a través de la drástica moderación salarial, impuesta mediante la fijación de incrementos en las remunera-

[5] Revista México Automotriz Nº 471, octubre de 1995

ciones mínimas por debajo de los índices inflacionarios, fue el argumento que la dirigencia sindical utilizó ante su complicidad con la brutal caída en este rubro, que alcanza hoy a más del 70 % del poder adquisitivo de los asalariados respecto del que se tenía en 1982. Otra consecuencia de la aceptación de esta estrategia gubernamental, fue la pérdida de capacidad de negociación sindical a nivel de la empresa, dada la extensión de los topes salariales a las remuneraciones fijadas en los contratos colectivos, tal como ocurrió en la industria automotriz.

En este sector , los contratos colectivos de las viejas plantas habían llegado a ofrecer condiciones de trabajo muy superiores a las legales instaurando, además, importantes espacios de intervención sindical en el manejo de los mercados laborales internos así como en el proceso de trabajo. La flexibilización contractual, a la par que se abrían las nuevas plantas en el centro y norte del país, llevó a un abatimiento generalizado de salarios y condiciones de trabajo en la industria al punto que en la actualidad no existen grandes diferencias entre las que ofrecen las empresas ensambladoras y las de autopartes (véanse los cuadros 1, 2 y 3) . Este proceso ocurrió con la complicidad de las dirigencias oficiales o después de derrotar a las pocas que intentaron oponer algún freno a la aspiración empresarial de conseguir un amplio margen de discrecionalidad para imponer las modalidades, el ritmo y el alcance del ajuste tecnológico y organizativo.

El papel del gobierno resultó fundamental para disciplinar a los inconformes, a quienes se impusieron castigos ejemplares que desalentaron cualquier posible solidaridad entre quienes eran sometidos a las mismas presiones en sus derechos adquiridos o cuestionaban a una dirigencia cada vez menos representativa. La historia de los conflictos en el sector durante los últimos quince años da cuenta de las consecuencias del autoritarismo laboral dominante en el país ante la ausencia de contrapesos al poder presidencial, bajo cuyo control se encuentran las Juntas de Conciliación y Arbitraje. (Arteaga, 1991; Herrera Lima, 1992; Bensusán y García, 1992)

El resultado de ello fue la consolidación en la industria de una estrategia de competitividad que combina alta productividad, bajos salarios y docilidad sindical. La recuperación de la hegemonía cetemista en el control de los sindicatos fue el factor que garantizó en gran medida el éxito de esa estrategia empresarial al dejarlos con muy escaso margen de maniobra y aislados dentro de una estructura vertical y autoritaria que acordaba cupularmente con los empresarios y el gobierno medidas que vulneraban los intereses de sus supuestos representados. Como lo reconoció un alto dirigente de esa organización, en la recuperación de esa hegemonía -apoyada tanto por el gobierno como por las empresas- estaba implícita la condición de respetar las políticas salariales y la unilateralidad de las estrategias empresariales de reconversión.[6]

[6] Entrevista con el Senador Juan S. Millán, Secretario de Educación y Comunicación de la CTM y Srio. General del Comité Ejecutivo Nacional del PRI, abril de 1997.

Aunque parte de la frustrada modernización laboral impulsada por la administración salinista (1988-1994) se refería precisamente a la necesidad de vincular los salarios a la productividad, de manera que los aumentos en las remuneraciones no fueran inflacionarios ni generalizados, este objetivo nunca fue alcanzado. Los procesos de concertación, a todos los niveles, no contaban con los interlocutores capaces de lograr un reparto mínimamente equilibrado de ganancias y pérdidas, como se demostró cuando desde el gobierno se impulsó el Acuerdo Nacional de Elevación de la Productividad y la Calidad (ANECyP), firmado en mayo de 1992 después de dos años de negociaciones.[7] Lejos de responder a las expectativas sindicales de dar previamente inicio a la recuperación del poder adquisitivo, o a las patronales, orientadas a conseguir una legislación laboral mas flexible, ofreció en cambio un marco muy general e impreciso de líneas de acción en torno a la productividad y a la calidad. Estas líneas debían particularizarse en convenios a nivel de cada empresa, lo que revelaba la imposibilidad de llegar a compromisos tangibles y exigibles entre interlocutores dotados de poderes marcadamente asimétricos.

Este nuevo acuerdo cupular proponía seguir en adelante los siguientes principios para modernizar las relaciones laborales en las empresas: 1. la mano de obra no puede ser considerada como un costo a minimizar; 2. el incremento de la productividad y la calidad no pueden ser impuestos y exigen del consenso y la participación de todos los actores; 3. la planeación eficiente y los recursos financieros y tecnológicos son condiciones a satisfacer por parte de las empresas y, 4. el clima adecuado de las nuevas relaciones laborales supone un reparto equitativo de los resultados que se obtengan.[8]

Como se desprende de estos principios, existía la intención de ampliar la bilateralidad y flexibilizar las remuneraciones fijadas rígidamente a partir de topes salariales acordados cupularmente para los ingresos mínimos en los pactos económicos. Sin embargo, el fracaso en el cumplimiento de estas metas fue evidente, mostrando nuevamente las limitaciones de los esfuerzos de modernización desde arriba, sin cambios acordes en la política laboral y económica -que mantenían a los salarios como principal variable del ajuste y ventaja competitiva frente al exterior- y sin la necesaria renovación de las dirigencias y estructuras de representación subordinadas al gobierno y a las empresas, obligadas a contener la movilización social y carentes de un poder autónomo de presión sobre su contraparte.

---

[7] Esta experiencia, surgida después de que en 1989 fracasara el intento patronal de reformar la legislación laboral con el propósito de flexibilizarla, buscaba promover entre sindicatos y empresas un comportamiento innovador orientado hacia la participación, el diálogo, la capacitación, la productividad y el reparto equitativo de sus resultados, en el marco de un discurso presidencial que planteaba la necesidad de contar para ello con un "nuevo sindicalismo" ajeno a las tradiciones de confrontación, más involucrado en el escenario de la producción, y sin la centralidad estatal propia del viejo arreglo corporativo.

[8] Véase el texto completo del ANEPyC en Excelsior, 27 de mayo de 1992.

En este contexto se firmaron los convenios de productividad en las plantas automotrices, los cuales, o bien no trascendieron el nivel de acuerdos formales o no condujeron a los resultados esperados. No hubo, por parte de la CTM, intento alguno por articular las negociaciones -mas que a través del diseño de un convenio tipo que debía suscribirse en cada planta- a pesar de controlar a la casi totalidad de los sindicatos de las ensambladoras y a más de la mitad de las empresas de autopartes. En consecuencia, al igual que sucedió con los contratos colectivos, las negociaciones se hicieron en total aislamiento, incluso entre plantas de una misma empresa.

En un caso que puede considerarse como excepcional -el de la ex-paraestatal DINA, privatizada en 1989 y con los ajustes mas drásticos en los puestos de trabajo-, la presencia de uno de los pocos sindicatos independientes del sector automotriz buscó ampliar su intervención en la producción a través de los convenios de productividad firmados en 1992 y 1993. Sin embargo, esta experiencia resultó en una nueva frustación debido a la falta de cumplimiento por parte de la empresa de los compromisos acordados en materia de bilateralidad, capacitación e incentivos económicos y a la debilidad del sindicato para presionar a su contraparte. Por el contrario, la estrategia de la empresa frente a este sindicato democrático y con una vida interna participativa, fue la de orillarlo al conflicto con el propósito de derrotarlo e imponer unilateralmente sus decisiones. (Bayón, 1997)

La posibilidad de alcanzar en esta industria paradigmática - y en el país, en general- una relación más directa entre el salario y la productividad se cerró abruptamente al estallar la crisis de diciembre de 1994, que se tradujo nuevamente en la adopción de una rígida política salarial destinada a contener la inflación y en la destrucción de fuentes de empleo. Aunque por primera y única vez la dirigencia cetemista evitó firmar un nuevo "pacto", avaló con su presencia y su voto la aplicación de los topes salariales en la Comisión Nacional de los Salarios Mínimos, donde ocupaba la totalidad de los puestos de representación obrera, para volver poco después a las negociaciones cupulares, como fue su costumbre desde 1987. El resultado fue nuevamente una caída salarial entre diciembre de 1994 y de 1996 de casi 30% en el poder adquisitivo de los salarios mínimos, a la par que sólo en 1995 se perdieron más de un millón de empleos manufactureros.

En la industria automotriz la estrategia cetemista de defensa del empleo se limitó presionar a los sindicatos para que aceptaran los topes salariales y firmaran acuerdos por plantas para realizar paros técnicos y evitar despidos, lo que de todas maneras no pudo lograrse. Un ejemplo del comportamiento de esta central frente a las decisiones de las empresas automotrices se dio cuando en 1995 la General Motors llevó a la práctica su decisión de cerrar la planta del Distrito Federal, donde estaba vigente uno de los pocos contratos colectivos que se había sustraido en cierta forma a la flexibilización salvaje ocurrida en los demás. Ese contrato estaba bajo la titularidad de un sindicato afiliado a la CROC, central igualmente corporativa y sometida al gobierno, pero enfrentada tradicionalmente a la CTM. Cuando la empresa General Motors optó por trasladarse a Silao, Guanajuato, la CTM logró la titularidad del nuevo contrato -mucho antes de que la planta comenzara siquiera a funcionar- bajo las condiciones decididas unilateralmente por la empresa: menores salarios y prestaciones que los que pagaba en el D.F., un contrato colectivo altamente flexible y escasa presencia sindical a nivel de planta. Por su parte, el sindicato de la CROC avaló esta situación sin intentar la mas mínima resistencia ni ofecer alguna salida alternativa al despido de los más de 1,000 trabajadores de la planta del D. F. (Lucio, 1994)

A mediados de 1995, la CTM anunció un "cambio de estrategia" frente a la grave situación de los trabajadores, después de una década y media de severos sacrificios y retrocesos y debido al nuevo contexto económico y político del país. Según su punto de vista, frente al deterioro de los salarios, la pérdida de participación de las remuneraciones en el PIB, el alto nivel de desempleo y subempleo y la drástica caída del mercado interno era necesario adoptar un nuevo esquema de relaciones laborales más participativo que dejara atrás la confrontación como recurso sindical encaminado a defender a los asalariados, estrategia que en realidad la CTM había abandonado por lo menos desde mediados de años cuarenta. En uno de los momentos de mayor gravedad de la crisis desatada en 1994 y cuando los trabajadores volvían a pagar los costos de las inversiones especulativas, la CTM y la Coparmex coincidían en que había llegado el "fin de la lucha de clases" y la necesidad de reducir la intervención del Estado en el mundo del trabajo. En un nuevo acercamiento directo con esa confederación patronal, después de que ésta retirara su vieja propuesta de reforma institucional, ambas organizaciones se comprometieron a elaborar un diagnóstico acerca de los problemas laborales del país, con el objetivo de "construir una nueva cultura laboral", suponiendo que un cambio de esas dimensiones puede "emerger" como producto de negociaciones cupulares.

Una vez más los resultados acordados fueron escuetos, vagos y escasamente originales. La CTM, al igual que las restantes organizaciones sindicales invitadas a última hora, no dieron a conocer ningún planteamiento que mostrara cuál era el punto de vista de los trabajadores, por lo que en lo fundamental se retomaron los planteamientos del ANEPyC en torno a la necesidad de una modernización laboral, incluyendo el cambio de valores, actitudes e instituciones como partes de ese proceso de cambio. Sin embargo, no se acordó ningún compromiso específico ni ninguna reforma institucional capaz de promover un nuevo modelo laboral con una menor presencia del Estado, basado en la cooperación y el diálogo entre sindicatos dotados de auténtica representatividad y capacidad propositiva y empresas humanizadas. Por el contrario, el énfasis fue puesto en el "cambio de mentalidades" y de las prácticas en torno a metas tales como la erradicación de la cultura empresarial de incumplimiento de la legalidad o de la corrupción de dirigencias dispuestas a lucrar con los derechos de sus representados. Como era de esperarse, esta "nueva" estrategia cetemista no se ha traducido hasta ahora en beneficio alguno para los millones de trabajadores que agremia, incluídos los trabajadores de la industria automotriz.

A su vez, la ausencia de estructuras sectoriales contribuyó al profundo debilitamiento del poder de los sindicatos automotrices; de esta manera la negociación cupular de los pactos nacionales ocurrió junto a una marcada atomización y escasa autonomía de los sindicatos a nivel de plantas y empresas. Paralelamente, los dirigentes locales siguen careciendo de la preparación y el asesoramiento técnico necesarios para negociar sobre temas tan complejos como la productividad y la calidad, dado que la asesoría de la CTM —como si nada hubiera cambiado en el escenario económico y productivo— se sigue limitando a aspectos legales de la contratación colectiva y, muy particularmente, se orienta a garantizar el apego a los lineamientos de la central así como a evitar o neutralizar la posible emergencia de liderazgos y corrientes sindicales alternativas. (Bayón, 1997)

En este contexto, las contradicciones entre un discurso "renovado" y las viejas prácticas autoritarias y cupulares propias del corporativismo tradicional, son evidentes. Sin fuerza propia de negociación y con gobiernos desinteresados en los mercados internos y comprometidos en crear paraísos laborales para atraer la inversión extranjera, la dirigencia sindical cetemista optó por el camino que le garantizaba, al menos en el corto plazo, su propia sobrevivencia, separándose cada vez más de sus supuestos representados.

De esta manera, fundamentalmente en sectores económicos claves de la economía mexicana como el automotriz, parece estarse produciendo un tránsito desde formas de corporativismo "estatal" (Schmitter, 1992) -el cual caracterizó a las relaciones del movimiento sindical con los gobiernos posrevolucionarios- hacia un "micro" corporativismo, en el que la pérdida de centralidad del Estado en la economía y su debilitada capacidad para asumir compromisos con los asalariados da lugar a la creciente subordinación de las dirigencias sindicales a las empresas, convertidas en el espacio privilegiado de las transformaciones económicas y sociales. Si hasta los inicios de los ochenta era muy difícil distinguir en México entre el discurso estatal y el de los dirigentes sindicales allegados al régimen, hoy es cada vez mas problemático diferenciar las concepciones empresariales sobre la competitividad y la productividad y las recetas apropiadas para conseguirlas, respecto de las que sostienen y proponen las dirigencias sindicales (Bayón, 1996). Sin embargo, más que una afortunada convergencia, el "nuevo discurso" sindical ha encontrado en la industria automotriz el terreno propicio para probar su aceptación acrítica de las metas y estrategias productivistas. De allí que se traduzca en la abdicación del papel que le corresponde a los sindicatos en la representación de los intereses de los agremiados, al carecer de la capacidad propositiva y de la autonomía indispensables para impulsar salidas equilibradas a las recurrentes crisis que afectaron al país y a la industria.

Cuadro 1
Regulación del proceso de trabajo

	EMPRESAS ENSAMBLADORAS			EMPRESAS DE AUTOPARTES		
	Ford-Hermosillo (CTM)	GM-R.Arizpe (CTM)	Dina (Indep.)	Tremec (CTM)	Kostal (CTM)	Sealed Power (FAT)
Definición de cargas y ritmos de trabajo	La empresa	La empresa	La empresa	La empresa	N/C	N/C
Movilidad horizontal	hasta 6 meses en áreas de línea	Abierta	Abierta	Abierta	N/C	Abierta
Programas de producción	N/C	N/C	Derecho del sindicato a ser informado, escu- chado y atendido.	N/C	N/C	N/C
Solución de conflictos a nivel de planta	2 instancias bilaterales	N/C	4 instancias bilaterales	2 instancias bilaterales	No existe bilateralidad.	3 instancias bilaterales
Cambio tecnológico	N/C	N/C	N/C	N/C	N/C	N/C
Trabajo en equipo	Sí	N/C	N/C	Sí	N/C	N/C
Supervisión del trabajo	Personal de confianza	Personal de confianza	Personal de confianza	Personal de confianza	Personal de confianza	Personal de confianza
Relación cliente-proveedor	N/C	N/C	N/C	N/C	N/C	N/C

Nota: N/C: no se contempla. CTM: Conferederación de trabajadores de México; Indep.: Independiente; FAT: Frente Auténtico del Trabajo.
Fuente: Contratos Colectivos de Trabajo 1994/96, 1996/98.

Cuadro 2
Regulación del mercado de trabajo

	EMPRESAS ENSAMBLADORAS			EMPRESAS DE AUTOPARTES		
	Ford-Hemosillo (CTM)	GM-R. Arizpe (CTM)	Dina (Indep.)	Tremec (CTM)	Kostal (CTM)	Sealed Power (FAT)
Ingreso de nuevos trabajadores	Propuesta del sindicato	Propuesta del sindicato	Propuesta del sindicato	Propuesta del sindicato	Propuesta del sindicato	Propuesta del sindicato
Cláusula de exclusión	Sí	Sí	Sí	Sí	Sí	Sí
Trabajadores eventuales	nº abierto	nº abierto	nº abierto	máximo 22%	nº abierto	nº abierto
Nº de categorías	1 (técnico de Ford)	47	21	10	3	22
Movilidad vertical	Certificación de habilidades. Ascenso posible cada 6 meses	Según LFT	Por capacidad para el desempeño del puesto	Por capacitación y certificación de habilidades	Aptitud y antigüedad	Según LFT
Reajustes y despidos	N/C	N/C	Estudio previo y acuerdo con el sindicato.	LFT. Información al sindicato.	N/C	N/C
Subcontratación	Sí.. Trabajos no relacionados directamente con el objeto de la planta	Sí.. Trabajos no relacionados directament e con el objeto de la planta.	Sí.. Trabajos ajenos al proceso de producción.	Sí.. Trabajos relativos a carga, descarga, construcción, reparación, ampliación y limpieza de instalaciones.	N/C	N/C

Nota: N/C: no se contempla; LFT: Ley Federal del Trabajo
Fuente: Contratos Colectivos de Trabajo 1994/96, 1996/98

Cuadro 3
Condiciones de trabajo

	EMPRESAS ENSAMBLADORAS			EMPRESAS DE AUTOPARTES		
	Ford-Hermosillo (CTM)	GM-R. Arizpe (CTM)	Dina (Indep.)	Tremec (CTM)	Kostal (CTM)	Sealed Power (FAT)
Jornada semanal	*D: 45 hs. *M:42.5 hs. *N: 40 hs.	D: 48 hs. M: 45 hs. N: 42 hs	D: 45 hs. M: 42 hs. N: 42 hs.	D: 48 hs. M: 45 hs N: 42 hs	D: 48 hs. M: 45 hs N: 42 hs	D: 48 hs. M: 45 hs N: 42 hs
Turnos de trabajo	8: 2 D 1M 5N	3	3	3 Libertad de la empresa p/ fijar turnos especiales	3	3
Vacaciones	De 10 a 14 días según antigüedad	De 8 a 18 días según antigüedad	De 13 a 22 días según antigüedad.	De 7 a 15 días según antigüedad	De 7 a 15 días según antigüedad	De 7 a 17 días según antigúedad
Días de descanso al año	12	13	13	12	12	10
Tiempo extra	Pago según LFT. Decisión bilteral	N/C	Pago según LFT. Decisión de la empresa.	Pago según LFT. Decisión de la empresa.	Pago según LFT. Decisión de la empresa	N/C
Salario promedio	$100 diarios (12.5 U$s)	$73 diarios (9.12 U$s)	$70 diarios (8.75 U$s)	$110 diarios (13.75 U$s)	$70 diarios (8.75 U$s)	$70 diarios (8.75 U$s)
Primas de asistencia y puntualidad	N/C	N/C	Mensual, trimestral y anual. Rifa anual de un automóvil p/trabaj.	Mensual.	Bimestral.	N/C

			sin inasistencias.			
Aguinaldo	36 días	32 días	33.5% del salario anual	39 días	31días	De 22 a 30 días según antigüedad
Reparto de utilidades	N/C	N/C	Cantidad anual como anticipo.	16 días anuales como anticipo.	N/C	N/C
Comedor	Sí	N/C	Sí	N/C	N/C	Sí. 55% a cargo de la empresa
Transporte	N/C	N/C	Sí.	Sí.	Sí.	Sí.
Despensa	17 % mensual	9% semanal	Cantidad fija semanal (apróx. 25% salario promedio)	7.5% mensual	cat.A: 3.66% mensual; cat. B y C: 7%	18.37% semanal

Nota: N/C: no se contempla. *D: diurna; M: mixta; N: nocturna
Fuente: Contratos Colectivos de Trabajo 1994/96, 1996/98

ACTORES, INSTITUCIONES Y SISTEMA DE RELACIONES LABORALES

El comportamiento del actor sindical en la industria automotriz se relaciona, entre otros factores, con las modalidades de sus vínculos con los demás actores: el Estado y las empresas. En este sentido, el caso mexicano se caracteriza por una ininterrumpida relación corporativa de subordinación y complicidad entre la dirigencia obrera y los gobiernos posrevolucionarios, iniciada hace más de cinco décadas. Esta continuidad no se alteró a pesar del drástico viraje en el modelo económico adoptado a mediados de los ochenta, cuando se dejaron atrás los compromisos tutelares con los asalariados.

A nivel institucional, a pesar de la mayor apertura en el proceso político después de las competidas elecciones de 1988, se han conservado intactos los candados jurídicos que permiten el control gubernamental del proceso organizativo y reivindicativo, en tanto la legislación no ha experimentado modificaciones tendientes a liberalizar la acción sindical. El control estatal sobre la movilización obrera depende en gran medida de los vínculos entre el gobierno y los sindicatos, ya que no está formalmente establecido el arbitraje obligatorio de las huelgas. Esto significa, por una parte, que cobra mayor significación la intervención gubernamental preventiva en procedimientos tales como el registro de los sindicatos así como de sus directivas y de la titularidad de los contratos colectivos, que dan acceso al ejercicio del derecho de huelga y, por otra, que existe una necesidad mayor de contar con una dirigencia subordinada, que acepte voluntariamente los límites a la acción reivindicativa que imponen las políticas gubernamentales y empresariales. Sin embargo, hay que advertir que aunque legalmente el gobierno no tiene la facultad de arbitrar obligatoriamente en los conflictos colectivos, otros mecanismos —como las declaraciones de inexistencia de las huelgas o el rechazo a tramitar los emplazamientos— pueden ser utilizados por las autoridades laborales para desalentar o reprimir el uso de esta medida de fuerza, dada la fragilidad del Estado de Derecho y la ausencia de contrapesos al Poder Ejecutivo.

Desde el punto de vista institucional, si bien los sindicatos disponen de importantes recursos de poder, dada la existencia de una legislación heredada de un proceso revolucionario que privilegió los derechos colectivos -de agremiación, contratación y huelga- por encima de las libertades individuales, el ejercicio de los mismos quedó condicionado al previo control gubernamental del nacimiento de la organización sindical y de sus decisiones claves -como la elección de sus directivas-durante toda su vida activa. De allí que el carácter coactivo del proceso de organización y contratación, bajo el control gubernamental, haya dado lugar a la formación de verdaderos monopolios de agremiación independientes de la voluntad real de las bases, sin legitimidad y representatividad real, puesto que la afiliación es obligatoria cuando existe un contrato colectivo con claúsula de exclusión, presente en la gran mayoría de los mismos. Además, la renuncia o expulsión a un sindicato provoca en tales casos la pérdida del empleo. Este poder coactivo de agremiación es en consecuencia un arma de doble filo: da mayor fuerza al sindicato pero, a la vez, demerita la calidad de la representación y no crea la necesidad de que la organización se preocupe por conservar o ampliar la afiliación. Además, esta modalidad eleva desmesuradamente los costos de un proceso de recomposición sindical desde abajo, situación que explica en gran medida el relativo inmovilismo de los trabajadores automotrices a pesar de la evidente incapacidad de la mayor parte de sus dirigencias.

De esta manera, se advierte que la variable político-institucional tuvo un papel decisivo en el comportamiento de los sindicatos mexicanos, puesto que el autoritarismo obstaculizó la modernización sindical y preservó la histórica "complicidad" de las dirigencias con el gobierno, extendiendo la relación de subordinación hacia las empresas, situación sumamente contrastante con la independencia y transparencia necesarias para implementar verdaderos procesos de cooperación y concertación.

Sin embargo, los cambios derivados del nuevo escenario político en el país después de las elecciones federales de julio de 1997 y la muerte del dirigente cetemista Fidel Velázquez, al provocar un debilitamiento aún mayor de los dirigentes vinculados al PRI y de la propia CTM, envuelta en la crisis sucesoria, son elementos que sugieren la extrema precariedad de la estrategia empresarial en la industria automotriz.

LA HEGEMONÍA CETEMISTA EN LA INDUSTRIA AUTOMOTRIZ: AISLAMIENTO Y SUBORDINACIÓN SINDICAL

Uno de los rezagos más importantes de la transición a la democracia en México es precisamente la falta de apertura del mundo sindical. Las organizaciones más importantes, como es el caso de la CTM —central que afilia a la mayoría de los trabajadores sindicalizados y que hoy hegemoniza a los sindicatos de la industria automotriz—, forman parte del sector obrero del partido oficial, el PRI, en tanto sus estatutos establecen la pertenencia colectiva al mismo, y se han preocupado por cerrar el paso a cualquier intento de liberalización de las reglas del juego en este escenario.

Ante la creciente presión por una mayor apertura política, la estrategia de las principales centrales ha sido la de defender a ultranza el statu-quo, dentro y fuera de ese partido, como único recurso para conservar sus cuotas de poder, en un contexto de creciente desprestigio ante las bases dado el alto costo de las políticas y planes gubernamentales y empresariales puestos en práctica con su complicidad . Esto ha llevado a la dirigencia sindical corporativa a evitar a toda costa cualquier reforma a la legislación laboral que pudiera poner en peligro los monopolios de agremiación.

Desde la perspectiva de la CTM, la estrategia seguida para recuperar el control de los trabajadores de esta rama clave por su lugar en el modelo de exportación resultó exitosa. A cambio de su evidente disposición a disciplinar cualquier inconformidad obrera y tolerar las medidas de ajuste del gobierno y de las empresas, consiguió convertirse en la contraparte preferida por las empresas automotrices trasnacionales, lo que le permitió obtener, a través de los respectivos sindicatos, la titularidad de la totalidad de los contratos colectivos de las plantas ensambladoras que se abrieron a partir de los ochenta.

Al respecto, es importante observar que en este proceso de organización no sólo no se tuvo en cuenta la opinión de los trabajadores -quienes compulsivamente tuvieron que afiliarse a los sindicatos cetemistas para obtener su empleo- sino que se reprimió con total impunidad cualquier intento de resistencia o de búsqueda de la más mínima autonomía frente a la CTM, como lo prueba el largo y costoso conflicto de los trabajadores de la Ford-Cuautitlán en aras de conseguir una elección democrática de su dirigencia.

Sin embargo, la hegemonía cetemista no se tradujo en un mayor poder de negociación frente a las empresas ni en una articulación de las condiciones de trabajo en torno a los contratos más favorables. Por el contrario, la homogeneización se dio a la baja y los sindicatos negociaron con las empresas a nivel de las plantas. Es precisamente el gran aislamiento y la debilidad de cada sindicato, lo que explica el éxito de las empresas y la fortaleza de la cúpula cetemista, quien controla a las dirigencias automotrices sin permitirles ningún desvío de los lineamientos de la central.

Es importante destacar que en el sector automotriz no pudo nunca formarse un sindicato nacional de industria, como existe en otros sectores económicos. Esta ausencia se debe tanto a problemas internos de las organizaciones sindicales como a la presión de las autoridades gubernamentales y las empresas. Estas últimas han tenido una gran injerencia en el proceso organizativo, no sólo al seleccionar con el aval de la autoridad laboral al titular del contrato colectivo -incluso desde antes que las plantas comenzaran a funcionar y a contratar trabajadores- sino interviniendo en la vida interna de las organizaciones.[9]

El siguiente cuadro ilustra la fuerte atomización de la estructura sindical de las empresas ensambladoras,donde predominan los sindicatos de planta, así como la clara hegemonía de la CTM sobre estas organizaciones.

Cuadro 4
Estructura sindical de las empresas ensambladoras

Empresa	Ubicación	Tipo de sindicato	Central Sindical
Ford	Edo. de México Chihuahua Sonora	De Empresa	CTM
General Motors	Edo.de México Coahuila Guanajuato	De Planta De Planta De Planta	CTM CTM CTM
Chrysler	D.F. Edo. de México Coahuila	De Empresa	CTM
Volkswagen	Puebla	De Empresa	FESEBES
Nissan	Morelos Edo.de México	De Planta De Planta	UOI

[9] Un claro ejemplo pudo observarse durante el conflicto en Volkswagen en 1992, cuando esta empresa obligó al sindicato a modificar sus estatutos y estructura interna (disminuyendo el número de delegados departamentales en la planta) y a vincularse a la Fesebes, organización de reciente constitución y hegemonizada por un liderazgo sindical entonces cercano a la Presidencia de la República.

	Aguascalientes	De Planta	
Dina	Hidalgo	De Empresa	Independiente
Renault	Durango	De Planta	CTM
BMW	Edo. de México	De Planta	CTM
Honda	Guadalajara	De Planta	CTM
Mercedes Benz	Edo. de México	De Planta	CTM

Nota. FESEBES: Federación de Empresas de Bienes y Servicios. UOI : Unidad obrero Independiente
Fuente: Elaboración propia

El sector de autopartes también presenta una marcada atomización sindical, pero una mayor heterogeneidad que en las empresas ensambladoras en lo que se refiere al tamaño de los sindicatos, producto de la coexistencia de empresas grandes, medianas y pequeñas. De acuerdo a la información obtenida en el Registro de Asociaciones de la Secretaría de Trabajo -la cual presenta serias deficiencias por la falta de actualización de los registros sindicales y a la ausencia de mecanismos adecuados para su procesamiento- el número promedio de afiliados por organización es de 556. En relación a la central de pertenencia se advierte una fuerte presencia de las centrales oficiales -CTM, CROC y CROM-, las cuales concentran el 64.5 % de los sindicatos, el 73% de los trabajadores y el 72% de las empresas. Dentro del sindicalismo oficial, la CTM se presenta como la central más importante, ya que controla casi el 50% de los sindicatos, el 65% de los trabajadores y el 60% de las empresas. El sindicalismo independiente ocupa un lugar minoritario en el sector, representando sólo el 16% de los sindicatos, el 9% de los trabajadores y el 15% de las empresas. La CTM no sólo agrupa a la mitad de los sindicatos del sector, sino que además concentra a los sindicatos de mayor tamaño; por el contrario los sindicatos independientes presentan la situación inversa: mientras que el 73% de los sindicatos cetemistas tiene más de 249 trabajadores, el 80% de los sindicatos independientes tienen menos de 249 trabajadores. La marcada atomización se expresa en el fuerte predominio de sindicatos de empresa -nacionales o locales-, los cuales representan el 65% de las organizaciones, y sólo un 36% pertenecen a sindicatos de industria.

Los factores endógenos que explican el aislamiento en que operan los sindicatos automotrices son de diversa índole. Por una parte, la estructura vertical y piramidal de la CTM que busca concentrar el poder en su cúpula ha impedido una mayor articulación horizontal entre los sindicatos. También existe en las dirigencias una concepción patrimonialista de los sindicatos, considerados como "cotos" de poder personal que se manejan a través de prácticas poco democráticas y discrecionales.

Hay, por otra parte, una marcada discontinuidad en las gestiones sindicales que se caracterizan por una visión inmediatista y restringida de la acción sindical, lo que ha impedido la elaboración de proyectos de largo plazo o capaces de traspasar los estrechos límites de cada planta. Incluso cuando se trata de sindicatos con diversas secciones correspondientes a plantas de una misma empresa, no hay una estrategia formulada para el conjunto, situación que obviamente es aprovechada e incentivada por las gerencias, al establecerse diferentes fechas de revisón contractuales y salariales para cada una de las plantas particulares. (Bayón, 1997)

El pragmatismo propio del corporativismo explica la escasa preocupación por disponer de diagnósticos claros y oportunos acerca de los procesos macro y microeconómicos en curso. Por lo general, se confía en los datos oficiales y, acostumbrados a negociaciones políticas de alto nivel, no ha existido la suficiente preocupación por formar cuadros sindicales con capacidad propositiva para ofrecer alternativas propias a los retos de la producción, en un contexto de creciente competencia económica.

Indiscutiblemente no se trata de un problema de recursos. La afiliación obligatoria a los sindicatos a través de las cláusulas de exclusión contenidas en la totalidad de los contratos colectivos, les garantiza un alto grado representatividad formal y fondos económicos importantes a través de los correspondientes descuentos en los salarios. Por su parte la CTM dispone, además de las cuotas de sus miembros, de muchas otras fuentes de recursos y de una considerable infraestructura -incluyendo centros de estudios y capacitación sindical de cierta envergadura- desarrollada en sus épocas de esplendor. Aunque por lo general esta central proporciona asesoría jurídica a los sindicatos en las negociaciones contractuales y ofrece diversos cursos de formación para las dirigencias con o sin financiamiento externo, estas contribuciones no han sido orientadas a fortalecerlas sino, por el contrario, a mantener su control sobre las mismas. Esto se debe a que en general los recursos institucionales y materiales de que se dispone no están al servicio de estrategias innovadoras y de la búsqueda de una real eficacia en las tareas de representación, sino del sostenimiento del viejo estilo subordinado de gestión sindical, el cual ha demostrado su fuerte incapacidad para defender los intereses de los agremiados en las actuales circunstancias.

Igualmente, la presencia de los dirigentes cetemistas en numerosos cargos de elección popular y en los órganos laborales tripartitos administrativos -por ej. en la Comisión Nacional de Salarios Mínimos- o jurisdiccionales -Juntas de Conciliación y Arbitraje- donde esa central tiene la mayor parte de los puestos de representación, no han servido para poner un freno a las drásticas estrategias empresariales o a las políticas gubernamentales, sino por el contrario, para hacerlas posibles.

La suerte de los trabajadores afiliados a sindicatos no controlados por la CTM no ha sido significativamente diferente. Las organizaciones más combativas y democráticas del sector hicieron a partir de los ochenta intentos de resistencia en forma aislada, lo que los condujo a una derrota que adquirió un carácter ejemplificador para el conjunto de los trabajadores. Es importante insistir en que la estrategia empresarial encaminada a debilitar a los sindicatos contó con pleno apoyo estatal. Así, mientras más combativos y democráticos eran los sindicatos, y mayores los niveles de bilateralidad conquistados previamente en el proceso de trabajo, más salvaje fue la ofensiva empresarial y el avasallamiento de los derechos laborales básicos. Las organizaciones sindicales independientes, respondiendo a un "instinto de sobrevivencia", desplegaron estrategias defensivas que, aunque con fuertes contradicciones y limitaciones, pretendían resistir los ataques que apuntaban a su aniquilamiento. Sin embargo, estos sindicatos - como los vinculados a la CTM- no contaron con diagnósticos y alternativas que tomaran en cuenta la profundidad e irreversibilidad de los cambios en la industria e intentaron defender los intereses de sus agremiados mediante costosas estrategias de confrontación, que si bien en los años setenta se tradujeron en resultados relativamente exitosos, en las últimas dos décadas condujeron a una profunda derrota ante una correlación de fuerzas fuertemente desfavorable para estas organizaciones.

Aunque tres de estos sindicatos, dos en el sector de ensambladoras -Dina y Volkswagen- y uno en autopartes -afiliado al FAT- se encuentran actualmente en el Foro "El Sindicalismo ante la Nación" formado en 1995 con el propósito de convertirse en el polo de atracción de un "nuevo sindicalismo", no se han hecho todavía esfuerzos para impulsar desde este nuevo espacio la renovación de las respuestas sindicales en la industria automotriz.[10] De la suerte de esta alternativa, junto a otras igualmente en formación, depende en gran medida la posibilidad de reorganizar el movimiento sindical mexicano en el futuro inmediato, con el propósito de dotarlo de la autonomía necesaria para que vuelva a ejercer su papel en la representación de los asalariados.

Sin embargo, en el corto plazo, la posibilidad de una renovación de la estrategia de los sindicatos automotrices seguirá fuertemente ligada de lo que ocurra dentro de la CTM como central hegemónica, donde las diferencias entre sus corrientes internas en torno al problema de la sucesión de una dirigencia anquilosada, amenazan con

---

[10] Este foro reúne a diferentes organizaciones convergentes en su crítica al corporativismo tradicional, aunque todavía no ha podido delinear un proyecto común. En su última reunión, a la que asistieron mas de setenta sindicatos, se discutieron diversos temas de la problemática laboral actual. Las divergencias mas importantes surgieron en torno a la posibilidad de que los sindicatos pertenecientes al CT (once de un total de 21 organizaciones) salieran de ese órgano para integrar con los restantes una nueva central. (La Jornada, 30 y 31 de enero de 1997).

desmembrarla y debilitarla en tanto que opción segura para los intereses patronales, tal como lo ha sido hasta la actualidad.

Otro factor de riesgo para las empresas y la CTM, al haber apostado casi exclusivamente al control de la indisciplina como sustituto del consenso activo de los trabajadores, es el efecto de una mayor democratización política. Si los métodos autoritarios dejaran de estar disponibles o tuvieran un costo muy alto para un gobierno democrático, difícilmente podría mantenerse en estado latente la conflictividad intersindical y obrero-patronal hoy contenida por los candados corporativos y el temor a la represión. Aunque en gran medida la restructuración automotriz estaría muy avanzada, las empresas tendrían que optar por otras estrategias, apenas hoy en ciernes -como el ofrecimiento de ventajas tangibles en prestaciones y salarios-, si se quiere conservar la paz laboral después de mas de quince años de severas pérdidas para los trabajadores en una de las industrias más competitivas del nuevo modelo exportador.

CONCLUSIONES

En un contexto caracterizado por recurrentes crisis económicas, programas de ajuste estructural, apertura comercial y reconversión productiva, se plantea la urgente necesidad para todos los interlocutores de lograr el clima de confianza necesario en los procesos de auténtica concertación de los intereses en juego, a fin de impulsar la adopción de respuestas equilibradas ante profundos cambios como los sufridos en el sector automotriz.

En este sentido, resulta decisiva la posibilidad de incorporar a las negociaciones a los distintos integrantes de la cadena productiva -ensambladoras, motores, autopartes, etc.- a fin de favorecer un reparto mas equilibrado de ganancias y pérdidas. Dicha posibilidad se encuentra indisolublemente ligada a la necesidad de institucionalizar un esquema de negociación colectiva articulado - a nivel nacional, sectorial, de empresa y de planta- a partir de un mínimo de condiciones de trabajo garantizadas por la ley . Por otra parte, el respaldo gubernamental se presenta como una condición necesaria para el funcionamiento del tripartismo en la definición de la política industrial.

Si lo que está en juego en el mundo actual es precisamente la posibilidad de combinar una alta competitividad y, a la vez, un orden laboral incluyente, es indispensable una regulación institucional apropiada que fortalezca el poder de negociación sindical a todos los niveles y muy especialmente dentro de la empresa, creando los incentivos positivos adecuados a una mayor corresponsabilidad.

En el caso mexicano, esta alternativa requeriría revertir las tendencias unilaterales de la reestructuración productiva y crear un clima laboral propicio a la cooperación .

Reemplazar la subordinación y la complicidad de las dirigencias sindicales por una auténtica capacidad de interlocución y proposición es una tarea que pasa igualmente por la adopción de cambios institucionales, sin que pueda eludirse por vías paralelas, como la negociación de acuerdos cupulares que no rompen con los arreglos corporativos previos.

Aunque constitucionalmente existe en México la libertad de asociación desde hace ochenta años, la remoción de los obstáculos legales —a nivel de las leyes reglamentarias— y políticos para renovar el sistema de representación —tanto de los trabajadores como de los empresarios— es una de las condiciones a cumplir para contar con interlocutores legítimos y con capacidad real de comprometer a sus representados. La existencia de un contexto democrático y con plena vigencia del Estado de Derecho resulta indispensable para propiciar un proceso gradual y pacífico de renovación de estructuras y liderazgos sindicales, de manera que en adelante los criterios y modalidades organizativas respondan verdaderamente a los intereses de las bases y no a razones de Estado que conducen a divisiones y unidades artificales como las que hoy caracterizan a las organizaciones sindicales mexicanas.

La posibilidad real de una intensa movilización de los trabajadores será también un requisito para crear en los medios empresariales el interés de contar con contrapartes sindicales dispuestas al diálogo y con capacidad propositiva, algo que no ocurrirá mientras dispongan de la capacidad represiva del gobierno y de las dirigencias afines.

Otra condición, además de la autonomía y transparencia, es la institucionalización de mecanismos bilaterales de definición de los cambios productivos, tanto de su ritmo como de su alcance, de manera tal que no sea necesaria una caótica proliferación de conflictos como único recurso para imponer en la empresa una negociación seria entre el capital y el trabajo o para obligar al primero a cumplir sus compromisos. Igualmente, la presencia de una dirigencia verdaderamente representativa y capaz de formular políticas alternativas a partir de sus propios diagnósticos será un factor imprescindible para reactivar los espacios tripartitos de determinación de la política económica, corrigiendo el actual desequilibrio en el poder de negociación de empresas y sindicatos y posibilitando el funcionamiento de otros de tipo sectorial, que tomen en cuenta los problemas propios de cada rama industrial.

No se trata, en consecuencia, de un simple cambio de mandos, de quedar en el aislamiento por la ruptura de las alianzas preexistentes o de hacer un nuevo arreglo entre las cúpulas, sino de una real transformación de las estrategias y recursos de poder sindicales tendientes a asumir el reto de ejercer una auténtica representación de las bases en un contexto marcado por la incertidumbre, el debilitamiento del Estado y el dramático impacto de los cambios tecnológicos y organizativos en la suerte de los trabajadores.

BIBLIOGRAFÍA

Arjona, E., 1990, "La industria mexicana de autopartes durante el auge exportador de los años ochenta" en Carrillo, J. (coord.), 1990, *La nueva era de la industria automotriz en México*, COLEF, México

Arteaga, A., 1991, "Ford: un largo y sinuoso conflicto" en Bensusán, G. y León, S. (coord.), 1991, *Negociación y conflicto laboral en México*, FES, FLACSO-sede México, México.

________ ,1992a "La reestructuración de la industria automotriz en México y sus repercusiones en el viejo núcleo fabril" en Arteaga, A. (coord.), 1992, *Proceso de trabajo y relaciones laborales en la industria automotriz en México*, FES, UAM-Iztapalapa, México.

________ , 1992b, "Industria automotriz: integración regional y repercusiones laborales. Algunas evidencias" en Bensusán, G. (coord.), 1992, *Las relaciones laborales y el Tratado de Libre Comercio*, FES, FLACSO-sede México, UAM-Xochimilco, México.

Bayón, M.C. , 1996 "Sindicatos y nuevas formas de organización del trabajo: entre el discurso y la realidad" en Rev. El Cotidiano Nº 80, Nov.-Dic. 1996, México

________ , 1997, *El sindicalismo automotriz mexicano frente a un nuevo escenario: Una perspectiva desde los liderazgos*, FLACSO-sede México, Juan Pablos Ed., México.

Bensusán, G., 1993, *La concertación social en los tiempos del ajuste estructural: El caso de México*, Documentos de Trabajo, OIT, Ginebra

________ ,1996, "Los sindicatos mexicanos en la transición política" en Rev. Argumentos Nº 24, UAM-X, México.

________ y García, C. (1992) "Entre la estabilidad y el conflicto: Relaciones laborales en la Volkswagen de México" en Arteaga, A. (coord.), 1992, *Proceso de trabajo y relaciones laborales en la industria automotriz en México*, FES, UAM-Iztapalapa, México.

Bueno, C. ,1995, "La cultura organizacional de las empresas de autopartes ante la globalización" en El Cotidiano Nº 73

Carrillo, J. ,1990, "Maquilización de la industria automotriz en México. De la industra terminal a la industria del ensamble" en Carrillo, J. (coord.), 1990, *La nueva era de la industria automotriz en México*, El Colegio de la Frontera Norte, México

________ , 1996, "Ford Hermosillo: Trayectoria y desarrollo de un modelo híbrido" en Micheli, J., 1996, *Japan Inc. en México: las empresas y los modelos laborales japoneses*, Porrúa, UAM-Azcapotzalco, Universidad de Colima, México.

De la Garza, E., 1990, "Siete tesis equivocadas acerca de la reconversión industrial en un país subdesarrollado: el caso de México" en Carrillo, J. (coord.),1990, *La nueva era de la industria automotriz en México*, El Colegio de la Frontera Norte, México

_____________, 1993, Reestructuración productiva y respuesta sindical en México, UNAM, UAM-Iztapalapa, México.

Herrera Lima, F. ,1992, "DINA: Reestructuración salvaje y conflicto laboral" en en Arteaga, A. (coord.), 1992, *Proceso de trabajo y relaciones laborales en la industria automotriz en México*, FES, UAM-Iztapalapa, México.

Katz, H. (1994) "The transformation of Industrial Relations in the United States" en Cook, M. y Katz, H. (coord.), 1994, *Regional Integration and Industrial Relations in North America*, Cornell University Press, Nueva York.

Lucio, R., 1994, *Las percepciones de los procesos de flexibilización. Un estudio sobre los trabajadores de la General Motors-México*, Tesis de Maestría, FLACSO-sede México, México

Regini, M. (1992) "Los empresarios frente al problema del consenso" en Rev. Sociología del Trabajo Nº 4.

Schmitter, P. (1992) "¿Continúa el siglo del corporativismo?" en Schmitter, P. y Lehmbruch, G., 1992, *Neocorporativismo I. Más allá del Estado y el mercado*, Alianza Editorial, México

MEETING "LEAN" COMPETITORS: FORD DE MEXICO'S INDUSTRIAL RELATIONS STRATEGY

P. Roberto Garcia and Stephen Hills[*]

INTRODUCTION

This study examines the industrial relations strategy of Ford de Mexico under conditions of regional economic integration. It is concerned with two of Ford de Mexico's automobile assembly operations, the Ford Hermosillo stamping and assembly plant (HSAP) and the Ford Cuautitlan assembly plant (CAP). The academic literature, the popular press, and our own field studies indicate that the state-of-the-art in manufacturing practice is the "lean production" system (Womack et al. 1990; Garcia 1996); therefore, we are focusing on the application of this management tool in Ford's Mexican operations.

Ford de Mexico has been adjusting to the very significant change in Mexico's auto industry regulatory environment. The regulatory changes of interest took place during the late 1980s and early 1990s as Mexico entered into a period of unilateral economic liberalization, leading eventually to the North American Free Trade Agreement (NAFTA) with the U.S. and Canada in 1994. In adjusting to a less restrictive and more competitive environment, the specific challenge for Ford de Mexico was to prepare all of its manufacturing operations for higher levels of internationally competitive performance. By 1990, Ford de Mexico's manufacturing operations exhibited two distinct levels of competitiveness: there were the older plants which were built in the early 1960s to serve the domestic market, and the newer assembly, engine, and parts plants which were built in the early and mid-1980s for the export market. Table 1 identifies the differences between old and new as exemplified in the Cuautitlan and Hermosillo plants.

---

[*] P. Roberto Garcia is an Assistant Professor at Indiana University. Stephen Hills is an Associate Professor at Ohio State University.

Table 1
Comparison Between Ford Plants

	Cuautitlan	Hermosillo
Target Market	Local	Export
Layout/Process Complexity	High: several models	Low: 1 or 2 models
Automation Level	Low	High
Machinery	Old, outdated	State-of-the-art
Work Organization	Seniority-based, rigid, many classifications	Team-based, flexible, few classifications
Union-Management Relationship	More combative	More cooperative
Competitiveness	Local market only	Global market

While the two plants were originally designed to serve different markets, NAFTA has forced them to compete for the same markets. It is in response to this demand that Ford-Cuautitlan has had to consider lean production as an option. While HSAP is a modern, lean production facility which is poised to compete in the global automotive industry, CAP is quite far from achieving global competitiveness standards. For example, in the 1996 Harbour and Associates productivity report, CAP still ranked last in productivity among all North American plants surveyed. Since 1995, the plant has experienced a significant amount of investment in automation and model complexity reduction. However, the sticking point is its inability to change its union-management relationship, and thus, its work organization toward the lean production system.

A high investment conversion strategy usually involves updating the machinery as well as the work organization. These are two key interrelated components, "hard" and "soft." Equipping a factory with the most up-to-date machinery may not achieve the highest levels of productivity —also necessary is a different type of work organization that can achieve higher quality and productivity standards. But to change the work organization in a pre-existing plant means gaining the cooperation and commitment of the workforce (Burawoy 1979), something Ford has yet to achieve at Cuautitlan.

RESEARCH QUESTION AND METHODOLOGY

This study addresses the following question: How has Ford attempted to implement the lean production system at Cuautitlan? Ford's subsidiary managers have two options: 1) closing down Cuautitlan and replacing it with a greenfield facility; or 2) managing both Hermosillo and Cuautitlan simultaneously while attempting to raise the capability of Cuautitlan to global levels. Preliminary fieldwork showed that the first option was not viable for Ford because of the cost of replacing Cuautitlan's infrastructure (plant, suppliers, communications, labor force, etc.). In addition, the Mexican government would not have looked kindly on a highly visible plant shutdown in the Mexico City area. Therefore, this study focuses the greatest attention on Ford's Cuautitlan conversion efforts.

The current study takes an inductive, theory-building, case-study approach. The rationale and techniques involved in this methodology can be found in the works of Piore (1983), Van Mannen (1983), Prahalad and Doz (1987), Eisenhardt (1989), Yin (1989), Denison (1990), Samuels (1990), Strauss and Corbin (1990), and Feldman (1989 and 1995). The primary data sources consist of interviews and direct observation of auto production practice at the plant level. Archival documents were also collected when available. The basis for the questions asked and issues explored were the result of preliminary field-based research, and literature reviews. Other sources included internal company documents, industry publications, general business publications, and government policies. Both company and government policies were studied in order to better understand the context of the research problem.

HISTORY OF THE UNION-MANAGEMENT RELATIONSHIP AT FORD DE MEXICO

Labor costs in Mexico tend to be a function of the plant location within the country and of the union-management history. By choosing to locate the greenfield HSAP plant in a predominantly agricultural region far away from Mexico City, Ford effectively reduced its compensation costs in dramatic fashion.[1] When HSAP was built, its isolated northern location made it one of the lowest-cost assemblers in the industry, while CAP was one of the high-

---

[1] Labor costs tend to be highest in the most industrialized areas of the country (i.e. Mexico City, Monterey, and Guadalajara).

est.[2] Since then, Ford has followed a strategy of reducing the disparity between the two plants by bringing both closer to the national industry labor compensation average. That is, CAP's considerably higher wages were lowered through hard negotiations with the union and by "buying out" the collective labor agreement in 1987 (described below). Simultaneously, HSAP's wages and benefits were allowed to increase at a faster rate than the industry average. Today, CAP's hourly compensation costs are slightly above the industry average while HSAP's are still slightly below. As will be discussed later, this pay scale disparity has contributed significantly to the deliberate separation of the two plants.

Ilan Bizberg, a Mexican labor relations expert, characterizes the Mexican labor movement as one based on control (Ilan Bizberg interview 1996). The centralized structure of the main labor federation, the Confederacion de Trabajadores Mexicanos (CTM), gives upper level leaders considerable control over the membership. Furthermore, the CTM supports the economic development policies of the various Mexican governments that have been in power continuously since the revolution. Garcia (1996) finds that in exchange for the CTM's political support, various presidential administrations have taken a pro-labor stance to enact strong Mexican labor laws, especially during the 1960s and 1970s. It was during this period that CAP's union leaders managed to wrest a significant degree of shopfloor control from management. This control has resulted in considerable countervailing power for CAP's union. Almost since its inception, CAP has experienced several difficult strikes and work stoppages.

A key episode in CAP's union-management relationship was the 1987 100-day work stoppage that coincided with the government's shift to a policy of economic liberalization. In the public sector, many state-run enterprises were either privatized or closed. In the private sector, many manufacturing firms were forced to deal with growing inflationary pressures by reducing costs. By 1985, Ford de Mexico identified CAP as one of the country's most costly assembly plants, and in 1987 the company initiated a major drive to lower costs at the plant. The union's opposition to these efforts led to the 100-day work stoppage. The strike ended when the company "bought out" the ex-

[2] The industry labor costs are calculated by surveying the automotive assembly and engine plants located in Mexico. The actual figures are collected by independent consulting firms to be shared by the participating firms. In 1993, one such report included detailed labor cost data for 18 automotive plants located in Mexico.

isting work contract, as permitted by law, and rehired 80 percent of the original workers.[3] To buy out the existing contract, Ford paid all the workers a severance amount of four months' wages, one month more than required by law. Those who were rehired began at zero seniority. The contract buyout resulted in an immediate payroll cost reduction of 40 percent. The CTM's national leaders acquiesced to these events and pressed the local union to sign a new contract that dismantled some of the previous restrictions on management action. As a result, CAP achieved a boost in efficiency due to a greater degree of shopfloor flexibility: the "Escalafon" system of job classifications, for example, was reduced from seventeen broad job categories to seven, permitting management greater discretion in the assignment of workers.

Ford de Mexico managers viewed the 1987 contract buyout as a necessary action and a preferable alternative to shutting the plant down completely at a later time. However, for the remaining workers, the terms must have been very difficult to accept. Given that NAFTA would require additional quality and productivity increases of CAP, future union-management negotiations would be colored by the difficult 1987 episode.

While HSAP's labor-management relationship is not entirely without strife,[4] it is not prone to the same levels of conflict as CAP.[5] A major reason for the difference is that the HSAP union's role in shopfloor issues was effectively limited, by design, at the time the plant was planned. By contract, one of the notable characteristics of HSAP is that there is wide management discretion in the union-management relationship.

THE WORK ORGANIZATION SYSTEM

The key difference between the two plants is their work organization system. When the two plants are compared, CAP's work organization is characterized as outdated, rigid, and inefficient, while HSAP's is considered modern, flexible, and highly efficient. Like the other traditional plants in Mexico, CAP's

---

[3] According to Ford de Mexico industrial relations managers, the firm exercised a legal separation clause at this time.

[4] There have been at least three strikes at the Hermosillo plant since 1986. Unlike Cuautitlan, however, the focus of these work stoppages was wages rather than issues of shopfloor control.

[5] While both plants fall under the same national CTM leadership, each union functions very differently at the local level. The relationship somewhat resembles the difference between most GM-UAW United States plants and the GM-UAW Saturn plant in Spring Hill, Tennessee.

work organization is still based on the "Escalafon" system, which dates back to the 1960s. The Escalafon is the formal pay and promotional ladder-type system used by many manufacturing firms in Mexico.

From the union's perspective, the Escalafon insures a considerable degree of job security for its most senior members. Each classification is linked to the one before, meaning that management must hire for entry level jobs only. A reduction in work force is achieved, correspondingly, from the lowest levels of seniority. The Escalafon also protects employment security through its narrow definition of jobs and its restrictions on who is to do the work.

By 1990 however, management regarded the Escalafon system, even as modified by the contract buyout of 1987, as an obstacle that blocked the transition to lean production. The Escalafon system still gave workers and the union a considerable amount of control over the shopfloor, and management therefore still viewed the labor agreement as too rigid. Workers believed their job classifications and differential pay were "sacred," and many still protested the abrogation of the old contract in 1987. The plant's troubled labor relations made it very difficult to forget the past and to change the nature of the union-management relationship in the plant.

HSAP, on the other hand, was created with a very different type of work organization. It is a Japanese-style flexible work organization —lean production— which attempts to overcome the rigidities of the traditional Escalafon system.

THE CONVERSION PROCESS OF CAP TO LEAN PRODUCTION

Implementation of a lean production system is far more difficult in a brownfield setting like CAP than in a greenfield setting like Hermosillo. While the eventual performance goal of both plants is the same, CAP is highly constrained by three decades of operational history (work routines, work organization, and union-management relations), the particular layout and process complexity of the location, and the outdated nature of most of the equipment. In effect, while the greenfield plant personnel have to learn the lean production system from scratch, the traditional plant counterparts have to first *unlearn* their past ways of doing things *and* then learn the new system of lean production. In many ways the interconnectedness of various aspects of the lean production system (work organization, technology, union-management relations, plant organization structure, training, role of communication, etc.) makes it very difficult to apply it as an overlay on top of an existing traditional system.

Furthermore, the lean production system implies a certain degree of trust that management will not exploit the flexibility it seeks in assigning employees to work "out of position." This degree of trust needs to be demonstrated incrementally as employees themselves help shape the new system. Management must prove that its aim is to improve competitiveness for economic survival and that job security ultimately depends on changing the work organization so that survival is possible.

Ford faces a significant challenge in its formulation of industrial relations strategy. On the one hand, the existence of many work rules and regulations implies a fairly high degree of distrust in the past. In asking the union to remove such restrictions, management must first demonstrate that it considers its employees worthy of trust. But in times of economic adversity, hard decisions must be made about reduction of all costs. Under such conditions, management often reverts back to previous authoritarian styles of decision-making and signals distrust. The sociologist Alan Fox refers to this pattern of management as "standard modern" (Fox 1974, 307). Trust is shown toward employees when competitive pressures are less intense, but when the pressure increases, trust is withdrawn and the tough decisions are made by a few managers. Yet, once the tough decisions about costs are made, trust is again required to meet the high quality expectations of competitive production. As Ford changes its patterns of management, it cannot show ambivalence in the level of trust extended either to employees or to their union.

Illustrative of the challenges facing Ford at Cuautitlan is the new round of labor-management conflict that came to a head in 1990. In response to Ford's modifications of the production system in 1987 and 1988, the local union at Cuautitlan initiated a campaign to democratize the larger union representing all Ford plants and to resist the lean production system. The clash of interests within the union and with Ford led to violence at the Cuautitlan plant in 1990, the death of a Ford worker, and Ford's firing of 1,600 employees. Quality circles, which were introduced in 1990, had all but disappeared by 1992 and production quality suffered (Paul Bernardo interview 1997).

A second challenge is strongly related to the first. In changing its work organization at CAP, Ford has been unwilling to create a corresponding system of compensation that would further raise labor costs and make CAP even more expensive compared to competing plants. Yet, if employees are willing to give up flexibility to enhance the company's success, they will expect to share in the benefits. When asked whether the Escalafon system at

CAP will eventually be replaced by something closer to the system at HSAP, a CAP industrial relations manager (who previously worked in the same role at HSAP) replied that such a change was resisted more by *management* than by labor. Apparently, the skill-based pay system at HSAP would be welcomed by the CAP workforce because there would be less of a brake on wage increases under the new pay regime than under the current, rigid Escalafon job classification scheme.

At HSAP, workers have the opportunity to move up to the next pay grade of the single job classification scheme as long as they have received the required amount of training and can demonstrate higher level skill by passing an exam. At CAP, workers increase their pay by moving upward through approximately 100 detailed job classifications grouped within seven broad categories. Movement depends on turnover in the positions above. Introducing a compensation system like HSAP's would allow all workers to advance in pay, not just those taking advantage of turnover-induced promotion. For Ford de Mexico's subsidiary level managers, changing the existing work organization in search of higher competitiveness, while allowing current labor costs to rise, becomes a difficult tradeoff.

There are four necessary ingredients for a successful implementation of the lean production system in an existing traditional plant: 1) supervision and direction by a group of external technically oriented experts in lean production techniques; 2) the support of an internal group of managers and technicians who know the history and the workings of the traditional facility; 3) the full commitment and cooperation of the various plant personnel (top managers, middle managers, supervisors, line workers, and union leaders) to carry out the changes required; and 4) a high degree of trust.

With respect to the conversion process at CAP, this study revealed that plant and subsidiary managers view the required change as involving two primary dimensions: 1) a *technological dimension* (machinery, automation, product and process complexity reduction, etc.); and 2) a *human dimension* (work organization, union-management relations, leadership style, etc.). The present study indicates that, of the two dimensions, the most difficult part of a traditional plant conversion involves the human dimension. Trust is a fragile asset and can be undermined by focusing on lowering labor costs without addressing the union-management relationship. A high commitment strategy requires the sincere cooperation of the workforce. In a unionized setting, sincere cooperation follows from step-by-step demonstrations that management trusts its workers and is committed to their long-term well being.

FORD'S DECENTRALIZED LABOR RELATIONS POLICIES IN MEXICO

When considering Ford's labor relations strategy, one must distinguish between rationalization of policy and centralization of decision making. While NAFTA has created certain pressures toward centralization of HSAP's and CAP's reporting relationship from Mexico City toward Dearborn, industrial relations has remained highly localized and decentralized at the subsidiary and plant levels.

A way to understand HSAP's split reporting structure is to consider that its technical activity is home-country (United States) driven while much of its support activity is host-country (Mexico) driven.[6] For their host-country specific activities, both CAP and HSAP report directly to Mexico City subsidiary managers. However, this is not to imply that the industrial relations function of both plants is standardized and centralized. In terms of industrial relations, the two plants are managed quite differently and are deliberately kept separate from each other. The current separation can be explained by considering that when HSAP was created, it was meant to be free of many of the work practices thought to be making CAP rigid and adversarial. The subsidiary level Ford managers were most concerned about keeping CAP and HSAP as separate as possible. The "contamination effect" was minimized when HSAP was sited as far away as possible from CAP and Mexico City. By locating HSAP close to the United States border where labor compensation costs were much lower, Ford de Mexico was able to reduce its wages and benefits dramatically at its second assembly plant. The move also brought the possibility of crafting a different union-management relationship than at its traditional CAP facility.

Ford's move northward resulted in a different union-management relationship than before. Although HSAP belongs to the same national union as CAP, it operates much differently at a local level. For example, HSAP's local union has almost no voice in work floor issues.[7] The labor contract was de-

---

[6] Yet another way to explain the structure is to say that Ford is employing a *global* approach to HSAP's technical activity (manufacturing/production, quality control, supplier relations) and a *multi-domestic* approach to its support functions (government relations, labor relations, taxes, finance, etc.).

[7] The CAP manufacturing manager expressed the danger in mixing the two plants' unions: "On a technical level there is total openness and communication. We can go to HSAP anytime we want and their doors are open. The union is another thing, we have to be more careful. We do not take workers to Hermosillo because the union sees what is most convenient for them, not what we want them to see." (Ford Interview: 7, 5).

signed so that management would have great flexibility in implementing a Japanese-style lean production work organization. These features of the HSAP work organization include one classification for all production workers, work in teams, and tremendous flexibility in assigning workers to various work floor locations.

From an industrial relations perspective, HSAP represents an incredible degree of managerial autonomy compared to CAP. For the subsidiary managers, the task of operating within the HSAP labor contract is much easier than at CAP. Consequently, they are still quite determined to prevent HSAP from relinquishing its managerial control and flexibility, as did CAP.

In recent interviews at Ford de Mexico (1996), labor relations managers were asked if labor relations policies were gradually becoming standardized between the two plants. The answer was a definite "no." Although the CTM represents workers in HSAP, CAP, and the Chihuahua engine plant (CHEP), the contracts that have been negotiated are quite different, reflecting the different work organization in each plant. Nevertheless, Ford de Mexico adheres to Ford's world-wide compensation policy of trying neither to be in the highest nor lowest pay ranges within the regions in which it is located. It tries to be at about the third quartile in pay wherever its plants are located.

A second piece of evidence regarding Ford's decentralized labor relations strategy is its tolerance of wide and continuing gaps in performance (productivity and quality) among its three main plants in Mexico. Over time, the gap between CAP and both HSAP and CHEP has narrowed, partly due to quality and productivity programs implemented in CAP. However, the other two plants continue to increase their levels of productivity as well. For the time being, Ford appears to be content to accept low performance at CAP, when compared to U.S. and Canadian standards, rather than insisting on a quick movement toward maximizing performance. This could mean that Ford is willing to wait for a system to emerge that is crafted by labor and management cooperation at CAP, or it could mean that the plant is in a "holding pattern" until an opportune time to close it permanently.

CONCLUSION

This study has covered Ford de Mexico's efforts to become more competitive in an economically integrated environment. At CAP, management has settled for a gradual conversion process which involves: 1) gradual reduction in production process complexity, 2) gradual introduction of robots and automation to increase productivity and quality, 3) continuous training of the existing workers, including CAP workers visiting other U.S. and Canadian Ford plants to study how certain things are done. What is missing is a comprehensive attempt to impose the "lean production" system at its traditional plant. Ford has decided on a gradual, give-and-take conversion process, involving the union in some of its decisions. In the face of government liberalization policies, Ford initially sought to reduce wage costs at CAP, but it has since then sought to maintain the trust of its union. We did not find evidence of a managerial strategy to force workers and the union to adopt the "lean production" system, as was the case in VW-Puebla. Rather, Ford is attempting to rationalize production information through its reorganization of reporting relationships while managing the adaptation of lean production methods through local, decentralized labor relations policies. The strategy is Ford's pragmatic implementation of "think global, act local."

BIBLIOGRAPHY

Burawoy, M. 1979. *Manufacturing Consent: Changes in the Labor Process under Monopoly Capitalism.* Chicago: University of Chicago Press.

Denison, D.R. 1990. *Corporate Culture and Organizational Effectiveness.* New York: John Wiley and Sons.

Eisenhardt, K.M. 1989. "Building Theories from Case Study Research." *Academy of Management Review* 14, no. 4: 532-550.

Feldman, M.S. 1989. *Order Without Design: Information Production and Policy Making.* Stanford: Stanford University Press.

——. 1995. *Strategies for Interpreting Qualitative Data.* Thousand Oaks, CA: Sage Publications.

Fox, A. 1974. *Beyond Contract: Work, Power and Trust Relations.* London: Faber and Faber.

Garcia, P.R. 1996. "Learning and Competitiveness in Mexico's Automotive Industry: The Relationship Between Traditional and World-Class Plants in Multinational Firm Subsidiaries." Ph.D. diss., University of Michigan.

Harbour and Associates. 1996. *The Harbour Report 1996: Manufacturing Productivity Company by Company - Plant by Plant.* Harbour & Associates Inc.

Piore, M.J. 1983. "Qualitative Research Techniques in Economics." In J. Van Maanen, ed., *Qualitative Methodology.* Beverly Hills, CA: Sage Publications.

Prahalad, C.K. and Y.L. Doz. 1987. *The Multinational Mission: Balancing Local Demands and Global Vision.* New York: Free Press.

Samuels, B.C. 1990. *Managing Risk in Developing Countries: National Demands and Multinational Response.* Princeton: Princeton University Press.

Strauss, A. and J. Corbin. 1990. *Basics of Qualitative Research.* Newbury Park, CA: Sage Publications.

Van Maanen, J. *Qualitative Methodology.* Beverly Hills, CA: Sage Publications.

Womack, J.P., Jones, D.T., & Roos, D. 1990. *The Machine that Changed the World: The Story of Lean Production.* New York: Rawson Associates.

Yin, R.K. 1989. *Case Study Research: Design and Methods.* Newbury Park, CA: Sage Publications.

Parte II
ENSAMBLE

Part II
ASSEMBLY

THE UNION ROLE IN TEAM CONCEPT: A CASE STUDY

*Michelle Kaminski**

INTRODUCTION

From a management perspective, lean production promises increased productivity and flexibility, at the risk of a fragile, unbuffered process.[1] From a union perspective, the same system promises more worker input, at the risk of increasing workplace stress and decreasing union solidarity.[2] The variation in how ideas of lean production are actually implemented in the workplace indicates the potential for the best —or the worst— of both worlds. The experience of the Ford Wayne Integrated Stamping and Assembly Plant and UAW Local 900 suggests that a proactive union, along with cooperative management, can create a work environment that has some of the competitive benefits of lean production, coupled with a work organization that is responsive to workers' needs.

Located in Wayne, Michigan, thirty miles west of Detroit, Ford's assembly and body-making operations employ a total of 3,600 workers in two plants producing the Ford Escort. The work organization in one of these plants, the stamping and body-assembly operation, has some features of lean production, although neither the workers nor the managers there consider this a

---

* Assistant Professor, Institute of Labor and Industrial Relations, University of Illinois, This work was supported by grants from the U.S. Department of the Air Force, contract number f33615-95-C-5512 and from the Air Force Manufacturing Technology program, contract number 94-5812-72-1.

[1] See James Womack, Daniel Jones, and Daniel Roos, *The Machine that Changed the World: The Story of Lean Production* (New York: Rawson Associates, 1990).

[2] Critiques can be found in Mike Parker and Jane Slaughter, "Unions and Management by Stress," in Steve Babson, ed., *Lean work: Empowerment and Exploitation in the Global Auto Industry* (Detroit: Wayne State University Press, 1995), 41-53, and John Paul MacDuffie, "Workers' Roles in Lean Production: The Implications for Worker Representation," in Babson, *Lean Work*, 54-69.

"lean" plant. The term they use to describe their work organization is "team concept." The distinction is more than a semantic one. The union contract incorporates some elements of lean production, such as teams, a single job classification for production employees, extensive training, and regular job rotation. But it also has other features that make the teams "worker-centered."[3] For example, team leaders are elected by hourly employees. Another feature —not usually found in lean plants— is that all hourly employees had input into the process of designing the team system.

Some background information about the Wayne plant is presented below, followed by a description of the team concept and workers' evaluation of it.[4]

GREENFIELD OR BROWNFIELD?

Whether a production facility is brand new ("greenfield") or has been in operation for many years ("brownfield") is a key factor in determining how teams are implemented. Teams are often more successful at greenfield sites because the company can hire a new workforce based on the applicants' interest in and ability to work in teams. In addition, greenfield sites usually have new technology, which can be designed specifically to complement the team form of work organization. The Saturn plant is perhaps the best known example of this in the United States. In contrast, brownfield sites usually have the advantage of having skilled and experienced workers who know how to get the most out of the existing equipment. But this advantage can sometimes be outweighed by a history of animosity between union and management that makes the transition to a new partnership difficult.

The Wayne facility cannot be described as either a brownfield or a greenfield site. Rather, it is a complex hybrid. Prior to 1987, the Wayne assembly plant was a single bargaining unit in a single building, represented by UAW Local 900. In 1987, Ford management approached the UAW about adding a stamping plant adjacent to Wayne Assembly. In exchange for the new jobs this would bring, management wanted a Modern Operating

---

[3] For a description of worker-centered teams versus supervisor-centered team, see Steve Babson, "A New Model Ford?" *Asia Pacific Business Review* (summer 1996): 82-98.

[4] Further information about the history and development of team concept at Wayne can be found in Michelle Kaminski, Domenick Bertelli, Melissa Moye, and Joel Yudken, *Making Change Happen: Six Cases of Unions and Companies Transforming Their Workplaces* (Washington, DC: Work and Technology Institute, 1996), 25-44. For a comparison of Wayne to other closely-related Ford plants, see Babson, "A New Model Ford?"

Agreement (MOA). An agreement was reached in 1988 that included teams, pay for knowledge, one classification system for production workers, and three umbrella classifications for skilled trades.

This agreement also split the existing bargaining unit in half. The new stamping plant and the body shop were combined into Wayne Integrated Stamping and Assembly (ISA), and formed one bargaining unit of Local 900. There are about 1,100 members of this unit. The other bargaining unit, Wayne Assembly, has about 2,500 members and includes the chassis, paint, and trim departments. It is also represented by Local 900. That unit does not have a team concept and is managed under a more traditional system. The assembly bargaining unit had the opportunity to vote on team concept, and rejected it by a 4-1 margin. The data reported below apply only to the ISA bargaining unit, and not to the traditionally managed assembly bargaining unit.

DESIGN OF TEAM CONCEPT

In 1988 and 1989, management and union leadership worked jointly to design the new work system. They visited other plants with team concepts, including NUMMI in California, and plants in Mexico and Japan. Many plant leadership groups conduct visits like this as they think about changing their work system. But the Wayne group also did something that few other plants of this size are able to accomplish: they got the input of almost the entire workforce about what they wanted the team concept to be.

They did this by taking advantage of a training program called "Zero Defects." The stated purpose of the jointly conducted training was to find out what barriers prevented people from producing a car with zero defects. The union leadership used this opportunity to create their bargaining agenda. For example, if workers indicated that lack of communication was a barrier, the union leader asked if having a team leader would help. Workers expressed concern that a team leader would be a company stooge. So, the union leader asked, "what if you elected them?" Workers were skeptical that management would allow this. The union's response was that they would bargain for what workers wanted. As a key union leader put it, "that's basically how we developed all our language. It was based on that class. I did not go into any negotiations with the company until I got a lot of communication from the plant." Management supported this process. For example, one manager who helped run the classes told workers, "we have the concepts on paper. We need you to draft the language."

A second aspect of the Zero Defects sessions was quite unusual —the selection and scheduling process. Everyone in the bargaining unit was ultimately invited to attend these sessions, in groups of about 20. But, according to both union and management, the first 20 people to attend were intentionally selected by the union as those who were expected to be most resistant to the team concept. That group of 20 selected the next group, and so on, until everyone had the opportunity to attend. Thus, after the first class, the union and management were not part of the scheduling. A primary advantage of this approach is that because they were able to offer their ideas and help shape the new system early in the process, even the most resistant workers would be more likely to support the ultimate design.

Worker involvement in design went even further in the stamping department. The manager of the launch team there had experience working with teams in other Ford locations. He insisted that the work process must be designed by the people who would ultimately work in that area. He delegated decisions, even when pressed to make them himself.

In 1990, the bargaining unit voted on the new contract language, including team concept. The contract was overwhelmingly ratified: 83 percent of skilled trades workers and 97 percent of production workers voted in favor of the MOA.

TEAM CHARACTERISTICS: CONTRACT PROVISIONS

In many workplaces, features of the work organization that are codified in the local union contract are likely to be followed more uniformly than those that are not. This has been an issue with teams, because some labor leaders and managers are hesitant to incorporate them into the local agreement. In such cases, there may be no leverage to enforce provisions of the team concept when commitment sags on one side or the other. At Wayne ISA, the team concept was first incorporated into the 1990 contract, and continued in the 1993 and 1996 contracts.[5]

Teams: All hourly employees are part of a team. Teams are formed based on natural work units, although on the assembly line the division points are

---

[5] Information is taken from UAW Local 900 and the Ford Motor Company, "Wayne Body and Stamping. Local Agreements, Letters of Understanding and Rates" for the years 1990, 1993, and 1996, and from the national collective bargaining agreement, UAW and the Ford Motor Company, *Agreements*, Volume I, 1993.

somewhat arbitrary. Approximately 10 to 15 employees are on each team, and there are approximately 60 teams in the plant. The contract also specifies the reason for creating teams: they are needed to be competitive, and will also provide opportunities for greater participation, improved quality of work life, and greater job security. Among other things, teams are responsible for scheduling job rotation, training, and vacations.

Job classifications. There is one classification for production workers ("technician") and three umbrella classifications for skilled trades: electrical, mechanical, and tool and die.

Pay-for-knowledge. As workers learn more tasks within their group, their pay increases. An employee progresses to the next rate level when the team members, team leader, and supervisor agree that the employee has demonstrated proficiency on those operations. Most employees are now at the top rate. In the 1990 contract the pay range for body stamping technician was from $16.12 to $16.73 per hour. In the 1996 contract, the range is from $18.975 to $19.60 per hour.

Team Leaders. Team leaders are elected by hourly employees. The 1990 contract called for a minimum term of three-months, although it has since been extended to six months. Team leaders are paid an additional $.50 per hour. The 1993 contract added a provision for an elected alternate team leader to stand in when the team leader is absent.

Job rotation. Employees are expected to learn all operations in their group. The team decides on the rotation schedule and a training plan to meet this goal. In practice, most teams rotate daily, while some rotate weekly. All production teams, except metal finishing (where the jobs are highly specialized), rotate jobs.

Transfers between teams. No employee can transfer from one team to another without the agreement of both management and the union. The purpose of this provision is to prevent the formation of cliques that exclude some team members.

Transfers from old bargaining unit at start-up. Body shop employees from the old plant were offered the opportunity to transfer with their work to the new ISA plant. Those who accepted the offer received a raise. (Union leaders report that all but two eligible employees did transfer.) Some of the additional openings were filled by volunteers from the old bargaining unit, using a "Best in Class" selection procedure. Attendance was an important criteria, along with seniority. The volunteer rate was reportedly low. Other openings were filled by laid-off employees with transfer rights from other Ford facilities, and some new hires.

TEAM CHARACTERISTICS: ADDITIONAL PRACTICES

Although the characteristics described below are not part of the local union contract, they are a regular part of how the team concept is practiced at Wayne.

Training. Workers attended a minimum of 40 hours of training as part of the launch process in 1990. Training was developed and conducted jointly. It covered both specific job skills and "soft skills," such as problem-solving and working in teams. Workers in some areas, such as stamping, received up to six weeks of additional training. In 1995, with the new model changeover, workers again attended a 40-hour training program. Of the 40 hours, 24 were devoted to team building and problem-solving. Mandatory topics such as health and safety were included as well.

Team meetings. Teams in the stamping area meet every day for 30 minutes, and teams in other areas meet once a week. The weekly meetings are 25 minutes long, with an additional five minutes allowed to travel back to the work station. Team leaders run the meetings.

Team leader meetings. All area managers are expected to hold weekly meetings with the team leaders from that area. In practice, most —but not all— areas hold these meetings.

Additional union roles in running the workplace. As the team concept has taken hold in the plant, the union has become increasingly involved in areas that were formerly the sole domain of management. The union sends a representative to weekly cost meetings, and has access to considerable financial information as a result. The union is also involved in strategic planning.

Model changeover. A joint committee was formed to plan the most recent model changeover for a major redesign (1996). Several hourly employees worked on this committee full-time. They were involved in setting up jobs, reviewing new equipment before purchasing decisions were made, and promoting good ergonomic design.

OTHER UNION ISSUES: CONTRACT PROVISIONS

One of the strengths of the union's role at Wayne is that it has defended strong contract language and practices about traditional union issues while simultaneously implementing team concept.

Overtime. Overtime opportunities are equalized among workers in each of eight areas within the plant. Hourly employees in each area elect one "overtime coordinator" per shift, who is paid the team leader rate. Once a week, overtime coordinators ask employees in their areas about their availability for overtime for the coming week, and keep records of overtime offered and accepted. This is a major change from the old system in which supervisors were responsible for overtime distribution. Under that system, overtime was a major source of grievances, and the goal of having elected overtime coordinators was to reduce their number. While grievances for all other issues have remained about the same under the MOA, the number of overtime grievances has, in fact, gone down substantially.

Annual area "bumping." Employees who want to transfer from one area to another sign up for that area. When job openings occur, they are filled based on the seniority of those who have indicated an interest in moving to that area. In addition, once a year management and the union administer a set of moves, or "bumps," throughout the plant, based on seniority. Under this system, high seniority employees are able to move to new areas even if there is not an opening. They must stay in that area for 12 months. Low seniority employees might be bumped from their job, and are moved to the area from which the more senior employee came.

Seniority interest survey. Job openings in preferred areas (material handling, environmental, quality weld surveillance) are filled based on a "seniority interest survey." The union surveys about 200 of the highest seniority workers annually to determine their interest in these jobs, should they become available. When openings occur, the union identifies the highest seniority worker who expressed interest in the job and informs him or her about the opening. The job is filled by the high seniority employee who is interested in that job. From the union's point of view, this eliminates complaints from high seniority employees that they did not see a job posting they would have been interested in, or that preferred jobs are given to the friends of union leaders.

ADDITIONAL UNION PRACTICES

Weekly plant walk-through. The union plant chairman and committee members conduct a regularly scheduled weekly plant walk-through, alternating shifts. In this walk-through, they go to every department and ask employees how things are going and if there are problems they can help resolve.

Union connection to teams. Union committee members attend many of the team meetings in their district. They attend when invited, or check in on a regular basis.

Grievances. Team systems are often associated with a decline in grievances. Except for a significant reduction in overtime grievances, that does not appear to be the case here. Managers and union leaders both report that grievances are only slightly lower than before.

EVALUATION OF TEAM CONCEPT

Worker assessment of team concept is measured by focus-group and survey data collected at Wayne ISA in the spring of 1995. Specifically, three focus groups were conducted with a total of 21 hourly employees on two shifts. Two supervisors, three managers and three union leaders were interviewed individually. Quantitative surveys were administered to a stratified random sample of hourly employees. Sixty-seven employees completed surveys on company time, with a response rate of 74 percent. The demographic characteristics of the survey respondents are shown in Table 1.

Table 1
Demographic Characteristics of Survey Respondents

Variable	Mean or Frequency		Valid Responses (N)
Gender	Men:	91.5%	59
	Women:	8.5%	
Race	White:	62.3%	53
	African American:	28.3%	
	Other:*	9.4%	
Age	Mean:	41 years	57
Years in Plant	Mean:	14 years	66
Job category	Skilled trades:	16.7%	66
	Production:	75.8%	
	Other:	7.6%	
Education	Some college or more:	26.6%	60
	High school graduate:	68.3%	
	Less than H.S. graduate:	5.1%	

* Data collection error.

Survey results shown in Table 2 demonstrate that hourly employees are, in general, very satisfied with the team concept. A sizable majority —71 percent— say they have benefited from team concept. In sharp contrast, only 7 percent say they have been hurt by it. When asked in more detail what they liked about teams, workers cited job rotation, reduced boredom, increased voice in what happens in the plant, and the opportunity to learn more skills. For example, one worker said about job rotation,

> That's the difference between the team concept and the old system. You could be stuck on a job for 30 years. Now you only have to do that bad job one day out of the week or one day every two weeks. It cuts down on absenteeism.

New equipment and attention to ergonomic issues has made many of the jobs less strenuous. Another worker compares his job before team concept to his current work:

> They had these manual weld guns that you had to tug and pull and lift, and you had to pick all your parts up by hand, even the big ones, and put them on. Now we've got push buttons. You put on small parts and for the big parts, the hoist comes over and puts it down and you just hit the buttons.

Workers, union leaders, and managers all report a significant reduction in job-related injuries —although figures were not available. The combination of improved ergonomics and job rotation seem to have contributed to this improvement. But some difficult jobs remain, and teams tend to rotate those jobs on an hourly basis.

Table 2
Worker Assessments of Team Concept

Survey Question	Agree or Strongly Agree	Neither Agree nor Disagree	Disagree or Strongly Disagree	Valid Responses (N)
The union should work with management to further develop the team concept here.	89.2%	4.6%	6.2%	65
I have benefited directly from the team concept.	71.1%	18.6%	10.2%	59
I have been hurt by the team concept	7.1%	26.3%	66.6%	57

Workers also report that they have more control over their work now. For example, one worker describes how the job has changed as a result of team concept.

> I can make decisions now as to 'is this stock any good, is this job running right, do I need to get a toolmaker or someone in here.' I can stop the line, cut the line off, say, 'This is not right. I need a toolmaker to fix this, and until it's fixed the line is going to sit.' Before we were all treated like we didn't have any brains, [like] we were dummies. Even though we did this job every day for eight to ten hours [management thought] we didn't know what was wrong, why there was a problem. Our input wasn't asked for, it wasn't needed, and if you gave it, it wasn't heard.

Another worker added,

> One of the best changes I've seen in my area [is that] the team decides who's doing what job. The [supervisor] does not come up and tell me who's doing what job . . . The team decides.

In spite of the success of team concept to date, workers also discussed some problems. For example, they report that there has been some backsliding in the years since teams were first implemented. In informal discussions, union leaders claimed that the training that was conducted during the 1995 model changeover (after the survey data were collected) helped to revitalize the teams.

A continuing issue is the variation in team responsibilities from department to department. In particular, the stamping area is seen as remaining true to the original team concept. Stamping is the area most removed from the assembly line, and as much as three days of inventory can be stockpiled. As a result, when repairs are needed, it is possible to shut down the stamping area without shutting down the entire assembly operation. In contrast, in those areas that are part of the assembly line, workers report that if you stop the line, "they're chewing your head off."

The small number of survey respondents who say they were hurt by team concept say that sometimes team members are not all treated equally, and that team concept is not fair to high seniority workers who have to rotate through all jobs in a team, instead of being able to do only their most preferred job.

Table 3
Team Concept Compared to Traditional Management

Compared to the way things were before there were teams here. . . .				Valid Responses (N)
... the pace of my job is	A little or a lot slower	About the same	A little or a lot faster	56
	21.4%	35.7%	42.9%	
... the amount of stress on my job is	A little or a lot lower	About the same	A little or a lot higher	58
	43.1%	24.1%	32.8%	
... I like my job	A little or a lot better	About the same	A little or a lot less	56
	69.6%	12.5%	17.8%	
... I feel the local union is	A little or a lot stronger	About the same	A little or a lot weaker	57
	40.4%	33.3%	26.3%	

In most lean production locations, workers are concerned about stress. The evidence at Wayne is mixed, as indicated in Table 3. In the survey, a sizable minority of workers report that the pace of their jobs is faster (43 percent). But in response to a separate survey question concerning the amount of stress on the job, 67 percent said that the level of stress they experience was about the same or lower. When workers were asked about the weaknesses of the team concept in interviews, none of them mentioned a problem with stress or with the pace. Instead, they emphasized that the work is less boring than it used to be.

Overall, workers give very high ratings to the work team system implemented at Wayne. In interviews, most —including some of those who had significant criticisms— said they would not want to go back to the old system. Workers also tend to give high ratings to their local union for its role in the team concept. Table 4 shows the survey results that specifically address the union's role. Sixty-four percent said that the local union represents their needs well. Almost three-quarters of respondents (72 percent) agreed that team concept strengthens the bargaining position of the local union. Some questions focused on negative outcomes. About one-quarter (24.1 percent) agreed that team concept weakens the position of the local union in processing a grievance. But only 10.2 percent agreed that team concept threatens the existence of the union.

Table 4
Union Outcomes

Survey Question	Agree or Strongly Agree	Neither Agree nor Disagree	Disagree or Strongly Disagree	Valid Responses (N)
The local union communicates well with members.	62.5%	15.6%	21.9%	64
The local union represents my needs well.	64.1%	18.8%	17.2%	64
Team concept strengthens the bargaining power of the union in contract negotiations.	72.2%	22.2%	5.6%	54
Team concept gives management more control over the union.	32.8%	25.9%	41.4%	58
Team concept weakens the union in processing grievances.	24.1%	25.9%	50.0%	58
Team concept threatens the very existence of the union.	10.2%	22.0%	67.8%	59

The union role in this facility is quite expansive. As one leader put it, "we've got a lot of say-so in everything that goes on. We basically know everything that's going on out on the floor." When asked how the job of union representative is different in this plant, one said,

> Everything that's done in the team concept ties into a union rep's job —job rotation, versatility. I'm basically involved in everything. We go to the team meetings. When we pass literature out, we don't stand at the front gate and wait for the people to come in and out of work. We take it right to the floor, one-on-one. We're all in contact with people....I believe that it's a lot more pressure as a union rep now [with the team concept] than it ever was. I don't think it's the type of pressure that makes you want to quit. I think it's just something that keeps everything going and churning. It makes you want to do it even more.

As further evidence of the members' approval of the union's role, the plant chairman, who is closely associated with the MOA, has been re-elected three times since team concept was implemented. Each time, he has run unopposed.

DISCUSSION

Critics of lean production and team concept raise several important concerns. First, lean production continually reduces the resources available to accomplish a task, and workloads increase accordingly. This is sometimes referred to as "management by stress."[6] Second, although teams and lean production promise that workers will have more input into decision making, many such workplaces remain Tayloristic, with a command-and-control style of supervision. Third, teams are seen as a threat to the independence of the local union and worker solidarity. On the other hand, proponents of teams believe that the promise of greater worker control and an expanded role for the union will create better work environments. What lessons can be learned from Wayne ISA about these issues?

First, as mentioned above, workers have a mixed view about stress and the pace of work. But even if the pace is quicker, workers report that equipment changes have made the work much easier physically and that teams have made it more challenging and interesting mentally. More challenging work can be a source of stress —but it is a tradeoff that many workers appear willing to accept.

Second, workers at Wayne ISA generally report that they do have more control over their jobs. Some of this stems from strong contract language. For example, because team leaders are elected, they are more accountable to workers. Teams decide on rotation schedules and vacations. Teams also de-

---

[6] Mike Parker and Jane Slaughter, "Managing by Stress: The Dark Side of Team Concept," *ILR Report* 26, no.1 (fall 1988): 19-23.

cide, with their supervisor, when workers have achieved the next level in the pay-for-knowledge system.

But, workers —especially in some departments— still report that they have less control than they would like. This might be inextricably connected to the technology in use. Assembly lines are not conducive to team work. Shutting down an assembly line, whether for team meetings or to solve quality issues, is very costly. Teams seem to work better where the technology lends itself to natural work groups of between 7 and 20 people who have a set of interdependent tasks, and whose product has both some connection and some separation from the next step in the production process.

Another limitation on workers' control at Wayne ISA is the lack of contract language defining a full set of responsibilities for the team and a clearly defined role for the team leader. Because these issues are vague in the contract, there is sometimes disagreement between teams and supervisors, and between management and the union, about who is responsible for what.

In spite of this issue, the contract language overall is quite strong. This can help counter one of the bigger problems with team concepts in practice: wavering management commitment. In many work sites, events such as a change in top management or new directives from corporate leadership can bring a fledgling team process to a halt. But if the parameters of the team concept are clearly specified in the contract, then the union has leverage to ensure that management lives up to it. This is one reason why even some management consultants believe that teams will last longer and are more likely to be institutionalized in unionized sites than in nonunion workplaces.[7]

The third issue typically raised by critics is the impact of teams on the local union. MacDuffie[8] identifies the dismantling of job control mechanisms as

---

[7] See Edward Lawler III and Susan Mohrman, "Unions and the New Management," *Academy of Management Executives* 1 (November 1987): 293-300. For research evidence, see John F. Witte, *Democracy, Authority, and Alienation in Work: Workers' Participation in an American Corporation* (Chicago: University of Chicago Press, 1980), especially the analysis of co-optation, misrepresentation, and structural impotence on joint committee. Witte concludes, "Although I agree... that a joint worker-management policy-level committee can coexist with a strong union, the union is absolutely essential. Without it, democracy at work will always be tilted against the worker, especially in those areas of greatest concern to the majority of employees." Witte, *Democracy, Authority, and Alienation*, 91.

[8] Issues cited are taken from MacDuffie, "Workers' Roles in Lean Production," 58. He raises a third concern, that of enterprise unionism. However, none of the data collected here specifically addresses that issue.

a key issue because it creates an opportunity for management favoritism and abuses. The ISA bargaining committee has been adamant about creating equal opportunities for overtime, bumping based strictly on seniority, and adherence to the job rotation schedule set by the team. Workers did not raise the issue of favoritism as a problem in any of the interviews.

Another concern raised by MacDuffie and others is that lean production and teams might lead workers to identify more with the company than with the union. There is no evidence of that at Wayne. In contrast, the union leadership's weekly plant walk-throughs help make the union leadership more accessible to members. Workers continue to turn to their union when they have problems to resolve.

The union at Wayne ISA played a strong, proactive role in both designing and implementing the team concept. It actively sought input from the membership, and used this to design a relatively worker-centered team system. In addition, the union leadership also continued to pay attention to traditional areas of union concern: overtime, seniority rights, bumping, and wages. In other work sites, union leaders sometimes become so swept up in their new roles that the traditional ones are neglected. By contrast, the Wayne example is evidence that a local union that plays a strong role in both traditional and non-traditional areas can help create a work environment that workers find more satisfying.

LA PRODUCTIVIDAD Y EL TRABAJO EN EL CONTEXTO DE LA PRODUCCIÓN ESBELTA EN VW DE MÉXICO

Huberto Juárez Núñez *

INTRODUCCIÓN

La reestructuración de la industria automotriz en México en la segunda mitad de la década de los años ochenta incorporó como uno de sus más preciados subproductos la versión de productividad que recién se consolidaba en los países industrializados occidentales y que, a la manera de una exitosa moda, se irradiaba a las plantas industriales de la periferia como parte del "paquete" de la modernidad en las relaciones industriales y en los sistemas de trabajo.

Bajo este tenor, las nuevas inversiones en instalaciones, en equipos, en nuevas tecnologías y en los diseños organizacionales, fueron acompañadas de una impresionante campaña para publicitar las buenas nuevas que la cultura productivista dejaría. En una escala descendente: para el país, para su economía, para las empresas -y en el último eslabón- para quien se pretendía como el beneficiario directo, el trabajador y su familia.

Ya en la carrera de la nueva cultura productivista, su difusión incluyó mensajes de todo tipo que de forma sistemática empezaron a circular en las fábricas automotrices instaladas en México. En la planta mexicana de VW registramos durante un buen período (1983-1990) una insistente campaña para incluir la productividad en el trabajo y en la vida cotidiana, que contenía los más diversos cortes: subliminales, directos, agresivos, religiosos, racistas. Para esto, las vía más socorrida fue el material impreso[1] pero incluyó materiales en video, conferencias, etc., donde se ponía siempre de relieve que la cultu-

---

* Profesor Investigador. Centro de Investigación y Estudios de Posgrado. Facultad de Economía-BUAP.

[1] Programa de Estudios de la Industria Automotriz. Archivo 1980-1996. FE-BUAP.

ra "mexicana" de trabajo, o como suelen llamarla, la del "ahí se va", debería ser sustituida por una nueva disposición laboral para lo que se daba como referencia, *el esfuerzo constante, la responsabilidad, la creatividad y la fidelidad* que los trabajadores japoneses, alemanes y americanos han mostrado en cada una de sus recientes proezas productivas. Sin mediar diferencia de corte económico, histórico, cultural y menos las de orden salarial, se ha buscado en todos los casos poner el acento en la necesidad de obtener cambios sustantivos en el comportamiento cotidiano en el trabajo, nuevas disposiciones volitivas frente a la nuevas materia de trabajo y también nuevas concepciones en torno a la eficiencia y la calidad.

De manera que en VW de México, en los años que van de 1984 a 1987, se probaron (induciendo y/o imponiendo) diversos métodos que enfatizaban la "integración activa", "participativa" y "voluntaria" del trabajador. Como en muchos lugares donde se probaron estos métodos, durante los primeros años de la campaña se destacan los *círculos de calidad* al final de la jornada de trabajo, donde un "moderador", siempre asignado por la gerencia, se esmeraba en encontrar el mejor procedimiento para integrar y comprometer a los asistentes con las conclusiones.

Después de un interregno (1986-1987), donde se mostró que los objetivos específicos de los círculos de calidad habían sido inaprensibles tanto para los *empleados-moderadores* como para los *trabajadores-reeducados*, se volvió al viejo y sencillo método vertical y autoritario de asignar tareas y ritmos de intensidad por medio de la omnipresente figura del *capataz* (vocablo muy usado en las fábricas automotrices mexicanas, originario del entorno rural porfirista) dentro de los límites que el Contrato Colectivo de Trabajo vigente (CCT) imponía a sus prerrogativas[2].

En esta vuelta al esquema vertical, por ejemplo, un buen día de 1988, la gerencia, escandalizada porque a su parecer un gran número de trabajadores consumían su tiempo de trabajo en lo que se podrían considerar "andanzas" por el interior de la fábrica, decretó que se aplicaría el despido bajo la modalidad de "abandono de área de trabajo" a todos aquellos que no justificaran debidamente su presencia en los pasillos de la factoría.

Transcurrida la primera semana de tal decreto, el saldo disciplinario era bastante magro. Los licenciados y capataces sorprendieron y despidieron a

[2] Esto fue bastante claro después de la huelga de 56 días en Junio-Julio de 1987, cuando VW acudió a la figura de "Conflicto de orden económico" donde intentó modificar el CCT y reducir personal.

unos cuantos, pero el tráfico en los pasillos no disminuyó. Todo el mundo tenía un salvoconducto en el bolsillo que lo autorizaba -so pena de afectar la producción del área a la que pertenecía- para desplazarce a los mas variados lugares de la fábrica al cumplimiento de tal o cual tarea: ir al almacén por materiales, al taller por refacciones, a la oficina por instrucciones o simplemente, porque era la pausa de alimentos, al comedor de la empresa.

Unas semanas más tarde las aguas volvieron a su nivel. No se volvió a escuchar de sanciones por "paseos" internos.

En resumen, la resistencia sindical a las iniciativas y formalidades productivistas de la gerencia llenó buena parte de los conflictos y negociaciones de los años que van de 1982 -año en que se inicia el cambio productivo en VW- hasta 1992, año en que mutan los contenidos de las relaciones laborales y se definen los nuevos parámetros para la aplicación de los esquemas organizacionales que descansan en el trabajo de equipo y que potenciarán en el corto plazo el crecimiento de la productividad.

En este trabajo se da cuenta de los diversos procedimientos que se están utilizando en la planta mexicana de VW para evaluar y aplicar los complejos esquemas de elevación de la productividad en el marco de los sistemas Lean Production.

PARTE 1

En la planta Puebla de VW los conceptos de productividad vigentes y las nuevas asignaciones de materias de trabajo y salarios se han establecido desde la definición política que sobre las relaciones laborales el gobierno mexicano tomó el 17 de Agosto de 1992. En esa fecha, la Junta Federal no. 15 emitió un *Laudo* donde aceptó la petición empresarial para desconocer las relaciones individuales y colectivas trabajo, y, a partir de la cual se establecen nuevas regulaciones laborales -sin consulta a los trabajadores- que tomaron forma como un nuevo Contrato Colectivo de Trabajo y un nuevo Estatuto sindical[3].

Esos cambios contractuales y estatutarios eliminaron la mayor parte de la prerrogativas sindicales relacionadas a la bilateralidad para determinar programas de producción y establecer ritmos de trabajo o detectar áreas de ries-

[3] Un procedimiento que inmediatamente fue considerado como un *modelo* a seguir por diversos segmentos de la patronal en la región y en diversas partes del país.

go; también eliminaron la regulación sobre el escalafón; desaparecieron a los *representantes seccionales* y cancelaron la figura de la *asamblea general* de trabajadores. Simultáneamente se incluyeron nuevas reglas para premiar, o en su defecto, penalizar las actitudes frente al trabajo, las faltas y los retardos y terminó por modificar la estructura de representación sindical para adecuarla a las nuevas necesidades productivas.

Junto a la reformas en las regulaciones laborales, se iniciaba una profunda reestructuración de sus relaciones industriales -de manera particular con los proveedores y subcontratistas que se instalarían en el nuevo corredor industrial- que permitió a la gerencia estar en posibilidades de proceder de manera inmediata a la reorganización del proceso productivo y de los sistemas de trabajo incorporando el sistema de Trabajo de Equipo, aquí llamados **"grupos de trabajo"**, y se instituyó un mecanismo de evaluación y aplicación de mejoras, el "Programa de Mejora Continua" (llamado PMC2), que se ejecuta y evalúa por medio de lo que se conoce como "Workshops internos".

Debe decirse que esta fase de la reestructuración del trabajo se dio en un período en el que la demanda doméstica de autos iniciaba su caída, cuestión que afectaba a VW en tanto que por muchos años fue este un nicho en que era líder. De esta forma, las definiciones generales de la nuevas reglas para establecer las mediciones de eficiencia, la productividad y la calidad, estuvieron siempre orientadas al desarrollo de los procesos productivos vinculados con los modelos de exportación, tipos A3 y ahora, con la versión A4 y el New Beetle (Concept One).

Los efectos de los cambios introducidos en los ámbitos -cambios en las relaciones laborales, reestructuración de las relaciones industriales, implementación de nuevos patrones de medición de eficiencia y productividad- tuvieron consecuencias de muy corto plazo. Para finales de 1993 estaba claro que el efecto combinado había propiciado resultados tangibles en el sentido de que los productos VW fabricados en México ya estaban incluidos en procesos que podían ser fácilmente homologados con sus equivalentes en las plantas del Consorcio en Europa y Brasil.

En primer lugar, veamos la relación *costos laborales totales/ Ingresos Totales anuales*, que durante la década de los 80 y los dos primeros años de los 90, se había mantenido en el rango de 8-12 puntos porcentuales (SHyCP 80-89), es decir, equivalentes a los valores que se registran en la gráfica 1 para los años 1990 y 1991, a partir de 1993 descienden sensiblemente hasta ser del orden del 3.1% en 1995 (véase gráfica 1). Los Costos Laborales totales que estamos relacionando se refieren a la suma de los Salarios y Prestaciones pagados a los trabajadores sindicalizados y a los Sueldos y Prestaciones correspondientes a todas las categorías del llamado "personal de confianza", concepto que agrupa a quienes realizan el trabajo de dirección y administración del proceso.

Gráfica 1

VW de México: Participación de los Costos Laborales Totales en los Ingresos Anuales.

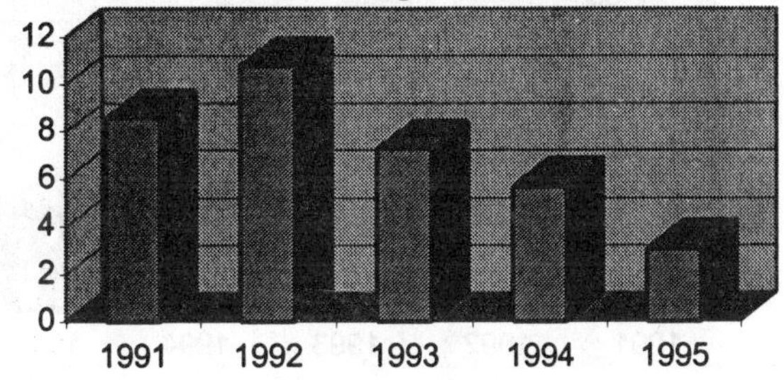

Costos Laborales incluye: Sueldos, Salarios y Prestaciones a todo tipo de personal.

Fuente: Elaborado por el autor con base en: Secretaria de Hacienda y Crédito Público. Estado de Resultados de VW de México, S.A de C.V. 1991-1996

Por su lado los *Ingresos* se refieren a las facturaciones anuales totales de ventas de autos, motores y partes al mercado nacional y al extranjero.

Dentro de esta relación general -que en realidad expresa un índice general de productividad- y procesando datos del Estado de Resultados de la empresa (SHyCP 80-96), podemos referirnos con mayor detalle a las variaciones que se dieron de manera especial en los *costos del trabajo sindicali-*

zado -costos que pueden definirse como los *costos del trabajo directo*[4]. Así tenemos que si en el mismo período (años 90) esta parte de los costos laborales la ponderamos con los valores que corresponden a los *Costos de Producción Totales*[5], resulta, tal y como puede verse en la gráfica 2, que a partir de 1993 se han estado deslizando hasta ser inferiores al 2% en el año 1995.

Gráfica 2

Fuente: *Ibid.*

[4] Estos costos Directos, de acuerdo a nuestras estimaciones representan en los últimos años alrededor del 45% de los costos laborales totales, que también se conocen como nóminas totales.

[5] Los Costos Totales comprenden: compras de materias primas y materiales de ensamble y subensamble; deducción de inversiones; sueldos, salarios y mano de obra; honorarios; previsión social; regalías y asistencia técnica; arrendamientos; fletes y acarreos; aportaciones a INFONAVIT, SAR, IMSS; devoluciones , rebajas y bonificaciones sobre ventas; pérdida inflacionaria; Intereses; Primas y fianzas; viáticos y gastos de viaje; otros gastos y otras deducciones. Conceptos que para efectos de análisis de estructura de costos se pueden agrupar como Costos directos, Costos Indirectos y Gasto Operativo (Juárez, 96).

En relación a este deslizamiento de la parte del costo que paga el trabajo que trasforma el producto, es necesario acotar que el fenómeno sucede dentro de una tendencia general que combina por una parte la disminución de la plantilla del personal sindicalizado y la aparición de categorías de empleados (no sindicalizados) de altos ingresos (más de 10 salarios mínimos) quienes, según los reportes de la empresa a las autoridades hacendaría mexicanas están obteniendo la mayor parte del desembolso en los costos laborales.

Con relación al comportamiento del la plantilla de personal y su composición, es un hecho que a partir de Agosto de 1992, la política de empleo ha variado substancialmente. Hemos calculado que de una plantilla de trabajadores sindicalizados equivalente a 14,100 personas hasta el mes de Junio del año 1992 (mes que precede al conflicto obrero-patronal), en Diciembre de ese mismo año, habían quedado alrededor de 12 mil trabajadores. Es decir el saldo inmediato del Laudo del 17 de Agosto de 1992 fue el desempleo para 2 mil 100 trabajadores. En 1995 la plantilla estaba por los nueve mil trabajadores, en 1996 había cerca de 8,500 y en 1997, ante el incremento de la producción para el mercada nacional y nuevos modelos y líneas para la exportación (Concept One, A-4), se ha registrado un incremento de 600 puestos de planta más una cifra de contrataciones eventuales que está moviéndose entre 800 y 1200 personas.

Así que la reducción de la plantilla ha ido de la mano con incrementos en la fabricación de unidades y partes (de este último rubro destacan en esta fábrica la producción de motores y ejes), y en esta tendencia, la reducción de personal ha tenido para la gerencia muchas justificaciones: despido de trabajadores considerados peligrosos políticamente, trabajadores viejos, trabajadores considerados indisciplinados y/o riezgosos para asumir los nuevos conceptos de trabajo. En realidad estos ajustes están directamente relacionados con los nuevos sistemas organizacionales que han potenciado la productividad del trabajo y que han permitido, de acuerdo al calendario de dispersión de la producción ejecutado por la empresa, que sean factibles las transferencias de partes del proceso a los proveedores y subcontratistas del nuevo parque industrial (Cluster FINSA).

El impacto más sobresaliente de este ajuste global en los costos laborales se ha revelado en los últimas como una drástica elevación de la relación que mide los *ingresos por trabajador*. La planta mexicana de VW que en la pasada década estaba muy por debajo dei promedio de los rendimientos del consorcio, en los años 90, especialmente en los años 93-94, ya supera el promedio general -y aunque no compite en el último año mostrado con las plantas españolas (SEAT)- supera a las plantas brasileñas y se acerca a los resultados que en este renglón tienen las plantas alemanas (VW-AG), tal y como puede apreciarse en la gráfica 3.

Gráfica 3

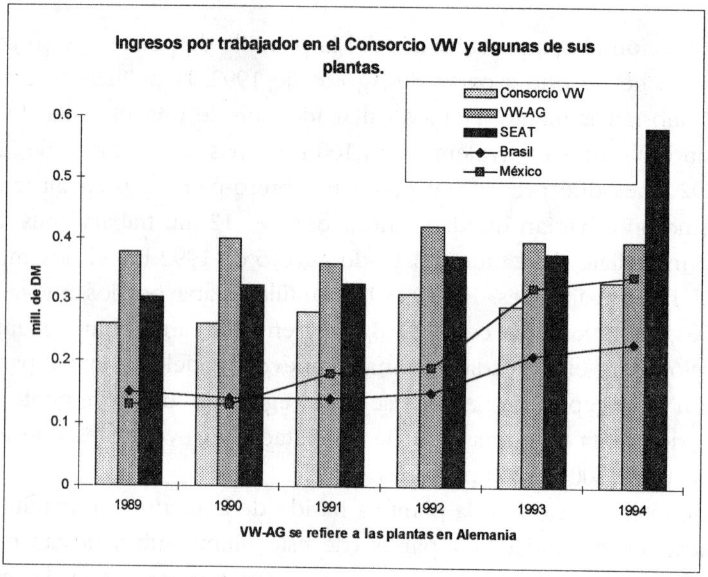

Fuente: VW-AG. Reports 1989-1995.

PARTE 2

Dentro de la tendencia del crecimiento de los indicadores globales de productividad, los indicadores micro, es decir, los que miden en la fábrica poblana la intensidad, la eficacia y las diversas expresiones de la productividad se volvieron muy puntuales. Las relaciones laborales se han saturado de exigencias cotidianas para cumplir con los objetivos relacionadas con la eficacia y la calidad. La estadística para el *autocontrol* y las mediciones en función de metas específicas fueron incorporadas como parte de la calificación de los equipos de trabajo de forma tal que sus integrantes -que por el sortilegio de las nuevas definiciones contractuales dejaron de ser obreros para volverse "técnicos VW"- agregaron nuevas calificaciones relacionadas al trabajo de inspección y control de calidad, la conservación y mantenimiento del equipo y a disposiciones para la búsqueda de mejoras al proceso.[6]

Todas y cada una de las áreas de trabajo fue sometido a un calendario de evaluaciones periódicas. Los nuevos indicadores para estas evaluaciones reflejaban la nuevas proyecciones de la gerencia en México: junto a la tradicional medición de "tiempos de tacto", se introdujeron cinco ponderaciones que permiten conocer avances reales en la productividad que se constituyen la base para otorgar premios salariales (que han ido del 4 al 6%), o también que sirven para presionar a los equipos de trabajo involucrados.[7] Los cinco indicadores en cuestión son: el indicador de *productividad* (piezas por operario por turno); *operarios en áreas de trabajo*; valor de las diversas piezas utilizadas en el trabajo de cada célula o área, también conocida como *"ahorros de materiales en proceso*"; *espacio* para ejecutar la operación medido en reducción de m2 y *rotación*, que se entiende como el producto resultante de multiplicar la cantidad de piezas por el tiempo de Tacto. De esta forma y teniendo como marco general los cambios en las nuevas relaciones laborales -que de inmediato permitieron un holgado ejercicio de las prerrogativas patronales- la política de inducir a nuevos ritmos de producción y hacia desempeños laborales que tienen a la productividad como pivote, los resultados para la estrategia gerencial fluyeron de manera positiva y prácti-

---

[6] Se incorporó al CCT una nueva cláusula denominada "Desarrollo de los Salarios" donde se establecen los requisitos generales y específicos para promociones salariales. Entre los del primer tipo tenemos "El trabajador escalará un nivel en reconocimiento a sus conocimientos, habilidades, experiencia, eficiencia y actitud en el trabajo hasta alcanzar el último nivel de la escala salarial que corresponde a su área". Para ascender de nivel es necesaria la certificación de habilidades técnicas en adición a las habilidades manuales...".

Como ejemplo del segundo tipo de requisitos estan reglamentados 8 exigencias que incluyen: antiguedad de "trabajos efectivos en el nivel"; "Haber cumplido y aprobado la capacitación y adiestramiento establecidos; desempeño satisfactorio de "cantidad y normas de calidad"; desempeño de "las actividades en base al plan de oportunidades de rotación con la eficiencia requerida"; "haber participado activamente en la implmentación de mejoras en los métodos de trabajo, organización de su área, medidas de seguridad, etc, con el fin de incrementar la productividad de su Departamento". "Haber Cumplido conlas normas de disciplina, seguridad, orden y limpieza; "Haber participado en la capacitación y adiestramiento a los demás trabajadores"; "haber cumplido con el noventa y ocho por ciento en puntualidad y asistencia". CCT. 1992-1996, p. 24-25.

[7] Los grupos de trabajo están coordinados por facilitadores y líderes cuyo nombramiento es prerrogativa de la empresa. Los procesos de evaluación incluyen figuras como "padrinos" y "moderadores", "responsables", "coordinadores de *control center*".

camente de manera automática. Con exepción de un corto período (otoño e invierno de 1992) cuando los trabajadores realizando diversos tipos de resistencias enfrentaron una política de "ablandamiento" centrada en el despido -con el saldo que hemos comentado- de todo aquel que se identificaba por la empresa como "incapacitado" para adaptarse a las nuevas materias de trabajo; la *producción esbelta* a los seis meses de haberse instalado en Puebla ya revelaba su éxito en las estadísticas de la gerencia de producción.

La medición de esos resultados se realiza desde 1993 a partir de una llamada "metodología general" donde el punto de referencia para evaluar y proceder a realizar los cambios y ajustes de los cinco indicadores que forman el cuerpo que define el *desempeño, la aptitud y la actitud* frente al trabajo, sería la situación que esos indicadores tenían *"antes"* de la evaluación. Por tanto el ajuste se hace a través de una simple división:

Fórmula para reconocer estado de indicadores:
nivel "después de la evaluación" x 100 /nivel " antes de la evaluación"
= Resultado para evaluar

En el cuadro 1 se presentan los resultados obtenidos en la evaluación para cinco áreas de trabajo que corresponden a tareas de ensamble y subensamble de modelos A3, Golf - Jetta para exportación, la fecha de evaluación corresponde a los meses de marzo y abril de 1994.

Cuadro 1

Programa de Mejora Continua PMC2 . Área de Ensambles y Subensambles. Nave 21

	ÁREAS				
	I	II	III	IV	V
	Productividad (piezas/operario/turno)				
Antes	11.6	14.4	13.5	11.6	32.5
Después	16.5	19.7	19.6	15.9	41.2
Variación %	42.2	36.8	45.2	37.1	26.8
	Operarios por día				
Antes	10	46	46	56	22

Después	8	28	42	52	20
Variación %	-20	-39.1	-8.7	-7.1	-9.1
Valor de las piezas diferentes para una misma función (Miles de N$)					
Antes	71.0	496.9	281.3	257.5	34.9
Después	69.4	152.5	216.1	199.4	32.1
Variación %	-2.3	-69.3	-23.2	-22.6	-8.0
Superficie m^2					
Antes	185	932	318	520	428
Después	PROVEEDOR	714	269	497	382
Variación %	_	-23.4	-15.4	-4.4	-10.7
Período de rotación (horas)					
Antes	7.18	30.1	20.6	17.2	11.2
Después	6.84	10.1	16.0	14.3	5.7
Variación %	-4.7	-66.4	-22.3	-16.9	-49.1

* La evaluaciones fueron hechas en el mes de marzo y abril de 1994. Fuente: VW de México. Planeación de Manufactura. Dirección de Control de Calidad. Junio de 1994.

** Áreas de Trabajo correspondientes al cuadro:

I. Subensamble y Montaje de amortiguador trasero para el tipo A3 (Golf-Jetta).
II. Ensamble de Tableros para el Tipo A3.
III. Ensamble de Puertas Tipo A3-Nave 21. Sala Kaizen.
IV . Subensamble de Puertas. Nave 21. Sala Kaizen.
V. Montaje. célula 1. Nave 21. Sala Kaizen.

Si se observa el comportamiento de los dos primeros indicadores, Productividad (piezas /operarios/turno) y Operarios por área de evaluación y se aplica *la fórmula para evaluación*, tendremos que mientras la productividad en las áreas mostradas tiene incrementos del orden de I (42.2%), II (36.8%), III (45.2%), IV (37.1%) y V (26.8%), el número de operarios presenta comportamientos negativos. Para las áreas I-V las cifras en este último caso son: -20%, -39%, -8.6%, -7.1% y -9% respectivamente.

El comportamiento de las otras tres variables nos indican que los ahorros en concepto de piezas diversas para una misma función, la disminución del espacio físico y la disminución del tiempo de rotación, significaron para la empresa elevar de manera importante los rendimientos y los aprovechamiento de la capacidad productiva.

Un año más tarde, es decir, tomando como referencia las evaluaciones de 1995, tenemos que los indicadores con más desarrollo —en el sentido de sus montos de variación y consistencia— están por el lado de las *economías de materiales* y de la *productividad por operario turno,* en tanto que los ajustes de personal *empiezan a llegar a sus límites* en el sentido de que profundizar en las disminuciones de trabajadores por tarea, célula o área, implicaría exponer el cada día más delicado equilibrio sobre el que están descansando la obtención de los altos estándares de eficacia y de calidad.

De las evaluaciones correspondientes al año de 1995 tenemos el registro de 24 áreas de trabajo, básicamente de procesos de ensamble y algunos procesos de pintura. Hemos concentrado nuestros resultados en una gráfica que expone el comportamiento de las cinco variables arriba mencionadas, las 24 áreas de trabajo están descritas en el cuadro 2 y la gráfica es la No. 4

Cuadro 2

Áreas graficadas: denominación y fecha de la evaluación.

I	Prueba de Ruidos.. Semana 03. 20/01/95
II	Retén de Mecánica. Semana 07. 24/02/95
III	Electromecánica. Semana 16. 05/06/95
IV	Área I. Célula. 24. Montaje A-3. N4. 13/01/95
V	Decorado. Molduras Onduladas. 20/01/95
VI	Cabina de Cera N-4 Montaje A-3. 27/01/95
VI	Área 1. Célula. 25. Montaje A-3. N4. 10/02/95
VII	Área I. Célula. 25-A. Montaje A-3. N4. 17/02/95
VIII	Área I. Célula. 27 Montaje A-3. N4. 03/03/95
IX	Área II. Cél. 28. Montaje A_3. N4. 17/03/95
X	Área III. Célula. 29. Montaje A-. N4. 31/03/95

XI	Área III. Célula. 30 Montaje A3. N4. 07/04/95
XII	Montaje Front-end. Célula. 41. A-3. N4. 14/07/94
XIII	Área III. Célula. 31. Montaje A-3. N4. 21/04/95
XIV	Área IV. Célula. 32. Montaje A3. N4. 28/04/95
XV	Banda Oval. Célula. 33. Montaje A-3. N4. 19/05/95
XVI	Línea Final. I/II. Célula 35.26/05/95.
XVII	Línea Final I/II. Célula. 36. Montaje A-3. N4. 02/06/95.
XVIII.	Línea Final. I/II. Célula. 37. Montaje A-3. N4. 16/06/95
XIX	Montaje de Asientos. Célula. 42. A-3. N4. 14/07/95.
XX.	Cabina de Filler III. N3. 03/03/95
XXI	Área II. Línea de Primer III. N3. 24/02/95.
XXII	Línea de Retrabajos. Pintura de Partes Negras. Sala PMC2. 1 Planeación. 11/11/94.
XXIII	Célula 9. Cristales. N21. A-3.25/11/94.

Fuente: Elaborado por el autor con base en: VW de México. Planeación de Manufactura. Dirección de Control de Calidad. 1995.

Gráfica 4

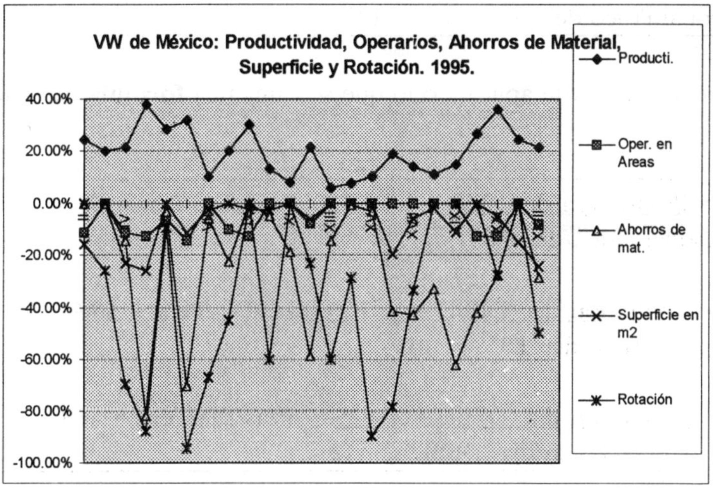

Fuente: Elaborado por el autor con base en: VW de México. Planeación de Manufactura. Dirección de Control de Calidad. 1995.

¿Cómo se han respaldado y garantizado estos resultados?. La relación "Después"/ "Antes", sigue un procedimiento simple pero efectivo: primero, se identifican los resultados que se están obteniendo para cada indicador, después, se fijan las metas a lograr y por último, se compara para en caso de ser necesario introducir los ajustes.

Por ejemplo el PMC2 correspondiente al área de ajustes mecánicos al motor (MCO) en la nave que construye los motores para el Jetta-Golf y para la exportación, antes de proceder a evaluar establece sus datos base como sigue:

a)

No de Técnicos	=	***14 x día***
Tiempo de Trabajo	=	***990 minutos***
Producción de Piez	=	***720 x día***
Tacto de Producción	=	***3.6' minutos***
Eficiencia	=	***90%***

En seguida se fija la diferencia entre la producción "ES" con la producción "DEBE":

b)

Producción/día debe:	825
Producción /día es:	720
Personal Físico/día es:	14
Personal Físico debe;	12

Y se procede al ajuste aplicando lo que se llama una **fórmula de "Factor"**

c)

Factor = <u>Producción/días "ES"</u> = <u>720</u> Pzas./Día/Pers.= *51.4*
Personal Físico/día "ES" 14

Factor= <u>Producción/día "DEBE"</u> = <u>825</u> Pzas/Día/Pers. = *58.9*
Pers. Físico/ día "ES" 14

Factor= <u>Producción/día "DEBE"</u>= <u>825</u> Pzas/Día/Pers. = 68.7
Pers. Físico/día "DEBE" 12

Establecido esto se identifican los aspectos relacionados a la calidad y a la intensidad del trabajo:

d)

En el caso de la calidad se identificó a los *retrabajos* como el factor con mayor participación en la definición de la calidad, se evaluó que ellos tenía un peso equivalente al 70% de la *función de la calidad.* Dentro de las causas de los retrabajos se identificó a las *variaciones del ángulo de encendido* como la causa principal. Se estableció disminuir el valor de los retrabajos hasta el 10%. El resultado obtenido al final fue una disminución al 12%.

e)

En el caso de los factores que obstruyen la intensidad del proceso se identificó a 17 causas importantes de las que sólo señalamos para ejemplificar: "sensores en mal estado y/o faltan", "monitores incompletos", "equipo se bloquea", "bulbo y conector de ventilador mal ensamblado", "falta estandarizar formatos", etc.

f)

Al final del Workshop se obtuvieron 20 propuestas de las cuales 16 se aplicaron de manera inmediata, y 4 quedaron "abiertas". Por ejemplo:

Inmediatas

Cambiar sensores de temperatura
Colocar a la misma velocidad las bandas
cumplir el programa de mantenimiento
estandarizar uso de formatos en el área
Los pisteros al entregar la unidad deberán apagar los consumidores eléctricos, etc.

Abiertas

Cambio en los equipos de ajuste de MCOS
Retén de mecánica verifica ensamble de conector ventilador
etc.

Transcurrido el proceso de aplicación de las propuestas, el resultado se evalúa y se concentra en la hoja *PMC2-Resumen.* En este caso, en el período Junio94-Marzo95 para el proceso Ajuste de MCOS se obtuvieron los resultados observados en el cuadro:

Cuadro 3

PMC2- Resumen. Proceso: Ajuste de MCOS

Fecha: 30/03/95

	Antes	Ahora	Resultado en %
Calidad (Casos) Retrabajos	70%	12%	8.3
Productividad (piezas/operarios/turno)	51.4	58.9	15
Operarios	14	14	0
Cantidad (pieza diferentes misma función) $	0	0	0
Lugar (m2)	0	0	
Período de rotación (horas)	1.375'	1.2'	13
Ahorros evaluados en 12 meses		$11,355.00	

Fuente: Elaborado por el autor con base en: VW de México. Planeación de Manufactura. Dirección de Control de Calidad. 1995.

En 1996, los resultados ya medían promedios generales para naves completas. Los *workshops* internos y la nueva cultura del PMC2 tienen ya una profunda integración con la producción diaria.

En los siguientes cuadros vamos a presentar las variaciones porcentuales resumen de los principales indicadores correspondientes una selección de áreas de cuatro grandes naves: ensamble, pintura, fundición y prensas.

Cuadro 4

KVP-VW de M. PROGRAMA DE MEJORA CONTINUA. (P M C 2)
Resumen de Resultados en variaciones % de workshops internos

Nave de Ensamble

Areas	Calidad	Productividad	Materiales en Proceso	Superficie	Tiempo de Rotación	Operarios (Número)
Banda Oval I L.I. (Pool-Team)	100	9	27	6	97	0
Banda Oval II L.II (Pool-team)	100	9	27	9	97	0
Conexiones de Motor Cel 35	100	28	4	3	76	-3
Célula 36 L-2 (Pool Team)	100	3	7	2	93	0
Célula 36 L.I (Pool Team)	100	13	26	1	97	-3
Area Célula 25 A Línea 1.	100	4	7	4	46	0
Area Célula 25 A Línea 2.	100	4	7	4	46	0

Célula 37 Línea 1.	100	4	6	4	0	0
Célula 37 Línea 2.	100	5	5	2	0	0
Ramal S-1. Célula 38/39.	100	13	5	7	75	0
Ramal S.1 Célula 32	100	11	7	4	5	0
Célula 33	100	11	4	4	6	0
Sub-Ens. Font-end. Célula 45.	100	17	7	1	10	0
Décorado Célula D-1	0	26	5	4	4	-3
Decorado Célula D-2	0	26	6	4	7	-3
Vestidura Célula 25 L-1	100	5	3	3	56	0
Vestidura Célula 25 L-2	100	5	3	3	56	0
Vestidura Célula 25 "Bota aguas" L-1	100	6	6	5	5	0
Promedio a 21 áreas de trabajo	90	11	8	4	38	-12

Fuente: Elaborado por el autor con base en: VW de México. Planeación de Manufactura. Dirección de Control de Calidad. Marzo de 1996.

Cuadro 5

KVP-VW de M. PROGRAMA DE MEJORA CONTINUA. (P M C 2)

Resumen de Resultados en variaciones % de workshops internos

Areas Seleccionadas de Nave de Pintura

Areas	Calidad	Productividad	Materiales en Proceso	Superficie	Tiempo de Rotación	Operarios (Número)
Retrabajos A-3 Línea especial	35	51	100	0	34	-9
Detallado Línea III	17	31	0	6	0	0
Gomas y Materiales en Datall.	100	3	6	0	88	0
Detallado "B" Línea II	100	0	40	0	12	0
Lamparazos L II	40	42	50	25	47	0
VBH Línea IV	30	15	50	0	6	0

Limpiesa de Cabinas S-3	40	48	0	35	55	0
Cabina de Esmalte III	100	14	30	5	11	0
A-III Golf/Jetta Retrabajos	50	0	100	20	4	0
KTL Sector I/Línea IV.	30	32	63	0	75	0
Lija de Filler. Línea III	54	10	0	83	19	-1
Lija de Retrabajos Sector 4	25	32	0	22	31	0
Lija de Filler III (interiores)	27	7	0	0	6	0
Lija de Primer- Línea III	45	22	10	0	30	0
Detallado III Retrabajos L-2	50	20	0	21	16	0
Cabina de Filler Línea III	50	10	26	0	100	0
Lija de Primer L-III	50	50	0	0	0	0
Sello Grueso L-III	50	50	0	0	0	0
Retrabajos A-3	0	11	0	0	10	0
Promedio Correspondientes a 23 Areas de Pintura	43	23	31	11	29	-10

Fuente: Elaborado por el autor con base en: VW de México. Planeación de Manufactura. Dirección de Control de Calidad. Marzo de 1996.

Cuadro 6

KVP-VW de M. PROGRAMA DE MEJORA CONTINUA (P M C 2)

Resumen de Resultados en variaciones % de workshops internos

Areas Seleccionadas de Nave de Fundición

Areas	Calidad	Productividad	Materiales en Proceso	Superficie	Tiempo de Rotación	Operarios (Número)
Ahorro Consumo de Electrodos	14	33	89	0	0	0
Variación medida 25.325 Diskus	0	0	82	0	95	0

Optimización Soporte de Motor	0	50	53	34	53	-3
Optimización Máquina Danobat	0	20	100	0	0	0
Sistema "Creed"	100	3	0	0	100	0
Adherencia d pernos a ejes	80	0	100	0	0	0
Optimizar Hueller 5	80	13	50	0	0	0
Unificar Calidad en Bielas	80	0	0	0	0	0
Conjunto Eje Trasero	49	5	74	29	47	0
Mejora de Calidad en Envíos	0	0	0	0	0	0
Arbol de levas Operación 70	100	1	74	0	74	0
Arena Preparada P/fabricación	0	0	50	0	0	0
Recuperación de Bielas	70	0	100	100	0	0
Opt. Máquinas Hueller Hille 2112	20	0	0	0	0	0
Reducción Gastos Herramienta	0	0	13	0	0	0
Estandarizar Informes ISO	33	0	0	0	0	0
Empaque y envío de Codos	25	0	0	0	0	0
Opyim. Cabina de encerado	61	0	0	0	0	0
Optim. Ensamble Zapata	70	32	66	18	65	-1
Optim. Mat. Aux. en Corazones	0	0	10	0	0	0
Promedio Correspondiente a 33 Areas de la Nave de Fundición	36	9	33	5	16	-4

Fuente: Elaborado por el autor con base en: VW de México. Planeación de Manufactura. Dirección de Control de Calidad. Marzo de 1996.

Cuadro 7

KVP-VW de M. PROGRAMA DE MEJORA CONTINUA. (P M C 2)

Resumen de Resultados en variaciones % de workshops internos

Areas Seleccionadas de Nave de Prensas

Areas	Calidad	Productividad	Materiales en Proceso	Superficie	Tiempo de Rotación	Operarios (Número)
Calle 15 Material dañado	28	14	3	0	0	0
Carga de Máquinas Nave 0	6	1	40	0	46	0
Planeación Serie	100	0	0	0	0	0
Eficientar Prensa 132	15	34	0	0	0	0
Material dañado Nave 1	52	28	1	0	0	-6
Prensa 161 C.16	33	46	0	0	0	0
Calle 3	0	23	0	0	0	0
Montaje de Herramientas	13	33	0	0	0	0
Carga de Máquinas N.1	43	9	0	0	0	0
Calle 15 (deshechos Ptas. Ext)	50	23	0	0	0	0
Mantenimiento Básico Nave 0	28	35	0	0	0	0
Larguero A-3 Calle 1	100	7	0	0	0	0
Calle 15 puertas tras. Inte.	60	2	0	0	0	0
Tapa delantera A-3	51	17	0	0	0	0
Recl. de Prov. y Hm/h6 809605/606	100	5	0	0	0	0
Reducción de Consumo Mat. Auix.	0	0	4	0	0	0
Tubo A-3	50	36	0	0	0	0
Calle 12 Costado A-3	19	3	0	0	0	0
Prensa 164	40	15	0	0	0	0
Promedio para 22 Areas de la Nave Prensas	38	16	2	0	0	-6

Fuente: Elaborado por el autor con base en: VW de México. Planeación de Manufactura. Dirección de Control de Calidad. Marzo de 1996.

Los cuadros 4-7 nos muestras que las mejoras en calidad, en productividad y ahorros de todo tipo no son homogéneos. Los mejores promedio de calidad están en las áreas de ensamble con un 90% y los promedios más bajos en la planta de fundición (36%) y la nave de prensas (38%). Seguramente el mejor comportamiento de la calidad en la nave de ensamble esta asociado con la generalización mayor de los *grupos de trabajo,* en tanto la planta de fundición con menos grupos de trabajo también es la nave con menos reacondicionamientos y mejoras técnicas en los últimos años.

Si se observan los promedios correspondientes a la productividad tenemos que el área de pintura tiene un crecimiento de 23%, la nave de prensas 16%, Ensamble 11% y fundición tiene 9%.

Los ahorros de Materiales en proceso siguen presentando un alto promedio para las áreas de pintura 31%, Fundición 33% y ya bajos para ensamble (8%) y prensas 2%. La eliminación de espacio es mayor en Pintura (11%) en tanto que en Prensas ya no se registra ninguna reducción[8].

Los tiempos de rotación siguen disminuyendo en Ensamble (38%), Pintura (29%), Fundición (16%) y es muy bajo en prensas.

El indicador correspondientes a los puestos de trabajo que se han suprimido en el período evaluado, de acuerdo al cuadro resumen para las cuatro naves, el mayor número corresponde a las áreas de Ensamble (12), después tenemos 10 en pintura, 6 en Prensas y 4 cancelaciones en Fundición. Es importante señalar que los ajustes de personal en 1996 están en su fase crítica, pues los conflictos internos tienden a reanimarse la constante presión par el adelgazamiento, la polivalencia y la flexibilización de las plantillas asignadas a las áreas.

Cuadro 8

KVP-VW de M. PROGRAMA DE MEJORA CONTINUA. (P M C 2)

Resumen de Resultados en variaciones % de workshops internos

Naves de Pintura, Ensamble, Fundición y Prensas

	Calidad	Productividad	Materiales en Proceso	Superficie	Tiempo de Rotación	Operarios (Número)
Nave de Pintura	43	23	31	11	29	-10
Nave de Ensamble	90	11	8	4	38	-12

[8] Buena parte de los procesos de prensas están en manos de un proveedor (TRW) ubicado en el "Cluster".

Nave de Fundición	36	9	33	5	16	-4
Nave de Prensas	38	16	2	0	2	-6

Fuente: Elaborado por el autor con base en: VW de México. Planeación de Manufactura. Dirección de Control de Calidad. Marzo de 1996.

Una recapitulación obligada sobre el comportamiento de los aspectos vinculados a la productividad y la situación del trabajo en esta planta nos indica que la *producción esbelta,* en efecto, puede mostrar resultados muy satisfactorios en el corto plazo dentro de un contexto de relaciones industriales y laborales donde las prerrogativas patronales prácticamente no tienen límites. En el caso de VW la máxima toyotista se ha cumplido al pie de la letra -desde la forma como se ha catalizado el conflicto laboral para desarticular la resistencia obrera, hasta las formas orgánicas en que la organización productiva se superpone a la organización sindical. La impresionante elevación de las curvas correspondientes a *piezas/operarios/turno, ahorro de materiales, economías de espacio, intensificación del tiempo de rotación,* todo dentro de la caída del número de trabajadores, nos indican que la nueva cultura de productividad puede tener altos costos para el trabajo - si se considera la pérdida de empleos y los aumentos en la intensidad del trabajo- y beneficiarios bastante localizados -si se consideran los resultados de los cinco indicadores de productividad para los tres años y para las diferentes áreas que hemos mostrado.

En este contexto, la resistencia de los trabajadores se ha expresado de diversas maneras: en protestas aisladas, intentos de negociación a nivel de área, en las primeras fases con actitudes de sabotaje a la producción y en general, con presiones a su dirección sindical para suavizar los efectos más graves de las nuevas directrices productivas. En el último episodio, se presentó una confrontación más o menos directa cuando las pretensiones de la transnacional para adoptar un nuevo esquema de horarios de trabajo enfrentó la opinión de los sindicalizados.

La gerencia mexicana vislumbró que como remate a sus éxitos productivistas se podría implantar nuevos horarios que flexibilizaran y racionalizaran el uso del trabajo (disminuir pagos de horas extras y eliminar el sistema de "pago de puentes"[9]) . Se dio a esa propuesta un nombre *ad hoc*: **"sistema**

---

[9] Como sucede en muchas fábricas en México y como un mecanismo general para sortear problemas derivados de expresiones religiosas y culturales de los trabajadores, en VW existen

alemán". En realidad se trataba de una propuesta que impone rotaciones de personal sobre la base de distribuir la jornada semanaria de 42 horas en cuatro días de trabajo y tener tres de descanso.

Desde 1995 se diseñó por la gerencia una campaña en forma para convencer a los trabajadores de las virtudes del nuevo esquema de horarios de trabajo, usando para eso dos o tres variantes del "Sistema Alemán". Por parte de los trabajadores el entusiasmo nunca fue muy manifiesto, porque era más o menos claro que cada una de las variantes implicaba un transtorno radical para adaptar el organismo a una nueva distribución de tiempos de trabajo y de descanso. Incluso ni la promesa del pago de una prima que podría ser equivalente al 120% de un día de salario fue suficiente para obtener consensos.

La propuesta se estuvo posponiendo hasta la primavera de 1997, cuando la nueva dirección sindical propuso un referéndum como mecanismo para aceptar o rechazar el dichoso nuevo sistema. Al parecer la respuesta de la empresa a la propuesta sindical para establecer un acuerdo estable respecto a los horarios de trabajo, aunque no fue muy entusiasta, se admitió sobre la base de la certeza de que, si bien los trabajadores no tenían mucho convencimiento para el cambio, tampoco en meses anteriores habían planteado formas alternativas o resistencias abiertas.

De esta manera el referéndum debía aprobar o rechazar el sistema alemán que se ilustra en los cuadros 9a y 9b donde están sintetizadas las variantes a y b que establecen las jornadas semanarias por turno, la rotación semanaria para cada turno, las pausas y la prima salarial.

Estas variantes se acompañaban con ejemplos concretos para la producción esperada en las diversas áreas de trabajo y que, como el que se ilustra en el cuadro 9c, establecían los nuevos resultados para variables específicas, en este caso para las áreas de pintura. En este último ejemplo es muy significativo observar cómo la empresa calculaba el incremento de la *producción por semana y por cinco días:* con menor producción diaria, y entonces, como el producto automático del simple cambio de forma de rotación de turnos.

La votación la ganó el sindicato. Los trabajadores rechazaron el nuevo sistema (80% de una votación que incluyó a cerca del 70% de los trabajadores sindicalizados) y ello representó el primer gran tropiezo en una larga cadena de eventos exitosos de la gerencia, lo cual, por otra parte ha

---

acuerdos para que en las fechas de alto ausentismo -semana santa, semana de muertos, 12 de diciembre etc.-, los obreros gocen el correspondiente "puente" de tres o cuatro días, a cambio de "pagarlos" aumentando proporcionalmente a su jornada de trabajo diaria efectiva, el tiempo de las jornadas que se volverán "puente".

significado que los trabajadores y su sindicato pueden estar en la ruta de nuevas negociaciones[10].

Cuadro 9a

Propuesta para nueva distribución de jornada de trabajo semanaria y rotación de turnos.

Cuatro días de trabajo por tres de escanso (Sistema Alemán A)

	Lunes	Martes	Miércoles	Jueves	Viernes	Sábado	Domingo
7-30 a 18.30 hrs	A	C	B	A	C	B	
20 a 6:00 Hrs	B	A	C	B	A	C	

Turno A= 42 Horas (2 de pausa)
Turno B= 42 Horas (2 de Pausa)
Turno C= 42 Horas (2 de Pausa)

Fuente: Elaborado por el autor con base en: Volkwagen de México, SA de CV. Departamento de Relaciones Laborales. 1997.

Cuadro 9 b

Propuesta para nueva distribución de jornada de trabajo semanaria y rotación de turnos.

Cuatro días de trabajo por tres de descanso (Sistema Alemán B)

	Lunes	Martes	Miércoles	Jueves	Viernes	Sábado	Domingo
7-30 a 18.30 hrs	C	A	A	A	A	C	
20 a 6:00 Hrs	B	B	C	C	B	B	

Turno A= 44 Horas (2 de pausa)
Turno B= 40 Horas (2 de Pausa)
Turno C= 42 Horas (2 de Pausa)

Fuente: Elaborado por el autor con base en: Volkwagen de México, SA de CV. Departamento de Relaciones Laborales. 1997.

[10] Que incluyen las correspondientes a la parte "dura" del clausulado del CCT y la titularidad de los Contratos de Trabajo en las nuevas empresas proveedoras.

Cuadro 9c
Ejemplo de aplicación del Sistema Alemán. Area de Pintura

	Situación Actual	Nuevo Sistema de Trabajo. 2 Turnos 10.5 Hrs x 6 días
Turnos por día	3	2
Tiempo de presencia	1440'	1260'
Pausa comida	2*30=60'	2*30=60'
Tiempo limpieza	4*20=80'	2*15=30'
Vaciado de cabina	------	2*20=40'
Tiempo efectivo de trabajo	1300'	1130'
Tiempo disponible para mantto.	140'	270' (+2.1 HRS/DIA)
Eficiencia de instalacion	88%	92%
Tiempo de tacto	1.5'	1.5'
Producción / día	762	693
Producción / semana	3810	4158
Producción promedio 5 días	762	831
Situación a capacidad máxima línea III		
Tiempo de tacto	1.4'	1.4'
Producción día	817	742
Producción / semana	4085	4452
Producción promedio 5 días	817	890
Personal adicional	39	39

Fuente: Elaborado por el autor con base en: Volkswagen de México, SA de CV. Oficina Técnica Pintura / EGR. J. Herrera. 1996-1997.

PARTE 3

Como hemos señalado, la adopción del sistema Lean Production en VW-Puebla ha pasado por la construcción del parque industrial FINSA en las inmediaciones de la Planta ensambladora. Este parque, llamado también "cluster VW" está diseñado para absorber buena parte de los procesos de fabricación primarios y de subensamble. En los aproximadamente cuatro años que tiene de funcionamiento ya han sido transferidos de la planta VW a los diversos proveedores una buena cantidad de procesos productivos: troqueles, estampados, subensamble de las diversas partes de las suspensiones, arneses y partes eléctricas, etc. Las diferencias de los criterios de acopio y funcionamiento de la cadena productiva son notables y se pueden apreciar solamente si mira con algún detenimiento la lista de los principales proveedores que funcionaban cuando el negocio principal era el mercado interno y VW de M era la empresa más importante en unidades producidas (1979-

1981) y si se compara con la lista de los principales proveedores FINSA en 1997 (cuadros 10a y 10b).

Obligada y naturalmente, los ingredientes de productividad eficacia y calidad, relacionados con la cadena general de producción se complejizan conforme se desplazan nuevas áreas de trabajo o las empresas proveedoras amplían sus radios de producción en función de los crecimientos de la producción. Si bien es cierto que estas empresas proveedoras en su mayor parte están aplicando sistemas de trabajo *just in time/kanban* probados con éxito en otras partes, la adopción de esos sistemas en esta región tiene peculiaridades que es necesario reconocer.

La primera veintena de empresas se instaló a la manera de una simple extensión de VW. Esto es, el proceso de dispersión de la fabricación fue en muchos casos transplantado sin mejoras o innovaciones, la gran fábrica empezó dispersando sus procesos de producción con criterios que tenían un acento organizativo y poco que ver con las nuevas tecnologías: las empresa proveedora que produce los troquelados y estampados tiene desde su instalación en 1993, la misma maquinaria y el equipo que existían en las naves de prensas de VW (Nave 0 y Nave 1). Maquinaria y equipo que virtualmente fueron arrancados de un lado y vuelto a sembrar en otro.

En otra parte, la producción del Bastidor Auxiliar y diversas Partes de Suspensión de los modelos de exportación (que estaban en Nave 5 en VW), se hacen en una nueva empresa con maquinaria "a consignación" de VW en adaptaciones muy simples para instalar las nuevas cadenas en la empresa proveedora.

En los últimos encontramos que en la mayor parte de los casos, lo que existe como elemento innovador son los nuevos conceptos de integración productiva donde la innovación tecnológica se localiza básicamente en el sistema informático para la coordinación logística que se extiende en algunos casos para verificar la eficacia del proceso.

Esto quiere decir que las cadenas productivas de empresas proveedoras de partes están directamente indexadas a las cadenas de ensamble de la fábrica ensambladora. El just in time/kanban es un hecho que ha generado delicados equilibrios entre la producción de partes y los tiempos de traslado y entrega. Esta cadena debe tener movimientos tan precisos como que un retraso de un minuto se penaliza en VW a un costo de 500-2000 Dls, dependiendo del punto de interrupción. En cuanto a las innovaciones tecnológicas, se ha introducido un sistema llamado *Hoja Electrónica Montis* que está conectada en una sofisticada red de informática y comunicación que coordina todos y cada uno de los movimientos de los proveedores de parte y los sincroniza con la marcha de los diversos flujos de montaje en la planta VW. En algunos casos (suspensiones, ejes, bastidores) la calidad ya empieza a ser controlada por el procedimiento *Poka Yoke* que revisa y audita las operaciones y mide micrométricamente los niveles de ajustes, aprietes, ensambles, etc.

En lo que corresponde a la política de empleo en el Cluster VW podemos encontrar, en primer lugar, que dentro del proceso de transplante y dispersión de la fabricación del automóvil, inicialmente las empresas admitieron a extrabajadores de VW bajo dos consideraciones: a) iniciar con trabajadores nuevos hubiera implicado gastos y tiempos de aprendizaje que no estaban a tono con las necesidades de la empresa ensambladora, y b), una rigurosa selección del personal, de tal forma que todos los admitidos aceptaran que ese cambio era el mejor trato dentro de un ambiente regional de desempleo, mismo que implica admitir que haber sido trabajador de VW es formar parte de una especie de *lista negra* de desempleados, inadmisible para las contrataciones en las empresas manufactureras de la localidad.

Fue así como en la punta de muchos de estos subprocesos productivos, de manera particular, en las fábricas proveedoras más importantes, están laborando extrabajadores de VW ganando los salarios más altos del promedio en el Cluster, pero menores a los salarios de sus camaradas en la gran fábrica. Se ha constituido un sistema salarial dual que se ha estado moviendo hacia los salarios bajos y que ha cancelado los movimiento a la inversa. En este sistema salarial los salarios de VW pueden ser entre 50% y 120% mayores que los de los trabajadores de las empresas de partes.

El tabulador salarial VW va del nivel más bajo de $70.00, hasta el más alto de $172.00. El promedio se ubica, en $85.00 diarios. En tanto, la mayor parte de los salarios en el cluster van desde 40 hasta 120 pesos, con un promedio que se mueve entre 55 y 60 pesos diarios[11].

Y por último, hablaremos sobre las consecuencias de las aplicaciones de la producción esbelta en el terreno de la organización obrera. En estas nuevas estructuras de proveedores se está imponiendo un esquema de contrataciones que de entrada aplica las vacunas contra la añeja tradición sindicalista de los trabajadores de VW y contra cualquier figura que presuponga el ejercicio independiente de derechos de organización sindical: lo obreros son afiliados, como parte de su trámite de contratación, a algunos de los *sindicatos de protección* que pululan en el ambiente -que como se sabe, son la cubierta para satisfacer la formalidad jurídica mexicana, pero perfectamente inútiles para actuar como mecanismos de lucha y resistencia obrera.

---

[11] Estos salarios son los vigentes hasta el primer semestre de 1997. A partir de agosto de 1997 los salarios VW aumentaron 23% (véase anexo 2) y en el "Cluster" FINSA en un promedio de 17%.

Al mismo tiempo que esto sucede, en el parque FINSA-VW se está probando un mecanismo de contratación más flexible: la contratación individual, *sin sindicatos*, que tienen la ventaja de eliminar para la patronal las negociaciones con los *dueños de los contratos de protección*, pero que deja a los trabajadores -en cuanto a la seguridad en el empleo y los derechos acumulados- pendientes de las evaluaciones gerenciales de *tres factores* que en orden de importancia son: actitud, aptitud y desempeño. Modernísima expresión que al decir de las gerencias laborales de las proveedoras[12] representa el futuro de la organización laboral y las asignaciones salariales en el cluster de VW.[13]

Pero esto no es todo, en otros casos el proceso de reorganización laboral transcurrió de manera más simple. Por ejemplo, los sistemas de empaque de refacciones para el mercado interno y para la exportación, que antes de agosto de 1992 se hacía con obreros sindicalizados, como consecuencia de los cambios laborales introducidos después del conflicto, toda la plantilla de estos departamentos fue recontratada con la categoría de "empleados de confianza". Eso liberó de presiones sindicales a los mandos y permitió que de 1993 a 1996 se hicieran ajustes de personal con bastante comodidad para la gerencia, que llegaron hasta puntos de esfuerzo críticos para los trabajadores. Recientemente, el mes de Junio de 1997, la nueva noticia para los empleados de estos departamentos fue que ¡sin cambiarse de lugar ni de sistema de trabajo! han dejado de ser trabajadores de VW y han pasado a ser empleados de un proveedor al que sólo se le conoce con el nombre de "El Instituto"[14].

---

[12] En una visita al Cluster un Director de producción de una empresa de partes eléctricas nos decía. "Mire, aquí, los tiempos del sindicato pasaron, ellos han echo mucho daño y talvez eran buenos cuando había explotación, pero ahora son otros tiempos y ahora lo que tenemos que hacer es trabajar, trabajar y siempre trabajar".

[13] Cuando menos en tres de estas empresas se ha probado que el incremento salarial anual, como se nos explicó, "se ha decidido por los propios trabajadores". El procedimeinto es una curiosa pero muy cuidadosa mescla de un paternalismo obsesivo y diversos candados para asegurar que nadie se "dispara". Se empieza por instalar un mecanismo donde la gerencia y "los trabajadores" deciden nombrar una comisiónque hará el estudio pertinente para el incremento. Después esa comisión hará la "evaluación de las necesidades y posibilidades de la empresa", simultáneamente al "reconocimiento justo al esfuerzo de los trabajadores" y por último, definirá "cuánto, cómo y a quién". El resultado es que estas empresas aal final se mueven dentro del mismo abanico salarial que ya hemos indicado arriba para las empresas proveedores del cluster,

[14] Que de entrada prometió respetar salarios y prestaciones pero no tuvo respuestas claras cuando se habló sobre los mecanismos de incremento a futuro, ni sobre los derechos de antiguedad en el trabajo.

En suma, una reflexión inicial acerca de las consecuencias de esta reordenación productiva especialmente en sus variantes organizativa y laboral, nos sugieren que los transplantes de los modernos sistemas de integración industrial están efectivamente provocando cambios profundos en regiones receptoras como Puebla. Lo peculiar de esos cambios está en que el transplante de los nuevos sistemas a nuestras tierras germina y desarrolla en capacidad de fabricación que se homologa muy rápidamente con los prototipos originales. Sin embargo, la enorme diferencia estriba en que no tenemos -cuando menos con la misma velocidad- transferencias de aprendizaje, know-how y tecnológicas[15].

En cuanto a los cambios en las culturas de trabajo, la productividad, la eficacia y la calidad, espero que en este trabajo haya sido explícito que, la obtención de los productos que compiten en los mercados más exigentes, se ha desplayado aprovechando una muy débil regulación laboral que ha permitido que no haya sido necesario recurrir a elevaciones salariales reales para obtener la flexibilidad y la polivalencia que son los preceptos pivote en las concepciones Lean Production.

Puebla, Ciudad Universitaria,1997.

Cuadro 10a

Relación de la Principales Operaciones Anuales de Compra (1981)
Proveedores

Empresa	Ubicación
Magneto SA de CV	Toluca Edo de México
Crinamex y/o Vidrio Plano de México SA	D.F.
Eléctro Optica	Tlalnepantla, Edo de México
Gocar SA	D.F.
Central de Industria SA	Tulyehualco
Productos Aurolín SA	D.F.
Cia Hulera Good Year Oxo	D.F.
Instituto Mexicano de Rehabilitación	D.F.
Condumex S.A.	Puebla
Triangel de México	Ciudad Satélite
Unirroyal	D.F.
Industria de Baleros intercontinental	Puebla
Nacional de Autopartes	Tultitlán, Edo. de México

[15] Véase: Juárez Núñez, Huberto. Impacto de los nuevos sistemas de integración industrial en regiones en desarrollo. Revista Aportes. 3-4. Enero-Abril. 1997. FE-BUAP:

Suspensiones Automotrices S.A.	Tlalnepantla
Barnices Aislantes S.A.	D.F.
Velcon S.A.	Celaya, Guanajuato
Oplex S.A.	Naucalpan, Edo. de México
Tebo S.A.	Naucalpan
Artifibras S.A.	Uruapan Michoacan
Kelsey Hayes de México S.A.	D.F.
Estaño y sus derivados	D.F.
Precisión Mecánica Nacional S.A.	Tlalnepantla
Arquimetálica S. A.	D.F.
Bujías Champion de México S.A.	D.F.
Industria de Hule Galgo S. A.	D.F.
Productos especiales metálicos S.A.	D.F.
Plásticos Creali S.A.	D.F.

Fuente: SH y CP. VW de México. Estado de Resultados. Anexo 5. 1981

Cuadro 10b
Principales proveedores-subcontratistas de VW de México (Cluster FINSA) 1996

Empresa	Rubro
Auxin de México (ext)	maquinado de vidrio
Duro Plast (ext)	partes de puertas
Electro Optica (ext)	módulos delanteros
Findlay Industries de México (ext)	revestimiento
Gedas Norteamérica (ext)	comunicación
Lear Corporation (ext)	asientos
Ayarep (ext)	facias o defensas
Productoras de Electrosistemas Santa Fe (ext)	bocinas
Refa Mexicana (ext)	troquelados y estampados
Rocwell Mexicana (ext)	módulos para puertas
Roth-Tecnica de México (ext)	sistema de escape
Siemens (ext)	arneses
Socop (ext)	luces interiores
Somer Allibert (ext)	tableros
Tramsnafv Technologies (ext)	partes plásticas
TRW (ext)	bastidor auxiliar y módulos de dir.
Turnkey (ext)	comunicaciones vía satélite
Siemens (ext)	eléctricos
Johnson Controls (ext)	asientos
Desarrollo del Vidrio (nal)	vidrio

Fuente: Dirección del Parque Industrial FINSA.

BIBLIOGRAFÍA

Asociación Mexicana de la Industria Automotriz (1993-1998). Boletines mensuales.

Juárez Núñez, Huberto. (1992) ¿Cómo llegaron los skeanheads a Puebla?. En VW de México, Nuevas Relaciones Laborales. Octubre. Coloquio Nacional de Sociología. Jalapa, Ver. Universidad Veracruzana.

_______ (1994). Paros Técnicos, nueva salida patronal. La Jornada Laboral. Febrero. No. 49.

_______ 1996-1997. Entrevistas Directas: Parque Industrial FINSA, Personal de Dirección de VW.

_______ (1997). Impacto de los nuevos sistemas de integración industrial en regiones en desarrollo. Revista Aportes. 3-4. Enero-Abril.. FE-BUAP.

Programa de Estudios de la Industria Automotriz. Archivo VW. FE-BUAP. 1983-1996.

Secretaría de Hacienda y Crédito Público. Estado de Resultados de VW de México. 1980-1996.

VW-AG. Anual Reports. Wolfsburg. 1980-1997.

VW de México (1995-1996). Cuadros Resumen del PMC2. Planeación de Manufactura, Dirección de Control de Calidad.

_______ Listado de personal sindicalizado: 1980-1996.

_______ Pospuestas para el "Sistema de Rotación Alemán". Departamento de Relaciones Laborales. Oficina Técnica de Pintura. 1997.

_______ Resumen de Resultados de Workshops internos. 1994-1996.

_______ Resultado de Ingeniería Industrial PMC2. 1996.

_______ Reportes periódicos. Relaciones Públicas. Información de la oficina de prensa. 1980-1997.

_______ Seguimientos al PMC2 en Fundición, Pintura, Ensamble y Estampados. 1996.

_______ Tabuladores Salariales. 1980-1996.

Anexo 1

Producción VW de México. Modelos y Líneas. Nacional y de Exportación.

	1993	1994	1995	1996
Producción Mercado nacional				
Golf 2 puertas	140	3,786	4	392
Golf 4 puertas	14,985	22,770	4,981	3,052
Total Golf	15,125	26,556	4,985	3,444
Golf GTI	452	2,259	259	562
Jetta 4 puertas	16,041	37,413	7,667	13,491
Derby	0	13	4,570	2,509
Sedán	98,236	78,276	15,933	33,099
Total Autos	129,854	144,517	33,414	53,105
				0
Combi	828	4,638	497	0
Panel	11,060	8,290	2,396	0
Comerciales	11,888	12,928	2,893	0
Total Produc. Merc. Nal.	141,742	157,445	36,307	53,105
Prod. de Exportación				
Jetta 4 Puertas	63,481	61,659	99,190	93,550
Golf 2 Puertas	5,226	17,817	16,380	9,734
Golf Cabrio	0	0	32	4,670
Golf 4 Puertas	28,554	19,396	39,529	65,172
Golf GTI	0	0	0	4,847
Total de Produc. Exportación	97,261	98,872	155,131	177,973

Fuente: Asociación Mexicana de la Industria Automotriz. 1993-1996.

Anexo 2

VOLKSWAGEN DE MEXICO: EMPLEO (30/04/97) Y TABULADOR Salarial 1997 (18 de Agosto de 1997)

Nivel	Personal	Personal (%)	Salario Tabulado. Agosto. 1997	1997 en Dls*	Planta Hombres	Planta Mujeres	Eventuales Hombres	Eventuales Mujeres	Total Hombres	Total Mujeres
A	655	6.3	81.92	10.20	44	3	598	10	642	13
B	143	1.4	85.60	10.70	60	3	78	2	138	5
C	357	3.4	89.78	11.20	144	12	194	7	338	19
D	146	1.4	93.73	11.70	86	3	57	0	143	3
E	685	6.6	98.01	12.30	496	30	151	8	647	38
F	364	3.5	104.67	13.10	295	15	52	2	347	17
G	600	5.7	112.34	14.00	557	20	21	2	578	22
H	1,054	10.1	118.95	14.90	980	42	32	0	1012	42
I	1,662	15.9	126.28	15.80	1,585	48	29	0	1614	48
J	740	7.1	132.43	16.60	698	33	9	0	707	33
K	2,056	19.7	139.25	17.40	1,958	90	8	0	1966	90
L	153	1.5	144.84	18.10	150	3	0	0	150	3
M	663	6.3	150.77	18.80	660	3	0	0	660	3
N	61	0.6	159.37	19.90	61	0	0	0	61	0
O	694	6.6	169.11	21.10	692	2	0	0	692	2
P	193	1.8	187.97	23.50	193	0	0	0	193	0
Q	15	0.1	199.53	24.90	15	0	0	0	15	0
R	209	2.0	212.41	26.60	208	1	0	0	208	1
Total	10,450	100.0			8,882	308	1229	31	10111	339

* Un dólar equivale a 8 pesos mexicanos.

Fuente: VW de México. Listados de personal sindicalizado. Abril de 1997. Tabuladores 1997.

CAMBIO TECNOLÓGICO Y APRENDIZAJE LABORAL EN GENERAL MOTORS: LOS CASOS DEL D.F. Y SILAO.

Alejandro García G.[*]
Arturo Lara R.[**]

INTRODUCCIÓN[1]

El propósito del presente trabajo es comparar los cambios observados en las pautas de aprendizaje de la planta del Distrito Federal con la de Silao Guanajuato, ambas pertenecen a la firma automotriz norteamericana General Motors.

La planta del Distrito Federal se inauguró en 1936 y se cerró en 1995, mientras que la de Silao inició sus operaciones en 1994. Ambas plantas responden a distintas orientaciones. La primera orientada a la satisfacción de la demanda interna y la segunda, orientada a la exportación. Modificación en el destino de la producción que expresa múltiples factores, que han venido modificándose en el tiempo, como el incremento, a fines de los años 70´s, en la intensidad de la competencia internacional que exige a las firmas del sector automotriz menores costos, mayor calidad y flexibilidad cuantitativa y cualitativa. Presiones que obligan a las empresas del sector automotriz a asimilar nuevos equipos como nuevas formas de organizar los flujos de bienes, servicios, información y conocimientos. Desde este horizonte de visibilidad, este trabajo reconstruye las formas del cambio tecnológico en estas dos plantas. La experiencia de planta del D.F. permite identificar las formas de aprendizaje asociadas al modelo fordista, en particular identificar la tensión a la que se ve sometida la empresa para transitar a nuevas formas de aprendizaje tecnológico. La historia de la nueva planta de Silao, historia todavía pe-

[*] Egresado de la Maestría en Economía y Gestión del Cambio Tecnológico, y Ayudante de posgrado en la Maestría de Salud en el Trabajo, Universidad Autónoma Metropolitana-Xochimilco.

[**] Profesor Investigador de la Maestría en Economía y Gestión del Cambio Tecnológico y del Departamento de Producción Económica de la Universidad Autónoma Metropolitana - Xochimilco.

[1] Agradecemos las críticas y sugerencias de Adriana Díaz-Berrio.

queña, puesto que cuenta con un poco más de tres años de antigüedad, permite identificar las nuevas estrategias de aprendizaje así como los perfiles del mercado de trabajo.

La estructura de esta investigación es la siguiente: en la primera parte se exponen brevemente las características tecnológicas, así como la forma de organización y las características del personal obrero empleado en la ensambladora instalada en la Ciudad de México.

La segunda parte describe la planta G.M. de Silao, empresa considerada una de las más grandes, de entre las que posee este grupo corporativo a nivel mundial. En este apartado, se enfatizan las mejoras tecnológicas más importantes identificadas durante nuestra visita de campo en julio de 1996. Asimismo, se destaca la importancia que tiene el entrenamiento y el conocimiento técnico en los procesos productivos, organizativos y en la calidad de la producción de esta planta. Finalmente se plantean las conclusiones.

ORIGEN, CARACTERÍSTICAS PRODUCTIVAS Y ORGANIZATIVAS DE LA PLANTA GENERAL MOTORS DE LA CD. DE MÉXICO

La historia de G.M. del D.F. puede dividirse en dos etapas: 1936-1980 y 1981-1995. La transición entre el primer periodo y el segundo se produce como resultado de tres factores: 1) la desconcentración de una parte de la producción de esta planta hacia el norte del país, 2) la reorientación del mercado hacia el mercado norteamericano y 3) la introducción de cambios tecnológicos y organizacionales novedosos.

a) Orígenes y Consolidación de la planta productiva, 1936-1980.

Esta planta inició su producción, en abril de 1936, con solo 36 trabajadores. El objetivo de la firma era producir la última fase del proceso de fabricación del automóvil o CKD´s para satisfacer fundamentalmente la demanda del mercado interno.

A partir de la transferencia de equipo y maquinaria especializada de origen estadounidense, General Motors de México produjo automóviles homogéneos y estandarizados basados fundamentalmente en economías de escala. Las formas de organización de la producción y las relaciones laborales se desarrollaron dentro de los principios del fordismo-taylorismo: producción en grandes lotes, medición rigurosa de tiempos y movimientos, profunda división del trabajo, bajos niveles de capacitación, realización de actividades monótonas. En esta estructura organizativa el salario dependía de la antigüedad en el trabajo, las tareas productivas eran repetitivas y se fijaban en función de las distintas categorías laborales.

En esta planta coexistían trabajadores muy calificados con otros trabajadores cuyos conocimientos y experiencias eran mínimos. El grupo de operadores calificados lo integraba regularmente personal de base, el cual había adquirido conocimientos y habilidades en la práctica; la empresa en raras ocasiones capacitaba a su personal. El conjunto de trabajadores poco calificado estaba compuesto por personal eventual en su mayoría (Cruz Guzmán, 1993).

Esta segmentación laboral al interior de la planta durante mucho tiempo permitió que un sector de los obreros gozaran de prerrogativas, las cuales se apoyaban en el monopolio y el dominio del conocimiento y del saber-hacer que era indispensable en el funcionamiento de las tareas productivas. Esta concentración del aprendizaje, al acumularse en un conjunto reducido de trabajadores, se volvió estratégica durante la negociación de las plazas de trabajo conquistadas a mediados de los años sesenta.

Por su parte, la amplia división jerárquica del trabajo entre la gestión de la producción y la ejecución-planeación contribuyen a concentrar la información y la toma de decisiones en la gerencia; bajo estas condiciones los operarios muy débilmente podían contribuir al desarrollo de las mejoras tecnológicas.

En el paradigma Taylorista el departamento de investigación y desarrollo es el área encargada de acumular y difundir el aprendizaje tecnológico. Sin embargo, las modificaciones que esta empresa logró hacer respondieron más bien a las exigencias de la matriz americana; estas mejoras tecnológicas estaban encaminadas sobre todo a cambiar las líneas y los modelos automovilísticos que se demandaban en el país (Arteaga A., 1993).

A mediados de los cincuenta, los trabajadores sindicalizados de esta firma lograron consolidar uno de los contratos colectivos de trabajo más importantes de la industria automotriz mexicana. El contrato de trabajo de esta planta normó durante muchos años el escalafón y la movilidad profesional a través de la antigüedad laboral y, asimismo, limitó la flexibilidad en la realización de las tareas. En este contrato se fijó una jornada de 40 horas en cinco días, incluyó prestaciones más altas que las de cualquier planta de filial mexicana.[2]

---

[2] Este contrato incluye prima vacacional, un fondo de ahorro, ahorro de navidad, vacaciones, transporte, descansos obligatorios pagados, IMSS, enfermedades profesionales, medico en la planta, seguro de vida, seguro de incapacidad permanente, gastos médicos y anteojos, riesgos de trabajo profesionales y no profesionales, bonos de puntualidad y despensa, apoyo a desarrollo cultural, gastos escolares, y becas de estudio, entre otros.

El sindicato, conformado en 1937, logró conquistar la "cláusula quinta" según la cual la firma se comprometía a ampliar los derechos laborales anteriormente citados, a cualquier trabajador del grupo corporativo, así como la obligación de consultar al sindicato en los momentos que la gerencia decidiese abrir otra planta. En 1963, a cambio de la eliminación de dicha cláusula, la empresa otorgó 250 plazas a trabajadores que habían laborado 15 años continuos en la empresa.

La eliminación de la cláusula quinta permitió la instalación, en 1965, de la planta de fundición y motores en Toluca.[3] La reacción del sindicato de la empresa instalada en el D.F. fue organizar una huelga, la cual tenía como meta reconquistar el derecho de los trabajadores a intervenir en la contratación de los trabajadores de las otras plantas. Sin embargo, solamente se logró que la empresa se comprometiera a: i) no retirar sus instalaciones del D.F., ii) respetar la materia de trabajo en dicha planta y iii) a mantener las prestaciones conquistadas (Carrillo y García, 1987; y Lucio Romero, 1994). Fueron estos y los subsecuentes movimientos sindicales los que frenaron, hasta principios de los ochenta, el proyecto empresarial de flexiblizar el proceso de producción y de desincorporar algunas etapas productivas de la planta de General Motors de la Ciudad de México.

RELOCALIZACIÓN GEOGRÁFICA Y MODERNIZACIÓN TECNOLÓGICA, 1981-1995.

En 1979, el grupo General Motors construyó un complejo automotriz en Ramos Arizpe-Coahuila, a partir de la puesta en operación de una planta de motores y otra ensambladora; consecuentemente la planta establecida en el Distrito Federal dejo de producir baterías, prensas, bujías, vestiduras, y chasises. La estrategia de la empresa consistió en reorientar su producción hacia el mercado norteamericano y en crear las condiciones para desmantelar progresivamente la fuerza del sindicato de la planta de Ciudad de México.

En las plantas del norte, debido la debilidad sindical, no solamente se pagaron salarios menores a los que prevalecían en el centro del país, además se introdujeron: maquinas reprogramables, grupos de trabajo, unidades estratégicas de negocios y el Just it Time. También se enfatizó la importancia de la calidad, la capacitación se convirtió en un eje central de la calificación

---

[3] En dicho artículo se expresa lo siguiente: "las estipulaciones del presente contrato colectivo de trabajo se extienden a todas las personas que trabajan en la empresa aún cuando no sean miembros del sindicato contratante y de acuerdo con lo dispuesto en el artículo 48 de la Ley Federal del Trabajo se aplicará a todas las dependencias actuales de la empresa y en las que se pudiera crear en lo sucesivo en cualquier parte del país" (Lucio Romero, 1994).

laboral y se abandonó el sistema de pago por antigüedad; éste ultimo se sustituyó por un sistema basado en el pago de remuneraciones por conocimiento, (Arteaga A.1993; y Micheli J., 1994).

A diferencia de las empresas del norte, la planta de General Motors del D.F. siguió concentrada en la demanda del mercado interno de camiones pequeños, medianos y grandes. En 1982, debilitado el sindicato, la dirección de G.M. del D.F. decidió tomar las siguientes acciones: reducir su planta laboral (de 3,225 se pasó a 2,200 trabajadores), incrementar los ritmos de trabajo, compactar las categorías laborales e introducir cambios tecnológicos (Carrillo y García, 1987).

Cuadro no. I

COMPARACIÓN DE LOS CAMBIOS TECNOLÓGICOS OBSERVADOS EN DOS ETAPAS DE LA PLANTA DE GM UBICADA EN EL D.F.

Tipo de Innovación	Primera Etapa,1935-1980	Segunda Etapa, 1981-1995
a) En Producto	- Carburador. - Lamina gruesa - Parrillas de metal cromado - Chasis remachado - Parabrisas y medallones sujeto por plásticos	- Encendido electrónico "fuel Inyection". - Lamina más delgada, menos corrosiva y más ligera - Parrillas de plástico - Chasis soldado - Parabrisas y medallones adheridos con cemento negro para reducir la resistencia al aire.
b) Maquinaria y Equipo	- Aplicación de fosfato y primer a través de un equipo pistola - Utilización de cepillo y tanque de gas para desprender la grasa de la lamina	- Instalación de transfer aéreo electrónico - Incorporación del mando central, el cual verifica el funcionamiento de todas las áreas y detiene la producción en caso de problemas. - Sistema ELPO, el cual incluye maquinaria y equipo electrónico que aplica el fosfato. - Cámara para el lavado de lamina a través de una lluvia de compuestos químicos - Horno de secado - Uso de computadoras en la calidad en el control y verificación de la calidad
c) Organizativos		- Justo a Tiempo - Manufactura sincronizada - Unidades operativas de negocios

Fuente: Elaboración propia a partir de Cruz Guzmán (1993) y Lucio Romero (1994).

Las innovaciones tecnológicas más importantes que se dieron durante el periodo de 1935-1995 se resumen en el cuadro número I. Los cambios tecnológicos más importantes son: a) mejora en los productos, modificación de los diseños y materiales de construcción de los automóviles; b) introducción de nueva maquinaria y equipo, sobre todo maquinas automatizadas, así como nuevos sistemas de limpieza en el laminado, e instrumentos electrónicos para el control de calidad; c) difusión de una filosofía de calidad y d) cambios organizacionales que tenían como propósito involucrar a los trabajadores en la dirección de los procesos y en la simplificación de las tareas a través del sistema de Manufactura Sincronizada; procedimiento a través del cual los obreros integrados con los ingenieros participan en la medición de los tiempos y movimientos de algunas tareas, y en la elaboración de gráficas de control de la producción. También, la empresa intentó formar grupos de trabajo, pero esta tentativa falló ante la percepción del sindicato de ser desplazado en algunas funciones que tenía sobre el control del proceso de organización y producción.

A pesar del cambio tecnológico señalado, la capacitación en el trabajo no se generalizó; solamente se capacitó a los trabajadores que se integraron al Sistema de Manufactura Sincronizada y a aquellos que estuvieron dispuestos a manejar el equipo nuevo. La estructura organizativa continuó centralizándose y los flujos de información permanecieron débiles. Las habilidades y conocimientos técnicos tenían como fundamento el aprendizaje sobre la marcha, la repetición y la especialización de las tareas, y la transmisión del saber de los trabajadores más antiguos hacia los más jóvenes.

Por su parte, algunos de los efectos que tiene la introducción de los cambios tecnológicos señalados en el cuadro número I son: i) eliminación de algunos riesgos de trabajo; ii) la sustitución de tareas simples y repetitivas por actividades de supervisión e interpretación de códigos y señales más complejas e inestables; iii) disminución del número de trabajadores; iv) aumento en los ritmos de trabajo y v) modificaciones en la composición de la fuerza de trabajo, incremento cuantitativo del personal joven y reducción del número de trabajadores antiguos (Cruz Guzmán, 1993).

Estas transformaciones tecnológicas se dieron con una débil oposición de los trabajadores, dada la desarticulación generada en el movimiento sindical a inicios de los ochenta. No obstante, los trabajadores opusieron resistencia a la persistencia de los bajos niveles de capacitación, al incremento acelerado de la productividad y de la intensidad del trabajo, observada a raíz de los cambios tecnológicos implementados, resistencia que toma forma del: tortuguismo, retardos y ausencias en la jornada.

Los obreros del área mecánica industrial protestaron al ver que sus conocimientos no eran suficientes para hacer frente a las nuevas condiciones productivas ya que la empresa solo ofrecía cursos de capacitación muy generales que no permitían obtener conocimientos técnicos suficientes para dominar la producción. Antes bien, los trabajadores debían asimilar espontáneamente y sin una estrategia sistemática los cambios que surgían en la practica diaria y de frente a los problemas que se iban presentando. Por su parte, los trabajadores del departamento de pintura se quejaron de que los cambios generados habían elevado el número de movimientos ejecutados de 100 a 150 por cada camioneta, provocándoles graves daños a la cintura; lo cual aunado al aumento de los niveles de producción se convirtió en un elemento importante en el estrés y el desgaste físico (Cruz Guzmán, 1993; y Lucio Romero, 1994).

En 1992, el sindicato y la empresa pactaron el cierre de la planta del D.F. y su traslado a Durango. En 1993 no se optó por esta ciudad, sino por Silao-Guanajuato. Posteriormente, en marzo de 1995, se llevaron a cabo cinco paros técnicos argumentando la caída de las ventas. Además se despidió a más de mil trabajadores, disminuyeron los turnos de trabajo de dos a solo uno y el número de unidades ensambladas se redujo de 216 a 100. Pero, no fue sino hasta el 8 de septiembre de 1995, cuando la planta de General Motors del D.F. decidió cerrar definitivamente sus instalaciones.

GENERAL MOTORS SILAO, UN PROCESO DE REESTRUCTURACIÓN EXITOSO.[4]

a) Origen y características productivas de esta ensambladora

La General Motors de Silao fue inaugurada en noviembre de 1994; en esta ensambladora se invirtieron 400 millones de dólares para producir el modelo Silverado y el camión pesado Kodiak. Aunque, esta empresa fue construida para ensamblar una gran variedad de modelos en la misma línea de producción, lo que era imposible prácticamente en las plantas tradicionales; en ésta se puede incrementar o reducir la producción de un modelo especifico con mayor rapidez y según el mercado lo demande. Dicha firma aplica procesos y prácticas tanto productivas como organizacionales similares a las de algunas empresas automotrices de Japón, Europa y Norteamérica.

La capacidad productiva de G.M. de Silao es de 25 unidades por hora, aunque a su máxima capacidad generará dos unidades por minuto; actual-

[4] Este apartado retomó una parte importante de la información presentada por Alejandro García G. (1997).

mente más del 80% de su producción se destina a la exportación y el resto al mercado interno. Para alcanzar esta meta la empresa mantiene estrechas relaciones con sus proveedores y con sus dos filiales: una ensambladora de motores, localizada en la Ciudad de Toluca, y la de carrocerías y sus partes establecida en Ramos Arizpe. De acuerdo con las estrategias de la empresa se espera que se instalen en los alrededores de la planta entre 60 y 80 empresas proveedoras.

La planta de Silao, situada al pie de la autopista Silao-Guanajuato, cuenta con 201 hectáreas en total. Esta ensambladora ocupa 14.8 hectáreas, de las cuales 10.7 hectáreas están destinas a carrocería, pintura, vestiduras de carrocerías, chasis y ensamble.

La planta esta dividida en tres áreas productivas básicas: ensamble, carrocería y pintura. Las camionetas atraviesan las distintas fases del proceso productivo a través de una "línea transfer" automatizada. La cadena de producción se basa en el estudio de tiempos y movimientos o "tiempos ciclos" como la denominan los trabajadores. De acuerdo con el gerente de Recursos Humanos, el movimiento programado de la cadena contempla un tiempo suficiente para que cada operario pueda realizar sus tareas. No existe ningún departamento de investigación y desarrollo; éste se ubica en los Estados Unidos, lugar de donde provienen las innovaciones tecnologías de diseño más importantes.

El puesto laboral más elevado dentro del organización corresponde al gerente de planta, persona en la que recae la mayor responsabilidad de la empresa. En los niveles medios se encuentran los gerentes de recursos humanos, de manufactura y de ventas. En el siguiente subnivel se localizan los coordinadores del área de calidad, de ensamble, de pintura y de estampado, entre las más importantes. En la base de esta estructura se sitúan los grupos de trabajo distribuidos en las líneas de producción; cada grupo, a cargo del "líder" o coordinador, se integra por 10 o 12 trabajadores.

b) Cambios Tecnológicos Introducidos, Habilidades y Conocimientos Requeridos por Trabajadores

Entre las mejoras tecnológicas implantados se encuentran las siguientes: introducción de maquinaria y equipo electrónico en las áreas de calidad, un sistema *transfer* aéreo automatizado, robots soldadores, robots pintores, el Kan-Ban, sistema logístico, Justo a Tiempo y el Sistema ANDON.[5] En el pla-

[5] Esta planta es la primera en usar una estación de monitoreo ambiental; este proyecto incluye un sistema de base de agua que reduce las emisiones y el uso de solventes, además cuenta con

no organizacional resaltan los grupos de trabajo autodirigidos y la Manufactura Sincronizada; esta última incluye grupos integrados por ingenieros y operarios que se organizan para, entre otras funciones, simplificar las tareas. Las tareas productivas realizadas en esta planta exigen técnicas de trabajo en equipo; la ampliación en la gama de conocimientos y de habilidades técnicas; un mayor involucramiento y una creciente responsabilidad del personal en las tareas de producción, de reparación, y de mejoramiento en la calidad de procesos y productos; el desarrollo de la capacidad para descifrar códigos y parámetros técnicos, así como de difundirlos a través de escritos o gráficas; y el de asegurar la continuidad de los flujos de información.

c) Mercado de trabajo y Movilidad Laboral

La ensambladora de Silao empleó a 1,700 trabajadores en julio de 1995. A mediados de 1996 trabajaban 2,000 personas, aunque se calcula que esta empresa generará 3,500 empleos directos y 11,000 empleos indirectos. De la planta del Distrito Federal, la de Silao únicamente recontrató al personal de confianza; no fueron permitidas las transferencias del personal de producción y de los supervisores que habían trabajado en la Cd. de México.

La G.M. de Guanajuato demanda técnicos y trabajadores con nivel educativo de secundaria, niveles de formación previo necesarios para integrar al trabajador dentro de un proceso de aprendizaje técnico, social y de comunicación exigente. El gerente de Recursos Humanos entrevistado señaló, respecto al papel de la educación: "para ser una empresa de clase mundial tenemos que tener a la mejor gente. Tenemos operarios con preparatoria, técnicos y con secundaria terminada; de lo contrario, es muy difícil que los trabajadores entiendan los conceptos que reciben durante el entrenamiento".

Dada la insuficiente oferta de trabajadores calificados en la región, la empresa firmó un acuerdo con el CONALEP para establecer un programa de cooperación mutua que permita capacitar a un mayor volumen de trabajadores y mejorar la calidad de su formación. El personal que trabaja en esta empresa esta compuesto básicamente por hombres, cuyas edades fluctúan entre los 22 y 25 años. Las mujeres en la planta de Silao regularmente trabajan en áreas administrativas. Sin embargo a mediados de 1996, la planta se vio obligada a modificar su estrategia de selección de personal integrando a mujeres en las líneas de producción dados los problemas de inestabilidad, ausentismo del personal masculino, y la débil oferta de personal masculino. Si los

---

tecnología de punta en el tratamiento y recirculación del agua residual que permite reducir el consumo de este liquido y provee un afluente de agua limpia.

resultados son favorables, señaló un gerente de esta planta, esta tendencia de *feminización* de la línea de ensamble continuará en el futuro.

Desde la perspectiva de la empresa, existen dos factores que explican el ausentismo y la rotación externa de los trabajadores. El primer aspecto es que, de acuerdo con un gerente, la planta está localizada a 3.8 k.m del principal poblado: "el lugar no es una zona industrial, aunque tenemos la de calzado cercas de aquí. No tenemos industrias pesadas alrededor, entonces básicamente el problema de la ausencia es que la gente vive en lugares retirados, por lo que estamos trayendo gente de zonas aledañas. Obviamente que si a alguien se le hace tarde no va a pagar un taxi que le cobra de 50 o 60 pesos".

El segundo factor se vincula a la débil disciplina laboral de los trabajadores, pues "la gente no tiene una cultura laboral, no sabe trabajar en una empresa seria donde se tiene una reglamentación y una disciplina en la hora de entrada, donde el trabajo es ordenado hasta para ir a los servicios sanitarios... Todo eso es educación, es trabajo en equipo, es adaptación y voluntad al cambio. La gente no esta acostumbrada a trabajar en horarios fijos, ni a la rotación de horarios".

La rotación externa de los trabajadores tiene profundas implicaciones sobre la estabilidad de la producción, en 1994, cuando arrancó la planta, algunas líneas de producción no podían comenzar a operar. De acuerdo a un ingeniero consultado, los costos-hora por parar la producción en una empresa ensambladora ascendían de 50 mil a 60 mil dólares por hora. La rotación del personal tiene un gran costo económico para la empresa toda vez que se ha invertido en la capacitación formal del trabajador 336 horas-hombre de 1994 a 1995, y a mediados de 1996, 280 horas-hombre; 42 días y 35 días respectivamente. Sin contar el costo de la capacitación informal, los costos de reclutamiento y selección de los mismos.

En empresas intensivas en capital y donde la cooperación entre los trabajadores y entre los grupos de trabajo resulta central la rotación de los trabajadores tiene graves implicaciones: 1) se elimina la tasa de retorno del capital humano que la empresa invirtió; 2) saber-hacer (know-how) que se pierde y se transfiere a otras plantas. Para la empresa la fuga de un trabajador calificado del centro de su mercado interno de trabajo y su contratación en una empresa rival, puede significar la transferencia de experiencia y conocimientos de la primera a la segunda firma. De manera que, dentro de la construcción de barreras a la competencia, una empresa necesita protegerse manteniendo cautiva a una parte esencial de su fuerza de trabajo, ante la imposibilidad de patentar la experiencia y los conocimientos adquirido; 3) provocan desequilibrios en la estructura de puestos y tareas; 4) inestabilidad y fragilidad en la forma como los grupos de trabajo se integran y comunican entre sí; 5) aspectos que en conjunto dañan los niveles de calidad, eficiencia y productividad de la planta (Lara Rivero, 1996).

d) Procesos de Aprendizaje

La base fundamental del aprendizaje depende de la forma en que interactuan y laboran los operarios al interior de cada grupo de trabajo. Cada grupo de trabajo, en esta planta, procuran su autodisciplina, decide quién es su líder, los periodos de rotación de sus integrantes, y así mismo, intentan resolver colectivamente problemas o errores de la producción o del desempeño individual o grupal; saben qué hacer cuando hay sobrecarga de trabajo, un elemento falta o hay problemas de calidad.

Los miembros del equipo también deben saber qué trabajo van a realizar, cuáles son sus metas y objetivos dentro de la empresa, y cómo y cuándo deben cumplir los lineamientos establecidos; en un momento dado, los trabajadores determinan si se quedan a trabajar más tiempo o no. La concepción medular de estos grupos autodirigidos es el "empowerment", la cual consiste en delegar la autoridad en los operarios de tal manera que puedan tomar decisiones, encontrar soluciones a sus problemas, lograr iniciativa y obtener un reconocimiento por los resultados obtenidos.

Hay reglas claras, por ejemplo, los trabajadores deben rotarse de turno cada 10 semanas; la movilidad laboral en cada línea de producción se acuerda con el líder del equipo. Asimismo, existen posibilidades de pasar del área de ensamble a la de carrocería, pero eso solamente sucede en raras ocasiones. En caso que algún trabajador solicite su cambio de área, solamente puede hacerlo a través de permutas; no sin antes tomar los cursos de capacitación específicos al área.

Este constante proceso de toma de decisiones en los grupos de trabajo fomenta la circulación de un flujo de información continuo entre el personal y su líder. A través de sus líderes de equipo los trabajadores pueden plantear a la gerencia sus deseos, dudas o problemas. Otros espacios de comunicación son el buzón de sugerencias y el sindicato. De acuerdo con la filosofía de esta empresa la circulación de la información es un aspecto medular para su buen funcionamiento: "la política es de puertas abiertas, la comunicación va desde arriba hacia abajo y de abajo hacia arriba".

Por otra parte, el sistema de pagos en esta estructura organizacional estimula la adquisición de los conocimientos adquiridos por los trabajadores, ellos pueden incrementar su salario por los siguientes motivos: a) conforme aumentan sus conocimientos; b) por que conocen y son capaces de ejecutar los diversos trabajos asignados al equipo que pertenecen; y c) por la disposición para reemplazar a cualquier miembro de su equipo en el momento requerido.

e) Capacitación Laboral

Antes de situarse en el piso de la planta, el personal debe tomar un curso básico que dura 280 horas, repartidas en treinta y cinco días, de entrenamiento teórico-práctico. En ese periodo, el trabajador recibe cursos teóricos y prácticos en simuladores. Posteriormente, el obrero ya en el piso continua con una semana de entrenamiento observando el trabajo de los operarios más experimentados.

Los temas principales del curso básico son: el funcionamiento y la integración de los equipos de trabajo; el uso de las filosofías, herramientas y procedimientos del aseguramiento de la calidad; la manufactura de los procesos productivos de la empresa; y la seguridad en el trabajo. En 1995 el temario de capacitación tenía una duración de 336 horas de entrenamiento básico, pero a mediados de 1996 la empresa optó por reducir el curso a 280 horas. En ambos cursos de entrenamiento, el eje fundamental está apoyada en la calidad y en el funcionamiento de los equipos de trabajo. En el curso de entrenamiento de 1994, los cursos de Estructura de Equipos de Trabajo, Interacción, Equipos Efectivos, Solución Organizada de problemas y Liderazgo constituían el 42% del número total de horas. En tanto en el programa de 1996 corresponde el 47%. Por su parte, los temas relacionados con la calidad -la Calidad Soy Yo, Herramientas Básicas de Calidad y Control Estadístico del Proceso- anteriormente constituían el 14% del total de horas impartidas y hoy corresponde el 18%. Los temas de capacitación que desaparecieron en 1996 fueron: Reconocimientos, Programas de Seguridad. Información General y sobretodo Formación de Instructores; este último contaba anteriormente con 16 horas (véase cuadro no. II).

Algunas de las razones que se esgrimen para justificar esta disminución del número de horas-hombre capacitadas y las modificaciones realizadas en algunas temáticas del Programa Básico de Entrenamiento son: la optimización de los recursos humanos y los altos costos financieros en los que ha incurrido empresa. A través de este programa de entrenamiento intensivo se ha intentado compensar las limitaciones y la escasa calificación que poseen los trabajadores guanajuatenses.

Cuadro no. II
TEMARIO DE ENTRENAMIENTO BÁSICO EN GM-SILAO

TEMA	CURSO 1995 (horas)	%	CURSO 1996 (horas)	%
1. Inducción	16	5	16	6
2. Administración de Controles de Piso	8	2	2	0.7
3. *Estructura de Equipos de Trabajo*	32	10	24	9
4. *Interacción*	24	7	24	9
5. La Calidad Soy Yo y Filosofías de Calidad	8	2	8	3
6. Herramientas Básicas de Calidad	16	5	16	6
7. *Equipos Efectivos*	60	18	56	20
8. Primeros Auxilios	4	1	4	1
9. Certificación de Operaciones	4	1	4	1
10. Sistema ANDON	4	1	4	1
11. Procedimientos	8	2	8	3
12. Básico de Seguridad	2	0.5	2	0.7
13. PARE	8	2	8	3
14. Solución Organizada de Problemas	8	2	8	3
15. El Líder	16	5	16	6
16. Bloqueo	4	1	4	1
17. Sistema contra Incendios	2	0.5	2	0.7
18. Control Estadístico del Proceso	24	7	24	9
19. Manejo de Materiales Peligrosos	4	1	4	1
20. T.P.M.	8	2	8	3
21. Manufactura Sincronizada	20	6	16	6
22. Sistema Jalar	4	1	4	1
23. S.P.S.	24	7	16	6
24. Procedimientos de Planta	2	0.5	2	0.7
25. Seguridad en el manejo de Montacargas	2	0.5	2	0.7
26. Reconocimientos	2	0.5	0	0
27. Programas de Seguridad	2	0.5	0	0
28. Información General	4	1	0	0
29. Formación de Instructores	16	5	0	0
TOTAL (Horas)	336	100	280	100
TOTAL (Días)	42		35	

FUENTE: Documento Interno de la Empresa.

CONCLUSIONES

Existe un conjunto de elementos que por último seria necesario rescatar y reflexionar:

1. La presión competitiva y la rígida tecnología de la planta del DF, aunado a relaciones industriales conflictivas que impedían la mutación tecnológica, condujeron a la General Motors al cierre de dicha firma.
2. Con el cierre de la planta del D.F y la construcción de una nueva en Silao, la empresa General Motors decide cancelar y transitar de: i) una estrategia de aprendizaje tecnológico que beneficiaba a un grupo selecto de obreros a una de mayor producción y difusión de información tecnológica, aprovechando las formas de aprendizaje utilizadas por las empresas japonesas; ii) pasar de una relación de confrontación sindicato-empresa a una relación de mayor cooperación; iii) disminuir o eliminar la influencia del sindicato en la regulación del proceso laboral y sobre todo de contratación; ampliando el grado de discrecionalidad de la gerencia en el establecimiento de niveles, movilidad escalafonaria, puesto y tareas, etc. iii) modificar la jerarquía de los estímulos económicos y no económicos de aprendizaje que unen y separan el mercado de trabajo y sobre todo que configuran el grado de disponibilidad de los actores de participar, o no, en los procesos de mejora tecnológica, por un concepto de integración que, asimilando los estímulos tradicionales, enriquece las nuevas formas donde los trabajadores participan en el procesamiento y consumo de la información (círculos de trabajo, grupos de trabajo, sugerencias, etc.). Transito que implicó en los hechos la construcción de una nueva planta, con trabajadores con una débil experiencia laboral y sindical previa; y con una fuerza de trabajo con relativamente mayores niveles de capacitación y educación que la vieja planta.
3. El transito de formas de organización fordista a una más flexible, más japonesa; tiene que descansar en dos grande pilares: la estabilidad y una elevada calificación y disciplina de la fuerza de trabajo. En este sentido la planta de Silao presenta dos grandes obstáculos. El primero, la elevada rotación del personal masculino que estaría conduciendo a la empresa a modificar la demanda cualitativa de fuerza de trabajo: reclutar a las mujeres por su mayor estabilidad que los hombres. En este punto de la historia breve de la empresa resulta difícil afirmar que se esta produciendo un

proceso efectivo de femenización de la fuerza de trabajo. Solo existen indicios.

4. Frente a los problemas de rotación, débil cultura y disciplina de las fuerza de trabajo de la región, la estrategia de la empresa es el de primero, pagar elevados costos financieros que significa impartir cursos de capacitación a contratar a los obreros con experiencia sindical de su planta del D.F. Estrategia agresiva de formación del personal de la planta que busca mejorar la calidad del proceso y la integración y funcionamiento de los equipos de trabajo, imprescindibles para competir en el mercado internacional.
5. Por último, la imagen de esta empresa viene a reforzar la tesis de que las nuevas tecnologías que se están difundiendo en el sector automotriz exigen un mayor esfuerzo empresarial a nivel económico, organizativo y de dirección para construir un capital humano de mayor calidad, más integrado y sobre todo con poderosos estímulos y condiciones para que su participación en los procesos de mejoramiento tecnológico sean cada vez más centrales y eficaces.

BIBLIOGRAFÍA

Arteaga Arnulfo (1985), "Innovación Tecnológica y Clase Obrera en la Industria Automotriz", en Esthela Gutiérrez, *Reestructuración Productiva y Clase Obrera*, pp. 146-169, Siglo XXI.

_______ (1993), "La Reestructuración de la Industria Automotriz en México y sus repercusiones en el viejo núcleo fabril", en *Procesos de Trabajo y Relaciones Laborales en la Industria Automotriz en México*, UAM-I y FFE.

Carrillo J. y García P. (1987), "Etapas Industriales y Conflictos Laborales: la industria Automotriz en México", en *Estudios Sociológicos*, vol. 5, no. 14, mayo -agosto, El Colegio de México.

Cruz Guzmán (1993), "Implicaciones del Cambio Tecnológico y Organizacional sobre la Fuerza de Trabajo en General Motors", en *Procesos de Trabajo y Relaciones Laborales en la Industria Automotriz en México*, UAM-I y FFE.

García Garnica A. (1997), "Cambio Tecnológico y Aprendizaje Laboral en la Industria Automotriz: algunos estudios de casos". Tesis de Maestría en Economía y Gestión del Cambio Tecnológico, UAM-X.

Lara Rivero A. (1996), "Competitividad, Cambio Tecnológico y Demanda Cualitativa de Fuerza de Trabajo en la Maquiladora de Exportación: el caso de las empresas japonesas en el sector electrónico de la televisión", Tesis para obtener el grado de Doctor en Ciencias Sociales, Colegio de México.

Lucio Romero (1994), "Las Percepciones de los Procesos de Flexibilización; un estudio sobre los trabajadores de General Motors de México", *Tesis de Maestría para obtener el grado en Ciencias Sociales*, FLACSO.

Micheli Jordy (1994), "Nueva Manufactura, Globalización y Producción de Automóviles en México", UNAM-FE, México.

GROWING PAINS:
LEAN PRODUCTION AT MITSUBISHI MOTORS

Lisa Jordan[*]

INTRODUCTION

In the Spring of 1989, Chrysler and Mitsubishi Motors entered into a joint venture to build automobiles in Bloomington-Normal, Illinois. Production and maintenance workers at the "Diamond Star" plant approached their jobs with great anticipation. Not only did these jobs offer significantly higher wages than most had previously made, but they came with promises of employee empowerment. Now, eight years after lean production and "employee teams" were introduced, worker expectations have dimmed substantially.

Previous research conducted at CAMI, Mazda, NUMMI, and the Ford Motor Company's Body and Stamping Plant in Wayne, Michigan, have examined the shopfloor dynamics created in a lean production facility.[1] Each study has challenged the simplistic conclusion of Womack, Jones and Roos[2] that "lean production" *automatically* results in worker empowerment and employee satisfaction. Rather, what emerges from this research is a more complex story in which worker perceptions of lean production and its impact on their working conditions differ by facility. "Lean production," then, manifests itself in different ways in the lives of workers. Based on this re-

[*] Director of Gender and Diversity Studies, Labor Education Services, University of Minnesota.

[1] James Rinehart, Chris Huxley and David Robertson, "Team Concept at CAMI," in Steve Babson, ed., *Lean Work: Empowerment and Exploitation in the Global Auto Industry* (Detroit: Wayne State University Press, 1995); Steve Babson, "Whose Team? Lean Production at Mazda U.S.A.," in Babson, *Lean Work*; Paul Adler, "Democratic Taylorism: The Toyota Production System at NUMMI," in Babson, *Lean Work*; Michelle Kaminski, this volume, and "Ford Wayne Stamping/UAW Local 900," in *Making Change Happen* (Washington: Work and Technology Institute, 1996).

[2] Womack, James, Daniel Jones and Daniel Roos, *The Machine that Changed the World*, (New York: Rawson Associates, 1990).

search, the specific nature of its impact in unionized workplaces seems to rest on the existence of contract language that protects worker rights, and on the specific supervisory practices that confirm or contradict worker expectations of empowerment. However, the particular relationship between the organization of work commonly known as lean production and employee satisfaction has remained unclear. This chapter examines that relationship by means of a unique survey instrument.

While the CAMI study surveyed worker attitudes over the course of a two year period, my research at Diamond Star examines the change in employee attitudes over eight years of operation. This analysis is made possible by the existence of a survey completed by a sample of workers at Mitsubishi Motors shortly after the facility opened in 1989. That survey data provides the baseline from which to measure changes in employee attitudes. To measure that change, I expanded the original survey and collected more thaan 1,000 returns from the plant workforce in the spring of 1997. This allows me to address some critical questions about lean production and worker empowerment. What, for example, is the interplay between the maturation of social and work organization, and employee attitudes? If change occurs in how workers feel, then how does it happen and what precipitates the new perspective? Finally, in a lean production setting, what organizational variables become key in determining employee satisfaction?

This paper is divided into five sections. I begin by providing a brief overview in section two of the history and operations of Mitsubishi Motors. A description then follows in section three of the social organization of the Bloomington-Normal plant. Section four explains the interview and survey methodology utilized to compile the data. In section five, preliminary survey findings are presented and there is a discussion of their implications.

BACKGROUND AND OPERATIONS

Originally called Diamond Star, Mitsubishi Motors began as a greenfield plant located in the Bloomington-Normal area of central Illinois. The site was chosen after an intensive competition among several midwestern states; in return for locating the plant in the community, Mitsubishi Motors received a variety of tax and other incentives.[3]

---

[3] For an extensive discussion of Diamond Star's decision to locate in Bloomington-Normal see Margaret Chapman, Arun Elhance and John Wenum, *Mitsubishi Motors in Illinois* (Westport, CN: Quorum Books, 1995).

Covering two million square feet, the plant is extremely compact and highly automated. The 3,204 production workers currently produce about 900 cars a day in six different styles: the Mitsubishi Galant, Spyder and Eclipse; the Dodge Avenger; the Chrysler Sebring and the Eagle Talon. The facility has its own stamping operation, but engine, seat and transmission production are located off site. The facility uses both Mitsubishi and Chrysler engines. Most suppliers deliver once a day on a just-in-time basis, but as the number of local suppliers continues to increase, deliveries are becoming more frequent. Much of the company's inventory is stored at GATX located next door to the Mitsubishi plant. Other inventory is stored in trucks in the plant parking lot. Tire and seat deliveries occur most often and arrive sequenced by vehicle specifications.

There are nearly 700 robots in the facility. While they operate throughout the plant, they are concentrated in the body shop and painting area. Robots were originally used to also install seats and dashboards in final assembly, but proved too slow and have been replaced by humans.

The facility has been solely owned by Mitsubishi Motors since the company bought Chrysler's 50 percent stake in 1991. This sale reportedly resulted from Chrysler's need to generate cash and boost profits during its recessionary crisis.[4] As noted above, Chrysler continues to contract with Mitsubishi to have several of its products produced in the Bloomington-Normal facility.

Mitsubishi has not been without its share of national attention. In the spring of 1996 the Equal Employment Opportunity Commission (EEOC) leveled sexual harassment charges against Mitsubishi Motors. Those charges have overshadowed other significant events at the plant, including its first reported profit in the spring of 1997. As a result of those charges, Mitsubishi employed former U.S. Secretary of Labor Lynn Martin to review working conditions at the facility. In her report, she referred to Mitsubishi Motors as a "company with Japanese parents and an American up-bringing ..." which "... as it moves from adolescence to maturity, ... has been buffeted by currents internal and external." While this paper addresses issues not directly related to the sexual harassment lawsuit, the culture of work at Mitsubishi and the evolution of work structures in the facility are certainly contiguous.[5]

---

[4] Clay Chandler and Bradley Streets, "Mitsubishi Buys Chrysler's 50% Stake in Their Diamond - Star Joint Venture," *Wall Street Journal,* 30 October 1991, Section A 4:2.

[5] In interviews, workers often noted the connection between these two.

THE SOCIAL ORGANIZATION OF PRODUCTION

The production and maintenance employees at Mitsubishi Motors are represented by UAW Local 2488. Like other joint-venture transplants, the company did not oppose union representation and the union was certified by card count in late 1988. The first collective bargaining agreement, signed in September of the following year, codified the plant's group-based production system and established a structure of shopfloor representation. As in Big Three plants, union members at Mitsubishi elect full-time representatives to district and plant-wide committees that monitor compliance with the contract and represent members in the grievance procedure. Unlike Big Three plants, however, the first collective bargaining agreement also recognized an additional level of union representatives called "line coordinators," each responsible for about 45 members in their immediate work area. Coordinators work at their regular plant jobs and cannot leave their work stations to represent members, but during breaks, lunch, and before or after work they serve as the first recourse for members seeking help. If the problem requires special attention, Coordinators pass it along to the appropriate union committee member. These full-time representatives —who answer to the union but are paid a regular wage by the company— try to settle disputes informally if possible, and by filing grievances when appropriate. Only about twenty grievances are filed per month.

The Japanese presence at Mitsubishi is manifested in the symbols and aesthetics of the facility. Employee life is bound by the rhetoric of work teams, quality in station, continuous improvement, and enterprise solidarity. As is typical in Japanese facilities, workers and managers wear the same uniform and eat in the same cafeteria. Also typical of Japanese-style management, terms like *Kaizen* are regularly used and workers are referred to as "associates." There is only one production worker classification and just two job classifications for skilled workers, compared to the dozens of specialized job classifications in a traditional Big Three plant. Work units are made up of approximately 15-20 workers and are called "groups," with line management the responsibility of a "group leader" (GL).

The contract at Mitsubishi focuses on labor and management's obligation to create and maintain a non-adversarial relationhship, but does little to set the precise terms of that relationship. Article I of the current contract lays the foundation for this objective:

> The Company and the Union pledge to maintain a genuine and unreserved spirit of cooperation between all parties concerned in order to achieve and promote harmonious labor relations. The bedrock of cooperation is respect and dignity for each person. To attain the highest degree of cooperation from all parties there must be unqualified trust in each other....[6]

The Company's responsibilities are understood to include:

> a safe work place, equitable wages and benefits and ... an environment based on the teamwork concept which establishes "Wa" or "harmony among people" in a non-adversarial environment that promotes mutual trust and respect.[7]

The Union's obligations include:

> long term cooperation in the recognition and commitment to the principal of flexibility that the Company must have to maintain and improve quality and efficiency, and to the implementation of work practices and flexible production systems.[8]

Thus, in the social organization of work at Mitsubishi Motors, concepts like trust, cooperation, flexibility and teamwork are said to be central to success. The company does have quality circles and Kaizen programs, both representing aspects of lean production which Womack, Jones and Roos see as guarantees of employee involvement and satisfaction. However, current research at Mitsubishi finds that these programs are actually the source of much worker discontent.

SURVEY METHODOLOGY AND A FRAMEWORK FOR ANALYSIS OF EMPLOYEE SATISFACTION

As part of an on-going research project examining employee attitudes about work at Mitsubishi Motors, I have surveyed the 3,500 member workforce and conducted interviews with selected union members and leaders. Combined with the 1989 survey conducted by Chapman, Elhance and Wenum,[9] this research provides the basis for examining the evolution of work at Mitsubishi Motors and defining what "lean production" has come to mean for workers

---

[6] MM-UAW Contract, Ratified August 27, 1995, 2

[7] Ibid., 3.

[8] Ibid., 3.

[9] Chapman et al., *Mitsubishi Motors in Illinois.*

at the Bloomington-Normal plant. Survey results and interviews were limited to bargaining unit employees since Mitsubishi Motors declined our requests to be involved in the project. This certainly limits my ability to address some questions; however, since the focus of the current study is employee satisfaction and not employer motive, the data is more than equal to the task at hand.

This research project was designed to provide both time series data and cross-sectional information. In other words, I wanted to look at both changes that have occurred at Mitsubishi Motors over time, and to be able to compare Mitsubishi Motors with other automakers in the U.S. and Canada. The research has been conducted in two phases. The first was a series of interviews with local union leadership and a select number of rank and file members. These interviews were focused on both issues of the technical organization of work and the social organization of production. Workers were asked about their involvement in quality circle programs and Kaizen projects. These one-on-one interviews were primarily intended to get a sense of how the productive process at Mitsubishi has changed over time. I interviewed approximately 20 individuals. The duration and depth of interviews varied depending on the individual's seniority in the plant, their role in the union, and their past experience with the quality circle program. The survey was essentially divided into three parts. The first replicated the survey done in 1989. The second included a variety of questions on work life that are also being asked of auto workers throughout Canada. The third focuses on issues that were prominent during the interview process, particularly quality circles and Kaizen. With the few exceptions noted below, the preliminary results reported in this chapter are taken from the first part of the 1997 survey.[10]

Because the primary focus of the current research is to replicate the previous study, we have used the same methodology for analysis. Workers were asked to rate their degree of satisfaction with a variety of workplace characteristics from 1 to 5, 1 being very negative and 5 very positive. Overall negative tabulations were made by combining "very negative" and "somewhat negative" responses. The same process was done for positive responses.

---

[10] The complete results from all three parts of the survey will be available by the spring of 1998. Those interested should contact the author at the Labor Education Service of the University of Minnesota, (617) 624-5020, or by e-mail: LJordan@csom.umn.edu.

The survey was sent to all bargaining unit employees. Our response rate was approximately 33 percent (or over 1000 respondents).

INTERVIEW AND SURVEY FINDINGS

When Diamond Star began operations in the spring of 1989, production and maintenance workers had reason to anticipate good things about their work. Throughout the hiring process, this anticipation was reinforced. As is typical in Japanese transplants, each employee was thoroughly screened for basic mechanical skills as well as their ability to work in a team. In reflecting on that period in the company, one production employee concluded, "I can't describe to you how proud I was to work in such a clean plant. I was told repeatedly during the first two weeks of orientation how special I was to be hired."[11] It was in the summer of that first year that Chapman, Elhance and Wenum surveyed a sample of employees for their opinion of the work environment at Mitsubishi, as summarized in Table 1.

Table 1
Diamond Star Motors, Worker Opinion, 1989*

Characteristic	Percent Negative	Percent Positive
DSM Wages	13.7	51.5
DSM Benefits	21.4	41.3
Working Environment	11.3	66.2
Supervisors	18.2	46.9
Managers	18.1	40.8
Asst. and Gen. Managers	14.1	43.8
Colleagues	3.0	74.2
Union Activity	37.0	21.0
Work Satisfaction	17.7	56.5
Pride at Work	8.5	79.3
Personal Growth	21.8	57.4
Promotion	38.1	30.4
DSM Products	5.6	87.8

*Percentages do not equal 100 because neutral responses are not included.

Source: Margaret Chapman, Arun Elhance and John Wenum, *Mitsubishi Motors in Illinois* (Westport: Quorum Books, 1995), 46

[11] Author interview with Mitsubishi employee, May 1997.

When set beside the research results reported by Chapman et al., the current interviews and survey results provide a provocative sketch of the evolution of lean work in this greenfield site. In the 1989 survey, workers were overwhelmingly positive about their experiences working at Diamond Star. Fully 66 percent of the respondents had a positive attitude about their work, nearly 50 percent had a positive attitude toward their supervisor, and 88 percent had a favorable impression of Mitsubishi's products. Eight years later, the same survey questions produced dramatically different results, as reported in Table 2. Interviews likewise revealed that employee attitudes had substantially changed in nearly every category evaluated in the earlier survey. Workers expressed frustration with what they perceived as poor quality parts, management's failure to follow through on promises, and a lack of voice in determining how work was done. Those characteristics like trust and cooperation that are seen to be the foundation of the social organization of work in lean production were viewed as nearly non existent.

A direct comparison of survey results is startling. While workers' satisfaction with their wages and benefits has increased significantly, in nearly every other area workers are less happy with their work lives. In 1989, nearly 50 percent of workers had a positive attitude about supervisors, but eight years later only 23 percent had a positive view of their group leader and just 4 percent had a positive view of mid- and upper-level management. On the other hand, attitudes towards union activity seemed to improve. By 1997, workers were less positive about promotion possibilities, pride in work, product quality, and personal growth.

When questioned about their evolving attitudes, employees focused on changes that had occurred at Mitsubishi over the course of the eight years. Workers who had been at the facility since it opened noted that they initially felt the company cared about their welfare. In the beginning, they had daily exercises and group meetings. On the line, they had full job rotations and the cycle times for completing their tasks seemed reasonable. However, according to several of the workers interviewed, as the company needed to increase production, much of this practice was discarded. One worker explained, "I started out driving a fork lift. Four years later, once I got on the assembly line I learned about the over-cycled jobs, parts that wouldn't fit, bad rotations and plain poor quality." Other workers said that it wasn't just that the company had changed, but that their positive expectations were never fulfilled. They had come into the company with high hopes —"that this manufacturing job would be different, better," as one put it— but the reality fell short of these expectations.

Table 2[12]
Diamond Star Motors, Worker Opinion, 1997* (1989)

Characteristic	Percent Negative	Percent Positive
DSM Wages	2 (13.7)	92 (51.5)
DSM Benefits	6 (21.4)	89 (41.3)
Working Environment	40 (11.3)	23 (66.2)
Supervisors**	49 (18.2)	23 (46.9)
Managers**	66 (18.1)	4 (40.8)
Asst. and Gen. Managers**	57 (14.1)	4 (43.8)
Colleagues	17 (3.0)	40 (74.2)
Union Activity	19 (37.0)	17 (21.0)
Union District Rep.***	19	38
Union Contract***	36	19
Work Satisfaction	38 (17.7)	38 (56.5)
Pride at Work	30 (8.5)	53 (79.3)
Personal Growth	38 (21.8)	26 (57.4)
Promotion	60 (38.1)	6 (30.4)
Quality Circles***	62	11
Kaizen***	72	9
DSM Products	9 (5.6)	55 (87.8)

* Percentages do not equal 100 because neutral responses are not included.
** These titles were used by Chapman et al. in the 1989 survey, but they are not used at Mitsubishi. To replicate the 1989 survey I defined each as follows in the 1997 survey: supervisors = group leaders; managers = upper management, such as the head of human resources and the head of employee relations; Asst. and Gen. managers = branch [area] managers.

*** Question only appeared on the 1997 survey

[12] Due to time constraints, 1997 results are based on a sample of the survey data collected and should be understood as preliminary. See footnote 10.

In our conversations with employees at Mitsubishi, there was frequent reference to the early promises of worker empowerment and the subsequent lack of genuine worker voice. Some 60 percent of the workers interviewed saw the selection process as the source of disappointment in this and other matters. The company's selection process continues to be an intensive procedure with several days of screening and testing before an individual is hired. During the process, the company continues to emphasize the involvement of employees in decision making and the role of "Kaizen" in the functioning of the plant. Workers at the facility indicated that the company hires a highly educated work force; indeed, many of the workers have college degrees. Workers explain that the company tells new hires that they will be asked for their input, but then, contrary to this promise, treats them as "beasts of burden." One worker who had held several factory jobs previous to coming to Mitsubishi summed up the situation in particularly blunt terms. "If you hire some dumb shit who is used to being a grunt, he'll come to work, work hard, take the paycheck and leave. But if you hire the folks the company seems to focus on, they're always on their way to a better job; and if not, they actually come in expecting the company to listen to them. They get real disappointed."[13]

Survey results reinforce these sorts of comments. Overall, workers seem frustrated with the rhetoric of empowerment in an environment they see as offering no real power. Sixty-two percent had a negative attitude about quality circles and 72 percent had a negative impression of Kaizen. When asked more specifically about these programs, 70 percent said you can never trust management and 80 percent said quality circles only benefit management.[14] Quality circles that were originally set up in the plant are currently fully functioning in only a couple of areas. In interviews and in survey comments, workers said they opted out because either the group leader was taking their ideas and relaying them upwards as his/her own, or because they felt favoritism was given to friends of the GL in determining who was assigned overtime for quality-circle activities —a way for "suck-ups to get some overtime."

---

[13] Interview with employee, May 1997.

[14] These preliminary findings are from the second and third part of the 1997 survey. See footnote 10.

In open-ended questioning on quality circles and Kaizen, workers often spoke of the broken promises that undermined their trust in management. One surveyed employee, to underline the point, provided a copy of a letter written by a group leader to upper management. In the letter, the GL described how his group had "Kaizened" their operation and rebalanced jobs to free a person who could serve as an utility worker, available to help other group members when needed. Based on the prospect that the utility worker could help trouble-shoot problems and provide spot relief, the workers increased their own work speed to support the new off-line position. Only three days later, the utility worker was removed from the area and transferred to another group. The group leader's impassioned letter of complaint to his superiors on this score stated that such behavior reduced the associates' willingness to participate in these projects.[15] This group leader was seen as a hero on the shopfloor, but many expressed the fear that he might suffer management reprisal. Incidents like this were repeatedly noted by workers, and seem to have significantly contributed to their negative attitudes. In cases where workers still participate in quality circles and group work, it seems to occur largely because of the trust between a particular GL and his or her group.

Moreover, "Kaizen" and quality circle projects have lost much of their daily relevance to continuous improvement of operations. The company continues to encourage quality circle presentations of new ideas, but these are now driven by a competitive imperative, with circles competing in company- and then national-level contests for a trip to Japan. Because the focus was turned to competition, smaller suggestions are often overlooked and the primacy of *continuous* improvement is lost. The company has recently undertaken an effort to encourage smaller projects, but is having little success.

Worker involvement has also been discouraged in a variety of other ways. While they still technically have the right to do so, workers have been discouraged from using their stop buttons to address quality problems through both formal and informal discipline. As a result, many employees felt that poor quality is being built into the vehicles they manufacture.

When surveyed about work pace and intensity, nearly 60 percent said that most of the time they have to work as fast as they can just to keep up, and 80 percent said they feel they have no control over their work.[16]

---

[15] Author interviews and letter addressed to general manager.

[16] These preliminary findings are from the second and third part of the 1997 survey. See footnote 10.

Employee interviews also revealed that the structure of the group served as a focus of discontent. While smaller "teams" exist in some areas to work on quality circle projects, the primary focus of operation is really the group, with upwards of 20 members. As members of management, group leaders chair meetings, assign work, and determine rotations. The exact nature of the relationship between the group leader and the group is determined more by the personality of the GL than by the general culture of the facility. Under the terms of the most recent contract, each group could also have an elected "team" leader who would be a bargaining unit member. The presence of a team leader is at the discretion of management, however, and the company has not exercised this option. Even if such a position existed, it is not clear what the role of the individual would be. As group members, the employees have no real voice other than through traditional union channels. In an interview, one employee told me that when he made suggestions about how to improve production, he was told by a group leader to "take your $20 an hour and shut up."

Unlike the lean production environments at Wayne Stamping and NUMMI,[17] workers at Mitsubishi have little input into designing or managing the productive process. While the facility continues to be lean in terms of technical organization and work intensity, it has little of the worker empowerment often associated with lean production,[18] and management practices seem to follow the top-down prescriptions of a traditional Taylorist model.

CONCLUSION

Survey results and interviews with employees of Mitsubishi Motors from August, 1996, through May, 1997, revealed a workforce severely disappointed in the quality of work life at Mitsubishi. This finding was in stark contrast to the attitudinal survey conducted in 1989. The question remains whether or not such an evolution in social organization and employee attitudes is inevitable. While preliminary, our analysis finds striking similarities with one key aspect of the CAMI study: as workers have more experience in a lean production environment, their positive estimations of the environment

[17] See footnote 1.

[18] Womack et al., *The Machine that Changed the World.*

decline. Based on our research, it appears that Mitsubishi maintained the technical organization of lean production and the rhetoric of employee involvement, but according to workers, the social organization of production lacks any real sense of *employee empowerment.* While Mitsubishi seems to operate in a lean way, it is largely devoid of the kind of positive features that lean production is said to entail for workers.

THE INTRODUCTION OF TEAM PROGRAMS AND COMPETITIVE MANUFACTURING AT GM LORDSTOWN: AN HISTORICAL PERSPECTIVE

John Russo[*]

INTRODUCTION

Since the plant's opening in 1966, labor-management relations at the GM complex in Lordstown, Ohio, have been marked by a singularly high level of conflict and controversy. Indeed, the public commentary and academic analysis that have followed events at Lordstown have shaped current theories of industrial sociology, anthropology, and labor relations. Specifically, the plant's 1972 strike was perhaps the most studied labor-management conflict in modern labor history, becoming a metaphor for an entire generation's socio-political struggle, and serving as a starting point for an attack on Taylorism and technological determinism.[1] So intense was the industrial conflict at Lordstown in the early 1970s that observers coined the term the "Lordstown Syndrome" to describe the varied worker responses to despotic management and repetitive, fragmented, and alienated work.[2]

In no small way, the conflict at Lordstown became the genesis for the reconsideration of adversarialism and the rethinking of personnel policy and labor relations in the United States during the 1970s. Especially in the auto industry, this rethinking of labor relations, together with growing competitive

---

[*] Director, Labor Studies Program, Youngstown State University.

[1] Stanley Aronowitz, *False Promises: The Shaping of the American Working-Class Consciousness* (New York: McGraw-Hill, 1973); Barbara Garson, *All the Livelong Day: The Meaning and Demeaning of Work* (Garden City, NY: Doubleday, 1975); David Moberg, "Rattling the Golden Chains: Conflict and Consciousness in Auto Work," Ph.D. diss., University of Chicago, 1978); John Russo, "The 1972 Lordstown Strike," in *Labor Conflict in the United States: An Encyclopedia* (New York: Garland Publishing, 1990); B.J. Widdick, ed., *Autowork and its Discontents* (Baltimore: Johns Hopkins University Press, 1976.)

[2] *Work in America. Report of the Taskforce to the Secretary of Health Education and Welfare* (Cambridge, MA: MIT Press, 1973).

pressures, led to early discussions between UAW officials and U.S. automakers which ultimately resulted in the development of Quality-of-Work-Life (QWL) programs, the Memorandum of Understanding in the 1973 GM-UAW Agreement, and various employee participation programs throughout the automotive industry.

Yet, at Lordstown itself, the introduction of "jointness" programs involving teams and lean manufacturing concepts was slow in gaining a measure of acceptance. To a large extent, this was a result of the plant's history of contentious labor relations, combined with the volatility of high-volume, small-car production and the perpetual crisis atmosphere this volatility has engendered.[3]

GM LORDSTOWN

The GM assembly complex at Lordstown is located 12 miles from Youngstown in Northeast Ohio. When it opened in March, 1966, it was characterized as the most technologically advanced plant in the GM Assembly Division (GMAD). Within five years, GM had expanded the complex to include both van and fabricating plants. Two UAW locals were chosen to represent the workers in the 1960s: UAW Local 1112 in the car and van assembly plants, and UAW Local 1714 in the smaller fabricating plant.

Following the 1972 "speed-up" strike, labor and management began to work more closely in the mid-1970s. The major concern for the two parties was to overcome Lordstown's image as a plant composed of "Gestapo" supervision (GMAD) and modern-day Luddites (autoworkers) who were producing an automobile (the Vega) which was known in trade journals for its molting parts. The local union leadership, under Marlin "Whitey" Ford, began making joint appearances with management at dealerships and at corporate headquarters to discuss quality issues. While not exactly détente, labor and management at Lordstown seemed to be making headway in establish-

[3] Given the complexity and sensitivity surrounding the issue of employee participation at the Lordstown plant, it was necessary to promise anonymity to all those who were interviewed either formally or informally. I would like to thank Jack Roberts and Ed Jones from General Motors and Bill Bowers and Al Alli from UAW Local 1112 for their time, assistance and cooperation in helping me research the period between 1987 and 1990. The results of this research was presented as a paper, "To Be or Not to Be: Semi-Autonomous Work Groups at GM Lordstown," at the Joint Conference of the University and College Labor Education Association and the AFL-CIO Education Department, April, 1990, in Nashville, Tennessee. For the research from 1990 to the present, I would like to thank Al Alli and Jim Basso from UAW Local 1112, and Tom Will, John Cordero, and Herman Maass from General Motors.

ing a better working relationship. In fact, the Lordstown complex was the first to reach a local agreement in the 1976 negotiations. In 1980-1981, labor and management were successful in gaining J-car production for the Lordstown complex. This was considered a major coup for Lordstown since the production of the J-car was central to GM's plan to recapture part of the compact car market from Japanese automakers.

But unlike other union locals at GM assembly plants, the UAW locals at Lordstown did not "buy into" the Quality-of-Work-Life programs that the company began to experiment with in the late 1970s. This was somewhat ironic, since QWL programs were jointly promoted by GM's top management and the UAW's national leaders (especially Vice President Irving Bluestone) as a collaborative effort to combat the very fragmentation, boredom, and alienation of assembly-line work that the 1972 Lordstown strike had highlighted. Yet at Lordstown, QWL's prescription for off-line meetings to discuss issues of work environment and group dynamics did not win membership support. In fact, Whitey Ford lost his presidency because of his support of QWL and of the concessionary National GM-UAW Agreement in 1982. According to local autoworkers, union members felt the program was a ruse and were skeptical of the sincerity of local management. They believed that while QWL programs might superficially improve working conditions, the programs were management-dominated and often undermined local union leadership. Consequently, local union members voted overwhelmingly against the introduction of formal QWL programs at Lordstown in 1982 and 1984, blocking their implementation. In these same years, the UAW Locals at Lordstown were at the forefront of the fight against concessions, voting against the national contracts of 1982 and 1984.[4]

The mid-1980s brought a "new era of labor relations" to the Lordstown complex as the members' fabled militancy was tempered by local economic conditions and the harsh competitive realities of the automobile industry. In the Youngstown-Warren region surrounding the plant, double-digit unemployment was a fact of life during the 1980s.[5] In fact, during the late 1970s and 1980s, the Youngstown-Warren area frequently led the nation with an unemployment rate which at times approached 25 percent as a result of its well known steel mill closings. GM's troubles now further destabilized the

---

[4] John Russo, "No Mood for Concessions: UAW Local 1112 Lordstown," *The Nation* (3 July 1982).

[5] Ohio Bureau of Employment Statistics, *1990 Annual Report* (Columbus, OH., 1991).

region's economy as the company began to feel the effects of international competition in the American market. In 1965, three companies had dominated the American market, but by 1985 over 20 companies vied for market share. In 1982, the combined impact of international competition and the Reagan recession led to layoffs of 125,000 GM employees nationwide. In the Youngstown-Warren area, there were major layoffs at Lordstown (the entire second shift), Packard Electric, and the 900 automotive jobbers within the area. The cumulative effects of unemployment and the decline of the American auto industry caused UAW locals at Lordstown to begrudgingly consider making the types of accommodations that were occurring at other GM plants.

REOPENING THE LOCAL AGREEMENT

In the mid-1980s, local leaders had to accept QWL despite the members' lingering distrust. There were at least three reasons for this. First, as demand for the J-car fell to 647,000 units in 1985, GM demanded the reopening of local agreements at the three plants —Lordstown, Janesville (Wisconsin) and Leeds (Missouri)— producing the model. In a context where the company had just announced four major plant closings, and with the three J-car plants now operating 75,000 units below capacity, GM's stated preference for plants willing to introduce "new concepts" to improve operations put Lordstown at risk of losing its second shift (about 3,000 jobs).[6] Furthermore, projected declines in J-car demand meant that the long-term consequences of not introducing new concepts was a total plant shutdown of J-car production in at least one plant. Since the competition to avoid such a fate, called "whipsawing" in union circles, was not prevented by the UAW International, Local 1112 felt compelled to reopen its local agreement and discuss the implementation of QWL at Lordstown.

Second, QWL programs at other plants had resulted in substantive improvements in working conditions, positive attitudes, and identification with corporate and union goals.[7] According to local union leaders, "We felt that we could enjoy the benefits of participation programs if we controlled the

[6] John Russo, "Saturn's Rings: What GM's Saturn Project is All About," *Labor Research Review* (fall 1986).

[7] The reported changes in attitudes may have been the result of the so-called "program effect." That is, no matter how superficial, many autoworkers perceived benefits from involvement in QWL programs. See Anil Verma, "Joint Participation Programs: Self-help or Suicide for Labor," *Industrial Relations* 28, no. 3 (fall 1989): 401-410.

process." At the same time, there was evidence that the unfavorable outcomes of participation programs for unions were due, in part, to lack of involvement by the union.[8] Local union leaders also understood instinctively that involvement programs were potentially empowering if the company was serious about providing information systematically to the union.

Third, management began to encourage bimonthly off-site meetings with local union leadership in late 1984 and 1985. In part, the purpose was to develop a closer working relationship with local union officials and to begin sharing information. Furthermore, a new plant manager had invited local UAW leadership to attend formal management production meetings. As a result of the meetings, the union appointed several autoworkers to begin training as QWL facilitators in 1985.

The following year, autoworkers at Lordstown reopened their local contract and incorporated several major changes, including an agreement to participate in employee involvement programs. These programs would include greater access to information, formal union participation in decision making, and the voluntary participation by assembly line workers in off-site training and shopfloor participation programs. The local leadership also agreed to changes in work rules that included elimination of the classification for inspectors. This resulted in the loss of 500 jobs, as each autoworker now became responsible for quality inspections and marking the production cards. Lastly, autoworkers were asked to learn seven jobs in their work area as part of a pay-for-knowledge program. Everyone who volunteered to participate in the program received an additional stipend. While additional pay was received, the autoworkers received little, if any, additional skill training or added job duties. That is, the pay-for-knowledge program functioned largely as a bonus payment.

Because of the changes in the local agreement, Lordstown retained its second shift and gained an edge in the fight for future J-car production. In turn, this led to limited shutdowns of J-car production at Janesville and sounded the death knell for J-car production at the Leeds plant. As a result, employee involvement programs became very closely associated with concessionary bargaining and layoffs in the minds of many autoworkers.

---

[8] Anil Verma and R.B. McKersie, "Employee Involvement: The Implications of Noninvolvement for Unions," *Industrial and Labor Relations Review* XL (July 1987): 556-568.

WORKER PARTICIPATION COMES TO LORDSTOWN

In early 1987, there were over 12,000 hourly and salaried employees at the Lordstown complex that produced J-cars (Chevrolet Cavaliers and Pontiac Sunbirds), full-size Chevrolet and GMC vans, and various fabricated parts for many GM plants. In addition, there were over 900 automotive jobbers within a 60 mile radius providing a variety of parts and services for Lordstown. Obviously, the Lordstown complex and associated jobbers were central to the viability of economically-strapped Northeast Ohio.

Given their past rejection of involvement programs, local union leaders at Lordstown feared a backlash if traditional terminology associated with QWL or Quality Circles was used. Consequently, autoworkers at Lordstown coined their own terminology for involvement programs, such as People Involvement Programs, Employee Participation Groups, and Discovery Teams. The change in names made it possible to deny involvement in those programs that may have been discredited in the past both locally and nationally. However, the use of varied names would ultimately add to the confusion among autoworkers over the purpose, direction, and responsibilities of union and management in the worker participation program.

The first step in the evolution of these programs was the identification and training of union representatives. The shop committee appointed local union members to be coordinators, many of them utility workers (higher seniority employees who covered for absentees and spot relief). The coordinators were taken offsite —often to the UAW education center in Black Lake, Michigan, or Detroit— to receive training. The second step was a massive training program for all employees. Individual "intact work groups" or "Employee Participation Groups" (EPG) from both shifts were taken off-site for formal educational training. These groups were composed of 15 to 20 individuals who would become the foundation of semi-autonomous work groups at Lordstown. The training program was voluntary and focused on group dynamics and basic awareness issues. The formal programs included instruction in communication skills, conflict resolution, principled negotiations, organizational behavior, and participative management. The basic awareness issues focused on the state of the auto industry and the recognition of a common ground between labor and management in an attempt to change the work culture at the plant. While jointly taught by labor and management, the programmatic designs and instructional materials were provided largely by management or its consultants.

From a management standpoint, a key concern was the many supervisors and middle-management employees who expressed both skepticism and hostility toward the training programs. Some did not believe in the program and continued to hold an adversarial philosophy. Others simply feared for their jobs and a loss of power at the worksite. Most reluctantly "went along" since GM headquarters had pushed the program and "put-up" enormous resources to fund the training.

Only a few autoworkers refused to participate in the voluntary training program. The reasons for the high level of participation were varied —from a commitment to the process, to simple curiosity, to a week away from the plant. Most autoworkers felt the programs were informative and "gave me time to think and contemplate." For others, it was a catharsis as they "spilled their guts" about their work lives at Lordstown. There were also challenges to both the programmatic content of the training and the "real" motivation of management. Most criticism was dealt with indirectly by admitting past labor and management mistakes and by stressing the need for "jointness" in the face of international competition, that is, by invoking a siege mentality. However, in several instances, individuals who were especially critical were asked to leave for disruptive behavior.

Overall, most autoworkers believed the programs were educational and not an overt threat to the union. In fact, many felt that the union's presence gave the program credibility and enhanced the union's prestige. Yet, other autoworkers expressed an uneasiness with the process and detected a subtle detachment by autoworkers from their union as a result of the program. In fact, some autoworkers felt that the work group activities highlighted in the training could result in real gains that could not be achieved by the union. This was especially true since many autoworkers believed that the grievance procedure was no longer an effective mechanism to settle disputes or to make changes in the work environment.[9] Put differently, to some autoworkers at Lordstown, work groups were seen as an alternative to the union.

In 1987 and 1988 as the training programs were completed, the Employee Participation Groups returned to the plant and began bi-monthly meetings.

---

[9] For example, it was not uncommon to have 3,000 to 8,000 grievances on file at Lordstown at any one time. Yet, very few cases ever went to arbitration —less than five in the decade of 1980s. Most were simply "horse traded" —trading good grievances for bad— which had the effect of undermining the grievance process.

EPG meetings were voluntary, semi-autonomous, and scheduled on company time. At first, the union closely monitored the meetings, fearing that work groups might abuse or infringe upon the collective bargaining agreement. EPG meetings focused on environmental concerns and quality issues using problem-solving methods learned during the training program, and incremental improvements in the environment and in maintenance practices did help improve working conditions. But the work groups frequently had concerns which had contractual or economic implications that were beyond their sphere of authority to implement. As a result, the program was temporarily stopped, only to be started again at a later time. This stopping and restarting process occurred a number of times in 1988. The result was a decision to have structured and fixed agendas for the EPG meetings.

However, the structured agenda caused problems as autoworkers and management had different priorities for the work group meetings. Autoworkers had more safety concerns and wanted better tools which would make their job easier; management, on the other hand, wanted to use the meetings for "propaganda purposes" (competition and the Japanese threat) and to criticize productivity, quality, and, indirectly, workers and the union. Soon, the work groups became disenchanted and attendance started to decline at meetings. As a result, the actual existence of functioning work groups and autoworker participation in any particular area became uneven. Even where union coordinators and management held the meetings and were committed to the program, attendance and participation were weak, at best.

To make matters worse, GM scheduled increased overtime. This amounted to regularly working 54-hour weeks in the assembly plant and over 60-hour weeks in the fabricating plant. When there were attempts to hold work group meetings at 5:00 a.m. before the day shift, few individuals came despite being paid time and one-half. Ultimately, the heavy overtime led to resentment, increased levels of absenteeism, worker compensation claims, and reduced quality audits. In turn, overtime, absenteeism, and quality control became the focus of work group meetings. Since work groups had little input into production scheduling, the key issue —excessive overtime— was not resolved. Yet, management continued to carp over the absenteeism and worker compensation claims that rose with the overtime hours.

While the shopfloor program was floundering, mid-level labor-management participation programs were temporarily more successful. The focus of these programs was union representation in decision-making on a series of issues concerning work reform, technology, supplier and customer needs, and quality. The most notable example was the development of the Discovery Process and Teams in late 1988. Discovery Teams were special-purpose groups composed of jointly chosen autoworkers and plant supervisors who were responsible for evaluating the organization and techniques of production and making recommendations for improving productivity and quality. More specifically, Discovery Teams studied material handling, preventive maintenance, tooling, and subcontracting, and evaluated their impact on product quality. The teams had authority to implement minor changes, but major recommendations that were costly or that could not be implemented easily became a "task force issue" for upper-level Discovery Teams or for GM's Simultaneous Engineering Program (SEP). As such, Discovery Teams functioned as kaizen or continuous improvement groups.[10]

However, as with EPGs, participation on Discovery Teams was mixed and little was actually accomplished for many of the same reasons mentioned earlier. In addition, utility workers and individuals who were in the job bank (a pool of excess workers who could be temporarily assigned to special projects or training) left the Discovery Teams when they were returned to production work to cover for the growing absenteeism. Consequently, a point was reached where the Discovery program ceased to function because no one was available.

THE RENEWED THREAT OF LOSING THE J-CAR

Throughout 1989, GM constantly reminded autoworkers at Lordstown of its decision to consolidate J-car production by the fall of 1990 and to discontinue the then current J-car model at the close of the 1993 model year. Beyond 1993, the Lordstown plant did not have a scheduled 1994 replacement model, even though a new 1994 J-car was to be introduced. While the threat of a plant closing within the next five years was real and Lordstown workers could not assume that GM would continue to build the J-car in the future,

[10] The Discovery Team concept also became synonymous with GM's "Quality Network," an overarching joint labor-management process that defines how GM is going to do business and whose basic goal is to involve all GM employees in a widening collaboration. SEP consists of largely salaried employees whose major concerns were the development of new parts, packaging and product design.

most industry analysis suggested "it's theirs to lose." At the same time, rumors began to circulate that GM's full-size van production would be consolidated and that the van plant would be closed at Lordstown. When Local 1112 officials and reporters asked GM about the rumors, the company described the hearsay as "insignificant."

With high absenteeism, declining quality, the disarray in the shopfloor participation program, and the uncertain future for J-car and van production, Local 1112's leadership decided to reopen the contract in the fall of 1989 for the purpose of considering changes in absentee policy, manning, and the full-scale implementation of semi-autonomous work groups. Meetings were scheduled for October 12 that would include union staff and corporate officials from Detroit. However, several hours before the scheduled meeting, word leaked from a GM Leadership Conference of top management officials in Traverse City, Michigan, that GM would build the 1992 Camero and Firebird at its Ste. Therese, Quebec, plant and that it would shift van production from Lordstown and Scarborough, Ontario, to GM's Truck and Bus assembly plant in Flint. The placement of the Camero-Firebird at the Ste. Therese plant, where the Canadian Government gave GM a $220 million interest-free loan to construct a new paint shop, meant that other GM assembly plants producing these cars (Pontiac, Oklahoma City, and Van Nuys) became candidates for plant closings and potential bidders for the 1994 J-car model. Specifically for Local 1112, the shifting of van production would result in the loss of 2,500 jobs at the Lordstown plant and would cost the already devastated Youngstown-Warren area another $100 million annually in lost manufacturing wages.

The announcement sent shock waves through the plant and local community. After all the talk about participation and information-sharing, Local 1112 leadership felt that they were blind-sided by GM. Even local GM management and their corporate liaisons in Detroit complained that there had been no warning about the impending closing of the van plant. The UAW International leadership was equally miffed at GM. Three days before the announcement, the UAW had held a meeting with over 100 local union officers to consider the expansion of team concept programs. Since the International union was a strong advocate of team concept and its stress on cooperation, UAW leaders felt betrayed and undermined. Stephen Yokich, UAW vice president at the time, said that the hasty announcement "suggests not only disarray but flagrant insensitivity and disregard for UAW represented GM workers who are meeting the challenge of boosting GM's quality and productivity." Furthermore, the closings cost both the UAW and GM additional credibility because of the assurances in 1987 negotiations that autoworker jobs would be safe if they cooperated with the company. In turn, the loss of credibility was sure to destabilize the climate for the upcoming GM-UAW national negotiations in 1990.

Needless to say, the October 12 meeting at Lordstown was short and heated. It would be impossible for Local 1112 to reopen the contract and receive a positive vote on any local agreement given the climate. Pending an investigation and assurances surrounding the actual timing of the van plant closing, Local 1112 postponed the reopening of the local contract negotiations until November. The purpose was to ascertain the actual van plant shutdown schedule and J-car production needs through 1994 so that any negotiation would include the reassignment of van plant employees to the J-car assembly plant.

On November 7, 1989, Local 1112 reopened its local agreement. GM told Local 1112 that the Lordstown plant must increase production to 425,000 vehicles by 1991 when all J-car production would be transferred to the Lordstown plant. That is, autoworkers at Lordstown would have to almost double 1988 production if they were to keep the J-car and win production of the 1994 version. To do this, GM management suggested increased line speed, reintroduction of tag relief (individual members taking breaks rather than "mass relief"), and a new system of production scheduling based on two ten-hour shifts a day, six days a week, with a third crew hired to cover the extra hours. The local agreed to these provisions, in part because tag relief and the three-crew schedule would create employment for the displaced van plant workers. Moreover, tag relief would be central to the conceptualization of intact work groups at Lordstown. That is, new work group would have 8 to 15 members with one worker filling a relief position; should someone be absent, the tag-relief worker would function as absentee relief for the group. At the same time, many supervisors believed that they would be eliminated or forced to return to the shop floor as production workers in the tag-relief positions.

To briefly summarize, after five years of formal and informal activities between labor and management at the Lordstown complex, work teams and special purpose teams were in place, but were largely inactive. As such, they functioned as an overlay for labor-management discussions about jointness and competitiveness, but lacked substance in actual practice. Despite these failings of the participatory programs, the labor-management meetings, information sharing, training, and limited team activities had improved the working conditions for production workers. In fact, everyone interviewed felt that Lordstown was a better place to work because of the worker participation program.

Yet, the overall support for worker participation programs and the introduction of teams was fragile. Often negotiated in times of crisis when job losses were imminent, and frequently overwhelmed in practice by the needs of production, the autoworkers at Lordstown remained ambivalent about the nature of work team activity and wondered openly if it was but a pretext for additional speed-ups or layoffs. To be sure, the situation was problematic and the ultimate acceptance of participatory programs at Lordstown remained very much in doubt.

FROM 1990 TO THE FALL, 1995

In the early 1990s as J-Car production was phased out at Janesville and Leeds, autoworkers at Lordstown faced steadily expanding work hours. To complicate matters, GM's market projections proved faulty and there was a sudden surge in demand for the J-car. Workers appreciated the dramatic boost in earnings as a result of overtime work, but the long hours —often ten- and twelve-hour shifts, six days a week— took its toll on what was an increasingly aging workforce at Lordstown.

As for the team programs, they were simply overwhelmed by the production schedule. The need to produce 400,000 vehicles overshadowed any commitment to team programs. Even when management offered time-and-a-half overtime wages if workers would come in for team meetings an hour before their shift began, there were few takers. Put simply, people rejected the incentive and preferred the rest time. Further, many autoworkers indicated this was additional evidence of GM's weak commitment to employee participation, which would always be seen as secondary to production demands.

While GM Lordstown was struggling to meet customer demand, GM began production of J-cars in Ramos Arizpe, Mexico, in 1990. To reassure Lordstown workers that Mexican production was not a threat to their job security, the J-cars produced at the Ramos plant were initially targeted for the Mexican and Canadian market. But the implications of J-car production in Mexico were not lost on the autoworkers at Lordstown. GM had not been successful in building a profitable small car in the United States. Even after seven years, its highly-touted and successful Saturn project had not become profitable. Further, the success of Ford Escort production in Hermosillo suggested that the future of profitable small car production lay in Mexico.

With the staggering workload, the Mexican threat, and a general dissatisfaction with the UAW International's handling of restructuring throughout GM, autoworkers at Lordstown felt compelled, as in the 1970s, to take action on their own. In late August, 1992, 2,400 autoworkers at the Fab Plant engaged in a nine day strike that eventually shut down six assembly plants and idled more than 40,000 autoworkers nationwide. Termed by the *Wall Street Journal* as "The Showdown at Lordstown," the main issue was GM's attempt to close the die shop at Lordstown and subcontract the work to a non-GM supplier.[11] While it was able only to postpone for two years GM's timetable for closing the die shop, the strike and its widening impact on GM's operations demonstrated that autoworkers could shackle the company's restructuring efforts. In this respect, the Lordstown strike became a model for other UAW-GM locals in fabricating facilities. Furthermore, the strike at the Fab plant helped avert a similar strike at the Lordstown assembly plant over its local agreement. The assembly plant agreement included guarantees for no reduction in volume unless the output in Lordstown exceeded the demand for J-cars in the U.S. and Canada, and agreement that cars produced in Mexico could only be sold in Canada if Lordstown was operating at full capacity.[12]

Following the 1992 strike, there was a strange quiet at the Lordstown plant. Production continued at high rates as the J-car continued to be GM's best selling model and the nation's fourth largest in 1993. In 1994, as so often happens in the year prior to a changeover to a new model sales, sales volume dropped and production became much less arduous. As some autoworkers observed, it was the first time in years that "I had a life." At the same time, there was a sense of anticipation and apprehension based, in part, on past experiences over what it would be like to produce the new J-car using team processes and lean manufacturing methods.

---

[11] Joseph B. White and Neal Templin, "Harsh Regimen: A Swollen GM Finds How Hard It Is To Stick With Its Crash Diet," *The Wall Street Journal*, 9 Sept. 1992, 1.

[12] Doron P. Levin, "Autoworkers End Walkout Against GM," *The New York Times*, 6 Sept. 1997, 1; Warren Davis, "What was behind the Lordstown strike," *The Vindicator* (Youngstown, Ohio), 17 Sept. 1992, A11.

COMPETITIVE MANUFACTURING AND 1995 J-CAR

The introduction of the new J-car at Lordstown required an overhaul of the production system as GM sought to build a profitable, low-cost, high-volume small car using modern design and manufacturing methods.[13] The new J-car was engineered using design-for-manufacturing methods to improve manufacturability and simplify production by reducing the number of parts. The new design also permitted the installation of a Robotgate system and the expansion of robots from 50 to 200. Overall, GM predicted that the design and engineering changes alone would reduce the build-time in man-hours by 30 percent.

Further, it was GM's intention to build the new generation J-car at Lordstown using a lean production system that had been patterned after the joint GM-Toyota (NUMMI) plant in Freemont, California. At Lordstown, this system was coined "competitive manufacturing." As with many lean production systems, competitive manufacturing involved the expansion of just-in-time systems, worker training, continuous improvement, quality at the source, online teams and flexible job classifications, and the reduction of supervisory and labor relations functions. Specifically, the plant was reengineered to minimize in-process buffering, to take advantage of the J-car's design simplification, and to introduce such work-flow monitoring techniques as Andon boards. The result was a significant reduction in the number of employees needed to produce the new J-car. Of 2,400 redundant workers, 750 were moved either to the stamping plant, loaned to the nearby supplier, Lear Seating, or transferred to other facilities. The remainder took early retirement.

However, GM immediately had trouble launching the new car. The problems were varied. Some related to poor planning and inadequate time allotted to debugging systems involving new dies. Others stemmed from poor engineering and communications between the Lansing Assembly Division and engineers at the Lordstown plant. The startup problems resulted in frequent line shutdowns and additional retooling in both the body shop and assembly line. Lastly, as has often occurred, GM had difficulty getting the new levels of tech-

[13] For a full discussion of the beginnings of new J-car production see Tim Keenan and David Smith, "What Went Wrong at Lordstown?: The Story Behind GM's Costly '95 J-Car Launch," *Wards Auto World*, April 1996.

nology and manning balanced correctly.[14] That is, GM has had a tendency to err too much on the technology side while manning at minimal levels.

The result was that production levels of the J-car through 1995 and 1996 were far below estimates. GM had predicted that, with the changes in design, engineering, technology, manning and three-crew work schedules, it could produce 1,600 cars per day. Yet, six months (February 1996) after the launch, GM was producing only 677 cars daily. After a year (August 1996), it was only producing 1,000 cars daily. Only in 1997 did Lordstown's daily production approach 1,400 cars, still 200 cars below original estimates.[15]

To make matters worse, in the midst of this debacle GM fired the UAW shop chairman at Lordstown in April, 1996, allegedly for not properly clocking into and out of the plant. (It is important to note that at other GM facilities there are few restrictions on the time and movement of shop chairmen.) The firing was seen by the Lordstown autoworkers as an act of provocation in anticipation of the 1996 GM-UAW national negotiations, and as retribution for the shop chairman's remarks during the 17-day Dayton strike in March, 1996, that "Lordstown could be next." Whatever the merits of the dispute, the firing resulted in a wildcat strike. After two days, a federal judge issued a temporary restraining order that forced employees back to work, and several weeks later the dispute was settled informally with the chairman's reinstatement.[16]

With the J-car production far behind schedule and with labor-management relations deteriorating, GM decided it was time to make a change in management at Lordstown. In August, 1996, Herman Maass arrived as the new plant manager. Previously, Maass had worked at Lordstown during the "war years" from 1966 through 1986. He left Lordstown in 1986 to become production manager at GM's Buick City Assembly Center in Flint, Michigan, serving there five years before moving to the Saturn plant in Tennessee, where he served as plant manager at the body systems plant until 1996. These two moves had profoundly changed Maass' ideas about manufacturing and labor relations. Buick City was one of the first GM facilities to embrace the team concept. Here, Maass had learned the difficulties of getting

---

[14] A good example is the GM Poletown plant in Detroit that, despite being technological advanced, was troubled by poor quality, production mishaps and marginal productivity gains.

[15] By way of reference, during the same period it took Ford only six weeks to ramp-up its redesigned Taurus to full production.

[16] Sandra Livingston, "Judge orders Lordstown workers back," *The Plain Dealer*, 17 April 1996, C1.

people, especially middle managers, to embrace team concept principles, and the need for the plant manager to become directly involved in developing mature concepts of problem-solving. While at Buick City, Maass gained notoriety as being one of the first plant managers at GM to shut down an assembly line for a half-hour every week for team meetings.[17] At Saturn, Maass had learned the necessity of working with the union as a full partner. Based on these experiences, he believed that full partnership and involvement by the union depended on expanded employee education and an expanded participatory decision-making process. While the latter was often slower than top-down rule making, Maass believed it would ultimately produce better decisions and long-term efficiencies.

When Maass returned to Lordstown in August, 1996, he found that adversarialism still reigned and that labor relations were still largely considered a zero-sum game. At the same time, the stakes were now much higher than in previous rounds of crisis management, since the J-car's troubled history raised the fundamental question of whether GM could ever produce a profit on a high-volume small car using lean manufacturing and team programs, and more specifically, whether it would try to do so at Lordstown when it came time to pick a site for a new generation J-car in the year 2001.

Maass saw his first challenge was to communicate a sense of urgency, which he did by frequently walking the line and asking his subordinates for hourly production figures. His physical presence and his expectation of hourly reports instantly resulted in a five-jobs-per-hour increase in production. If a simple showing of supervisory accountability and direct management involvement could increase production, Maass concluded that the plant could achieve additional improvements through employee participation. His first major initiative was to have work teams study the causes of down time. In the past, this task had largely been left to managers who frequently ignored engineering or design problems, only to blame the union or employees. Further, to attack quality problems, Maass instituted a "no-ship" policy when workers found such "customer disatisfiers" as poor door fits, electrical problems, or leaks. In the later part of 1996, as the rail lines at Lordstown filled with cars waiting for repair or incoming material waiting for quality

[17] See *Industry Week* story on Herman Maass, May 1990. In no small part as a result of the foundation laid by Maass, Buick City became "GM's Mecca" for quality car production and its model for labor-management cooperation.

problems to be resolved, the plant pressed ahead with the no-ship policy despite pressure from GM headquarters and dealers for shipments.

By June, 1997, with production rising to approximately 1,400 cars daily, the remaining quality problems and line stoppages were primarily the result of equipment breakdowns or bad parts. Yet, formal employee involvement lagged, and remained, at best, uneven throughout the plant. Further, management insisted that productivity (in terms of build man-hours) was still not at levels that made the car profitable. That is, there was further need to cut the workforce and/or increase line speed. But it was clear that GM Lordstown was approaching its goal of producing a profitable small, high-volume car using lean production and design-for-manufacturing methods.[18]

SUMMARY

The overall effect of lean production's gradual introduction at the Lordstown assembly plant is evident in the dramatic change in plant demographics. Between 1987 and 1997, the hourly workforce was cut almost in half, from 11,000 to 6,000. Production workers took the brunt of the job cuts, with the percentage of skilled trades employees rising to over 10 percent by 1997; in some parts of the plant, even the absolute number of skilled workers increased with the arrival of new technologies and the need for preventive maintenance. While the number of production job classifications has been reduced from 39 to 3, skilled trades classifications have only been reduced by two. The proportion of minority workers in the total plant population (salary included) has remained constant at 15 percent, but the proportion of women has grown from 12 percent to 28 percent. The average age of the workforce is now 47 and suggests that further downsizing may be possible through attrition.[19]

In terms of labor-management relations, there has been a steady decline in the number of grievances filed. For example, from the plant's opening through the late 1980s, there were roughly 5000 grievances on file at any

---

[18] It should be remembered that it took the Saturn Corporation's greenfield site seven years before it turned a profit.

[19] The UAW-GM Master Agreement includes a "30-and-out" provision that allows retirement after 30 years of service. Since many workers at Lordstown were hired between 1966 and 1972, these workers are approaching the qualifying years of service.

time. This number has been reduced to 500, most of these concerning disputed workloads during the new-model changeover. Meanwhile, plant-wide joint programs seem most effective in relation to quality, health and safety, ergonomics, and apprenticeship training. For example, the occupational injury-illness summary suggests that there has been a drop of almost 50 percent in each category. However, while on-line teams have been organized, with one coordinator for every seven employees, their distribution and operation throughout the plant is still uneven. The team coordinators are selected on the basis of seniority, and supervisors only attend team meetings occasionally, usually when they are invited. The lack of adequate infrastructure, such as meeting rooms and regular meetings and times, has contributed to ambivalence toward on-line team programs. Consequently, on-line teams, when they function, operate as ad-hoc problem-solving groups.

In terms of plant operations, the just-in-time system has been largely implemented using both electronic signaling and pull cards. The number of suppliers has been reduced from 900 to 441 and the average in-process buffers have been reduced to four hours. In terms of process technology, the plant has 239 robots used in the body shop (230), paint shop (4), and trim (5). The engine-powertrain installation has been fully automated, and five automated inspection devices have been added in the body shop. On the horizon is the expansion of cellular manufacturing systems throughout the plant.

Quality has also improved significantly since ramp-up of the new J-car. The J.D. Powers and Associates Quality Survey found a drop from 136 problems per 100 cars in 1996 to 93 problems in 1997. In reporting the drop, J.D. Powers noted that it was unusual because it came at a high-volume plant producing entry-level cars. Herman Maass attributed the improved quality to project teams composed of engineers and production workers who focused on each of the 12 areas judged in the Powers survey. At the same time, the quality mark is still behind the top-rated small cars, the Saturn and Toyota Tercel, which average 65 problems per 100 cars.[20]

---

[20] "Local Cars Make Gain in Quality," *The Vindicator*, 15 April

The cumulative effect of the introduction of team programs and competitive manufacturing at Lordstown has been to dramatically cut costs. Yet, Lordstown management insists that the J-car is still being produced at a loss. While costs have been cut by $600 per car in the last year, GM holds that it must cut at least another $250 per car to reach the break-even point. Much of the savings in recent months have come from the reduction of overtime, fewer repairs, reduced scrap, and downsizing. While GM publicly suggests that further cost savings can be made by the on-line teams, it is well understood that significant future improvements can only occur through increased production or downsizing the workforce. It is in these areas that future conflict between labor and management could occur at Lordstown. In the short term, what is at stake is a proposed $300 million paint shop which GM will decide on in early 1998. In the long term, the focus of concern is the future of new J-car production in 2001.

No doubt, what happens at Lordstown will be closely followed by those studying the automobile industry —not only for placement of the new J-car, but for the future of small car production by GM in the United States. GM has shown at Saturn that it can make a high-quality small car and, after years of initial losses, generate a small operating profit. The question is whether this will be enough to persuade management that continued production of small cars in the United States is a viable option when more profitable alternatives beckon. At the Ford's Hermosillo plant, the Escort model is produced at the same level of productivity and quality as at Ford's assembly plant in Wayne, Michigan —but with labor costs that are one-tenth of those in the United States. In this context, the real issue for workers at Lordstown, as well as those studying the auto industry, is whether any degree of commitment to lean production and team programs can outweigh the wage differential available to GM at Ramos Arizpe. Currently, the Ramos plant is using antiquated manufacturing methods and technology to supply an 11 percent share of the J-car market, and the plant is in need of significant new tooling and investment. How GM handles its future investment and production decisions involving the Ramos and Lordstown plants will go long way in describing, not only production of J-cars, but the future of small car manufacturing in the U.S. itself.

CHRYSLER CANADA'S WINDSOR ASSEMBLY PLANT: LEAN PRODUCTION THROUGH BARGAINED INCREMENTAL CHANGE

*John Holmes and Pradeep Kumar**

INTRODUCTION

Across the world automobile industry, production and management strategies to achieve competitiveness are converging around variants of lean production, a combination of manufacturing methods and human resource/labour management practices designed to reduce cost and produce the highest levels of product quality, productivity, and flexibility (Womack et al. 1990, Fine and Clair 1996, Kochan et al. 1997). The authors of the influential book *The Machine That Changed the World* (Womack et al. 1990) claimed that lean production was the *one best way* to organize production in the automobile industry. They argued that there was one particular group of labour-management and human resource practices (so-called high-performance work organization systems) associated with effective lean production practices.

Contrary to the monolithic and idealized version of lean production presented by its proponents, our research on the Canadian motor vehicle assembly industry (Holmes and Kumar 1995, Kumar and Holmes 1997a) has demonstrated that the actual changes in work organization associated with lean production remain diverse and plant and enterprise specific. Such diversity is especially striking with regard to employment practices. Similar findings have recently been reported by researchers in the MIT-based International Motor Vehicle Program who conducted two surveys of auto assembly plants around the world (MacDuffie and Pil 1997). They found that although globalization and foreign direct investment have promoted a certain convergence in work and human resource practices, many factors across and

---

* John Holmes is a Professor in the Department of Geography, Queen's University. Pradeep Kumar is a Professor at the School of Industrial Relations, Queen's University.

within companies continue to produce a diversity of outcomes. The diversity is particularly marked among the Big Three (GM, Ford and Chrysler) plants in Canada and the United States (Pil and MacDuffie 1996). Such findings have led Kochan et al (1997, 4) to remark that "...employment practices are shaped not in a deterministic fashion by methods of production, or by some singular technological or economic imperative, but by a multiplicity of factors." Our own research (Kumar and Holmes 1996, 1997a) has shown that in the highly unionized Canadian vehicle assembly industry the union response to management's lean production strategies and the distinct organizational/institutional cultures and histories of local labour-management relations are two of the most important factors shaping workplace change in particular plants.

The objective of this paper is to describe the incremental and bargained introduction of lean production practices at Chrysler Canada's Windsor Assembly Plant (WAP) in the context of broader workplace change in the Canadian motor vehicle assembly industry.[1] Since the early 1980s this plant has built one of Chrysler's most successful products —the Dodge Caravan and Plymouth Voyager minivans. We make no claim that the experience and outcomes of workplace change at this plant can be generalized to other Canadian assembly plants. In fact, our broader research project has stressed the considerable diversity that exists between companies and plants with regard to changes in work organization and workplace relationships. However, we believe that the case of WAP provides a very good illustration of what can be achieved by a strong and confident union negotiating the terms under

---

[1] We do not claim that this paper is an exhaustive and in-depth case study of the Chrysler Windsor Assembly Plant. Rather it uses information that was gathered in May 1994 during a visit to WAP and interviews with plant management and the local union leadership. These interviews formed part of a much broader research project examining recent workplace change in the ten Canadian assembly plants owned by the Big Three. We also interviewed senior industrial relations management personnel at Chrysler Canada and the CAW Chrysler National Representative. Some of the factual data were collected from secondary sources, including the *Harbour Report*, *Ward's Automotive Yearbook*, collective agreements, and reports and documents provided by the CAW. Chrysler Canada kindly supplied data on grievances, absenteeism rates and work refusals. We would like to thank the management and union representatives at Chrysler Canada who agreed to be interviewed and who provided us with other data and information. Financial support for our research was provided by the Social Science and Humanities Research Council of Canada.

which lean production is to be introduced into a plant. Furthermore, it provides a vivid illustration of the way in which present industrial relations and employment practices in Canadian assembly plants reflect both *change* and *continuity* with past practices.

The remainder of the paper is divided into two sections: the first summarizes some of the general conclusions flowing out of our broader project regarding the nature of workplace change stemming from the introduction of lean production methods into Big Three assembly plants in Canada, and the second draws on concrete examples from the WAP case study to illustrate our general argument about continuity and change.

LEAN PRODUCTION AND WORKPLACE CHANGE: THE CANADIAN CONTEXT

The Big Three have been engaged in a massive restructuring of their production and management systems since the early 1980s (see Kumar and Holmes in this volume). One important aspect of this process of restructuring has been a drive by management to implement changes guided by the philosophy of lean production. External to their assembly plants, the Big Three have emphasized supply chain management focused on rationalizing their supplier base, reducing the number of first-tier suppliers, forcing suppliers to achieve continuous cost reductions, and contracting out the assembly of modular components. Internal to the assembly plants, management has sought changes in work processes and labour-management relationships with a view to improving productivity, product quality, and management flexibility. Such changes are designed to reduce non-value-added work, reduce work-in-process, promote continuous improvement and the better use of worker knowledge, and achieve more managerial flexibility with regard to the scheduling and assignment of work.

Given the highly integrated nature of the North American automobile industry and the Big Three's common drive to implement lean production, the changes desired by management in Canadian assembly plants have been very similar to those sought in plants in the United States. The outcomes of the process of change, however, have been quite different in the two countries, especially as they pertain to changes in work organization and labour-management relationships. A key factor accounting for this difference is the divergent responses of the two autoworker unions —the Canadian Auto

Workers (CAW) and the United Auto Workers (UAW)— to industry restructuring.[2] In the United States, each of the Big Three in the 1980s forged, to a greater or lesser degree, a "partnership" with the UAW to facilitate the introduction of new forms of work organization and contingent compensation. Such commitments to partnership became enshrined in the contract language of the UAW's Master Collective Agreements with the Big Three. In Canada, the automakers encountered considerable resistance to such changes from the CAW.[3]

While reaffirming its commitment to "an efficient and productive workplace producing quality products" and recognizing "the potential benefits of new technology and new work processes to workers," the CAW has been vehement in its opposition to Japanese-style management techniques. It regards lean production and new technology as a potential source of job losses, deskilling, work intensification, job stress, repetitive injuries, and increased management control. The union is not only concerned over loss of worker autonomy and control, but is also fearful of the erosion of the independent workplace role of the union under lean production. The union opposes concepts of "jointness" and "partnership" for shopfloor governance

---

[2] Two broad categories of explanation have been advanced for the difference in union response. One links the more militant response of the CAW to historical and contemporary differences in the political culture and ideological underpinnings of unionism in Canada as compared to the United States. The second argues that the CAW was able to adopt a more militant bargaining stance because, after 1980, the Canadian vehicle assembly industry not only enjoyed a significant labour cost advantage over the United States, due to the declining value of the Canadian dollar and the lower cost of health insurance benefits, but also because Canadian assembly plants were building products which were both in high demand and generating higher profit margins. In other words, although the pressures for change were very similar in the two countries, the economic terrain was uneven and enabled the CAW to more effectively bargain the terms under which lean production practices were introduced. There is substance to both these explanations but their relative weight is not important in the context of the present paper. See Holmes and Rusonik 1991, Kumar 1993, and Kumar and Holmes 1996 for a fuller discussion.

[3] Resistance first surfaced in 1982 and 1984 when the then Canadian wing of the UAW refused to reopen contracts and grant concessions to the Big Three. In 1989 the CAW produced its first statement on work reorganization which strongly opposed the introduction of Japanese-style work practices and lean production. Following experimentation with workplace change at CAMI and other assembly plants, the statement was modified in 1993 to articulate a position of ideological resistance to lean production and a more pragmatic approach to work organization. This statement was reaffirmed at the 1996 CAW National Bargaining Convention.

and performance-related contingent compensation; these two issues were the predominant reasons behind the CAW's 1985 breakaway from the UAW, which, largely to save jobs, had accepted them in its agreements with the Big Three in the United States.

Instead, the CAW has argued for the development of "close working relationships" with management at both the corporate level and, especially, at the plant level; relationships which nevertheless recognize the different objective interests of management and labour with regard to issues of compensation and conditions of employment, and emphasize the importance of an independent base for negotiating with management. This has led the CAW to combine ideological resistance with a pragmatic willingness to negotiate workplace changes that benefit both workers and employers. The union has developed a proactive agenda to make the system more human-centered, to preserve and expand jobs, make work more comfortable, ensure a safe and healthy work environment, and enhance workers' skills and capacities. While opposing formal employee involvement programs and team concept structures, it has supported informal and incremental changes that use "workers' experience, knowledge and skills to produce good quality products," with group structures that do not involve responsibility for traditional management functions, and representation on joint committees concerned with such issues of mutual benefit as training, new technology, health and safety, ergonomics, production standards, and employment equity/human rights. In the same vein, the union has been supportive of changes in work schedules and work arrangements.

Thus, the CAW has developed a distinctive approach to workplace change, one which has reinforced the divergence in auto industry labour relations and human resource management systems between Canada and the United States (see Kumar and Holmes 1997a for a discussion of the key areas of divergence). This "accord" has produced a stable labour relations environment and has been mutually beneficial to both employers and workers. Employers have found that they can work around the CAW's opposition to labels such as "team concept" and "partnership" and have not been unduly hindered in their quest for increased operational flexibility. They have been able to considerably increase flexibility in work rules and work arrangements and incrementally introduce movement towards employee involvement and group-based work systems. There have been relatively few interruptions to production in the Canadian industry, as compared to the United States where flexibility-related issues have become a constant focus for struggle between management and UAW locals. The most important benefits, from management's perspective, have been the impressive gains in productivity and product quality made by Canadian plants. Workers have benefited from the accord through greater job security, improved health and safety provisions, and increased protection and representation as a result of the strengthened role of the union at the workplace level. Many commentators point to the "positive" working relationship between management and labour as one of the key reasons behind increased investment in the Canadian auto industry during the 1980s and 1990s.

Workplace reforms and changes in work organization in Canadian assembly plants can be best characterized as having been *experimental, incremental and evolutionary*, reflecting both *continuity* and *change* in past practices. The changes that have taken place have been dictated by the pragmatic needs of employers and employees taking into account considerations of both the need to ensure the competitive survival of specific plants and the previously unfulfilled aspirations of workers. Comparative data collected by the MIT International Motor Vehicle Program (Pil and MacDuffie 1996) reveal that, compared to their sister plants in the United States, Big Three assembly plants in Canada score low on measures of the "high performance work practices" that proponents of lean production claim as an integral part of a lean production system —HRM philosophy, formal team concept, Employee Involvement, Quality Circles, and job rotation (Table 1). This is what one would expect given the very different stances taken by the CAW and UAW with regard to work reorganization. But, Canadian plants on average consistently score higher than US plants on measures of productivity, product quality, and levels of perceived worker influence. These data call into question the claim made in *The Machine That Changed the World* that high performance work organization systems are necessary to effectively implement lean production. In fact, they suggest that within the broader framework of lean production, the desired twin objectives of high economic efficiency and product quality can be achieved in plants characterized by more traditional work practices and adversarial relationships between union and management.

Table 1
Competitive Position of Big Three Plants: Canada and the United States, 1994

		U.S.	Canada
Number of Plants Surveyed		19	8
Productivity (hours/vehicle)		23.2	19.8
Quality (defects/100 vehicles)	1995	62.2	56.1
	1989	86.8	80.7
	Change	-28%	-31%
Inventory level (days)		1.4	1.3
Paint/assembly buffer (% of one shift production held)		38.5	25.4
Automation (% direct production steps automated)		33.8	32.2
Robots/Vehicle/Hour		3.3	3.1
Work Systems Index (100 = Multi-skilling; 0 = Specializing)		27.8	26.9
HRM Policy Index (100 = High Commitment; 0 = Low)		30.0	19.9
Number of Plants with Teams		8	1
% Workforce in Teams (if teams present)		52.4	25.2
% Workforce in EI or QC Groups		38.0	6.1

Source: Pil and MacDuffie 1996

Our research has focused on the process and nature of workplace change in the ten Big Three assembly plants located in Canada (see Appendix in Kumar and Holmes in this volume). We have found that, although corporate strategies to achieve competitiveness are converging across the North American auto industry and that all assembly plants are to some extent "lean," there are some marked differences between different companies and, especially, between plants regarding the extent to which work has been reorganized and relationships changed. These differences arise from the distinct organizational/institutional corporate cultures of each of the Big Three, and the specific histories of labour-management relationships and cultures in different assembly plants. Both GM Canada and Chrysler Canada, for example, have an avowed and explicit goal of becoming "lean."[4] The approaches of the two companies have been quite different, however. Since the introduction of Synchronous Manufacturing (GM's term for lean production) in 1989, management at GM Canada, which has elected not to foster a good working relationship with the CAW, has moved aggressively and unilaterally to try to implement lean production in its three Oshawa assembly plants and at Ste. Thérèse. They have promoted the use of Andon boards for process control, visual line balancing systems, pull systems and just-in-time production methods, flexible work cells, and "Best People Practices." GM documents openly refer to the company's drive to implement lean production, and point to the UAW-GM partnership in the United States as the preferred template for change in Canada. On the other hand, Chrysler Canada has been much less aggressive in pushing lean production at its two plants in Windsor and at its Bramalea car plant. Although the Chrysler Operating System (COS) maps out a strategy for reorganizing all Chrysler operations around the principles of lean production, the company has adopted a far more incremental approach to introducing change, especially in the two Windsor plants —WAP, which builds the very popular minivan series, and the Pillette Road Truck Plant (PRTAP), which builds full-size vans and trucks. Although Chrysler management's objective is to change the culture of these plants, they are pursuing it through a process of negotiation and bargaining, building upon their established excellent working relationship with CAW Local 444.

In summary, and as we have argued elsewhere (Holmes and Kumar 1995, Kumar and Holmes 1996, Kumar and Holmes 1997a), a number of lessons can be drawn from the Canadian experience:

* whatever the idealized vision of lean production, the nature and scope of workplace change depend crucially on the union response;

[4] Ford Canada is also pushing the philosophy of lean production through its Ford 2000 program. There is a significant difference, however, between the degree to which changes have been introduced in the two Oakville assembly plants and the St. Thomas assembly plant, which remains much more traditional in its production methods.

* labour and management have different visions of work reorganization;
* there are no immutable core values for management, other than the imperatives of improving the "bottom line." The actual forms assumed by workplace innovations are based on the concrete needs and mutual interests of employers and employees and are pursued for pragmatic reasons;
* change in Canadian plants has been guided by both management considerations of efficiency and flexibility and union concerns for equity, fairness and security;
* to effectively participate in and shape workplace reforms, unions have to be not only strong and independent, but also capable of articulating a clear vision, agenda and strategy for change;
* there is more than "one best practice" with respect to labour relations practices within the broader framework of lean production. Rather than completely dismantling the traditional (Fordist) system of labour relations, the latter can be maintained and modified through bargained incremental changes to meet the feasible efficiency and flexibility needs of management.

BARGAINED, INCREMENTAL WORKPLACE CHANGE AT CHRYSLER CANADA'S WINDSOR ASSEMBLY PLANT

As stated in the introduction, we believe that Chrysler Canada's Windsor Assembly Plant (WAP) provides a good illustration of both the *continuity* and *change* that characterizes workplace reorganization in the Canadian motor vehicle assembly industry in the 1990s. It clearly demonstrates what can be achieved by a strong and confident union negotiating the terms under which lean production is to be introduced into a plant.

The Plant Context

Windsor, Ontario, which faces Detroit across the Detroit River, has been home to Canadian automobile production since the turn of the century. Vehicle assembly has taken place on the WAP site since 1929. This is, then, a plant and community with a long history and well-developed culture of auto industry work and unionization.[5] One of the conditions of the Canadian

---

[5] The first Ford assembly plant in Canada opened in Windsor in 1904. Chrysler Corporation of Canada was incorporated in 1925 and in 1929 completed a new passenger car assembly plant

government's contribution to the bailout of the near-bankrupt Chrysler in 1980 was that the company should commit new investment and employment to Canada. The most visible outcome of this commitment was the modernization of the WAP to launch the new line of minivans in 1983. Until the early-1990s, when the St. Louis South plant was added to meet the soaring demand for minivans, WAP was the sole North American source of these popular vehicles. The new NS series minivans were launched in the summer of 1995 and WAP builds two models (Voyager and Caravan) on one platform in four body styles. WAP contains single body, paint and assembly lines, and has no on-site stamping, die construction, engine assembly or seat assembly. Engines are sourced from Chrysler engine plants in Trenton, Michigan, and Saltillo, Mexico; transmissions come from Kokomo, Indiana; 80 percent of major body stampings are sourced from Chrysler's central stamping plants in Michigan and Ohio; and seating is outsourced from Magna International's Windsor Seating plant. Tables 2, 3 and 4 provide further information on WAP's production characteristics, workforce, and employment and labour relations practices.

As noted earlier, Chrysler Canada has been less aggressive than GM in pushing lean production in Canada. Nevertheless, during our interviews at WAP, management placed considerable emphasis on the overall goal of increasing efficiency through continuous process improvement. They identified three principal strategies to achieve this goal. The first is the implementation of the Chrysler Operating System, the company's variant of lean production. The plant manager pointed to efforts to move production towards one-piece flow, reduce lead times and work-in-process, redesign work stations to reduce operator travel distance and floor space, and the use of visual line balancing ("The Wall") to increase labour productivity. The second is the general push to reduce all non-value added time to a minimum. This is especially evident in the drive to reduce the number of line supervisors and quality inspectors. The third strategy, given the strong demand for the vehicles being built at WAP, is to increase capacity utilization by implementing an alternative work schedule (AWS).

---

which became the nucleus for the present Windsor Assembly Plant. Today, Windsor is home to two Chrysler vehicle assembly plants, two Ford engine plants, a GM transmission plant, a former GM Trim plant now owned by Peregrine, and scores of independent automotive components plants.

Table 2
Chrysler Windsor Assembly Plant: Labour Force Characteristics

	1989	1992	1995
Size of Workforce			
Hourly	4434	4358	4917
Salaried	53	43	302
Total	4487	4401	5219
Demographics			
Women: Hourly	119	128	—
Salaried	6	7	—
Average Age	42.3	43.8	41.6
Average Seniority	13.5	19.5	14.3
Hours Worked ('000s)			
Straight time	7,698	7,479	11,987
Overtime	1,339	1,476	2,832
Total	9,037	8,955	14,819

Source: Collective Bargaining Documents

Table 3
Chrysler Windsor Assembly Plant: Production Characteristics

Line Speed	1996:	72.0 vehicles/hour (three 7.5 hour shifts)
	1993:	69.0 vehicles/hour (two 8 hour shifts)
	1990:	64.0 vehicles/hour (two 8 hour shifts)
Daily Output	1995:	1,470
Capacity	1996:	325,000 - 3 shift, 270,720 - 2 shift
Production	1996:	373,171
Robots:	1995:	409
	1993:	157
	1990:	142
	1987:	133
Labour Productivity (worker/vehicle)	1996:	3.42
	1992:	3.75
	1989:	4.39

Source: *Ward's Automotive Yearbook, Harbour Report*

Table 4
Chrysler Windsor Assembly Plant:
Employment Practices and Labour Relations Measures

Classifications		1989	1992	1995	
Non-skilled		42	36	36	
Skilled		16	16	15	
Supervisor/Hourly (ratio)		1:29	1:38	1:42	
Training Hours		1990	1995		
Production		2.8	17.11		
Skilled Trades		7.7	53.93		
Quality Processes:	Inspect own work and SPC				
Job Rotation:		No			
Pay for Knowledge:		No			
Transfers:		By Seniority			

Compensation: COLA, AIF (No profit sharing, merit pay, or bonus)
Wage rates by classification:
Wages (1995) : Production $CAN 22.02
Trades $CAN 26.49

Grievance, Absenteeism and Work Refusal Rates

	1990	1991	1992	1993	1994
Grievances	347	287	176	140	127
Absentee Rate*	5.17	5.10	5.81	5.27	4.68
Work Refusals	101	136	70	84	68

$$\text{*Absentee Rate} = \frac{\text{Straight Time (ST) Lost Hours}}{\text{ST Hours Worked + ST Lost Hours}} \times 100$$

Source: Collective Bargaining Documents; Chrysler Canada, Labour Relations Department

The Union-Management Relationship

Local 444 of the CAW represents Chrysler workers at both WAP and the Pillette Road Truck Plant. The local union has a strong and confident leadership, with a reputation for political stability and well-developed lines of succession.[6] It was patently obvious during the 1996 round of collective bargaining that among the Big Three, the CAW's best relationship is with Chrysler Canada, a relationship reflected in the following two quotations from the company and the union:

> We are committed to nurturing the best labour relations in the industry. In 1996, for the third consecutive set of negotiations, Chrysler Canada reached a win-win agreement with our labour partners, the CAW, without any work interruptions. This is testimony to our continuing policy of consultation, not confrontation, inclusion as opposed to exclusion, empowerment and open, honest dialogue on all issues with our workforce —something we can be proud of. (President's Message, *1996 Annual Report*, Chrysler Canada)

> In the context of [this] relationship, there is more respect between both sides. There is more a desire to be open, to confront our problems in an open way, to sit down and share information, to try and find a resolution .... when you look at the number of workplace problems, take a look at the grievance load, all of the traditional signs point to something must be going right here. There is a different relationship .... we still exhibit tremendous shopfloor power, but we don't use it all the time. We don't have to. We don't have to resort to the actions that we used to take before to get minor things corrected. (Interview, CAW Chrysler National Representative, June 1996.)

How does this relationship manifest itself at the local level in Windsor? While they subscribe to and embrace the general framework and agenda on workplace change promulgated by the CAW National Office, the leadership of Local 444 prides itself on its autonomy and has demonstrated willingness to work with plant management to fashion pragmatic responses to the competitive pressure for workplace change. Present plant management at WAP is viewed by the union as being progressive and enlightened. The plant manager has considerable respect for, and in turn, is respected by the local union leadership. In our interviews with the plant manager and the president of the local union, both spoke warmly of the open dialogue that existed between them. Management spoke of the relative ease of negotiating change with the CAW at the plant level, as compared with their experience with the

[6] The political stability and strong leadership of Local 444 contrasts sharply with the disruptive factionalism and lack of unified leadership which characterize the politics of CAW Local 222 at GM's Oshawa complex.

UAW in U.S. plants, because within the CAW there is clear leadership and a unified position on any particular issue.

Thus, during the 1990s a well developed and responsive working relationship has existed between the union and the company, a relationship which has produced an excellent labour relations environment and provided a firm foundation on which to pragmatically bargain changes in work and employment practices at WAP and PRTAP.[7] It is worth noting that in a recent benchmarking study of working conditions in Canadian auto assembly plants the WAP was the plant judged to have the best physical and social conditions of work (CAW 1995).

Continuity in Workplace Practices at WAP

In order to emphasize that the process is not only one of change but also one of continuity with past practices, we will first briefly outline two key areas in which there has been virtually no change: pay systems, and the job-control focus of post-war industrial unionism built around job classifications and seniority rights. For the last half-century, these last two features of the collective bargaining agreement have regulated movement within the plant's internal labour market.

The traditional post-war wage setting formula established in national pattern bargaining, with a cost-of-living-agreement (COLA) increase plus an annual improvement factor (AIF), continues to prevail in unionized auto plants across Canada.[8] Unlike the United States, Canada's Big Three plants (including WAP) have no contingent compensation schemes, such as lump-sum bonuses, profit sharing, or pay-for-knowledge.[9]

Across the North American auto industry, management would like to have much more flexibility with regard to moving workers between jobs, and reorganizing work across existing job boundaries. At the same time, management would like to have more power to restrict or reduce the amount of "job

---

[7] In our broader research project we found this relationship to be quite specific to Chrysler's Windsor plants and far less well developed, for example, at Chrysler's Bramalea Assembly Plant.

[8] For all practical purposes, this statement can be extended to include the Japanese transplant assemblers as well, since CAMI (itself unionized), Toyota, and Honda all set their wages in accordance with prevailing union rates within the Big Three.

[9] The only bonus of any kind found in Canadian assembly plants are relatively small bonuses offered for good attendance or as incentives for workplace suggestion schemes. There is no bonus-based suggestion scheme at WAP.

churning" that annually takes place within a plant's internal labour market as senior workers exercise their contractual right to bid on other jobs. Such churning results in significant additional training costs, impedes productivity, and can compromise quality. To these ends, management would like to see a reduction in the number of job classifications, the weakening of seniority rights with regard to job assignments and distribution of overtime, the formal acceptance of job rotation, and restrictions on job bidding by workers. In our interviews both at WAP and other Canadian assembly plants, managers repeatedly mentioned these as changes that they desired. They acknowledged, however, that they had been able to make virtually no progress towards achieving their desired objectives because of the intransigence of the union on the key issue of seniority, which is the lynch-pin of job-control unionism. The CAW has fiercely protected seniority rights to ensure that workers can move over time from "bad" jobs to "good" jobs.[10] At WAP the union has rejected formal job rotation, retained the practice of opening every single job in the plant to bids by seniority on one particular day a year,[11] and successfully defended the "city-wide" posting of jobs in Chrysler's Windsor plants despite management's desire to limit job posting and seniority rights to individual plants.[12]

Similarly, management has had relatively little success in efforts to reduce the number of job classifications in Canadian assembly plants. At WAP a 1986 proposal to introduce an alternative work assignment system, which included reducing the number of unskilled classifications from 50 to 9 and

---

[10] "Good jobs" are regarded as those that are not subjected to the unrelenting pace of the line. They include such jobs as end-of-line inspection, janitorial jobs, and off-line sub-assembly work; jobs that are highly prized by those with high seniority or partial injury related disabilities. It is precisely these jobs which are targeted for elimination or contracting out under lean production.

[11] Clearly this traditional and contractually entrenched practice (known alternatively as "open season" or "Sadie Hawkins day") which has existed at both WAP and PRTAP since the 1940s gives rise to very high levels of "job churning" in these plants —management and union estimates range from 50-65 percent of workers changing jobs each year.

[12] The impact of city-wide job posting can be dramatic. When Chrysler added the third shift at WAP in 1994, for example, the majority of new openings were taken by workers with varying degrees of seniority at the Pillette Road Truck Assembly Plant and new hires moved into the open jobs at Pillette Road, resulting in a very large number of workers who needed to be either trained or retrained. The union president estimated that besides the 800 new hires, over 4000 workers had switched jobs during the phasing in of the third shift.

skilled classifications from 16 to 8, was rejected. So too was a 1993 proposal to introduce a newly combined "welder repairer" classification.[13]

Negotiated Workplace Change at WAP

We now turn our attention to areas where change has occurred at WAP. These changes have been bargained between Chrysler and CAW Local 444 in such a way that each party sees innovation as serving, in some measure, its own interests and objectives. The following are some of the most important examples of negotiated workplace change at WAP.

a. Work Groups, Production Coordinators, and Quality Alert System Facilitators.

Teamwork has been one of the most complex and controversial issues in Canadian auto plants over the last ten years, and one that illustrates well our general argument regarding the nature of workplace change in the Canadian auto industry. Attempts by the Big Three to introduce team concept into their Canadian plants have been met with stiff and well orchestrated opposition from the national office of the CAW.[14] In 1989 the CAW issued a statement on work reorganization (CAW 1989) which rejected what it perceived to be management's agenda for teamwork and lean production. However, following its experiments with work organization at CAMI and several other plants, the union produced a revised statement on work reorganization which allows enough flexibility and autonomy for union locals to engage in informal experiments with group-based forms of work organization (CAW 1993a).[15] Irrespective of the particular form assumed by these experiments in different

---

[13] The same is true of Ford plants and GM's plants in Oshawa. Only at Chrysler Bramalea, a new greenfield plant opened in the late 1980s, and at GM Ste Thérèse are there significantly fewer classifications (Kumar and Holmes 1997a).

[14] By contrast, during the 1980s team concept became a formalized and central element in what came to be known as "modern operating agreements" in many U.S. auto plants; local agreements which were seen to be a necessary condition for the successful implementation of lean production and competitive survival. Team concept received the formal endorsement of the national leadership of the UAW and it spread rapidly but unevenly through companies such as GM. Only one of the ten Big Three assembly plants in Canada —GM Ste Thérèse— has a formal team concept provision in its collective agreement.

[15] "Team" remains a dirty word in Canadian auto plants. In our interviews we were told by management that "sure we have teams, we just don't call them teams." Union representatives were blunt in stating their continued opposition to the U.S.-style team concept.

companies and plants, they share a number of common characteristics. The groups are informal and experimental, in the sense that they can be canceled by either the union or management on relatively short notice; their primary function is to focus on quality issues, and they rarely if ever address productivity or continuous improvement (Kaizen); group or team leaders mainly help solve quality problems, deliver training, and provide relief to other members of the group, but do not engage in matters pertaining to production standards; and the selection of group leaders or production coordinators —as well as the absence of formal job rotation within the work groups— enshrines the fundamental principle of seniority.

WAP provides a very good example of such experimentation. After hard bargaining in 1994, plant management negotiated memorandums of understanding with Local 444 which allowed for two new positions —"production coordinator" and "quality alert system (QAS) facilitator"— which are intended to provide "leadership" and support for work groups. An hourly-paid position that is filled by seniority, the production coordinator is responsible for a work zone consisting of up to forty workers and performs many of the duties previously carried out by first-line supervisors (distributes tools and gloves, records attendance, starts shift, etc). They are not allowed to dispense discipline, assign or reassign work, or redesign work stations, and can only fill in for absent workers if absolutely necessary. Meetings are convened between production coordinators and managers during breaks, but these meetings are voluntary and the union discourages participation by the production coordinators.[16] The responsibilities of QAS facilitators, who were put in place for the launch of the new NS minivan, focus on quality, repair, and training workers for their work assignments. The aim of the position is to have "floating" repair people to monitor and correct quality problems on the line, and the facilitator has the power to stop the line if necessary. Once again, the positions are hourly-paid, posted, and filled by seniority, with training provided by the union to ensure that the people filling the position understand the boundary between their responsibilities and those of supervisors.

These informally negotiated changes benefit management by helping reduce the number of inspectors and first-line supervisors (the introduction of production coordinators reduced the ratio of supervisors to hourly-paid

---

[16] We were told that originally management had wanted the meetings to be mandatory, for the production coordinators to be actively involved in kaizen-style activities, and to fill in for absent workers. These demands had been successfully resisted by the union.

workers at WAP from 1:25 to 1:42), thus reducing non-value-added activity. However, the changes also benefit the union by empowering workers around the issue of quality improvement, a mutual objective of both management and union, without blurring the necessary distinctions between supervisors and workers.

b. Work Time Arrangements

Although management would like to have much more discretion and flexibility in scheduling overtime, the union has not been very accommodating.[17] The CAW favors a strategy which would not only limit overtime but actually reduce the amount of time worked by individual workers in order to force the creation of new jobs, or at least the retention of as many existing jobs as possible. This policy has not only underpinned the union's opposition to relaxing restrictions on mandatory overtime, but has also shaped their approach to negotiating particular kinds of alternative work schedules (AWS) in plants where companies are seeking to maximize capacity utilization in the face of strong product demand. This is well illustrated by the negotiation in 1993 of the AWS at WAP, which added a third shift by moving to a six-day, three-crew, three-shift system, and establishing a shorter work day for full pay; a production worker now works a 7.5 hour shift but is paid for 8 hours. The AWS also established a weekend maintenance crew which works 32 hours for 50 hours pay.[18] This locally negotiated outcome increased capacity utilization and provided more production flexibility for management, while for the union it maintained a six-day production schedule, provided for less time worked by individual workers for the same pay, and at the same time generated more jobs (a minimum of 650) in aggregate than alternative three-shift systems. As the union noted in announcing the AWS (CAW 1993b):

> the new third shift at the minivan plant is a tremendous achievement for Chrysler workers, their families and the community ... we have shown

---

[17] Provincial labour standards in Ontario provide individual workers with the legal right to refuse overtime beyond a 48-hour work week. In the United States there are no legal restrictions whatsoever with regard to mandatory overtime. With the advent of lean production, and particularly JIT techniques, the ability of managers to extend shifts on short notice to meet daily production schedules has become increasingly critical.

[18] An almost identical AWS agreement was also negotiated in 1993 for the Chrysler Bramalea plant but has yet to be implemented.

> that there is an alternative [to double-digit unemployment]. By more equitably sharing existing work, everyone will benefit. In addition, we are retaining work opportunities including the six-day production schedule and premium working hours for all trades ... Our members, families and the community will reap the benefits and you can be proud of what you have done.

c. Training and Ergonomics

There has been a steady increase in the amount of training provided to workers in Canadian assembly plants over the last decade, and the union has not only negotiated minimum training time and joint control of training with management, but has also played a major role in the design and delivery of the training. In contrast to the United States, where training in all areas is conducted *jointly* by both the union and management, in Canada training is delivered by the union in *consultation* with management. Broadly, one can distinguish two types of training. The first, which is related to restructuring, involves technical and work-culture training associated with major plant modernization projects and the launching of new models. The training that preceded the introduction of the new NS minivan model at WAP in 1995 is a good example.[19] The second type of training is much more continuous and ongoing and encompasses training around issues such as quality, ergonomics, literacy, human rights and mandated health and safety training. At WAP, where the union reported to us that a staggering 85 percent of workers retire with some kind of disability, the union has negotiated an ergonomics checklist and alternative work assignments for injured workers. Once again, we emphasize that these changes have been achieved because they are of mutual benefit to both management and the union. Training improves quality and reduces injuries, both mutual goals of management and labour. It helps management reduce costs due to such things as poor quality or injury, and provides workers with protection against injury. The union has emphasized

---

[19] By its very nature this training tends to be cyclical and discontinuous and its longer term impact at some plants has proven problematic. During the downtime prior to the new model launch there is ample time available to deliver training. This produces heightened expectations with respect to the introduction of a new shopfloor work culture. Once the model goes into production, however, the time to continue and follow up on training becomes increasingly squeezed by the need to move product, and if the promises and heightened expectations are not met then the whole training initiative becomes severely compromised and trust is destroyed. This certainly happened at Ford Oakville following the launch of the Windstar.

the need for more generic portable training which improves the employment prospects of workers in the wider job market in the event of layoffs.

CONCLUSION

During the 1990s the CAW has enjoyed a remarkable degree of success in building a strong union which provides the resources and direction at the national level to strengthen the ability of leadership at the local level to negotiate pragmatic changes in work organization. The union's development of a *cadre* of strong local leaders and activists, its emphasis on the continuous education of the rank-and-file with regard to work reorganization issues, and its commitment to open and democratic debate within the union have all been central to the effort to shape the changes going on in local plants and to link these changes to a coherent national strategy on work reorganization.

The Chrysler Canada Windsor Assembly Plant provides a good illustration of this strategy. The relationship between union and management remains fundamentally an adversarial one and the basic elements of the traditional post-war labour relations system —formula-like wage rules in multi-year contracts, centralized pattern bargaining and connective bargaining between plants, and a job-control focus linking workers' employment rights to detailed job classifications and seniority— have remained intact. However, a strong and productive working relationship with extensive communication and information sharing has developed between plant management and local union leadership. This has created a very good industrial relations climate with low rates of grievances, absenteeism, and work refusals. It has also enabled Chrysler to bargain incremental changes in work practices and to achieve sustained improvements in quality and efficiency. In particular, the company has made significant strides towards reducing the number of first-line supervisors by shifting many of their responsibilities to hourly-paid production coordinators. While pragmatically agreeing to those changes in work practices which it perceives as providing tangible benefits to its membership, the union has successfully resisted any change that would weaken or breach seniority rights. Although some jobs have been lost through continuous improvement efforts, these have been more than offset by the adding of the third shift to meet product demand.[20] Workplace changes inspired by the

---

[20] This underscores the importance of the contextual fact that for the last ten years WAP has produced a highly successful product. This has provided the union with bargaining power and has enabled progressive improvements in productivity without threatening the employment security of its members.

lean production model have taken place at WAP and have resulted in significant gains in productivity. However, the changes have been achieved through local bargaining between management and a strong and confident union leadership. The experience of workplace change at Chrysler's Windsor Assembly Plant— and across the Canadian auto assembly sector —demonstrates that a strong union with an independent and well articulated agenda for workplace change and rank-and-file solidarity is able to defend worker rights and play a significant role in shaping the form taken by lean production.

BIBLIOGRAPHY

CAW. 1995. *Working Conditions Study: Benchmarking Auto Assembly Plants.* North York ON: Canadian Auto Workers.

——. 1993a. *Hard Times, New Times: Fighting for Our Future. Report to the National Collective Bargaining and Political Action Convention.* North York, Ontario: Canadian Auto Workers.

——. 1993b. *Third Shift Becomes Reality.* Broadsheet. North York, ON: Canadian Auto Workers.

——. 1989. *CAW Statement on the Reorganization of Work.* North York, Ontario: Canadian Auto Workers.

Fine, Charles and Richard St. Clair. 1996. *Meeting the Challenge: US Industry Faces the 21st Century — The US Automobile Manufacturing Industry.* Washington D.C.: U.S. Department of Commerce Office of Technology Policy.

Holmes, John and Pradeep Kumar. 1995. "Harmonization and Diversity? North American Economic Integration and Industrial Relations in the Automobile Industry." In Bert van der Knapp and Richard Le Heron, eds., *Human Resources and Industrial Spaces: A Perspective on Globalization and Localization.* New York: John Wiley & Sons.

Holmes, John and Anthony Rusonik. 1991. "The Break-up of an International Labour Union: Uneven Development in the North American Auto Industry and the Schism in the UAW." *Environment and Planning A* 23.

Kochan, Thomas, Russell Lansbury and John Paul MacDuffie, eds. 1997. *After Lean Production: Evolving Employment Practices in the World Auto Industry.* Ithaca: Cornell University Press.

Kumar, Pradeep. 1993. *From Uniformity to Divergence: Industrial Relations in Canada and the United States.* Kingston, ON: IRC Press.

Kumar, Pradeep and John Holmes. 1997a. "Continuity and Change: Evolving Human Resource Policies and Practices in the Canadian Automobile Industry." In Kochan, MacDuffie and Lansbury, *After Lean Production.*

——. 1997b. "The Canadian Automobile Industry in the Context of North American Integration" (mimeographed). Kingston, ON: School of Industrial Relations, Queen's University.

——. 1996. "Change, But In What Direction? Divergent Union Responses to Work Restructuring in the Integrated North American Auto Industry." In Frederick C. Deyo, ed., *Social Reconstructions of the World Automobile Industry.* New York: St. Martin's Press.

Lewchuk, Wayne and David Robertson. 1996. "Working Conditions under Lean Production: A Worker-based Benchmarking Study." In Paul Stewart, ed., *Beyond Japanese Management.* London: Frank Cass.

MacDuffie, John Paul and Frits K. Pil. 1997. "Changes in Auto Industry Employment Practices: An International Overview." In Kochan, MacDuffie and Lansbury, *After Lean Production.*

Pil, Frits K. and John Paul MacDuffie. 1996. "Canada at the Cross-Roads: A Comparative Analysis of the Canadian Auto Industry." A paper presented at the Canadian Workplace Research Network Conference in Vancouver, October.

Womack, James, Daniel Jones and Daniel Roos. 1990. *The Machine That Changed the World.* New York NY: Rawson Associates.

Parte III
PARTES Y COMPONENTES

Part III
PARTS AND COMPONENTS

DE LA PRODUCCIÓN NACIONAL A LA COMPETENCIA GLOBAL: EL CASO DE LA INDUSTRIA MEXICANA DE AUTOPARTES

Carmen Bueno[*]

INTRODUCCIÓN.[1]

La industria automotriz y en particular la industria de autopartes instalada en México ha experimentado cambios significativos a lo largo de su historia. En este ensayo se presentarán las implicaciones que ha tenido el haber surgido como una industria orientada a abastecer productos para el consumo nacional, para posteriormente pasar, en un lapso relativamente corto, a integrarse dentro de un sistema industrial-comercial globalizado. De tal suerte, que esta rama industrial se enfrenta en la actualidad, ante el reto de fabricar productos que puedan competir en precio, calidad y entrega oportuna bajo los estándares internacionales.

Las empresas de autopartes ejemplifican con claridad las alternativas y los obstáculos que algunos sectores industriales en México han tenido que enfrentar ante los procesos de globalización.[2] Estas empresas forman parte de la industria automotriz que ha sido pionera en implementar cambios a nivel internacional.[3]Hoy día, la tendencia de esta rama industrial es configurar un

---

[*] Centro de Investigación y Estudios Superiores en Antropología Social (CIESAS)

[1] Este ensayo presenta resultados preliminares de una investigación titulada: "La industria de autopartes en México: de la producción nacional a la globalización.

[2] En 1996 el sector automotriz ocupa el segundo lugar en exportaciones, después del petróleo.

[3] En este ensayo, sobretodo cuando se referiere a las relaciones con el gobierno no se hará distinción entre industria automotriz e industria de autopartes. En cuanto a política económica, ambas industrias mantienen la misma posición. Un informante cometó: "La industria de autopartes está dentro de un mercado de segunda pues dependemos directamente de lo que sucede en el plano de la industria automotriz. Si la industria automotriz logra seguir colocando sus modelos, es decir vendiendo, la industria de autopartes enfocada a los productos de utilización directa, seguirán vendiendo; si la industria automotriz detiene su avance económico, la industria de autopartes será afectada directa y proporcionalmente."

sistema productivo que trascienda los límites de la empresa individual y se convierta en una fábrica global (Blim 1992) que rebase incluso, las fronteras nacionales. Como afirma Ianni "La empresa global es una totalidad compleja y problemática, articulada y fragmentada, integrada y contradictoria, desigual y antagónica. Todo esto se da de manera simultánea. (1996 :7)

La "fábrica global" producto de la nueva configuración económica internacional, ha impuesto nuevos mecanismos de transacción cuya característica central es la integración productiva a nivel internacional, en la cual se redistribuye el papel de cada país y de cada empresa dentro del mapa mundial del comercio y de la industria. A esta cadena de relaciones se le suele llamar técnicamente "encadenamiento productivo" cuyo propósito es formar organizaciones sistémicas cuya estructura pretende articular las partes con el todo y con esto, optimizar recursos tecnológicos, planear directrices generales para el sistema, dinamizar y modificar el desempeño de las partes involucradas.

La empresa global supone integrar un macroproceso industrial, fragmentando la producción, trasladando subprocesos a empresas independientes o a maquiladoras que mantienen entre sí diversas modalidades de dependencia administrativa, financiera, tecnológica y comercial. Por tanto, se forja una interdependencia entre ensambladoras, empresas de autopartes, socios tecnológicos y abastecedores de insumos, donde circulan productos, maquinaria, información, dinero y patrones de organización de la producción. Tal parece que la frontera de las empresas en esta orquestación ya no es espacial-territorial sino lógica, de acuerdo a los intereses supranacionales de la industria automotriz. Chase-Dunn, uno de los estudiosos de las economías mundiales, afirma que el sistema económico mundial integra complejos subsistemas productivos que se sustentan en la desigualdad social a partir de la división internacional del trabajo. Esta estructura tiene múltiples centros de control, cuya dinámica se mantiene a través de diversas modalidades de apoyo y confrontación. Este control multicéntrico al que alude el autor lo define como una jerarquía de fronteras organizacionales y múltiples niveles regionales que se sobreponen entre sí (1989:9).

Sin embargo, y a pesar de la naturaleza global de este sector industrial, las plantas productivas siguen enmarcándose dentro del ámbito político de una nación. En este sentido y siguiendo la propuesta de Wallerstein (1979), una de las características que ha permitido a la economía mundial ajustar sus estructuras a los cambios lógicos de la economía capitalista ha sido la ausencia de un mecanismo político central que pueda incidir en corregir la mala distribución de los beneficios a todo el sistema. En sustitución, los estados-nación mantienen una posición de subordinación dentro del sistema de economía-mundo, legitimando, a través de marcos jurídicos circunscritos al plano nacional, las reglas de la producción y sobretodo las reglas del intercambio a nivel global. Bajo este paradigma, las empresas de autopartes están ubicadas en dos planos de acción: uno, político espacial y otro logístico de los intereses supranacionales de la industria automotriz. Como se expondrá a continuación, las empresas de autopartes, en sus diversas etapas han tenido que dar respuesta a las estrategias de la producción mundial automotriz, a la vez que regirse por la política industrial del Estado mexicano.

Derivado de las discusiones de Chase-Dunn y Wallerstein, el cuestionamiento obligado es si este nuevo paradigma de integración mundial está reforzando relaciones de intercambio desigual y desarrollo dependiente o bien si efectivamente estamos frente a una verdadera reestructuración de la planta industrial mexicana que se incorpora en condiciones de mayor igualdad tecnológica, productiva, financiera y de mercado. Para poder contestar a esta interrogante se presentará información sobre los cambios experimentados por la industria de autopartes a lo largo de cinco etapas históricas importantes: la primera es el momento de despegue de esta industria, la segunda se distingue por ser una etapa de integración. La tercera se caracteriza por ser la etapa de compensación de importaciones por exportaciones. La cuarta es la consolidación de un modelo de integración global de este sector industrial y por último, la situación actual de esta industria.[4] Los elementos que se abordarán tienen que ver con las relaciones que las empresas de autopartes han mantenido con las plantas ensambladoras, con las empresas proveedoras de insumos, con las grandes corporaciones a las que en ocasiones pertenecen, con los socios tecnológicos que son empresas generalmente ubicadas en los países donde se originó la industria automotriz y con el gobierno mexicano.

EL MOMENTO DE DESPEGUE

La primera ensambladora que se establece en el país en 1925 fue Ford Motor Company. En ese primer momento prácticamente todas las autopartes y componentes se importaba y sólo se ensamblaban algunas piezas en México.

[4] Esta periodización fue tomada de los trabajos de Arteaga (1992), Carrillo et al. (1987) y Morales (1992).

Diez años más tarde, otras dos ensambladoras abren sus plantas en México, General Motors y Automomex[5]. Desde esta primera etapa, son las empresas norteamericanas las que van a tener una posición predominante en el mercado automotriz mexicano. Es hasta la tercera década del presente siglo que se instalan las primeras plantas de autopartes y componentes, en particular fabricantes de neumáticos, amortiguadores y cristales.

El verdadero momento de despegue de la industria automotriz se da a fines de los cuarentas. Es cuando se aprecian los primeros frutos del modelo económico de sustitución de importaciones. Para el año 1948 se presenta la primera modificación de ley, en la cual se controla la importación directa de vehículos. A cambio de esto, el gobierno mexicano ofreció diversos apoyos para incentivar a capitales extranjeros y nacionales a invertir en plantas productoras de automóviles. Uno de las medidas más importantes fue la ampliación de la infraestructura carretera, también se permitió la libre importación de maquinaria, el reembolso del 100% de los impuestos indirectos sobre exportación, la regulación del costo de mano de obra, etc.

El resultado de estas medidas fue que, alrededor de dos docenas de empresas automotrices de Estados Unidos y Europa se instalaron en el país, trayendo, según el comentario de un gerente, "fierros viejos y caducos pero que aquí se rehabilitaron para darle vida a la naciente industria automotriz en México". Como asunto excepcional a lo largo de la historia de la industria automotriz en México, en esta primera etapa, industriales mexicanos tuvieron el interés de producir una marca nacional de automóviles. Esto último es el caso de la marca Vorguar en Monterrey o de Automex que produjo la línea Rambler y que fue inversión mexicana.

La planta industrial de autopartes estaba en manos de inmigrantes europeos o norteamericanos, muchos de ellos profesionistas, visionarios[6] que buscaron apoyo tecnológico en Europa y Estados Unidos para instalar fábricas que tendían a diversificar su producción hacia bienes de consumo doméstico y de oficina, así como a la fabricación de autopartes. Este primer

---

[5] Automex fue una empresa automotriz mexicana de capital público que se apoyo fuertemente en tecnología americana.

[6] Un ejemplo ilustrativo de esto es un hijo de inmigrante alemán a Estados Unidos, estudió en M.I.T. ingeniería metalúrgica. Él vino de paseo a México, le gustó el ambiente y la oportunidad de negocio. En un principio puso una ferretería y aprovechando la política de sustitución de importaciones, compró una representación de una firma austríaca para vender acero y posteriormente compró otra licencia tecnológica en Inglaterra para producir máquinas de escribir, autopartes y línea blanca.

momento no repercutió significativamente en el desarrollo de la industria de autopartes. Flores nos indica que antes de 1962, el valor agregado a los vehículos ensamblados en el país representaba aproximadamente el 20% del total del costo directo de producción de cada unidad. (1987:58)

A partir del despegue de la industria de autopartes en México y hasta la fecha, otro de los grandes problemas que tiene que sortear esta industria es el hecho de que gran parte del acero, el hule y el plástico se tienen que importar de Estados Unidos, Europa o Japón.[7] Esto los ha sometido a constantes presiones en los costos de producción, porque los insumos se cotizan bajo precios internacionales, lo cual resulta muy oneroso para algunos fabricantes de autopartes.

En esta primera etapa de despegue se pudo apreciar el lento e incipiente desarrollo de la industria de autopartes en México. Esto fue producto de una naciente industria automotriz que tenía como objetivo central cubrir la limitada demanda nacional y se veía poco presionada a integrar componentes producidos en México.

ETAPA DE INTEGRACIÓN

Esta etapa arrancó con el decreto presidencial de 1962 que impulsó fuertemente a la industria de autopartes. Este decreto obligó a las empresas armadoras a incorporar como mínimo el 60% del costo directo de fabricación de insumos nacionales a los vehículos producidos en el país. Esto trajo dos consecuencias importantes: la decisión de muchas armadoras de irse del país, considerando que la planta industrial mexicana no tenía el suficiente desarrollo para producir autopartes. La segunda, limitó la oportunidad de las ensambladoras a fabricar ellas mismas la mayoría de las partes fuera de México, estableciéndose una estrategia de desarrollo horizontal de la planta automotriz en el país. El resultado fue las ensambladoras comenzaron a fabricar directamente algunas partes de motores, aunque se vieron obligados a demandar autopartes producidas de manera independiente.

Sin embargo, cabe mencionar que en los sesentas, las empresas norteamericanas mantenían una política productiva de controlar la mayor parte de su

[7] Uno de los grandes proveedores de aceros en México tiene su casa matriz es Austria, comenzó a desarrollar estos insumos desde 1857. Actualmente cuenta con 36 subsidiarias, 2 compañías de venta internacional, 51 tiendas y 100 agencias. En México tiene una agencia que dentro de la corporación es considerada del más bajo rango.

producción al interior de la firma. Comenta un ejecutivo que, Ford y Chrysler compraba los lingotes de acero, lámina y vidrio, fabricando ellos mismos los componentes. Tanta concentración mostró ser incosteable y poco productiva por lo que para las subsecuentes etapas, la tendencia de las armadoras fue precisamente centralizar los procesos medulares y apoyarse en la generación de una red de empresas independientes que les surtieran de componentes y autopartes.

El desarrollo de la industria de autopartes no sólo estuvo en manos de extranjeros, sino que también el gobierno mexicano jugó un rol activamente intervencionista. Durante el gobierno del Presidente Miguel Alemán se compraron industrias no estratégicas, que se encontraban en crisis económica o bien se crearon nuevas fábricas de productos que requerían de fuertes inversiones. También se procuró reforzar el desarrollo industrial, invirtiendo en plantas productivas que eliminarían cuellos de botella en cadenas productivas. Estas estrategias de política económica justificaban el interés de la inversión pública por la industria de autopartes.

El resultado concreto de este periodo fue: una mayor diversificación de la planta industrial. Se comenzaron a producir partes eléctricas, ejes traseros, partes para motor, frenos, carrocerías, sistemas de enfriamiento, transmisión y embrague y partes de suspensión.[8] Esta gran expansión en la variedad de partes fabricadas en relación a la época anterior no tuvo repercusiones positivas en la calidad de la producción. Esto fue reflejo del carácter proteccionista que imperaba en ese momento en la política económica de México. La planta industrial permaneció aislada de la competencia externa. Cualquier componente de importación que hubiese querido colocarse en el mercado mexicano requería de permisos de importación, así como del pago de impuestos muy elevados. Además de que la competencia interna entre las fábricas de autopartes era casi nula. Cada una de las plantas instaladas abastecía por igual a todas las armadoras del país. El mercado interno seguía siendo reducido, comparado con la creciente demanda de los países del primer mundo.

---

[8] Algunos datos que ilustran la situación del momento son los siguientes: Había alrededor de 15 ensambladores, éstas junto con la industria de autopartes ampliaron su mercado de trabajo de 25 mil trabajadores en 1962 a 135 mil en 1972, o sea que la proporción casi se sextuplicó en diez años. El mercado también creció, en 1965 se vendieron 96,359 unidades mientras que en 1973 alcanzó una cifra de 259,074 unidades, teniendo una tasa de crecimiento anual de 13,2%. (Flores 1987:59).

El ambiente productivo de esta época era el siguiente: La materia prima no pasaba por una medición rigurosa de calidad por parte de la industria de autopartes. Esto se derivó en una falta de presión sobre los pocos proveedores de materia prima a nivel nacional para que procuraran surtir insumos de óptima calidad. Al igual que en la época anterior, la mayoría de las empresas habían comprado licencias tecnológicas en el extranjero. Para mediados de los sesentas además de la tecnología norteamericana y europea, entró la japonesa. Las sociedades tecnológicas se convirtieron en una asociación estratégica: el capital extranjero ponía la tecnología, ofreciendo la maquinaria y el "know how" y los empresarios en México abrían el camino al mercado nacional. Así, las sociedades tecnológicas durante todo el desarrollo de la industria de autopartes, se convirtieron en una estrategia eficaz de minimizar riesgos y de penetrar con más éxito al mercado.

A diferencia de etapas posteriores, las ensambladoras y las empresas de autopartes tenían una relación puramente comercial, en donde sólo fluía el componente, sin mayor intervención de las ensambladoras. Esta situación permitió que los abastecedores de autopartes tuviesen una cierta independencia tecnológica, pudiendo desarrollar mayor inventiva y creatividad. Algunos trabajadores que vivieron ese momento comentan que se vieron forzados a improvisar y a innovar tecnología al punto de que, algunas piezas se fabricaban para ajustarse al mercado mexicano. Por ejemplo, los amortiguadores eran especiales para las condiciones de las carreteras mexicanas, al igual que las llantas que tenían seis cuerdas en lugar de cuatro, como se utilizaba en Europa.

En resumen, la etapa de integración provocó, sin lugar a dudas, una diversificación de la producción de autopartes. Sin embargo, el rendimiento y la calidad seguían enfocados a un mercado cautivo y altamente protegido.

ETAPA DE COMPENSACIÓN DE IMPORTACIONES POR EXPORTACIONES

Durante los setentas se manifiesta una fuerte preocupación del Estado mexicano por el déficit en la balanza de pagos. Esto provocó que se introdujeran nuevos reglamentos para compensar las importaciones. Por tanto, para el caso que aquí nos ocupa, se exigió que la cuota básica de importaciones se debería de compensar con la exportación de un 40% de componentes fabricados por la industria nacional de autopartes y un 60% por la producción de empresas terminales en México.

Esta reglamentación fue determinante y estratégica para la fabricación integral de motores y para arrancar la fase exportadora de la industria automotriz. General Motors, Chrysler y Nissan propusieron instalar fábricas de motores, ubicadas en los estados del centro y del norte del país. Esto efectivamente contribuyó a la consolidación de fabricantes de partes y componentes. Su aplicación reforzó el plan de integración de autopartes mexicanas para cubrir principalmente el mercado nacional, aunque comenzó a alentar a la planta industrial en México hacia la exportación. La entrada al mercado internacional estaba prácticamente monopolizada por las ensambladoras. Las empresas de autopartes sólo exportaban de manera indirecta a través de las primeras.

Durante los setentas, se mantuvo la protección al mercado interno. Además se acentuó la participación directa del gobierno en el sector productivo. La modalidad de ese momento fue la de acordar inversiones conjuntas entre capital privado y gobierno. Se afianzaron las mismas relaciones que se originaron en etapas anteriores con los socios tecnológicos, con los proveedores de insumos y con las ensambladoras instaladas en el país.

Todavía en este período la producción estuvo básicamente orientada a cubrir la demanda nacional. Las empresas de autopartes tenían el control de la situación, avalados por una política proteccionista que obligaba a las armadoras a comprar sus productos. Además las plantas paraestatales no prosperaban pues muchos de sus dirigentes las utilizaban para sus intereses políticos y generalmente eran fábricas que trabajaban con fuertes déficit. El perjudicado era el cliente que tenía que comprar autos con partes y componentes de baja calidad por la falta de competencia tanto interna como externa.

LA PRODUCCIÓN MEXICANA EN EL MERCADO INTERNACIONAL

Preámbulo al modelo neoliberal orientado a la apertura comercial y a la integración de México a los mercados internacionales, fue el decreto de 1977 donde se formularon diversas disposiciones gubernamentales que apoyaban la formación de una infraestructura exportadora de la industria automotriz en México. Aunada a esta situación, durante los primeros años de la década de los ochenta, la industria automotriz norteamericana y europea entraron en un proceso de reestructuración a nivel internacional como respuesta a las presiones competitivas de las empresas japonesas. Además por los efectos que tuvo el alza del precio del petróleo sobre el mercado automotriz a nivel internacionnal.

A partir de este momento, la política exportadora de México quedó envuelta en las presiones sobre las normas productivas del mercado internacional, presiones que aún en la actualidad son difíciles de enfrentar por la mayor parte de empresas de autopartes, si se considera que en el momento de arranque y consolidación, esta industria tuvo un desarrollo altamente protegido. A pesar de ello, las empresas de autopartes han participado activamente en el proyecto de exportación más ambicioso de la industria automotriz: la colocación de motores principalmente en el mercado norteamericano. En 1982 se exportaron 320 mil unidades, cuatro años más tarde, la producción se cuadruplicó y se llegaron a exportar 1,386,359 motores. (Flores 1987:62)

Para las empresas que se habían desarrollado en los sesentas fue un momento de reestructuración.[9] Algunas de las empresas modificaron su producción diversificada orientada al mercado nacional de bienes de consumo para especializarse en aquellos nichos donde podían tener más oportunidades de desarrollo en el plano internacional.[10] Para ello, negociaron con sus socios tecnológicos para que los últimos invirtieran de manera más agresiva, en algunos casos esto provocó que la inversión extranjera se convirtiera en mayoritaria. Esto fue puesto en práctica principalmente por empresas independientes que no pertenecían a ningún consorcio pero que habían surgido asociándose con empresas reconocidas en el mercado internacional.

En otros casos sucedió lo contrario, puesto que en las etapas anteriores, los socios tecnológicos habían convenido en participar ofreciendo la licencia tecnológica, asesoría de proceso y de producto a cambio de que la contraparte mexicana se responsabilizara de la penetración al mercado exclusivamente nacional. Estos socios tecnológicos al tener intereses globales, han establecido diversas modalidades de participación en fabricas localizadas en diversas partes del mundo, ya sea directamente o de manera asociada. Este predominio en el mercado es lo que les da prestigio y credibilidad en el ámbito internacional. Sin embargo, protegen mucho los mercados que ellos han podido mantener cautivos y por lo tanto se han dado casos en que, prácticamente "aplastan a los socios mexicanos" en el interés de la contraparte mexicana por participar en los circuitos internacionales.

Otras consecuencias del proceso de la reestructuración industrial fueron: Se dieron fusiones entre empresas formando corporativos. Estos consorcios

---

[9] Zapata et al. (1994) realizan un estudio sobre los cambios en el proceso productivo de empresas de autopartes que participaron activamente en este modelo de reestructuración.

[10] Una de las empresas estudiadas comenzó fabricando refrigeradores, máquinas de escribir, planchas y autopartes para el consumo nacional. Su estrategia de reconversión se orientó hacia la especialización en la industria de autopartes, exportando de manera indirecta los engranes de bombas de aceite, partes internas de amortiguador y otras pequeñas partes estructurales.

ampliaron su rango de influencia y consolidaron cadenas productivas, monopolizando ciertos nichos en la fabricación de autopartes. Estos grandes consorcios alteraron sus formas de financiamiento acorde a las transformaciones de los sistemas financieros y a la redistribución internacional de los flujos de capital por la vía de las inversiones bursátiles. Por otro lado, las empresas estatales de autopartes fueron vendidas al sector privado. El gobierno tomó medidas para vender, liquidar, fusionar y transferir más de setecientas empresas. Algunos autoparteros aprovecharon la oportunidad de comprar a muy bajo precio estas empresas, sobretodo para integrar cadenas productivas. Pero también se dieron casos en los que las paraestatales se vendieron a otros capitales de manera indiscriminada, capitales que aprovecharon el "remate" pero que desconocían la operación de una fábrica de este giro. En el rama automotriz, las empresas públicas afectadas fueron VAM y Renault Mexicana, 9 firmas del consorcio Diesel Nacional y seis empresas de autopartes. (Vidal 1993-104).

Para algunas de las empresas pequeñas o medianas de autopartes, esto significó su desaparición, sobretodo para aquellas que se habían mantenido inamovibles durante la política proteccionista del modelo de sustitución de importaciones y que no vislumbraron su capacidad de exportar a otros mercados. Además de ver amenazada su posición dentro del mercado nacional. Esto les implicaba en principio y como algo inevitable, realizar fuertes inversiones en tecnología para poder competir en volumen, calidad y precio en los mercados internacionales, lo cual les resultaba incosteable. Además consideraron que no podían competir con productos que iban a ser importados de manera directa, que tenían calidad superior y precios altamente competitivos en el mercado internacional. Otra estrategia para evitar el cierre total de la empresa fue cambiar de giro y convertirse en distribuidores de partes importadas. Esto, sin embargo, trajo como consecuencia el despido masivo de trabajadores manuales.

En este periodo proliferaron parques industriales ampliamente socorridos por las empresas automotrices, situados en los estados del centro y norte del país que "huyeron" de la saturación del espacio físico y de la fuerza de los sindicatos de la Ciudad de México.[11] Otro resultado significativo de este

---

[11] Uno de los más grandes consorcios de la industria de autopartes en México comenzó en esta época su proyecto de descentralización, aunque las oficinas centrales del corporativo se ubican en el D.F. En un principio sus plantas industriales estaban localizadas en el D.F., en una de estas plantas se suscito una huelga de gran trascendencia. Actualmente tienen plantas en Aguascalientes, Chihuahua, Celaya, Tlaxcala donde aplican programas de desarrollo comunitario y de capacitación para los familiares de los obreros. Sobre la aplicación de estos programas

momento fue el nacimiento de un fuerte programa maquilador en los estados fronterizos del norte del país. En 1981 había en la frontera 41 plantas maquiladoras de autopartes que ocupaban al 8.7% del total de la mano de obra de las maquiladoras. A fines de los ochentas había más de un centenar de plantas fabricando autopartes y empleaban a una quinta parte de la mano de obra de este ramo.(Morales 1992:83).

Como resultado de estas transformaciones, la producción de autopartes nacional se puede dividir en los siguientes rubros: la venta de componentes originales para la producción nacional de vehículos, la producción de refacciones también para el mercado nacional. La exportación indirecta de autopartes, es decir que se introducen al mercado internacional al integrarse a motores o vehículos que se ensamblan en México para la exportación. Esto último es lo que más fuerza tiene hasta la actualidad en el proyecto exportador. Otro tipo de exportación también importante es la exportación promovida, que es una exportación directa al extranjero, aunque bajo la intermediación de alguna empresa armadora y por último la exportación directa que se divide en mercado de refacciones y la venta a mercados internacionales ya sea a plantas ensambladoras o a empresas de autopartes que compran de México algún componente de un subproceso.[12]

Estos cambios organizacionales se proyectaron en relaciones cualitativamente distintas con las empresas ensambladoras, los socios tecnológicos y con los abastecedores de insumos.[13] Esto será motivo de análisis en el siguiente apartado.

---

en las plantas del D.F., uno de los ejecutivos comentó que "el problema central que tienen en las plantas que instalaron hace 30 años en la zona industrial de la Ciudad de México es la actitud de los líderes sindicales que todo lo ven mal".

[12] La exportación directa implica un proceso largo de negociación, por ello, la capacidad de respuesta de la industria de autopartes no puede ser automática. Comienza por que la fábrica de autopartes sea aceptada por las ensambladoras como candidato a proveedor. Esto es demostrado por su capacidad productiva, por haber producido para el mercado nacional, por los premios en calidad que le han sido otorgados por las ensambladoras. A partir de ese momento, puede pasar un periodo de 18 meses que empieza por la elaboración de un prototipo a mano, si este es aceptado se fabrica el prototipo con herramentales, posteriormente se ofrece una muestra de producción, en este punto de la negociación, la empresa de autopartes ya tuvo que realizar una fuerte inversión en la tecnología para producir en cantidad y calidad el producto requerido. Generalmente los contratos se hacen por modelo, así es que cada modificación implica una nueva negociación.

[13] Un director de un gran consorcio de autopartes comentó: "Los que nos hemos dedicado a las autopartes somos muy operativos, somos fierreros que venimos desde abajo, ahora se nos pide ser más de relación, todo se convierte en negociación".

LAS AUTOPARTES EN EL UMBRAL DEL SIGLO XXI

El desenvolvimiento de la industria de autopartes ha aumentado la brecha entre las empresas que han podido participar en la lógica de reconversión industrial a nivel internacional y aquellas que tienen una presencia marginal exclusivamente en el mercado nacional.[14] Además en la última década del presente siglo, se presentó un comportamiento errático de la economía mexicana en lo general, lo cual tuvo efectos dramáticos para la planta industrial instalada en el país. Las empresas de autopartes, sobretodo las que se mantienen cautivas al mercado nacional han vivido una severa crisis porque la demanda nacional se ha reducido, como reflejo de la reducción en el poder de compra en la sociedad mexicana.

Esta crisis se acentúo a principios de 1994, cuando la venta interna de automóviles ya sufría los embates de la recesión. En el momento de la devaluación del peso y del colapso económico a fines de 1994, tanto las empresas pequeñas como las grandes pararon parte de su producción, algunas tuvieron que cerrar o se declararon en moratoria de pagos[15], sobretodo aquellas que habían adquirido préstamos en dólares.[16] Muchas siguieron estrategias de sobrevivencia, reduciendo costos principalmente, reduciendo el número de horas trabajadas, liquidando personal,[17] o bien, reforzando líneas de producción destinadas a la exportación.

---

[14] Hoy día se pueden encontrar empresas localizadas en las zonas industriales de la Ciudad de México que parecen fotografías vivas de los años sesentas, se mantienen produciendo para el mercado de refacciones prácticamente con la misma maquinaria y con los mismos sistemas administrativos manuales que introdujeron al iniciar sus actividades durante el modelo proteccionista por la vía de sustitución de importaciones.

[15] Una de las empresas visitadas había comprado en 1993 maquinaria en Alemania, tenía una deuda en marcos y se mantenía aún cautiva del mercado nacional. En 1995 al bajar las ventas de automóviles en un 75% tuvo que declararse en moratoria de pagos, despedir a mitad de su personal y trabajar sólo dos semanas al mes para abatir costos. A mediados de 1996 renovó el pago de la deuda, incrementó las horas de trabajo pero no ha podido recontratar al personal que despidió.

[16] Durante los primeros años de esta década, los industriales en México comenzaron a prepararse para la "entrada triunfal" al mercado internacional. Los bancos nacionales e internacionales ofrecían programas especiales para incentivar la inversión en el cambio tecnológico.

[17] Una de las corporaciones estudiadas mandó a su personal de vacaciones, posteriormente se recortaron los días de trabajo, trabajando sólo tres días a la semana. Algunas empresas de este corporativo se cerró temporalmente aunque no optaron por despedir a los obreros de planta porque querían mantener a su personal capacitado para cuando volvieran a tener niveles de crecimiento buenos.

Después de este periodo de crisis, una agencia de consultoría americana, reportó que hay 474 empresas grandes de autopartes, de éstas, 155 son compañías propiedad mayoritaria de capital mexicano, 155 son plantas propiedad de capitales extranjeros y 164 maquiladoras (Ward 1996). Además hay un número subregistrado de empresas menores que según la fuente antes señaladas asciende a 40. Por otro lado, la revista Expansión publicó que hay 831 empresas, de las que 531 fabrican partes originales y unas 200 son maquiladoras (Expansión 1997: 25). Independientemente de las discrepancias en el número de empresas registradas, dirigentes de este sector afirman que el 805 del total de ventas esta controlado por 115 empresas y que el nuevo modelo de integración global no le ha dado cabida a la pequeña empresa.

Además los noventas marcan una penetración vertiginosa a los mercados internacionales. Una de las características centrales de la globalización en este periodo, ha sido la participación de México en las economías regionales integrales. Tal es el caso del Tratado Trilateral de Libre Comercio de Norteamérica(TLC)que pone en ventaja el flujo de mercancías entre Canadá, Estados Unidos y México en relación a otros países del orbe,[18] a partir de la liberación de aranceles y tarifas. A diferencia de la manera como eran elaborados los decretos por el gobierno mexicano en periodos anteriores, en relación a la política industrial nacional, en los que se daba poca injerencia en su formulación a los empresarios de autopartes; en el TLC se invitó a estos últimos a participar en la negociación, pidiéndoles que presentaran un perfil del sector y que estuvieran presentes en una sala adjunta para ser consultados a lo largo del proceso. Ellos consideran que fue un gran logro. Sin embargo reconocen que el sector de autopartes que no tiene una participación de capital directa de las ensambladoras, se mantiene en desventaja con relación a la capacidad de *lobbying* de estas últimas, quienes efectivamente pudieron defender sus peticiones en la mesa de negociación.[19]

Derivado de la integración al mercado mundial, existe una gran preocupación por consolidar estrategias globalizadoras en un plazo relativamente corto, por parte de las empresas que controlan la producción de autopartes en México. Una situación importante es que según los acuerdos pactados en el TLC, para el año 2004, el mercado de autopartes y vehículos se abre a la

---

[18] El apoyo del gobierno para la integración con otros mercados parece ir acorde a los objetivos de la política económica liberal vigente en México, prueba de ello son las continuas negociaciones para integrar la economía del país a otros mercados como sería el Mercosur o la Comunidad Económica Europea.

[19] En 1996 se estima exportar un millón de vehículos por tres millones de motores. Toda esta exportación esta directamente en manos de las plantas ensambladoras.

desregulación y la apertura total entre México, Estados Unidos y Canadá, con lo cual desaparece la frontera entre el comercio interno y externo. Esto está implicando una resignificación territorial y logística de la producción automotriz. Esta medida es un indicador trascendental de la manera como el Estado mexicano ha apoyado los intereses de los grandes capitales mundiales, poniendo aún mayor presión sobre la capacidad productiva de muchas empresas de autopartes instaladas en México.

Por el momento, la participación de México en el TLC ha provocado mayor concentración, casi una monopolización de la relación comercial con Estados Unidos (cuadro 1). Además México exporta a 64 países, los más importantes después de Estados Unidos son Canadá, Alemania y Brasil. Además de las autopartes que se integran directamente a las cadenas productivas de las ensambladoras, Estados Unidos es el país que se encarga de comprar y a su vez distribuir refacciones y autopartes originales producidas en México hacia otros mercados, incluyendo el pulverizado e inestable mercado centroamericano. Según comentarios de un director de un consorcio, el vender autopartes a un distribuidor en Texas garantiza la venta hecha a 15 países del Caribe y Sudamérica. Algunos ejecutivos mencionan que el mercado norteamericano es el más fácil de penetrar por ser el consumidor más grandes de automóviles en el mundo, además de la avasalladora relación que se ha mantenido desde el inicio con la producción norteamericana. El producto mexicano entra a otros mercados por el precio, sobretodo en aquellos procesos que no están tan tecnificados.[20]

Cuadro 1

Valor de las exportaciones de autopartes mexicanas. 1990-1995. (Dólares)

	1990	1991	1992	1993	1994	1995
Alemania	50,506	110,878	88,384	49,581	19,802	19,644
Brasil	3,628	9,671	20,344	13,681	53,054	82,024
Canadá	4,787	147,547	279,069	390,027	387,949	116,010
U.S.A.	2,649,174	3,896,623	3,759,674	512,183	1,121,580	272,806
Japón	635	9,301	2,267	40,515	119,202	329
Total	2,708,730	4,174,020	4,149,738	1,005,987	1,701,587	490,813

Fuente: Banco Nacional de Comercio Exterior.

20 La diferencia en salario entre un obrero alemán y un mexicano es de 9 a 1, esto sin incluir prestaciones. Una empresa japonesa ubicada en Aguascalientes surte directamente de asientos a ensambladoras en Japón, su competitividad radica en los costos de operación de la planta mexicana, en relación a la casa matriz que se ubica en uno de los suburbios de Tokio.

Por el lado de la importación y producto de los apoyos que el gobierno mexicano ha brindado a la apertura del mercado, está la introducción de lo que se denomina material de ensamble o CKD, que son autopartes desensambladas, que entran directamente a las plantas ensambladoras ubicadas en el país. Esto ha traído consecuencia negativas, por un lado en lo económico, el material de ensamble deja nulo o poco valor agregado a México. Por el otro y a pesar de los grandes esfuerzos que la planta industrial mexicana está haciendo por pertenecer al grupo privilegiado de empresas de "calidad mundial", las interconexiones entre empresas mexicanas se ha debilitado por esta competencia desleal, provocando mayor vulnerabilidad y mayor presión a las fábricas en México, teniendo que castigar sus costos operativos.

Otro asunto estratégico en las relaciones con el gobierno mexicano es la constante negociación de la industria automotriz para contar con mejores condiciones para vender en el deprimido mercado nacional y por ello, han luchado por conseguir apoyos fiscales. A principio de los noventas se implementaron modificaciones a la miscelánea fiscal, se incrementó la carga de impuestos en la compra de automóviles nuevos. Finalmente y derivado de la severa crisis que ha vivido esta industria durante los dos últimos años, en 1996 se eliminó, el ISAN (impuesto sobre automóviles nuevos) y se consiguió la deductivilidad fiscal en la contabilidad de las empresas en la compra de vehículos nuevos.

En cuanto a la participación en los circuitos de producción y distribución mundiales, la presencia de estas empresas de autopartes ha sido bastante heterogénea. Las que han tenido mejores oportunidades son aquellas empresas de autopartes que son filiales de grandes corporaciones internacionales que mantienen una política de producción integral. Así cada una de las plantas se especializa en un producto que se fabrica en gran escala para ser colocado en cualquier parte del mundo. Esto significa que la planta en México debe demostrar que tiene la capacidad técnica para fabricar determinados productos. En todo el proceso cuenta con el apoyo de la corporación para la compra de maquinaria, la capacitación de sus técnicos en cualquier parte del mundo y mejores niveles de negociación a escala mundial.[21] La

[21] Una de las empresas estudiadas surte directamente a Europa y Estados Unidos, las plantas de esta misma corporación instaladas en España y Bélgica también surten a VW México. Sin embargo, la planta de México se ve obligada a recibir y resolver cualquier queja de VW México, independientemente de que la autoparte no haya sido producido directamente en México. Por lo que la proximidad física sirve para hacer enlaces y negociaciones que están implicando una relación cara a cara para la solución de problemas.

especialización les significa incrementar la competitividad de sus plantas, elevando la calidad y bajando costos por la escala de producción.

Otro cambio en las relaciones productivas que ha impuesto la actual estrategia global es que toda empresa de autopartes que surten a las ensambladoras ya sea a las plantas localizadas en México o cualquier otro destino, forman parte de lo que se le llama *global sourcing*. Esto quiere decir que tienen que cubrir los requisitos en calidad, cantidad y tiempo de entrega de un producto global. A diferencia de las etapas donde la producción estaba orientada exclusivamente al consumo nacional, la relación con las empresas ensambladoras se mantiene a través de una serie de controles a lo largo de todo el proceso productivo. Para ello se han desarrollado múltiples manuales de calidad[22], estos han sido elaborados por las ensambladoras para que las empresas de autopartes conozcan y fabriquen de acuerdo a las políticas de calidad de las primeras.

Para las plantas de autopartes en México que surten directamente al mercado nacional e internacional es el QS9000 el que predomina a partir de los noventas.[23] Este es un certificado de calidad que dicta las normas del producto y del proceso para la producción de las "tres grandes" Ford, Chrysler y General Motors y que se ha convertido, para el contexto mexicano, en el parámetro universal de evaluación. Para que las ensambladoras hagan el seguimiento de calidad se aplican continuamente auditorias a las fábricas de autopartes.

Sin embargo, la más compleja es la auditoría del QS9000. Para ello existen compañías instaladas exclusivamente en los Estados Unidos, especializadas en auditar el cumplimiento de este manual de calidad. Las auditorías se llevan a cabo cada seis meses por tres años y posteriormente de manera más esporádica. En estas auditorías se hace una rastreabilidad del producto a través de todo el proceso donde se vigila lo técnico y también el desempeño de la fuerza de trabajo. En el proceso previo a las auditorias, las empresas de autopartes concentran todo su esfuerzo en detectar fallas potenciales en el diseño, en el proceso y en el producto final. La evaluación es extremadamente rigurosa y se les da un periodo de gracia de tres meses para poder subsanar inconformidades. Si no se cumple con lo propuesto quedan fuera

---

[22] Entre estos está el Q1 para Ford, el VDA6 para los automóviles europeos, los manuales de calidad de NISSAN.

[23] El QS9000 es el certificado de calidad especializado en la industria automotriz, derivado del ISO9000 que es más universal.

de la integración al encadenamiento productivo global de la industria automotriz. Un técnico comentó: "Nosotros no nos preguntamos si nos gustan o no las auditorias del QS9000, tenemos que cumplir porque es el mercado de exportación el que nos da de comer y todos, incluyendo los obreros, estamos conscientes de esto".

El QS9000 es un procedimiento que exige llevar registros rigurosos de todo el proceso, por ello es muy laborioso, altamente burocratizado, lo que les implica un gran esfuerzo, tensión interna y una altísima inversión.[24] Ante esta situación es comprensible la estrategia de aquellas fábricas de autopartes de convertirse en distribuidores de productos importados. Al ser representantes de productos que se fabrican en alguna otra parte del mundo evitan cubrir los múltiples requisitos de calidad. En estos casos, las representaciones sólo muestran el certificado de calidad otorgado en el país de origen con lo que avalan que el producto vendido responde a las exigencias de los estándares globales.

Algunos resultados concretos que ilustran las dificultadesque la planta industrial de autopartes en México está enfrentando por cubrir las exigencias de calidad de la producción global fueron destacados por algunos gerentes y mandos medios: Las piezas defectuosas, el desperdicio y el retrabajo siguen siendo una práctica usual en el proceso de producción. Es interesante percibir que en estas plantas se han logrado innovaciones tecnológicas propias para resolver estos problemas. En una de las plantas estudiadas había defectos en el acabado de pintura lo cual estaba provocando que las piezas se oxidaran. Para remediar esto limpiaban la pieza con pulque[25] para volverla a meter a los hornos de pintura.

Otro elemento que ha sido difícil de sortear es la oferta nacional de materia prima de alta calidad. Si bien las compañías de acero, aluminio, hule, plásticos y vidrio instaladas en el país también comienzan a implementar programas de "calidad Global", todavía no cuentan con proyectos de investigación y desarrollo, ni con la asistencia de universidades y clientes, que les permita mantener una calidad óptima para todos los insumos requeridos por la industria automotriz. Esto refleja que la estrategia de buscar en las relaciones un apoyo a la calidad, no es una práctica usual en el contexto mexicano,

---

[24] Esta lucha por ingresar exitosamente a las redes de la producción internacional ha sido muchas veces superada por los socios tecnológicos del país de origen, quienes ahora están más preocupados por asuntos tales como minimizar los efectos negativos al medio ambiente, el uso óptimo de energía, evitar el desperdicio, etc.

[25] El pulque es una bebida embriagante que se extrae del aguamiel del maguey.

como lo es en los grandes centros industriales del mundo. Además de que los proveedores de materia prima compiten en calidad con empresas que llevan hasta más de un siglo produciendo insumos para esta industria, empresas de reconocido prestigio y que abastecen al mundo entero.

La inversión en tecnología es elevada. En muchas de las plantas de autopartes en el país existe una combinación de tecnología avanzada, versátil que se adecua fácilmente a la variedad de productos. Esta tecnología es el orgullo de la empresa, sin embargo, aún se siguen importando máquinas que son obsoletas en los países altamente industrializados y que en México se habilitan y se adaptan. El argumento es que haciendo un análisis de la estructura de costos, hay maquinaria que responde perfectamente bien a la demanda productiva de las plantas mexicanas que sigue siendo reducida y por tanto resulta más costeable y menos riesgoso mantener subprocesos intensivos en mano de obra.[26] Además para los socios tecnológicos esto es un negocio redondo, son máquinas que ya fueron ampliamente utilizadas, se venden al exterior y con esto el retorno de la inversión es mayor.

Además a lo largo de la historia de la industria de autopartes en México se ha podido constatar la dependencia tecnológica del extranjero. Esta brecha se siguen ensanchando si se toma en cuenta que las máquinas y por tanto la tecnología son importadas. Hoy en día la maquinaria para la industria de autopartes cuenta con sistemas electrónicos, hidráulicos, neumáticos y de censores, así como máquinas de control numérico. Esta gran complejidad tecnológica sólo se diseña en países altamente industrializados y se exporta a todo el mundo. Si bien antes en México, los obreros podían modificar algunas partes de la maquinaria para adaptarla a sus necesidades, hoy, ante la sofisticación tecnológica, sólo diseñan en las mismas empresas de autopartes, dispositivos mecánicos auxiliares y se adecuan troqueles, bovinas y herramentales. La injerencia en la tecnología se limita a dar mantenimiento e inclusive reparar la maquinaria. Sin embargo, para problemas mayores se tiene que recurrir a los centros de investigación y desarrollo de origen.

Ante la globalización y las condiciones económicas actuales, la respuesta de los socios tecnológicos ha sido diversa. Unos pocos han invertido capital de riesgo, ampliando su participación financieras. Otros consideran que la situación actual del país no es propicia para nuevas inversiones directas. Un

---

[26] Una de las plantas estudiadas fabrica mil marchas diarias, mientras que en Alemania se fabrican 32 mil diarias. Haciendo un análisis costo-beneficio, les convino mantener procesos intensivos en mano de obra más que introducir máquinas muy sofisticada.

elemento que enfatizan es el hecho de que no existe una mezcla equilibrada entre exportaciones y ventas para el mercado local. Uno de los ejecutivos de empresa de autopartes comentó que en 1996 México exportaría el 85% de su producción en la industria automotriz y sólo se consumiría localmente el 15%,[27] lo cual demuestra la crisis de la demanda interna. Ante esta situación, los socios tecnológicos sólo se limitan a seguir ofreciendo asesoría técnica y financiera. Además, como se mencionó en el apartado anterior, algunos de estos socios sienten amenazada su posición en el mercado internacional, al pretender las empresas instaladas en México entrar directamente en los circuitos de producción global. En algunos de estos casos, estas plantas han optado por cesar la relación con los socios tecnológicos, compitiendo de manera independiente por conseguir un espacio en estas nuevas relaciones productivas.

Otro problema es que hay un rezago significativo en la capacitación, los obreros en lo general no han recibido la información ni el entrenamiento adecuados para familiarizarse con la calidad ni con la participación grupal.[28] Esto es un proceso que lleva tiempo, dinero y esfuerzo, tres elementos que sólo pueden atender las empresas con gran capacidad financiera y que ya tienen una posición privilegiada en el mercado. Empresas que pueden invertir y esperar ver frutos a mediano plazo.

En este apartado se pudo apreciar que los bloques de integración regional, que se consideran ejemplos de la globalización, incrementaron la presión internacional por implementar cambios significativos en cuanto a, la inversión en mejores herramientas de trabajo, mejores insumos y por ende mejor respuesta a las demandas del consumidor. Esto se ha derivado en un rejuego de poder, en el que las cadenas productivas por un lado, ampliaron y afianzaron cierta interconexiones pero, por el otro, generaron nuevas rivalidades.

---

[27] Sólo para ilustrar este desbalance, el Volkswagen es un coche de alto consumo en México. En 1996 la planta en Puebla producía mil unidades diarias, de las cuales 800 se exportaban a Estados Unidos y Canadá.

[28] Una empresa de autopartes iba a tener la visita de tres inspectores para evaluar la implementación de QS9000. Como parte del procedimiento, los inspectores hacen preguntas a los obreros. Como la inducción a la filosofía de calidad había sido deficiente, se prepararon carteles sobre el QS9000, se les dio unas calcomanías con la filosofía de la empresa, pidiéndoles que se aprendieran de memoria el lema de la compañía y se les dio una plática rápida para que pudieran responder adecuadamente a los inspectores, haciéndoles notar que si no contestaban correctamente, la empresa podía cerrar y ellos se quedarían sin trabajo, pues dependía su futuro de esa dictaminación.

REFLEXIÓN FINAL

En este ensayo se tomó como punto de análisis los cambios experimentados por la industria de autopartes en México. Se puede afirmar que efectivamente no sólo se dio un mayor grado de complejidad sino que se pudieron apreciar diferencias cualitativamente significativas en la integración de esta rama productiva instalada en México dentro del sistema económico mundial. En las diversas etapas por las que ha atravesado la industria de autopartes se destacan dos niveles de integración.

El primero orientado hacia la producción de autopartes para el consumo nacional dentro de la política de sustitución de importaciones. Esto provocó la transnacionalización de la producción orientada exclusivamente a cubrir la demanda de los países receptores. En ese momento fabricando productos basados en prototipos uniformes pero con calidad diversa, de acuerdo al mercado que cubrían. El gobierno mexicano coadyuvó a esta situación protegiendo la producción interna de la competencia internacional, incluso participando directamente como empresario en las cadenas productivas. Este primer nivel de integración arrancó y se consolidó con una fuerte dependencia en la obtención de materias primas e insumos diversos además de la tecnología de los países altamente industrializados. Sin embargo, la base tecnológica era principalmente mecánica lo que permitió un mayor margen de maniobra en la adecuación de ésta al contexto mexicano.

El segundo nivel de integración se distingue por la reestructuración internacional de la industria automotriz. Para México, esto significó abrir la frontera productiva y comercial nacional y tener que competir en el plano mundial. La propuesta era participar directamente en el encadenamiento productivo de la industria automotriz, con productos que compiten en calidad, precio y tiempo de entrega dentro de los estándares globales. La estrategia ha sido una mayor especialización en los procesos productivos. El estado mexicano propició la libre competencia, producto de su política económica neoliberal. En este tenor, el gobierno, para fomentar la exportación de productos mexicanos, implementó medidas buscando posicionar a la planta industrial en condiciones de mayor competitividad internacional. Lo más significativo fue la integración a las economías regionales. En el último apartado se pudo apreciar como, a partir de la expansión del sistema productivo automotriz a escala mundial, aparecieron fuerzas integradoras, a la vez que, fuerzas fraccionadoras que han irrumpido la estabilidad del sistema a nivel de la planta productiva ya existente en México.

La industria de autopartes ha realizado grandes esfuerzos para poder introducirse a las redes del mercado global. Las estrategias han sido múltiples: aglutinarse en grandes corporaciones para poder optar por mejores condiciones tecnológicas, financieras y de mercado. Abandonar su papel productor para convertirse en representante de autopartes que se importan directamente del extranjero. Participar en el programa maquilador que los sitúan en una posición de mayor dependencia del exterior.

La ventaja competitiva se concentra en el bajo costo de los salarios. En estas plantas se encuentra una combinación de procesos altamente tecnificados con procesos intensivos en mano de obra. Sin lugar a dudas, la cercanía al mercado consumidor más grande del mundo hace de México una base industrial atractiva. Sus desventajas, los bajos volúmenes de producción, que limita su posibilidad de realizar inversiones tecnológicas costosas ; La dependencia de materia prima internacional que repercute directamente en los costos, la subordinación a la tecnología de punta y a socios tecnológicos que en ocasiones han frenado la posibilidad de las plantas de autopartes en México de entrar directamente a los mercados internacionales.

Las grandes empresas de autopartes en México siempre se han movido dentro de las fronteras organizacionales de la empresa automotriz. Los dos niveles de integración responden a cambios cualitativos de las economías de escala en el sistema mundial contemporáneo, participando dentro de una dinámica de apoyo y confrontación por el control diferenciado de los recursos. Este control se vuelve multicéntrico si se considera el acceso diferenciado a la tecnología, a los insumos y al mercado. Para las plantas de autopartes en México la integración a la cadena productiva de vehículos los ha sometido a relaciones heterogéneas de complementación y competencia. Variaciones en las relaciones que definitivamente no han alterado su situación subordinada, no central en las redes productivas y comerciales de la industria automotriz.

BIBLIOGRAFÍA

Arteaga, Arnulfo (coordinador) 1992 *Proceso de trabajo y relaciones laborales en la industria automotriz en México,* Universidad Autónoma Metropolitana-Iztapalapa y la Fundación Friedrich Ebert, México.

Blim, Michael l. 1992 *Introduction: The Emerging Global Factory and Anthropology, Anthropology and the Global Factory,* Bergin and Garvey edit, U.S.A.

Carrillo, Jorge y Patricia García 1987 Etapas industriales y conflictos laborales: La industria automotriz en México", *Estudios Sociológicos,* núm. 14, mayo-agosto.

Chase-Dunn, E.d. 1989 *Global Formation Structures of the World-Economy,* Edit. Basil Blackwell.

Flores E., Cesar 1987 "Evolución de la industria automotriz en México" en *La reconversión industrial en América Latina. La industria automotriz.* Fondo de Cultura Económica, México, pags. 58-64.

Ianni, Octavio 1996 *Teorías de la globalización,* Siglo XXI editores, México.

Mateyca, James 1987 "Reconversión de autopartes en México"_*La reconversión industrial en América Latina. La industria automotriz.* Fondo de Cultura Económica, México, pags. 132-59.

Morales, Josefina 1992 "La reestructuración industrial"en *La reestructuración industrial en México. Cinco aspectos fundamentales".* En Editorial Nuestro Tiempo, Instituto de Investigaciones Económicas, UNAM, México. págs. 55-98.

Revista Expansión, 1997, Autopartes. "La última oportunidad", México, octubre 22.

Revista Imagina, "Imagen de la Industria Nacional de Autopartes, México, Año 2, Núm. 14, julio-agosto.

Scheinman, Marc, 1996, México's Auto Industry in Transition: Recession Hastens Globalization Michigan: A Special Report from Ward's Communications.

Vidal Bonifaz, Francisco Javier 1992 "Lo que el viento se llevó: la industria paraestatal", en *La reestructuración industrial en México. Cinco aspectos fundamentales.* Editorial Nuestro Tiempo, Instituto de Investigaciones Económicas, UNAM, México. Págs. 99-130.

Wallerstein, Emmanuel 1974 "The Rise and Future Demise of the World Capitalist System: Concepts for Comparative Analysis", *Comparative Studies in Society and History,* The Cambridge University Press, vol.16, núm. 4, septiembre, págs. 387-409.

1979 *El moderno sistema mundial. La agricultura capitalista y los orígenes de la economía-mundo europea en el siglo XVI,* Siglo XXI Editores, México.

Wolfe, Alvin 1977 "The Supranational Organization of Production: an Evolutionary Perspective", *Current Anthropology,* vol. 18, no.4, diciembre.

Zambrano, Carlos 1987 "La industria mexicana de autopartes: su situación y proceso de reconversión", *La reconversión industrial en América Latina. La industria automotriz.* Fondo de Cultura Económica, México.

Zapata, Francisco, Taeko Hoshino y Linda Hanono 1994 *La reestructuración industrial en México. El caso de la industria de autopartes.* Cuadernos del CES, el Colegio de México, no. 37.

LEAN PRODUCTION AND THE SPECTER OF MEXICO: A CASE STUDY OF A U.S. AUTO PARTS PLANT

*Susan Helper**

INTRODUCTION

After years of growth and relative stability following World War II, the North American auto industry has been transformed in the past two decades by two major changes: the globalization of competition and the spread of lean production techniques. This chapter analyzes the relation between these two trends in a supplier plant where both have been particularly apparent.[1]

The operation in question is headquartered in a medium-sized Ohio town, and is a wholly-owned subsidiary of a U.S. automaker; I will call it "Brookline."[2] In the late 1960s, the Brookline operation employed 13,500 workers in one huge complex approximately one and a half miles long and a quarter of a mile wide. This vertically integrated complex provided the parent company with all of its wiring harnesses —the bundled wires that distribute electrical signals throughout the car. Workers were represented by an international union, and received wages and benefits comparable to those who worked in automobile assembly plants.

During the next decades, Brookline underwent a series of related, but separable changes. First, competition in its product market increased, as Brookline's parent began to turn to lower-wage, nonunion competitors for wiring harnesses. In response, Brookline's divisional management began in 1973 to open new plants in lower-wage areas, first in Mississippi, then in

---

* Associate Professor of Economics, Case Western Reserve University.

[1] Thanks to Steve Babson, John Russo, Tony Budak, Frank Budak, Alice Lynd, Staughton Lynd, Charlotte Ingalls, and Don Wells for many helpful discussions about the issues discussed in this paper.

[2] See Kochan, Katz, and Mower (1984) and Gillett (1992) for much useful information on this division.

Mexico and Asia. By 1997, Brookline had 37,000 employees in Mexico,[3] and bargaining-unit employment in Ohio had fallen to 7,000. Second, Brookline management adopted several of the tenets of what came to be called "lean production." For example, management sought a larger voice for the division in designing its products; management and the union set up several mechanisms for employee participation in decision-making; and some managers (particularly in Mexico) actively studied Japanese quality assurance techniques, aided considerably by tutoring from a Japanese rival.

These changes came to Brookline earlier than they did in many other manufacturing plants, both automotive and non-automotive. Understanding the causes, consequences, and interrelationships of these changes may help others to understand —and to change— their environments. In particular, understanding the linkages between the nature of product-market competition and the ways in which new production techniques are implemented will help to answer the question of whether lean production is, or can be, beneficial to workers.

THE DEBATE OVER LEAN PRODUCTION

Womack, Jones, and Roos (1990) coined the term "lean production" to signify a system in which empowered work teams minimize buffers, boost productivity, and correct defects through continuous-improvement activities (see Babson, this volume, for a summary of the key elements of lean production.) According to Womack et al., lean production benefits everyone: for consumers, managers, and workers, it is simply "a superior way for human beings to make things." Workers necessarily benefit because lean production depends on their commitment to continuously improve a system that runs with minimal —"lean"— resources; their withdrawal of commitment will therefore shut the system down. In fact, Womack and his research team initially called lean production "fragile production" to emphasize its vulnerability to disruptions of this and other types.

In contrast, Parker and Slaughter (1995) argue that lean production is "management by stress," in which workers are forced to come up with ways to eliminate any slack time from their jobs. Lean production puts workers into deliberately understaffed teams and pushes them to identify with man-

[3] Ringler 1996, 1.

agement goals. Peer pressure replaces supervisors in monitoring output, blurring the line between management and workers at great cost to union values of solidarity. Lean production weakens or removes seniority rights and job classifications which protected the "industrial citizenship" that workers had won through their unions, replacing due process with management fiat (Wells 1995, 1997).

Adler (1996) admits that lean production can take the form of "despotic Taylorism," in which workers indeed suffer. However, lean production can also take the form of a "democratic Taylorism," in which workers have a significant say in the design of their jobs and in plant governance. Even though the jobs are repetitive and must be done in a standardized way, this type of production has a lot to recommend it because it provides an acceptable balance between workers' need for creativity and control (met through collective design and improvement of standardized work methods), and society's need for efficiency.

For Applebaum and Batt (1994), the "high performance" or "high road" workplace incorporates many elements of lean production: an emphasis on quality, training, and employee participation. The skills needed to run such a workplace ensure workers high wages and protection against an excessively fast pace of work; the productivity, high quality, and responsiveness achieved by these workers enables management to make profits as well.

Babson (1997) and Kaminski (this volume) take a middle road: lean production has some potentially good aspects for workers, but a strong, vigilant union is necessary to ensure that these gains are realized. Babson (73) notes that this state of affairs should not be surprising; unions fought hard to humanize mass production and achieved a fair amount of success in "tam[ing] the most oppressive inequities of Fordism." Lean production is not "inherently any worse for workers than the Fordist system of mass production."

What explains these different perceptions? Two key questions are:

1. How easy is it for a worker to find another job of equivalent quality? Womack implicitly assumes it is quite easy; a worker has nothing to fear if she pulls the stop cord. It is management which has to worry about keeping workers happy enough that they work hard in ways that are tough to monitor: making suggestions, running to fix problems before the (very small) buffer runs out, etc. Applebaum and Batt's high performance workplace has institutions in place that prevent managers from acting capriciously: unions which enforce the use of grievance procedures, or training which makes workers hard to replace; Adler's view is that NUMMI has such institutions. In contrast, Parker and Slaughter (1995) and Wells (1997) argue that auto workers don't have good employment alternatives if they should lose their current job, so they will acquiesce to speed-ups and other concessions (and pressure their peers to do the same) to keep their plant open. Babson and Kaminski seem more contingent; if unions are strong (with capable leaders, active members, and favorable product and legal environments), then lean production will be implemented in a way more beneficial to workers.

2. *Should workers in a capitalist economy accept responsibility for the quality and cost of production?* Womack et al. implicitly assumes that the answer is yes. Adler also believes that in situations like NUMMI, where workers have a say in governance, they are not "just dupes if they accept some responsibility for reducing costs. I hear workers saying 'Why should American consumers have to pay an extra $2,000 a vehicle just because we can't learn to work effectively in the plant?' I don't think that they say this just because they have been brainwashed." Adler also points out that competitive pressures don't always benefit capitalists at the expense of workers; sometimes consumer demands for quality, in particular, force managers to give workers more power than they would like.

The other authors, to varying degrees, find this idea problematic. Wells (1995, 1997) finds that lean production aims to create a new form of Gramscian hegemony, in which lower classes internalize managerial norms, to the benefit of dominant classes. Local unions which adopt such goals as their own may win some temporary benefits for their plant, but ultimately will weaken their collective strength and endanger "union autonomy, worker solidarity, and the future of labor politics." (1997, 190).

In the sections that follow, I will examine how these factors of external competition and internal identification with managerial goals affected the ways in which lean production has been implemented (or not) in Brookline's Ohio operations.

RESPONSES TO COMPETITION AT BROOKLINE

The 1950s and 1960s: The Good Old Days?

In the post-World War II years, Brookline was a traditional mass production factory. Thousands of workers labored together under one roof, producing a relatively standard product from beginning (raw steel, copper, and plastic resin) to end.

There were four parts to the production process. The first was making the cable; the second was making the components (brass terminals and plastic connectors) that eventually were attached to the cable; the third was lead prep, in which cables were cut to the proper length and had a terminal placed on one or both ends; the final step was assembling the harness, in which connectors were snapped on to the cut leads, which were then bundled together with tape.

The first two steps were long-characterized by a high degree of automation. The third, lead prep, began to be automated in 1980s, while the last step, harness assembly, still remained quite labor-intensive even in the 1990s. Assembly is done by a group of about twenty people working on large peg boards with many posts to guide the routing of leads, and holders for attaching connectors. The boards are attached to conveyors; each worker attaches a few wires or connectors as the board passes her station. The work can be learned in a few hours, and is very tedious. There are many opportunities to create a defect —for example, by not inserting a lead into the connector far enough to establish an electrical connection.

Relations between union and management were adversarial until the end of the 1970s. For example, according an oral history compiled by a union member, work rules in the 1950s stated that "no more than two people were allowed to speak to one another at the same time, lunch time was limited to 20 minutes, and no tables and chairs were provided." It took a wildcat strike in 1959 to get fans installed in the factory, despite intense heat from plastic molding machinery. There was a fair amount of worker militancy expressed on the shopfloor, including wildcat strikes (Sachs 1994).

The 1970s and 1980s: The Rise of Low-Wage Competition

In the 1970s, unionized autoworkers were able to maintain their real wages despite stagflation. However, workers at their nonunion competition steadily fell behind the rising cost of living, creating an ever larger wage gap (Herzenberg 1991, ch. 5). This gap had a particularly noticeable impact on prices of a labor-intensive product like wiring-harness assembly, and nonunion competitors began to pose a threat to Brookline's monopoly of the parent's wiring-harness business. In response, Brookline undertook a two-pronged strategy: it sought both to find lower-wage workers, and to innovate in products and service to the customer.

The low-wage strategy began with a 1973 announcement of "no more bricks and mortar" (i.e., investment) in Brookline's Ohio operations (Kochan et al. 1984, Sachs 1994). Instead, Brookline met growing demand for its product by turning to nonunion subcontractors (often owned by current or former Brookline supervisors), and by opening two plants in Mississippi in 1973 and 1975. The Mississippi plants were eventually organized (in 1979 and 1982) by the same union that represents Brookline workers in Ohio. These southern plants included not only harness assembly, but cable making and molding of connectors. In 1975, Brookline opened its first plants in Mexico, for harness assembly only. The Mexican factories paid one-tenth of the wages paid in Ohio, a percentage which has declined over time. The Mississippi factories started out low-wage, but are now covered by the same master agreement as the Ohio operations.

However, Brookline management decided that the low-wage strategy "was not a sufficient response." According to a senior executive, "nobody is profitable at build-to-[blue]print wiring, your margin is like a grocery store, just a few percentage points. Wiring is not perceived as hi-tech and has lots of labor content. So you're a low-wage chaser, a continual price chaser" (Gillett 1992, 79-80). Brookline therefore decided to increase the engineering content of its products. Rather than build connectors according to blueprints provided by the car divisions, Brookline began to design proprietary connectors with improved features, such as increased impermeableness to water, and ability to carry a higher voltage without overheating. The supplier invested early and heavily in benchmarking the competition and reverse-engineering their designs. (Gillett 1992; divisional web site; engineering headquarters visit, 1992)

Brookline also began to emphasize responsiveness to the customer. This strategy was attractive to the buyer for several reasons. First, wiring, while unglamorous, can be the source of many headaches for the final consumer; it's very difficult to find a loose connection once a harness is installed in a car. Also, wiring is subject to frequent engineering changes, since it is relatively cheap to shorten a wire or change a connector in response to a quality problem. For example, perhaps the designer of a new car model has left so little space in an area that it is hard for a worker to fit his hand in to install a part. Changing sheet metal would require new tooling, an expensive and time-consuming proposition. Automakers would pay a premium for a wiring supplier who would not only quickly respond to engineering changes, but would also station an engineer at their assembly plant to help improve quality and reduce long-term costs. In the early 1980s, Brookline began stationing such "resident engineers" inside the customer's assembly plants to provide a quick response to quality problems and design changes. While resident engineers are common in Japan, this was perhaps their first use in the United States. (Gillett 1992, 44).

Meanwhile, more harness assembly work was moved to Mexico, and the Ohio workforce was gradually shifted to the making of components for the Mexican operation. At first, according to one worker, "we were happy to see the conveyors go —we hated that work" (interview, June 1997). But as the movement of work continued, job security became a major concern. "Every discussion or complaint [met with the response] 'We can always move your job to Mexico' .... It was the first time I heard 'be grateful you *have* a job.' Fear took hold ...." (interviews with shopfloor workers in Sachs 1994, 11). As indicated in Table 1, job loss was already evident by 1977.

In that year, the winning candidates for union shop chairman and local president ran on a platform that promised to "try to save jobs and have closer cooperation with management" (interview with shop chairman in Kochan et al. 1984, 34). Because of the growth in demand for its products, Brookline managers felt they "needed the continued cooperation of its existing workers as it sought to lower its overall wage costs" (Gillett 1992, 76). Both parties therefore agreed on a plan to increase employee involvement in Ohio.

The shop chairman offered the union's participation in a task force that management had set up to improve performance. The result was a joint Jobs Committee (Sachs 1994; Kochan et al. 1984, 34-35). The work of this committee resulted in the first hiring in Ohio since 1973, and three new plants were opened at the complex between 1978 and 1980 —marking the end of the "no more bricks and mortar" pledge (union newsletter, 1979). The employee involvement process also called for committees of rank-and-file employees, and there were 60-65 such committees operating by the summer of 1983. These committees dealt with issues such as substance abuse, health and safety, and defect prevention using Statistical Process Control. In one of the new plants, three production lines operated as "Semi-Autonomous Work Groups," meaning that they had no direct supervisor. The plant's "Quality of Work Life" program was praised by industrial relations experts Kochan, Katz, and Mower (1984, 33), who noted that "the program has gone considerably farther than most of the QWL activities" at other plants in their study.

Table 1
Employment at Brookline

Year	Number of Active Bargaining Unit Employees
1973	13,500
1977	12,000
1979	12,500
1982	9,000
1984	8,900
1992	6,500
1994	8,000
1997	7,500
1998	5,900 est.
2000	5,000 est.

Sources: Kochan, Katz, Mower (1984); union newsletter; *Employee Benefit Plan Review*, 1985; interviews with union officials.

However, the company still felt that costs were too high, and in 1977 management proposed that new workers be hired at $4.50 per hour in wages, compared to the $12 per hour wage of the incumbent workforce. The union voted this proposal down in 1978, but in the recession year of 1982, the Jobs Committee again proposed a two-tier wage structure, along with an early retirement program. After much debate, the membership agreed in 1984 to the two-tier proposal. Under this "Progressive Hiring Plan" (PHP), new employees would be hired at 55 percent of the $19.60 hourly base compensation (including benefits) of senior employees. The new hires would reach parity after ten years. In addition, the contract stipulated that anyone in the bargaining unit who was employed by Brookline in 1982 would not lose their job due to movement of work to new plants.[4] Under this agreement, 1,500 people were hired. (*Business Week* 1983)

The two-tier wages remain a source of controversy in the union. Some argue that the second tier created a second class of worker, which is inconsistent with union solidarity. Others felt that the lower wage was the only way that new workers would be hired.

[4] In a later contract, it was agreed that those hired under the PHP would gain this protection after ten years with the company.

At first, many workers were enthusiastic about the employee involvement program. At least a third of the union dissidents interviewed by Sachs served as coordinators in the first years of the program, but this group of workers gradually grew disillusioned, feeling that they had lost sight of their own interests. One union representative, who had been involved in joint decision-making for years, said that "if you spend too much time with management, you begin to think like management .... Looking back I was wrong to do this" (Sachs 1994, 24). The union leadership was so closely tied to management and its ideology of competitiveness that they no longer did a good job of defending workers' interests, he felt.

Management also grew frustrated with employee involvement in Ohio: its principal result, they felt, was not cost reduction, but more jobs paying uncompetitive wages (Gillett, personal communication, 1991). There was also frustration with the union, which management saw as blocking progress and failing to recognize the realities of the marketplace. There was also resentment: a senior worker with overtime made more than some mid-level managers, and these salaried personnel sometimes complained that "no one gives me any job security." Engineers who were told to learn Spanish and prepare to move away from their homes in the Midwest to El Paso also felt that the "selfish union" was causing the decline of Brookline's hometown (interviews, 1997).

However, Brookline's operations in Mexico had adopted many principles of lean production, and the new products and services sold well. The division was given high marks in a 1986 study that classified each of the parents' division as red (not competitive), yellow (potentially competitive) or green (world class). Brookline was deemed to be "green," with the cautionary note that the division tended to be high cost. Brookline succeeded in winning some business to supply rival automakers; the major problem the division faced, joked some managers, was that it was tied to a "red" customer —its parent, which was losing record amounts of money and market share (Gillett, personal communication, 1991).

The 1990s: Brookline Emerges as A High-Tech, Low-Wage Competitor

As we have seen, Brookline was able to simultaneously implement a high-tech and a low-wage strategy. This ability to combine the two strategies appears to contradict the prescription of those who argue that management must choose only one of two ways to compete: the high road, producing high-quality, innovative products with a high-wage and therefore motivated labor force, and the low road, paying low wages and, therefore, producing lower quality products with unmotivated workers.

In fact, Brookline was able to separate its products from its production process. As the new customer service strategy took hold, many more resources in Ohio were devoted to product engineering, and many fewer to industrial engineering (Gillett 1992, 42; interviews, 1997). In contrast, industrial engineering became a high priority in the Mexican plants in the mid-1980s; a former plant manager in Mexico felt that this emphasis helped to explain the high quality performance of the Mexican plants (interview, April 1997). It is possible that a high-wage, high-commitment strategy might have been more profitable, since it could have been even more responsive to customers, involving shopfloor workers in problem-solving and shortening supply lines (Helper 1995). However, it is hard to know, since Brookline's rivals also adopted a low-wage strategy, eliminating the possibility of comparing results.[5]

In 1994, many of the "PHPs" reached parity with the senior workers. In contract negotiations that year, management said that it would hire new workers only if a third tier of wages were introduced. After much debate, the union approved the "Competitive Hiring Plan" (CHP), under which workers would be hired at $9.68 per hour with limited benefits. They would receive the job security and pay package of the incumbent employees only after 85 percent of those hired before 1973 had retired. In return, the union was promised 2,000 new jobs assembling particularly complex harnesses. (The harnesses went into a car which was both high-end, meaning lots of electronics, and small, meaning not much space to put all the wiring.)

In December 1994, management again went to the union with a proposal for hiring 1,000 new workers, this time if the union agreed to reductions in job classifications. The new work would be focused on Bussed Electrical Centers (BEC), a significant departure from traditional wiring harness design.

---

[5] A partial exception was Sumitomo, the company that helped Brookline's Mexican plants learn about lean production. At Honda's request, Sumitomo set up its North American operations in Kentucky and had a fair amount of success, though the firm eventually built a Mexican plant as well (MacDuffie and Helper, forthcoming).

In a traditional harness, a wire is required for each switch. With the huge number of electronic gadgets in today's cars, these wires take up a significant amount of space, creating problems in fitting all the harnesses inside car doors, for example. In a BEC, multiple switches are placed inside a box, with a harness attached at either end. A car has about 4 BECs, replacing up to a mile of wiring. This technology was invented by Brookline. Because BEC production is less labor-intensive, it offers the possibility that more production could be profitable in Ohio.

Whether or not the hiring pledge has been fulfilled is a matter of disagreement. BEC production began in June 1996; but the previous January, the company announced that 1,800 wire-cutting jobs were being transferred to Mexico. The union thought management had promised to hire 1,000 new employees; managers thought they had agreed that 1,000 people who would have been laid off due to the movement of work to Mexico and elsewhere, would still have jobs. In addition, in November 1996, management announced that the BECs for pickup trucks would be made in Mississippi, not Ohio —a loss of 468 jobs— and that the harness assembly for the small high-end car would be moved to Mexico by September (Klayman 1994; Christian 1996; Ringler 1997, 1).

Meanwhile, the union had been working without a local contract for ten months. A tentative agreement was finally reached in March, 1997, but 68 percent of the membership voted against it. The union therefore went on strike on May 13, 1997. This turn of events was a surprise to many, including the company and some employees, since the walkout came from a union "with little history of strikes or militancy" (Adams and Vanac 1997).

The opposition to the tentative agreement was based on two factors: a feeling among older workers that retirement incentives were not sufficiently generous in a year of record profits for the corporation, and fear of continued job loss among younger workers. Both groups were united in feeling that the leadership had given too much to management.[6] Of the 7,500 active

---

[6] Particularly troublesome was the union leadership's willingness to go along with a 1994 management proposal to move to "continuous run" in some areas, without calling for a vote of the membership. Continuous run meant that workers worked three 12-hour shifts in three days, and then had the next three days off. This system had some benefits for management: better machine usage (higher quality and lower energy costs because the machines were less fre-

workers at the Ohio operation at the time of the strike, 45 percent were "traditional" (i.e., pre -1973) employees making $20 per hour plus benefits and guaranteed against layoffs due to movement of work to other Brookline plants. One thousand were CHPs, who made $9.68 and had no job security; the rest were PHPs, who did have job security and earned an intermediate wage. The average age of the work force was over 45 years, and average seniority was 28 years. (At thirty years' seniority, an employee may retire at full pension.) Despite the protection that many workers have against layoffs, hiring and no-layoff guarantees remained important issues. Many members want to see their children and grandchildren work at Brookline; others are concerned about the economy of the region if Brookline's operations shrink further. (Adams and Vanac 1997; union's unofficial web site; interviews).

The strike resulted in a victory for the union after only 26 hours on the picket lines. Most importantly, the CHPs were given no-layoff guarantees, and retirement incentives were increased.

VARIETIES OF LEAN PRODUCTION IN THE OHIO OPERATIONS

The previous section showed the development and flowering of mutual mistrust, due in large part to the rise of low-wage competition for Brookline's products. It is against this background that efforts to adopt lean production at Brookline should be understood.

In 1992 visits to Brookline's operations, I observed a striking difference between the division's Ohio and Mexican plants (Helper 1995). The Mexican plants (which assembled components made in Ohio) had adopted much of the lean production menu. There was minimal work-in-progress inventory in the plant, and great attention was paid to minimizing wasted motion by designing special racks to hold wires and connectors. Although operators did not participate much in these activities, industrial engineers were actively involved in continuous improvement, including organizing evening study groups to read the latest on just-in-time production. In contrast, the Ohio

---

quently turned off, and therefore spent less time producing bad parts as they were warmed up), and reduced overtime payments.

Another issue was that the international union had agreed to not oppose Brookline management's building a plant in Alabama in 1993, where the workers would be paid $6.50 per hour. In return, management would not oppose the union's efforts to organize the plant.

operations were squarely rooted in the mass production era. Large, expensive, and not particularly reliable machines made huge batches of components and wires, even when the next processing step was to be done not in Mexico, but a few hundred yards away.

By 1997 lean production techniques were more in evidence in Ohio, but adoption was very uneven in different parts of the complex.[7] The most traditional operation was wire drawing, in which copper wire was stretched thinner by a series of different machines. Most of the machines were decades old. Because the machines had different capacities, workers spent a great deal of time loading wire onto a spool, welding the ends from the new and old spools together, and then breaking apart the welds so the wire could wait in inventory until its turn on the next machine. Two years ago, two new "multidraw" machines were introduced. Each of these has computer controls and can draw several types of wire at once, but they don't eliminate the inventory, loading, and unloading of the old system.

Running these machines requires a fair amount of skill: to thread the wire through the maze of brackets and fixtures in the machine; to use the right amount of lubricant to keep it cool; and to avoid injury from the rapidly spinning wire. Many of the tricks about how to do these things were only inside the heads of the operators, who were all men with decades of experience. As one of them put it, "the corporation may own the machine, but I own the knowledge." No standardized work instructions were visible.

This knowledge is important to the plant's performance. The plant superintendent explained that high uptime was the key to making money in the business; he was proud of the increase in capacity utilization from 92 percent to 94 percent over the last year. (Less attention was paid to the rework numbers, which at 3.6 percent seemed to represent significant lost output.)

Like his colleagues in the wire drawing plant, the vinylite machine operator also had a fair amount of autonomy in the way he did his job. His years of experience helped him in changeovers to a different color, which he did every 20 minutes to 8 hours, and in knowing when to start the next batch. "Usually," he said, "I start a new color with 7000 feet of wire left in the reel, but I'll run a bit more scrap this time because we're talking."

He had become reluctant to share with management the improvements he had figured out, because he had previously experienced a similar line being

[7] I visited the main Brookline complex in April 1997, before the strike.

videotaped before the work was sent to Alabama. Recently, he had run a sample for the division's plant in China to use as a model. As a "traditional" employee, his own job was not threatened by these actions, but he worried about the impact on the town.

In this area, there are meetings of operators and supervisors to discuss production issues. These are not regularly scheduled, but held "when the corporation wants you to run quality." According to a union representative, these meetings are held "in the guise of health and safety meetings, which the union wants, and the contract dictates —but they slip efficiency in there because the men won't go to efficiency meetings."

The other areas of the plant had more elements of lean production. However, some of the new machines had been designed more with a mass production philosophy in mind. That is, they were complicated, embodied a lot of skill in the machine rather than the operator, and were capable of producing a large volume of output when they were up (which wasn't always, due to the complexity). One example was a slitter, a $3 million machine introduced three years before, which cut up steel to be used in making terminals. The operator said, "I love this work —I like to be busy." Every 3 minutes she changed a roll of steel, threaded it in a complicated way, walked 20 feet to other end of machine, and pushed on the roll with a stick to align it correctly ("that's because I'm short").

Kaizen techniques were being used to improve the performance of the machine, with most of the effort apparently done by engineers. A chart on the wall showed increasing capacity utilization (though it was still only 70 percent) and some of the reasons why: using bigger rolls of steel (which had to be changed less often), improved stock availability, etc. While no one has worked on eliminating the time to walk to the end of the machine and adjust the steel with the stick, some aspects of the operation were quite worker-friendly. The area was carpeted with a cushioned floor mat which was much easier to stand on all day than the cement floor, and a light curtain improved safety. Asked if she had ever made a suggestion to improve the operation, she laughed and said she didn't think it would be worthwhile.

The BEC area has three types of jobs. One job is tending machines making components; these machines are complicated plastic injection molders which can make very precise patterns. A second job was working on an assembly line of about 20 people, putting together the boxes. A third job (held by only about four people) was inspecting the final product.

The assembly jobs had the least autonomy. Cycle times were under a minute, and there was no buffer between stations. There were photos above each station indicating how to do each job, and the assemblers seemed to be being following the prescribed procedure. There was also a sign explaining what to do about quality problems: "If you find a defect, attempt to repair. If you can't, document and properly dispose of the part." (That is, don't stop the line, don't personally do a root-cause analysis, and don't keep the part for analysis of what might have gone wrong.) One machine had a big sign above it saying "gloves must be worn on this job"; it was being operated by someone not wearing gloves.

The machine operators spent a lot of their time stacking parts as they came off of the machine, inspecting as they went. They were also responsible for some set-up and maintenance. For example, a common problem was that the machine ejected the part before it was cooled, leaving a mark. Operators were trained to adjust the timing so that this didn't happen. One operator kept a notebook of fixes that technicians had made to her machine. No one had suggested she do this; "I just don't want to have to bother them for every little thing that goes wrong."

The inspectors performed a number of tests to make sure that the product worked. On the day that I visited the plant, they seemed to be idle at least half of the time.

All of the workers on the day shift were supposed to receive a 24-minute break in the morning. The machine tenders were accustomed to turning their machine off, or calling for a "floater" when they took their breaks. However, to increase output, the supervisor wanted the operators to leave the machines running, and catch up on stacking parts when they returned. To the supervisor, this seemed like effective time management; to the operators, this was changing a negotiated part of the contract without due process. It also seemed unfair that the workers on the assembly line and those whose machines needed frequent tending continued to have their machines turned off while they were on break.[8]

Workers found ways to withhold cooperation, consciously or not. The day I visited the area, one of the molding machines was down. A "floater" came

[8] What was at issue here was not workers' physical ability to catch up (the pace of work in the molding area was fairly relaxed) but rather the principle of how that pace was to be determined.

over from the assembly area (which was not located where the machine operators could see it, frustrating visual control) to say that they had run out of parts. She stopped to talk a little with the operator and myself, while the operator filled a container with parts, working at a measured pace. (This was the same operator who on her own initiative kept a notebook of how to adjust the machine.) After the container was full, we talked a few more minutes, and then the floater walked back to the assembly area. About fifteen minutes was lost in this procedure; multiplied by the 20 people on the line yields 5 lost person-hours —time for a lot of 24 minute breaks, especially since it seemed that under normal circumstances, the molding machines were not the bottleneck process.

The most "lean" part of the complex was a harness-assembly plant which I visited in June 1997. Almost all assembly had long been done in Mexico, but the need to hold particularly tight tolerances led management to see if it couldn't be done in Ohio. This operation was very impressive. A lot of incremental improvements had been made by both engineers and operators, with the result that components were readily available to the worker on the conveyor without stooping, turning, or walking. Inventory was very low, and many procedures were in place to prevent defects.

The plant's high performance was recognized in a November 1996 letter to employees from the Director of Ohio Operations, which said "All performance measures within the plant's control have been excellent. The customer relationship is unparalleled." Unfortunately, these statements were made in a letter announcing the plant's closing, because "the fact remains that Ohio Operations is unable to compete [with Mexico] in high labor content products."

Despite the plant's scheduled closing three months after my visit, relations between workers and managers seemed cordial. (During the strike, the plant superintendent came out to the picket line every few hours to offer coffee and doughnuts.)

THE FUTURE OF OHIO OPERATIONS

Both management and the union seemed internally divided about the future of Brookline's Ohio operations. On the management side, one group was in favor of closing the complex completely in the next few years. Moving the entire operation to Mexico was consistent with lean production principles because 1) quality was higher (only one defective part per million in Mexico, compared with 66 for Ohio operations), and 2) just-in-time could be more effectively carried out if all parts of the value chain were near each other. Jim Womack, who served as a consultant to the company, described the Mexican operation as "world-class lean," with the exception of its long supply lines. This all-in-Mexico management group seems to have lost, because the 1997 strike settlement gave lifetime security against layoffs due to movement of work to the CHPs, most of whom are in their twenties. (However, 45 percent of the "traditional" workforce is eligible for retirement in five years, making it relatively easy to shrink the operation significantly.)

A second management group seemed to be in favor of using the threat of moving work to win concessions from the union. An example of this was the visit of the head of automotive component production for Brookline's parent, in early 1997. He came to tour the BEC area, accompanied by bodyguards. At one point he asked a supervisor in a loud voice, "so when are we moving this to Mexico?"

A third management group believed that components production should be kept in Ohio, while assembly was done in Mexico. This group of managers appeared to accept that the "high road" argument did apply to part of Brookline's operations: that is, that high-wage production could be profitable if enough technology could be applied to the problem. Customer demands for wiring that takes up less space, and advances in software that make it possible to respond to engineering changes without changing the assembly process, both increase the viability of a high-tech option. Consistent with this strategy, Ohio Operations recently announced a $25 million investment in highly precise injection molding equipment, which needs a clean-room environment and reliable power supply. Whether the profitability of this option is increased by high wages is an open question, particularly given the ambivalence of both sides about employee involvement. An alternative place to locate the high-tech production would be the U.S. South, where some of the BEC work is indeed scheduled to go. (Because these plants are newer, more hiring was done under the CHP and PHP agreements, making the average wage there lower.)

Within the union, there were also several points of view (sometimes expressed by the same person). One view, dominant in the leadership from 1977 to 1996, held that cooperating with management in making suggestions for improvement and accepting lower wages for new hires was the only way to preserve jobs in Ohio.

A second view, dominant in the people interviewed by Sachs (1994), was that employee involvement *caused* job loss. EI did this directly, by leading to productivity gains, and indirectly, by sapping the union of the militant, grass-roots tradition that had won many gains in the 1950s and 1960s. Like the first two groups of managers, these workers did not believe that there was a "high road," in which high tech, high profits, and high wages all went together. A member of the 1986 shop committee described what he had learned on a (management-sponsored) trip to Mexico: "You cannot compete with a buck and a half an hour. And if you could, they'd move to Haiti, or Sri Lanka, or Bangladesh and pay 30 cents an hour" (Sachs 1994, 25). The implication of this view seems to be the same as its management counterpart: the closing of Ohio operations. Despite the brave words of Sachs, it is hard to see why militancy would lead management to hire more people in Ohio if it is so easy to move.

A third view combines an emphasis on skill upgrading in Ohio with efforts to raise wages at competitors in the South and in Mexico. As one union member put it in August 1997, "the only way we can compete is with skill. They can continue to use us for de-bugging, and then send the work to Mexico or Mississippi when the bugs are worked out. But just as computers keep advancing, from 286 to 386 to 486, there will always be a new thing that needs to be de-bugged." However, the same person also expressed reservations about sharing ideas with management, because they could be used to speed up or move the work.

Key to the success of this view is figuring out a way that workers can share their knowledge with management in a way that both sides feel they can benefit. However, the individual security generated by the no-layoff pledge combined with bitterness toward management for continually trying to erode the bargained agreement, makes this tough on the labor side. On the management side, frustration has also built up over the years; managers are tired of the bureaucracy involved in making productivity-enhancing changes to work rules. Instead, some de-bugging work is now done at a new technical center, staffed by technicians who are not members of the bargaining unit.

CONCLUSION: MACHINE-CENTERED LEAN PRODUCTION MEETS JOB CONTROL UNIONISM

Brookline management has succeeded in adopting some aspects of lean production in their Ohio operations. However, lack of trust between management and workers has frustrated the employee involvement component of the system. In some conceptions of lean production, the key source of its success in increasing quality and productivity is that it unleashes employee creativity (Adler and Cole 1993, Florida and Kenney 1993). Paradoxically, Brookline either relies on workers' craft skill that mangers can't figure out how to standardize (wire-drawing and vinylite coating), or standardizes with little organized input from workers (BEC and slitter operation).[9]

How much to participate is a source of confusion within the union as well. One very thoughtful union leader said, "of course we want to cooperate and turn out high quality. There are other ways to compete besides competing in wages —tap into people's creativity." But later in the same conversation he added, "I'm not sure how much I want to get into producing high quality for management. Management should manage. Unless they want to give us the capital and let us run it, we shouldn't do their work for them."

In any case, it is important to note that this discomfort with lean production stems not so much from "old attitudes" or "resistance to change," but from a perception that the change hasn't been big enough —that workers do not share enough in the benefits created by sharing knowledge with management.

Perhaps the key difference between the two sides is a difference in values. With few exceptions, management believes that the discipline of the market will and should prevail. It is seen as self-evident that the company needs to do what will make the most profit;[10] government and unions should

---

[9] It is interesting to note that the former areas are populated exclusively by "traditional" male workers; the latter are populated by "traditional" female workers, and younger workers of both sexes.

[10] A partial exception to this view was the superintendent in the harness assembly plant, who believed that some kind of local content rule should protect the incomes of those who couldn't get enough education to compete on a global market. He had also sacrificed his own career advancement because he didn't want to move out of the Midwest.

not try to interfere in this process. In contrast, many of the workers do not believe that the company should try to maximize its profits; a positive profit should be enough. Instead, the company should show loyalty to them, since, as one 33-year employee put it, "I've given a lot more to GM than I have to any of my ex-wives." Another worker expressed the same thought about GM less flippantly: "we broke our legs, smashed our fingers, and breathed copper dust to make you what you are."

I argued above that lean production's impact on workers would depend on a) how easy it is for workers (and their communities) to find alternative employment, and b) how much workers and managers share the same values. As the case of Brookline shows, increased opportunities for management to globalize production have led to negative impacts for workers on both these counts. The result is an increasing divergence between the interests of top management (whose ability to make profits is not dependent on the motivation of the Ohio workforce) and workers (who have strong ties to their community). The firm and its workers are caught in a vicious circle, in which increased managerial efforts to exit from Ohio lead to reduced worker loyalty and willingness to work hard, which leads to increased managerial efforts to exit.

It is important, however, not to blame a production method for outcomes that are really the result of increased global competition and the decline of unionism in the United States. Increased competition by itself would have produced negative results for Brookline's workers under any production regime. True, more competition causes lean production to be adopted in a way that makes workers worse off (faster pace of work, less protection from management capriciousness). But speed-ups might have happened even if Jim Womack had never lived —though perhaps without lean production's emphasis on low inventories (meaning a strike can produce management concessions quickly), or its rhetoric of employee involvement.

BIBLIOGRAPHY

Adams, D. and M. Vanac. 1997. "Electrical Workers Pull Plug." *Akron Beacon Journal*, May 14, A1.

Adler, P.S., B. Goldoftas and D. Levine. 1997. "Ergonomics, Employee Involvement, and the Toyota Production System: A Case Study of

NUMMI's 1993 Model Introduction." *Industrial and Labor Relations Review* 50 (April): 416-417.

Adler, P.S. and R. Cole. 1993. "Designed for Learning: A Tale of Two auto Plants." *Sloan Management Review* 34 (fall): 85-94.

Adler, P.S., and P. Landsbergis. 1996. "Dialog on Lean Production and Workers' Health." U.S.C. Working Paper, November 1996.

Applebaum, E. and R. Batt. 1994. *The New American Workplace.* Ithaca: ILR Press.

Babson, S. 1997. "When 'Empowerment' Means 'Exploitation': Negotiating the Terms of Lean Production." *Working USA.* (May-June): 69-76.

Business Week. 1983. "Revolutionary Wage Deal." *Business Week* (August 29): 54-56.

Christian, N. 1996. "GM's Most Cooperative Union to Fight Loss of Jobs to Mexico." *Wall Street Journal,* May 22,.

Gillett, Frank E. 1992. "The Integrating Supplier: A Study of an Auto Industry Supplier's Relations Across Several Customers." Master of Science in Management and Master of Science in Technology and Policy Thesis, MIT.

Helper, Susan. 1995. "Can Maquilas Be Lean?" In Steve Babson, ed., *Lean Work: Empowerment and Exploitation in the Global Auto Industry.* Detroit: Wayne State University Press.

Herzenberg, Steven. 1991. "Towards a Cooperative Commonwealth? Labor and Restructuring in the US and Canadian Auto Industries." Ph.D. diss., MIT Department of Economics.

Kenney, M. and R. Florida. 1993. *Beyond Mass Production.* New York: Oxford University Press.

Klayman, Ben. 1994. "Workers Say They've Earned Right to Add Jobs." *Youngstown Vindicator,* 1 December.

Kochan, T., H Katz, N. Mower. 1984. *Worker Participation and American Unions.* Kalamazoo, MI: Upjohn Institute Press.

MacDuffie, John Paul, and Susan Helper. "Creating Lean Suppliers: The Honda Way." In P. Adler, M. Fruin, and J. Liker, eds., *Remade in America.* Oxford: Oxford University Press.

Parker M. and J. Slaughter. 1995. "Unions and Management by Stress." In Babson , *Lean Work.*

Ringler, Larry. 1996. "Plant Jobs to Go." *Tribune Chronicle* (Warren), 19 November.

Sachs, B. 1994. "The Disappearance of Local 717." photocopy, July.

Wells, D. 1997. "When Push Comes to Shove: Competitiveness, Job Insecurity, and Labour-Management Cooperation in Canada." *Economic and Industrial Democracy* 18:167-200.

——. 1995. "Origins of Canada's Wagner Model of Industrial Relations." *Canadian Journal of Sociology* 20:193-225.

Womack, J., D. Jones, and D. Roos. 1990. *The Machine that Changed the World.* New York: Rawson Associates.

THEN AND NOW: OBSERVATIONS ON NEW WORK ORGANIZATION AT GM POWERTRAIN

Danny Hoffman[*]

INTRODUCTION

Even in a context of "jointness" between labor and management, the union has to decide how it will contend with management's unilateral imperative to "get lean." Does the union wait until management acts, then the union reacts through the grievance procedure, collective bargaining, or perhaps strike action? Or does the union look for other ways, perhaps through the joint labor-management process, to actively deal with the organizational change objectives of management, including widespread process changes on the shop-floor? To what degree can these two strategies co-exist, or even be seen as connected —that is, the collective bargaining *agreement* seen as a kind of "joint" process, and labor-management "partnership" seen as a kind of continuous bargaining?

In recent years, these questions have been raised to a special prominence in the auto industry. As a labor educator at the University of Michigan, I have been especially interested in the experience of GM and the UAW. I worked at the GM transmission plant near Ypsilanti, Michigan, for thirteen years and was active in the union throughout, serving as a committeeperson (grievance representative), editor of the local union newspaper, and first vice president (a full-time position at the local).

I came to work at the University of Michigan Labor Studies Center in the mid-1980s, and while I worked with a number of joint union-management organizations over the subsequent years, I had not heard much about what was going on at my old plant (now part of the GM Powertrain Division) or the UAW Local which represents the hourly workforce there, Local 735. In

[*] Coordinator, Labor Studies Center, University of Michigan.

the spring of 1997 I therefore began a study of new work organization in the three GM Powertrain Division transmission plants located in the United States: Toledo Powertrain in Ohio, Warren Powertrain in Detroit's northeast suburbs, and Ypsilanti, my old workplace, located in Detroit's western suburbs.[1] What I found surprised me.

MORE WITH LESS

The changes in output and plant population in the three plants compared to ten years ago are dramatic. In the case of the Ypsilanti plant, the plant population now stands at 5,320, down from 6,400 —but according to the local union bargaining chairman, the current workforce produces about *fifty percent* more parts per day than in 1987.[2] At the Warren facility, the local union president estimated that production output is "the same or slightly higher" than in 1987, but it is being achieved with 2,500 workers, compared with 3,500 ten years ago. At Toledo, the Quality Network Coordinator appointed by the local union stated that the workforce actually increased by two hundred over the last ten years —but the plant now turns out double the production of 1987.

These incredible productivity increases are consistent with GM's goals. Like most American manufacturing firms today, the name of the game is getting "lean." In a presentation in May of 1996 at the University of Michigan's "Lean Manufacturing Conference," the plant manager from Warren Powertrain defined management goals in terms drawn explicitly from the "menu" of lean production: pull systems, small-lot production, containerization, level schedules, one-piece flow, Andon systems, process control, and so on. Many other components of lean systems were discussed as part of the presentation.[3]

---

[1] My primary focus has been the Ypsilanti plant, which I know best and where I have friends and family who still work there. In addition to several walking tours of the complex, I have relied on interviews with union leadership, plant management, and individual workers at their jobs, as well as the available documentary evidence —collective bargaining agreements, training manuals, planning guides, and joint labor-management reference material. I have had less exposure to the Warren and Toledo plants and have used them primarily to sketch contrasting or complementary cases. In both cases I have relied on plant visits and discussions with union leadership.

[2] Employment numbers were provided by the union at each location.

[3] Larry Spiegel, "Lean Manufacturing: A GM Perspective," Presentation at the Lean Manufacturing Conference, May 1996, sponsored by the University of Michigan. For the lean production "menu," see Babson, this volume.

It is important to note that the UAW and GM have worked together for the past ten years on a program called Quality Network which also contains elements commonly found in lean production systems. Formally recognized in the 1987 UAW-GM National Agreement, the Quality Network program was initiated primarily to address product quality issues. It was further defined in the 1990 National Agreement's Document 119, which stated that the

> General Motors process for total quality is the Quality Network —the one process for customer satisfaction. Although management has the ultimate responsibility for the Quality Network, it is recognized that UAW leaders and members are valuable partners in the development process, the action strategies, and its implementation plans.[4]

Among the Quality Network's "tools and techniques" are "lead time reduction, pull systems, small-lot strategies, workplace visual controls, quick setup processes, people focused practices" and other elements of lean production that the UAW and GM include in their initiative to "synchronize the organization."[5]

In two of the three transmission plants I visited, Ypsilanti and Toledo, the local union appeared to view the Quality Network program as an opportunity to involve workers in the redesign of the work processes and to perhaps soften the blow of the pending "leanness." In the case of the Warren plant, according to the local union president, the union leadership pulled out of all locally controlled joint programs, including any involvement in the Quality Network program, shortly after the union's 1996 elections. A strike followed in 1997, sparked in part by membership complaints over work loads, excessive overtime, and the company's refusal to hire more workers.

In the case of the Ypsilanti and Toledo plants, some view the changes taking place as nothing more than workers, involved in "joint" processes, helping to do management's dirty work and figuring out ways to increase productivity by reducing the number of jobs. On the other hand, many view it as a way for workers to have some say in making the plants more productive by eliminating a lot of wasteful practices left over from the days of management's "our way or the highway" mentality —practices that never made sense to the workers to begin with.

---

[4] Thomas Weekley and Jay Wilber, "United Auto Workers and General Motors Quality Network," in Edward Cohen-Rosenthal, ed., *Unions, Management and Quality* (Chicago: Irwin Publishing, 1995).

[5] *UAW-GM Action Strategy Summary* (Detroit: UAW-GM, 1993).

In the case of the Warren plant, it is evident that management has implemented many of the same "lean" practices visible in the technical organization of the other two plants, but with this difference: instead of workers having input up front, the process changes occur unilaterally and the union protests the changes through the grievance procedure.

MAJOR CHANGES IN TECHNICAL ORGANIZATION: INVENTORY AND PARTS FLOW

My memories of the Ypsilanti plant are not fond ones. During the time I worked there the plant population soared to over 14,000 employees, over 10,000 being rank and file UAW members. In the late 1970's, the Ypsilanti plant produced over 10,000 automatic transmissions each day. Since it was the world's largest transmission producing facility, it also produced more gears than any factory on earth, contained dozens of enormous heat-treating furnaces, used thousands of solvents and other types of chemicals, and as a result, was a hot, dirty, mist-filled hell hole. Building parts for inventory was the order of the day. Department after department was full of parts tubs or racks, filled with parts waiting to move on to the next process. It was common to see row after row of tubs stacked twenty to thirty feet in the air, cluttering the already crowded plant and creating very hazardous conditions. Today, with the just-in-time (JIT) "pull" system, the stock buffers have been virtually eliminated. As a result, one of the first things to catch my attention when I began studying the plant after a ten-year absence was how much brighter and open it seemed. The towers of parts bins blocking light and access were gone.

The change in parts flow was especially evident in the assembly rooms. In this area, a parts "supermarket" with clearly marked isles and addresses had been moved next to the assembly line, in sharp contrast with the previous practice of stockpiling parts in a different building. This move greatly reduced the amount of line-side stock necessary at each assembly work station, because now it is only a matter of getting stock from the nearby supermarket. The job of deciding when to restock a work station was once the responsibility of the area supervisor, who would call the stock chaser when more parts were needed. Now the "stock-chasers" in the area, usually a forklift driver or tug operator, are responsible for stocking each work station when they see it is necessary. Stock chasers I spoke with agreed that the supermarket system made their job easier. Now there was a central location from which to get parts, whereas in the past they had to chase all over the plant to retrieve parts for the assembly room.

Signs throughout the huge Ypsilanti plant read "Andon is coming," referring to the overhead digital sign-boards used in many plants to call stock chasers for parts, to call skilled trades for maintenance work, or to simply call attention to the particular work stations that are having problems or are causing delays. Andon boards are being installed in all three assembly rooms in the plant, with the first function brought on line being the digital display of targeted production per shift and, next to it, the actual up-to-the-minute production count. These "visual controls" are supposed to improve the response time to problems as they are identified and displayed on the Andon. One high-level production manager in the Ypsilanti plant had another way of explaining the Andon's role. When asked what management's goals were with respect to their use, he offered a sports analogy: "It's one thing for the referee to call a penalty against a team. It's another thing to call out the number of the particular player who committed the penalty." No individual worker, he explained, wants to be singled out as the "cause" for production delays that may lead to mandatory overtime at the end of the shift if the targeted production level is not reached. According to this manager, "the Andon makes everyone aware of the overall process and creates a kind of team atmosphere."[6]

Another noticeable change in parts flow is evident in sub-assembly. For years, the Ypsilanti plant contained large sub-assembly areas that were physically separate from the assembly lines that they fed. Today, the goal is to move sub-assembly as close to the assembly process as possible, with many sub-assembly benches located next to the main line and feeding it stock on a JIT/demand-pull basis.

At the Toledo plant, the pull system is almost identical to that in Ypsilanti, with the same trend towards consolidating the previously separate manufacturing, sub-assembly, and assembly areas. It is common to see an assembly

---

[6] This does not mean that the Andon, alone, necessarily has the effect of increasing peer pressure by highlighting troubled work stations. It may reinforce a potential for peer pressure, but other social and technical factors create or negate such a potential, including the nature of the bargaining relationship, the relative strength of the union, the demographics of the workforce, and the reward systems that encourage or discourage peer pressure.

area not only flanked by a parts supermarket and sub-assembly operations, but also by some elements of parts fabricating. With this set-up, if an assembly worker finds a manufacturing problem, he or she can immediately walk to the nearby manufacturing process and show it to the operator or job-setter. This is in contrast to the old system where many of the parts were produced at the opposite end of the plant.

In the case of the Warren plant, however, the production areas, sub-assembly areas, and assembly areas were still largely separated in the spring of 1997. The JIT pull system was also significantly different. Instead of the stock-chaser deciding when to re-stock a job from the neighboring supermarket, at Warren each assembly line worker has a push-button hanging above the work station that is used to signal a central computer when more parts are needed. Hi-lo operators are stationed near the read-out station in the assembly supermarket in the adjoining department, not at the line. The computer prints the order for the parts needed and where they are to go. The hi-lo driver then puts a card through a swipe-reader which records his/her ID and documents the time they left the station. They go to the parts supermarket and retrieve the appropriate pallet and take it to the line. When they return to the supermarket, they run their card through the swipe-reader. As a result, there are fewer hi-lo drivers and line-side inventory is much smaller. The local union is protesting the system as a possible means for conducting on-going time study, and as a means for singling out workers for disciplinary action. The union also feels that there is a safety hazard for workers throughout the plant as hi-lo drivers rush to stay within the time limits prescribed by the computer.

THE NOT-SO-VISIBLE TECHNOLOGICAL CHANGE

In the early 1980s it was common to hear workers in the Ypsilanti plant discuss the highly publicized influx of new technology, especially robotics, being installed at many GM facilities. In the few cases where the company brought robots into the Ypsilanti plant, workers would stand and marvel at the glittery new high-tech wonders. The earliest robot I recall was installed to load a lathe —it was down for repairs nearly every time I walked by. I also recall a robot which caused a stir in the case division of the Ypsilanti plant. The case division is the area where the castings for the transmission housing —the "case" as it is called— are machined to exact tolerances. Scattered around the division were several inspection conveyor belts, where a series of workers inspected the quality of the cases. The expected work standard was known to all who worked in the area: fifty cases per inspector per hour. If you had a five-person line, you could expect 250 cases per hour. The person at the first station on this line was responsible for loading the cases onto the conveyor. Every so often he would hesitate for a few seconds so all the "downstream" inspectors could take a sip of coffee or light a cigarette. As long as the line turned out the expected number of cases, the workers and the bosses stayed happy. When the first robot showed up in the case division, to no one's surprise, it was installed at the first station on one of these case inspection lines. Now all of the line inspectors would be forced to work at the pace set by the machine, or more accurately, set by management. There would no longer be any time for the cigarette or the sip of coffee, so long as the machine was running properly. It soon became obvious, however, that it wasn't going to be running properly too often. I would often enter that area of the plant and notice the robot shut down, with the repair staff trying to de-bug the problems. Eventually they gave up and the device sat idle while a worker was once again put back loading the line.

It was examples like this, multiplied across GM's many plants, that finally led the company to re-think its high-tech approach. Today, although there is much high-technology in use in the Ypsilanti plant, the huge facility has no robots. Only two robots remain in use in the Toledo plant. At Warren, although a new machining operation under construction will use several pick-and-place robots, the situation in mid-1997 was much the same as the other two plants, with no robots in use, and with workers in some parts of the plant performing their jobs next to abandoned robots.

NON-VALUE-ADDED LABOR: INSPECTORS AND FOREMEN HIT HARDEST

In terms of job cuts, the two most at-risk positions in the transition to lean production are inspectors and supervisors, both of them targeted as "non-value-added" positions.

In all three plants, probably the most widely used computer-based technologies are the automatic inspection devices installed in the newest generation of machine tools and assembly lines. For example, in the "Second Clutch Build Line" in the Ypsilanti plant there are two different lines for sub-assembly of the same part. Both lines have the same number of workers doing the actual assembly work, and both lines produce the same number of parts. The difference is that the older line has three inspectors at the end of the process who perform a series of quality-control checks. In contrast, the new line has computer-based inspection capabilities built right into it, with a separate automated device immediately following each work station on the line. There are no human inspectors.

In fact, throughout the plant the quality-control inspection classification has been virtually wiped out. Part of this change is accounted for by new technology, as in the clutch line, and part of it results from the implementation of statistical process control, where machine operators periodically gauge the quality of the parts coming off their machines, rather than waiting for inspectors to catch problems later. When I was elected UAW committeeman at the Ypsilanti plant in the late 1970s, I represented all of the parts inspectors on the day shift, numbering over 500 workers; there was nearly the same number on the afternoon shift and half as many again on the midnight shift, for an in-plant total of about 1,200 to 1,300 inspectors. Each part manufactured in the plant was individually examined by this small army of inspectors. As recently as ten years ago, there were still between 700 and 800 inspection jobs according to union estimates. Today, with advanced technology and process changes, only about 100 workers remain in the inspection classification. Most are roaming audit inspectors who go from department to department, spot checking parts. The inspection classification has seen similar reductions in the other two transmission plants, with Toledo now having only about 100 inspectors, down from around 400 ten years ago.

During my years as a union representative in the Ypsilanti plant, the number of foremen was staggering. The inspectors I represented were broken into large departmental groups, each with between seventy and eighty workers who equalized overtime and vacation scheduling; for each one of those groups, it was typical to find seven or eight foremen, a general foreman, and a superintendent. As recently as 1987, there was still an average of one foreman for every ten (or fewer) workers. By 1997, that ratio had widened to just one foreman for every 40 to 50 workers. At Warren and Toledo, the ratio is roughly one foreman for every 20 to 30 workers.

There are some who argue that this dramatic reduction in the number of bosses is due to the increase in worker decision-making power and the input workers now have in the joint processes. A somewhat different perspective is suggested by my experience at Ypsilanti, from the days when it was common to see a foreman stand in a single location and watch over a handful of workers: higher management, prodded by intensifying competition, finally realized that they didn't need all those bosses in the first place.

JOINT LABOR-MANAGEMENT PROGRAMS

Joint programs are certainly nothing new at the Ypsilanti plant. When I served my initial term as first vice president of Local 735, the president and bargaining chairman were very aggressive in pursuing joint programming that involved union members in very non-traditional roles. At one point in 1986, there were as many as 187 hourly workers —UAW members— working full time in appointed jobs in joint programs. They had 53 salaried counterparts, for a total of 240 employees working full time in joint programs focused on such things as worker suggestions, product awareness, ergonomics, training, customer satisfaction, job placement, and plant communications.[7]

Today, under guidelines set forth in the UAW-GM Quality Network Program, the joint labor-management process incorporates an even more expansive agenda of workplace change, yet there are far fewer full-time appointees attached to the program. In the Ypsilanti plant there are now less than 70 UAW members working in full time joint-program jobs —apparently these "non-value added" positions have been downsized with the same urgency as inspectors and supervisors. At Toledo there are 110 full-time "joint" appointees. At Warren, where the union has withdrawn from Quality Network, the only union appointees still functioning are six individuals who work on the joint ergonomics committee.

Three Quality Network initiatives are of special interest:

1) The commitment to the provisions of Document 40 of the UAW-GM National Agreement, which gives workers an opportunity and a means to raise their own concerns about quality; 2) the planned maintenance program, established to increase up-time and reliability of machinery; and 3) the commitment set forth in the Quality Network program which gives workers a right to have a say in the design or re-design of their jobs.[8]

Do Union Members Really Care About Quality?

Because of the management-rights clause in the UAW-GM National Agreement, management has the exclusive authority to determine quality levels. In my final year as a committeeman at the plant, prior to being elected vice

---

[7] Denise Tanguay-Hoyer and Gregory Huszczo, *Forging A Partnership Through Employee Involvement: The Case of the GM Hydra-Matic Willow Run Plant and UAW Local 735 Joint Activities* (Washington D.C.: U.S. Department of Labor, 1988)

[8] Weekley and Wilber, "UAW and GM Quality Network."

president, the single most common protest call I received from the inspectors I represented was that they were being ordered to pass along what they considered to be poor quality parts. Most of the time I felt as though my hands were tied because of the contract language. At a minimum, I would document what was going on so that if any parts were returned to the department for quality problems, at least the workers had evidence that it was no fault of theirs. In many cases I would write a grievance, knowing we had no real contractual grounds for it, simply to let management know that the union and its members were protesting poor quality decisions which impacted our job security.[9]

One case which stands out in my mind concerned a worker who was facing an unpaid suspension for refusing his foreman's direct order to pull a red tag off a tub of bad parts, and to ship them to assembly. As this worker's representative, I had to threaten management that I would go to the press to tell them how a GM worker was disciplined and suspended without pay for refusing to accept poor quality parts. It was only then that the worker was returned to his job and the parts were never shipped.

Today, as part of the commitment to quality there is "Document 40," intended as a review system outside of the grievance procedure. If the worker raises an issue about quality, the process calls for attempts to first resolve the issue within the department; if it is not resolved, it is referred to a committee within the plant which includes the plant manager and the union bargaining chairman. In the rare instances where the issue still cannot be resolved, it is then referred to a division-level committee of union and company staff. I was informed that in the earliest days of the Quality Network program at Ypsilanti, a case was referred to this division-level committee; the high-profile review which followed was so unpleasant for in-plant personnel that all concerned now prefer to resolve quality problems internally rather than air their "dirty laundry" to outside parties. The union people I toured the plants with said that this attitude has led to major quality improvements at all three locations.

---

[9] In some cases it was a matter of the worker being trained to gauge the parts in a particular way, insuring that variations remained within certain tolerances, and to reject those parts which gauged outside of those standards. In reality, many parts that fell slightly outside of the gauge specifications would still function normally in the transmission. The problem, of course, was that workers were not trained in "engineering permissibilities" or "deviations," as management referred to them. All the inspector knew was, "the gauge reads outside the limits I was given, so this must be a bad part." Many of them were bad, while others were usable —in either case, the boss would tell them to ship the parts to assembly.

Planned Maintenance

When I worked at the Ypsilanti plant, there was no planned maintenance of machinery. As one current skilled trades worker reminded me, "We used to run the machine, day after day, shift after shift, until something went wrong. Then it was anyone's guess as to how long it would take to figure out what was wrong, fix it, and get it running again."

Today, as a result of the Quality Network provisions for planned maintenance, things are very different. Through the use of high-tech monitoring equipment, skilled trades workers at the Ypsilanti plant conduct tests and gather data on such things as vibration and heat problems while the machine is still operational. The data is then turned over to a small group of high seniority journeyman trades workers for analysis. By the time they have completed their task, these trades workers have put together a kit with all of the parts needed to do the necessary maintenance on the machine, along with a list of tools needed for the job.

The same program is in place at the Toledo plant, and in one area where the Quality Network staff have tracked the results, they have increased uptime on some machines by as much as 80 percent. In Warren, the local union president says that there is no planned maintenance program in place.

Worker Input in Job Design

When I read the highlights of the Quality Network program, the part which made me most skeptical was a section which addressed the need for workers to be involved in the design or re-design of their jobs. In an article by Thomas Weekley, Assistant Director of the UAW Quality Network, and Jay Wilber, Executive Director of General Motors Quality Network, they write:

> Today there are quality and productivity improvement teams that are comprised of experts in all facets of the production operation, specifically including job setters and operators. Quality Network action strategies are their tools for effective change .... A commitment to a redeployment plan for affected workers is fundamental. In fact, cooperation and understanding is critical on the part of all affected functional groups: operators, job setters, the skilled trades, engineers, financial planners, schedulers, material handlers, health and safety representatives, and so on.[10]

---

[10] Weekley and Wilber, "UAW and GM Quality Network," 116-

There was no such commitment in the early 1980s, when I represented a worker who was threatened with discipline for making a minor adjustment to an inspection device. His modification not only made the job more comfortable, but, as he proved to me and to members of management in the department, it allowed him to run the device faster so he could actually inspect more parts. What was management's rationale for ordering him to put the device back the way it was? I still recall the general foreman's angry face as he blurted out, "We have never done it that way before, and we're not going to start doing it any differently today." Had the worker continued to defy management, he would have been suspended without pay. We ended up writing a grievance to try to get the change implemented, but again, the "management rights" clause in the contract gave supervision another victory. Under that old Taylorist system, management had total control over the processes used in the plant.

I was therefore surprised to find many workers at Ypsilanti who told me that they were very involved in the ways that their jobs were re-designed. One assembly line worker who I had known for many years told me that when they were preparing to make some major adjustments to the line processes, several engineers and skilled trades workers spoke with him at length. If he could adjust his movements to do his job in the way he thought best, he was asked, how would he do it? He said he couldn't believe how much of what he told them was actually integrated into the new processes once his job was re-designed.

I came upon a another high seniority worker who I once represented, and who I remembered to be very skeptical of the joint programs in their early days. "Ah, you know how it is," he observed. "Nothing ever really changes." But when I asked specifically about whether or not he had any say in how his job had been re-designed, he answered, "well now, I will say as far as that's concerned, when they made all these changes we had a lot of meetings and judging from the way things ended up, they listened to a lot of what we said. I was surprised." I heard many similar comments throughout the Ypsilanti plant and got the same impression from my visits to Toledo.

In the case of the Warren plant, when I asked the union president about workers having a say in the re-design of their jobs, he painted a different picture. "Here the engineers use a program called ESP," he answered. "You know, 'extra-sensory perception.' The engineers think they know everything about what's going on with the machines without ever having to ask the people who work on the shop floor."

LEAN WITHOUT TEAMS

One of the most advertised elements of the "lean" model is the use of work teams or "self-directed" work groups. Yet, even in the two transmission plants that are most involved in joint programs and "lean" methods, there was little evidence of such formal teams or groups. The closest thing to any "team" arrangement was in the Toledo plant, where small groups of five or six workers rotate jobs in the assembly room. When I asked the union if these "groups" ever held formal meetings to discuss issues about their work, I was told that they do not. Workers in this assembly area report the same: these are rotation groups only, with no role —"self-directed" or otherwise— in coordinating or improving the production process. At Ypsilanti and Warren, there is no formal designation of work groups that even remotely resembles team concept.

I also asked if any of the departments ever held departmental meetings, or if they had employee involvement meetings, or any type of formal meeting structure. At Ypsilanti, very few departments ever hold any type of meetings. At Warren, the union president speculated that "they might have a meeting when the job goes down." And at Toledo, some areas hold regular "informational" meetings, with good attendance.

While there is no formal structure of work teams in the Ypsilanti plant, there are informal arrangements that mark the changing nature of the plant's work organization. Job-setters seem to play an especially prominent part in these changes. Traditionally, the job setter was responsible for setting up the machines with proper tooling, making minor adjustments when necessary, and alerting the supervisor when there was a significant problem. Today, with the huge reduction in the number of supervisors in the plant, the job setter's responsibilities have expanded accordingly to include such matters as giving job assignments to co-workers, scheduling maintenance and repair of machines, and training new workers assigned to their area. In this respect, the job setter serves as a de facto "team leader." This approach may serve the purposes of both management and the union better than the formal "team concept" approach that was piloted in one assembly area but later abandoned when controversy arose over the role and selection process for the team leader. Rather than impose this controversial structure on a skeptical workforce, plant leaders may prefer the "informal" role played by the job setter, who is usually a somewhat older and more experienced worker chosen by seniority.

CONCLUSION

For many years I was a skeptic when it came to joint union-management work arrangements, and to some extent I still am. When I was editor of my local union paper I filled my monthly column in the early 1980s with numerous attacks on the joint processes in the UAW-GM system. Many of the things I have seen in recent years have made me more open-minded. I see the great successes of the planned maintenance programs at Toledo and Ypsilanti, and the many improvements in overall product quality in all of the plants. I also see how people take great pride, and find great pleasure, in feeling that they helped shape those success stories.

Heading into the 1996 contract negotiations at the three locations, the two plants that were involved in the Quality Network program and joint programs in general, Ypsilanti and Toledo, saw their grievance loads greatly reduced. At Ypsilanti, the bargaining chairman estimated that the 500 unresolved grievances they had going into negotiations was, by far, the lowest number in the over two decades that he had been involved in the bargaining process. He pointed out that over those past twenty years, the local union never had fewer than 2,000 grievances going into contract talks. The union leaders I spoke with at the Toledo plant could not give exact numbers, but indicated that their grievance load was also much lower heading into contract negotiations than in years past. At Warren, however, with a workforce less than half the size of the Ypsilanti plant, the local union president said they went into the 1996 negotiations with about 1,500 grievances. The largest single category, in his estimate, were "speed-up" grievances under article 78 of the UAW-GM National Agreement. As GM continues to implement their new work systems, he observed, the workers in the Warren plant were feeling over-loaded. At Ypsilanti and Toledo, however, such grievances are rare, and union leaders attribute this to the Quality Network program and the opportunity workers have for input into the design of their jobs.

This would appear to vindicate those who see lean production as a boon for workers, so long as its provisions for employee participation are protected in a collective bargaining agreement. However, there is good reason to cross-examine this kind of evidence before drawing overly generous conclusions. The decline in grievances might indicate that the conditions that give rise to grievances have improved, but it might signify something different —that legitimate grievances are simply discouraged, or that conflict over working conditions, rather than disappearing, has been transposed to different arenas. This latter possibility was evident in an assembly room I visited in one of the plants where Quality Network is a prominent feature of the change process. Here I was told that workers not only have control over the way the work is set up, they also control the speed of the actual production process. This is possible because the assembly line consists of moveable skids that remain stationary at each work location until the operator sends them along to the next work station —a technical feature that gives operators some discretion over how long each transmission remains in front of them. Because management allows, or encourages, such behavior, the majority of workers have decided that rather than abide by the 55-second job cycle that is supposed to prevail on this line, they will each perform their tasks in 45 seconds or less, meaning they will hit their production target early. When they finish early, the entire workforce from this particular assembly operation can roam around the plant or get a pass to go home without pay for the remainder of the shift. A minority of workers object to this self-imposed speed-up, some because they find the pace too tiring, some because they see the likelihood that management will eventually tighten the production standard and cut the number of people on the line. But when these workers asked their union representative to write a speed-up grievance, the union rep said that he could not because grievances can only be written against management. Since the pace of the work was being set by other hourly rated (UAW) people, there was no grievance.

Although this was the only case I saw of collectively self-imposed speed-up, it highlights the potential for management abuse of the joint labor-management process. In this case, despite the emphasis on "standardized work" and explicitly prescribed "best people practices," management condoned and probably welcomed the fact that "empowered" workers had accelerated their work pace to the point where these few may eventual "kill" the job for those who follow.

The potential for this kind manipulation accounts for some of the Warren plant's troubled history with respect to Quality Network and joint programs. Proposals for "team concept" and far-reaching changes in union representation had polarized the local union in the late 1980s, provoking bitter election campaigns between caucuses that favored or opposed these innovations. When the smoke cleared, the opponents held the high ground and the advocates were discredited as management toadies. Afterwards, limited efforts to implement joint programs met with some success (in health and safety especially), but these modest initiatives were jeopardized in 1995 by the company's threat to outsource several hundred jobs making wheel rims. The local union leadership decided that at least part of their strategy to counter this threat would be a boycott of the joint processes. After local negotiations dragged on into 1997, the union called a strike over this and other issues, shutting the plant for five days and, by starving GM's JIT supply system, immediately forcing the shutdown of four other plants. Rather than risk yet another destabilizing confrontation with a local union (see Babson, this volume) GM agreed to add 420 jobs to the plant workforce and to keep the wheel jobs at Warren until at least the year 2002. So perhaps the old-style adversarial approach is not totally dead just yet.

On the other hand, at least in the case of the transmission plants at Ypsilanti and Toledo, the local unions have had enough success with Quality Network and programs to make labor-management partnership a viable option, at least for the time being. The question remains, will they be able to sustain those successes through the long-haul? Based on my past experiences, I'm still awaiting that "crash-and-burn" final chapter.

In any case, what these three plants have in common, no matter how different their particular bargaining history, is that General Motors is going to implement as much of the "lean" production menu as possible, with or without the union's involvement. In this context, it is still too early to say for certain which union approach is the best response.

MODERNIZACION EMPRESARIAL Y ORGANIZACION DEL TRABAJO EN GENERAL MOTORS DE MEXICO: COMPLEJO TOLUCA (MOTORES)

Sergio González López
*Selene Villa Méndez**

El presente documento tiene como objetivo identificar las estrategias de modernización empresarial que se implementan en el *Complejo de motores de General Motors en Toluca* (GMT) y las formas de organización del trabajo que se desarrollan. La importancia de un estudio de caso con las características de GMT en las situaciones actuales tiene por lo menos tres aspectos relevantes sobre el análisis de los factores promotores e inhibidores de: la transferibilidad centro-periferia de las nuevas formas de organización de la producción; el "margen de maniobra local" para implementar cambios hacia esa dirección; y la capacidad de reestructuración de una planta para adecuarse de formas productivas *fordistas-tayloristas* hacia "*flexibles*".

Como se podrá observar a lo largo del trabajo, por lo menos para el caso específico que se analiza, no se puede hablar de modelos únicos y unidireccionales, sino de configuraciones particulares en las que se combinan, hibridizan; conceptualizaciones, estrategias, acciones y reacciones. El concepto de "configuración" se toma en el sentido planteado por *De la Garza (1993)*, según el cual se aleja del concepto de "sistema", pero no equivale a la fragmentación total; es, por el contrario, coherencia junto a discontinuidades, a contradicciones, a fragmentaciones parciales.

En el país, *General Motors de México* (GMM) es la principal empresa automotriz y exportadora-importadora manufacturera. En sus cerca de 60 establecimientos da ocupación a más de 50 mil personas. Sus actividades las desarrolla en diversos giros, como automotriz, maquiladoras automotrices y electrónicas e informática, las cuales operan de manera relativamente independiente.

* Coordinador de Posgrado y Coordinadora de Difusión respectivamente, de la Facultad de Planeación Urbana y Regional, Universidad Autónoma del Estado de México.

Temporal y territorialmente, se pueden notar varias fases en las formas de penetración de la empresa en el país. Desde los treinta y hasta principios de los sesenta, el ensamble de vehículos en base a partes importadas en el complejo en el Distrito Federal (DF); en los sesenta y setenta creciente integración nacional, con la producción de autopartes en el complejo del DF y la creación del complejo de motores en Toluca; en los setenta desarrollo de la planta maquiladora en la frontera norte; en los ochenta y hasta la fecha creciente orientación hacia las exportaciones a través del complejo de Ramos Arizpe y diversificación de actividades.

En la rama automotriz, exceptuando a las plantas maquiladora, los establecimientos de la empresa son: en el Distrito Federal las oficinas generales, hasta finales de 1995 contaba con planta de camiones que fue desconentrada hacia Silao, Guanajuato; el complejo de motores y ensamble de automóviles en Ramos Arizpe; y el complejo de motores en Toluca, al que desde 1994 se incorpora la planta de camiones Kodiak..

CONSIDERACIONES GENERALES

GMT surge a principios de la década de los sesenta, en un periodo de crecimiento del mercado e integración nacional de la industria automotriz.

Frecuentemente se relaciona a las fases de desarrollo de esta industria con la política económica sectorial implementada, que tendría como principal expresión a los decretos emitidos por el gobierno mexicano. En este sentido, la planta de motores GMT sería producto de la convergencia de dos políticas: integración nacional del sector (Decreto de 1962) y desconcentración territorial de la economía (Política de Industrias Nuevas y Necesarias).

Estas, si bien incidieron, debido a que restringía la importación de motores y otorgaba estímulos fiscales a empresas que se localizaran fuera del DF, son insuficientes para explicar la instalación de la planta en Toluca (*González, 1992*).

Al respecto deberían considerarse adicionalmente que un año antes del decreto en cuestión la empresa había adquirido el terreno donde se instalaría en Toluca; un año después del decreto y uno antes del inicio de operaciones de la planta, la empresa consigue negociar con el Sindicato de la planta en el DF que no tenga la titularidad en esta planta y en otras, que posteriormente se instalarían en otras localidades. Esta estrategia de la empresa propició conflictos con el sindicato del D.F., en los sesenta y los ochenta.

Asimismo, en 1962 es ampliada la carretera México-Toluca e introducidas líneas de alta tensión y gasoductos. En 1963 se decreta la Zona Industrial del Valle de Toluca. Finalmente, durante este periodo y hasta finales de los setenta la industria automotriz estaba orientada hacia el mercado interno y que en la planta del DF se ensamblaban autos y camiones, por lo que la cercanía a la Ciudad de México era estratégica

Toluca es la capital del estado de México y es uno de los principales centros industriales del país, se ubica a sesenta kms. al poniente de la ciudad de México y tiene una población de aproximadamente un millón de habitantes. Cuenta con más de mil establecimientos industriales que ocupan a alrededor de 60 mil trabajadores (*González, 1993*). La principal rama productiva es la automotriz que con cerca de 50 establecimientos emplea a unas 20 mil personas, sobresaliendo empresas como *Chrysler, Nissan, Mercedes Benz, BMW, y General Motors*, entre otras (*González, 1994*).

CRONOLOGÍA

GMT inicia operaciones en 1964 sobre un terreno de 42.4 has., contando con dos plantas productivas: una de fundición de monoblocks y partes de motor y otra de maquinado y ensamblado de motores, así como un edificio de oficinas administrativas e ingeniería. La planta de maquinado y ensamble sólo contaba con la línea de *motores L6* para camiones del tipo 130, 250 y 292 plg3 (pulgadas cúbicas), destinadas para abastecer a la planta ensambladora en el DF.

En 1969 se incorporó la producción de motores de 153 y 161 plg3 para exportación, con el objeto de hacer uso completo de la capacidad instalada.

En 1971 fue adicionada la producción de *motores V8* para ventas domesticas y de exportación, misma que se aumentó en 1985 para satisfacer la demanda del Grupo de GM de Venta de Refacciones (GMSPO).

En 1987 fue reemplazada totalmente la línea 1 de moldeo en planta de fundición por una nueva línea automatizada y moderna.

En 1988 cambió la estructura operativa del staff de la planta y la mano de obra sindicalizada, constituyendo un cambio hacia la "*calidad total*".

En 1989 se introduce el *motor HO* (alto rendimiento) de 3.0 lts. reemplazando al 153 y 181 plg3 (GM, 1991).

Más recientemente, desde 1994 se iniciaron los trabajos para poder producir el motor del Chevy, para lo que se hicieron movimientos en las líneas de maquinado para dejar espacio; se inicia el ensamble del camión *Kodiak*, utilizando para ello la antigua nave de almacenamiento (2.5 miles m2.); y en el presente año entra en operación el Almacén General de Refacciones para el corporativo en el país y laboratorios de ingeniería en una nueva nave con 3 has. de construcción.

Por otra parte, en la planta se construyó en agosto de ese año la Planta de Tratamiento de Aguas, con una inversión de 4 millones de dólares (MDD), con capacidad para un millón de litros que permite reciclar el 50% del agua utilizada. (*FINANCIERO, 4 agosto 1994*)

PRODUCCIÓN

GMT tiene una producción anual promedio de 140-150 mil motores y de 33,500 toneladas de metales de hierro fundidos, aproximadamente. Los motores son para camiones, usos industriales, comerciales y marinos. El último motor utilizado para automóviles fue para el *Montecarlo* que dejó de producirse en 1984. Una característica importante de los motores producidos en el Complejo es que a pesar de no ser de "alta tecnología" y no producirse a gran escala, ésta planta es la única que se dedica a ellos dentro del Corporativo. Precisamente, estas características de tipo y volúmenes de motores hacen que GMT sea rentable para el Corporativo.

El primer motor fue producido en marzo de 1965, para 1980 ya se había alcanzado la cifra de un millón, para 1988 el motor 2 millones, para 1991 el 2.5 millones (GM, 1991) y el 20 de enero de 1995 produjo su motor 3 millones. Prácticamente, desde su inició ha exportado al implementar un plan para tal fin en 1966 (*FINANCIERO, 2 abril 1990*). Hacia 1980 las exportaciones representaron el 76.5% del total, para 1990 se redujo al 50% (*FINANCIERO, 20 septiembre 1990*) y actualmente es del 65.6%.

Para 1994, produjo alrededor de 140 mil motores, distribuidos de la manera siguiente:

V8 101 mil unidades, para camiones y camionetas, 60% para exportación y el resto para la planta en el DF.

L6 31 mil unidades, para camionetas, 80% para exportación y el resto para refacciones.

L4 8 mil unidades, para uso industrial (montacargas) y marino, 80% para exportación y el resto para el mercado de refacciones.

Comparada esta producción con la de 1991, con un total de 158.5 miles, de los cuales 90 mil fueron *V8* y 68.5 miles de *L4* y *L6* (*FINANCIERO, 10 diciembre 1991*), se nota un ascenso los primeros y retroceso en los segundos.

No obstante que el Complejo abastece el 60% de la demanda de motores de 4 cc. del mercado de EU, teniendo como clientes a *Mercury Marines, Marine Power y Outboard Marine*, y para Japón es el principal abastecedor de *Yamaha*, orientando exportaciones de este tipo de motor hacia Canadá, Latinoamérica, Suecia, Israel, Irak, 'Gran Bretaña, Kuwait, Arabia Saudita y Australia, (*FINANCIERO, 2 abril 1991*).

Recientemente se han introducido dos nuevos productos: El camión *Kodiak* para el mercado interno del que se tiene planeado alcanzar en un año cinco mil unidades, mitad a gasolina y mitad a diesel, derivado de una estrategia competitiva de la empresa; y el fundido de monoblock y cabeza de motor para el *Phaser* que produce *Motores Perkins*, derivado de las dificultades tenidas por esta empresa con *SIDENA y CIFUNSA*, que anteriormente se los proveían.

Asimismo, desde 1995 se preparó la línea para producción para motores del *Chevy*, vehículo importado originalmente de la planta en Zaragoza, España, y que ya se ensambla en la planta de Ramos Arizpe.

No obstante, ser una planta poco automatizada, ha alcanzado elevados niveles de calidad, de manera que en 1990 recibió el premio "*Fundición de Excelencia*" otorgado por la Sociedad Mexicana de Fundidores, A.C., Capítulo México de la *American Foundryment's Society*, en ese evento *Richard C. Nerod*, presidente y director ejecutivo de GM México, declaró que es la mejor planta fundidora en el país, en el corporativo y con destacado lugar en el mundo entero", (*FINANCIERO, 14 enero 1991*).

Para GMT 1991 fue un año significativo, obtuvo el premio "Nacional de Calidad", otorgado por el gobierno mexicano, premio que según *Gonzalo García*, director general de la planta, "es fruto de la cultura de calidad que se tiene en la planta y que responde al esfuerzo conjunto de directivos, empleados y obreros" (*FINANCIERO, 10 diciembre 1991*); también, recibió el "Premio Estatal de Seguridad", a raíz de los bajos índices de accidentes registrados; y alcanzó 23 auditorias del Corporativo con cero discrepancias, lo que implicó que a partir de dicha fecha el Corporativo ya no realiza en el Complejo auditorias, pasando estas a realizarse internamente.

Esto se explica por las intensas acciones de la empresa por desarrollar formas de organización del trabajo orientadas hacia la productividad y la calidad a las cuales han sido participativos sindicato y trabajadores.

EMPLEO Y RELACIONES LABORALES

Siguiendo a *Dombois y Pries* (1993), dos son los aspectos centrales de la relación asalariada (capital/trabajo): las relaciones contractuales y las relaciones laborales. Donde las primeras definen las condiciones de empleo -ante todo salario, horarios y estabilidad laboral-, en otros términos, el carácter de la mano de obra como mercancía que se intercambia con el capital en la forma contractual; y, las segundas, que definen las condiciones y exigencias "legítimas y razonables" en el proceso del trabajo -sobre todo las de trabajo, cooperación y autoridad-, es decir, la transformación de la fuerza de trabajo en trabajo dentro del proceso laboral.

No obstante, en diversos trabajos a las "relaciones contractuales" se les denomina "relaciones laborales", y a las "relaciones laborales" como "organización del trabajo". Con el objeto de tener homogeneidad con los conceptos predominantes se utilizarán éstos últimos, pero refiriéndonos a las características planteadas por *Dombois y Pries.*

Durante la presente década, sobre todo a partir de 1993 se evidencia una reducción del personal ocupado en el Complejo, derivado, por un lado del deterioro económico del país, como del mejoramiento de los niveles de productividad, (CUADRO 1).

CUADRO 1
G.M.T.: PERSONAL OCUPADO

PERIODO	TOTAL	TRABAJADORES	ADMINISTRATIVOS
1993 (finales)	3,200	2,200	300
1994 (principios)	2,500	2,250	250
1994 (finales)	2,362	2,030	302
1995 (principios)	2,332	1,554	ND

No obstante, estos retrocesos significativos del personal ocupado no han propiciado desde su inauguración ningún estallamiento de huelga, en buena medida por la colaboración entre empresa y sindicato, siendo indicativo que el secretario general del mismo es la misma persona desde el inicio de labores del Complejo. En lo que respecta a las remuneraciones, adicional al salario, los trabajadores reciben como compensaciones: sobresueldos por realizar temporalmente actividades que rebasan su categoría, premios, y sobresueldos por desempeño y participación en cursos.

De acuerdo al Contrato Colectivo de Trabajo 1994-1996, signado en mayo de 1994 entre la empresa y el *Sindicato Nacional de Trabajadores de la In-*

dustria Metalúrgica y Similares, Sección 9, miembro de la CTM, existen nueve categorías: Primera a cuarta especiales y primera a quinta. Los trabajadores para las primeras son elegidos por la empresa y los trabajadores para las segundas acordados entre ambas partes.

El nivel salarial de acuerdo a las categorías es, considerando a la más baja como 1.00:, es el siguiente:

Primera Especial	2.64
Segunda Especial	2.41
Tercera Especial	2.14
Cuarta Especial	2.03
Primera	1.88
Segunda	1.61
Tercera	1.40
Cuarta	1.17
Quinta	1.00

Para el acceso a cada una de las categorías tienen preferencia los trabajadores que laboran en el departamento donde se abre la categoría.

Otras prestaciones y estímulos recibidos por el trabajador son:

Días de descanso obligatorio con pago de salario íntegro.- 17, Más el primero de diciembre cuando haya cambio de Presidente de la República y cuando haya elecciones electorales ordinarias.

Vacaciones a trabajadores de planta con pago íntegro Más 188 %.- 10 días a los trabajadores con un año de antigüedad, **12** a los de **2, 14** a los de **3, 16** a los de **4, 17** a los de **5 a 8**, **18** a los de **9** a **13, 20** a los de **14** a **19**, **22** a los de **20** a **24**, y **24** a los de **25** a **29** años.

-- Premio de puntualidad (un mes sin retardo).- un día.

-- Premio de asistencia (un mes sin falta).- 3 días.

-- Récord perfecto (un mes sin retardo ni falta).- 15 días.

Por participación en seminarios, cursos, propuestas de mejoramiento, etc., el trabajador sólo recibe reconocimientos simbólicos. Actualmente está en análisis el darle un premio monetario en proporción al ahorro que para la empresa represente la aplicación de las propuestas de los trabajadores.

Por otra parte, en su mayoría los trabajadores de producción tienen una edad promedio entre 25 y 35 años, superior al de otras plantas automotrices en la zona. Debido en parte por la propia antigüedad de la planta y por el compromiso implícito de la empresa de procurar mantener a los trabajadores, sobre los cuales han hecho importantes inversiones en capacitación.

Aparentemente se han dado cambios en los criterios de reclutamiento, privilegiando en los últimos años al personal con escasa experiencia, oficio y edad, y mayor escolaridad.

De manera sintética las características que son relevantes para interpretar las relaciones laborales que se desarrollan en GMT son: a) El carácter funcional de las relaciones sindicato- empresa; y b) La "tranquilidad" laboral en la zona.

Un funcionario de GMT decía "Las buenas relaciones obrero-patronales están vinculadas con las buenas relaciones que existen entre el sindicato y la empresa". Esto tiene varias implicaciones, como que finalmente estos tipos de relaciones no se dan en abstracto sino a partir de experiencias y expectativas concretas entre los agentes sociales que, si bien en absoluto no cancelan relaciones de poder entre ambos, sí plantean formas de acción que para el caso de GMT han sido de colaboración y por tanto de control "unificado" hacia el trabajo. Este nivel de "identificación sindicato-empresa se expresa en la inexistencia de huelgas en el complejo y en la permanencia del secretario general del sindicato desde el origen del complejo y su intervención cercana en las decisiones tomadas por la empresa, entre las que destaca la incorporación de Equipos de Trabajo (ET) y Unidades de Negocios (UN).

Por otra parte, Toluca ha sido tradicionalmente una de las zonas industriales del país con menores emplazamientos y estallamientos de huelgas. Esto nos remite, creemos a cuestiones "culturales", que constituyen una veta de investigación sobre la que debe profundizarse.

ESTRUCTURA ORGANIZATIVA

Al formar parte GMT de un corporativo internacional y dedicarse a la producción de un componente (motores y sus partes), el análisis de su estrategia empresarial de modernización que influye a su vez sobre su estructura organizativa requiere intentar la identificación de las determinantes externas e internas del Complejo que configuran las formas específicas de organización, producción y trabajo bajo las cuales opera. Por ello, de manera breve se hará una referencia a modificaciones estratégicas del corporativo en lo internacional y nacional para, con mayor detalle abordar las condiciones internas del Complejo Toluca.

ESTRATEGIA CORPORATIVA

En el primer nivel, se puede mencionar que ante la crisis financiera del corporativo, derivado de la fuerte competencia de las empresas automotrices japonesas, GMC desde los ochenta desarrolló cambios de estrategia, que se expresó tanto su incursión en otros sectores, como de informática, aeoroespaciales y de robótica, a través de adquisiciones y *joint ventures*; alianzas con otras empresas automotrices; reducción de plantas y personal ocupado en Estados Unidos y Canadá; y el desarrollo de plantas maquiladoras y automotrices sobre todo en el norte de México. Más recientemente, ante la negociación y puesta en operación del Tratado de Libre Comercio de Norteamérica (TLC), el corporativo modificó su estructura regional incorporando a México en la Gerencia de Norteamérica cuando anteriormente estaba en la de América Latina.

De estas estrategias se pueden distinguir dos momentos significativos en cuanto a la organización del trabajo en las plantas en México, a principios y a finales de los ochenta que tienen que ver con intentos de incorporar conceptos de *calidad total*. Para el primer momento exploraron pero no pudieron generalizarse en el Complejo de Toluca y se introdujeron en el recién creado Complejo de Ramos Arizpe; para el segundo, se alcanzó la operación generalizada en Toluca y fracasó su introducción en el DF.

Por otra parte, las decisiones de producción, mercadotecnia y proveduría está n definidas a nivel de las oficinas centrales, a partir del que se coordinan las operaciones necesarias en cada uno de los complejos productivos. En función de esto, GMT establece distintos vínculos con los otros establecimientos de la empresa nacional e internacionalmente, y también con proveedores, por medio del sistema de cómputo "Olympic", operado por *Electronic Data System* (EDS), quién se instaló en la planta desde 1989. A través de este sistema se relacionan EU-México (cada planta y oficinas centrales). La interconexión de información está diseñada de manera tal que cada planta tiene solo niveles de acceso a las otras de acuerdo al tipo de requerimientos preestablecidos centralmente.

GMT abastece todos los motores demandados por la planta del DF, cigüeñales (de hierro nodular) al de Ramos Arizpe, funde monoblocks para otras empresas automotrices y exporta motores sobre todo a Estados Unidos (EU) a través del Grupo de GM de Venta de Refacciones (GMSPO). Con sus proveedores se aplica la técnica "80/20", que distingue y privilegia aquellas materias primas e insumos que representan mayor valor. De acuerdo a ella y a la evaluación de proveedores enmarcadas en "Objetivos para la Excelencia

(TFE)", según calidad, liderazgo, tecnología, confiabilidad de la entrega, estructura corporativa y capacidad financiera, se les clasifica y se establecen diferentes tipos de relaciones con ellos.

Con los del rango mayor, se trabaja en sus plantas a través del "Grupo Dinámico GM", quien estima su calidad. Este grupo es del corporativo en el DF, e incluso las compras son realizadas centralmente a través del "Grupo Coordinador de Materiales Directos" en el DF, no pudiendo hacerlas las plantas directamente.

Por lo anterior, se puede señalar que se presenta una fuerte verticalidad de las directrices diseñadas por el corporativo hacia cada una de las plantas, asimismo, que se refuerza una integración en las relaciones entre ellas. Por otra parte, la incorporación de formas de organización del trabajo tienen como "detonador" estas estrategias, no obstante, esto último no significa homogeneidad en las implementaciones ya que a nivel de planta inciden las particularidades internas de cada una de ellas. Esto puede constatarse en Cruz (1995) y en GM (1993), para los casos de GM en el DF y en Ramos Arizpe, respectivamente, y para Toluca lo cual se verá continuación con mayor detalle.

Para mostrar de una manera clara la forma en que está organizado GMT se presenta separadamente la estructura administrativa formal, como aquella que funcionalmente está operando, tratando de reconstruir en el segundo caso las vías que se exploraron hasta llegar a la vigente forma de funcionamiento.

ESTRUCTURA ADMINISTRATIVA

Administrativamente, GMT está organizado de la manera siguiente:

Dirección General
Operaciones de Maquinado
Operaciones de Fundición
Finanzas
Calidad
Ingeniería de Manufactura
Recursos Humanos
Materiales
EDS
Kodiak
Almacén General de Materiales

De estas áreas, las tres últimas son las más recientes. La de EDS que fue contratada para la planta en 1989 y, en 1994 la del *Kodiak* y el Almacén General de Refacciones. En el caso de EDS se trata de una consultora, adquirida por el corporativo en 1984 pero que opera de manera independiente, y se encarga de diseñar y operar los sistemas de cómputo (sistema Olympic), para establecer intercambios de información de la planta Toluca con EU-México (DF, Ramos Arizpe)

Kodiak es una área implementada para ensamblar CKD un camión pesado, segmento en el que no participaba GM en México, que se aplicar para carga comercial y de servicio. Actividad que se realizar nacionalmente solo en Toluca, adaptando para tal efecto la antigua nave de almacén.

El Almacén General de Materiales, con 150 trabajadores, fue establecido para abastecer al corporativo a nivel nacional y es resultado de la desconcentración de la planta en el DF, operando de manera independiente del complejo, no obstante que se ubica en los terrenos de ella, y está relacionado verticalmente con las oficinas centrales en el DF, desde donde se deciden los abastecimientos para los otros complejos en el país.

ESTRUCTURA FUNCIONAL

Dos son los aspectos centrales de funcionamiento de GMT a su interior, la constitución de Unidades de Negocios (UN) y de Equipos a distintos niveles. Ambos enmarcados en el "Programa Integral de Operación" (PRINDO), que constituye el "Plan de Calidad" del Complejo.

De acuerdo a (G.M., 1991), funcionalmente, GMT está organizado a partir del *PRINDO*, el cual integra a todos los programas que se orientan hacia la consecución del Plan de Negocios, que es diseñado cada cinco años.

La estructura *PRINDO* se fundamenta en "la participación, involucramiento y satisfacción personal bajo la relación cliente-proveedor, dando con ello mayor fortaleza y claridad en la fijación de objetivos, eficiencia en la administración y efectividad en la comunicación de todo el Complejo". Este programa empezó a operar de manera limitada desde 1980, debido a que estaba orientado principalmente a la aplicación de técnicas estadísticas para el mejoramiento de la calidad, y estaba orientado hacia mandos medios.

Es hasta 1987 que se toma la decisión de generalizar dichas técnicas para todo el personal y se introduce el concepto de Equipos de Trabajo (ET). Para tal efecto se inician equipos experimentales, uno por cada planta con la participación del sindicato. Siendo en 1988 cuando se inicia la operación generalizada de ET y una reorganización de todo el Complejo, dividiéndolo en UN, propiciando una descentralización económico- financiera.

Así, está constituido por equipos a diferentes niveles que tienen comunicación entre sí, y son:

Equipo Coordinador, integrado por el *staff*, sindicato, presidentes de equipos operativos y lidereado por el director del Complejo.

Equipos Operativos, integrados por los gerentes y representantes de los departamentos de servicio y lidereados por los presidentes de las unidades operativas o de servicio.

Equipos de Apoyo, integrados por los supervisores de operaciones, supervisores o representantes de áreas de servicio y lidereados por el supervisor general del área.

Equipo de Trabajo, integrados por los miembros operarios ya sea de línea de producción o del área de servicio y son lidereados por un "coordinador" elegido por el propio equipo.

De esta manera, actualmente existen 1 equipo coordinador, 6 equipos operativos, 13 equipos de apoyo y alrededor de 200 equipos de trabajo, de los cuales 140 están en las áreas productivas y los restantes en las áreas administrativas.

A partir de la Unidad Coordinadora (Gerencia/sindicato), se desprenden las seis UN: hornos, moldeo, corazones y limpieza, maquinado sur (monoblocks), norte (partes de motor), y ensamble motores; seis unidades de operación, una para cada UN y posteriormente los ET.

A continuación se presenta de manera esquemática la cronología seguida en GMT hasta llegar a su estructura funcional actual. Como se mencionaba, si bien los intentos de modificación de la organización fueron desde 1980, hasta 1987 se desarrollan importantes acciones para tal fin.

En 1987 se conforma un equipo exploratorio (con la participación del sindicato), que visita distintas plantas; se aprueba el modelo de ET de GMT; se contrata a expertos externos; y se imparten cursos bajo el "modelo cliente-proveedor" a los equipos coordinadores, operativos y de implantación

En 1988 se aplican dos ET de manera experimental en las líneas de maquinado y fundición; se realiza la primera Junta de Negocios (JN) con todo el personal donde se les informa sobre la situación del Complejo; se realiza la primera junta de Coordinadores (13 coordinadores); y se dan cursos a ellos de desarrollo de habilidades y liderazgo en la supervisión, y de desarrollo de programas de capacitación técnica. Finalmente se generalizan los ET y UN.

En 1989-1990 se realizan cuatro juntàs de negocios, donde a partir de la cuarta se abordan temas específicos, siendo el primero "Productividad"; se inician las "Caminatas de Calidad" (una cada semana); se imparten cursos de mejoramiento de calidad en las líneas y m quinas críticas (aquellas que requieren mayor exactitud); cursos gerenciales *Deming* a gerentes; cursos de proceso de mejora continua a todo el personal; y se desarrolla la "Mansión de la Madurez" para analizar la situación de operación de los ET.

En 1991-1992 se realizan otras cuatro juntas de negocios, con temas como "Mantenimiento y Seguridad, Cliente, y Competitividad"; se desarrolla un programa de formación integral para favorecer la madurez de los ET; se dan más de 70 cursos técnicos y conceptuales; se inicia la secundaria abierta y el tecnológico GM en las instalaciones del complejo; se realiza la medición del ambiente laboral, con el objeto de analizar la involucración del personal a los programas de calidad.

En 1993 se realiza la evaluación de coordinadores; se redefine la estrategia hacia los ET; se lleva a cabo la décima junta de negocios con el tema "Manufactura Sincronizada"; se implementa el Plan Integral de Educación de la Excelencia; se da entrenamiento a todo el personal sobre manejo de material peligroso; y se reduce el número y tiempo de los cursos a la vez que se escalonan.

En 1994 se da un proceso de reentrenamiento con el curso de evaluación del desempeño, con el que se aplica una encuesta sobre la mentalidad del trabajador sindicalizado y un informe sobre el ambiente laboral.

Un aspecto clave de la forma de organización del Complejo es la independencia relativa para decidir la forma específica que asume. Si bien existe una decisión corporativa de incorporación de la "calidad total" y "equipos de trabajo", estas son exploradas, implementadas y evaluadas internamente, adquiriendo una forma particular, distinguible de las otras plantas del Corporativo.

En este sentido, se puede mencionar que conceptualmente en GMT se analizaron, exploraron y aplicaron distintos planteamientos sobre control total de la calidad, incluyendo a *Deming, Crosby, Juran, Ishikawa* y otros. De acuerdo a funcionarios de la planta "se aplica lo mejor de ellos, dependiendo de que tanto se adecuan a las condiciones específicas del Complejo"; asimismo, durante el trayecto de implementación seguido se han hecho nuevas adecuaciones.

Si bien los diferentes autores sobre "*calidad*" y la propia GMT resaltan en lo general la relación calidad-productividad- competitividad, entre ellos y la empresa hay diferencias. En *Santos y García* (1987) se puede encontrar un excelente análisis comparativo entre las distintas "corrientes de la calidad". Para este caso lo que interesa resaltar es la hibridez que se desarrolla en GMT.

Así, a pesar de retomar la definición de *Crosby* sobre calidad como "cumplir los requisitos del cliente", y el "estilo gerencial"; incorpora de manera fuerte la relación "cliente-proveedor" de *Juran e Ishikawa*, y de éste último el "*kaisen*" y "*kanban*"; enfatiza en las técnicas de medición de la calidad de *Deming*. En lo que respecta a la organización del trabajo, GMT asume una manera vertical de equipos de trabajo, al restarles el carácter voluntario de su constitución, no obstante que da libertades en formas de selección del coordinador y de reunión.

Por otra parte, probablemente dos son las principales adecuaciones en torno a los ET desarrolladas a partir de 1993. Antes había total libertad para elegir al coordinador y el problema a desarrollar, ahora para ser coordinador se requiere aprobar un examen de conocimientos y el problema lo delimita la empresa.

ORGANIZACIÓN DEL TRABAJO

GMT, bajo el esquema PRINDO, opera en su conjunto (áreas productivas y administrativas) a través de UN y equipos a distintos niveles, siendo los últimos los ET.

En lo que respecta a las áreas productivas éstas se encuentran organizadas en equipos de tres tipos: operativos, de apoyo y de trabajo, siendo 6 los primeros, 13 los segundos y 140 los últimos. A cada uno de los operativos corresponde una UN, relativamente autosuficientes en los términos señalados anteriormente. El número de trabajadores y equipos por planta y UN se indican en el (CUADRO 2).

Esta es la situación cuantitativa de la organización del trabajo, pero, cómo funcionan. Para tal efecto, se combinaron los planteamientos de *Dombois y Pries* y los indicadores de *Durand* (1994).

Según los primeros autores la organización del trabajo ("relaciones laborales", para ellos) se refieren al proceso de trabajo y de producción, remitiendo en su conjunto al valor de uso de la fuerza de trabajo, e incluyendo cuatro aspectos sobre todo: diseño técnico del proceso, organización del trabajo (propiamente dicha), asignación del trabajo y control y rendimiento del trabajo. Para el segundo, los aspectos centrales sobre la organización del trabajo a considerar la vida interna de los ET, el trabajo de producción, la forma en que son controlados los ET, y la implicación obrera.

CUADRO 2

GENERAL MOTORS: COMPLEJO DE MOTORES DE TOLUCA, MEXICO
PERSONAL OCUPADO Y EQUIPOS DE TRABAJO POR PLANTA
Y UNIDAD DE NEGOCIO.

PLANTA -- UNIDAD DE NEGOCIO	*PERSONAL OCUPADO*			*EQUIPOS DE TRABAJO*			
	TOTAL	*TRA-BAJ.*	*SU-PERV.*	*TO-TAL*	*OP-ERAT*	*APOYO*	*TRA BAJ.*
TOTAL	*1,554*	*1,465*	*89*	*159*	*6*	*13*	*140*
MAQ. Y ENSAMBLE	*913*	*864*	*49*	*120*	*3*	*10*	*107*
-- MAQUILADO NORTE	*293*	*276*	*17*	*31*	*1*	*2*	*28*
-- MAQUILADO SUR	*360*	*342*	*18*	*28*	*1*	*4*	*23*
-- ENSAMBLE	*132*	*128*	*4*	*38*	*1*	*2*	*35*
Turno matutino				*18*		*1*	*16*
Turno vespertino				*20*		*1*	*19*
Taller mecánico	*128*	*118*	*10*	*23*		*2*	*21*
FUNDICION	*641*	*601*	*40*	*39*	*3*	*3*	*33*
-- HORNOS	*97*	*81*	*16*	*19*	*1*	*1*	*17*
-- MOLDEO	*174*	*164*	*10*	*12*	*1*	*1*	*10*
-- CORAZONES Y LIMPIEZA	*370*	*356*	*14*	*8*	*1*	*1*	*6*

Fuente: G.M.T.

COMPLEJO EN SU CONJUNTO

Para el caso de GMT en sus áreas productivas, en general pueden identificarse, en los términos de *Dombois* y *Pries*, que en el diseño del proceso predominan las formas legales negociadas de "concertación institucionalizada", al existir tanto en la implantación como operación de los ET de una participación directa y organizada por parte del sindicato. No obstante, tanto la intención original como el seguimiento de ellos tienen una fuerte carga gerencial.

La organización del trabajo (propiamente dicha) es ante todo en términos de flexibilidad e involucramiento mas potencial que activa, lo que significa que no obstante existir la capacitación y adiestramiento en el personal para realizar actividades polivalentes, en la práctica esto sucede esporádicamente, principalmente ante ausencias o vacaciones de los trabajadores, más que una practica regular de rotación, debido en parte a la rigidez escalafonaria que implicarán los cambios y a que se sigue privilegiando la habilidad individual del trabajador (especialización).

En relación a lo anterior, la asignación de las tareas corresponde principalmente al escalafón, antigüedad y especialidad del trabajador, que a pesar de ser una decisión que puede tomar la empresa, procura recurrir al sindicato y al ET para realizarla, con el objeto de seguir manteniendo las buenas relaciones laborales existentes, que es una de las principales características en el complejo.

En cuanto al control sobre el trabajo, si bien formalmente se pretende alcanzar el autocontrol, y en este sentido una fuerte participación del ET o de su coordinador (elegido por el ET), el supervisor (designado por la empresa) es quien ejerce el papel controlador a nivel de línea.

Ahora, siguiendo el esquema de *Durand*, para el conjunto del Complejo (CUADRO 3), se puede observar que la organización del trabajo en términos de funcionamiento de los ET, presenta como principales características: Los ET se encuentran en una fase de generalización, ya que la fase exploratoria o de arranque fue en 1987 y para el año siguiente ya operaron en la totalidad del complejo. Asimismo, la constitución de ellos, a pesar de ser una decisión del corporativo, tuvieron una fuerte participación del sindicato en la forma de arranque y de operación generalizada.

En lo que respecta a la vida interna de los ET se puede notar, por lo menos hasta 1993, que existe un elevado grado de organización del trabajo, ya que son los miembros de los ET los que deciden formas de reunión y como se coordinan, aunque a partir de ese año el problema que desarrollan ya es elegido por la empresa cuando antes era por el ET.

El grado de polivalencia es elevado pero sustancialmente mayor a la rotación efectiva de los operadores, porque esta, exceptuando cuando hay ausencia de trabajadores principalmente es esporádica más que rutinaria.

En cuanto al líder (coordinador) del ET, su elección por los miembros y su rotación entre ellos, aunque siguen teniendo capacidad los miembros, desde 1993 se ha venido restringiendo a que el coordinador apruebe un examen de conocimientos diseñado por la empresa. Por otra parte, no obstante que para ser coordinador no existe relación jerárquica, funcionalmente quien tiene un papel de "líder real" es el supervisor (designado por la empresa) quien formalmente en los ET tendría solo un papel de "monitor". El trabajo de producción es el aspecto donde tienen menor participación los ET, debido a que la ayuda de equipo de cómputo es sobre todo a nivel de consulta, prácticamente no tienen incidencia sobre los estándares de calidad, es mínimo el control de calidad al interior de los ET, y aun menor en el mantenimiento de equipo y maquinaria y fijación de stocks por el ET.

Debido a que los ET se enmarcan en UN, al interior de cada una de ellas se da una cierta autonomía en cuanto a las maneras específicas de administrar recursos financieros y humanos, y al ubicarse esta UN más próximas a las áreas productivas predominan formas negociadas de decisión.

En lo que respecta a la implicación obrera, esta cuestión es la más difícil de evaluar por la fuerte connotación subjetiva y cultural que supone. No obstante, se podría señalar, por un lado, que ante la estrecha relación sindicato-empresa, se da el interés de la empresa por promover la participación y calificación del trabajo (acorde a los nuevos modelos de organización del trabajo); y por el otro lado, la existencia de salarios superiores a los de la media local y el creciente desempleo que implica la crisis, se da una tendencia hacia la implicación obrera, que no es mayor tanto porque las remuneraciones se otorgan en gran medida según el puesto más que por una evaluación objetiva del trabajo y los estímulos que reciben los trabajadores son sobre todo simbólicos, como porque es aun reducida la incidencia del trabajo sobre las formas concretas de trabajo como estándares de calidad, control, flujos y mantenimiento

Con el objeto de pormenorizar en los procesos productivos y en la organización del trabajo que se desarrollan en GMT, a continuación se presentan una descripción del proceso productivo en cada una de las plantas y las particularidades de la organización del trabajo en dos lineas productivas, obviando algunas de las formas ya mencionadas para el Complejo en su conjunto cuando no hay diferencias significativas.

CUADRO 3
GENERAL MOTORS: COMPLEJO
DE MOTORES DE TOLUCA, MEXICO

FECHA Febrero 1995 PLANTA Complejo en General

CARACTERISTICAS DE LA ORGANIZACION DEL TRABAJO	*RANGO*	*CALIF.*
Puesta en funcionamiento de los ET. (año de arranque: 1988)	0..........10	10
% de la fabrica que se encuentra en ET (Experimentación o Generalización)	0..........10	6
Constitución de ET por la dirección (0), o por negociación (10)		
VIDA INTERNA DEL ET		
Grado de organización propia del trabajo (débil: 0 ; fuerte : 10)	0..........10	8
Grado de polivalencia de las operadores (débil: 0 ; fuerte : 10)	0..........10	6
Grado de rotación de los operadores (débil: 0 ; fuerte : 10)	0..........10	3
Denominación (0) elección (10) del líder. Denominación del líder.	0..........10	9
Grado de rotación del líder (ausencia : 0; frecuencia : 10.)	0..........10	10
Ausencia de relación jerárquica del ET (ausencia : 10)	0..........10	7
EL TRABAJO DE PRODUCCION		
Grado de utilización de sistemas por computadora en el proceso (información: 0 ; consultado por el ET: 10)	0..........10	2
Longitud de los ciclos (cortos : 0; muy largos : 10)	0..........10	8
Estándares impuestos por el BM (0) o negociados hasta en el modo de calculo (10)	0..........10	1
Control de la calidad asegurado solamente por un servicio exterior a la linea (0) o concebido por los operarios (10)	0........ .10	5
Mantenimiento asegurado solamente por un servicio exterior a la linea (10) o confianza en la concepción de instalación por el ET (10)	0..........10	3
Flujos sin stock (0) o gestión de la PRODUCCION negociada (10)	0..........10	3

ROL DE ENMARCAMIENTO (Forma en que los ET son controlados).		
Trabajo administrativo repetitivo (0) o trabajo de anticipación con medios financieros y/o humanos (10)	0....... ..10	8
Gestión de los hombres para el servicio del personal (0) o autonomía de medios locales : modos de escalafón (10)	0........ 10	9
Mandos autoritarios (0) o decisiones negociadas (10)	0..........10	9
IMPLICACION OBRERA		
Fuerte subempleo local (0) o pleno empleo (10)	0..........10	4
Inseguridad del empleo (0) o garantías de empleo en la firma (10)	0..........10	8
Salarios iguales a la media local (0) o netamente superiores (10)	0..........10	6
Remuneraciones según el puesto de trabajo (0) o según la evaluación objetiva del trabajo (10)	0..........10	5
Rechazo de la implicación individual (0) o compromiso mutuo en el trabajo (10)	0..........10	9
Rechazo sindical de la nueva organización (0) o compromiso sindical (10)	0..........10	10

Esquema de trabajo de Jean Pierre Durand (1994)

PLANTA DE FUNDICIÓN

Esta planta cuenta con cinco hornos de cinco toneladas cada uno (dos de inducción y tres de electricidad). Se obtienen cuatro tipos de metales: duro, suave, nodular y aleado.

El proceso productivo de la planta es:

A. Recepción y disposición de chatarra.

B. Recalentado de chatarra.

C. Mezclado de ferroaleaciones.

D. Horneado.

E. Vaciado en moldes.

F. Corazones.

G. Limpieza de piezas fundidas.

H. Traslado a planta de maquinado.

Los inventarios del material para fundición antes cubrían las necesidades para un lapso de 10 a 12 días, ahora para 1.5 días, lo que supone una organización *justo a tiempo*.

También se han dado cambios en cuanto a la calidad de chatarra, consistente en una reducción de las especificaciones. Antes se solicitaba que no tuviese pintura, oxidación, etc. y que estuviese compactada, y ahora no existen esas restricciones, debido a la dificultad para contar oportunamente con el material. No obstante, la calidad no ha variado, debido a que las especificaciones necesarias se alcanzan por medio de las ferroaleaciones.

Las principales materias primas son: chatarra industrial, proveniente del DF y en menor medida de Monterrey y Toluca, aunque en situaciones de emergencia se ha recurrido a su importación. Arena Silícica, utilizada para los moldes, proviene de la empresa nacional Istmo ubicada en Veracruz. Ferroaleaciones, importadas de EU y Brasil por una empresa nacional importadora localizada en el DF.

La planta de fundición ocupa actualmente a 641 personas, de las cuales 601 son trabajadores y 40 supervisores, asimismo esta organizada en tres unidades de negocios (hornos, moldeo y corazones y limpieza) en torno a los cuales se desarrollan equipos de trabajo: 3 operativos, 3 de apoyo y 33 de trabajo.

La organización del trabajo en la línea de corazones y limpieza, en la que por las características propias del proceso productivo el tipo de trabajo en la línea es predominantemente monótono, poco calificado y que da poco espacio a la incorporación de iniciativas que supongan cambios sustantivos en el proceso. De acuerdo a los planteamientos de *Dombois* y *Pries* no presentan diferencias sustantivas a las características del complejo en su conjunto. Aplicando el esquema propuesto por *Durand* (CUADRO 4) se pueden desprender las particularidades siguientes:

Se tiene una percepción fuerte de que la constitución de ET es promovida por la empresa y por tanto existe escaso margen de negociación.

La participación de los ET en el trabajo productivo es menor al promedio, debido a que es esencialmente poco calificado y dominado por las especificaciones incorporadas a la maquinaria, asimismo, ante los elevados niveles de ruido la comunicación entre trabajadores es escasa.

El control de calidad internamente es reducido, detectándose por el ET sobre todo las fallas visibles o notorias. Por otra parte, cuando se presentan estas fallas son debidas principalmente a deficiencias en las aleaciones, que corresponden a la línea de hornos.

El control sobre el ET es mayor por parte de la empresa a través del supervisor debido a la escasa calificación del trabajo y a mínima comunicación durante el proceso.

También por la escasa calificación y marcada significación del escalafón, y la situación critica de la economía que ha propiciado desempleo, se da una tendencia hacia un involucramiento formal mas que real, con el objeto de mantener la fuente de empleo.

PLANTA DE MAQUINADO Y ENSAMBLE

Tradicionalmente se ha ocupado en la planta maquinaria de reuso. A ultimas fechas es que se ha introducido maquinaria más sofisticada, aunque no de punta, y solamente en líneas de producción específicas, como la maquinado de motores L6 y V8, y la de cigüeñales.

El proceso de maquinado y ensamble parte de dos flujos: piezas fundidas en la planta y piezas compradas.

Las piezas fundidas pasan al desbaste, inspección, acabado e inspección final.

Las piezas compradas pasan al almacén, inspección y nuevamente a almacén.

Ambos flujos se reúnen en el proceso de subensambles, donde se realiza el ensamble de ellas.

CUADRO 4

GENERAL MOTORS : COMPLEJO DE MOTORES DE TOLUCA, MEXICO

FECHA Febrero de 1995 PLANTA Fundición (corazones y limpieza)

CARACTERISTICAS DE LA ORGANIZACION DEL TRABAJO	*RANGO*	*CALIF*
Puesta en funcionamiento de los ET. (año de arranque: 1988)	0............10	10
% de la fabrica que se encuentra en ET (Experimentación o Generalización)	0............10	2
Constitución de ET por la dirección (0), o por negociación (10)		
VIDA INTERNA DEL ET		
Grado de organización propia del trabajo (débil: 0 ; fuerte : 10)	0............10	6
Grado de polivalencia de las operadores (débil: 0 ; fuerte : 10)	0............10	6
Grado de rotación de los operadores (débil: 0 ; fuerte : 10)	0............10	3
Denominación (0) elección (10) del líder. Denominación del líder.	0............10	9

Grado de rotación del líder (ausencia : 0; frecuencia : 10.)	0............10	9
Ausencia de relación jerárquica del ET (ausencia : 10)	0............10	7
EL TRABAJO DE PRODUCCION		
Grado de utilización de sistemas por computadora en el proceso (información: 0 ; consultado por el ET: 10)	0............10	2
Longitud de los ciclos (cortos : 0; muy largos : 10)	0............10	8
Estándares impuestos por el BM (0) o negociados hasta en el modo de calculo (10)	0............10	1
Control de la calidad asegurado solamente por un servicio exterior a la linea (0) o concebido por los operarios (10)	0............10	4
Mantenimiento asegurado solamente por un servicio exterior a la linea (10) o confianza en la concepción de instalación por el ET (10)	0............10	3
Flujos sin stock (0) o gestión de la PRODUCCION negociada (10)	0............10	3
ROL DE ENMARCAMIENTO (Forma en que los ET son controlados).		
Trabajo administrativo repetitivo (0) o trabajo de anticipación con medios financieros y/o humanos (10)	0............10	8
Gestión de los hombres para el servicio del personal (0) o autonomía de medios locales : modos de escalafón (10)	0............10	6
Mandos autoritarios (0) o decisiones negociadas (10)	0............10	6
IMPLICACION OBRERA		
Fuerte subempleo local (0) o pleno empleo (10)	0...........10	3
Inseguridad del empleo (0) o garantías de empleo en la firma (10)	0...........10	4
Salarios iguales a la media local (0) o netamente superiores (10)	0...........10	6
Remuneraciones según el puesto de trabajo (0) o según la evaluación objetiva del trabajo (10)	0...........10	3
Rechazo de la implicación individual (0) o compromiso mutuo en el trabajo (10)	0...........10	7
Rechazo sindical de la nueva organización (0) o compromiso sindical (10)	0...........10	9

Esquema tomado de Jean Pierre Durand (1994)

En el proceso de ensamble, primero se realiza una inspección de los subensambles, se realiza el ensamble, que pasa a inspección, banco de pruebas y al vestido final.

Las lineas de maquinado son siete, y una la de ensamble, las primeras son:

A. Cigüeñal.

B. Árbol de levas. C. Monoblock y cabeza de motor V8 y L4.

D. Bombas de agua.

E. Válvulas.

F. Monoblock y cabeza de motor L6.

G. Volantes, anillos, cubiertas, embrague, empaquetadora y bombas de aceite.

H. Bielas.

El volumen de producción y de inventarios se realiza *justo a tiempo*, operándolo el área de ingeniería de manufactura, en coordinación con los departamentos de operación (maquinado y fundido) por medio del Sistema PISCIK, el cual transmite los requerimientos y volúmenes alcanzados a través de letreros electrónicos a cada una de las líneas. Las programaciones son diarias, mensuales y anuales.

Para el análisis de la organización del trabajo se tomó la línea de cigüeñales, por ser ésta una de las mas "críticas" en cuanto a grado de precisión que debe alcanzar el componente, asimismo porque esto exige una mayor calificación y participación del trabajador en el control de la calidad, a diferencia de la de moldes y limpieza en la planta de fundido. No obstante, siguiendo los planteamientos de *Dombois* y *Pries* no muestra diferencias sustanciales con respecto al complejo en su conjunto. En lo que respecta al esquema de *Durand* (CUADRO 5), se puede mencionar como particularidades las siguientes:

En la constitución de los ET se nota una mayor participación de los miembros, aunque se reconoce como determinante la acción de la empresa. Esto, debido a la mas fuerte vida interna del ET, derivada a su vez por la existencia de mayores formas de comunicación entre ellos durante el proceso. Asimismo, es mayor la polivalencia y rotación de puestos entre los trabajadores, por la propia calificación de ellos y que existen menores restricciones por parte de la empresa para efecto de la rotación. Por otra parte, también es mayor la ausencia de relación jerárquica, debida a la mayor comunicación entre miembros del ET y supervisores.

CUADRO 5
GENERAL MOTORS: COMPLEJO DE MOTORES DE TOLUCA, MEXICO

FECHA Febrero de 1995 PLANTA Maquinado (Cigüeñales)

CARACTERISTICAS DE LA ORGANIZACION DEL TRABAJO	*RANGO*	*CALIF*
Puesta en funcionamiento de los ET. (año de arranque: 1987)	0.........10	10
% de la fabrica que se encuentra en ET (Experimentación o Generalización)	0.........10	4
Constitución de ET por la dirección (0), o por negociación (10)		
VIDA INTERNA DEL ET		
Grado de organización propia del trabajo (débil: 0 ; fuerte : 10)	0.........10	7
Grado de polivalencia de las operadores (débil: 0 ; fuerte : 10)	0.........10	7
Grado de rotación de los operadores (débil: 0 ; fuerte : 10)	0.........10	4
Denominación (0) elección (10) del líder. Denominación del líder.	0.........10	10
Grado de rotación del líder (ausencia : 0; frecuencia : 10.)	0.........10	10
Ausencia de relación jerárquica del ET (ausencia : 10)	0.........10	9
EL TRABAJO DE PRODUCCION		
Grado de utilización de sistemas por computadora en el proceso (información: 0 ; consultado por el ET: 10)	0.........10	4
Longitud de los ciclos (cortos : 0; muy largos : 10)	0.........10	7
Estándares impuestos por el BM (0) o negociados hasta en el modo de calculo (10)	0.........10	2
Control de la calidad asegurado solamente por un servicio exterior a la linea (0) o concebido por los operarios (10)	0.........10	6
Mantenimiento asegurado solamente por un servicio exterior a la linea (10) o confianza en la concepción de instalación por el ET (10)	0.........10	3
Flujos sin stock (0) o gestión de la PRODUCCION negociada (10)	0.........10	3
ROL DE ENMARCAMIENTO (Forma en que los ET son controlados).		
Trabajo administrativo repetitivo (0) o trabajo de anticipación con medios financieros y/o humanos (10)	0.........10	8

Gestión de los hombres para el servicio del personal (0) o autonomía de medios locales : modos de escalafón (10)	0.........10	8
Mandos autoritarios (0) o decisiones negociadas (10)	0.........10	8
IMPLICACION OBRERA		
Fuerte subempleo local (0) o pleno empleo (10)	0.........10	3
Inseguridad del empleo (0) o garantías de empleo en la firma (10)	0.........10	4
Salarios iguales a la media local (0) o netamente superiores (10)	0.........10	5
Remuneraciones según el puesto de trabajo (0) o según la evaluación objetiva del trabajo (10)	0.........10	4
Rechazo de la implicación individual (0) o compromiso mutuo en el trabajo (10)	0.........10	8
Rechazo sindical de la nueva organización (0) o compromiso sindical (10)	0.........10	9

Esquema tomado de Jean Pierre Durand (1994)

El proceso productivo posibilita una mayor participación del ET, resolviéndose al interior de ellos buena parte de los problemas que se presentan, para lo cual cuentan con equipo de cómputo, lo mismo sucede con el mantenimiento de la maquinaria que periódicamente realiza el ET. Sin embargo, los estándares de calidad y ritmos de los flujos son impuestos por la empresa.

El control sobre el trabajo es menor que en la línea de corazones y limpieza, debido a la mayor y mejor comunicación con los supervisores.

La implicación del trabajo también es mayor que en la otra línea, pero existe con respecto a esta una más clara inconformidad con los niveles salariales, debido a que los trabajadores la perciben como insuficiente de acuerdo a la calificación del trabajo y a las exigencias que impone el proceso productivo.

CONCLUSIONES

GMT constituye un ejemplo interesante de como un complejo dedicado a la elaboración de un componente automotriz (motores y sus partes) de escasos nivel tecnológico y volumen de producción entra a un proceso de cambio productivo hacia el mercado internacional con calidad, productividad y competitividad. Con las limitaciones que impone el análisis de un estudio de caso, pueden desprenderse algunas ideas generales sobre el grado de transferibilidad de conceptos y estrategias organizacionales que tienen como sustentos la flexibilidad productiva y el involucramiento del trabajo.

Entre el tránsito de conceptos y estrategias a formas concretas de acción existen una multitud de posibilidades, combinaciones que hacen que cada configuración especifica lograda sea un caso prácticamente único. ¿Hasta que punto se puede ponderar la generalidad y especificidad de los cambios, particularmente los referidos a la organización del trabajo?

En GMT los cambios productivos están fuertemente relacionados con los presentados a nivel corporativo. en ese sentido, las estrategias de modernización son impulsadas por el proceso de reestructuración que se siguen centralmente. En un primer momento (la primera mitad de los ochenta) con carácter exploratorio y en uno posterior (de 1988 a la fecha) con gran intensidad para su generalización.

La estrategia diseñada por el corporativo parece mostrar una marcada verticalidad en lo que respecta al tipo y especificación de productos y tecnología dura (maquinaria y equipo), y cierta adecuación de la organización del trabajo a las condiciones internas de los complejos, posibilitando marcadas diferencias entre los complejos que operan en México. En otros términos, para el segundo caso plantea la creación de ET, pero no la forma especifica de como operaran.

En GMT se evidencia un amplio "margen de maniobra local" para seleccionar e hibridar conceptos, estrategias y practicas sobre la organización del trabajo. Los cuales han sido favorables para la empresa, ya que le han permitido alcanzar elevados niveles de calidad y productividad. Esto, debido en gran medida a la estrategia de la empresa de hacer participar al sindicato en la toma de decisiones, y a la notoria identificación de objetivos del sindicato con la empresa que ha posibilitado una relación funcional entre ambos. Este tipo de buenas relaciones antecede a los cambios ocurridos en los ochenta y es uno de los factores determinantes que ha posibilitado cambios organizacionales sin fuertes conflictos y con un relativo involucramiento de parte de los trabajadores.

La relatividad del involucramiento de los trabajadores en el proceso de trabajo, organizados en ET, presenta aspectos "favorecedores" como "inhibidores". Entre los primeros se puede señalar al intenso trabajo por parte de la empresa para calificarlos conceptual y técnicamente en la "nueva cultura del trabajo", en las intensas relaciones gerenciales personales con los trabajadores, y en el compromiso implícito por tratar de mantener la fuente de empleo. Entre las segundas, la rigidez escalafonaria para funcionar polivalentemente de manera mas regular, y que los estímulos a la productividad, calificación e involucramiento privilegian lo simbólico sobre lo monetario.

También la autonomía de trabajo de los ET es relativa, ya que mientras, por una parte, la empresa estimula la participación de los trabajadores en ellos y les brinda calificación en tal sentido, por la otra, los supervisores (designados por la empresa) desempeñan un papel efectivo superior en el proceso de trabajo al del coordinador del ET (elegido por los trabajadores), asimismo, los ET no determinan volúmenes ni secuencias de la producción, solo la capacidad para optimizar los procesos.

Las relaciones hacia el exterior que establece GMT se encuentran fuertemente condicionadas por el corporativo a nivel nacional. El decide tipos y volúmenes de producción, califica y selecciona a proveedores, dosifica el intercambio de información entre los complejos, etc. Constituyéndose de esta manera en un marco rígido que, por lo tanto, prácticamente solo permite maniobrar al interior del complejo sobre la organización del trabajo.

BIBLIOGRAFIA

Crosby, Philip B.,(1987), *La calidad no cuesta. El arte de cerciorarse de la calidad*, CECSA, México, 1992.

De la Garza Toledo, Enrique (1993), "Estilo de desarrollo y nuevos patrones de relaciones laborales", DOMBOIS y PRIES (eds.), *Trabajo industrial en transición: experiencias de América Latina y Europa*, Nueva Sociedad-FFEM-Colegio de Puebla, Venezuela, pp.13-26.

Deming, W. Edwards (1989), *Calidad, productividad y competitividad. La salida de la crisis*, Díaz de Santos, España.

Dombois, Rainer y Ludger Pries (1993), "Modernización empresarial y cambios en las relaciones industriales en América Latina y Europa", DOMBOIS y Pries (coords.), *Modernización empresarial: tendencias en América Latina y Europa*, FESCOL, Colombia, pp. 11-40.

Durand, Jean-Pierre (1994), *Indications pour remplir la grille synthetique d'interpretation*, (paper).

González López, Sergio (1992), *Proceso de configuración territorial de la industria automotriz terminal en México 1964-1989*, UAEM, México.

_____ (1993), *Proceso de industrialización en la Zona Metropolitana de Toluca: situación actual, perspectivas y lineamientos de política para su desarrollo*, Reporte final de investigación, UAEM, México.

_____ (1994), "Reestructuración tecnológica e integración regional: el caso de la industria automotriz en Toluca, México", en *Ciencia ergo Sum*, vol. 1, número 2, agosto, UAEM, México, pp. 111-127.

GM (1991), *Sistemas y herramientas de calidad total: Complejo Toluca*, General Motors de México, México.

_____ (1993), "Complejo Ramos Arizpe", en *Actualidades*, año 1, núm. 0, abril, Premio Nacional de Calidad, México, pp. 3-10.

_____ (1994), *Contrato Colectivo de Trabajo, Complejo Toluca 1994- 1996*, General Motors de México, México.

Ishikawa, Kauro (1988), *¿Qué es el control total de calidad ?*, Norma, Colombia, 1992.

Juran, J. M. (1990), *Juran y la planificación para la calidad*, Díaz de Santos, España.

Santos Corral, Josefa y Susana García Salord (1987), *Los círculos de calidad. Experiencias en la empresa mexicana*, UNAM-CONACYT, México.

MAQUILADORAS EN REDES: EL CASO DE DELPHI-GENERAL MOTORS

*Jorge Carrillo**
*Alfredo Hualde***

INTRODUCCIÓN[1]

La industria maquiladora de exportación (IME) se estableció en México hace ya treinta años. En la última década ha sido la principal fuente de generación de divisas después del petróleo, y es la principal generadora de empleos dentro del sector manufacturero. Desde la década pasada mantiene altas tasas de crecimiento[2], mientras que la industria manufacturera no-maquiladora mantiene tasas muy bajas. La evidencia empírica muestra claramente que se trata de una industria dinámica, moderna y heterogénea (Carrillo, 1993).

No obstante su crecimiento meteórico, su importancia relativa, su modernización y los efectos económicos multiplicadores, siempre han existido fuertes críticas a esta industria. Sobresalen la falta de integración productiva[3] (como una debilidad para lograr un desarrollo más equilibrado y endógeno), la escasa inversión en capital, tecnología y alta dependencia de personal de escasa calificación[4] (como una muestra de su característica de ser intensiva en mano de obra) y el deterioro que generan.

---

* Investigador de El Colegio de la Frontera Norte. Profesor Invitado en la UAM-I

** Investigador de El Colegio de la Frontera Norte

[1] Toda la información referente a las empresas GM proviene de las entrevistas realizadas por los autores con gerentes de plantas de Delphi en Ciudad Juárez, durante noviembre de 1995 y junio de 1996. Los autores agradecen toda la cooperación brindada por la empresa.

[2] La tasa de crecimiento promedio anual fue de 14.9% entre 1984 y 1990; y de 7.9% entre 1991 y 1996 (Cimex-Weffa, 1995).

[3] El grado de integración de insumos nacionales fue de 1.08% entre 1984-1990 y de 1.55% entre 1991 y 1996 (Cimex-Weffa, 1995).

[4] Los trabajadores de producción representaron el 81.6% del total de empleados en 1984-1990 y el 81.2% en 1991-1996 (Cimex-Weffa, 1995).

Mientras que la investigación muestra que la IME es una industria heterogénea en donde coexisten tanto actividades económicas tradicionales como otras más sofisticadas, con sectores productivos muy diversos, y con empresas de origen de capital muy distinto, las críticas se dirigen más hacia un estereotipo de maquiladora inspirado en las primeras maquiladoras que a la realidad industrial-productiva de la IME. Por ello, deseamos proponer una clasificación de tipo de empresas maquiladoras, con el fin de entender ciertas pautas en esta industria diversa con rasgos comunes que parece estar frente a una nueva encrucijada con la emergencia de un nuevo tipo de empresas. La importancia de esta tipología es que permite entender con mayor claridad las trayectorias del modelo de industrialización para la exportación en el caso de México.

El trabajo expone en la primera sección lo que hemos denominado la tercera generación de maquiladoras. Y en la segunda sección exponemos el caso Delphi-Juárez como muestra de la emergencia no sólo de un nuevo tipo de empresa maquiladora sino de una nueva relación entre empresas.

UNA NUEVA GENERACIÓN DE MAQUILADORAS

El análisis de la IME se ha desarrollado, desde mediados de los ochenta, bajo lo que podemos denominar dos grandes enfoques: uno que muestra la heterogeneidad de la industria y que intenta construir diferentes tipologías de empresas, y otro que resalta sus rasgos comunes y que presenta a esta industria en una forma unívoca. Dentro de estos enfoques, existen por supuesto distintas percepciones sobre las debilidades y los aciertos de dicha industria. Estos dos enfoques, tan dispares entre si, conviven en muchas de las ocasiones en un mismo discurso. Así por ejemplo, mientras que cualquier estudioso o actor social o institucional involucrado en la administración, promoción, regulación o estudio de la IME sabe que existen realidades muy distintas dentro del conjunto de las empresas maquiladoras en México, al mismo tiempo le da un tratamiento estadístico, analítico o discursivo como si se tratara realmente de una sola industria.

La IME no es una industria en el sentido literal, ni tiene un significado productivo, tecnológico o laboral. Se trata fundamentalmente de un régimen arancelario en el cual se inscriben las empresas con el fin de poder importar temporalmente libre de impuestos, los insumos, componentes, maquinaria y equipo necesarios (así como el traslado de personal técnico extranjero) para producir un bien o servicio en México y re-exportarlo hacia Estados Unidos. Sin embargo, **sí existen rasgos comunes significativos** dentro de esta heterogeneidad estructural de las empresas maquiladoras, sobresaliendo tres de ellas: i) su orientación al mercado estadounidense (casi por definición)[5]; ii) su localización primordial en el segundo eje de industrialización "norteño-fronterizo" con centros especializados como Ciudad Juárez y Tijuana (Alegría, Alonso y Carrillo, 1995), y iii) la utilización intensiva de los recursos humanos como competencia central[6]. Por tanto, analizar a las empresas maquiladoras como si pertenecieran a una sola industria si es de gran utilidad, pero no por el poder explicativo del concepto, sino porque permite contrastarlas con empresas surgidas bajo un modelo de industrialización distinto: el de la situación de importaciones, caracterizado por la orientación al mercado interno, la ubicación de las empresas alrededor de tres principales áreas metropolitanas (Ciudad de México, Monterrey y Guadalajara) y una mayor combinación de los factores tecnología, capital y trabajo[7].

En este sentido **si es factible y útil identificar grandes conglomerados de empresas** de acuerdo a rasgos comunes referentes a la actividad económica, la tecnología y la organización de la producción y el trabajo. La construcción de tipologías de empresas maquiladoras ha sido una fuente de riqueza empírica y ha desencadenado una mayor rigurosidad analítica. Dicotomías construidas como empresas tradicionales y modernas (Mertens y Palomares, 1988), viejas y nuevas (Gereffi, 1991), de escasa o avanzada tecnología (González-Aréchiga, Ramírez, y Suárez-Villa, 1989), han mostrado sólidamente la existencia de al menos dos tipos de maquiladoras. Wilson (1992) propone que las maquiladoras pueden ser de tres tipos de acuerdo al "modelo productivo": ensamble tradicional manufactura y "posfordistas".

Sin duda, esta tercera categoría, la del posfordismo, es la que más debate ha suscitado, ya que para algunos autores como Wilson (1992) o Shaiken y Browne (1991) se trata, en palabras nuestras, de una mala copia del sistema

---

[5] Las empresas maquiladoras exportan en su inmensa mayoría el 100% de su producción, aunque pueden vender un 40% al mercado nacional. En el 2,001 podrán vender el 100% al mercado interno.

[6] Todas las actividades económica maquiladoras son intensivas en mano de obra (U. S. Congress, 1992).

[7] Estas características del modelo de industrialización por sustitución de importaciones se presentaron también en varios países latinoamericanos.

de producción japonés, por su limitada y parcial aplicación que enfatiza la intensificación y la degradación del trabajo. Mientras que para otros autores se trata de una nueva etapa de la IME caracterizada por un proceso de modernización industrial, con un mayor enriquecimiento del trabajo y una mayor competitividad (Alonso, Carrillo, Contreras, 1994; Carrillo 1993). Los analistas de los transplantes asiáticos en norteamérica complementan la anterior afirmación al señalar que se trata de empresas con un excelente desempeño logrado a través de un proceso de hibridación (Abo, 1994); y de sectores con mucho potencial para aumentar la competitividad y desarrollar cadenas productivas pero con urgentes debilidades por abatir (Choi y Kenney, 1994; Kenney, Romero y Choi, 1994).

Bajo este enfoque de construcción de tipologías se logra, por un lado, mostrar la gran heterogeneidad de la IME en períodos específicos y, por otro lado, examinar las empresas de distintas actividades económicas bajo la óptica del modelo dominante de industrialización exportadora. Por tanto la elaboración de tipologías permite analizar la diversidad fabril, no al interior de "una industria" o sector sino de mayor importancia, de un modelo de industrialización. Es en este sentido que proponemos para su discusión la existencia de **tres tipos de empresas** en la industria maquiladora, con base en lo que consideramos la característica central de la IME, el uso intensivo de la mano de obra: las empresas de primera generación las podemos bautizar como **"basadas en intensificación del trabajo manual"**, las de segunda generación como **"basadas en la racionalización del trabajo"** y las emergentes o de tercera generación **"basadas en competencias intensivas en conocimiento"**.

Por generación estamos entendiendo un tipo ideal de empresas con rasgos comunes y con tendencias a predominar durante un tiempo específico. Sin embargo en un mismo período se encuentran distintos tipos de empresas e, incluso, un mismo establecimiento puede contar con diferentes rasgos pertenecientes a diferentes generaciones (proceso que podemos denominar de hibridación). Por tanto, al hablar de generaciones nos estamos refiriendo **al alcance en el aprendizaje** logrado por empresas particulares a partir de sus propias trayectorias tecnológicas y organizacionales.

Veamos la tercera generación de maquiladoras[8].

---

[8] Para una descripción de la primera y segunda generación véase Carrillo y Hualde, 1996.

EMPRESAS MAQUILADORAS DE TERCERA GENERACIÓN: BASADAS EN COMPETENCIAS INTENSIVAS EN CONOCIMIENTOS

Antes que nada debemos señalar que existe muy poca evidencia empírica para delinear este tipo de empresas. Pero consideramos que la existencia de una empresa como Delphi-Juárez (o el complejo Samsung que se desarrolla en Tijuana) es suficiente para formular la hipótesis de la emergencia de una tercera generación de maquiladoras[9]

Las maquiladoras de tercera generación las podemos caracterizar por una mayor presencia de corporaciones transnacionales. Se trata de plantas ya no orientadas ni al ensamble (como la primera generación) ni a la manufactura (como en la segunda) sino al diseño, investigación y desarrollo. Las empresas siguen manteniendo escasos proveedores regionales, pero se desarrollan importantes "clusters" intrafirma y se potencializan las cadenas inter-firma. Esto es, se inicia un proceso de integración vertical centralizada a través de la conformación de complejos industriales en el lado mexicano, los que a su vez potencializan los vínculos con proveedores nacionales. Los complejos encadenan, dentro del mismo territorio, centros de ingeniería que proveen a maquiladoras de manufactura, los cuales a su vez mantienen proveedores directos-especializados y proveedores indirectos como talleres de maquinado o de inyección de plástico, además de importantes proveedores de responsabilidad total en distintas áreas de Estados Unidos.

El nivel tecnológico aumenta considerablemente en estos centros, pero no precisamente por la adaptación de procesos automatizados, sino por la compleja y diversa maquinaria y particularmente por los sistemas electrónicos para el diseño de prototipos. La dependencia tecnológica hacia la matriz en estos centros de investigación, diseño y desarrollo (I&D&D) practicamente desaparece y la toma de decisiones es autónoma, aunque evidentemente siempre evaluada y certificada por los clientes. Estas empresas de tercer tipo se caracterizan principalmente por contar con trabajo altamente calificado, esto es, constituida por ingenieros y técnicos de alto nivel. Desaparece en estos centros el trabajo intensivo y se privilegia el conocimiento y la creatividad tanto en el diseño y la manufactura, así como en la manufacturabilidad de los productos y procesos. La responsabilidad, discreción y el conoci-

[9] Esta generación probablemente será la última en tanto tipo de maquiladoras, ya que en el 2,001 desaparecerá el régimen de maquiladoras (no los establecimientos). Como industria exportadora seguramente veremos el desarrollo de nuevos tipos de empresa.

miento involucrados en estos nuevos trabajos es de muy alto nivel. Se trabaja por proyectos conformados por equipos de ingenieros y un soporte técnico, los cuales operan bajo una constante presión por alcanzar mejores resultados que los de sus competidores.

Se trata de centros de investigación, diseño y desarrollo de clase mundial, no sólo por el personal altamente calificado que ocupan, preocupado por concluir en el menor tiempo posible los proyectos de manera completamente satisfactoria para los clientes, sino por su trabajo en equipo por las empresas maquiladoras de manufactura a las cuales surten desde productos prototipo hasta líneas de ensamble. En este caso la fuente de competitividad está dada en la reducción de la duración de los proyectos, los costos de operación, y la rapidez de manufacturabilidad. En otras palabras, por la capacidad de ingeniería y tecnología los salarios relativos del personal calificado, y la comunicación y cercanía con su eslabón (en este caso empresas maquiladoras). En estas empresas de nueva generación los salarios vuelven a emerger como una principal ventaja comparativa y competitiva (tomando en cuenta las competencias laborales y los ingresos recibidos en México versus Estados Unidos), ya que el principal insumo de los proyectos son precisamente los ingenieros y su equipo de soporte[10].

En estos centros se diseñan y aplican los principios de flexibilidad que reestructuran tanto el *lay out* como los puestos de trabajo de las empresas manufactureras. La hipótesis central es que bajo este tipo de empresas de tercera generación se privilegian los clusters productivos. Su localización en territorio mexicano es resultado de decisiones transnacionales estratégicas de largo plazo que parten de la existencia de aglomeraciones industriales competitivas. Estas empresas de tercera generación representan "un salto de frontera" (*break through*) industrial. Como señaló un informante del primer centro de I&D&D maquilador: "... en las maquiladoras se siguen las recetas, aquí las hacemos... estamos frente a la industria del diseño".

En este tipo de empresas persiste, sin embargo, una debilidad añeja: la falta de proveedores locales, aunado a la falta de personal altamente calificado.

Veamos a continuación la caracterización del centro técnico Delphi-Juárez, o empresa maquiladora de tercera generación.

---

[10] Un trabajador de Delphi-A en México obtiene en promedio de 1.65 a 3 Dólares la hora más prestaciones, comparado con el promedio en Vandalia, Ohio de 10 Dólares la hora o de 17 Dólares en el caso de un miembro de la UAW (Wall Street, Junio 3, 1996).

EL CASO DE DELPHI-GM EN JUÁREZ

El centro de ingeniería de autopartes Delphi-Juárez es parte de la firma Delphi Automotive Systems (Delphi-A) la cual a su vez es una de las seis divisiones de la transnacional General Motors. Delphi-A tiene a su cargo la producción de autopartes dentro del complejo transnacional (un auto regular contiene tres mil autopartes) y está conformada por manufactura, investigación y desarrollo, y productos químicos[11]. La firma está especializada en cuatro grandes áreas: baterías, sistema de fuel injection, sistemas de purificación atmosférica y energía y sistemas de motor. La matriz de Delphi-Juárez se encuentra en Detroit y está representada por Delphi Energy & Engine Systems (Delphi-E). En junio de 1996 ésta contaba con 5,500 empleados.

A partir de la visión de autopartes como una industria estratégica dentro de la industria automotriz mundial para elevar la competitividad de las ensambladoras, se han incrementado las presiones de globalización y racionalización desarrolladas al respecto por el famoso director Super López. Después de cuatro años de reestructuración Delphi-A es actualmente una firma muy rentable. Bajo esta estrategia la matriz Delphi-E decide reubicar afuera de Estados Unidos, por primera vez en su historia, uno de sus siete centros de investigación y desarrollo. Se trata del traslado de la planta de Anderson, Indiana[12] hacia Ciudad Juárez[13]. Esta decisión estratégica obedece a la necesidad por reducir los tiempos de entrega y los costos globales. Mientras que en promedio el número de empleados en cada centro de ingeniería de Delphi-E es de 500 personas, en Delphi-Juárez se ocupan 860 y han logrado disminuir, tan sólo en un año de operaciones, un 60% los cos-

---

[11] Es el jugador más grande la altamente fragmentada industria de las autopartes cuyas ventas son de 720 mil millones de Dólares anuales. Delphi-A tuvo ventas del orden de 26.4 mi millones de Dólares en 1995 (15% del total de GM) y cuenta con 179,000 empleados en el mundo. Delphi es tres veces más grande que su competidor más cercano (*Wall Street Journal*, junio 3, 1996).

[12] El centro de Anderson aún persiste pero quedó asignado con otras familias de productos.

[13] Existen muchas plantas maquiladoras de arneses de GM en Juárez, pero pertenecen a la división Packard, la cual cuenta aproximadamente con 33,000 empleados en el norte de México (la mayoría en Juárez). Además existe otra división, DEPSA, la cual tiene maquiladoras que fabrican vestiduras también en esta ciudad. Delphi-A tiene actualmente una enorme importancia en México. En términos de empleo, Delphi-Juárez la tercera parte (63,000) del total de empleados (175,000) de esta compañía en este país, siendo además el principal de GM en México (con un total de 75,000 empleados), según información del *Wall Strett Journal* (3 de junio de 1996).

tos globales (comparados con la planta de Anderson), y un 20% los tiempos de entrega.

Delphi-Juárez abre sus puertas el 2 de junio de 1995 en esta ciudad siendo "una maquila más". Pero en este caso, se trata del primer centro de I&D&D en su tipo, no sólo en esta ciudad "maquiladora por excelencia", sino en todo México. Con una inversión inicial de 150 millones de Dólares (un poco menos de la mitad en equipo) Delphi-Juárez se dedica a producir solenoides y sensores[14].

Durante varios meses fueron enviados ingenieros y técnicos mexicanos al centro de GM en Anderson para recibir la capacitación necesaria en áreas críticas, ya que se trataba de una operación totalmente nueva para México, en donde el rol principal de esta maquiladora no es la producción de autopartes especializada propiamente dicho, sino la fabricación integral. En el centro de desarrolla desde una idea general (incluso hasta antes del papel) hasta el desarrollo de todo el producto, incluyendo su manufacturabilidad (las líneas de producción). Este sistema lo denomina como *full package*.

La decisión de relocalizar este centro de I&D&D en Ciudad Juárez fue estratégica para GM. Según los gerentes entrevistados los factores principales de localización fueron tres: a) la cercanía con Estados Unidos; b) la experiencia de 15 años de aprendizaje de las firmas maquiladoras productoras en Juárez (desde hace años reconocida como una zona con prestigio mundial y reconocido producto); y c) la calidad de las competencias de los ingenieros mexicanos[15].

Con el fin de reducir los tiempos de entrega, Delphi Juárez se trasladó a esta ciudad para lograr la máxima cercanía posible con su **eslabón principal: una empresa maquiladora de la misma división**. De tal manera que

---

[14]Los solenoides van en diferentes partes del motor y son válvulas (para aceite, agua, aire, etc.) que permiten tanto los flujos de aire en los sistemas de combustión como la regulación de combustión. Por su parte los sensores identifican y transmiten señales eléctricas (aunque de flujo electrónico), se trata de partes con electromagnetos y están altamente tecnologizadas. En promedio, un automóvil lleva 40 solenoides y 60 sensores.

[15] Algunos factores particulares fueron la infraestructura necesaria en telecomunicaciones, carreteras, transportes, hotelerías, etc., así como los servicios especializados al productor, y los servicios gubernamentales como agentes aduanales especializados. Otro factor fue la posibilidad de que los extranjeros vivan en el "lado americano" y crucen diariamente para laborar en Juárez. Otros factores cruciales fueron la existencia de proveedores cercanos y la potencialidad de desarrollar proveedores con calidad certificada, así como la disponibilidad de ingenieros y técnicos competentes (entrevistas con gerentes).

en lugar de mover los prototipos y el proceso de manufactura 1,800 millas dese Anderson hasta Juárez, ahora están a sólo unos cuantos minutos. Ciudad Juárez cuenta además con una localización geográfica estratégica para abastecer a distintas plantas ensambladoras a lo largo de la Unión Americana, y mantiene una mano de obra no calificada y semicalificado diez veces de menor costo que en plantas automotrices en "el otro lado". Asimismo, esta localidad es la zona industrial con mayor tradición exportadora. Mantiene en mayor número de establecimientos maquiladores de autopartes, con una reconocida especialización en los arneses y con una amplia experiencia en el ramo de las autopartes. Desde 1979 en que se estableció la primera planta de Chrysler, ha proliferado el establecimiento de plantas tanto de las "Tres Grandes" como de algunos transplantes japoneses. Todo lo cual ha favorecido el desarrollo de economías de aglomeración.

Referente al mercado de trabajo, Juárez cuenta con una amplia mano de obra con muchos años de experiencia en el sector de autopartes. Si bien la producción de ingenieros y técnicos no es suficiente para entender la demanda de empleo calificado por parte de la industria maquiladora, la alta movilidad laboral ayuda a encontrar a la gente. Por su parte en materia educativa, el estado de Chihuahua cuenta con universidades y tecnológicos que imparten diversas carreras de ingeniería muy vinculadas con la industria, e incluso existe un importante centro de investigación de materiales. La actividad de calidad de los ingenieros no sólo es apreciada en estas empresas, sino que GM evaluó a los ingenieros disponibles y potenciales para ser ocupados en este centro de I&D&D, llegando a la conclusión de que se trataba de ingenieros sumamente competentes.

Lo anterior no significa, de ninguna manera, que no haya problemas de mano de obra para esta y muchas otras empresas, ya que aún no ha sido resuelta la necesidad de una mayor oferta de personal calificado. Siguen existiendo carencias en la infraestructura en comunicación (aeropuerto insuficiente y cruces de frontera muy tardados), entre otras. En particular Delphi-Juárez requiere una mayor agilidad en las visas por el alto número de técnicos e ingenieros visitantes y una mayor flexibilidad legal (por ejemplo para probar los prototipos dentro de la ciudad en autos en circulación y para agilizar diversos permisos). Incluso la falta de una estructura legal para el establecimiento de centros de I&D&D hace que Delphi-Juárez tenga que afiliarse al régimen de maquiladoras.

Veamos tres áreas de gran importancia en este centro: producción, recursos humanos y eslabonamientos productivos.

PRODUCCIÓN

El valor de solenoides y sensores está en función del costo del proyecto. Un prototipo, por ejemplo, "vale lo que un ingeniero y su equipo de soporte, es decir, 80,000 dólares y eso es barato debido a que está hecho en México". La producción de 20 piezas junto con la manufactura de 14 celdas (manufactura celular) pueden representar millones de dólares de costo (y el producto sigue siendo un solenoide para inyector, por ejemplo). Al iniciar el centro contaba con 130 proyectos; para julio de 1996 tenía 107. Aproximadamente 10 son terminados anualmente (esto es, listos para su producción). La duración promedio de un proyecto es de 20 meses, pero Delphi-Juárez ya ha tenido un récord mundial en 13 meses. Se producen *commodities* que serán manufacturados en 1998. Se están construyendo, por ejemplo, 100 piezas que serán puestas en los motores de clientes para su certificación, y una vez aprobadas serán producidas un millón de ellas en las plantas de Juárez y Chihuahua en 1988.

El centro trabaja de acuerdo al desarrollo de equipos de trabajo según proyectos, bajo un plan estratégico de *full package* compuesto en cuatro fases. La primera fase es el inicio de idea. El cliente hace su solicitud en la cual muchas veces ni siquiera en sabe con exactitud lo que quiere, sino que tiene una idea aproximada de lo que necesita. Aquí empieza el intercambio de información, negociación, etc. En esta fase se trabaja muy independiente del cliente, "... se labora con 'Ciros Peralocas' " que trabajan por proyecto en grupos de trabajo. Estos se constituyen por un ingeniero de producto, uno de prueba, uno de proceso, un líder coordinador, un ingeniero de manufactura y cada uno con área de soporte y laboratorio de ensamble. Se trata de proyectos muy adelantados que serán producidos aproximadamente en el año 2,004.

La segunda fase es la conformación del diseño. El proyecto está definido, esto es, hay una propuesta de concepto inicial y la constitución de diferentes equipos de trabajo. Aquí se trata más cercanamente con el cliente. Posteriormente se pasa a la etapa de concepto aprobado. Es decir, ya se han producido de uno a cinco piezas o juegos, por ejemplo. En esta fase las piezas construidas son muy costosas. Una vez creado el prototipo se busca la aprobación del cliente.

La tercera fase es la validación del producto. Ya probado el prototipo se compra o adapta el equipo necesario para la construcción y validación del concepto. Ahora ya no son muestras sino decenas de piezas (500 por ejemplo). Se trata de la manufacturabilidad de los diseños. Se hace y/o diseña el equipo de producción (se valida el equipo, gieches-equipo de medición) y se instala la manufactura. Se diseña el layout, los manuales, etc. En otras palabras, se diseñan, construyen, adaptan e implementan las líneas de ensamble con equipo, maquinaria, herramental, etc. Aquí por ejemplo se diseñó la manufactura celular (celdas en U) de la empresa SEC.

La cuarta fase consiste en la mejora continua de sus diseños y prototipos así como de la manufacturabilidad de los mismos.

Este centro compite internacionalmente con otros centros proveedores de GM tanto en Estados Unidos como en Japón (Nipondenso) y en Alemania (Siemens). Uno de los entrevistados mencionó que este centro "no tiene comparación con otros, ni en EU ni otros países, ya que aquí somos más eficaces y se generan más ganancias"[16] . En todo caso Delphi-Juárez es el primer centro que aplica el QS-9000 dentro de Delphi-A.

RECURSOS HUMANOS

Referente al empleo el centro inició contratando un 20% de ingenieros extranjeros y un 80% de ingenieros y técnicos mexicanos. Al comienzo empleaba 370 personas (75 ingenieros venidos de Anderson, a quienes se les hizo una oferta para trasladarse a Juárez, vivir en El Paso y contar con mejores salarios). Del total de los 370 empleados el 90% son ingenieros. De los ingenieros mexicanos muchos de ellos vienen de Chihuahua. Varios ingenieros tienen maestría y doctorado. En septiembre de 1996 ocupaba 860 personas en Ciudad Juárez, aunque no todos pertenecen a Delphi-E.

Los ingenieros y técnicos requieren ciertos conocimientos (como Autocad versión 12 si están directamente encargados del diseño) para poder manipular el sistema de Unigraphics de GM. Se trata de un "trabajo muy nuevo para todos ... el trabajo, la maquinaria, los equipos...", en donde las competencias centrales son, mecánica, electromecánica y magnética, y evidentemente la creatividad. Por ello algunos ingenieros y técnicos mexicanos

[16] En una de las visitas a Delphi-Juárez se estaba llevando a cabo una reunión con un gran número de gerentes de otras empresas tanto subsidiarias de Delphi-E como de las otras divisiones de la firma, con el fin de que conocieran la variedad de los productos que realiza toda la compañía, así como las operaciones de Delphi-Juárez. En otras palabras, este centro se está constituyendo en uno de capacitación y ejemplo para otros centros técnicos.

fueron enviados al centro en Anderson por ocho meses. Este centro ofreció, en 1995, tres meses de capacitación a sus ingenieros y técnicos en diversos lugares, ochenta horas a sus trabajadores de producción y cuarenta horas a sus gerentes y administradores. En particular todos se vieron envueltos en la norma QS-9000 (ya fueron certificados) que, según menciona un gerente "fue muy difícil obtener, ya que normalizar los procedimientos en un centro de investigación es una tarea muy complicada, dado que los procesos no son estandarizados".

No obstante que el problema de oferta de ingenieros y técnicos especializados ha sido identificado, no hay ninguna vinculación con universidades y tecnológicos mexicanos, sino que las relaciones las han establecido con universidades estadounidenses cercanas (como las universidades de El Paso, de New Mexico y de Austin). Los estudiantes de esas universidades realizan prácticas profesionales en Delphi-Juárez. Vienen aquí por períodos cortos y se les encarga parte de los proyectos; "ellos mismos hacen muchos diseños, la idea es que aprendan a poner sus conocimientos teóricos en la práctica". Sin embargo, estos nuevos ingenieros no serán contratados por Delphi-Juárez ya que sus exigencias serían sin duda mayor a los 7,000 pesos que les pagan a los ingenieros mexicanos de recién ingresos.

En relación a los salarios, el centro mantiene 4 bandas y muchos rangos dentro de cada banda. Si bien los salarios son relativamente altos para el contexto local, no hay punto de comparación en la región por no existir otros centros similares. En el contexto local un dato de referencia es que en una encuesta mantenida con 50 ingenieros (Hualde, 1994 y 1995) de distintas edades y experiencia en 1994, el ingreso promedio mensual se acercaba a los 6,000 pesos mensuales, por lo que la cifra mencionada anteriormente puede ser (teniendo en cuenta la inflación y la devaluación) algo más elevada que la media actual pero no parece sustancialmente mayor.

Como menciona un entrevistado, "es muy probable que sea la maquila que mejor paga, pero esto debe ser muy variable en función del tipo de personas que aquí se emplean". En todo caso, un entrevistado menciona que no es sólo por cuestión de salarios que muchos ingenieros quieren trabajar en Delphi-Juárez. Los técnicos al salir de los centros educativos "desean un puesto de trabajo en mantenimiento o ingeniería dentro de las empresas, y no de supervisores, como lo tienen la mayoría". "Su trabajo de supervisión consiste en vigilar los procesos, controlar inventarios, etc., pero no pueden hacer nada de diseño, porque un cambio en manufactura -aunque sea mínimo- sería muy costoso. Esto es, "... aunque veas el problema no puedes hacer nada. En cambio aquí si: si estas en diseño puedes cambiar lo que sea.

Aquí, por el contrario practicas lo que estudiaste". Mientras que la capacidad de decisión, iniciativa, etc., está totalmente reducida en las de manufactura por el factor de los costos, en los centros de investigación no es así. Los ingenieros pueden en una maquiladora de manufactura, si acaso, hacer cambios en procesos y en sistemas, pero no en producto, porque esto significa cambios en las herramientas de trabajo. Mientras que aquí... no hay nada fijo, todo es flexible para poder cambiarse y estar probando".

ESLABONAMIENTOS PRODUCTIVOS

Delphi-Juárez, como la gran mayoría de maquiladoras en México tiene un bajo nivel de integración nacional (1%). La mayoría de los proveedores están en EU, aunque cuentan con un sistema de proveedores globalizados en donde participan 30 países. Sus principales proveedores en México se localizan en Toluca, Chihuahua y Puebla. Cuentan además con una maquiladora como proveedor que le surte de magnetos. Están en negociaciones para desarrollar dos proveedores de alambre-magneto con Condumex. También existen diversos tipos de talleres vinculados al centro como los de maquinado. A pesar de su corta vida en Juárez, este centro asistió a la primera exposición de insumos (INTEREXPORT) en su tipo en México. "Deseamos incrementar sustantivamente los proveedores en México, pero es imposible encontrar uno que satisfaga nuestros requerimientos. Por eso la tarea es desarrollarlos a mediano plazo". Para ello cuentan con una visión estratégica para desarrollar proveedores en México.

En una industria madura como la automotriz lleva mucho tiempo desarrollar proveedores. "El proveedor tiene que empezar a desarrollarse a partir de que ha sido aprobado. No puede llegar al momento, los que tenemos ya han sido desarrollados en un largo y complejo proceso de relación. Hay que recordar que se trabaja con mucho tiempo de antelación para la elaboración de un producto.

No obstante esta pobre integración nacional del 1%, este centro no es una *isla tecnológica*. Localmente Delphi-Juárez está altamente integrada en un sistema intra-firma, ya que el desarrollo de proyectos incluye hasta la manufactura la cual es realizada por una empresa maquiladora de la misma división, la empresa SEC con plantas en Ciudad Juárez y en Chihuahua. Estas dos empresa maquiladoras (Delphi-Juárez y SEC) funcionan como un sólo complejo industrial. La empresa SEC establecida en Juárez en 1980 fue la primera planta que empezó a ocupar más hombres, que implantó nuevas ideas de manufactura sincronizada (JIT, administración por celdas, empresas dentro de la empresa) y que diversificó sus productos. Actualmente manejan 18 rotaciones de inventarios semanales. Cuentan con 4,200 empleados que reciben 70 horas de capacitación promedio anual. SEC ya ha sido certificada en la QS-9000, y ha recibido otros premios como el Q1 de Ford. Esta empresa tiene cerca de 100 clientes, siendo los principales dos plantas de Ford y dos de GM en Estados Unidos. Particularmente interesante para nuestros propósitos, es que esta empresa tiene proyectadas alianzas estratégicas con empresas tanto nacionales (Condumex) como extranjeras al igual que Delphi-Juárez para el desarrollo de proveedores, y que sus principales competidores están precisamente en Ciudad Juárez.

Respecto a los eslabonamientos "hacia adelante", los clientes de Delphi Juárez son empresas transnacionales del automóvil e incluyen firmas como Toyota, Honda, Ford, Isuzu, Mercedes y BMW. El principal cliente es GM (67% de las ventas pero se trata de distintas ensambladoras a lo largo de la Unión Americana.

CONCLUSIONES

El establecimiento de Delphi-Juárez tiene un importante significado para México, Se trata de un nuevo tipo de empresas que se integra productivamente con otra empresas (aunque los insumos nacionales sigan siendo pobres), generando economías de aglomeración y potenciando la conformación de clusters. Como menciona el director de Delphi-Juárez "... es el salto más grande que se ha dado en años en la industria maquiladora en México". Por tanto, no se trata ni de una nueva maquiladora con mayor tecnología, ni de una maquiladora más avanzada, se trata de un nuevo tipo de empresa, que hemos bautizado como basada en competencias intensivas en conocimiento o de tercera generación.

Delphi-A ya estableció otro centro técnico en esta misma ciudad. La proliferación de estos nuevos centros técnicos tiene un importante significado para la industria automotriz en México no sólo en términos de la creación de empleos calificados y de la generación de empresas que aportan mayores divisas , en términos relativos, sino también por el desarrollo de la ingeniería industrial para la región. Sin embargo, desde la perspectiva estadounidense, estos traslados representan la pérdida de empleos bien remunerados y la desvalorización del trabajo calificado sindicalizado. Aún existen 68,000 trabajadores en estados Unidos de Delphi-A (73% sindicalizados por la UAW).

El fenómeno de globalización de la producción de Delphi-A viene también acompañado de un importante proceso de racionalización de la producción consistente en la reducción de plantas en Estados Unidos, en la concentración de empresas en México integradas vertical y horizontalmente, y en la futura y posible autonomía de Delphi de General Motors, lo cual provocaría que la principal sede de operaciones de la firma sea México y no Estados Unidos[17]. Todo indica que este proceso de especialización regional (dentro TLCAN) está integrando distintas fases dentro de la cadena global del producto, añadiendo más valor a las operaciones en México. La paradoja central es que mientras haya un proceso de enriquecimiento productivo, tecnológico y en las competencias laborales, el cual genera una mayor competitividad internacional de las empresas, se sigue desvalorizando el trabajo en general, ahora también el calificado.

BIBLIOGRAFÍA

Abo, T. (1994). Hybrid Factory. The Japanese Production System in the United States. Oxford University Press. New York/Oxford.

Alegría, T., Alonso, J. Y Carrillo, J. (1995). "Reestructuración Productiva y Cambio Territorial en el Norte de México: Consolidación de un Segundo Eje de Industrialización". Ponencia. Seminario Internacional Impactos Territoriales de Procesos de Reestructuración, Instituto de Estudios Urbanos, Santiago, Julio 12-14.

Alonso, J., Carrillo, J., Contreras, O., (1994) "Mercados laborales y condiciones de trabajo en la transición de la industria maquiladora". Ponencia Seminario Internacional Las Maquiladoras en México: Presenta y Futuro del Desarrollo Industrial, El Colegio de la Frontera Norte y International Institute for Labour Studies OIT, Tijuana, del 23 al 25 de mayo. 29 p.

Carrillo, J. (Coord.) (1993). Condiciones de empleo y capacitación en las maquiladoras de exportación en México, STyPS y El Colegio de la Frontera Norte, Tijuana, 1993, 287 p.

[17] De hecho Delphi mantiene en México el mayor número de empleos (72,000), con lo cual se convierte en el principal empleador privado en el país.

Carrillo, J. y Hualde, A. (1996), "Delphi-General Motors: ¿Centro de Investigación y Desarrollo o Maquiladora de Alta Tecnología?". Ponencia. Coloquio Internacional Aprendizaje Tecnológico, Innovación y Política Industrial: Experiencias Nacionales e Internacionales, UAM-Xochimilco, México, Septiembre 25-27.

Carrillo, Mortimore y Alonso (1996), Competitividad, capacitación y movilidad laboral en empresas de autopartes y de televisores en el norte de México, El Colegio de la Frontera Norte, Tijuana (avance).

Cimex-Weffa, (1995), Maquiladora Industry Analysis, Vol. 8, no. 1, Bala Cynwyd, January.

Choi Won, Dae and Martin Kenney, (1994), The Globalization of Korean Industry: Korean In-bond assemblers in México, University of California, Davis, August (Document).

Gereffi, G. (1991). "The 'old' and 'new' Maquiladora Industry in Mexico: What is their Contribution to National Development and North American Integration?" en Nuestra Economía, año 2, no. 8, Facultad de Economía, Universidad Autónoma de Baja California, mayo-agosto, pp. 39-63.

González-Aréchiga, B., Ramírez, J. C. y Suárez-Villa, L. (1989). La industria electrónica en la frontera norte de México: competitividad internacional y efectos regionales. Ponencia. Neigghbors in Crisis: A call for Joint Solutions, Irvine, CA, enero.

Hualde, A. (1994). "Mercado de trabajo y formación de recursos humanos en la industria electrónica maquiladora de Tijuana y Ciudad Juárez, El Colegio de la Frontera Norte, Tijuana, (Reporte de Investigación/CONACYT).

-------(1995). Técnicos e ingenieros en la industria maquiladora de exportación: su rol como agentes innovadores, en Gallart. M. A. (Coord.), La formación para el trabajo en el final de siglo. Entre la reconversión productiva y la exclusión social. CIID-CENEP, México-Buenos Aires.

Kenney, Martin, Jairo Romero and Dae Won Choi, (1994), "Japanese and korean investment in the In-bond assemblers: What Role in Global Commodity Chains?", Paper for International Conference on the In-bond assemblers in México: Present and Future prospects of industrial Development, El Colegio de la Frontera Norte, Tijuana, April.

Mertens, L. y Palomares, L., (1988). "El surgiendo de un nuevo tipo de trabajador en la industria de alta tecnología. El caso de la electrónica" en

Estela Gutiérrez (compiladora) Reestructuración Productiva y Clase Obrera, México, S. XXI-UNAM.

U.S. Congress, Office of Technology Assessment, (1992), U.S.-Mexico Trade: Pulling Together or Pulling Apart?, U.S. Government Printing Office, ITE-545, Washington, D.C. October.

Shaiken, H. And Browne, H. (1991). "Japanese work organization in Mexico", in Manufacturing Across Borders and Oceans, Monograph Series 36, Center for US-Mexican Studies, University of California, San Diego, La Joya. pp. 25-50.

Wilson, P. A. (1992). Exportes and Local Development. México's New Maquiladoras, University of Texas Press, Austin, 161 p.

Parte IV
ORGANIZACIÓN DEL TRABAJO

Part IV
BENCHMARKING WORK ORGANIZATION

WORK REORGANIZATION AND THE QUALITY OF WORKING LIFE IN THE CANADIAN AUTOMOBILE INDUSTRY

*Wayne Lewchuk and David Robertson**

INTRODUCTION

In recent debates over the merits of different forms of work organization, advocates of lean production promote this variant of the Toyota production system as a more humane and productive alternative to Fordism.[1] Lean production is portrayed as a system of work organization which achieves higher levels of productivity through flexible, empowered workers and a team-based production system.[2] Fordism is portrayed as a hierarchically organized production system in which management controls decision making and workers simply respond to orders issued by managers. The debate has been structured to have us believe that the choice is between one system where workers generate productivity gains by working smarter versus the alternative where workers can only produce such gains by working harder. In our view this is a false portrayal of both the primary managerial objective in adopting lean production, and of lean production's impact on workers.

We have two fundamental disagreements with the existing characterization of lean production and Fordism. First, there is little evidence that workers have been empowered in any meaningful way as a result of the spread

* Wayne Lewchuk is Director of the Labour Studies Programme at McMaster University. David Robertson is Director of Work Organization and Training for the Canadian Auto Workers.

[1] Much of this debate has focused on the work of James Womack, Daniel Jones and Daniel Roos, *The Machine That Changed the World: The Story of Lean Production* (New York: Rawson Associates, 1990).

[2] See, *OECD, Technology, Productivity and Job Creation* 2 (Paris: 1996), 129-75 for an example of how the empowerment debate is now dominating policy analysis.

of lean production.[3] Second, by focusing on productivity through empowerment, the discussion has been deflected from the real transformation which is underway in the North American vehicle industry, namely, the undermining of accepted production standards and the wage-effort bargain implicit in the post World War II compromise reached by automobile companies and the UAW.[4]

As part of this compromise, the UAW backed off from its demand to have more say in running the shops, and management's right to manage in the pursuit of higher productivity was enshrined in the collective bargaining agreement. It is easy to exaggerate the nature of this compromise. Management obtained a degree of compliance from the union in its pursuit of higher productivity, in return for an agreement to share the gains with workers. Management did not receive a blank cheque to do as it pleased. Seniority agreements, job classifications, job posting arrangements, grievance procedures, and recognition of the union created a complex system of checks and balances, some formal and some informal, which regulated acceptable management practices and effort norms. Maintaining worker compliance was contingent on management keeping to these norms. We argue that it is this historical compromise over production standards which is under attack in the transition to lean production, not the Fordist system of production.

---

[3] See Wayne Lewchuk and David Robertson, "Working Conditions under Lean Production: A Worker-Based Benchmarking Study," *Asia Pacific Business Review* 2 (summer 1996): 60-81; Wayne Lewchuk and David Robertson, *Production Without Empowerment: Work- Reorganization from the Perspective of Motor Vehicle Workers* (Capital and Class, forthcoming, 1997). There are now a number of studies which suggest that the actual practice of lean production is fundamentally different from the system described in management texts. See, CAW-Canada Research Group on CAMI, *The CAMI Report: Lean Production in a Unionized Auto Plant* (Willowdale, Ontario: Canadian Auto Workers, 1993); Joseph Fucini and Suzy Fucini, *Working for the Japanese: Inside Mazda's American Auto Plant* (New York: The Free Press, 1990); Philip Garrahan and Paul Stewart, *The Nissan Enigma: Flexibility at Work in a Local Economy* (London: Mansell, 1992); Steve Babson, ed., *Lean Work, Empowerment and Exploitation in the Global Auto Industry* (Detroit: Wayne State University Press, 1995); William Green and Ernest Yanarella, *North American Auto Unions in Crisis, Lean Production as Contested Terrain* (Albany: State University of New York Press, 1966); Laurie Graham, *On the Line at Subaru-Isuzu* (Ithaca: Cornell University Press, 1995).

[4] See Sam Gindin, *The Canadian Auto Workers: The Birth and Transformation of a Union* (Toronto: Lorimer, 1995), 108-24.

In what follows, we will test the "smarter but not harder" hypothesis against survey responses from 2,290 production workers employed in the Canadian assembly and powertrain plants of General Motors, CAMI (a joint GM-Suzuki venture), Chrysler, and Ford. (Details of the research methodology can be found in Appendix 1.) We first describe the workplace environments and plant populations that we surveyed, before turning to the key questions of how hard people are working and the extent to which workers have been empowered under the new forms of work organization.

WORK ORGANIZATION IN THE CANADIAN MOTOR VEHICLE INDUSTRY

The nine assembly plants and five manufacturing plants involved in this survey have been organized into eight divisions: an assembly division for each of the four companies; GM engine; Ford engine (representing the two older Ford engine plants); GM transmission; and the Ford truck modular engine plant. The GM transmission plant and the Ford truck engine plant are new plants employing up-to-date technology and work organization. Both are in their ramp-up phases and are operating at less than half their rated capacity.[5]

Table 1 provides some basic information on workforce characteristics within the eight divisions. The only division that stands out as being different is CAMI, which has a younger workforce and employs more women than most of the other divisions.

Table 1
Characteristics of the Workforce by Division

	Percentage Male	Average Age
GM Assembly	90	43
CAMI Assembly	79	33
Chrysler Assembly	82	37
Ford Assembly	94	41
GM Engine	88	44
Ford Engine	81	41
GM Transmission	91	41
Ford Truck Engine	79	40

[5] Details of how the plants have been subdivided can be found in Appendix 1.

Since the implementation of the Canada-U.S. Free Trade Agreement in 1989 and the North American Free Trade Agreement in 1993, Canadian assemblers and manufacturers have responded by investing in new capital equipment, tightening up work practices, and experimenting with various forms of work reorganization.[6] Most of these changes have been guided by the philosophy of lean production. External to the workplace, all four companies have moved aggressively to rationalize their supplier base by contracting out major components, consolidating work under fewer first-tier suppliers, relying on them more for design and innovation, and forcing them to cut costs. Internal to the workplace, management has searched for ways to reduce buffers and work in progress, remove surplus labour, implement JIT systems, promote continuous improvement, and make better use of worker knowledge of the production process. The main interest of this paper is the internal changes in work practices.

While all plants are getting lean, there are important differences in the experience of each company and each workplace. The first of the Canadian plants to make the transition to lean production was CAMI.[7] Workers at CAMI are organized into "teams," but the teams have little authority. Most of the decisions about workload and design are made in advance by industrial engineers. In our estimation, CAMI is not the leanest workplace examined in this paper. That distinction goes to GM assembly. Here, the shift to lean production began in the late 1980s under the name "Synchronous Manufacturing." Management moved aggressively to reduce staffing levels and maximize the use of available time. They promoted the use of Andon boards for process control, pull systems to discipline the delivery of parts, material supermarkets, material-card pull systems, visual line balancing processes (also referred to as the "wall"), just-in-time production, flexible work cells, and "best people practices." At the GM manufacturing plants, the technical rigidities inherent in the somewhat older manufacturing technology limits the extent of workplace reorganization. Hence, there have been fewer changes at the St. Catherines engine plant, which employs capital equipment from the

[6] For a review of trends in work practices in North American vehicle plants, see Pradeep Kumar and John Holmes, this volume, and *Continuity and Change: Evolving Human Resource Policies and Practices in the Canadian Automobile Industry* (Kingston: Queen's University, 1996).

[7] See James Rinehart, Christopher Huxley, David Robertson, *Just Another Car Factory? Lean Production and its Discontents* (Ithaca: Cornell University Press, 1997); CAW-Canada Research Group on CAMI, *The CAMI Report.*

1960s, relative to the General Motors Windsor transmission plant, which was retooled in 1993. There are no teams at the transmission plant, but efforts are made to involve workers in continuous improvement and to get them to use their knowledge of the production process to reduce the non-value-added components of existing jobs.

Chrysler has been less aggressive in pushing lean production in Canada, in part because the demand for its product at its largest Canadian facility, the Windsor minivan plant, exceeds supply. This does not mean that Chrysler has been unaffected by the managerial interest in lean production. The Chrysler Operating System charts out a strategy to reorganize all Chrysler operations around the principles of lean production. At Ford, the push towards lean production is spelled out in the Ford 2000 programme. However, the one Ford assembly plant from which data is drawn for this paper, was also the least lean site we visited. Part of the plant was retooled in 1990, but much of the technology is of an older vintage. As with GM, work reorganization at Ford manufacturing sites tended to be associated with major investments in new capital equipment. The plant with the oldest technology, Windsor engine plant #1, was also the least affected by workplace reorganization associated with lean production. The Windsor Essex engine plant, which opened in the 1980s and has experienced substantial investment in the last five years, had also made more changes designed to tap worker knowledge of the production process. Workers are not formally organized into teams, but there are regular communication meetings and weekly Dimensional Control Planning meetings which act as problem solving forums. The most far-reaching change had taken place at the Ford Windsor truck modular engine plant, which had just undergone a major investment in new capital equipment. The plant has a "modern operating agreement" with the union which allows a number of departures from operating arrangements found at other Ford plants, including the use of teams.

While to some extent all of the plants in the study are lean, none have adopted the human resource practices associated with lean production in Japan. Neither age-based nor merit-based pay systems have taken root in Canada. Nor are profit sharing or bonus schemes employed. Workers continue to be paid an hourly rate determined by the job they perform, and most job openings are allocated on the basis of seniority. Job rotation and teams are only found at the CAMI plant and the Ford truck modular engine plant. However, the failure to implement these human resource practices should not be taken as evidence that Canadian plants are not lean. Here we find ourselves in agreement with a recent study by Oliver et al., who found that high productivity was virtually uncorrelated with human resource policies intended to modify the attitude of workers towards their employer. They concluded that success was based not on the innovative human resource practices found in Japan, but rather process discipline and control.[8] This focus on control stands in sharp contradiction to the picture painted by supporters of lean production who argue that authority will become more diffuse within the organization and that workers will be empowered to improve their working lives. The Oliver study indicates that successful lean plants are controlled plants; whether they empower workers is secondary.

WORKLOADS IN ASSEMBLY AND MANUFACTURING PLANTS

Figures 1 and 2 present data on two aspects of overall workload in Canadian automobile plants, physical load and work pace.[9] Figure 1 reports results from a question which asked workers about their physical workload. Approximately one in three direct production workers reported their workload was too heavy, ranging from nearly half at GM assembly to just over one-tenth at GM transmission. On average, workers in assembly plants were more likely to report physical load was a problem than were workers in manufacturing plants. The impact of new forms of work organization varied. The assembly plants of GM and CAMI, where work reorganization has proceeded the furthest, stand out as reporting some of the heaviest workloads. Within the manufacturing plants, GM transmission and the Ford truck engine plant, which have also experimented with new forms of work organization, were less likely to report heavy workloads. Given that these two plants were in their ramp-up phases, and that there were long periods of inactivity during most shifts, it is somewhat surprising that they did not report much lighter physical workloads. Workers at Ford assembly, which has made the least progress in moving towards new forms of work organization, reported lower workloads compared to the other assembly plants.

Figure 2 reports results from a question which asked workers about their current work pace. More than half of all workers reported their work pace was too fast, ranging from 80 percent at GM assembly to 19 percent at GM

---

[8] Nick Oliver, Daniel Jones, Rick Delbridge, James Lowe, Peter Roberts, and Betty Thayer, *Worldwide Manufacturing Competitiveness Study: The Second Lean Enterprise Report* (Anderson Consulting, 1994), 21.

[9] The key for these tables: ASS = assembly; ENG = engine; TRA = transmission; and TME = truck modular engine.

transmission. Other than GM assembly and transmission, the probability of workers reporting that their work pace was too fast was about the same. The impact of work reorganization on work pace was similar to what was found above. GM assembly stands out as being most likely to report work pace was too fast, while GM transmission was the least likely to report this was a problem.

Figures 3 and 4 examine how physical workload and work pace have changed in the last two years. In both figures, the experience of assemblers at General Motors stands out as different from all other workplaces. Figure 3 reports results from a question which asked workers if their physical workload had changed in the last two years. Just over one-third of all direct production workers surveyed reported their workload had become physically heavier. At GM assembly over 53 percent reported increases in physical workload, while at the new Ford truck modular engine plant, which was still in ramp-up, only 12 percent reported such increases. Workers employed in assembly were more likely than workers employed in manufacturing to report increases in physical workload.

Figure 4 reports results from a question which asked workers if their work pace had changed in the last two years. Just under 60 percent of all workers reported their work pace had increased in the last two years. This ranged from a high of nearly 88 percent of all direct production workers at GM assembly to 39 percent at the GM engine plant. Unlike the previous three questions which indicated conditions were less severe in manufacturing than assembly, the results for change in work pace indicate that other than GM assembly, assemblers and manufacturers were equally likely to report their work pace was increasing.

Figure 1
Percentage Reporting Physical Workload Too Heavy

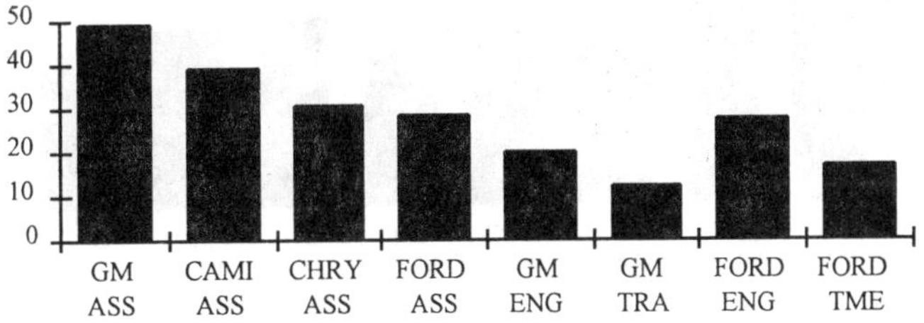

Figure 2
Percentage Reporting Work Pace Too Fast

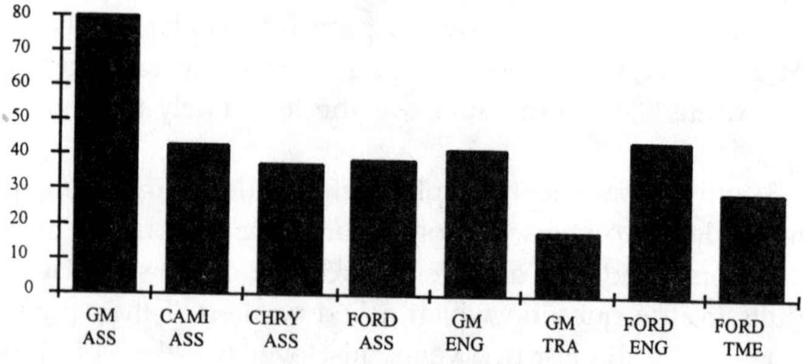

Figure 3
Percentage Reporting Workload Heavier

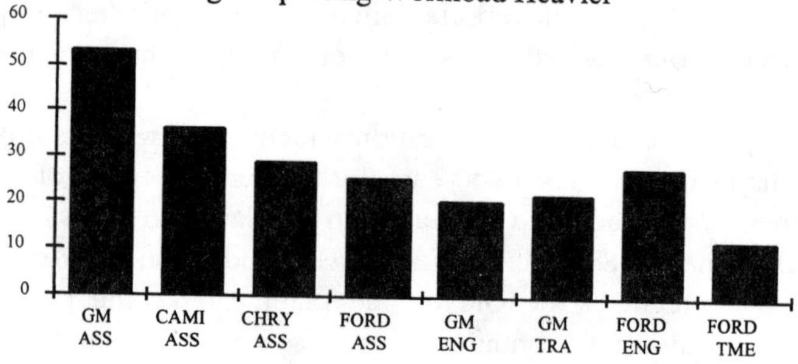

Figure 4
Percentage Reporting Work Pace Faster

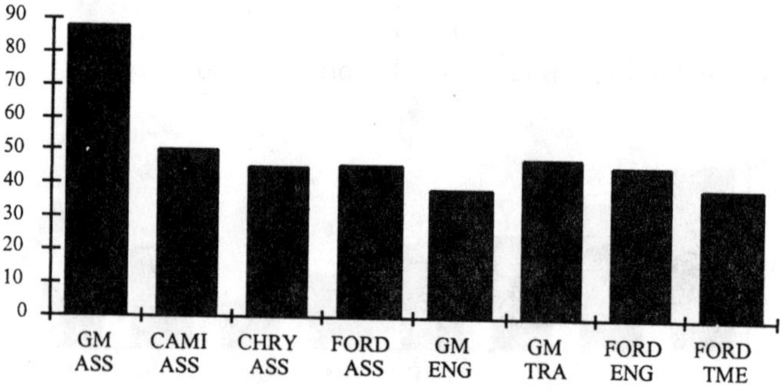

Figure 5
Percentage Reporting Difficult to Change Job Features

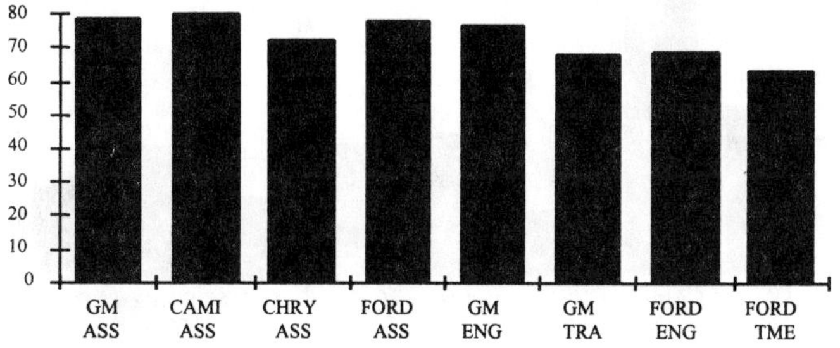

Figure 6
Percentage Reporting Difficult to Vary Work Pace

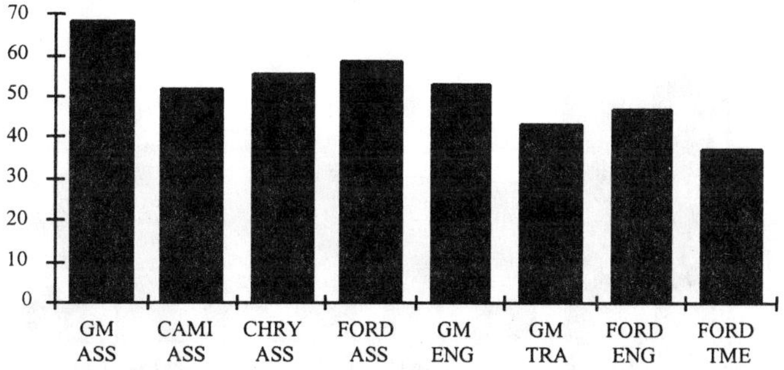

Figure 7
Percentage Reporting Difficult to Leave Work Station

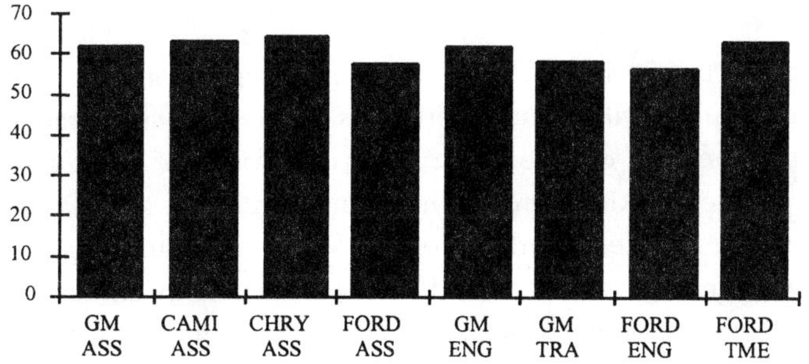

Figure 8
Percentage Reporting Difficult to Get Time Off

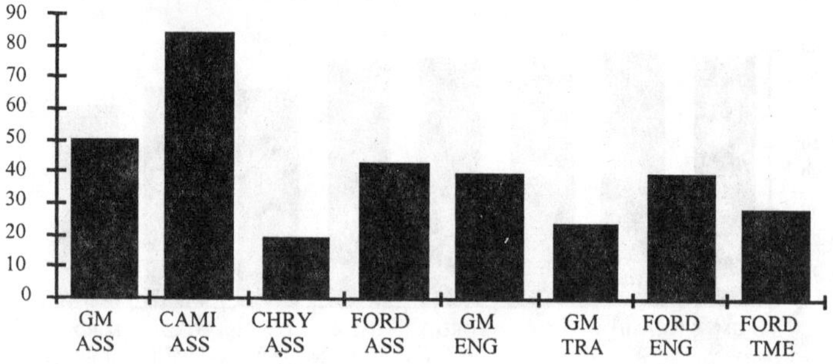

Figure 9
Percentage Reporting Increased Monitoring

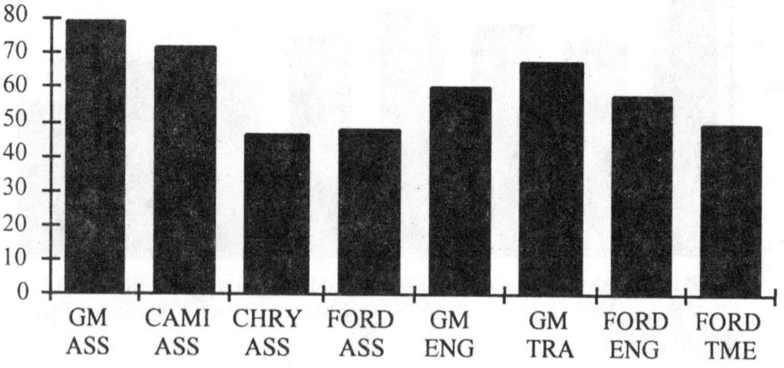

WORKER EMPOWERMENT IN ASSEMBLY AND MANUFACTURING PLANTS

The previous section casts doubt on the simple hypothesis that new models of work organization will reduce workloads. There was significant evidence that at least in the case of assembly plants, new forms of work organization resulted in people working harder. This section will look at the other half of the equation. Are workers working smarter? It is important to place the debate over worker empowerment and lean production in context. Not even the most ardent supporters of lean production are suggesting that this new system of work will result in a return to the level of worker empowerment enjoyed by skilled craft workers in the nineteenth century. There is, however, a strong suggestion that workers will participate in day-to-day problem solving, will have some influence over how they should perform their work, and through this will be able to enhance the quality of their working life. Hence, the focus of this section is on day-to-day decisions over how and when work should be performed, rather than decisions over corporate policy, choice of technology, or product design. A minimum level of empowerment would enable workers some choice over how they work, the rhythm of work, and the time spent at work.

It is hard to conceptualize that workers would be "working smarter" unless they have some ability to change things that they do not like about their jobs. As can be seen in Figure 5, there is little evidence of worker empowerment at any of our workplaces. On average, 75 percent of all direct production workers reported that it would be difficult to change things they did not like about their job. The gap between different workplaces was relatively small. Workers at CAMI and GM assembly, the two leanest categories, reported the greatest difficulty in changing things. This is exactly the opposite of what the proponents of lean production have argued. At GM transmission and Ford truck engine, workers were only marginally less likely to report that it would be difficult to change things that they did not like about their jobs.

Another important indicator of empowerment is the ability to influence when work is done by varying the rhythm of work over the course of the day. Figure 6 indicates that new models of work organization have done little to empower workers in this area. Fifty-eight percent of all direct production workers reported having little or no control over the work pace during the day. Workers in assembly plants were marginally more likely to report it was difficult to vary their workplace than those working in manufacturing plants.

Another important aspect of worker empowerment is control over time itself, including the ability to leave a workstation to attend to personal matters, such as going to the toilet, or getting time off to leave work and attend to personal matters, such as caring for a sick child or going to the doctor. Figure 7 is based on a question which asked workers how easy it was to find a relief worker so they could leave their workstation. For almost two-thirds of the sample it was difficult to find a relief worker to attend to personal matters. Figure 8 examines the flexibility workers have in getting time off work to attend to personal matters. Here we see a major difference between workplaces. CAMI workers reported that it was much more difficult to get time off, despite the fact that in the last year the market for the product CAMI manufactures has been relatively soft. Despite this lack of demand, CAMI workers had the second highest number of overtime hours. GM assembly's production workers also reported that it was relatively difficult to get time off, followed closely by Ford assembly and Ford engine workers. Workers at Chrysler assembly were the least likely to report having trouble getting time off when requested, even though Chrysler workers work more overtime than workers at any of the other companies.

A factor explaining inter-company differences in access to time off the job is differences in contract language. Workers at Ford, Chrysler, and GM are all entitled to Personal Paid Absences, while at Chrysler an agreement has also been reached to allow Temporary Part-Time employees to cover for absences between Fridays and Mondays. The CAMI contract lacks these provisions. During interviews with workers at lean plants it was not unusual to hear that management was less flexible in granting time off. At GM, management has been particularly aggressive in demanding changes to provincial legislation which would make it easier for management to impose mandatory overtime on workers.

Figure 9 examines the extent to which workers reported that managerial surveillance had increased in the last few years. The manufacturing plants in general, as well as GM assembly and CAMI, were more likely to report increases in monitoring. This suggests that the lean model, rather than providing a space where workers might act independently in their personal interest, is a system in which the range of autonomous action may actually be reduced.

CONCLUSIONS

This study has presented the results of a survey of over 2,000 Canadian motor vehicle workers employed at plants in various stages in the transition to lean production. Overall, there was little evidence that new forms of work organization resulted in "working smarter but not harder." Workloads remained heavy, and for many workers, had increased in the last few years. The majority found it difficult to modify their jobs, vary their work pace, or leave their workstation to attend to personal matters. Workers at CAMI and GM assembly, where management has been the most aggressive in reorganizing the work process, reported high workloads but little potential for modifying working conditions or controlling the rhythm of work; they also reported the greatest increase in monitoring. Within the manufacturing sector, the two plants which have invested heavily in new equipment and experimented with new models of work organization did report generally lower workloads and a higher level of empowerment. Progress here needs to be kept in context, however. Both the GM transmission plant and the Ford truck modular engine plant were still in ramp-up to full production, yet nearly two-thirds of the workers at these two locations still reported it would be difficult to change things they did not like about their jobs, and approximately 40 percent reported having little scope for varying their work pace during the day.

Most of the results presented in this paper contradict predictions by the proponents of lean production that this new model of work organization empowers workers, allows them to work "smarter," and otherwise enhances their quality of working life. These results thereby raise the fundamental question of what it is that makes modern motor vehicle plants more productive relative to older plants. Issues such as capacity utilization, manufacturability, and equipment age almost certainly play an important role. There is also evidence in this paper that at lean plants managerial control of workers has actually increased. Direct production workers at lean plants continue to have little scope to change things they do not like about their jobs, often find it difficult to vary the rhythm of work, and often find it difficult to get time off to attend to personal matters. These results are consistent with the work of other authors who make the case that workers in lean plants have less, not more control, over the quality of their work life.[10]

A careful reading of the various company documents intended to guide the shift to lean production reveals they may pay lip service to empowerment, but the real focus is process control. At GM, lean production is synonymous with concepts of control and standardization. Worker empowerment is not only irrelevant, it may be counterproductive once a workplace is error proofed and standardized. Rather than solving the social and health problems associated with Fordism, lean production may actually compound them.[11]

---

[10] See footnotes 3 and 7.

[11] On worker health, see the contributions by Landsbergis et al., Ferris, and Graham in this volume. See also Robert Karasek and Tores Theorell, *Healthy Work: Stress, Productivity and the Reconstruction of Working Life* (New York: Basic Books,

APPENDIX 1: SURVEY METHODOLOGY

The study was made up of two components, a survey distributed to workers at each workplace, and a site visit. The site visit allowed us to inspect the production process and to interview members of the union executive committee. All workplaces assembling vehicles and manufacturing engines and transmissions in Canada and organized by the CAW were originally included in the study. The Ford Oakville assembly complex had to be dropped due to a combination of funding problems and awkward timing. The survey was distributed to approximately one out of every six production workers. Surveys were randomly distributed by local union members. Each person was asked to distribute 25 surveys to ensure an even distribution throughout the plant. Surveys targeted at different areas of the workplace and different shifts were pre-bundled by the research team based on rough estimates of the proportion of people in each area of the plant. Surveys were filled out by workers on their own time and were returned to their local union representative, or the union office, in unmarked sealed envelopes. Respondents were asked not to identify themselves on the survey. The surveys were returned to the national office of the CAW and then sent to McMaster University for coding and data analysis. Response rates from each workplace and for the study as a whole are reported below.

Table A-1
Response Rates: Direct and Indirect Workers

	Population	Surveys Distributed	Surveys Returned Total	Surveys Returned Direct*	Response Rate
Chrysler Assembly					
Bramalea	2,600	450	305	226	67.8
Pillette Road	1,700	270	206	164	76.3
Windsor Minivan	5,600	750	357	231	47.6
GM Assembly					
Oshawa Car #1	2,841	450	335	249	74.4
Oshawa Car #2	3,172	450	301	198	66.9
Oshawa Truck	3,600	450	107	80	23.8
St. Thérèse	2,841	450	382	272	84.9
Ford Assembly					
St. Thomas	2,600	450	325	239	72.2

CAMI Assembly					
Car and Truck	2,500	550	106	85	19.3
GM Engine					
St.Catherines	1,450	250	159	138	63.6
GM Transmission					
Windsor	1,358	225	155	98	68.9
Ford Engine					
Essex	1,244	250	217	163	86.8
Windsor #1	700	200	113	74	56.5
Ford Truck Engine					
Windsor Truck	611	150	102	73	68.0
Total	32,817	5,345	3,170	2,290	59.3

* Direct production workers in entire sample.

IS LEAN ENOUGH? BENCHMARKING WORKER OUTCOMES AND PRODUCTIVITY IN SMALL MANUFACTURERS

Brad Markell[*]

INTRODUCTION

Studies of lean production in the North American automobile industry usually examine the major producers, their assembly plants, and the business and production outcomes at these facilities. Less is known about work organization in the small shops that feed the "supply chains" of the auto industry. Even rarer are studies of work organization and worker outcomes in these small and medium-sized facilities. This study will use a data set from the Performance Benchmarking Service (PBS) of the Industrial Technology Institute in Ann Arbor to examine worker outcomes as well as business performance in the small shops at the base of the supply system.[1]

Examining what is going on in these small shops allows us to approach the related question of why productivity in small manufacturing facilities has not increased at the same pace as in larger facilities.[2] Are there plausible explanations for this in the business, production, and workforce data we have collected? Or is it simply that many small and mid-sized manufacturers are consigned to those parts of the supply chain where low value-added production is all that is available, the better work having been captured by those higher on the value chain?

---

[*] Program Manager, Industrial Technology Institute.

[1] The Performance Benchmarking Service at the Industrial Technology Institute in Ann Arbor, Michigan, has for many years collected an annual data set of business and production metrics from small and medium-sized manufacturing facilities.

[2] *U.S. Census of Manufacturers*, 1992.

BRAVE NEW AUTOMOBILE INDUSTRY

The importance of small and mid-sized shops in the automobile industry is perhaps greater than it has been in a long time, as the industry remakes itself in an ever more rationalized and cost-conscious ideal. One of the salient features of this remaking is the redistribution of tasks involved in conceiving, designing and producing automobiles, which can be seen on several levels. These tasks have been redistributed among the automakers and their various suppliers, geographically, and certainly on the shop floor.

The prominence of outsourcing as a strategy in the remaking of the industry has focused attention on the small, or relatively small, firms that have a chance to gain business as a result. Indeed, from 1992 to 1995, the shops in the PBS data set increased their sales 32 percent, while manufacturing output in that period increased only 14 percent.[3] The price squeezing that the original equipment manufacturers (OEMs) apply to their suppliers is well known, and Ron Blum's analysis elsewhere in this volume provides a useful framework for understanding the larger drive to remove resources from every facet of car making, from the money needed to finance the design of new products, to the cost of direct labor. Some suppliers have the size and positioning in the supply chain to resist the worst of this squeezing and to capture some of the high value-added work from the OEMs.[4]

The firms likely to be able to sustain these positions in the auto industry have sales ($U.S.) in the hundreds of millions per year, operate in several nations, and serve many customers. Lear Corporation and Johnson Controls, which supply seating and interior components, are well known examples. Such firms often supply the capital and the engineering talent needed to design and deliver sophisticated vehicle systems in high volumes to the OEMs. These firms now sit at the figurative crossroads of the supply chain, casting about for the most desirable work, looking upwards to their still more powerful OEM customers, but turning to their suppliers with the same squeezing, attempting to knit together a coordinated production system through supply chain optimization.

---

[3] Dan Luria, *Toward Lean or Rich? What Performance Benchmarking Tells Us About SME Performance, and Some Implications for Extension Center Services and Missions* (Ann Arbor, MI: Industrial Technology Institute, 1996).

[4] John Couretas, "Survey: Suppliers Can Win Adult Game of Chicken," *Automotive News*, 22 November 1997, 43.

Yet, in the second and third tier of the automotive supply chain, small manufacturers with the highest productivity and quality don't necessarily capture the most work. A fair number of small shops win contracts with a "low-road" strategy that features low productivity and low unit labor costs, producing "commodity" products not of their own design.[5] The smallest manufacturers in the U.S. are thus the objects of growing attention from those concerned with how outsourcing will affect the automobile industry, the U.S. economy, and the employees of these firms.[6]

Any attempt to understand what is going on in small manufacturing firms must first confront the falling relative productivity and pay levels of small manufacturers in the United States. From 1967 to 1992, the value-added and payroll per employee of small shops fell from nearly 80 percent of that of large manufacturers to 67 percent.[7] A twenty-five year trend of growing productivity and wage gaps between large and small manufacturers raises important questions for all concerned. There is evidence that price-squeezing combined with lackluster productivity has driven profit margins for the smaller auto suppliers below five percent —too low for long-term survival.[8] Are these small firms capable in any way of becoming more productive, or of capturing more of the value chain? Will they have the productivity and market position to generate the amount of value-added per employee that will support a "good job" —well compensated, safe, satisfying to the psyche, and so on?

From the point of view of the workers employed by these firms, these are critical questions. A large number of small manufacturers in the U.S. are on the low-road path, and their employees must suffer along the road as well. This brings us to a consideration of lean production and lean practices. Does better work organization offer a path away from the low road? The lean production system was developed in high-volume auto assembly plants, and for the most part that is where it has been studied. While lean practices have been adapted for many types of manufacturing, in small firms and for certain kinds of manufacturing, many questions remain about how and when to use lean practices. How, for instance, might one apply "lean" principles to a

---

[5] Luria, *Toward Lean or Rich?*

[6] *U.S. Census of Manufacturers*, 1992. There are well over 350,000 such small manufacturers in the United States employing over 11 million people.

[7] *U.S. Census of Manufacturers*, 1992.

[8] Tom Murphy, "Seeking the Perfect Mate," *Ward's AutoWorld* 33, no.12, 59.

manufacturer of high-priced, low-volume tooling? What would it mean to implement work teams in a firm with 17 shop employees, as has one of the PBS respondents?

Can small firms that adopt lean practices be productive enough to support high compensation and good jobs? The question raised in this paper is whether, in shops like the ones represented by the following data, lean practices in and of themselves can raise value-added per employee high enough to support such employment. In a fair number of shops, lean or not, other organizational capabilities which could contribute to high value-added work, such as design expertise, are missing. Employees of such shops often face the prospect of low wages, dirty, dangerous and boring work, and a future of productivity increases wrought by speed-up. The aim in this chapter will be to describe outcomes of interest to workers (pay and benefits, safety, etc.) and productivity as they are found in this sample of small firms, and then to make preliminary assessment of whether new forms of work organization are as empowering as advertised.

THE DATA SET

Each year, early in the first quarter, PBS renews its data set with a "wave" of fresh data collected through a facility-level questionnaire. Firms are sent one of nine industry or process based questionnaires, and in 1997 each firm also received a twelve-page human resource questionnaire. There were 244 firms that responded by answering both the regular PBS questionnaire and the human resource questionnaire.[9] It should be noted that the PBS questionnaires are in the main completed by the managers at the firms surveyed, and this presents obvious limitations in assessing production systems and work organization —put bluntly, the workers are likely to see things differently from the boss.[10] This becomes especially important in evaluating how managers describe decision sharing in their firms.

Although the firms in the sample were not chosen to represent small shops in the automobile sector, the resulting data set leans in that direction. Twenty percent of the firms make more than 90 percent of their sales to the

---

[9] The response rate for firms that answered both questionnaires was 22 percent.

[10] See, for example, Adrienne Eaton, "The Survival of Employee Participation Programs in Unionized Settings," *Industrial and Labor Relations Review* 47: 371-389; and Tom Juravich, Howard Harris, and Andrea Brooks, "Mutual Gains? Labor and Management Evaluate Their Employee Involvement Programs," *Journal of Labor Research* 14: 165-185.

auto industry, and 42 percent have over one-third of their sales to auto. The sample firms are heavily weighted toward Michigan and the other Great Lakes states. The industry composition in the sample under represents consumer goods generally, and in particular apparel, electronics and printing. In turn, metalworking and plastics firms, tool and die shops and machine builders, firms in sectors which support metalworking, and makers of intermediate goods are over represented.[11]

The facilities which responded to the human resource questionnaire indeed represent small manufacturing: the median employment is just 78. The middle 50 percent of respondents reported that between 62 and 82 percent of their employees were assigned to the shop, while the proportion of shop employees considered skilled ranged from 8 to 33 percent. This data is more interesting in light of another finding: 34 percent of the respondents make no clear distinction between production and skilled employees. The data set we have does not enable us to investigate by whom the work normally considered skilled (e.g. machine repair) is performed in these shops; finding this out would provide interesting insights into work organization and productivity in small shops. In keeping with the Great Lakes geographic skew, 17.9 percent of the respondent firms have employees who are represented by a union. Table 1 presents the employment profile of the median respondent firm.

Table 1
Employment Profile of the Median Respondent Shop

	Percent
Non-Skilled Shop	59.4
Skilled Shop	15.3
Managers	8.8
Other	16.7

[11] Performance Benchmarking Service, "Supplemental Report on Human Resource Management" (Ann Arbor, MI: Industrial Technology Institute, 1997).

WORKER OUTCOMES

In assessing how valuable or desirable a job may be for an industrial worker, one need not stray too far from the essentials of compensation and safety. Adequate compensation is the first and mandatory hurdle on the path to a good job, the essential building block in a sort of Maslow's hierarchy of job attributes. Especially at the wage rates observed in this particular sample of firms, the level of compensation does more to affect a person's overall quality of life than the more intrinsic benefits which managerial and professional employees, and the more well-compensated industrial employees, seek in their work.

When one makes under $20,000 a year, as do many of the full-time employees of the respondent firms, a wage increase of a few dollars per hour is much more important than, say, whether the boss seeks your input on some matter. More than any other measure, how well a worker is compensated determines where a person lives, whether they or their family members have adequate access to health care, and whether one looks forward to a retirement of poverty or one of at least a modicum of comfort. Wages, medical insurance and pension coverage are thus straight forward measures of how "good" a job is. Safety and occupational well-being are an obvious concern to workers, and by any plausible standard should be included in a discussion of worker outcomes. I will add turnover as a measure of whether workers find employment with a particular firm desirable: at what rate do they vote with their feet by leaving?

Wages in the Respondent Firms

Wages in small shops tend to vary considerably from employee to employee, and that is confirmed in the PBS data set. We asked employers to provide us with information on wage rates in three ways: lowest production wage, highest production wage, and highest skilled wage. These allowed us to have a fair idea about wage rates in these shops without over-burdening the respondents. The highest average production wage was 70 percent greater than the lowest average production wage, and in 25 percent of the respondent shops the difference was at least 100 percent. The wage data are summarized in Table 2, with the respondent firms ranked by what they pay their employees in each category.

Table 2
Distribution of Hourly Wages in Respondent Shops

Rank of Firms by Wages (U.S.) in Percentiles		Lowest Production	Highest Production	Highest Skilled
Lowest	10th	$5.50	$ 8.82	$11.69
	25th	$6.00	$10.25	$15.00
	Median	$7.00	$12.50	$17.00
	75th	$8.06	$15.00	$19.50
Highest	90th	$9.80	$17.26	$22.00
Average		$7.66	$13.01	$17.07

At the opposite end of the value chain from these small shops, in the unionized assembly and component plants of the Big Three, the distribution of wages is strikingly different, in at least two respects: first, as expected, hourly wages are much higher ($19.00 for production workers in 1996); second, the differentials are far smaller, with less than $1.50 separating the lowest and highest paid production workers, and $3.50 separating the skilled from the lowest-paid production worker. On a straight-time basis, the Big Three UAW member grossed roughly $38,000 a year in 1996. Among PBS respondents, in contrast, fewer than ten percent of the lowest paid production workers earned even $20,000 per year in straight-time wages, and only half of the highest paid production workers earned as much as $25,000 per year. We did not ask for a complete wage-rate distribution, so we can't say with more specificity how many workers are at each wage level, but the table provides some guidance. Clearly, most of the shop employees of firms in this sample are not making a good income. Only a few of the highest paid skilled workers match the Big Three's wage rates, while even the *highest* paid production worker in the average PBS firm ($13.01) is paid less than the average for *all* production employees in durable goods manufacturing ($13.62).[12]

[12] U.S. Department of Labor, *Employment and Earnings* 10, no. 44 (October 1997): Table B-15.

Medical Coverage and Pensions

The PBS human resources survey asked some basic questions about benefits, primarily health insurance and pension coverage. It does not require a great leap of faith to suppose that many or most workers would consider these benefits important or desirable attributes of any job, particularly given the problems with the social provision of these benefits in the United States. The information collected by PBS about insurance and pension coverage is consistent with data published by the U.S. Department of Labor.[13]

Most of the firms in the PBS sample provide some medical insurance to some of their employees, and a slight majority of the firms surveyed provide medical insurance to all their employees. Comparable data from the U.S. Department of Labor for small private establishments indicates that 42 percent of employees must pay part of the cost of insurance for themselves, and 67 percent contribute to the cost of medical insurance for family members.[14] Further, as indicated in Table 3, the value of what covered employees receive varies greatly among PBS respondents, as, presumably, does the level of care offered and the employee's satisfaction with it.

Table 3
Medical Insurance and Pensions in Respondent Shops

Rank of Firms by Benefit, in Percentiles		Yearly Medical Premium (U.S.) per Covered Employee	Percent of Employees with Pension Coverage
Lowest	10th	$ 884	0
	25th	$1,716	32
	Median	$2,816	98
	75th	$4,000	100
Highest	90th	$5,218	100

As for pension coverage, while the top 50 percent of firms cover the vast majority of their shop employees, in the bottom 50 percent the number of employees with an employer provided pension drops off sharply. Many shop employees in the respondent firms have no pension, and 12 percent of the

[13] Bureau of Labor Statistics, U.S. Department of Labor, *Monthly Labor Review* 120, no. 6, 79.

[14] Ibid.

respondent firms provide no shop employees a pension. This is to say nothing about the type of pension, the risk associated with it, or its eventual value to the employee. PBS did not collect information on pension costs to the employer, but a look at the pension coverage profile of the respondent firms helps fill out the picture. The median values for percent of all employees with no pension is 35 percent, for employees with a defined benefit plan 18 percent, and for those with defined contribution coverage 47 percent. Even given this limited data, it seems clear that the retirement income of many of the employees of respondent firms is less than adequate and secure. In fact, very few shop employees retire from the firms in this survey. The bottom 50 percent of firms on this measure had no retirements in the year preceding the survey, and even the 90th percentile had only 2 percent retire in that period. As a cause for turnover, retirement is dwarfed by other reasons.

Turnover

Turnover rates have been identified as an important determinant of productivity and often figure in discussions about work organization and employee satisfaction.[15] In this sample, average annual turnover is 32 percent, while the median for turnover is just 17.5 percent, and the best 5 percent of firms on this measure had no turnover.[16] Conversely, the worst 25 percent of firms had a turnover rate over 36 percent and the worst 10 percent, incredibly, over 60 percent.[17]

Turnover itself is in some ways an employee outcome, since changing jobs is not without transaction and opportunity costs to an individual. More importantly for our purposes, the rate at which employees quit is a very direct indicator of how much they value their employment. Not withstanding

---

[15] Mark A. Huselid, "The Impact of Human Resource Management Practices on Turnover, Productivity and Corporate Financial Performance," *Academy of Management Journal* 38: 653.

[16] The respondents provided information on the number of persons employed as shop employees during the year and average "position count" in the same period. The turnover rate is a calculated figure representing "bodies per slot."

[17] Which turns out to be bad news for just about everyone involved: in the data from the 1997 PBS wave collection, turnover is negatively correlated with productivity at an .07 significance level. For those interested in this and other features of the study, PBS makes the data set available to researchers on request. Contact Julie Darman at the Performance Benchmarking Service, Industrial Technology Institute, Ann Arbor, Michigan; email, jad@ITI.org.

the employee's reasons for quitting, in this instance the PBS data provides a reliable indicator of shop employee behavior —a certain number of them voluntarily left their job.

Voluntary quits are by far the most common reason for turnover in the respondent firms, followed, but not closely, by discharges and layoffs. We calculated a quit to discharge ratio for firms reporting at least one of each: 57 percent of the firms had at least two quits for every firing, and 25 percent had at least five quits for every discharge. Just six percent of the firms in the sample had no shop employees quit during the prior year, while the worst five percent had 39 percent or more of their shop employees quit. (Only 19 percent managed not to fire anyone.) The median firm had ten percent of its employees quit during the year, and quits accounted for more than half of all turnover in 44 percent of the respondents. If quit rates are any indication of the desirability of a job, or any measure of a job's perceived instrumentality in meeting one's needs, then clearly, many of the jobs provided by the shops in this sample are not making the grade.

Safety

The right to a safe and healthy work environment is established in the law of the United States, but workers continue to be killed and injured on the job in large numbers. In 1996, there were 6,112 fatal occupational injuries in the United States, a level which has varied only slightly since a new monitoring program was established in 1992.[18] The PBS human resources survey collected information on accident rates which allows a comparison to the basic data reported by the government on manufacturing workers in general.

For the workers in the respondent firms, the data are not encouraging. The injury rate at these firms is 172 percent of that reported for durable goods manufacturers overall, an average of 19 injured per 100 workers compared to 11 per 100 workers for all firms.[19] The news appears to be better when it comes to the more serious injuries that cause the worker to take time off work, but this results from different reporting standards. The average in our sample is 5.0 lost-time injuries per 100 employees, while for durable goods manufacturing overall the rate is 4.9 injuries per 100 employees; how-

---

[18] http://stats.bls.gov/oshfat1.htm, accessed 5 December 1997.

[19] http://www.osha.gov/oshstats/bls/manuf5.html, accessed 13 January 1998.

ever, the overall figure (4.9 percent), unlike the PBS data, also includes accidents which caused the worker to be placed on light duty, but not to miss any days of work.

The PBS data presents solid evidence that the workers in the respondent shops, and other like shops, work in environments which are markedly less safe than manufacturing firms as a whole when it comes to injuries. The PBS data does not contain information which would allow us to make statements about the relative frequency of other occupational health hazards, such as chemical exposure or repetitive strain injury, but there is no reason to believe that these shops perform better, relative to all manufacturing firms, than they do with respect to injuries. A partial explanation for their poor safety record, and an indication of the importance these firms place on their employees' safety, is found in the PBS data: 22 percent of the respondents had no health and safety budget at all, and only 32 percent spent as much as $100 per employee on health and safety each year.

WORK ORGANIZATION

Perhaps no feature of manufacturing production operations has been discussed and debated more than the set of ideas grouped around the term "work organization." The popularization of this subject in the business press has increased the public's familiarity with terms and concepts long relegated to academic obscurity. What in many ways began with a small cadre of investigators asking how Japanese automobile manufacturers achieved higher conformance quality and manufacturing productivity than U.S. firms has grown to be an industry in and of itself. The academic and business press bustle with analysis and advice about teams and task redistribution, engineering and reengineering, and so on, the parade of acronyms and agenda never ending. Many of the most propagated concepts have lodged themselves in the American psyche; we're all team players now, and "getting lean" is as much an imperative in the workplace as in the fitness center.

Yet, agnostics and naysayers have persisted in asking damning questions about the new "improvement" gospel, particularly concerning its impact on workers. Automobile assembly plants with lean practices generally report higher productivity than those with none, but some investigators report that work intensification is an under-reported and ill-considered part of the lean recipe, one that promoters were slow to acknowledge. Is the ugly underbelly of lean manufacturing a healthy dose of good old-fashioned speed-up?[20] Some analysts have gone so far as to question whether lean production is simply a modified form of Taylorism, giving it such titles as "Intensified Taylorism," or "Democratic Taylorism."[21]

In keeping with the desire to approach these questions from the view of the workers, one might ask: "What do the shop employees of the respondent firms find when they report for work each day?" We've already detailed part of the answer; they find a small shop where most of them earn pay well below the manufacturing average, work in relative degrees of unsafe conditions, and will over time watch many of their colleagues leave the firm.

The PBS survey did not probe the issue of work intensity, but it did ask questions concerning work organization, mainly in the areas of teams and job rotation. Recording the presence of "teams" tells only part of the story, for it often begs the question of what should be considered a team, and what do the team members do that is different from non-team members. The results of this survey do not equip us to answer all such questions. As noted earlier, the PBS questionnaires are in the main completed by managers, who are likely to see and describe things differently than the workers. For example, the data supplied by managers indicates that in some areas, particularly shopfloor decisions, workers said to be in teams were also said to exert more decision making authority than non-team members. There is no way of knowing, however, whether that means they are occasionally asked their opinion, or they are formally consulted, or they are included in a consensus-type decision making process.

Teams

In asking about teams, the PBS staff decided to define them for the purpose of the question as "formal groups that include shop employees and assume

---

[20] See Lewchuk and Robertson, this volume. An internal General Motors analysis (in author's possession) of Japanese assembly plants in Japan done in 1990 estimated the work intensity to be 50 percent greater than in American assembly plants, which would mean that work intensity accounted for a majority of the hours per car differential (e.g. 20 vs. 30 hours per car).

[21] Mike Parker and Jane Slaughter, "Managing by Stress: The Dark Side of Team Concept," *ILR Report* 26, no. 1 (fall 1988): 19–23; Paul Adler, "Democratic Taylorism: The Toyota Production System at NUMMI," in Steve Babson, ed., *Lean Work: Empowerment and Exploitation in the Global Auto Industry* (Detroit: Wayne State University Press, 1995), 207-219.

responsibilities traditionally reserved for staff and management." The use of teams is not widespread among or within the shops in this sample, although in a substantial minority, 18 percent, all the shop employees are in teams.

Table 4
Shop Employees in Teams in Respondent Shops

Percentage in teams	Percentage of firms reporting
100	18
75 - 99	6
50 - 74	4
25 - 49	9
1 - 24	8
0	55

We also collected extensive data about decision making in these firms, especially which "classes" of employees have influence over particular types of decisions. The diffusion of decision making responsibilities in an organization is a stated hallmark of so-called "post-Taylorist" work organizations, whether they be of the high-performance or lean variety. Exploiting the knowledge that workers have about the process in order to "improve the system" is central to the continuous incremental belt-tightening these new forms of work organization are said to bring about. In the PBS respondent firms, manager's *perceptions* about decision making indicate distinct differences between shops with and without teams. The shops with teams claimed to give notably higher levels of decision-making influence to shop workers than did shops without teams. This higher level of influence carried across the three categories of decisions we asked about: day-to-day shop activity (such as changing machine settings), human resource decisions (such as when to train), and business operation decisions (such as tracking department performance). What exactly managers mean by *influence* could be anything from an actual "seat at the table," to a casual consultation on the order of "what do you think?"

Each manager was asked to estimate the decision making influence of different "classes" of persons in the organization, as if each group controlled a certain percentage of the "votes" needed to make a decision. The groups we asked about were production employees, skilled trades employees, team (if any), union (if present), first-line supervisors, and higher management or staff. The totals were to always come to 100 percent, distributed among the various categories.

In analyzing the data, we decided that one useful construct might be to make a distinction between the decision influence held by hourly employees and that held by management employees. This resulted in combining the reported influence of production workers, skilled trades employees, teams, and the union to come up with "hourly worker influence," with the balance of the decision-making influence retained by management. It should come as no surprise that management personnel have most of the decision-making influence. Yet the managers report quite clearly that shops with teams give more decision-making influence to hourly employees than shops without teams. Table 5 shows the percent of influence hourly employees have over decisions in the mean and median firms, for shops with and without teams.

Table 5
Hourly Worker Influence, Teams vs. No Teams[22]

	Hourly Worker Influence as a Percentage of Decision Authority In Respondent Shops:			
	Without Teams Mean/Median		*With* Teams Mean/Median	
Day-to-Day Shop Activities				
Set job schedule	7	0	13	0
Decide how much overtime	4	0	13	0
Stop/slow production for quality	40	40	59	60
Stop production for safety	39	40	53	50
Setting volume standards	6	0	15	0
Redesign process for ergonomics	24	20	39	40
Redesign process for quality	20	20	35	34

[22] These are preliminary results of a study to be completed with correlations and measures of confidence in 1998. Those interested can contact Brad Markell at the Industrial Technology Institute in Ann Arbor; email, BXM@iti.org.

Change machine settings	52	50	58	60
Initiate blueprint change	17	0	29	25
Determine task order	12	0	32	25
Determine part routings	11	0	23	0
Determine characteristics measured	10	0	19	0
Allocate tasks among workers	12	0	27	20
<u>Human Resource Decisions</u>				
Use temporary workers	4	0	11	0
Set training budget	3	0	13	0
Decide when to train	3	0	13	0
Select new supervisors	1	0	3	0
Select new shop employees	4	0	11	0
Evaluate shop employees	4	0	16	0
Determine shop employee discipline	3	0	6	0
Decide to use subcontractors	2	0	8	0
<u>Business Operations Decisions</u>				
Select business performance criteria	2	0	7	0
How to track plant performance	3	0	12	0
How to track dept. performance	3	0	17	0
Decide new technology	6	0	10	0
Decide equipment purchase	7	0	17	10
Select subcontractors/suppliers	2	0	10	0
How to resolve customer complaints	4	0	7	0
Meet with vendors	5	0	14	0
Estimate costs/Prepare quotes	3	0	7	0
Decide which jobs to quote	1	0	5	0
Help make sales calls	1	0	3	0
Develop new product designs	6	0	11	0

In almost every instance, and certainly in the aggregate, the managers responses indicate that workers in shops with teams have more decision making influence than in shops without teams. Whether this reflects real power sharing is open to further investigation, but it's likely that teams and other participatory schemes are in fact a system for exploiting worker knowledge without letting hourly workers actually make important decisions, which is exactly the understanding in Japan.[23] This likelihood is suggested by the difference between day-to-day decisions, where team members have more (but still modest) influence, and human resource and business decisions, where management retains the preponderant authority. In any case, the evidence here is clear and broad enough to suggest that decision making *processes* are different in shops with teams, even if management still retains decision making *authority*.

Unanswered is the extent to which workers would differ from their managers in assessing their own influence, and whether they believe that they benefit at all from having limited decision making influence. In shops that have teams, do managers fashion their perceptions to fit the ideology that teams by their nature make for a more democratic and egalitarian workplace? What happens if the workers and the managers disagree on a decision? None of these questions can be answered with the data we have, but they are all worth investigating.

Whatever the purpose of teams and their activities, the survey responses indicted that workers in teams enjoy a substantial amount of team time. The median shop with teams allotted three hours per month for each employee in a team for off-line "team activity." One in four shops with teams allot more than five hours a month per employee for such activity, while the bottom 25 percent allow no more than an hour and twenty minutes per month. It would be interesting to know if workers report the same amount of off-line time provided for team meetings. We didn't collect data on what this time is used for; perhaps the sample contains a subset of firms in which the nature of the work, say building machine tools, demands that workers spend time planning and coordinating their work. It also seems that it would be difficult to maintain so much team time in the face of production pressures. We did not ask whether this time is taken at the cost of lost production or on overtime.

---

[23] It is worth noting that in Japan, teams and participation are not meant to increase decision making authority for workers. See Robert M. Marsh, "The Difference Between Power and Participation in Japanese Factories," *Labor and Industrial Relations Review* 45: 250. Also instructive is a quote by Haruo Shimada of Keio University in Japan from *Business Week*, 10 July 1989: "(In Japan), team concept is not intended to increase workers' autonomy but to help find out the problems in the production line so that no defective goods will be produced. In the U.S., workers tend to take participation as having a voice in all kinds of things that in Japan are determined by management and engineers."

Job Rotation

Job rotation is an increasingly familiar feature of work organization in factories. The benefits of job rotation are said to accrue to both employers and employees, to the later through job enrichment, to the former through multi-skilling and labor flexibility, and to both through reduced injuries. We asked questions about how many production workers rotate, among how many positions, and how often.

Job rotation is practiced to some degree in 85 percent of the respondent firms; the median respondent reported that 74 percent of its production employees rotate their jobs, while the *mean* figure for percent of employees that rotate is 60 percent. When asked, with respect to those who do rotate, how many "positions" each employee rotates across, the shops reported that 48 percent of the workers rotate 2-3 jobs, 30 percent rotated 4-6, and 22 percent rotated 7 jobs or more. We were also curious about how often the workers rotated, since avoiding injury and maintaining skills requires more than periodic stints on other jobs. As the table below details, most workers rotate at least once per shift, and the vast majority within one week.

Table 6
Average Hours Between Job Rotations in Respondent Shops

	Hours Between Job Rotations				
	1 - 1.99	2 - 3.99	4 - 7.99	8 - 39.99	40+
Percentage of Workers:	15	22	27	34	2

Interesting findings emerged about teams and job rotation: they are not as linked as we expected. Job rotation is a frequent component of team-type work systems, and the data do show that facilities using teams are more likely to practice job rotation than those with no teams, by 72 percent to 57 percent. However, of the firms using job rotation, only a bare majority, 51 percent, were also using teams. Job rotation is therefore occurring independently of teams.

PRODUCTIVITY

The Performance Benchmarking Service (PBS) has collected information on value-added from small manufacturers since 1992, calculated as sales minus purchased inputs. PBS uses value-added per employee, i.e. labor productivity, to rank and describe performance in manufacturing facilities. Edith Wiarda of the PBS staff has written a convincing monograpf explaining why using a single measure is the best way to evaluate small-firm performance, and why value-added makes the most sense as the single best performance measure for small manufacturers.[24]

Understanding productivity levels in small shops is important to workers and unions, for firms with low productivity cannot support good jobs. Although many other factors intervene in the determination of how much compensation the employees of a small firm will receive, including labor market conditions and whether the employees have a union, without high productivity the economic wherewithal to support decent compensation is missing. The median value-added per full time employee reported by the respondents was (U.S.) $56,174 per year, with only 21 percent of the firms reporting value-added per employee above $80,000; by comparison, the mean value-added per employee for all manufacturers in the U.S. was $91,202 for 1995, placing the respondent firms well below the productivity of all manufacturers combined.[25] Thirty-seven percent of the PBS firms had value-added per employee below $50,000 a year and 19 percent below $40,000 per year. The multi-year trends found in the PBS data show that some firms are improving productivity rapidly, while others stagnate or fall behind.[26] Between 15 percent and 20 percent of the small shops in the data set are increasing their productivity rapidly, at about 10 percent per year on average. Yet, for one-half of the respondents, productivity is flat or falling, and in about 15 percent it is falling rapidly.

Further, analysis of the PBS data set indicates that the productivity performance for small firms tends to vary from year to year, driven in large part by swings in sales and capacity utilization. Between 1992 and 1994, half the shops in the PBS data set had sales changes of more than 25 percent. This environment drives many firms to favor business strategies which maximize the use of variable-cost production factors, mainly labor, over fixed-cost

---

[24] Edith Wiarda, "The All-Around Competition: What Does It Mean to be Best Overall?" (Ann Arbor: Industrial Technology Institute, 1996).

[25] U.S. Department of Commerce, *1995 Survey of Manufacturers*, Table 1a, 11.

[26] The analysis of productivity trends is largely drawn from the work of my colleagues at the Performance Benchmarking Service, including Luria, *Toward Rich or Lean?*, 2-3.

factors such as machinery and product development efforts —in other words, to travel the low road, and to take their employees along for the rough ride.

Over the years, the PBS staff has analyzed the determinants of productivity in these small shops. Much of the story starts with the sales figure in the value-added formula. A firm is more "productive" if it is able to command a price premium for what it produces, based perhaps on proprietary factors or the product being difficult to manufacture. Firms producing what are essentially industrial commodities —for example, simple stampings or molded products— cannot command a high margin on their sales because so many other firms can also do the work. Other, straight forward determinants of productivity which emerge from the PBS data set are not surprising. Value-added per employee is positively correlated with capital per full time employee, percent union, lower turnover, higher seniority, and use of computers.

For the workers, though, the firm's productivity is a means to the end of better compensation. The question naturally arises, how much productivity does it take to support a job with decent compensation? Without entering too deeply into the debate over what exactly comprises decent compensation, in my view that level is far above the official poverty line ($16,036 for a family of four in 1996) by at least 75 percent and perhaps as much as 100 percent.[27] One recent analysis suggests that each household needs at least one worker earning at least $27,000 per year for a reasonable standard of living, and that in the U.S. there is a deficit of 15.7 million such jobs.[28]

The PBS data on small shops suggests that perhaps 55 percent of the value-added per employee can be used for employee compensation, typically 80 percent wages and 20 percent in benefits. This in turn leads to the proposition that it takes value-added per employee of about (U.S.) $60,000 per year to support a job paying $13.00 per hour plus benefits. Forty-five percent of the respondent firms have at least that much value-added per employee. Given the distribution of value-added per employee reflected in the PBS data, it seems clear that many small manufacturers just plain don't have the means to supply well paying jobs. Still, a quick comparison of the value-added and wage data, applying the proportions suggested above,

---

[27] http://www.census.gov/hhes/poverty/threshld/thresh96.html, accessed 10 January 1998.

[28] John E. Schwarz, *Illusions of Opportunity: The American Dream in Question* (W.W. Norton and Co., 1997).

leads one to the conclusion that many of the shops in this survey can afford to pay more than they now do.

CONCLUSION

Seen from the point of view of workers, the news about small manufacturing establishments is not good. Many small manufacturers, perhaps half or more, do not have the underlying productivity to provide well-compensating jobs. Without a doubt, some firms have the economic wherewithal to support better jobs than they are now inclined to, but for those shops without the productivity to support high wages, the point is moot. Unfortunately for the employees of these shops, the firms don't seem to be in a position to buck the trend and drastically increase productivity. Indeed, as the trends for value-added per employee suggest, many small manufacturers are on a slow slide to oblivion, apparently less and less able to muster some combination of products and capabilities which will pull them out of the productivity dungeon.

The restructuring of the automobile industry is creating a business ghetto of low value-added production which is meted out by the OEMs and, increasingly, the large first-tier suppliers who are in a position to mediate the distribution of the work the OEM's don't want. Indeed, Chrysler and Dana have struck a deal in which they consciously manipulate the amount of value-added work assigned to Dana in order to justify a new Dana facility close to a Chrysler assembly plant.[29]

In fact, it appears that the purchasing policies of large firms are "enabling" low productivity manufacturers by favoring those that can deliver continual price cuts on high-volume, easy-to-make goods. These firms are competing as undifferentiated suppliers of what are essentially commodity inputs, winning ugly with a strategy that sweats labor and skimps on investment.[30] Since these firms are producing industrial commodities, they compete on the basis of price and increasingly must bid against a higher number of competitors to win the job. Indeed, the PBS data shows that two-thirds of the respondents must quote against five or more other firms to win their contracts.

---

[29] Mark Phelan, "Chrysler's Global Blueprint for Small Assembly Plants," *Automotive Industries*, December 1997, 48.

[30] Luria, *Toward Lean or Rich*, 2 -3.

When one's customers focus on price cuts, offer short-term contracts, and present fluctuating schedules, then low-wage workers and under investment make business sense. Unfortunately, since it takes high value-added to support high wages, this formula is just the opposite of what decades of economic literature suggest is needed for high productivity: more capital per employee and highly skilled workers. Incremental improvements resulting from lean practices will sooner or later revert to the customer who, remember, is buying industrial commodity products on short-term contracts.

Further, the environment that these firms find themselves in is becoming even more harsh with the growth of the supplier base in Mexico. How does one fashion a plan to compete in a U.S. or Canadian facility on the basis of keeping labor costs low in the era of NAFTA? For example, U.S. unionists traveling to Juarez in December, 1997, found GM paying workers in its parts plants $3.30 per day. When one is selling industrial commodities at a market bid price, it is very difficult to be productive enough to overcome compensation ratios of 8:1 or 10:1.

Small manufacturers in the U.S. face a period of profound difficulty. The majority with flat or falling productivity will find it difficult to stay in business over the long term. They cannot continue to fall behind in productivity without losing the ability to attract even the lowest skilled workers. Another increase in the minimum wage could even kill off some of the worst shops, forcing the price of labor above what they can afford to pay. This, in fact, would be a good thing: social policy should not be tailored to keeping sweatshop managers in business.

Whether better forms of work organization are useful in these shops, when so many lack the market position to capture the resulting efficiency gains, is doubtful. The pressure to deliver selling price reductions will continue, and the less able firms are likely to be hurt further as global overcapacity and OEM dictates to share warranty costs on defective parts grow.[31] The employees of these firms are unlikely to see improvements in the outcomes most important to them unless and until the firms they work for can become more than market price suppliers of industrial commodities. Lean is not enough.

---

[31] See, for example, Tim Moran, "Overcapacity is also a Supplier Problem," *Automotive Industries*, January 1998, 26; Marjorie Sorge, "Bad Parts: Who's At Fault?," *Automotive Industries*, July 1997, 36; and Mark Plelan, "Twenty Suppliers Lay out Their Future Strategies," *Automotive Industries*, December 1997, 87.

Parte V
SALUD Y CONDICIONES DE TRABAJO

Part V
HEALTH AND WORKING CONDITIONS

NEW SYSTEMS OF WORK ORGANIZATION: IMPACTS ON JOB CHARACTERISTICS AND HEALTH

Paul A. Landsbergis, EdD, MPH;
Janet Cahill, PhD; Peter Schnall, MD, MPH[*]

INTRODUCTION

We live in a period of time in which new systems of work organization are being introduced throughout the industrialized world, raising the question of whether these systems impact on the prevalence of job strain (that is, work combining high demands and low control). We are intrigued by this question due to our own work, and that of our colleagues (for example, Robert Karasek, Tores Theorell, Tage Kristensen, and Jeff Johnson), linking job strain with hypertension and heart disease.

In Karasek and Theorell's 1990 book *Healthy Work*[1] they not only discuss the evidence linking job strain and illness, but also discuss experiments in work organization which might possibly create healthier jobs —for example, Quality of Work Life programs, Scandinavian socio-technical systems, or Japanese management techniques, also known as "lean production." They described the debate around these systems, and posed a question about lean production. They said: "The unresolved question is the amount of *control* really afforded" to workers in Japanese-owned plants in the United States. In other words, do workers have greater or lesser job decision latitude (job control), or more or less job strain and risk of illness under lean production than under other systems?

---

[*] Paul Landsbergis is Assistant Professor of Epidemiology at Cornell University Medical College. Janet Cahill is Professor of Psychology at Rowan College of New Jersey. Peter Schnall is Associate Professor of Medicine at the University of California at Irvine.

[1] Robert Karasek with Tores Theorell, *Healthy Work: Stress, Productivity, and the Reconstruction of Working Life* (Basic Books, 1990).

The 1990 text from MIT which had assessed lean production in auto manufacturing, *The Machine that Changed the World*,[2] had argued that, in the best Japanese auto companies, "multiskilled" workers can solve quality problems at their source and boost productivity. The "freedom to control one's work" replaces the "mind numbing stress" of mass production. Armed with "the skills they need to control their environment," workers in a lean plant have the opportunity "to think actively, indeed proactively," to solve workplace problems. This "creative tension" makes work "humanly fulfilling." Much has subsequently been written about this subject but, until recently, very few empirical studies had been conducted. Today, we have some data than can help to answer this "unresolved" question about lean production's impact on job dimensions and health.

Lean production is an attempt to reduce impediments to the smooth flow of production through techniques that include continuous improvement in productivity and quality ("Kaizen"), "just-in-time" (JIT) inventory systems, and training workers to conduct quality control through quality circles. In Table 1 we provide, from earlier case studies, models of the extent of job-decision latitude under lean production, socio-technical systems, and the U.S. human resources approach. Lean production does seem to provide for more job enlargement, cross-training, and problem-solving opportunities than traditional manufacturing job design. However, quality circles are not autonomous work teams, nor are they empowered to make managerial decisions. Cycle-time in lean production is still very short (often one minute or less in auto assembly). Following highly standardized steps at each narrowly defined task is mandatory. Reliance is placed on time studies and standards to ensure maximum workloads (e.g., working 57 seconds out of a minute vs. 40-45 seconds in a traditional plant). JIT inventory systems remove the buffer stocks between operations, leaving workers' personal time and flexibility to serve as buffers. Consequently, long work hours and involuntary overtime are common.

---

[2] James Womack, Daniel Jones, Daniel Roos, *The Machine that Changed the World* (New York, 1990).

Table 1
Some Common Models of New Work Systems

	Lean Production	Human Resources	Socio-Technical Systems
* Origin	Japan	United States	England, Scandinavia
* Worker Teams	Supervised	No	Self-directed
* Group Decision Making/ Problem Solving	Yes, through QCs	No	Yes
* Cycle Time	Short	Short	Long
* Skills:			
Vertical Tasks	Just QC process	No	Yes
Horizontal Tasks	Yes	Some	Yes
Knowledge Depth	Trade off depth for greater breath	Limited	Team characteristic, not individual
* Autonomy	No	No	Yes
* Jobs Rotate	Yes	Some	Yes
* Cross-Training	High	Some	High
* Unions	Company unions	Anti-union	Strong unions
* Components	JIT, TQM, QC	QWL, EI	

Source: Eileen Appelbaum and Rosemary Batt, *The New American Workplace* (Ithaca: ILR Press, 1994).

However, many earlier reports promoting lean work have not discussed the potential for work stress (due to high demands and limited latitude), or injuries and illness. While the debate continues on lean production and important issues such as productivity, quality, labor relations, worker solidarity, and the spread of low-wage supplier jobs, we focus on the critical but relatively neglected area of employee injuries (including upper extremity musculoskeletal disorders [UEMDs]), and on job characteristics related to job strain (i.e., job demands, control, social support). We focus on this issue because lean work and other team-based methods are spreading to many industries. Thus, a careful empirical assessment of the impact of new work systems on job characteristics is critical in understanding trends in worker health, not just in auto manufacturing production, but throughout Western economies.

METHODS AND RESULTS

The surveys and case studies we review (Table 2) are primarily from North America and include several recently conducted surveys. We do not claim that this is an exhaustive review of this topic; however, the major surveys and case studies that we know of are included (citations are listed at the end of the chapter). We carefully reviewed each study and rated associations between lean work, job characteristics and health outcomes. So, what do these studies indicate?

Table 2
Lean Production and Health Outcomes:
Surveys and Case Studies Reviewed

Lean production in auto, upper extremity musculoskeletal disorders (UEMDs) and stress

* 3 surveys by Canadian Auto Workers, 1993-1996
* 4 U.S. case studies, 1993-1996

Lean production in auto, and job characteristics

* 3 surveys by Canadian Auto Workers, 1993-1996
* 1 survey by United Steelworkers in Canada, 1995
* 1 survey by United Auto Workers in Michigan, 1993
* 2 U.S. case studies, 1991-1995

New work systems in other industries, and job characteristics

5 surveys and 3 case studies from electronics, garment, health care and other industries in England and the U.S.

Associations between lean production in auto manufacturing and UEMDs, fatigue, stress, and tension are summarized in Table 3. Authors of case studies of Japanese-owned auto assembly plants in the U.S. (including the 1990 visit to six such "transplants" by Christian Berggren and his colleagues at the Swedish Royal Institute of Technology) reported high levels of perceived stress and of musculoskeletal disorders, such as tendinitis and carpal tunnel syndrome, due, in their opinion, to the fast work pace, long work hours, highly repetitive work, and limited rest breaks. Other factors mentioned were lack of early treatment due to peer pressure to "work in pain" and not report injuries, and the denial of work-relatedness by management —with the comment that "there are weak and there are strong people."

Table 3
Associations Between Lean Production in Auto and Health Outcomes

	Sample N	UEMDs	Fatigue, Stress, Tension
Canadian surveys			
16 Auto Parts Suppliers	1,670	0	?
CAMI (GM-Suzuki)	100 (4x)		+
CAMI, GM, Ford, Chrysler	2,424	?	?
U.S. case studies			
Auto Alliance (Mazda-Ford)		+	
6 Japanese "transplants"		+	+
NUMMI (GM-Toyota)		+	
Subaru-Isuzu		+	+

0 = no association, ? = equivocal association, + = modest association, ++ = strong association

While we could locate no studies which specifically assessed the prevalence or incidence of musculoskeletal disorders in lean workplaces, the three surveys conducted by the Canadian Auto Workers Union suggest a worsening problem. Among the auto parts supplier workers, survey data indicated that increases in job tension and fatigue over the past two years were significantly greater in lean companies than in traditional companies. At General Motors, the most lean of the four companies surveyed, 67 percent of workers reported working in pain at least half of the days in the last month. At the Japanese joint venture, CAMI, 42 percent of workers reported working in pain. Across the four companies, a majority reported more job tension and fatigue than several years ago.

Associations between lean production in auto manufacturing and job characteristics are reported in Table 4. More detailed information is available from these surveys on the job characteristics which comprise job strain. Job demands were fairly consistently reported to be elevated. Among auto parts workers, those in lean companies reported significantly heavier workloads, and "too few people," than in traditional companies. Seventy-nine percent of GM workers and 54 percent of Ford workers said they could "not keep up without working as fast as you can"; 73 percent of Mazda workers reported "I will likely be injured or worn out before I retire."

Table 4
Associations Between Lean Production in Auto and Job Characteristics

	High Job Demands	Low Decision Authority	Poor Skill Development
Canadian surveys			
16 Auto Parts Suppliers	++	?	0
CAMI (GM-Suzuki)	?	+	+
CAMI, GM, Ford, Chrysler	+	+	
Walker Exhaust (Canada)	0	0	0
U.S. survey			
Auto Alliance (Mazda-Ford)	+	+	+
U.S. Case studies			
6 Japanese "transplants"	+		
Subaru-Isuzu (Indiana)	+	+	

0 = no association, ? = equivocal association, + = modest association, ++ = strong association

Low or decreasing decision authority was also consistently reported. At CAMI, while 51 percent reported at Survey 1 being "actively involved in making decisions at work," 1.5 years later at Survey 4 this proportion fell to 33 percent. The role of teams in providing a place for "influence over the job" similarly fell from 79 percent to 45 percent. During early start-up periods, "participation" and job rotation were practiced, but during production, dissatisfaction rose. At Survey 4, 60 percent reported that teams "get us all to pressure one another" compared to only 19 percent at Survey 1. At Mazda, participation was also very limited. As the local union president put it, "They promised us a rose garden. They gave us a desert."

The promise of lean production in producing highly trained "multiskilled" workers was also challenged by the survey data. At CAMI, the proportion of workers who felt that "as a result of training, I'm no more skilled since all the jobs are about the same" rose from 53 percent at Survey 1 to 72 percent at Survey 4. At Mazda, 89 percent of respondents said that "the actual training I have received is fair or poor." Only 6 percent reported it as excellent.

Associations between new work systems in other industries and health outcomes are reported in Table 5. Some additional small-scale surveys have also been conducted in other industries. The British surveys show similar (although not always consistent) effects of JIT work systems as the North American auto plant surveys. In the U.S. health care industry, experiments in team-based decentralized work have been called "patient-focused care."

Table 5
Associations Between New Work Systems
in Other Industries and Job Characteristics

	Sample N	Psych. Strain	Low Decision Authority	Job Demands
Cross-sectional surveys				
123 cos. (Pennsylvania)	537	0	0	
British prospective surveys				
Car seat manufacturer	35	+*	0	+*
Electronics assemblers	56	0	(increase in control)	?
Electronics assemblers	44	0	?	?
U.S. Case studies				
Patient-focused health care		?**	(increased authority for aides - if staffing reasonable)	?**
Modular mfg. (garment)		+	(some increase in authority)	0

*if no worker participation in implementation of system **if understaffing
0 = no association, ? = equivocal association, + = modest association, ++ = strong association

Surveys show some increase in decision-making authority and job satisfaction, mainly for nurse aides, if staffing levels are kept reasonable. Professional nurses (RNs) are concerned since some of their work is being transferred to poorly trained lower-paid aides, and since such programs are often designed to save health care costs by eliminating professional nurse positions, causing understaffing and greater stress for nurses.

It was also apparent that, in unionized facilities, it was impossible to study a "pure" form of lean production. In most of the cases we examined, collective worker resistance to the stress of lean production occurred through strikes, strike threats, collective bargaining, and requesting government safety inspections (Table 6). These efforts have "humanized" lean

Table 6
Response of Workers/Unions to Lean Production

5-week strike (Canadian Auto Workers - CAMI, 1992)
2-hour strike (UAW - NUMMI, 1994)
Strike threat (UAW - Mazda, 1991)
OSHA inspection and settlement (UAW - NUMMI, 1992-4, and GM, Ford and Chrysler)
Surveys to document conditions
Collective bargaining

work to some extent —through moderated work demands (more staff, and control over line speed and job standards), increased latitude (electing team leaders, ability to transfer, joint committees), fairer access to training, and ergonomics programs (Table 7).

Table 7
Modification of Lean Production Through Union Efforts

* Improved staffing through a Temporary Assignment Pool of workers to fill in for absent or injured workers. (Undermines one purpose of teams: peer pressure to discourage absenteeism and encourage working while injured.)
* Fairer access to training
* Increased transfers between departments
* Joint committees on health and safety, ergonomics, training
* The right to elect or recall team leaders
* Team leaders' duties in contract
* Increasing work loads due to absenteeism is forbidden
* Temporary assignments offered to workers on the basis of seniority
* Some limits on line speeds and work loads
* Ergonomics programs

Job analysis, worksite evaluations
Engineering controls, task rotation, rest periods
Review models before production
Better medical management
Reduce line speed
No reprisals for reporting injuries

CONCLUSIONS

Recent surveys tend to confirm some earlier case studies that lean production does create an intensified work pace and work demands, and that increases in decision authority and skill levels are very modest. Decision latitude remains low. Thus, such work can be considered to have high job strain. In jobs with physical ergonomic stressors (such as auto manufacturing), this intensification of labor appears to lead to increased musculoskeletal injuries.

Since fast-paced repetitive short-cycle work with few rest breaks, long work hours and low authority are risk factors not only for musculoskeletal injuries —they also, in effect, define job strain— we suggest that high rates of musculoskeletal injuries in lean workplaces may be a warning sign of chronic job strain. Therefore, they may well be predictors of illnesses with longer latencies, such as hypertension and heart disease. If we are correct in our analysis, the potential for dramatically increased rates of hypertension and heart disease exists if lean methods (including outsourcing, longer work hours, understaffing and insecure work) are widely implemented in the labor market. Forms of lean production are by no means limited to Japanese-owned companies nor just to manufacturing, but are promoted in many sectors, including health care.

We have also provided some evidence that unions are a countervailing force to this trend, that they have modified, humanized to some extent, the lean production system. Alternatives to lean production exist. Christian Berggren has written persuasively about socio-technical system efforts in Scandinavia and the increased latitude provided by autonomous work groups.[3] However, many questions remain. We need better data from prospective studies. We need to know the impact of lean production on:

---

3 Christian Berggren, *Alternatives to Lean Production: Work Organization in the Swedish Auto Industry* (New York,

1) Worker skills. Is it memorizing standardized company-specific procedures or true skill development? Who controls access to training or the content?
2) Co-worker support and worker solidarity? Is peer pressure used to increase work pace?
3) On health in nonunion workplaces, especially supplier firms.
4) On workforces that are older and not so highly selected.
5) What is the time period of the effect of lean methods? In some cases, employees were very satisfied with their participation in planning production. However, once the system was in operation, they felt betrayed by the speed-up and lack of participation.

We also need better data on alternatives, such as socio-technical systems:

1) Are there alternatives which promote healthy work —which reduce job strain, injuries, or blood pressure?
2) What about the health impact of related work systems such as Total Quality Management (TQM), re-engineering, modular or cellular manufacturing, or agile manufacturing?

STUDIES REVIEWED

Surveys co-sponsored by the Canadian Auto Workers

Lewchuk, Wayne, and David Robertson. 1998. "Work Reorganization and the Quality of Working Life in the Canadian Automobile Industry." This volume.

Lewchuk, Wayne, B. Roberts, C. McDonald, and David Robertson. 1996. "Working Conditions Study: Benchmarking Auto Assembly Plants." Willowdale, ON: Canadian Auto Workers.

Rinehart, James, Chris Huxley, David Robertson. 1995. "Team Concept at CAMI." In Steve Babson, ed., *Lean Work: Empowerment and Exploitation in the Global Auto Industry.* Detroit: Wayne State University Press.

Robertson, David, James Rinehart, Chris Huxley, Jeff Wareham, Herman Rosenfeld, Alan McGough, Steve Benedict. 1993. *The CAMI report: Lean production in a Unionized Auto Plant.* Willowdale, ON: Canadian Auto Workers.

Survey by the United Steelworkers in Canada

Murphy, Colette, Doug Olthuis. 1995. "The Impact of Work Reorganization on Employee Attitudes Towards Work, the Company and the Union."

In C. Schenk and J. Anderson, eds., *Re-Shaping Work: Union Responses to Technological Change.* Don Mills, ON: Ontario Federation of Labor.

U.S. survey of autoworkers

Babson, Steve. 1993. "Lean or Mean: The MIT Model and Lean Production at Mazda." *Labor Studies Journal* (summer): 3-24.

U.S. case studies of autoworkers

Adler, Paul. 1995. "Democratic Taylorism: The Toyota Production System at NUMMI." In Babson, *Lean Work.*

——. 1996. "Ergonomics, Employee Involvement, and the Toyota Production System: A case Study of NUMMI's 1993 Model Introduction." *Industrial and Labor Relations Review* 50 (April): 416-417.

Berggren, Christian, Torsten Bjorkman, and Ernst Hollander. 1991. *Are They Unbeatable? Report from a Field Trip to Study Transplants, the Japanese Owned Auto Plants in North America.* Stockholm: Royal Institute of Technology.

Division of Occupational Safety and Health. 1994. "Special Order" (NUMMI inspection). Department of Industrial Relations, State of California. 8 January.

——. 1993. "Citation and Notification of Penalty (Citation R1D4-4014)." Department of Industrial Relations, State of California. 6 January.

Graham, Laurie. 1995. *On the Line at Subaru-Isuzu: The Japanese Model and the American Worker.* Ithaca: ILR Press.

Surveys of other industries

Jackson, Paul, Robin Martin. 1996. "Impact of Just-in-Time on Job Content, Employee Attitudes and Well-Being: A Longitudinal Study." *Ergonomics* 39: 1-16.

Mullarkey, Sean, Paul Jackson, S. K. Parker. "Employee Reaction to JIT Manufacturing Practices: A Two-Phase Investigation." *International Journal of Operations and Productions Management* (in press).

Parker, Sharon. 1995. "How Do Modern Manufacturing Systems Affect Shop-floor Jobs and Well-Being?" Presented at the APA/NIOSH Conference on Occupational Stress. Washington, D.C., 13-16 September.

Parker, Sharon, Paul Jackson, Toby Wall. 1995. "Autonomous Group Working Within Integrated Manufacturing: A Longitudinal Investigation of Employee Role Orientations." In Gavriel Salvendy and M.J. Smith, eds., *Human-Computer Interaction: Application and Case Studies.* Amsterdam: Elsevier.

Parker, Sharon, Toby Wall. 1978. "Job Design and Modern Manufacturing." In Peter Warr, ed., *Psychology at Work.* London: Penguin Books.

Parker Sharon, Toby Wall, Carol Myers. 1995. "The Effects of a Manufacturing Initiative on Employee Jobs and Strain." In S. Robertson, ed., *Contemporary Ergonomics 1995.* London: Taylor and Francis.

Case studies of other industries

Greiner, Ann. 1995. "Cost and Quality Matters: Workplace Innovations in the Health Care Industry." Washington, D.C.: Economic Policy Institute.

Richardson, Trudy. 1994. "Reengineering the Hospital: Patient-Focused Care." In Mike Parker and Jane Slaughter, eds., *Working Smart: A Union Guide to Participation Programs and Reengineering.* Detroit: Labor Education and Research Project.

Wunderlich, Gooloos, Frank Sloan, Carolyne Davis, eds. 1996. *Nursing Staff in Hospitals and Nursing Homes: Is it Adequate?* Washington, DC.: National Academy Press.

ACCIDENTES DE TRABAJO EN VW DE MÉXICO

*Ma. Cristina González García**
*Huberto Juárez Núñez***

Accidente de trabajo es toda lesión orgánica o perturbación funcional, inmediata o posterior, o la muerte, producida repentinamente en ejercicio, o con motivo del trabajo, cualesquiera que sean el lugar y el tiempo en que se presente.
Quedan incluidos en la definición anterior los accidentes que se produzcan al trasladarse el trabajador directamente de su domicilio al lugar de trabajo y de éste a aquel.

Art. 474. Ley Federal del Trabajo

"Al bajarse de la unidad se le trabó el pie izquierdo entre la puerta y el estribo en el momento que el transfer adelantó la carrocería cayendo al piso.
Nota del servicio médico: paciente que a la exploración física *no presenta signo de contusión en cráneo, presenta reacción psicótica con obnubilación, signos de depresión nerviosa, diaforesis con hiporreflexia, irritabilidad, bradifagia, incoherencia crisis conversiva, ...*
Solicitamos a medicina del trabajo *valoración e investigación* en este caso."

Texto de la descripción de un accidente de trabajo y nota del servicio médico de la empresa. 15 de Nov. de 1993.

INTRODUCCIÓN

Dentro del binomio social *salud y trabajo*, sin duda, los accidentes laborales representan el aspecto más grave y dramático de lo que podríamos denominar *el costo* en salud y vida para los trabajadores. Las condiciones de trabajo, la intensidad del trabajo, el nivel de los sistemas de prevención y protección corporal, las tecnologías, el equipamiento, los sistemas de trabajo y el tipo de producto y de industria, son entre otros, el conjunto de factores que están

* Médico especialista del Instituto Mexicano del Seguro Social.
** Profesor Investigador. Centro de Investigación y Estudios de Posgrado. Facultad de Economía-BUAP

detrás de los diversos niveles de frecuencia conque los accidentes laborales se presentan en la fábricas mexicanas.

En el caso de la gran industria —y en ella la industria automotriz— la asociación entre el trabajo cotidiano, las sobrecargas de trabajo y los riesgos de accidentes por desempeño, son una cuestión que ha permanecido sin grandes modificaciones en los últimos años a pesar de que en el ámbito oficial y empresarial -y dentro de la cobertura de los cambios en la Ley del Instituto Mexicano Seguro Social (IMSS)- se habla de mejoras substanciales.

En este último sentido, las nuevas regulaciones de la Seguridad Social en México (véase: Mussot, 1997; Luna y García 1997; Laurell 1996) —aprobadas en diciembre de 1995, y con vigencia a partir de julio de 1997— en lo que toca a las condiciones y accidentes de trabajo, parten del presupuesto de que los riesgos de trabajo en la industria de punta, pueden disminuir sensiblemente como resultado de la modernización del equipamiento y la maquinaria y de los cambios organizacionales del proceso productivo[1].

A manera de corolario se ha establecido en la nueva Ley del IMSS —como una especie de compensación a los desembolsos patronales en nuevas tecnologías y equipamientos asociados a la seguridad en el trabajo— un conjunto de mecanismos que prevén la reducción de las cotizaciones patronales a las empresas que demuestren disminuir riesgos de trabajo. Este procedimiento introduce cambios no sólo en las asignaciones de cuotas patronales, especialmente se consolidan las formas de atención y cuidados a la salud que al desvincularse del las instituciones públicas, provocarán un mayor uso de los servicios médicos privados[2], es decir, mecanismos de atención donde las evaluaciones y las ponderaciones sobre enfermedad y salud pue-

[1] El IMSS "que en 1990-1991 cubría aproximadamente a 38 millones de mexicanos, 47.5 de la población, muestra un ligero aumento de la mortalidad de la población derechohabiente de 1985 a1990..." (Villegas y Noriega. 1996).

[2] La sustitución de entidades públicas por privadas es parte de una tendencia que se hizo explícita en las formulaciones y recomendaciones de instituciones como el Banco Mundial. El informe de 1993 establece entre otras directrices que: "...el gasto público debería orientarse hacia programas más eficaces en función de los costos que contribuyan en mayor medida a ayudar a los pobres...Se gastan fondos públicos en intervenciones de salud de escasa eficacia en función de los costos, como la cirugía de los casos de cáncer...Los gobiernos tienen que facilitar mayor diversidad y competencia en el financiamiento y la prestación de medidas de los servicios de salud. Si los gobiernos financiaran un conjunto de medidas de salud pública y servicios clínicos esenciales, el resto de los servicios de esta índole se podría cubrir mediante el financiamiento privado" (Banco Mundial, Informe 1993, p iii).

den estar bajo control de las empresas contratantes[3]. Este sería el caso de la industria manufacturera con mayores ingredientes de reestructuración y de manera especial, es el caso de las plantas de ensamble de autos.

Sin embargo, al considerar las evidencias que cotidianamente se presentan en los consultorios y unidades medicas de las instituciones públicas (todavía) responsables de atender los diversos tipos de problemas de salud y riesgo, el supuesto oficial y empresarial parecen no tener mucho sustento. Los accidentes de trabajo en la gran industria se siguen presentando, posiblemente en un número menor y dentro de una tendencia que configura nuevos perfiles.

Estos perfiles (padecimientos nerviosos, por ejemplo), pueden no ser susceptibles de clasificación si se toman las agrupaciones tradicionales, incluso, muchos de ellos no son concebidos como accidentes (agotamientos y crisis nerviosas) porque las obligaciones productivas, que ahora evalúan y califican desempeño, aptitudes y actitudes, están normadas por nuevas regulaciones laborales que tienden incluso a inhibir su registro ante las instancias oficiales, cuestión que afecta de entrada el número de los registros existentes.

En el contexto de esta hipótesis general, nuestro trabajo indaga las expresiones más características de los accidentes de trabajo en una gran fábrica mexicana, a saber, la planta VW en Puebla, filial del consorcio alemán VW-AG.

PARTE 1

Hace algunos años (1986-1987), cuando por primera vez estudiamos los reportes empresariales y sindicales sobre la frecuencia de accidentes, encontramos que en la planta VW de México, la mayoría de los accidentes de trabajo afectaban básicamente las partes del cuerpo que están más expuestas, en el sentido de su función directa en el trabajo manual y por tanto, en conexión con las herramientas, los equipos y los diversos dispositivos necesarios para el ensamble de los autos (Juárez, Garduño, 87).

---

[3] Es público y un tema muy desglosado en México el hecho de que los cambios en las regulaciones en la seguridad social: pensiones, atención a la salud, calificación y atención a los accidentes de trabajo, indemnizaciones, etc., han seguido muy de cerca el modelo de privatización de estos servicios introducido en Chile en los años de la dictadura. Muchos de los efectos en el mediano y largo plazo pueden ser vislumbrados si se considera que las prerrogativas del capital han sido salvaguardadas en la misma forma e intensidad que en el modelo chileno (Sapag Ch. 1995, Díaz. 1996)

Junto a esto, los reportes observados para estos años indicaban que de los 250 accidentes anuales promedio en fábrica registrados por la parte sindical de la Comisión Mixta de Higiene y Seguridad y por la Secretaría de Previsión Social del Sindicato VW, las áreas de trabajo donde se presentaba la mayor frecuencia de este tipo de accidentes eran las nave de ensamble de carrocerías, la nave de prensas y la nave de ensamble final.

La explicación más recurrente en el ámbito sindical era que los accidentes de trabajo se producían como resultado de presiones para obtener las cuotas productivas diarias y de operaciones repetitivas, inseguras y bajo débiles sistemas de protección y prevención.

Por su lado, la explicaciones de la gerencia y de los diversos jefes de naves y áreas, discurrían en el sentido de que los accidentes eran parte de una cultura de trabajo que asumía con poca responsabilidad y con hábitos inadecuados, el uso de los implementos, de la ropa y el equipo de seguridad para la ejecución de las diversas operaciones (por ejemplo se argumentaba que muchos trabajadores no usaban adecuadamente las mascarillas, las caretas, los guantes, las herramientas, etc.) .

El procesamientos de esos reportes[4], nos indicaban que las extremidades superiores (dedos, manos, brazos) eran las partes más vulnerables. En 86 ocupaban el 36% de total anual y en 1987 el 26%, en ambos casos, seguidos por las afectaciones a las extremidades inferiores (muslos, rodillas, espinillas, pies, dedos) que representaron el 26% y el 25% respectivamente.

Sobre la base de la estadística sindical y considerando cinco áreas de localización (en función de la información a la que se tuvo acceso), en las gráficas 1 y 2 mostramos la distribución porcentual de los accidentes registrados correspondiente a los años 1986 y 1987.

---

[4] Que tal y como se observa en las gráficas 1 y 2, agrupaban los accidentes en cinco grandes grupos que identifican a cuatro partes del organismo y el resto se agrupa en la categoría de "otros".

Gráfica 1

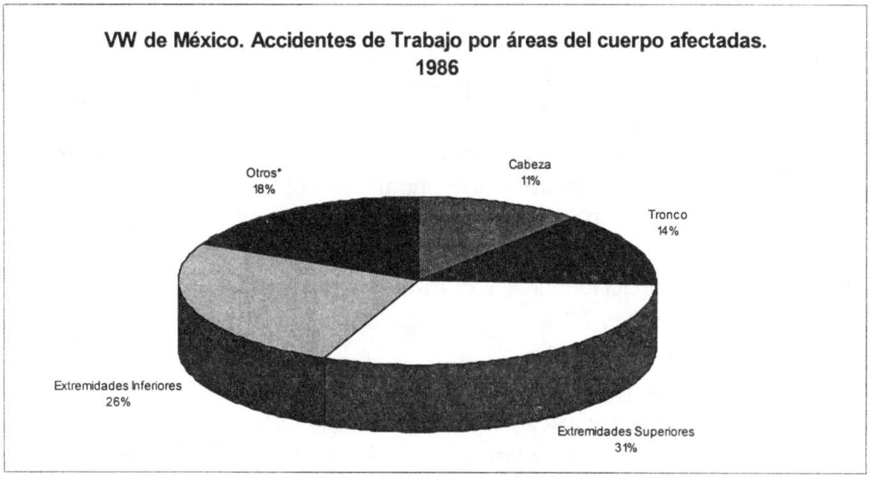

Fuente: Elaborado sobre la base del Reporte de Accidentes de Trabajo en VW de México. Secretaría de Previsión Social del Comité Ejecutivo del SITIASCVWM. 1986.

Gráfica 2

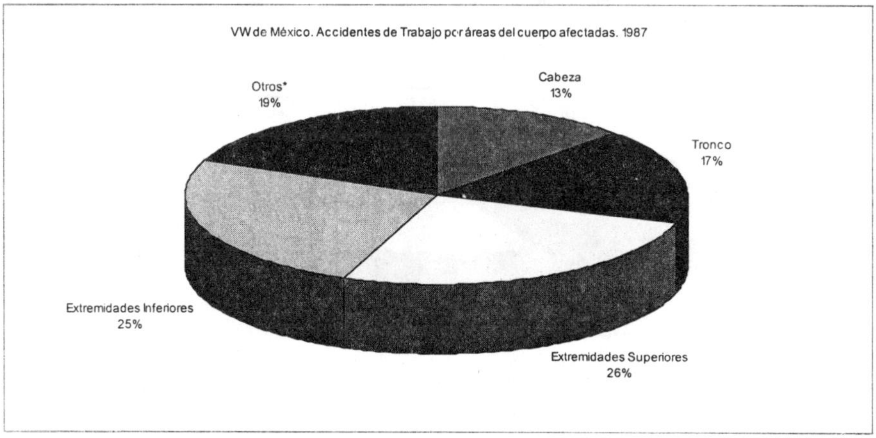

Fuente: Elaborado sobre la base del Reporte de Accidentes de Trabajo en VW de México. Secretaría de Previsión Social del Comité Ejecutivo del SITIASCVWM. 1987.

Algunos años después (1993), tuvimos acceso a otra muestra, más pequeña -un reporte de 54 casos- donde los accidentes ocurrían en un ambiente de cambio organizacional y tecnológico que incorpora como nuevos ingredientes, el "trabajo de equipo" y el desplazamiento de diversas áreas productivas y materias de trabajo a proveedores instalados en las cercanías de la gran fábrica (Juárez, 1996).

Procedimos a analizar y a comparar los datos sobre los accidentes de trabajo en esta nueva situación. En un primer momento utilizamos la misma metodología de agrupación de 1986 y 1987 (esto es, concentrados los datos en cinco áreas) y el resultado fue más o menos sorprendente: las extremidades dejaron de ser la región mas accidentada y el rubro "Otros" que ocupaban 18% y 19% en los registros de 86 y 87 se desplazó hasta ocupar el primer lugar con una cuota de 44% (véase gráfica 3).

Al considerar que para 1993 el personal sindicalizado estaba disminuyendo como producto de los reajustes por la dispersión de algunos procesos hacia los nuevos proveedores de VW y también por los incrementos de productividad generado por la introducción de los nuevos sistemas de trabajo, pensamos que el nuevo lugar de los "Otros" accidentes de trabajo estaban manifestando nuevas situaciones que deberían indagarse para una mayor comprensión acerca de las afectaciones a la salud de las nuevas condiciones de trabajo.

Gráfica 3

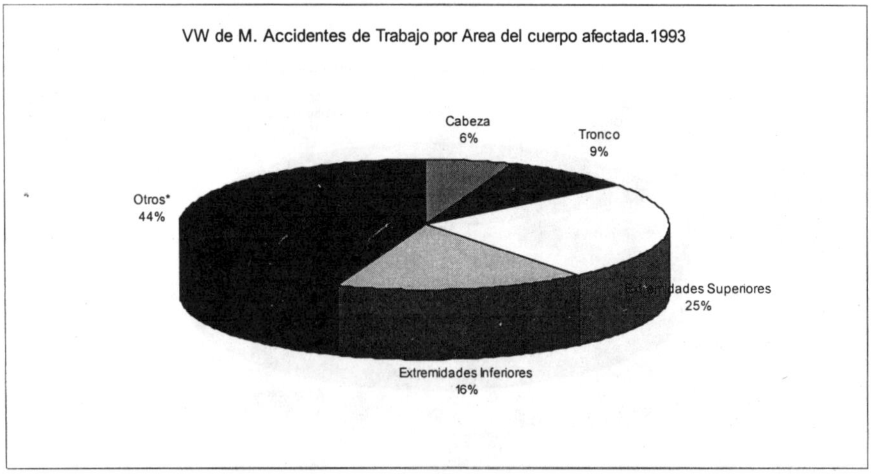

Fuente: Elaborado sobre la base del Reporte de Accidentes de Trabajo en VW de México. Secretaría de Previsión Social del Comité Ejecutivo del SITIASCVWM y Comisión Mixta de Higiene y Seguridad. 1993.

PARTE 2

Por tanto, la modificación del espectro estadístico de los accidentes en VW, nos obligó en primer lugar a revisar el procedimiento de agrupación utilizado -el diseñado con los responsables de la Secretaría de Previsión Social del Comité Sindical de VW en 1986- y después, a buscar una ampliación del universo de análisis.

En esta fase del análisis pudimos integrar un conjunto de registros puntuales (la forma MT1 que es el reporte empresarial de los accidentes de trabajo al IMSS[5]) para 15 meses correspondientes a los años 1993 y 1994. Al mismo tiempo tuvimos acceso a los reportes mensuales y anuales para períodos similares elaborados por el Departamento de "Seguridad Industrial" de VW de México, que aunque no están desglosados por casos, en sus totales mensuales nos permitieron establecer comparaciones y corroboraciones de nuestras estimaciones.

Un hallazgo adicional fue localizar la agrupación estadística de los accidentes en estos quince meses en función de las edades de los trabajadores afectados.

Los resultados obtenidos son los siguientes

Edades y número de accidentes:
En el período analizado hemos encontrado que los grupos de edad con más frecuencia son los que correspondes a los trabajadores con edades que fluctúan entre los 22 y los 30 años, seguidos por el grupo que se ubica entre los 32 y los 35 años (ver gráfica 4). Los trabajadores que acumulan el mayor número son los que tienen 25, 26 y 24 años (entre 35 y 46 accidentes) con una antigüedad laboral promedio de 5 a 6 años de operarios de planta[6].

---

[5] Esta forma, que es la base básica para el registro oficial de accidentes de trabajo, en los años 80 siempre llegó a las instancias sindicales ya procesada, utilizando los cinco grupos que están en las gráficas 1,2 y 3. Para nuestro análisis de 1993 y 1994, es necesario aclarar que no pudimos obtener el reporte médico del responsable del IMSS, contenido en el reverso de la forma MT1. Por tanto la información básica que nos proporciona el documento puede calificarse en muchos caos como descriptivo y desde el punto de vista médico, deficiente. Se percibe que existe siempre una preocupación a describir más el mecanismo del accidente que las lesiones que se ocasionan al trabajador y en muchos casos se señalan las regiones afectadas en lenguaje coloquial, no médico.

[6] Los trabajadores de VW al igual que la mayor parte de los trabajadores de la industria automotriz en México, cubren períodos de trabajo con la modalidad de contratos temporales

Gráfica 4

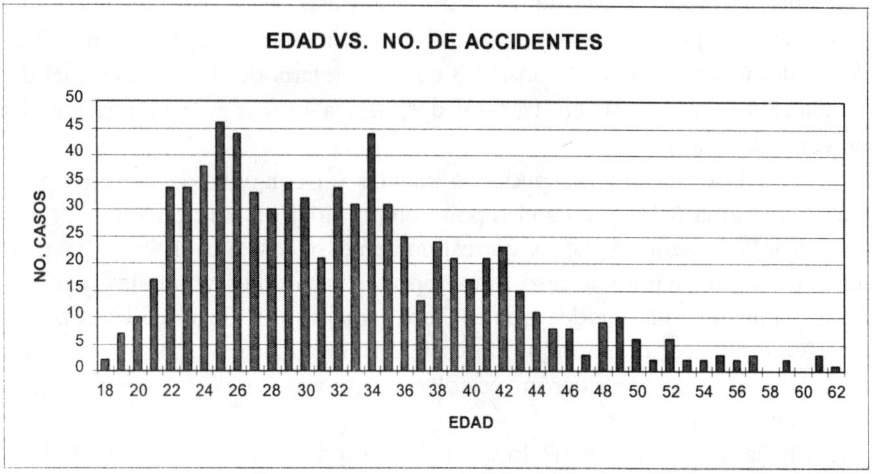

Podemos decir que los accidentes de trabajo durante el período de estudio se presentaron con mayor frecuencia entre obreros jóvenes. Esto puede tener una explicación si desglosamos dos cosas, el tipo de accidente y las regulaciones laborales vinculadas al desempeño cotidiano.

Para abordar el problema, en primer lugar procedimos a desglosar el rubro de "Otros accidentes de trabajo" que en la clasificación tradicional da cuenta de accidentes considerados como poco frecuentes, porque están localizados en regiones del cuerpo aparentemente poco expuestas o porque se refieren a afectaciones consideradas atípicas en la industria automotriz: glúteos, testículos, cintura, cuero cabelludo, tobillos, crisis nerviosas, etc. En segundo lugar, adoptamos como criterio de agrupación una topografía anatomo-funcional que permite establecer cuadros nosológicos más adecuados desde el punto de vista médico. Bajo este enfoque establecimos 17 modalidades a partir de los cuales agrupamos y procesamos la información sobre los accidentes reportados en los 15 meses. Los resultados pueden verse agrupados en los cuadros 1-4

(eventuales). Este, es un tiempo de trabajo que en VW era de dos años, en los años 90 se ha vuelto difícil de promediar porque la duración de los contratos temporales tiene variaciones que dependen de coyunturas asociadas a estímulos a la productividad, por tanto son a discreción de las gerencias.

Nuestro análisis empezó por distinguir los reportes que se refieren a los accidentes en trayecto al trabajo de los ocurridos en el área de trabajo en la fábrica en las horas de jornada. Los registros preliminares de 1993 indicaban que el número de los accidentes en trayecto eran cada vez mas frecuentes y la clasificación de "otros" debía su crecimiento a la acumulación de este tipo de casos.

Accidentes en Trayecto al Trabajo:

Los accidentes en trayecto al trabajo representan un gran porcentaje en el total de percances registrados en los años 1993-1994. En el primer año sumaron el 45.9% y en 1994 el 42.4%. En los cuadros 1 y 2 podrá observarse que los accidentes ocurridos en este espacio se concentran en los conceptos "Policontundidos", "Lesiones de Manos", "Lesiones en los Pies", "Lesiones en Rodillas" y "Esguinces de Tobillo". Es decir, en la mayor parte de los casos, al parecer, las lesiones y las policontusiones son producto de las prisas para el abordaje de las unidades de traslado a la fábrica y a accidentes viales por exceso de velocidad. Los trabajadores de VW inician su día laboral además de la presión para llegar puntualmente a la fábrica, en función de un sinnúmero de factores: las distancias, el estado de las unidades de transporte, la vialidad de la ciudad y las zonas conurbadas, cuestiones que provocan que sea muy difícil establecer tiempos de traslado estandarizados y seguros.

Y lo importante en esto es, tal como hemos mencionado arriba, que a partir de agosto de 1992 las regulaciones laborales premian o castigan de manera especial la puntualidad y la asistencia. La regulación sobre el tiempo de ingreso a la fábrica se ha vuelto puntillosas, un obrero puede llegar tarde una vez por semana (con una tolerancia de quince minutos), pero un segundo retardo o rebasar la tolerancia establecida, le da el derecho a la empresa a no permitirle la entrada al trabajo.

Por ejemplo la cláusula 31 del Contrato Colectivo de Trabajo establece que:

"Los trabajadores ***estarán obligados a presentarse en su lugar de trabajo a la hora en punto****; sin embargo, se establece una tolerancia para casos imprevistos, de quince minutos una vez por semana, en el sentido de que el trabajador que llegue tarde, pero cuyo retraso no exceda de quince minutos, se le permitirá la entrada al trabajo siempre y cuando no se haya producido otro retraso en la misma semana. Cuando el trabajador durante la semana ya haya llegado con retraso una vez o cuando llegue después de*

transcurrido el término de tolerancia, la empresa podrá no permitirle la entrada al trabajo"

Pero el asunto de la puntualidad tiene una acotación adicional (que es un cambio fundamental respecto a la anterior regulación), el tiempo de la jornada discurre no a partir de que se ingresa a la fábrica, sino a partir de que con el uniforme de trabajo puesto se está presente en la estación de trabajo.

La cláusula 32 del CCT dice: "*Los trabajadores se cambiarán de ropa de trabajo en los vestidores* ***antes de iniciar sus labores y ya con la ropa de trabajo marcarán su tarjeta*** *o cualquier otro documento personal establecido por la Empresa u observarán cualquier sistema que la empresa señale como parte integrante del procedimiento para el control de la puntualidad y asistencia, a fin de que puedan estar a la hora en punto en su lugar individual de trabajo"*

Dados estos textos del CCT, existe otro conjunto de normas para otorgar "estímulos" a los trabajadores con récord de asistencia perfectos o cercanos a esto. Si bien es cierto que la existencia de los "premios" mensuales y anuales datan desde antes de agosto de 1992, lo característico ahora es que los premios se otorgan a trabajadores puntuales y sin ningún tipo de ausencias al trabajo, esto último significa que quedan fuera de los premios aquellos trabajadores que tuvieran incluso faltas justificadas. Dice el CCT:

"Los trabajadores que en cada mes de calendario no tengan más de dos retrasos, cada uno de ellos no superior a quince minutos, y además no tengan ni una falta de asistencia, ***justificada o injustificada****, recibirán un premio equivalente a un día de salario tabulado. El premio les será entregado el segundo viernes del siguiente mes.Para los efectos de esta cláusula, se consideran falta de asistencia, la ausencia del trabajador por todo un día de trabajo"* (Cláusula 33 del CCT)

"A aquellos trabajadores que en el período de un año, comprendido del 1o de septiembre al 31 de agosto del año siguiente, ***hayan ganado 10 de los premios mensuales*** *a que se refiere la cláusula inmediata anterior, la Empresa les cubrirá, en el curso de la segunda semana del mes de octubre de cada año,* ***un premio adicional anual equivalente a treinta y dos días de salario tabulado****, pagado con el salario vigente a la fecha de pago.*

"A aquellos que hayan ganado ***once premios mensuales, el premio anual será equivalente a treinta y cuatro días de salario tabulado vigente y para los trabajadores que hayan ganado doce premios mensuales,***

el premio anual será equivalente a treinta y ocho días de salario tabulado vigente. *Todos estos premios pagados en el mismo período*"(Cláusula 34 del CCT, énfasis nuestros).

Esta normatividad ha sido motivo de sistemáticas campañas de difusión de parte de la empresa para recordar a los trabajadores "lo que les cuesta faltar". En los últimos meses la gerencia ha publicado un texto "recordatorio" sobre el tema, que es batante ilustrativo de lo que aquí decimos y por ello a continuación los reproducimos:

EN LA CUERDA FLOJA[7]...

LO QUE TE CUESTA FALTAR

- PERDER EL SALARIO DEL DIA CON LA PARTE PROPORCIONAL DEL 6o Y 7o DIA.
- PERDER EL PREMIO MENSUAL (1 DIA DE SALARIO)
- POSIBLE PÉRDIDA DEL PREMIO ANUAL SI NO COMPLETAS LOS 10 PREMIOS MENSUALES (32,34 O 38 DÍAS)
- PERDER UN DIA DE AGUINALDO POR CADA FALTA
- TU PARTICIPACION EN EL REPARTO DE UTILIDADES SE VE REDUCIDA PROPORCIONALMENTE A TUS FALTAS
- PERDER LA OPORTUNIDAD DE ASCENDER CADA NUEVE MESES
- PERDER EL TRABAJO SI TIENES MÁS DE TRES FALTAS EN 30 DÍAS

CUIDA TU ECONOMÍA
NO FALTES CUIDA TU EMPLEO
VW RELACIONES LABORALES

Dentro de este conjunto de reglas y el celo de la empresa para aplicarlas resulta bastante explicable porque la fracción de tiempo que implica el traslado a la fábrica se vuelve un asunto de la mayor importancia, cada uno de los trabajadores de VW necesita obtener el premio mensual y de ser posible la prima anual de los 38 días tabulados.

[7] Nuestra reproducción del afiche de la oficina de Relaciones Laborales de VW, es textual, sólo falta una ilustración que va entre las leyendas finales signada con la palabra ausentismo y un obrero caricaturizado perdiendo el equilibrio sobre la cuerda.

Cuadro 1

VW de México. Accidentes en trayecto al Trabajo

1993

Áreas del Cuerpo	Ene	Feb	Mar	Jul	Ago	Sep	Oct	Nov	Dic	Totales en áreas	Por Distrib. %
Lesiones de Manos	4	2	2	3	4	5	3	6	0	29	13.0
Policontundidos	3	5	3	6	6	3	0	4	4	34	15.2
Contusiones Lumbo-Sacras	0	1	2	2	1	0	2	1	2	11	4.9
Lumbalgias de Esfuerzo.	0	0	0	1	0	3	1	0	0	5	2.2
Esguinces de Tobillo	1	3	6	3	7	4	2	4	2	32	14.3
Lesiones en Rodillas	3	1	1	1	6	3	1	4	4	24	10.8
Lesión en Muslos y Piernas	0	2	0	1	1	1	3	4	0	12	5.4
Lesiones en los Pies	1	5	1	1	4	7	2	5	4	30	13.5
Lesiones de Brazos y Antebrazos	0	1	1	0	0	1	1	0	2	6	2.7
Lesiones de Hombros	1	1	0	0	0	0	1	0	1	4	1.8
Lesiones de Cabeza	1	2	0	4	3	2	0	1	1	14	6.3
Lesiones en los Ojos	0	0	1	0	0	0	0	1	0	2	0.9
Esguince de Cuello	0	1	0	2	0	0	0	0	2	5	2.2
Contusiones Cadera	0	0	0	0	0	0	0	0	0	0	0.0
Contusión de Tórax	0	0	0	0	0	0	0	0	0	0	0.0
Quemaduras	0	0	0	0	0	0	0	0	0	0	0.0
Varias	0	2	1	0	0	4	3	0	2	12	5.4
Datos Incompletos	0	0	0	1	2	0	0	0	0	3	1.3
Total por mes	**14**	**26**	**18**	**25**	**34**	**33**	**19**	**30**	**24**	223	100.0

Elaborado con base en: VW de México. Forma MT1. 1993

Cuadro 2
VW de México. Accidentes en trayecto al Trabajo
1994

Áreas del Cuerpo	Jul.	Ago.	Sep.	Oct.	Nov.	Dic	Totales en áreas	Por Distri. %
Lesiones de Manos	0	5	3	3	5	4	20	11.4
Policontundidos	6	9	10	10	5	8	48	27.4
Contusiones Lumbo-Sacras	3	0	3	1	2	1	10	5.7
Lumbalgias de Esfuerzo.	0	1	1	2	0	0	4	2.3
Esguinces de Tobillo	0	7	4	1	1	1	14	8.0
Lesiones en Rodillas	1	5	2	3	4	2	17	9.7
Lesión en Muslos y Piernas	0	1	0	0	2	1	4	2.3
Lesiones en los Pies	3	6	12	1	4	4	30	17.1
Lesiones de Brazos y Antebrazos	0	4	0	2	2	0	8	4.6
Lesiones de Hombros	2	0	1	1	1	2	7	4.0
Lesiones de Cabeza	1	1	1	0	0	0	3	1.7
Lesiones en los Ojos	0	0	0	1	0	0	1	0.6
Esguince de Cuello	0	0	0	1	0	0	1	0.6
Contusiones Cadera	0	0	0	0	0	0	0	0.0
Contusión de Tórax	0	2	0	0	0	0	2	1.1
Quemaduras	0	0	0	0	0	0	0	0.0
Varias	1	0	1	2	2	0	6	3.4
Datos Incompletos	0	0	0	0	0	0	0	0.0
Total por mes	17	41	38	28	28	23	175	100.0

Elaborado con base en: Volswagen de México. Forma MT1. 1994.

Accidentes de Trabajo en Fábrica

En nuestra muestra de análisis los accidentes de trabajo en fábrica representaron el 54.1% y el 57.6% (cuadros 3 y 4). Si dentro de esto consideramos el tipo de accidentes ocurridos y las partes del cuerpo que han sido afectadas con mayor frecuencia, tenemos que la incidencia es más recurrente en: "Lesiones de manos" (ocupando en los dos años más de un tercio del total de accidentes ocurridos en fábrica), "Lumbalgias de esfuerzo" (con más del 10% del total), "Lesiones en los ojos", "Lesiones en los pies", "Policontundidos" y "Contusiones Lumbo-Sacras".

Para los nueve meses analizados correspondientes al año 1993, se registraron 263 accidentes y para los seis meses de 1994, 238; lo que significa que el promedio mensual de accidentes en el primer año fue de 29.2 y de 39.6 en 1994.

La relación entre accidentes y cargas de trabajo-materia de trabajo, no es fácil de ubicar dado el tamaño de la fábrica y lo incompleto de la estadística. En esta relación intervienen muchos factores, la mayor parte de ellos asociados al desgaste físico y mental de una jornada ordinaria, a los diversos niveles de esfuerzo aplicado en las diversas áreas de trabajo, a los factores de riesgo mayor en áreas con mucha intervención de manos (fundición, soldadura, ensamble), las presiones diarias de la gerencia para obtener la producción, la competencia que se genera a nivel de equipos de trabajo, etc.

Sin embargo, dentro de las limitaciones que nos impone la información primaria y a partir de una revisión cuidadosa tanto de la evolución del número de accidentes, de perfiles con más recurrencia y de las constataciones de caso directas, todo nos indica que si por una parte el número de accidentes a aumentado con relación a los años 80' (cuando menos a los años de los que pudimos obtener registros confiables) a pesar de que en los años 90' el número de trabajadores es menor; por otra parte, encontramos que las nuevas regulaciones contractuales pueden tener una incidencia directa en el aumento de la frecuencia de accidentes en tanto de una lado se han eliminado muchas prerrogativas sindicales vinculadas a las calificaciones de la intensidad del trabajo, la determinación de área peligrosa[8], los cambios de

[8] Por ejemplo, en las ediciones de CCT antes de agosto de 1992 había una cláusula (76) que decía: "si el trabajador estima que el equipo de seguridad lesiona o pone en peligro sus órganos o su salud, lo manifestará por escrito por escrito con los responsables del área". Esta cláusula (ahora la 65) suprimió esa frase que permitía evaluaciones sindicales sobre riesgos en el equipo de se seguridad y precisó las obligaciones del trabajador en la conservación del equipo.

horario, turno y materia de trabajo[9]; y porque también se presiona para que a lo largo de la jornada de trabajo la prioridad sean la eficiencia y la calidad de la producción[10].

Cuadro 3
VW de México. Accidentes de Trabajo en Fábrica
1993

Áreas del Cuerpo	Ene	Feb	Mar	Jul	Ago	Sep	Oct	Nov	Dic	Totales por área	Por Distri. %
Lesiones de Manos	8	11	8	7	12	17	16	10	8	97	36.9
Policontundidos	2	1	0	0	2	1	5	0	2	13	4.9
Contusiones Lumbo-Sacras	1	2	2	1	0	0	1	1	3	11	4.2
Lumbalgias de Esfuerzo.	1	0	3	2	2	5	10	2	3	28	10.6
Esguinces de Tobillo	1	2	2	3	1	2	1	1	1	14	5.3
Lesiones en Rodillas	0	2	3	0	2	1	0	0	2	10	3.8
Lesión en Muslos y Piernas	3	2	0	2	1	0	1	2	0	11	4.2
Lesiones en los Pies	1	2	0	0	3	6	0	0	2	14	5.3

---

[9] Puede leerse la cláusula 55 del CCT: "La Empresa queda facultada por necesidades de trabajo, para cambiar a los trabajadores transitoriamente de puesto, actividad, turno y lugar de trabajo. Estos cambios transitorios se sujetarán a las siguientes reglas: 1. Los cambios hasta por 15 días los podrá hacer la Empresa libremente . 2.- Los cambios transitorios de 16 a 45 días serán notificados por escrito al Representante Sindical en la última hora de la jornada. Por un lapso mayor deberán ser convenidos con el representante del Sindicato".

[10] La más clara de estas prioridades se encuentra en la cláusula 54 "De la Normas de Calidad": "Estando sujeta la producción a normas concretas y a bien definidos requisitos de calidad y seguridad, todo trabajador está obligado a cumplir rigurosamente las instrucciones que reciba de sus jefes, relativas al procedimiento que deba seguir para garantizar la calidad del trabajo y del producto, así como efectuar las operaciones y correcciones que se le ordenen durante el proceso, haciendo uso adecuado de los medios y registros de control que para este fin determine la empresa".

Lesiones de Brazos y Antebrazos	3	1	0	0	1	2	0	0	0	7	2.7
Lesiones de Hombros	0	1	0	1	1	0	1	1	2	7	2.7
Lesiones de Cabeza	2	2	1	1	0	1	0	0	1	8	3.0
Lesiones en los Ojos	3	1	2	1	2	2	2	1	1	15	5.7
Esguince de Cuello	0	1	0	0	0	1	0	0	0	2	0.8
Contusiones Cadera	0	0	0	0	0	0	0	0	0	0	0.0
Contusión de Tórax	0	1	2	1	1	1	2	1	4	13	4.9
Quemaduras	1	0	0	0	0	0	0	0	0	1	0.4
Varias	0	0	0	0	0	0	0	2	1	3	1.1
Datos Incompletos	1	0	1	1	1	2	1	0	2	9	3.4
Totales por mes	27	29	24	20	29	41	40	21	32	263	100.0

Elaborado con base en: Volswagen de México. Forma MT1 1993.

Aunque existen cláusulas que establecen la intervención de las instancias sindicales, por ejemplo, en la Comisión Mixta de Higiene y Seguridad, Exámenes Médicos en el IMSS, provisiones de equipos de seguridad (Cláusulas 63, 64 y 65), en la práctica estas funcionan como regulaciones administrativas que establecen procedimientos y niveles para solucionar controversias entre representantes del Sindicato y la empresa, recomendaciones para el buen uso de equipos de seguridad o enunciados para acudir a servicios IMSS.

Ahora, más que en los años setenta y ochenta, el carácter limitado que se asigna a la parte sindical en estos aspectos, ha impedido -dentro de la coyuntura de incrementos de la producción y de la productividad para unidades de exportación-, establecer medidas preventivas reales para evitar accidentes. En la mayor parte de las experiencias conocidas, hemos constatado que los intentos serios de abordar una política global de prevención ha chocado con la resistencia empresarial que remite el caso a verificaciones e inspecciones oficiales que han sido muchas veces verdaderos trámites.

Cuadro 4

VW de México. Accidentes de Trabajo en Fábrica

1994

Áreas del Cuerpo	Julio	Agos	Sep.	Oct.	Nov.	Dic.	Totales por área	Por Distri. %
Lesiones de Manos	8	22	14	15	13	10	82	34.5
Policontundidos	3	3	2	1	1	1	11	4.6
Contusiones Lumbo-Sacras	1	5	1	3	0	1	11	4.6
Lumbalgias de Esfuerzo.	0	10	6	5	6	6	33	13.9
Esguinces de Tobillo	1	3	1	1	0	1	7	2.9
Lesiones en Rodillas	2	3	1	3	1	0	10	4.2
Lesión en Muslos y Piernas	1	1	0	2	0	0	4	1.7
Lesiones en los Pies	0	3	1	1	7	5	17	7.1
Lesiones de Brazos y Antebrazos	1	1	0	3	0	0	5	2.1
Lesiones de Hombros	0	3	0	2	1	1	7	2.9
Lesiones de Cabeza	1	4	1	3	1	1	11	4.6
Lesiones en los Ojos	4	1	5	3	4	1	18	7.6
Esguince de Cuello	0	0	0	0	0	0	0	0.0
Contusiones Cadera	0	2	0	0	0	0	2	0.8
Contusión de Tórax	0	1	5	1	3	0	10	4.2
Quemaduras	0	1	0	0	0	0	1	0.4
Varias	0	1	0	0	0	3	4	1.7
Datos Incompletos	0	3	0	0	1	1	5	2.1
Totales por mes	**22**	**67**	**37**	**43**	**38**	**31**	238	100.0

Elaborado con base en: Volswagen de México. Forma MT1. 1994

De esta forma los accidentes en fábrica se presentan como una asociación cuasi obligada entre el desempeño eficiente y los costos en salud (un concentrado de los casos analizados puede verse en el cuadro 5).

Si ahora procedemos a un análisis integral de los accidentes de la muestra este nos revela lo siguiente.

En las lesiones de las manos que incluyen algunas de muñecas encontramos contusiones, heridas contusas, fracturas, quemaduras, amputaciones de dedos, de falanges y de manos, machacamiento de dedos, esguinces de dedos, manos y muñecas.

En los renglones de brazos y antebrazos, muslos y piernas encontramos: contusiones, heridas, fracturas, quemaduras.

En los pies: contusiones, esguinces, fracturas de ortejos, quemaduras por metal líquido, heridas.

En la cabeza se detectaron: traumatismo craneo-encefálicos, conmoción cerebral algunas veces con pérdida del estado de alerta, contusiones simples, heridas, fractura de nariz, quemadura por sosa caústica.

Las lesiones más frecuentes en los ojos fueron: contusiones y heridas en los párpados, cuerpos extraños, conjuntivitis por sustancias químicas y por luz de soldadura.

En varios: trauma acústico, hernias, etc.

En lo tocante a las rodillas tenemos heridas, contusiones y esguinces.

Cuadro 5

Volkswagen de México, SA. Accidentes de Trabajo. Resumen.

	1993 Núm.	Participación %		1994 Núm.	Participación %
En Tránsito	223	45.9	En Tránsito	175	42.4
En Fábrica	263	54.1	En Fábrica	238	57.6
Total para 1993 (9 meses)	486	100.0	Total para 1994 (6 meses)	413	100.0
Promedio por mes	54		Promedio por mes	68.8	

Fuente: Anverso de la forma MTI que la empresa VW de México, SA de CV reporta al IMSS.

Y finalmente, al margen de cuántos de estos accidentes de trabajo hayan sido legalizados por el Departamento de Medicina del Trabajo del IMSS, la revisión de los casi 900 casos de nuestros registros y los testimonios de trabajadores en consulta, mostraron las circunstancias que rodean estos riesgos sufridos por los obreros de esta planta automotriz.

En primer lugar sobresale la política delineada por la empresa hacia la minimización del registro de accidentes de trabajo. Para ello existe toda una mecánica que se inicia con la intervención del personal del Departamento de Seguridad Industrial, quienes "en caliente" valoran la gravedad del daño y si calculan que este no amerita atención especializada, tratan de convencer al accidentado de "tomarse unos días para componerse", desde luego, con su sueldo pagado, inclusive se le "sugiere" al trabajador "ver un médico particular" para su atención. Es célebre el comportamiento ligero de estos "evaluadores" en los casos de crisis nerviosas o golpes con traumatismos internos.

Entonces, el procedimiento empresarial para clasificar y calificar accidentes justo se inicia en el momento que los responsables del Departamento de Seguridad Industrial de la empresa se presentan en el área del accidente y califican la gravedad. Debe decirse que este personal puede tener algún entrenamiento paramédico pero en ningún caso son profesionales o especialistas. De esta manera sus auscultaciones y diagnósticos son superficiales, especialmente en los casos donde no observan "evidencias" de daños corporales.

El otro eje de esta política "de atención" es el papel del médico de la empresa cuya misión es paliar al máximo los daños producidos por el accidente en forma inmediata con analgésicos, antipiréticos, ácido acetilsalicílico, masajes, aplicación de ultrasonido y hasta cambios de puesto para que los turnos sean terminados y también, para evitar que por lesiones "pequeñas" los trabajadores acudan al IMSS a reportar sus accidentes.

Además, se busca que la presencia de este personal vaya "educando" a los obreros en el sentido de que primero está el médico de la empresa antes de que los del IMSS, puesto que es él quien autoriza los "permisos" para que los accidentados y los enfermos por otras causas puedan salir de la planta a buscar su atención médica.

Es muy común encontrar en los reportes de la forma MT1 el hecho de que un accidentado se reporte en primer lugar con el médico de la empresa y no busque su primera atención en los servicios médicos del IMSS. La presión para inhibir el mecanismo legal para el tratamiento del accidente es muy notorio en los casos de las Lumbalgias de Esfuerzo, para las que usual-mente el médico de la empresa solicita al Departamento de Medicina de Trabajo del IMSS "investigaciones para confirmar" pues para él es éste un caso que siempre le genera dudas respecto de su veracidad.

Dentro de esta calificación, es claro que no se consideran los casos de daños por esfuerzos repetitivos sobre un órgano o sistema, o de las situaciones en donde, por ejemplo, tratándose de columna, un esfuerzo aparentemente moderado puede ser el detonador que haga aparecer la suma de esfuerzos de muchos años.

Con todo, la empresa genera su propia estadística por intermedio de su Departamento que levanta accidentados, el Departamento de Seguridad Industrial. Cuando revisamos sus reportes sobre accidentes de trabajo (véase cuadro 6), encontramos que en 1993 registraron en un año, un total de 359 accidentes en fábrica (nosotros en nueve meses registramos 263). El promedio mensual en los dos casos es muy parecido: para nuestro procesamiento el dato es de 29.2 accidentes por mes y para Seguridad Industrial de VW es de 29.9.

Para 1994 obtuvimos una serie de cinco meses (Enero-Mayo) que al compararla con la nuestra (de seis meses) nos arroja para el primer caso 31.6 accidentes mensuales (158 casos) y para nuestros cálculos ese promedio es de 39.6.

Cuadro 6

Accidentes de Trabajo. 1993-1994

Fuente de Reporte	1993	Promedio mensual	1994	Promedio mensual
VW de México. Departamento de Seguridad Industrial.*	359	29.9	158	31.6
Juárez y González. Formas MT1**	263	29.2	238	39.6

* El número de accidentes para 1993 corresponde a 12 meses. El dato de 1994 corresponde 5 meses (Enero-Mayo)

** Los datos de 1993 corresponden a accidentes en fábrica para nueve meses y los de 1994 también en fábrica para seis meses.

Fuentes: Departamento de Seguridad Industrial. "Accidentes de Trabajo 1993-1994" y Formas MT1 procesadas en los cuadros 4 y 5.

CONCLUSIÓN

Nuestro estudio de caso muestra que los accidentes de trabajo en VW de M, aún considerando que nuestro período de estudio es corto, derivan en su mayor parte de la ausencia de una política real de prevención y que las normas de seguridad en el trabajo y los equipos de protección son muy débiles, tal y como la apreciación sindical lo califica..

En los años noventa, con el desarrollo de la producción de exportación, el desempeño cotidiano exige en muchos casos tareas polivalentes: producir, cuidar la calidad, mantener el equipo, limpiar, observar las curvas de rendimiento. Es muy probable que esto está detrás de la existencia de padecimientos nerviosos, que en los casos de su manifestación aguda no se les da la connotación de accidentes de trabajo. Por su parte los accidentes típicos tienden a diversificarse y los accidentes productos de esfuerzos repetitivos difícilmente son identificados.

En este contexto las regulaciones contractuales tienen un peso muy importante. Dentro del ambiente regional- nacional de desempleo, bajos salarios y pérdida de la capacidad adquisitiva salarial, conservar el trabajo y obtener dinero adicional vía primas de puntualidad y asistencia, o vía "desarrollo de salarios", son dos cosas fundamentales para los jefes de familia. El impacto de estas regulaciones sobre la productividad del trabajo es un hecho constatado[11], los planes del consorcio alemán para una plataforma de exportación al mercado estadounidense y canadiense se están desarrollando sobre esa base (modelos A4, Concept One), y al mismo tiempo, para nosotros, ha sido también bastante claro que la modernización tecnológica y organizacional no tiene como parte de sus prioridades la salud y la calidad de vida de los trabajadores mexicanos de esta gran corporación.

BIBLIOGRAFÍA

Banco Internacional de Reconstrucción y Fomento/Banco Mundial (1994)."Informe sobre el Desarrollo Mundial 1993. Invertir en Salud". Banco Mundial. Washington D.C.

Díaz, Alvaro (1994). "El Mercado de las ISAPRES en Chile". Salud y Cambio.

[11] Al respecto, puede consultarse nuestro estudios de caso en este libro.

García, Héctor (1996). "Economía y Salud". Trabajo y Democracia Hoy. Diciembre.

Instituto Mexicano del Seguro Social. "Nueva Ley del Seguro Social". 1996.

Laurell, Asa Cristina (1995). "El autodiagnóstico del IMSS: en el pecado lleva la penitencia". Trabajo y Democracia. No. 26. Julio-Agosto.

Ley Federal del Trabajo. Ed. 1990.

Luna, Jesús. García, Salvador (1997) "La Nueva Ley del Seguro Social y las Afore". Cuadernos de Trabajadores No. 15. Ed. CENPROS.

Mussot L., Ma. Luisa (coordinadora) (1996). "Alternativas de Reforma de la Seguridad Social". UAM-X. Fundación Friedrich Ebert Stiftung.

Juárez Núñez Huberto (1996). "Cambios en el Sistema de Seguridad Social. Escenarios para México". Tercer Foro: El Sindicalismo Ante la Nación.

Juárez Núñez, Huberto y Garduño, Arturo (1987). "Reconversión Industrial: Dos significados opuestos". Ed. UAP-STIASCVWM.

Ordenes, Jorge (1996). "El sistema previsional chileno". Revista Trabajo y Liberación.

Sapag Chain, Reinaldo (1995). "Evolución del Sistema Privado de Pensiones en Chile". IPCTT.

Villegas Rodríguez, Jorge. Noriega Elío, Mariano (1996). "Vida y salud de los trabajadores y sus familias en el neoliberalismo mexicano". Trabajo y Democracia Hoy. Octubre.

Volkwagen de México: "Contratos Colectivos de Trabajo". 1972-1998.

-Departamento de Seguridad Industrial. "Reportes sobre Accidentes de Trabajo". 1993-1994.

-Accidentes de Trabajo. Formas MT1 para el IMSS. 1993-1994.

LEAN PRODUCTION AND WORKPLACE HEALTH AND SAFETY

David Fairris[*]

INTRODUCTION

The workplace reform movement in the U.S. has made rapid progress in the past two decades. A 1992 survey of manufacturing establishments with over fifty workers found that roughly half of the surveyed plants had embarked on experiments with quality circles, work teams, job rotation, and total quality management techniques (Osterman 1994, 177). Employee involvement schemes such as quality circles (QCs) and work teams are being combined with programs such as total quality management (TQM) to improve product quality and eliminate production inefficiencies. Efforts such as these, which are based on Japanese management techniques and which solicit worker input to improve productive performance, are commonly referred to under the heading "lean production."[1]

The primary research focus of scholars who have studied the workplace reform movement in the U.S. has been the impact of employee involvement schemes and the new quality and quantity control measures on labor productivity (see the review by Ichniowski et al., 1996). Productivity improvements reduce unit labor costs and raise profits; they may also lead to greater employment security for workers and to enhanced wages and benefits. Productivity enhancement is often seen as a necessary ingredient in the struggle of U.S. enterprises to become and remain competitive internationally. America's fixation on productivity is also arguably related to the alarm over the productivity slowdown which emerged during the late 1960s and early 1970s.

---

[*] Associate Professor of Economics, University of California Riverside.

[1] The lean production model is not the only one currently being implemented at American workplaces, but Appelbaum and Batt's (1994) exhaustive survey of the state of the workplace transformation movement leaves little doubt that it is the dominant approach.

However, productivity and its rate of growth over time are not uncontroversial measures of social welfare. Productivity enhancement may be brought about by practices that worsen worker welfare —for example, speed ups in production and reduced levels of health and safety. Indeed, amidst the wealth of research activity suggesting that moderate productivity improvements emanate from transformed work places, there has been very little energy devoted to exploring the impact of lean production techniques on the working conditions of America's workers.

Case study evidence, much of it from Japanese transplants in the U.S. auto industry, suggests that this inattention to the impact of workplace transformation on working conditions is unwarranted. Lean production plants appear to demand a higher level of work intensity from workers than other untransformed or less-transformed plants. Fucini and Fucini (1990, 37) note that most Japanese auto transplants attempt to run as close to 60 seconds of work per minute as possible —presumably the explanation for why they are able to assemble vehicles with an average of 21.2 hours of labor compared to 25.1 hours for Big Three auto plants (Womack et al. 1990, 92). Babson's survey of workers at the Mazda plant in Flat Rock, Michigan, revealed that three-quarters of the surveyed workforce felt that their work pace was so intense that they would be either injured or worn out before they reached retirement (Babson 1993, 13).

Pushing people to produce may result in worsened workplace health and safety. Berggren, Bjorkman, and Hollander (1991) visited a number of Japanese transplants in the U.S. and found growing health and safety complaints related to the intense pace, repetitive job tasks, and long hours. At Mazda they found extremely high levels of repetitive strain injuries and an injury rate three times the level of other U.S. auto plants (Berggren, Bjorkman, and Hollander 1991, 55).

Wokutch's (1992) case study of health and safety at another Japanese auto transplant utilizing various features of the lean production approach yielded similar findings. In 1988, the injury and illness frequency (44.4 per 200,000 hours worked) was 91 percent higher than the rate for the industry, and 66 percent higher than the rate for auto plants similar to this one, employing at least 1,000 workers (Wokutch 1992, 192). Strains, sprains, and cumulative trauma disorders (CTDs) —which can be attributed to the stress of the production system— accounted for a large share (almost 50 percent) of the reported injuries and illnesses in the plant for 1988 (Wokutch 1992, 195). For CTDs alone, the rate was roughly five times as high as the rate for comparably large auto plants in the industry (Wokutch 1992, 195).

Lest it be thought that these problems are confined to wholly owned Japanese transplants, consider the recent experience at NUMMI, the highly-touted joint venture between GM and Toyota based in Freemont, California, which utilizes a lean production work organization. Following the 1993 model change, there was a 12 percent increase in worker absences due to health and safety problems. The apparent cause was the prescribed time standards for job tasks under the new model. Although injuries began to increase long before the new standards were met, management failed to respond to the problem and continued with its plan to increase line speeds in order to meet prescribed standards. Cal-OSHA was finally summoned to the plant, resulting in a citation which concluded "serious employee injuries due to repetitive stress, as well as employee symptoms of impending stress injury increased alarmingly" following the model changeover (quoted in Levine 1995, 33).

In the present paper I explore the association between workplace transformation and worker health and safety across a broad range of manufacturing industries. Utilizing a recent survey of manufacturing establishments with information on the extent and amount of experience with transformed workplace practices, in combination with industry-level data on injury and CTD rates over the late 1980s and early 1990s, this study offers the only statistical findings yet available on the association between lean production and workplace health and safety. While, contrary to the findings of recent case studies, I find no evidence that lean production plants are more prone to increased rates of CTDs, injury rates do appear to have increased more rapidly over this period in lean production settings, and specifically where TQM techniques are employed intensively.

DATA

The Organization of Work in American Business Survey was conducted in 1992 among employers with more than fifty employees in an attempt to measure the extent of workplace reform efforts in the U.S. (see Osterman 1994). Among other things, establishments were asked questions about those workers composing the core occupational work group in the plant, and the extent to which this group was involved in practices such as work teams, QCs, and TQM techniques at the time of the survey. From the survey I extracted for analysis those manufacturing establishments whose core work groups are blue-collar occupations. Using each establishment's reported 3 digit SIC industry code, the average annual change in injury rates and CTD rates between 1986 and 1991 for the industry in which each establishment resides was computed and imported into the data set. The year 1986 was chosen as the starting date for computing rates of change in workplace health and safety because this was the year that the average establishment in the survey had introduced quality circles among its core work group.

The data are far from ideal. The extent of experimentation with workplace reform among the core work group of an establishment at a particular point in time fails to capture important information about both the pervasiveness of the reform movement among the larger plant work force and the years of experience the work force has had with the new organizational approaches to production.[2] We take some comfort in the fact that workplace reform appears to spread rather slowly through any experimenting plant (Appelbaum and Batt, 1994), and so there is likely to be a fair degree of correlation between these various measures of the intensity of experimentation.[3]

A second major concern with the data is that proxying establishment level injury and CTD rates by the industry rates in which establishments reside introduces considerable measurement error into the analysis. This presents no particular econometric problem because both injuries and CTDs appear as dependent variables in the analysis, but the integrity of the results is undeniably compromised by this procedure. Unfortunately, it is the best we can do given the health and safety data that are currently available.

In addition to specific measures of the extent of workplace transformation, the Organization of Work in American Business Survey contains information on a variety of establishment characteristics that are used as control variables in the statistical analysis. The full set of variables, their definitions, and sample means appear in Table 1. Restricting the analysis to the manufacturing/blue-collar sample left us with 295 observations.[4]

---

[2] While the survey contains information on the number of years each establishment has experimented with particular workplace reforms, there is no information on the extent of such experimentation in any but the survey year. We make use of the "years of experience" information in results reported in footnote three below.

[3] For example, roughly a third of the establishments in our sample report having had no experience with workplace reform in the form of QCs; another third report having had some experience, but four years or less; and the remainder report having had QCs in place for more than four years. The simple correlation between years experience with QCs and the extent of QC participation among the core work group in the survey year is significant at the .01 level, independent of whether or not the "no experience" group is present in the analysis.

[4] Because of differences in the availability of reported data on injuries and CTDs, the sample for the analysis of injury rates differs very slightly from the sample used to analyze CTDs. It is only by chance that the number of observations is the same for both samples. The means and stan-

The average annual injury rate increase between 1986 and 1991 was 4 percent for this sample of establishments, a trend which is consistent with that of the manufacturing sector as a whole (Smith 1992, 560). The rate of CTDs has grown dramatically in recent years in manufacturing —quadrupling, for example, between the years 1986 and 1991. For our sample of establishments, the annual average rate of change in CTDs over this period was 65 percent. While CTDs are fast becoming a major health concern, they affect a much smaller percentage of the manufacturing labor force than do injuries. For the period 1986-91, the average yearly lost workday injury rate was roughly fifty workers out of a thousand. By contrast, CTDs affected roughly six workers out of a thousand, little more than one-tenth the injury rate.

RESULTS

The results of an ordinary least squares regression of injury rate changes on various features of the lean production model of workplace reform are contained in column (1) of Table 2. The results suggest that lean production has contributed significantly to the worsening of workplace safety in manufacturing over the period of the late 1980s and early 1990s. While three of the four lean production variables —namely, quality circles, teams, and job rotation— are not statistically associated with injury rate movements during these years, the extent of experimentation with TQM is significantly related to rising injury rates. Roughly 10 percent of the average rise in injury rates over this period can be accounted for by the spread of TQM.

It is not surprising that, of all the aspects of the lean production model, TQM is the one most significantly related to increased workplace injuries. Whereas quality circles and teams are purported to be attempts at increasing worker participation, TQM focuses almost exclusively on process changes such as the elimination of wasted time and motion, increased throughput (i.e., speed), simplification of tasks, and reduced cycle times. It is a top-down, management approach to production reminiscent of the Taylorist principles of scientific management which were introduced into U.S. manufacturing during the early 20th century (Appelbaum and Batt 1994, 88-91).

---

dard deviations reported in Table 1 are for the injury rate sample. Rounded to the nearest whole number, however, the independent variable means for the two samples are virtually identical.

Table 1
Variable Definitions and Descriptive Statistics

	Definition of Variables	Mean (Standard Deviation)
Injuries	The average annual change in the lost-workday injury rate (injuries per 100 workers) from 1986 to 1991.	3.93 (4.93)
CTDs	The average annual change in the cumulative trauma disorders rate (CTDs per 10,000 workers), 1986-1991.	65.50 (54.01)
QC	The percentage of the establishment's core work group involved in quality circles.	37.80 (39.27)
Teams	The percentage of the establishment's core work group involved in self-directed work teams.	30.04 (39.08)
TQM	The percentage of the establishment's core work group involved in total quality management.	41.96 (44.80)
Rotation	The percentage of the establishment's core work group involved in job rotation.	31.99 (38.03)
Skill Change	A dichotomous variable equaling one if the establishment reported that skills involved in doing the jobs of the core work group had changed in the past few years, and zero otherwise.	.64 (.48)
Plant Size	The number of employees at the establishment.	1862 (3301)
% Union	The percentage of the establishment's eligible blue-collar workers covered by collective bargaining agreements.	50.46 (48.53)
% Female	The percentage of the plant workforce that is female.	32.44 (28.52)
% Blue Collar	The percentage of the plant workforce composed of blue-collar workers.	64.52 (23.00)
Years Experience	The number of years that the establishment has possessed quality circles.	4.20 (4.40)

Looking at the other control variables, we see that injuries increased more rapidly over the period in establishments where the blue-collar percentage of the workforce was the greatest; where the percentage of the workforce was male; where the plant size was large; and where the skills of the core work group underwent significant change over the period. The first two results are not very surprising. The last two results are interesting enough to warrant some discussion.

There are two aspects to the plant size result that bear noting. First, recall that no establishment in the sample contains fewer than fifty workers. Thus, the experiences of the smallest manufacturing plants, which have grown disproportionately in recent years and among which there are a significant number of health and safety offenders, are not represented in our results.

Second, the results of the quadratic specification suggest that the largest plants in the sample underwent less deterioration in safety, and indeed that the very largest plants witnessed safety improvements. Very large plants are more likely than small and medium size plants to have their workers' compensation insurance premiums reflect past safety experience, which may offer an added incentive for these establishments to monitor closely their health and safety performance.

The positive and statistically significant relationship between changing skills and injuries is arguably the most surprising of these results. Changing skills in the workplace account for, on average, roughly twenty percent of the average annual rise in workplace injury rates over this period. The development of new skills on the job may lead to increased workplace injuries in the short run as workers adjust to their new job tasks.[5] Once greater confidence and familiarity are attained, however, the impact of changing skills on injuries ultimately rests on the degree of danger inherent in the new production processes. It is impossible to say whether this finding represents short-run or long-run effects. Interestingly, however, there is little correlation between changing skills and our various measures of lean production workplace reform.

Table 2
Estimated Coefficients (Standard Errors) from Health and Safety Regressions

Independent Variables	(1) Injuries	(2) CTDs
Constant	-1.27	34.93*
	(1.06)	(11.91)
QC	6.08 E-3	1.77 E-1**
	(8.04 E-3)	(9.22 E-2)
Teams	-7.20 E-3	-2.39 E-1*
	(7.64 E-3)	(8.78 E-2)
TQM	9.93 E-3**	-1.53 E-3
	(6.61 E-3)	(7.58 E-2)
Rotation	3.22 E-3	-3.56 E-3
	(7.23 E-3)	(8.33 E-2)
Skill Change	1.21**	6.27
	(0.56)	(6.43)

[5] Milkman (1997, 152-53) cites the increased hazards associated with the introduction of robots at the GM-Linden plant in the mid-1980s.

Plant Size	6.84 E-4* (1.62 E-4)	6.79 E-3* (1.85 E-3)
Plant Size^2	-1.75 E-8* (6.24 E-9)	-1.59 E-7** (7.14 E-8)
% Union	6.61 E-3 (6.09 E-3)	-6.63 E-2 (6.94 E-2)
% Female	-1.78 E-2** (9.57 E-3)	-7.24 E-2 (1.08 E-1)
% Blue Collar	4.82 E-2* (1.20 E-2)	3.56 E-1* (1.34 E-1)
R^2	.19	.11
N	295	295

* indicates significance at the .01 level.

** indicates significance at the .05 level.

Injury rate data do not capture the strains and other health-related disorders increasingly associated with jobs that possess short cycle times and which require repetitive movements and a fast work pace. These "repetitive motion disorders" or "cumulative trauma disorders" as they are variously labeled have been growing rapidly in recent years. In column (2) of Table 2 we present the findings of the analysis of CTD growth over the period and its relationship with lean production techniques.[6] The results reveal that quality circles are positively associated with the growth of CTDs and that teams are negatively associated with CTD growth.

The negative association between the extent of team production and CTD growth runs counter to what one might expect given the existing case study evidence. However, the greatest freedom that work teams are granted is the self-determination of job assignments. To the extent CTDs are more likely to occur where workers engage in lengthy stays at very repetitive job tasks, teams can reduce the incidence of CTDs by rotating workers through the various job tasks performed by the work team. (The job rotation variable, which represents management's assessment of the extent of worker job rotation, will not capture job rotation that is initiated by teams unbeknownst to management.)

[6] These results are corrected for heteroscedasticity. Heteroscedasticity was not present in the injury rate results.

Another possible explanation, however, is that team settings provide a context within which workers are discouraged from reporting CTDs.[7] In team settings, the team is held collectively responsible for seeing to it that the work is completed. When a team member reports a debilitating repetitive motion disorder and, as a result, receives a restricted work status, an added burden is thereby placed on other team members. Injured workers, anticipating feelings of guilt or perhaps social ostracism by fellow team members, may therefore be reluctant to report such disabilities. Both Besser (1996) and Graham (forthcoming) have found some evidence for this dynamic in their analyses of production at Japanese auto transplants in the U.S.

Various explanations also may be offered for the positive association between quality circles and CTDs. Quality circles may diminish worker solidarity —as several critics have charged (e.g., Parker 1985) —thereby making it easier for management to increase work pace and shorten cycle times for jobs, which in turn may lead to increased rates of CTDs. This explanation seems consistent with the empirical findings relating QCs to enhanced labor productivity.

However, there exist other plausible explanations as well. The recent and very rapid growth in reported CTD rates probably reflects, at least in part, growing acceptance of prior-existing disorders as legitimate, and thus now recordable, workplace-related illnesses. If so, the growth rates in reported CTDs across industries may reflect differences in the perceived legitimacy of such disorders —owing perhaps to differences in the power of workers to influence the recording of injuries and illnesses or to differences in the progressivity of management thinking on this issue. In this case, the positive association between QCs and CTDs may be based on the greater likelihood of an accurate reporting of CTDs in settings where workers are given the opportunity to discuss issues related to the quality of work life.[8] Weighing against this explanation is the finding that CTD growth and teams —which offer somewhat similar opportunities for worker input as QCs— are negatively as opposed to positively related.

Another possible explanation for the positive association between QCs and CTD growth is one based on selection. (Note that this serves as an alternative explanation for the positive association between TQM and the growth

---

[7] Thanks are due to Laurie Graham for suggesting this interpretation.

[8] When a term capturing the interaction between QCs and percent union is added to the specification of the CTD equation, the interaction term is positive and significant at the .10 level, lending some support to this interpretation of the QC result.

in injury rates as well.) Suppose worsening workplace health and safety is a sign of problems in the process of production (including perhaps inadequate productivity) which management eventually comes to view as profitably addressed through QCs (or TQM techniques). In this case, workplace reform may result from worsening health and safety instead of being its cause.[9] Given this explanation, we might also expect to observe a negative association between QCs (TQM techniques) and labor productivity —something which is rarely found in the literature.

Looking briefly at the other results of the CTD analysis, we see that both establishment size and percent blue collar are positively and significantly related to CTD growth, just as they were in the injury rate analysis, and presumably for similar reasons. However, unlike in the case of injury rates, neither skill changes nor the percentage of the work force composed of females appears to have a significant bearing on the rate of growth of CTDs across industrial establishments. Cumulative trauma disorders have been rising across a variety of jobs, apparently independent of both the gender and the changing skills demanded of the workers who occupy them.

The results of our empirical analysis reveal that quality circles account for roughly ten percent of the average annual rise in CTD rates over this period, while teams reduce the growth rate in CTDs by roughly eleven percent. Overall, the workplace transformation movement thus has served to reduce the growth of CTDs on the order of about one percent. Work teams generally represent a further stage in the evolution of workplace reforms, typically following a period of experimentation with quality circles. These results suggest that the progression to team production is beneficial for workers.[10]

---

[9] However, when a similar analysis is conducted using a select sample of establishments whose experience with workplace reform dates back to before 1988, the estimated coefficients on the QC variable in the CTD equation and the TQM variable in the injury equation roughly double in size. This is at least suggestive evidence against the selection explanation.

[10] Among our sample of establishments, the number of years of experience with QCs is significantly and positively correlated with the existence of teams in production. Roughly a quarter of the sample possesses QCs but no work teams, whereas the opposite is true for less than ten percent of the sample. Suggestive evidence on the interaction between QCs and teams can be obtained by adding an interactive term to the CTD equation. When this is done, the estimated coefficient on the QC variable is positive and significant at the .01 level, and the coefficient on the interactive term is negative and significant at the .01 level. The bad effects of QCs appear to be significantly alleviated by the existence of teams in production.

CONCLUSIONS

The findings of this study suggest that lean production methods accounted for a ten percent rise in injury rates and a one percent decline in CTD rates over the period 1986 to 1991. Given the greater prominence of injuries in the overall numbers of health and safety problems in the workplace, these results suggest that lean production methods be viewed as having contributed to the worsening health and safety record of American manufacturing during the period of the late 1980s and early 1990s. In establishments where the movement towards work teams has been blocked by either union or management recalcitrance, leaving, for example, QCs and TQM techniques as the only components of workplace reform, workers appear to pay a huge price indeed in the form of worsened workplace health and safety.

This is the first study to offer empirical findings on the relationship between workplace transformation and workplace health and safety across a broad range of manufacturing industries. The results should provide researchers with the impetus to explore further the impact of the lean production model of workplace reform on working conditions. More light needs to be shed on the causal relationship between lean production and workplace accidents and illnesses. Better data on the extent of experimentation with lean production techniques, both over time and across the entire work force, would be enormously helpful, as would plant-level data on injuries and CTDs.

BIBLIOGRAPHY

Appelbaum, Eileen and Rosemary Batt. 1994. *The New American Workplace.* Ithaca: ILR Press.

Babson, Steve. 1993. "Lean or Mean: The MIT Model and Lean Production at Mazda." *Labor Studies Journal* (summer): 3-24.

Berggren, Christian, Torsten Bjorkman, and Ernst Hollander. 1991 *Are They Unbeatable? Report from a Field Trip to Study Transplants, the Japanese Owned Auto Plants in North America.* Stockholm: Royal Institute of Technology.

Besser, Terry L. 1996. *Team Toyota.* Buffalo: State University of New York Press.

Fucini, Joseph, and Suzy Fucini. 1990. *Working for the Japanese: Inside Mazda'a American Auto Plant.* New York: Free Press, Macmillan.

Graham, Laurie. Forthcoming. "Permanently Temporary: The Japanese Model and the Reproduction of Social Control." In Randy Hodson, ed., *Research in the Sociology of Work: The Globalization of Work.* Volume 7. JAI Press.

——. 1995. *On the Line at Subaru-Isuzu.* Ithaca: ILR Press.

Ichniowski, Casey, Thomas A. Kochan, David Levine, Craig Olson, and George Strauss. 1996. "What Works at Work: Overview and Assessment." *Industrial Relations* 35(3): 299-333.

Levine, David I. 1995. *Reinventing the Workplace.* Washington, D.C.: Brookings Institution.

Milkman, Ruth. 1997. *Farewell to the Factory.* Berkeley: University of California Press.

Osterman, Paul. 1994. "How Common is Workplace Transformation and How Can We Explain Who Adopts It?." *Industrial and Labor Relations Review* 47(2): 175-88.

Parker, Mike. 1985. *Inside the Circle: A Union Guide to OWL.* Detroit. Labor Notes/South End Press.

Smith, Robert. 1992. "Have OSHA and Workers' Compensation Made the Workplace Safer?." In David Lewin, Olivia S. Mitchell and Peter D. Sherer, eds., *Research Frontiers in Industrial Relations and Human Resources.* Madison: Industrial Relations Research Association.

Wokutch, Robert. 1990. *Worker Protection, Japanese Style.* Ithaca: ILR Press.

Womack, James, Daniel Jones, and Daniel Roos. 1990. *The Machine that Changed the World.* New York: Rawson/Macmillan.

WORKER HEALTH IN TWO AUTO ASSEMBLY PLANTS: A COMPARISON OF POLICY IN UNION VS. NONUNION ENVIRONMENTS

*Laurie Graham**

INTRODUCTION

Work related repetitive strain injuries (RSIs) such as carpal tunnel syndrome are a growing problem for workers in the United States. RSIs have emerged as the number one cause of occupational illness (Labor Research Association 1996a, 5), representing 62 percent of all workplace illnesses in 1995 (Bureau of National Affairs 1997a). RSIs have reached an especially critical level in the automobile industry as assembly line workers have come to account for two-thirds of all repetitive strain injuries and illnesses in this country (Patch 1997).

Because RSIs are not visible, workers are vulnerable to efforts by their employers to restrict benefits (Patch 1997). Employers and their insurers dispute most carpal tunnel claims despite the fact that the overwhelming majority of such claims are finally upheld. For example, researchers at Mount Sinai hospital found that insurers fought or did not respond to more than 80 percent of workers' compensation claims involving carpal tunnel syndrome, yet a judge later upheld 97.5 percent of those claims (Labor Research Association 1996a, 5). Workers also experience a delay in needed treatment. According to one study, an average of 414 days pass before a carpal tunnel claim is ruled on, and an average 226 days pass from the time a doctor requests treatment for a worker until it is authorized by a judge (Labor Research Association 1996a, 5). Additionally, because the extent of soft-tissue injuries cannot be quantified, workers fall prey to benefit cuts (Patch 1997). As the incidence of RSIs grows, compensation costs for employers are driven upwards by rising claims and insurance company profits, the latter increasing at an average annual rate of 7.9 percent between 1992 and 1995 (Labor Research Association 1996b).

---

* Associate Professor of Labor Studies, Indiana University, Kokomo.

It is well documented that lean production increases work intensity and heightens workers' fears of being injured at work (Parker and Slaughter, Robertson et al., Rinehart et al., Babson, Graham). Among Mazda workers surveyed at the company's Michigan assembly plant in 1990, 73 percent reported that "if the present level of work intensity continues I will likely be injured or worn out before I retire" (Babson 1996). At CAMI, the GM-Suzuki joint venture in Ontario, workers surveyed in 1990 and 1991 also reported mounting concerns about the intensity of work: in the latter year, 70 percent agreed with the statement that "working in teams is a way to get us to work harder" (up from 40 percent who agreed in 1990, when the plant began production), and 61 percent believed that CAMI wanted them to "work harder," not smarter (up from 39 percent the year before). (Robertson et al. 1993, 29, 35)

At the same time, the team structure in lean production plants has been found to encourage under-reporting of RSIs. In Japanese transplants, healthy workers often come to resent injured teammates because they have to pick up any slack caused by their injury-related work restrictions. At Subaru-Isuzu in Indiana, injured workers were accused by teammates of faking their injuries in order to get an easier job (Graham 1997).

At Toyota in Georgetown, Kentucky, a decrease in injury rates was attributed to an emerging pattern of under-reporting (Besser 1996). Several factors were involved. First, once a team member was put on restriction, he or she was refused any transfer out of that group. Second, company-team ideology acted as a disincentive for reporting injuries by stigmatizing such reports as a sign of nonconformity. Third, the nature of RSIs puts the burden of reporting squarely on the injured worker, as RSIs are not acute, visible injuries. Workers fear they will not be believed. They try to put off reporting and hide the injuries from others so they can transfer to a safer job before their injuries become apparent. In this way, they avoid both the social stigma of being on restriction and, hopefully, permanent disability (Besser 1996, 122).

Recent studies suggest that the presence of a union has a positive effect on workers' health and safety. For example, in their case study of injury rates during a recent model change at the GM-Toyota joint venture (NUMMI) in California, Adler et al. (1997) found that, unless prompted by union intervention, management did not sufficiently address ergonomic issues. Another study involving workers' compensation recipiency rates found that union members were substantially (60 percent) more likely to receive workers' compensation benefits for their work-related injuries and illnesses than were their nonunion counterparts (Hirsch et al. 1997, 233). Both these studies provide supportive evidence that union intervention is beneficial to workers. However, neither specifies the particular differences between a union approach and its nonunion counterpart in lean production.

This chapter attempts to unearth these differences through a comparison of two automotive final assembly plants. One is a nonunion Japanese transplant, the other is a unionized Big Three (General Motors, Ford, or Chrysler) assembly plant. The framework for comparing the two is the concept of "worker control." From this perspective, we examine what role worker empowerment plays in improving plant health and safety. Japanese auto transplants espouse a company philosophy of worker empowerment through involvement in a team structure (Womack et al.); conversely, unions provide a mechanism for worker empowerment through collective bargaining, grievance procedures, and worker solidarity.

METHODOLOGY

Data were collected through telephone interviews with workers from the Japanese transplant and the unionized plant. Supportive data from newspaper interviews, company and union publications, and conversations with state labor department and unemployment compensation representatives are used to specify the nature of each company's approach to health and safety.

Many similarities exist between these two plants. Both are located in a single midwestern state, they began production at new facilities during the 1980s, and each employed about 2,500 production workers during the spring of 1997, the time of this study. At both plants, assembly line production is organized around teams; quality circles function to improve the product and increase efficiency; and each plant has implemented some level of just-in-time inventory control and in-house worker training.

Both companies express concern over issues of health and safety. Each have some type of in-house medical program and an ergonomics or health and safety team. Additionally, the transplant boasts a "work hardening" program for injured workers to help them gradually increase their work hours when they return to their jobs.

More important than these similarities, however, are the differences in how the concept of worker control is operationalized in each plant's approach to health and safety. Based on these preliminary results, the transplant's approach can be described as one aimed at disempowering its workforce. The company has avoided the issue of RSIs by exploiting a more vulnerable, secondary workforce. In contrast, the unionized plant structurally empowers workers through a negotiated contract which includes the right to strike over issues of health and safety.

EXPLOITATION OF CONTINGENT WORKERS: A NONUNION TRANSPLANT'S APPROACH TO CONTROL

In order to protect its core workforce from injuries which have the potential of undermining worker loyalty to the company, the transplant employs a large contingent workforce contracted through a temporary agency. According to one group leader (the equivalent of a foreman), the proportion of contingent workers (referred to here as "temps") to core employees tends to be fairly constant over time. He provided the following figures: during March, 1996, there were 480 temporary workers at the transplant, representing about 22 percent of the total workforce. Temps have worked at this transplant for years with little hope of becoming part of the core workforce (Graham 1997). Even more relevant to the case at hand is the evidence that temps end up in the least desirable and most injury-prone jobs. The following interview with a group leader suggests the ways in which temps play a vital role in lowering injuries among core workers:

> Q: I am interested in the experience of the temporaries. Do you know if temps were routinely put on the most dangerous jobs or jobs with the highest injury rates?
>
> A: (Group Leader) Temps definitely ended up in the less desirable jobs. This occurred because of the transfer policy. A [core worker] would transfer in if it was a better job before a temp could be called. So yes, they [temps] ended up in the jobs with higher injury rates.

According to the state labor department, if any temps are injured at the transplant, the temporary agency is responsible for workers' compensation and insurance costs, not the transplant.

Exploitation of contingent workers is not a new practice for Japanese automakers. During his research at Toyota in Japan, Kamata reported (1982, 67) that reinforcement and seasonal workers were usually assigned the hardest jobs. The company reportedly hired about 2,000 seasonal workers a year, with the vast majority not finishing their contracts (only 30 percent in Kamata's workshop [172]). Kamata attributed the high turnover to work intensity and injuries. The injury rate was proportionately much higher among new seasonal and reinforcement workers than regular workers (209).

In addition to ending up in injury-prone jobs due to the transfer system, temps are generally given little or no training and are put on the line at full line speed. This gives them no time to become "work hardened" so that their bodies might adjust to the fast pace of the assembly line. Many temps refuse to work under such conditions and simply walk away from the job, as described by this team member:

> Usually, if the work bothers their hands, or if they can't take the line speed pressure, there is a high turnover, they say "this is a bunch of crap." On our team, we've had them leave at lunch and at second break. One girl just walked out with the line moving. Two times temps left at lunch and didn't come back.

The following excerpt from an interview with a Group Leader supports the team member's observations. Many temps could not keep up the fast pace:

> I had two or three walk out while I was group leader. I went after them and talked them into coming back. Why did they leave? It was because of the line speed. But I hear a lot of stories from other group leaders about temps walking out. There was a very high turnover in temps.

Businesses hire temps for many reasons. One is lower hourly wages — about one-third lower than core employees in the transplant according to workers interviewed (Graham 1995, 64, 85-86). For a flat fee, temp agencies take on the job of filing the necessary paperwork for taxes, unemployment insurance, and on-the-job injury insurance for the temporary workers. Temp agencies also screen, test and check the backgrounds of applicants. During a recent newspaper interview, the Vice President of Human Resources at the transplant confirmed that temps are hired to protect core employees:

> Keeping such a large temporary presence is a part of the company's corporate culture. Auto plants in Japan use temporary workers as a tool to protect their core workers. (Hao 1997).

In Japan, contingent workers are used to promote the expectation of lifetime employment among core workers. Temps are regularly exploited to offset the rigidities of the permanent employment system by providing a "buffer" for regular workers from market uncertainties (Lincoln and Nakata 1997, 38). At Japanese auto transplants in the U.S. a similar pattern has emerged. For example, according to research by Kim (1995) at Nissan in Tennessee, American transplant workers believe they can count on "lifetime employment" despite the absence of any contractual obligation in this regard, and temps are used to maintain that belief. Continuation of such a myth is intimately connected with a worker's belief in his or her ability to stay healthy on the job.

WORKER EMPOWERMENT: A UNIONIZED PLANT

In auto assembly plants organized by the United Auto Workers (UAW), injured workers are protected by union contracts and jobs can be changed or adjusted through safety representatives chosen from the plant floor and trained by the union. The strategy is not only to protect workers from additional harm, but to enforce workplace safety —even if it means refusing to work. In the present plant, workers retain the right to strike over safety issues. In this way, workers' interests may take priority over company interests.

During the spring of 1997, workers at the unionized plant staged a two-week strike while negotiating their new local contract with the company. Strike issues focused on overwork and the inability to take time off —a central problem of lean production and a contributing cause of RSIs. Through their direct action, workers forced the company to create an additional 276 permanent jobs focused at gaining relief for workers and cutting back on job injuries. The settlement provides for periods of rest from injury-prone, repetitious jobs. A replacement worker is assigned to fill in for ten minutes of every continuous hour on designated jobs. Jobs are analyzed by the plant safety committee, which includes workers from the shopfloor. According to the union bargaining chairman of the local union:

> The purpose is to remove that worker from the operation for physical relief. The goal is to get the job fixed and hiring permanent people to fill in gives the company incentive to fix it.

The new jobs created under the local collective bargaining agreement included:

1. Replacement workers: 83 jobs to fill in for people requesting contractual time off, such as vacation time.
2. "Front loading" jobs: 10 jobs to speed up the transfer process so that workers who put in for a transfer to another area are able to do so faster.
3. Ergonomics replacements: 22 jobs to fill in for any job designated as injury-prone or having an injured person on it. A replacement worker will fill in ten minutes of every continuous hour on the job.

4. Trainers: 40 jobs to establish trainers for worker enrichment. The trainers will survey workers to see what training they want to receive. The worker decides and the company pays up to 32 hours of training that is not job specific to the plant.

Workers at the unionized plant also addressed a divisive issue within teams that indirectly pertains to health and safety. Previously, teams would meet and if one person felt he or she was doing too much work, then the team had the authority to decide to shift some of that work to another person on that team. While this provision sounds empowering on the surface, it actually disempowered workers by pitting them against each other. The local union took that language out of the contract. Now it is up to the company to shift work around and the union retains the right to file grievances in cases of overwork.

Temporary workers at the unionized plant are covered by the union and company's Master Agreement. Temps are generally used as summer vacation replacements. According to the UAW shop chairman:

> If they (temps) are needed for any purpose other than short-term use such as summer vacation replacements it must be agreed upon by the union and company. It requires the signature of the personnel director and the bargaining chair of the local and then it has to go to a national authority. After a certain period of time, if a temp is still on the payroll he becomes a union member and regular employee. The goal is to make everyone what we call "whole," or as equal as the rest of us as possible —the same protections.

CONCLUSION

When Milkman (1991) completed her exhaustive study of California's Japanese transplants, she cautioned that one should not underestimate the desire of transplant companies to remain nonunion. As we examine the role that unions can play in safeguarding worker health and safety through increasing worker control, a picture emerges as to why transplants desire their nonunion status.

In order to support a rhetoric of safety and trust, it has apparently become necessary for this lean production transplant to exploit the bodies of contingent workers. By assigning temporary workers to the worst jobs, core employees are made to feel less insecure about potential injuries which could lead to job loss. While core employees are protected from injury-prone jobs, the surrounding community is also made to feel more secure in its support of the plant and the tax incentives and other subsidies provided to the company. Overall injury rates for the transplant appear to be lower as injured temps are attributed to the injury rate of their employer, which in this case is the temporary agency, not the transplant. As the nonunion variant of lean production relies on the exploitation of temporary workers to protect core workers, it transfers the cost if its injured workers to society while also exploiting a vulnerable, contingent workforce.

The transplant creates a "socially constructed" injury rate to obscure the actual dangers that are present in its production system. Otherwise, the company would be vulnerable to an outwardly rippling wave of apprehension: individually, the worker's fear of injury would undermine loyalty and commitment to the company; organizationally, the collective apprehension of workers would undermine the process of work intensification that is central to lean production's success; socially, transplant workers re-entering the surrounding community with permanent disabilities would undermine the company's reputation and political support. The extensive use of temporaries protects the transplant from these potential outcomes.

To summarize, a policy that relies on temporary workers creates a false image of working conditions in a nonunion lean production plant. Hidden from scrutiny are the injurious results of speed-up and overwork. Core workers and community leaders are manipulated with the false impression that the transplant will provide workers with lifetime employment and that management truly puts the safety of workers first. On the other hand, the union and the company at the Big Three plant have created an environment where workers are empowered by the right to strike over safety and health issues during the life of the contract, and where such issues can therefore be addressed in a direct and forthright manner during negotiations. Through this bargaining structure, injury-prone jobs are not shifted to other more vulnerable workers, but are dealt with directly by measures —ergonomic improvements, additional staffing, relief time, and training— that confront lean production's agenda of continual work intensification.

BIBLIOGRAPHY

Adler, Paul, Barbara Goldoftas, and David Levine. 1997. "Ergonomics, Employee Involvement, and the Toyota Production System: A Case Study of NUMMI's 1993 Model Introduction." *Industrial and Labor Relations Review* 50 (April): 416-437.

Babson, Steve. 1996. "UAW, Lean Production, and Labor-Management Relations at Auto Alliance." In William Green and Ernest Yanarella, eds.,

North American Auto Unions in Crisis: Lean Production as Contested Terrain. Albany: State University of New York Press.

Besser, Terry. 1996. *Team Toyota: Transplanting the Toyota Culture to the Camry Plant in Kentucky.* Albany: State University of New York Press.

Bureau of National Affairs. 1997a. "Union Labor Report" 51 (3 April).

——. 1997b. "Union Labor Report" 50 (12 December).

Graham, Laurie. 1997. "Permanently Temporary: The Japanese Model and the Reproduction of Social Control." In *Research in the Sociology of Work* 6: 129-147.

——. 1995. *On the Line at Subaru-Isuzu: The Japanese Model and the American Worker.* Ithaca: Cornell University Press.

——. 1993. "Inside a Japanese Transplant: A Critical Perspective." *Work and Occupations* 20 (May): 147-173.

Hao, Sean. 1997. "Temporarily in Work." *Journal and Courier* (Lafayette, Indiana), 8 February.

Hirsch, Barry, David Macpherson, and J. Michael Dumond. 1997. "Workers' Compensation Recipiency in Union and Nonunion Workplaces." *Industrial and Labor Relations Review* 50 (January): 213-236.

Kamata, Satoshi. 1982. *Japan in the Passing Lane.* New York: Routledge.

Kim, Choong Soon. 1995. *Japanese Industry in the American South.* New York: Routledge.

Labor Research Association. 1996a. "Workers' Comp and Carpal Tunnel." *Economic Notes* 64 (December): 5.

——. 1996b. "Workers' Comp Trends." *Trade Union Advisor* 9 (December): 5.

Lincoln, James, and Yoshifumi Nakata. 1997. "The Transformation of the Japanese Employment System: Nature, Depth, and Origins." *Work and Occupations* 24: 33-55.

Milkman, Ruth. 1991. *Japan's California Factories: Labor Relations and Economic Globalization.* Los Angeles: University of California, Institute of Industrial Relations.

Parker, Mike. 1985. *Inside the Circle: A Union Guide to QWL.* Boston: South End Press.

Parker, Mike, and Jane Slaughter. 1995. "Unions and Management by Stress." In Steve Babson, ed., *Lean Work: Empowerment and Exploitation in the Global Auto Industry.* Detroit: Wayne State University Press.

——. 1988. *Choosing Sides: Unions and the Team Concept.* Boston: South End Press.

Patch, Kimberly. 1997. "Workers De-Compensation: Benefits Evaporate for Repetitive Stress Sufferers." *Dollars and Sense* 209 (Jan.-Feb.).

Rinehart, James, David Robertson, Christopher Huxley, and the CAW Research Team on CAMI. 1996. "CAW, Worker Commitment, and Labor-Management Relations Under Lean Production at CAMI." In Green and Yanarella, *North American Auto Unions in Crisis.*

Robertson, David, James Rinehart, Christopher Huxley, Jeff Wareham, Herman Rosenfeld, Alan McGough, and Steve Benedict. 1993. *The CAMI Report: Lean Production in a Unionized Auto Plant.* Willowdale, Ontario: Canadian Auto Workers.

Womack, James, Daniel Jones, and Daniel Roos. 1990. *The Machine that Changed the World.* New York: Rawson Associates.

Parte VI
TLC Y SOLIDARIDAD A TRAVÉS DE LAS FRONTERAS

Parte VI
NAFTA AND CROSS-BORDER SOLIDARITY

BUILDING TRANSNATIONAL COORDINATIVE UNIONISM

Don Wells[*]

People in our plant are very upset about our jobs leaving. However, we know that it is the employer, not Mexican workers, who are creating the problem. We have an international problem and we need an international solution based on workers' solidarity. Sooner or later we will have to get to the point of joint collective bargaining that includes both the company's Canadian and Mexican workforce. That's the goal.

Ravinder Singh Grewal,
President, United Steelworkers of America Local 1090,
Custom Trim Ltd., auto parts plant in Waterloo, Ontario, Canada.[1]

Money has no heart, no soul, no conscience, no homeland.

Frank Stronach,
owner, Magna International,
international auto parts manufacturer.[2]

Capitalism is in business for profit, and wherever it is going to realize the most profit out of human blood, there it is going.

Mother Jones

INTRODUCTION

In the past, labour has faced a choice between internationalism and nationalism. Today, when global neoliberalism is attacking labour rights and weakening the welfare state, the choice is between internationalism and a new feudalism built around workers' loyalty to "their" firms. Thus employers are increasingly pressuring workers to engage in an ever-deepening competitiveness alliance with management. The rationale, in the context of lean production, is that only an active partnership between workers and managers

---

[*] Associate Professor, Labour Studies and Political Science, McMaster University.

[1] *Working Together: Labor Report on the Americas*, September-October 1997, 2.

[2] Quoted in Canadian Labour Congress Policy Statement, *The Jobs Crisis*, May 1994.

can generate sustained improvements in productivity. Many workers and union leaders regard such competitiveness alliances as soft tyrannies backed up by market forces over which they have little or no control. Often their greater fear is the harder tyranny of job loss. The threat of capital flight to low-wage, high-repression regimes, such as Mexico, shackles unions. Breaking these chains requires a new transnational coordinative unionism that combines participatory mobilization at the local union and community levels with strategic coordination at national and international levels. Such unionism is already emerging through growing transnational labour solidarity. In North America, unions are building this solidarity, particularly in the auto, steel, trucking, clothing, and telecommunications sectors and in parts of the public sector.[3]

BACKGROUND

Under pressure from neo-liberal trade policies and global competitiveness, workers and local unions in Canada and the U.S. are entering into increasingly elaborate productivity alliances with management (Wells 1997a). Spurred by continental economic integration since the 1980s, such productivity alliances have also increased in Mexico, most notably in the auto sector (de la Garza Toledo 1994; Arteaga Garcia 1994). These productivity alliances center on hybrid forms of lean production, marked by total quality management, teams, multi-tasking, flexible working hours, and a host of other efficiency/speedup innovations. Not coincidentally, these productivity partnerships are being imposed in a context of high unemployment and underemployment, deregulation and privatization, and massive attacks on labour rights and the welfare state. Increasingly, managers are linking these alliances, as well as wage and benefit concessions, to (usually vague) promises of improved job security. It is under these circumstances of labour market coercion that deepening labour-management productivity alliances are emerging as the heart of a new industrial relations of fragmented, decentralized corporate fiefdoms. Workers' dependency on "their" firms threatens to

---

[3] Research for this paper was partly funded by a research grant from the Labour Studies Program at McMaster University. For generously providing me with information and insights, I am grateful to Robin Alexander, Steve Babson, Peter Bakvis, Gerry Barr, Steve Benedict, Gary Cwitco, Alex Dagg, Barbara Eastman, Marty Glaberman, Sheila Katz, Annie Labaj, Judith Marshall, Benedicto Martinez, Robert O'Brien, Marta Ojeda, John Riojas, Jose Santos, Ali Shah, Sid Schniad, Mary Tong, Ken Traynor, Fern Valin, Ron Verzuh and Tony Wohlfarth.

become the atomized basis of a twenty-first century industrial-relations feudalism that has broad and disturbing implications for the future of democracy.

The significance of these labour-management alliances is perhaps most apparent when we look back to the late 1960s and early 1970s. Those were years of low unemployment combined with what the mass media dubbed "blue-collar blues" and "white-collar woes." Many workers, autoworkers especially, rejected much milder productivity alliances by carrying out wildcats, sabotage, concerted absenteeism and other direct action, frequently against their union leaders as well as managers. By contrast, today is an era of job fear —fear of being fired, of being laid off, of not making it to retirement, of falling into poverty and marginalization in a "new economy" of part-time, insecure, low-paid jobs, in neo-liberal societies that denigrate the "losers" in the global "competitiveness" game (Mishel 1997, Wells 1997b).

Little wonder that managers find it relatively easy to intensify work and maintain an iron discipline among those fortunate enough to have "real" (full-time, permanent, more-than-minimum-wage) jobs. Beyond big pools of excess labour at home lies an ocean of over a billion adults around the globe who are unemployed or seriously underemployed. Managers' power is also enhanced by growing wage inequality, increasing opportunities to move to places where labour is weak and cheap, and by a popular perception that firms can move at the hint of a union drive (Bronfenbrenner 1996). Management's power is also bolstered in Canada and the U.S. by the extraordinarily decentralized nature of the industrial relations systems. This fragmentation grows as bargaining units become smaller due to flexible technologies, downsizing and contracting out, and the rise of small-scale service sector organizations. Critical too is the increasing productive overcapacity in sector after sector. Before the new millennium arrives, the global auto industry, for example, is expected to be able to produce nearly 80 million vehicles for fewer than 60 million buyers.[4] It is under these circumstances that corporate power in Canada and the U.S., and around the globe, is more one-sided than at any time since the 1930s.

Thus it is that many union locals and workers enter into these productivity alliances. Many fear that if they do not do so they risk losing their jobs to competitors that are increasingly nonunion and located in low-wage, high-

---

[4] "The Coming Car Crash," *The Economist* (10 May 1997).

repression labour regimes. Yet many locals that have entered into such partnerships find themselves on an endless conveyor belt to more speedup, worsening health and safety, lower or stagnating wages, multi-tier workforces, contracting out, and a host of other wage and work concessions.

This is a truly bizarre world for workers. Multinational firms in northern countries are much less willing to share the benefits of increased labour productivity than they were in the aftermath of World War II, when labour was strong. Now employers are imposing on labour in northern, developed economies the authoritarian and hyper-exploitative industrial relations that they have been forcing on labour in the southern parts of the world. And yet protectionist, even xenophobic workers are expected to remain loyal to their rootless, denationalized, authoritarian management "partners." This is an ideology of one-sided cooperation that cannot hold.

Responding to these new, contradictory realities, some unions are already building part of a new foundation for a stronger, more democratic and transnationalist labour movement. This is visible in the new networks of unions and labour and community activists whose primary goal is to reduce the global labour inequalities which give transnational firms the leverage to whipsaw concessions and maintain discipline. These networks are taking advantage of new opportunities that management strategies are creating for labour. In particular, production that is increasingly fragile, due to just-in-time production and lean inventories, is vulnerable to local work stoppages that effect production on a transnational scale.[5] In order to take full advantage of these strategic openings, however, labour will need to rebuild itself by creating a new kind of unionism.

TRANSNATIONAL COORDINATIVE UNIONISM

Labour's best hope is a *coordinative unionism* which combines the mobilization capacity of the workplace and community with the scope of national and transnational strategies (Wells 1996). This model extends unionism horizontally while deepening its democratic roots through renewed mechanisms of class mobilization, communication, representation, and participation (Lynd 1997; Lynd and Lynd 1988; Glaberman 1980; Wells 1995a, 1995b). It includes

[5] A recent example is the 1996 General Motors strike in Dayton, Ohio, which quickly shut down GM production in both the U.S. and Canada. See Babson, this volume.

what Staughton Lynd (1992) calls "solidarity unionism." It means "rank and file" unionists continuously bargaining with managers over reorganization of the labour process, and using direct action tactics (e.g. work stoppages, collective absenteeism, etc.) as well as official strikes to build solidarity, participation and bargaining leverage. It means unionized workers helping unorganized workers to organize themselves. It means local labour bodies working with their communities to build local economies that are more democratically accountable.

To weaken corporate pressures for local unions to react to the immediate survival needs of "their" individual workplaces, high priority must also be given to the horizontal coordination of strategy among locals in the same sector, and among communities with the same employers. This coordination among unions, community groups and social movements is critical to building mass democratic power against global corporate rule.

Governments throughout the world are becoming increasingly neo-liberal. So, too, are the key corporate-dominated international organizations, including the World Trade Organization, the World Bank and the International Monetary Fund. These institutions, together with international trade and investment agreements such as the Canada-U.S. Free Trade Agreement, the North American Free Trade Agreement, and the Multilateral Agreement on Investment all have at their core the reduction of state capacity to regulate global capital. Since all these institutions lack public accountability, they cannot be an immediate strategic focus of labour internationalism. Borderless capital cannot be countervailed without borderless unionism.[6]

Following is a discussion of growing links between Canadian unions and labour in the U.S., Mexico, and elsewhere in the Americas.[7] These international labour links have the potential to help build a more democratic base from which to launch more state-centered (not state-dominated) strategies later on. In order for this to happen, transnational union links need to develop far beyond the fraternal tourism of labour elites that still characterizes much international labour solidarity. Transnational solidarity needs to be

---

[6] For a very helpful discussion of organizing steps toward a North American Auto Workers Network, see Moody and McGinn 1992, 51-58.

[7] Because of its Canadian focus, this paper neglects key U.S.-Mexico-centered developments such as the United Electrical Workers' Strategic Organizing Alliance with the independent Authentic Labour Front (FAT) in Mexico; the partnership between the Farm Labour Organizing Committee in Ohio and the Union of Agricultural Workers and Peasants in Mexico; and the solidarity work of the Union of Needletrades, Industrial and Textile Employees (UNITE!) in Mexico, the Caribbean and Central America.

based at the local level, and rank-and-file members need to be the core activists. Otherwise, local union leaders run the risk of attack by their own members as absentee leaders who put international solidarity junkets ahead of their members' concerns on the job. The longer term vision is that transnational labour links need to be the institutional foundation of new labour and popular alternatives to global corporate control. Transnational coordinative unionism needs to be a practical alternative to the fantasy that a core of highly skilled, highly paid workers in countries such as Canada and the U.S. can protect their jobs at the expense of super-exploited, sweated labour around the world (Wells 1997c).

TRINATIONAL AND HEMISPHERIC WORKS COUNCILS

Given the growing capacity of transnational firms in such sectors as auto, electrical appliances, and clothing, to whipsaw concessions from workers, an initial goal of coordinative unionism might be a *more democratic, collective-bargaining version* of the European Works Council. The European Union requires multinational firms to create European Works Councils where employers consult with employee representatives. Because this model is hierarchical and focused on consultation instead of collective bargaining, its use for the kind of coordinative unionism proposed here can only be transitional. More useful examples are the German model where unions control most employee representatives on the works councils, and the Swedish model, which is also based on strong unions (see Muller-Jentsch 1995, and Brulin 1995 respectively). While these have not been transformed into formal transnational models, they have influenced the formation of "voluntary" European Works Councils (Streeck and Vitols 1995).

Even these union-based councils will require reform. A recent study of twenty union-based councils concluded that all were limited in their ability to deal with managerial prerogatives, and that workers' representatives had more "voice" than "ear." The councils "more resemble international union committees for multinational companies than works councils proper" (Streeck and Vitals 1995, 261). The powerful German metalworkers' union and Volkswagen have built the most progressive model. In 1992, Volkswagen agreed to a Pan-European Works Council representing workers in Germany, Spain and Belgium, soon to be joined by representatives of Volkswagen's Skoda works in the Czech Republic (MacShane 1996, 57).

Although works councils have often been a paternalistic substitute for genuine unionism, Denis MacShane, former adviser to the International Metal

Workers Federation, contends that works councils and genuine, independent unions are not mutually exclusive.

> Much depends on whether they follow the German *Betriebsrat* model, which is a worker-only Works Council with rights to have representatives on the board of big companies, or the French *comité d'entreprise* format, which is a joint worker-management council open to employer manipulation. Also, the role of the unions is vital. Where they are sectarian and politically divided, and have low membership, as in France, the works council can drift off into independent existence. Where they are organized on a one-workplace, one-union system and under social democratic hegemony as in Germany or Austria, they reinforce the class consciousness of works council delegates by constant education and mobilization (MacShane 1996, 61).

Works councils can also be pre-union formations, according to prominent social scientists, Rogers and Streeck:

> While originally intended to be no more than consultative bodies, councils may be captured by workers seeking not just consultation on production matters, but a chance for articulating distributional interests different from the employer's. Councils may also be used by external forces, such as unions, as an entryway into the workplace, where they may insert themselves between employer and the workforce (Rogers and Streeck 1995, 16).

At a minimum, a progressive variant would require collective bargaining functions and would need to be based on elected worker representatives who were democratically accountable to their constituents. However, in the absence of other institutions that bring workers together from different subsidiaries of the same firm, the European models are a useful starting point.

In North America, where works councils have been central to corporate "union avoidance" strategies, transnational coordinative unionism could be built partly out of union structures that are already in place. A partial Canadian precedent is the Canadian Auto Workers Council where local union delegates meet from across the union. The CAW has separate councils for local delegates from each major automaker. Both the union-wide and company-wide councils provide a forum for communication among local and national leaders. However, they need to be based more on the active participation of members at the local and workplace level. This will require major changes in the nature of unionism in Canada and the United States.[8] In

[8] Reflecting the centralization of power in most unions after World War II (Wells 1995a, 1995b), most delegates to the councils are elected at local "general membership" meetings that are al-

Mexico, local unions created a now-defunct Solidarity Pact among three Ford plants, a General Motors plant, Nissan plant, Volkswagen plant and a Mexico-owned National Diesel (DINA) truck plant, to coordinate their responses to concession demands. This pact lost momentum when the Mexican government's Confederation of Mexican Workers (CTM) blocked support for Ford workers in the late 1980s (Middlebrook 1991, 284). Yet it provides a potentially valuable precedent, particularly now that Mexican workers are building more autonomous unions.

A hybrid of such union councils and the better European works councils could be the basis for a North American Automotive Federation (NAAF). Since the biggest competitive threat to low-wage countries usually comes from other low wage countries, the NAAF should later be expanded into a World Auto Federation that includes union representatives from the rest of Latin America, Africa, Oceania and Asia, as well as Europe. Such a transnational autoworkers' federation would be made up of locally elected delegates from unions in each country. Delegates representing workers from the same firms would be organized into international councils for each firm. Where feasible, these union councils could coordinate union relations with labour-management works councils for the same firms. This dual council model, a mix of union councils and works councils, would give unions more control over labour's agenda in works councils.

Reflecting national and union political realities, each union in the NAAF and in the works councils would be autonomous. Coordination would focus initially on minimalist common goals. As confidence builds, common agendas could broaden. Initial NAAF agendas would center primarily on non-wage issues such as union rights to organize and bargain collectively, workplace health and safety, hours of work, technological change, outsourcing, employment equity, work reorganization, training, workplace representation structures, grievance processes, etc. More progress can probably be made, at first, in reducing the unevenness of continental industrial relations in these areas rather than substantially reducing the wage and benefit chasm between Mexican autoworkers and autoworkers in the north. Beyond a certain point, wage and benefit improvements for Mexican workers expose the zero-sum job competition based on labour cost differentials that bedevils labour solidarity across the Rio Grande. A NAAF would need to accept the fact that lower wages in Mexico will mean that in a continentally managed system of trade, some jobs in Canada and the U.S. will be lost. However, differentials

---

most invariably poorly attended. This weakens the councils' capacity to mobilize and it reflects deeper relations of power within unions and between unions, employers and the state.

in labour costs should not be exaggerated by a state policy to keep wages artificially low or by an authoritarian politics which denies workers' rights to independent unions, free collective bargaining, legal due process, free elections and government accountability to the electorate. Moreover, northern job losses should be offset by active, state-initiated employment policies (Wells 1997b). Given such broader goals, a NAAF would necessarily be a highly politicized continental federation of social unionism.

AN EMERGING TRANSNATIONAL COORDINATIVE UNIONISM

At present, the principal Canadian mechanisms for transnational union solidarity are "international solidarity funds." Since 1985, five major unions in Canada have established such funds. With the exception of the Canadian Auto Workers' fund, which is paid for by company contributions, the other funds are based on payroll deductions of a cent an hour from each member. In each case, the funds are sponsored at the level of supportive local unions. If the funds meet certain criteria, these monies are matched with funds from Canada's foreign aid arm, the Canadian International Development Agency, thereby doubling the funds. Canada's main central labour body, the Canadian Labour Congress, and four unions with international solidarity funds, have set up a Labour International Development Committee. Over the next three years, the Committee will channel over five million dollars (Canadian) into strengthening North-South labour ties.

The Committee also creates a forum for union coordination at a time when relations among many unions are competitive. In the wake of President Bush's NAFTA proposal in 1990, auto unions in Canada, the U.S. and Mexico have held several meetings to discuss common interests. At a meeting in 1991, autoworkers from General Motors, Ford and Chrysler agreed to set up a North American committee to cooperate on a continental scale (Moody and McGinn 1992). Among other actions, the CAW and UAW locals have conducted corporate campaigns against GM, Ford and Honeywell for violating labour rights in Mexico (Alexander and Gilmore 1995). Through the North American Ford Workers' Solidarity Network (Carr 1996, 217), UAW locals and the CAW have supported Ford workers in Cuautitlan, Mexico, where thugs from the state-dominated labour federation killed a union activist in 1990 (Barry et al. 1994, 328-329). This support led Ford to demand that severance pay for fired Mexican unionists be contingent on ending the solidarity campaign (Barry et al. 1994, 340). A Trinational Observer Committee of unionists, lawyers and activists was unable to ensure democratic elections at Ford-Cuautitlan, but management rescinded the firing of union militants.[9]

Along with UNITE!, the United Electrical Workers, Teamsters, UAW, Steelworkers, and other unions, the CAW is actively supporting maquiladora workers in Mexico, Central America and the Caribbean.[10] In particular, the CAW has been linking workers from the same firms in Canada and Mexico (Canadian Labour Congress 1996, 80). In addition, the CAW is teaching a "women's activist program" to Mexican workers, and has delivered a health and training course to fourteen independent Mexican unions. This course, taught jointly by Canadian and Mexican instructors, was the first of its kind provided to Mexican unions by a Canadian union.[11] These activities, together with exchange of information concerning wages, benefits, working conditions and bargaining strategies,[12] are preconditions for continental collective bargaining in the auto industry.

Continental solidarity is also building in telecommunications. Canada's Communications, Energy and Paper Workers Union (CEP), together with its U.S. counterpart, the Communications Workers of America (CWA), and the CAW, coordinated transnational collective bargaining with Northern Telecom in 1989 (Pomeroy 1991, 93-94; Cohen 1991, 90-91). The CEP and CWA are coordinating transnational organizing activities. The CEP has also entered a mutual defense alliance with the CWA and the Mexican Telephone Workers' Union (Barry et al. 1994, 340). This alliance centers on top union leaders but there have also been meetings among local leaders from the three unions (Groff 1994, 10-11). Local links are facilitated by international telephone operators who speak English and Spanish as part of their jobs.[13] This alliance is limited, however, in particular by the business unionist character of the Mexican union and its support for NAFTA (Cook 1994, 150-151). Nevertheless, the links among telephone unions are broadening. In 1996 nine unions in North America met at the Second International Telecommunications Workers Conference in Tijuana, Mexico. These alliances parallel the Inter American Council of the Postal, Telegraph and Telephone (PTTI) International, a federation coordinating telecommunications unions in 115 countries.

---

[9] Interview, Jose Santos Martinez, Ford Workers Democratic Movement, 18 April 1997.

[10] Interview, Mary Tong, Support Committee for Maquiladora Workers, 20 April 1997.

[11] Interview, Annie Labaj, CAW National Office, 24 April 1997.

[12] Interview, Barbara Eastman, UAW Local 1292, 18 April 1997. The Transnationals Information Exchange, a European-based organization, has also played a key role in building union networks in the continental auto industry (Moody and McGinn 1992, 50-51).

[13] Interview, Gary Cwitco, Communications, Energy and Paperworkers Union, 24 April 1997.

Among other things, the PTTI is setting up a Northern Telecom Council of Unions.[14]

Continental labour solidarity is also being built in the transportation sector. In 1996 the Teamsters hosted a Trinational Truckers Summit to discuss common concerns about NAFTA provisions deregulating continental trucking.[15] In 1997 the Teamsters met with unions from eleven countries in Europe and North and South America representing workers at United Parcel Service. They agreed to create a UPS World Trade Union Council, which would, among other things:

*devise a Global Code of Corporate Conduct and Social Responsibility;
*establish an international network of union officials and stewards within UPS to exchange bargaining strategies on a continuous basis using the Internet, electronic mail, etc.;
*establish international labour standards in areas such as health and safety and human rights;
*pressure the company to set up works councils along the lines of the European Works Councils.[16]

In Canada, the Steelworkers have been most active in international projects involving "linkage visits" between local union activists from Canada and the south (Marshall 1997, 62). In Mexico they have been working closely with the independent Authentic Labour Front (FAT). Projects include a growing solidarity campaign with Mexican workers concerning health and safety and other issues at branch plants of Custom Trim, a Canadian auto parts manufacturer whose plants in Canada are organized by the Steelworkers.[17]

Canadian Steelworkers have initiated solidarity links with workers elsewhere in Latin America as well, including a growing link between Canadian and Chilean miners who work for the Canadian multinational, COMINCO. According to union sources, COMINCO managers have begun to take notice of the ongoing exchange visits and conference calls between the two unions. The Canadian local has been working with the Chilean local to build the latter's organizational capacity in areas such as collective bargaining, repre-

---

[14] In this case, international labour solidarity was not initiated as an alternative to enterprise unionism. Union leaders at Northern Telecom in Mexico asked their Canadian counterparts to team up with management to make Nortel more competitive (Marshall 1997, 59).

[15] Interview, John Riojas, Teamsters Union, 18 April 1997.

[16] *Convoy Dispatch*, March 1997, 5.

[17] Interview, Marta Ojeda, Coalition for Justice in the Maquiladoras, 18 April 1997.

sentation systems, grievance procedures, etc.[18] By pressuring COMINCO from Canada, the Steelworkers also helped fired Chilean workers get their jobs back. Similar ties are being built between miners at Placer Dome in Canada and Chile.

Another interesting example concerns the Gerdau Group, a Brazilian multinational corporation. Recently Gerdau bought two steel plants in Canada where the workers are represented by the Steelworkers. Partly because of strong ties with Europe, Brazilian unions have a works council at Gerdau. The Brazilian unionists have invited the Steelworkers to join their council, and even posed the possibility of helping the Steelworkers bargain with Gerdau.[19] This case is especially significant because it exemplifies *mutual* support among unions on a North-South basis, rather than one-way assistance to solve southern "problems."[20] The Steelworkers teach this two-way international solidarity in week-long courses for union activists (Marshall 1997, 61).

Recently, teachers unions in English-speaking Canada, Quebec, the U.S. and Mexico formed a coalition to, among other things, monitor the impact of NAFTA on public education (Canadian Labour Congress 1996, 81). The Ontario Secondary School Teachers Federation has also set up an international labour solidarity fund. All the major Canadian public sector unions and the postal workers have also built links with their U.S. and Mexican counterparts in opposition to the privatization of public services. Canada's largest public sector union, the Canadian Union of Public Employees, has an international solidarity fund and, among other links, has a partnership with municipal workers in Mexico City (Verzuh 1997, 24, 28).

Finally, in Quebec, the Confederation of National Unions (CSN) has a partnership with Mexico's progressive, independent union, the Authentic Labour Front (FAT), focused mainly on organizing and education.[21]

INTERNATIONAL TRADE SECRETARIATS

International Trade Secretariats (ITSs) are global federations of unions (affiliated to the International Confederation of Free Trade Unions) in the same

---

[18] Interviews with Judith Marshall, Fern Valin, and Gerry Barr, Canadian Steelworkers, 22 April 1997.

[19] Interview, Sheila Katz, Canadian Labour Congress, 25 April 1997.

[20] Interview, Gerry Barr, Canadian Steelworkers, 22 April 1997. In 1990 Brazilian unionists also helped the Service Employees International Union obtain a contract for janitors working for the International Service System, the largest cleaning contractor in the world (Frundt 1996, 397.

[21] Interview, Peter Bakvis, Confederation of National Unions (CSN), 23 April 1997.

sectors in different countries. They are an increasingly important component of transnational unionism. Most of the fourteen ITSs have few resources and are highly bureaucratic, but a few provide important help in setting up company councils and in union organizing. For example, the International Union of Food, Agricultural, Hotel, Restaurant, Catering, Tobacco and Allied Workers Associations have created company councils. Similarly, the International Metalworkers Federation has set up World Auto Councils to exchange information on working conditions and contracts at each of the major auto firms in order to present a more united front against corporate whipsawing. The Councils are campaigning to harmonize transnational contracts in areas such as union rights, work time, rest periods, wages, etc. Moreover, several ITSs have created data bases to track various operations and bargaining practices of multinational firms. These data bases have been used to help coordinate corporate campaigns (Herod 1997).

ORIT (the Inter-American Regional Workers Organization), an organization of unions affiliated to the International Confederation of Free Trade Unions, has underlined the importance of establishing cross-border agreements among unions negotiating with the same transnational firms in different countries (ICFTU/ORIT 1994, 11). ORIT, non-government organizations, and social movement activists have called for a "hemispheric social alliance to confront free trade" (International Centre for Human Rights and Democratic Development 1997, 4). ORIT and ITSs could become a major impetus for transnational bargaining against global whipsawing.

Codes of Corporate Conduct and Conventions of the International Labour Organization

In the absence of unions, campaigns to improve, extend and enforce corporate codes of conduct can lead to coordinative pre-bargaining. Or, as in Germany, where Daimler-Benz and Volkswagen granted the same union rights to South African workers as to German workers (MacShane 1996, 62-3), codes of conduct can reinforce collective bargaining. Campaigns to strengthen and enforce corporate codes of conduct tend to be more effective among apparel manufacturers who charge a premium to consumers who buy apparel as an identity symbol. These firms know their "labels" can be seriously tainted by negative images. As a Levi Strauss executive responsible for international sourcing explained, the firm is willing to pay more for better labour practices abroad that "maintain the brand image" (Compa and Darricarrere 1996, 187-8).

Thanks to international labour campaigns, Levi Strauss,[22] Reebok, Wal-Mart, Sears Roebuck, Home Depot, Timberland, J.C. Penney, Nike and Starbucks have all agreed to improve the enforcement of their codes of conduct. Policing of the codes has often been a travesty. For example, Levi Strauss, accused of using child labour, unsafe working conditions, and failing to pay workers, argued that it did not enforce its code to "avoid offending" its suppliers (Forcese 1997, 26). Even when enforced, many of these codes do not include the right to unionize and merely mandate suppliers to pay minimum local wages instead of a living wage. Usually the codes are intended to improve public relations rather than industrial relations.

Perhaps the biggest victory thus far has been the international GAP campaign. "Gapatistas" from unions and religious and community groups pressured the GAP to agree to *independent* monitoring of labour standards. Although the GAP Code is still not enforced adequately,[23] it can be used as a benchmark for labour standards elsewhere in the industry. Recently, Students Stop Sweatshops, a coalition of over 50 student organizations, supported by the rock band Rage Against the Machine, launched a boycott of Guess clothing, a firm which the U.S. Department of Labour has repeatedly cited for underpaying workers and refusing to pay overtime. The boycott is being conducted in conjunction with an organizing drive by the Union of Needletrades, Industrial and Textile Employees (UNITE!). In Canada, the Labour Behind the Label Coalition and UNITE! are heading up a campaign against retailers selling clothes made in domestic and international sweatshops (Yanz and Jeffcott 1997, 27).

The GAP campaign, which is also leading to union organizing, may be more effective than the highly publicized "no sweatshop" Workplace Code of Conduct signed by President Clinton in 1997. Firms subscribing to the code have the right to "no sweat" labels on their clothes to mislead customers into believing they are buying goods not made in sweatshops. However, the code omits the right to a living wage and fundamental labour rights. It allows firms to employ 14 and 15 year-olds for more than 60 hours a week at below-poverty wages. It allows "external" monitors of the code to be accountable to firms hired by the very firms being monitored (Weiss 1997, 2).

---

[22] Levi Strauss agreed to enforce a comprehensive code (Forcese 1997, 22) and invited the Amalgamated Clothing and Textile Workers Union (now the Union of Needletrades, Industrial and Textile Employees, i.e., UNITE!) to organize its plants in Mexico (Frundt 1996, 391).

[23] For example, GAP denied well-documented code violations at its Mandarin supplier plant in El Salvador, and then pulled out, thus punishing the workers there (*NACLA Report on the Americas*, Jan.-Feb. 1996, 37).

In effect, the sweatshops remain. The code sets no new standards and no new levels of enforcement. Elaine Bernard, Director of the Harvard Trade Union Program, quipped that the code gives a "Good Housekeeping Seal of Approval to a kinder, gentler sweatshop."

More comprehensive than these corporate codes-of-conduct campaigns is the campaign by the International Confederation of Free Trade Unions, the largest global federation of unions, to have a social clause enforced by the World Trade Organization (WTO). As a substitute for such add-ons as the notoriously weak and largely unenforceable labor side accord to NAFTA, the social clause would be added to all international trade agreements. The Canadian Labour Congress, Canada's largest central labour body, supports this campaign. The clause would include International Labour Organization (ILO) conventions to abolish forced labour, protect freedom of association, maintain free collective bargaining, outlaw child labour, and prevent employment discrimination. The advantage of having these ILO conventions integrated into the WTO is that they could be backed up with trade sanctions. The ILO lacks enforcement mechanisms for its conventions, while the WTO is dominated by developed northern states which tend to reflect the interests of the northern political elites and dominant multinational firms. The effectiveness of this campaign to create an enforceable social clause thus appears to hinge on the democratization of the WTO.

CONCLUSION

While little progress has been made through state and corporate institutions, gains through an incipient transnational coordinative unionism are appearing. After many efforts to unionize maquilas in Central America and Mexico failed due to intimidation (e.g. mass dismissals of union supporters and death threats) and to state failure to enforce basic labour rights, a Van Heusen plant recently became the first maquiladora in Guatemala to have a union contract. The contract addressed all major union demands including significant wage increases, a grievance procedure, and protection against outsourcing and discrimination by supervisors.[24] This victory is credited in important part to the International Textile, Garment and Leather Workers Federation (an ITS), UNITE, and a non-governmental organization, the U.S.-Guatemala Labor Education Project.[25] With strong international support,

---

24 Campaign for Labor Rights, *Labour Alerts, Labour News*, 19 August 1997.

25 Interview, Monica Felipe Alvarez, Secretary General, Union of Modern Shirts Workers (STE-CAMOSA), 7 September

workers at a Fortex plant in Nicaragua also recently won the first agreement ever negotiated in Managua's free trade zone. In Tijuana, Mexico, workers at Han Young, a truck parts supplier for Hyundai, won certification by the independent, progressive union, the Authentic Labour Front. This victory, in the face of massive intimidation, was won with the support of unions in Canada and the U.S., and with help from a boycott of Hyundai products that was mounted by the energetic U.S.-based Support Committee for Maquiladora Workers. Similarly, unions from Canada and the U.S. are supporting the struggle of workers at an auto parts plant outside Mexico City who want to affiliate with the Authentic Labour Front. The plant is a subsidiary of Echlin, Inc., a multinational firm based in the United States.

It is too early to predict how far these transnational coordinative union tendencies will develop. It is clear, however, that these trends are growing not just at the level of labour leaders but among union members, albeit unevenly. Transnational coordinative unionism is consistent with new labour mobilizations in countries, such as Korea, Poland, South Africa, and Brazil, that are most threatened by neo-liberal globalization. Transnational coordinative unionism is also linked to the globalization of feminist, human rights, religious, community, environmental, and other social movements and popular coalitions. Although labour's links to this "new politics" are strained by a clash of organizational cultures and by differing perceptions of the importance of party politics, labour's openness to social movement politics appears to be growing (Carroll and Ratner 1995). Furthermore, the end of the Cold War has freed many from the old ideology of "national interests" that made many unions pawns of political and corporate elites, particularly in the Third World (Sims 1992). Not least significant is the creation of an independent labour federation in Mexico, the 1.5 million strong and growing National Union of Workers —the first major opening toward autonomous unionism in Mexico in seventy years (La Botz 1997).

All this suggests that in the face of the global corporate and state offensive against labour, transnational coordinative unionism is becoming a realistic basis for a stronger, more democratic labour movement in the 21st century.

BIBLIOGRAPHY

Alexander, Robin and Peter Gilmore. 1995. "Trade Unionism Across the Border." In F. Rosen and D. McFadyen, eds., *Free Trade and Economic Restructuring in Latin America*. New York: Monthly Review Press.

Arteaga Garcia, Arnulfo. 1994. "The Restructuring of the Automobile Industry in Mexico and its Repercussions for Labor." In Maria Cook and Harry Katz, eds., *Regional Integration and Industrial Relations in North America*. Ithaca: Cornell University.

Barry, Tom et al. 1994. *The Great Divide: The Challenge of U.S.-Mexico Relations in the 1990s*. New York: Grove Press.

Bronfenbrenner, Kate. 1996. "The Effect of Plant Closing or Threat of Plant Closing on the Right of Workers to Organize." Report submitted to the Labor Secretariat of the North American Commission for Labor Cooperation. September 11.

Brulin, Goran. 1995. "Sweden: Joint Councils Under Strong Unionism." In Joel Rogers and Wolfgang Streeck, eds., *Works Councils: Consultation, Representation and Cooperation in Industrial Relations*. Chicago: University of Chicago Press.

Canadian Labour Congress. 1996. *Social Dimensions of North American Economic Integration*. Ottawa.

Carr, Barry. 1996. "Crossing Borders: Labor Internationalism in the Era of the NAFTA" in Gerardo Otero, ed., *Neo-liberalism Revisited: Economic Restructuring and Mexico's Political Future*. Boulder: Westview.

Carroll, William and R. Ratner. 1995. "Old Unions and New Social Movements." *Labour/Le Travail* 35.

Cohen, Larry. 1991. "An International Mobilization Strategy." In Steven Hecker and Margaret Hallock, eds., *Labor in a Global Economy*. Eugene Oregon: Oregon University Books.

Compa, Lance and Tasha Darricarrere. 1996. "Private Labor Rights Enforcement Through Corporate Codes of Conduct." In Lance Compa and Stephen Diamond, eds., *Human Rights, Labor Rights, and International Trade*. Philadelphia: University of Pennsylvania Press.

Cook, Maria. 1994. "Regional Integration and Transnational Labor Strategies." In Cook and Katz. *Regional Integration and Industrial Relations in North America*.

de la Garza Toledo, Enrique. 1994. "Industrial Democracy, Total Quality and Mexico's Changing Labor Relations." In Cook and Katz. *Regional Integration and Industrial Relations in North America*.

Forcese, Graig. 1997. *Commerce with Conscience?* Montreal: International Centre for Human Rights and Democratic Development.

Frundt, Henry. 1996. "Trade and Cross-Border Labor Strategies in the Americas." *Economic and Industrial Democracy* 17.

Gapasin, Fernando and Michael Yates. 1997. "Organizing the Unorganized." *Monthly Review* (July-August).

Glaberman, Martin. 1980. *Wartime Strikes: The Struggle Against the No-Strike Pledge in the UAW During World War I.* Detroit: Bewick Editions.

Groff, Ruth. 1994. *Mexico: Not Quite How We Imagined I.* Etobicoke, Ontario: Communications, Energy and Paperworkers Union.

Herod, Andrew. 1997. "Labor as an Agent of Globalization and as a Global Agent." In Kevin Cox, ed., *Spaces of Globalization.* New York: Guilford Press.

International Confederation of Free Trade Unions/ORIT. 1994. *Final Document.* Labour Rights and Economic Development Conference, Panama, April.

International Centre for Human Rights and Democratic Development. 1997. *Libertas* 7:1.

La Botz, Dan. 1997. "Mexico: Is a New Labor Movement Being Born?" *Labor Notes* (October 1997).

Lynd, Staughton. 1997. "The Possibility of Radicalism in the Early 1930s: The Case of Steel." In Staughton Lynd, ed., *Living Inside Our Hope.* Ithaca: Cornell University Press).

——. 1992. *Solidarity Unionism: Rebuilding the Labor Movement from Below.* Chicago: C.H. Kerr.

Lynd, Alice and Staughton Lynd. 1988. *Rank and File: Personal Histories of Working-Class Organizers.* New York: Monthly Review Press.

MacShane, Denis. 1996. "Human Rights and Labor Rights: A European Perspective." In Compa and Diamond. *Human Rights, Labor Rights and International Trade.*

Marshall, Judith. 1997. "Globalization from Below: The Trade Union Connections." In Shirley Walters, ed. *Globalization, Adult Education and Training.* London: Zed Press.

Middlebrook, Kevin. 1991. "The Politics of Industrial Restructuring: Transnational Firms' Search for Flexible Production in the Mexican Automobile Industry." *Comparative Politics* 23:3.

Mishel, Lawrence et al. 1997. *The State of Working America 1996-97.* Armonk, NY: M.E. Sharpe.

Moody, Kim and Mary McGinn. 1992. *Unions and Free Trade: Solidarity vs. Competition*. Detroit: Labor Notes.

Muller-Jentsch, Walther. 1995. "Germany: From Collective Voice to Co-management." In Rogers and Streeck, eds., *op. cit.*

Pomeroy, Fred. 1991. "Mobilizing Across Borders." In Steven Hecker and Margaret Hallock, eds., *Labor in the Global Economy*. Eugene Oregon: University of Oregon Books.

Rogers, Joel and Wolfgang Streeck, eds. 1995. *Works Councils: Consultation, Representation and Cooperation in Industrial Relations*. Chicago: University of Chicago Press.

Sims, Beth. 1992. *Workers of the World Undermined: American Labor's Role in U.S. Foreign Policy*. Boston: South End Press.

Streeck, Wolfgang and Sigurt Vitols. 1995. "Europe: Between Mandatory Consultation and Voluntary Information." In Rogers and Streeck, eds., *op. cit.*

Verzuh, Ron. 1997. "Worker to Worker: CUPE's Grassroots International Solidarity." *Our Times* (May-June 1997).

Weiss, Larry. 1997. "Sweatshop Taskforce Report Fuels Controversy." *Working Together: Labor Report on the Americas* (May-June).

Wells, Donald. 1997a. "When Push Comes to Shove: Competitiveness, Job Insecurity and Labour-Management Cooperation in Canada." *Economic and Industrial Democracy* 18:2.

——. 1997b. "Why Canada Needs an Active Jobs Policy." *Policy Options* 18:3.

——. 1997c. "Why the 'High Road' to Competitiveness is the Wrong Road." *Canadian Dimension* (July-August).

——. 1996. "New Dimensions for Labor in a Post Fordist World." In Yanarella and Green, eds., *North American Auto Unions in Crisis*. Albany, New York: State University of New York Press.

——. 1995a. "Origins of Canada's Wagner Model of Industrial Relations." *Canadian Journal of Sociology* 20:2.

——. 1995b. "The Impact of the Postwar Compromise on Canadian Unionism." *Labour/ Le Travail* (fall).

Yanz, Linda and Bob Jeffcott. 1997. "Fighting Sweatshops, Building Solidarity." *Canadian Dimension* (September-October).

TLC, LEGISLACIÓN Y POLÍTICA LABORAL

*Oscar Alzaga**

INTRODUCCIÓN

Nuestro tema es la legislación laboral en el marco del TLC, lo que requiere que incursionemos en otras disciplinas que, sin ser nuestra especialidad, las tomemos en cuenta, como lo es el TLC, la política que lo animó y el contenido económico, comercial y su impacto en el trabajo. El centro de nuestro trabajo es la legislación laboral mexicana, el modo en que influye a ésta el Acuerdo de Cooperación Laboral firmado por los tres países, hacer un cuadro mínimo comparativo entre la legislación laboral mexicana y la de Estados Unidos (EU), para mejor comprender sus diferencias y coincidencias y el impacto de la nueva Ley de Inmigrantes Ilegales y de Responsabilidades de Inmigrantes de EU que entró en vigor el 1º de abril de 1997. En conjunto pretendemos advertir los cambios que del exterior vienen a condicionar la administración e impartición de justicia que afecta a los trabajadores de México y sus derechos, en la nueva situación que abre el TLC.

Ciertamente en México no hemos tenido una reforma a la legislación laboral, como en el caso de muchos países latinoamericanos y europeos, aunque mucho se ha insistido en esa reforma por el gobierno, empresarios y organismos internacionales, pero en los hechos, de facto, se han impuesto cambios en detrimento de los derechos de los trabajadores y de la legislación vigente. Sorprende a propios y extraños el grado de inseguridad jurídica que prevalece, la arbitrariedad de las autoridades. Por ejemplo, las empresas denominadas franquicias contratan trabajos al margen de la legislación; los registros sindicales se otorgan con criterios políticos, no legales; la contratación colectiva ha sufrido múltiples mutilaciones a pesar de que constitucio-

---

* Abogado laboralista. Presidente de la Asociación Nacional de Abogados Democráticos (ANAD).

nalmente se prohibe, etc. Así, muchas empresas extranjeras aceptan la *práctica* con la que e aplica la legislación, al margen o en contra de ella. Pero también debemos decir que las fuerzas políticas y sociales avanzan hacia la transición democrática, al dejar de tener el país un sólo partido gobernando y ahora hacerlo con tres principalmente (PRI, PAN Y PRD). Por lo que se abren mejores posibilidades también para la seguridad jurídica, la libertad sindical y el reconocimiento y respeto de los derechos del trabajo.

EL TLC Y LAS PROMESAS DE UN MEJOR PORVENIR.

Con la aprobación del Tratado de Libre Comercio (TLC o NAFTA) en noviembre de 1993, la relación económica y comercial de México con Estados Unidos (EU) se volvió más cercana y amplia, que la previamente existente, pues si bien históricamente México ha tenido una relación muy fuerte con EU, la más importante, del orden del 75% de sus relaciones económicas externas que ahora, con el TLC se profundizan, en particular las comerciales y se vuelven más complejas y cercanas, con repercusión en múltiples aspectos.

El grado de dependencia, por ser una relación entre economías desiguales, marcadamente desiguales (ver anexo I: TLC comparación entre socios), también se profundiza e influye en la economía interna de México. Esa influencia ha quedado demostrada my pronto: después de la entrada en vigor del TLC el 1º de enero de 1994, cuando la economía mexicana entra en crisis como en estallido, con la devaluación del paso frente al dólar, el 19 de diciembre del mismo año, apenas a 11 meses del TLC, quién "rescata" a México con un préstamo de 20 mil millones de dólares en febrero de 1995, es EU, a cambio de la factura petrolera de México. Así, pareciera que nuestro país queda atado a EU por un buen tiempo, significando el TLC un mecanismo fundamental en tal sentido.

Sobra decir que el TLC repercute en la soberanía nacional, en todos los órdenes: político, económico, energético, social, etc. Junto con las presiones del FMI y el Banco Mundial se llega a modificar el texto Constitucional para adecuarlo a los nuevos tratados en materia de comercio e inversiones extranjeras, facilitando la entrada de éstas.

No obstante la profunda repercusión del TLC, debemos decir y recordar que su contenido es exclusivamente comercial (tarifas y aranceles aduanales) y económico, incluyendo normas al respecto, que durante su negociación los representantes se negaron a incluir temas tan importantes como los sociales, laborales, migratorios, derechos humanos y ambientales. Sería hasta la campaña de Clinton en 1973, cuando por las presiones sindicales y de grupos ecologistas de EU, se aceptó incluir sólo dos temas: laborales y ambientales, pero cuyo contenido resultó limitado y principalmente de beneficio para las empresas y no para los trabajadores como se verá más adelante.

En efecto, en septiembre de 1994 se incluyó como parte del TLC, los Acuerdos paralelos en materia ambiental y laboral (ver anexo II: los Acuerdos Paralelos). El TLC siempre se promovió publicitariamente como la creación del mercado más grande del mundo, que permitiría un gran desarrollo a los tres países y, al menos a México, pasar del tercer al primer mundo al volverse "socio" del país más poderoso del mundo.

A tres años y cuatro meses de la entrada en vigor del TLC, el atraso del país y los daños de la crisis de diciembre de 1994 sitúan la economía en condiciones peores a las previas a ese año. Tan sólo en materia de empleo, en 1995 la crisis provocó la pérdida de casi 2 millones de empleos, de los cuales 850 mil eran inscritos del IMSS y hasta el momento no se han recuperado sino sólo una parte, casi 600 mil. En el lapso 1995-1997, no se han generado los empleos para las nuevas generaciones que en un número mayor al millón de jóvenes acceden anualmente al mercado de trabajo mexicano.

Adicionalmente, para que México entrara al TLC se realizó de 1989 a 1993 una serie de cambios substanciales que incluyó desde las reformas constitucionales (en inversión extranjera en áreas estratégicas, educación, propiedad agraria, privatizaciones, etc.) hasta cambios de flexibilización laboral, modificando y mutilando por la vía de los hechos los contratos colectivos de trabajo, como una medida para alcanzar los estándares de "productividad" y como condición previa a la privatización de empresas públicas, en su caso.

El cambio más significativo que provocó el TLC en tres años, fue en los sectores de importación y exportación del país, ligado a EU, con pocas ligas con el mercado interno -donde el ejemplo más ilustrativo es la industria del automóvil.

En efecto, los beneficiados han sido ese localizo segmento de empresas exportadoras, principalmente empresas transnacionales que operan en México, quienes a través de la figura del comercio intrafirma definen la dirección del flujo de los capitales y el destino de las utilidades de la actividad económica. Se ha mostrado que las más grandes operaciones de importación y exportación son circuitos cerrados, quedando en la mayor parte de los casos, los beneficios al margen del país.

En resumen el TLC ha significado para México:

- Una más grande y estructural relación económica de México con EU, mayor a la previa que de suyo ya era considerable.
- Una relación nueva profundamente asimétrica entre los dos países, sin cláusulas ni medidas compensatorias, para el país más débil.
- La integración de esas economías nacionales en condiciones de supuesta igualdad, sólo puede llevar a que las asimetrías aumenten.
- Tales consideraciones, a la vez, repercutirán en la soberanía nacional de México, debilitándose frente a EU.
- Las crisis económicas de México crecientemente serán acompañadas también de los efectos del TLC, por su influencia en la economía interna, a la vez que México dependerá del auxilio de EU para salir de ellas, con los costos y condiciones que imponga el "socio" del norte.
- El TLC es un negocio casi exclusivo de las grandes empresas principalmente transnacionales y maquiladoras, expresa una nueva y más cercana relación entre ellas en el marco de la globalización en América del Norte.
- Sólo de manera secundaria tienen importancia los Acuerdos Paralelos, en el caso laboral como instrumento en manos de los empresarios y gobiernos.
- Quedan excluidos temas como los sociales, derechos humanos y migratorios.

LOS ACUERDOS PARALELOS Y EL DE COOPERACIÓN LABORAL DE CANADÁ, MÉXICO Y ESTADOS UNIDOS

El 14 de septiembre de 1993 se aprobó el Acuerdo de Cooperación Laboral (ACL) entre los tres países, como parte del TLC, este último aprobado el mes de noviembre del mismo año y con vigor desde el 1º de enero de 1994.

El ACL tiene como objetivos, según declara el documento, los siguientes: contribuir al bienestar de los trabajadores de los tres países, promover la aplicación efectiva de cada legislación laboral, el intercambio de información, evaluar la productividad y la calidad. A través de medidas de inspección y vigilancia del cumplimiento de leyes, investigando violaciones, creando comisiones para impulsar la mediación, la conciliación y el arbitraje, que garanticen la transparencia de los procedimientos. Desafortunadamente estos objetivos sólo son declarativos y genéricos, sin que obligue a las partes a su cumplimiento. Las medidas concretas y particulares acordadas en el ACL se refieren sólo a tres aspectos: prohibir la labor de los menores, que los salarios mínimos establecidos en cada país se respeten y que las medidas de seguridad industrial se cumplan.

Por lo tanto, el ACL limita la posibilidad de que el primer objetivo sea realmente cumplido, pues además las medidas de mediación, conciliación y arbitraje, quedan en manos de los respectivos gobiernos, por ello hasta ahora la aplicación del ACL ha quedado en las denuncias que los trabajadores o sus sindicatos han presentado, con muy escasa eficacia jurídica para evitar las violaciones que se cometen con los derechos laborales en cada país.

Podemos dividir en tres partes el ACL: los aspectos declarativos del enunciado de la primera parte, sin fuerza legal pera su cumplimiento; los aspectos concretos a los que sí se obligan los tres países y las instancias de mediación legal para hacer valer las quejas y violaciones que se cometan.

Sin embargo, para el cabal conocimiento del alcance del ACL debemos tomar en cuenta dos aspectos que condicionan dichas normas, a saber: las diferencias existentes entre las tres legislaciones laborales de cada país, así como las diferencias que se presenten en la realidad del trabajo (salario, empleo, productividad, etc.). Puesto que el ACL se pretende montar en las legislaciones existentes en cada país y en las propias realidades, que distan mucho de parecerse.

LAS LEGISLACIONES LABORALES DE MÉXICO Y ESTADOS UNIDOS

Nos referiremos principalmente a las diferencias que existen en el sistema jurídico de México y Estados Unidos, que se expresan en distinto nivel en la rama del derecho, mismas que arrastran desde sus orígenes diferencias históricas y culturales.

En Estados Unidos a partir de la dominación inglesa se adoptó el *Common Law* como sistema jurídico, mientras que en México en el periodo de la Colonia, se impuso el sistema neoromanista mezclado de algunas costumbres establecidas por el derecho indígena.

El sistema legal que predomina en la mayor parte de EU tiene implícita la tradición inglesa que se caracterizó por la protección de las libertades de los ciudadanos y la independencia de los jueces respecto a los demás poderes. En sus orígenes, el *Common Law* fue ante todo un derecho de juristas prácticos, formados en la resolución de casos y en la aplicación de precedentes, juristas que no codificaban sus normas y no utilizaban la distinción clásica de los romanos de derecho público y privado. Es el sistema que le atribuye al poder judicial el control de constitucionalidad y la defensa de los derechos individuales frente a los demás poderes.

Por lo contrario, el sistema jurídico que se impuso en México a partir del siglo XVI, arrastra una tradición de codificación de normas ligada a la doctrina y la filosofía. En el derecho romano los resultados se alcanzan por juristas académicos y no por jueces, se desprendían del estudio de conceptos y dogmas, desdeñando los precedentes judiciales.

Tal marco macrojurídico se reproduce en las diversas áreas del derecho. Como correctamente señala la doctora María Teresa Guerra: "a la fecha en Estados Unidos el derecho laboral es visto y apreciado bajo la óptica comercial, reconociendo el derecho de asociación, de huelga y contratación colectiva con el propósito de eliminar obstáculos al libre flujo de mercancías y no agravar los daños al comercio, mientras que en México la legislación laboral mantiene una óptica y fundamentación social, sin que figuren las razones comerciales, por el contrario, el reconocimiento de los derechos individuales y colectivos del trabajo se hace bajo el entendido de que algunos de esos derechos pueden deteriorar el interés comercial.

La diversa concepción, impacta el conjunto de criterios jurídicos y normas laborales de cada uno de estos países, como puede apreciarse en el análisis de cada uno de los aspectos fundamentales del sistema jurídico laboral en ambos países." [1]

Asimismo otras diferencias más habrá que considerar, empezando por las de orden constitucional, pues mientras que en México el artículo 123 es amplio en su reconocimiento de derechos laborales y protector de los mismos, en el caso de EU los derechos del trabajo no están reconocidos en ese nivel, salvo la prohibición de la esclavitud y la servidumbre. Cuestión que en EU no sólo es de origen sino también de cultura e historia. En México al estar incluidos en la Constitución los derechos laborales, como garantías sociales que el Estado se compromete a garantizar, su observancia no corresponde únicamente a los particulares, sino que es de interés público y responsabilidad del Estado garantizar su cumplimiento.

Otra diferencia, se ubica en el carácter primordialmente federal de la legislación laboral mexicana, que se deriva del artículo 73 fracción X de la Constitución, y que da lugar a que las principales leyes laborales mexicanas estén bajo control del Congreso de la Unión. Mientras que en el derecho laboral estadounidense las leyes estatales juegan un papel relevante. El cumplimiento de compensaciones de los trabajadores, los beneficios para los

---

[1] Ver revista Trabajo y Democracia Hoy, Núm. 34. nov.-dic. de 1996.

empleados por motivos de lesiones relacionadas con el trabajo, el seguro de desempleo, y los estatutos, entre otros asuntos, son materia de ley estatal. Sin embargo, el carácter estatal de la legislación de EU es relativo, porque importantes legislaciones, como el Acta Nacional de Relaciones Laborales, así como el Acta de Estándares Mínimos, el Acta de Salud y Seguridad en el Trabajo y el Acta de Seguridad de Ingresos del Empleado Retirado rigen a nivel federal. De igual forma la Junta Nacional de Relaciones Laborales está bajo el poder federal.

El Acta de Relaciones Laborales fue aprobada en 1935 y confirmada por la Suprema Corte en 1937 como constitucional bajo el poder del Congreso. Con esta ley se busca eliminar obstrucciones al libre flujo del comercio, garantizando el derecho de los empleados del sector privado a hacer huelgas, a autoorganizarse, a designar sus representantes y a llevar a cabo negociaciones colectivas, bajo el argumento de que la protección de dichos derechos salvaguardaba al comercio de daños y desordenes. Esta Ley solo se aplica a los empleados del sector privado cuyo negocio afecte al comercio, con excepción de la industria del transporte, también rige las actividades del sindicato prohibiéndoles restringir o coaccionar a los empleados en el ejercicio de sus derechos.

La legislación laboral norteamericana parte del principio de que el Estado no debe imponer normas que al proteger al trabajador, o sus organizaciones, vulneren los derechos y libertades del empleador o del propio trabajador. Por lo mismo, no se obliga al empleador (del sector privado) a conservar un trabajador, ni se le impone la firma de contratos de trabajo, no se afecta su libertad de selección de empleados (es ilegal pactar preferencias o exclusividad de contratación), ni se le obliga a prorrogar en forma indefinida los contratos de trabajo, no se permite la terminación por resolución sindical, no se generan derechos por permanencia, ni se le obliga a pagar salarios por días no laborados, no se dan ventajas en juicio al trabajador, ni se le impone al empleador la carga procesal.

En Estados Unidos se considera contrario a la libertad personal que el empleador no pueda iniciar o rescindir libremente una relación de trabajo, que no pueda seleccionar a la empresa de la seguridad social o a sus trabajadores, se considera discriminación para el trabajador que se obligue al empleador a contratar exclusivamente a los miembros del sindicato o preferir a quienes realizan actividad sindical y que se obligue a terminar una relación laboral por disposición sindical. Por otra parte, la condición de subordinado del trabajador en ese país, se expresa no solamente en su carácter de receptor de órdenes, sino que subyace la idea de servidumbre en la relación laboral, expresándose en un trato preferencial para el empleador al extremo de considerarse legal la terminación de la relación de trabajo sólo por voluntad patronal. Bajo la premisa de igualdad de las partes la legislación estadounidense esconde el trato desigual para el trabajador, dando ventajas al patrón al considerar de interés público y de primer orden la no afectación del interés comercial e industrial.

En la legislación mexicana, por el contrario, prevalece la idea de que los derechos del trabajador y sus organizaciones representan el interés colectivo y que por lo tanto es interés social proteger sus derechos por encima de los derechos individuales del patrón. Con esta idea se guió el constituyente de 1917 al romper con los esquemas de la teoría constitucional e incorporar los derechos laborales en la Carta Magna. La legislación laboral parte de considerar como desiguales a las partes, capital y trabajo, en la relación de trabajo, en tanto que en EU se considera una relación de iguales, incluso con protección al comercio.

TAMBIÉN DISTINTAS REALIDADES

El empleo y desempleo en México es un problema tan grande y especial que trastoca las bases de la misma legislación, veamos: se calcula que de 36 millones de población económicamente activa (PEA) para 1996, sólo 16 tenían en empleo estable o seguro, 12 estaban en la economía informal y 8 en empleo precario o temporal y en el desempleo, es decir, 20 millones de trabajadores quedan fuera del marco legal laboral, porque éste sólo rige el empleo formal y asalariado. Peor aun, es la situación de los protegidos por la seguridad social, ésta sólo llegan 12.5 millones de trabajadores (en el IMSS e ISSSTE), de los 36 que son en total.

Uno puede imaginar la presión que el desempleo y subempleo ejerce sobre el empleo, la forma en que los empresarios aprovechan la sobre oferta de mano de obra y el escaso empleo, que de igual forma presiona el salario a la baja y a la inestabilidad en el empleo. De tal manera, que aun si las leyes en México se cumplieran, éstas se verían rebasadas por la realidad social y económica.

Desde luego el problema del empleo en México no se compara con el de EU y Canadá, aunque en ellos el desempleo también muestre tendencias al crecimiento. Porque el problema en México es de magnitudes muy diferentes. Lo cual vuelve el tema de la estabilidad en el empleo en uno fundamental como derecho, lo mismo la protección de los puestos por parte de los sindicatos, temas cuya base legal es distinta en EU.

En México la estabilidad en el empleo la determinan un conjunto de normas vigentes en la Ley Federal del trabajo (LFT), que son la base y el corazón del sistema jurídico laboral, consiste en que la regla señala el derecho al empleo estable y la excepción el empleo eventual (por obra o tiempo determinado), con la obligación del patrón a la reinstalación en el puesto si un trabajador es despedido sin causa justa, todas esas medidas son protectoras de la estabilidad y continuidad en el trabajo. Por el momento protege a cerca de 12 millones de trabajadores, del total de 16. No obstante, con las reformas a la legislación laboral que se presentan como proyectos, este capítulo se ve en peligro, como ha sucedido en otros países.

Así por un lado, las legislaciones de EU y México se encuentran distantes, mientras que por otro, la mexicana se haya amenazada de perder lo positivo de ella, para los trabajadores, por las reformas a las que se le quiere someter. Dificultando ambas razones el acercamiento de los trabajadores para la identidad de causas comunes en materia de empleos y salarios, de derechos comunes para un frente común.

En el merco de las diferencias, debemos anotar también las que se refieren al derecho laboral internacional, pues los convenios de la OIT no están suscritos del mismo modo por los tres países del TLC, para Canadá sólo están en vigor 26; para EU 11 y para México 68. Con lo cual el panorama se dificulta para armonizar derechos a favor de un frente común de trabajadores. Sin embargo, el ejemplo lo muestran los sindicatos europeos que lograron establecer la Carta de Social de los Trabajadores, con derechos tales como los de migración y trabajo en cualquiera de las naciones de la Comunidad Europea. En torno a los convenios de la OIT, en lugar de buscar su cumplimiento se buscan las llamadas cláusulas sociales y ambientales, que debilitan el frente común internacional, por otro sólo regional, ya que éstas sólo resultan banderas de un sector de sindicatos de EU, mientras que las de la OIT son respaldadas y reconocidas por la mayor parte de los sindicatos del mundo.

LA JUSTICIA LABORAL EN MÉXICO

Hemos apuntado que la legislación laboral mexicana es más protectora del trabajo y que ofrece una serie de normas favorables a la estabilidad en el empleo, lo mismo que en el derecho de contratación colectiva y huelga, que los convenios de la OIT en mayor número están suscritos y ratificados por nuestro país, cuyo rango en le jerarquía de leyes es el mayor, el Constitucional. No obstante, el nivel de aplicación de las leyes deja mucho que desear, sobre todo cuando la materia es colectiva - sindical, huelga y contratación colectiva -. Debemos apuntar en primer término la debilidad de los poderes judicial y legislativo frente el ejecutivo, la falta de autonomía de éstos ante el poder ejecutivo, principalmente el presidencial. Luego, que las autoridades laborales más importantes las nombra el ejecutivo, con lo cual las resoluciones en materia colectiva suelen ser más de orden político que jurídico, aun a costa de violar flagrantemente las leyes y la propia Constitución. Recuérdense los casos de la huelga del SME en 1987, el cierre de la Ford Cuautitlán en 1987, la huelga de Aeroméxico en 1988, el conflicto de enero de 1990 en Ford Cuautitlán, VW en 1992, entre otros casos.

Sin duda los derechos más vulnerados en el país son los de orden colectivo, que además por su trascendencia afecta al conjunto de los trabajadores, la norma colectiva es del derecho laboral su parte más dinámica, la que arrastra al conjunto de las demás normas, tal y como la estabilidad en el empleo se significa por ser la base del conjunto de derechos en materia laboral.

Apuntaremos de la legislación laboral mexicana sus principios al menos en el texto, que además son fines o metas constitucionales y legales, esos principios orientan y rigen las relaciones de trabajo, individuales y colectivas, son los puntos cardinales de la legislación, entre otros:

- La justicia social.
- El carácter protector o tutelar de la ley a favor del trabajador.
- El equilibrio de derechos en la relación trabajo - capital.
- La estabilidad en el empleo.
- La irrenunciabilidad de los derechos adquiridos de los trabajadores.
- La igualdad de derechos por igualdad de trabajo.
- El trabajo como medio para garantizar la vida, la salud y un decoroso nivel económico para el trabajador y su familia.
- los derechos de la mujer que trabaja, jubilados y pensionados, trabajadores del campo, minusválidos, emigrantes, menores.
- La autonomía y libertad sindical, como derechos exclusivos de los trabajadores.
- Prohibición expresa al gobierno y empresarios de intervenir en el sindicato.
- La bilateralidad reconocida en la contratación colectiva.
- Libertad de huelga.

Para muchos estudiosos la legislación mexicana en su texto resulta muy protectora del trabajo, en algunos casos sin embargo existen normas secundarias que contradicen y niegan algunos principios, como el de la huelga que con las calificaciones que de ellas hacen las autoridades la limitan, o con disposiciones de otras leyes, como la requisa, la anulan; la bilateralidad en la contratación colectiva con la intervención de la autoridad, la limitan, lo mismo que la libertad de negociación entre las partes.

La parte más débil de los sujetos jurídicos de la legislación laboral de México es la que corresponde a la organización de los trabajadores, a los sindicatos. Prevalece la organización corporativa subordinada al Estado y al partido oficial, el PRI, teniendo como la primera representante de los trabajadores a la GTM, la principal organización colectiva del país, cuyos dirigentes oscilan sus edades entre los 80 y 90 años. En parte la legislación apoya esas estructuras corporativas, a través de la intervención de las autoridades en el registro de los sindicatos, de las directivas sindicales, en la administración de justicia y las negociaciones colectivas. Pero también las autoridades lo hacen al margen y en contra de la ley, como es el caso de la afilición forzosa de los sindicatos al PRI; con la aplicación de leyes indebidas para declarar quiebras fraudulentas (como Ruta 100, Aeroméxico, Cananea, etc.), la aplicación de la requisa dispuesta en leyes secundarias como la Ley de Vías Generales de Comunicación y la de Telecomunicaciones, contra la disposición de la huelga en el artículo 123 Constitucional, entre otros casos.

Está aun lejano el deseo de los trabajadores de que sus organizaciones más importantes sean democráticas y autónomas. Las mismas autoridades aprueban los estatutos de la CTM (ley interna) en 1992, que establecen la obligación individual y colectiva de sus miembros de afiliarse al PRI, de militar en él y comulgar con su ideología, a la vez que sanciona a los trabajadores que no lo hagan, no obstante que todas esas normas son contrarias a las garantías fundamentales de la Constitución del país, la ley suprema.

No obstante, en el país nunca han dejado de existir luchas sindicales que buscan cambiar ese tipo de organizaciones. Recientemente las experiencias del Foro, el Sindicalismo ante la Nación, de la nueva central la Unión Nacional de Trabajadores (UNT), la Coordinadora Intersindical Primero de Mayo, los foros regionales sindicales y las corrientes democráticas en sindicatos nacionales muestran hasta que punto sigue vigente esa necesidad de cambio, acorde con los tiempos políticos que vive el país, con la declinación del partido oficial como única opción para la ciudadanía. Nuevos vientos anuncian la transición democrática del país, que sin duda alcanzará el ámbito laboral y sindical.

La ley de EU contra los emigrantes

El 1º de abril de 1997 en EU entró en vigor la nueva Ley de Inmigrantes Ilegales y de Responsabilidades de Inmigrantes, que resultó una verdadera declaración contra la emigración, entre sus medidas destacan las del uso de violencia, que si ya antes existían, ahora tiene la autorización en el trato de los emigrantes ilegales, asimismo se integran otras medidas como la deportación sin previo juicio, además de el contenido de discriminación, xenofobia y racismo, todo lo cual culminará con el muro que se extenderá en la frontera, para evitar no sólo la migración del sur, sino también la comunicación entre las comunidades y culturas del norte y del sur del continente.

Es evidente las violaciones a los derechos humanos que se cometen, además de ser contraria de los convenios de la OIT, los relativos a los trabajadores emigrantes: el 97, 100, 111 y 143. Esta ley se suma a otras medidas previas como fue el intento de la Iniciativa 187 de California, la Ley Helms-Burton y la certificación del narcotráfico de los países, que en conjunto pretenden juzgar a los otros países con leyes y jurisdicción propia.

Así, por un lado, profundiza México con EU sus relaciones comerciales y económicas con el TLC, ahonda la presencia de empresas transnacionales y de maquiladoras en México; pero en cambio, en materia de emigración, derechos humanos y laborales se pone un muro entre el norte y el sur, para privilegiar las relaciones empresariales, no así las humanas, ni las laborales. La última palabra la tendrán los trabajadores de ambos países, y los de México también con los del sur, con quienes la identidad cultural es mayor.

Anexo 1

T.L.C Comparaciones entre Socios

CONDICIONES DE VIDA

	CANADA	EEUU	MEXICO
Condiciones de vida (rango según los indicadores de desarrollo humano)	1o.	6o.	46o.

DEMOGRAFIA

	CANADA	EEUU	MEXICO
Habitantes por Km. Cuadrado (1990)	3	27	45
Edad promedio de la población (1991)	33.5	33	19
Procreación de hijos por mujer (1990)	1.7	1.8	3.3
Muertes por cada mil habitantes (1990)	14	17	27
Superficie en Kilómetros cuadrados	9 976 140	9 372 610	1 958 200

DATOS BASICOS ECONOMICOS

	CANADA	EEUU	MEXICO
Producto interno bruto (PIB) en millones de dólares	492 987	5 208 004	208 558
Producto interno bruto (PIB) por habitante en dólares	17 680	19 850	5 320
Porcentaje de crecimiento del producto interno bruto (PIB) 1980-1990	2.8	2.4	1.3
Porcentaje del producto interno bruto (PIB) mundial	2.4	25.5	1.0

LABORAL

	CANADA	EEUU	MEXICO
Porcentaje del producto interno bruto (PIB) destinado al pago de prestaciones sociales a los trabajadores	18.8	12.3	2.4
Salario mínimo por hora (en dólares)	4.25	4.25	0.46

SALARIO POR HORA PROMEDIO (EN DOLARES)

	CANADA	EEUU	MEXICO
Industria Textil	11.5	9.8	1.5
Quìmica-petroquìmica	17	17	1.5
Ind. Electrónica y Automotriz	14	14.2	1.2

Anexo 2

ACUERDOS PARALELOS AL TRATADO DE LIBRE COMERCIO DE AMERICA DEL NORTE

ACUERDO SOBRE COOPERACION LABORAL

1. El TLC, la Competitividad y el Empleo.

El T.LC propiciará un mayor intercambio económico en la región. La complementariedad de los tres países generará condiciones de mayor competitividad frente al resto del mundo. El aumento de la competitividad generará mas empleos en México ; empleos productivos y mejor remunerados.

2. Objetivos del Acuerdo Laboral.

Reafirmar los principios laborales plasmados en el marco legal mexicano. Mejorar las condiciones de trabajo y los niveles de vida. Apoyar los objetivos generales del T.LC. Promover la aplicación efectiva de las leyes laborales en los tres países.

3. Obligaciones de las Partes

Cada país mantiene y determina de manera Independiente sus legislaciones, disposiciones y reglamentos internos en materia laboral. Las partes mantendrán niveles elevados de protección laboral. Ningún lado laboral será objeto de revisión o apelación. Las Partes darán difusión a sus leyes, reglamentos y procedimientos administrativos. Además, se notificarán entre si sobre su status normativo. Habrá acceso público a la información relevante, de acuerdo a las legislaciones nacionales respectivas. Las acciones de cada parte para asegurar el cumplimiento de sus leyes incluirán : inspecciones, incluyendo el nombramiento y la capacitación de inspectores, la creación de comités mixtos y trabajadores y averiguaciones y medición y arbitraje.

4. Comisión Laboral

Consejo Ministerial, Será la instancia superior de la Comisión estará integrada por Secretarios de Estado encargados de la materia laboral. Se reunirá por lo menos una vez al año. Sus decisiones será por lo general por consenso. Sus funciones incluirán : supervisar, la aplicación del Acuerdo Laboral, dirigir los trabajos del Secretariado, establecer prioridades para las medidas de cooperación, facilitar las consultar entre las partes y tratar las controversias sobre la interpretación y aplicación del Acuerdo, y promover la difusión de información comparable sobre la aplicación de leyes laborales, normas de trabajo e indicadores del mercado laboral. En particular, el Consejo Ministerial promoverá actividades de cooperación en áreas como : seguridad e higiene en el trabajo, trabajo de menores, trabajadores migratorios, prestaciones laborales, programas sociales para los trabajadores, compensaciones laborales, programas sociales para los trabajadores, compensación por accidentes o enfermedades, igualdad entre mujeres y hombres en el lugar de trabajo y asistencia técnica sobre normas laborales.

Secretariado: Será presidido por un Director Ejecutivo. Dará apoyo técnico al Consejo Ministerial. Su presupuesto y programa anual será aprobado por el Consejo. Prepara periódicamente informes descriptivos sobre : legislación y procedimientos administrativos en material laboral, condiciones del mercado laboral y desarrollo de recursos humanos.

Oficinas Administrativas Nacionales : Cada parte establecerá una Oficina Administrativa Nacional (OAN). Serán los puntos de contacto entre los tres países y el enlace nacional con el Secretariado. Proporcionarán información al Secretariado sobre su legislación laboral, así como datos estadísticos en materia laboral.

CONSULTAS Y CONTROVERSIAS

Consulta entre Oficinas Administrativas Nacionales : Una OAN podrá solicitar consultas con otra OAN sobre legislación laboral, su administración o las condiciones del mercado laboral.

Consultas Ministeriales : Las Partes se podrán consultar entre si sobre temas relacionados con las obligaciones del Acuerdo.

Comité Evaluador de Expertos : Si un asunto no se resuelve en las consultas ministeriales, las Partes podrán solicitar la creación de un Comité Evaluador de Expertos (CEE), siempre y cuando se trate de un asunto que : no involucre derechos colectivos, esté relacionado con el comercio, esté amparado por leyes laborales mutuamente reconocidas e involucre la falta persistente, sistemática e injustificada en la aplicación efectiva de la legislación laboral. El CEE presentará un informe preliminar para consideración del Consejo Ministerial en el plazo máximo de 120 días, a partir de su establecimiento. Dicho informe podrá contener recomendaciones. El CEE presentará un informe final al Consejo en un plazo máximo de 60 días, a partir de la presentación del informe preliminar. El informe final se publicará 30 días después de su presentación. Las partes proporcionarán al Secretariado sus respuestas o las recomendaciones contenidas en el informe final en un plazo de 90 días, a partir de su publicación.

Consultas entre las Partes : Si el Informe final del CEE no resuelve la controversia, las Partes podrán solicitar consultas, siempre y cuando se trate de un asunto sobre seguridad e higiene, trabajo de menores y el pago de salarios mínimos que cada Parte, de manera independiente, establezca. Las consultas no resueltas en 60 días podrán turnarse al Consejo Ministerial, que tendrá 20 días para reunirse y 60 más para resolver. Si el Consejo no resuelve la controversia, podrá formar un panel arbitral.

Pánel Arbitral. El procedimiento arbitral, así como los mecanismos de ejecución de las decisiones arbitrales, serán iguales a los descritos en el Acuerdo Ambiental.

ENTENDIMIENTOS ADICIONALES

1. Financiamiento de Proyectos Fronterizos.

México y Estados Unidos han convenido en desarrollar un programa de financiamiento para mejorar la infraestructura en la frontera común. El programa dará atención al tratamiento de aguas, al manejo de desechos sólidos y a otras áreas relacionadas con el mejoramiento ambiental. Se creará una institución coordinadora de proyectos. Se establecerán fuentes de financiamiento, incluyendo un fondo bilateral aportado por los gobiernos federales. Se definirán criterios para aplicar los recursos y otorgar viabilidad financiera a los proyectos.

2. Salvaguardas.

Se creará un grupo de trabajo, que reportará a la Comisión del Tratado de Libre Comercio de América del Norte, para fungir como foro de consulta cuando una Parte considere que existe un crecimiento anormal de las importaciones, o prevea el recurso a una salvaguarda. El grupo estudiará la evolución de variables relevantes para la aplicación de salvaguardas en casos específicos. El grupo también podrá atender las apelaciones de salvaguardas que una Parte haga ante el GATT.

THE UE-FAT STRATEGIC ORGANIZING ALLIANCE

Robin Alexander[*]

Given the growth of transnational corporations, it is imperative that U.S. trade unionists begin to think about developing meaningful working relationships with unions in other countries. If we face our common employers together, we can succeed in improving wages and benefits everywhere. However, if we permit the transnationals to pursue a low-wage strategy and play us off against each other, we share a future of common misery.

The alliance between my union, the United Electrical Workers (UE) with the Frente Auténtico del Trabajo (FAT) represents one model of how labor organizations in different countries can work together. We offer this information in the hope that it will serve to inspire other trade unionists to establish relationships with sister unions, either using this model or developing alternatives themselves.

THE LABOR MOVEMENT IN MEXICO

With an estimated 10,000 of its members losing their jobs as U.S. plants moved to Mexico, the UE had good reason to seek a new kind of relationship with unions to the south. The first step occurred in 1992 when the union entered into a "Strategic Organizing Alliance" with FAT in an effort to build international solidarity focused on organizing.

We initially met FAT representatives at a tri-national meeting in Zacatecas, Mexico, which came about as part of the fight to oppose NAFTA. Although labor and environmental organizations in the U.S. and Canada were strongly against the agreement, in Mexico it took great courage to speak out in opposition. At that time, Mexico was doing well economically and the Mexican government was spending huge amounts of money to convince the Mexican people that NAFTA was the necessary step to make Mexico a "first world" country.

---

[*] Director of International Labor Affairs, United Electrical Workers.

Opposition was also difficult because virtually all Mexican unions at that time strongly supported NAFTA. This was the case because there was no real separation between the Congress of Labor and the government. Membership in the major labor federations that make up the Congress of Labor, including the Confederation of Mexican Workers (CTM) and the Revolutionary Confederation of Workers and Peasants (CROC), carried with it mandatory membership in the ruling Party of the Institutional Revolution (PRI). Because of government domination and corruption, the "official unions," as they are known, are undemocratic and generally provide little in terms of benefits for their members. For example, "ghost unions" and "protection contracts" are prevalent both in the interior and in many border cities. Companies, often prior to the time workers are hired, will purchase contracts from one of the official unions. The workers will have no idea a union exists and the contract will remain in a drawer and will be brought forward in the event that the workers attempt to organize.

Although Mexican laws are generally stronger than those in the U.S. and appear to provide ample protection for workers, government hostility renders them virtually meaningless where workers are attempting to organize independent unions. The Mexican government has enormous power to intervene in the labor movement, to remove and replace union leaders, to declare strikes "illegal," to militarily seize work places, to grant or withhold legal recognition, and to delay the proceedings by which workers can change union representation. Basic human rights such as freedom of speech and association are frequently violated with impunity. These practices are particularly notable in the border area where the government has assured special "protection" to the maquila plants.

The challenge which has confronted independent unions in Mexico for more than half a century is disheartening in itself: how to effectively organize in the face of opposition by employers, official unions and the government. When you add to this the issues of globalization, the decimation of national industry, and the imperative to organize transnationals, the work ahead appears daunting indeed.

Yet, in situations of crisis there are also opportunities. In the 1997 elections, the center-left Party of the Democratic Revolution (PRD) swept Mexico City, winning both the post of Mayor and virtually all of the assembly seats, while on the national level the National Action Party (PAN, the right opposition party), PRD, and other smaller opposition parties broke the PRI's stranglehold, taking control of the lower congressional house for the first time. Adding to the sense of change, Fidel Velasquez, the 97-year old leader of the CTM, finally died, ending a 56-year reign as Mexico's most prominent labor leader. During his half-century in power, Velasquez had subordinated the Mexican labor movement to the PRI, creating a system of domination and corruption for which Mexican workers have paid dearly.

Also on the labor front, in November of 1997 the Foro (Forum) Group transformed itself from a coalition which analyzed the problems facing the Mexican labor movement, into a new labor federation, the National Union of Workers (UNT). The UNT is composed of some 200 labor and peasant organizations which together comprise 1.5 million members. One of the principles which unites the unions is a determination to operate in a manner which is independent of government control. Indeed, UNT unions have harshly criticized NAFTA and the government's neo-liberal policies, and have called for major changes in social and economic policy. The federation's collective leadership is composed of three presidents and seven vice presidents, and its statutes provide for one-third of the leadership to be women. (These last points are a bit problematic, however, as the statutes provide that this more democratic form of leadership will exist only during the first year; of the initial officers, none of the three presidents and only one of the seven vice presidents is a woman.)

All of the Foro's affiliates did not immediately join the UNT, and whether it lives up to its promise remains to be seen. Nevertheless, the founding of the new federation is a very positive step, and if it really stands its ground and breaks the historic ties with the government it will be a tremendous advance for working people in Mexico. It should be noted that in May of 1997 the Foro Group, together with a more left coalition of insurgent union and community groups, organized a May Day march of 250,000 people. For many hours, and with tremendous enthusiasm, hundreds of thousands of marchers paraded to the Zócalo to criticize the President, rather than to applaud him as had been the practice of the CTM and Congress of Labor for many decades.

THE STRATEGIC ORGANIZING ALLIANCE BETWEEN UE AND FAT

The Pittsburgh-based United Electrical, Radio & Machine Workers of America (UE) unites a diverse membership —from assembly workers and welders, to social workers and scientists— on the basis of working together in a democratic, rank-and-file union. The union's commitment to democracy is encapsulated in its slogan, "The members run this union." UE has been on the cutting edge of the effort to establish meaningful relationships between U.S. and Mexican workers, and the same principles of solidarity and democracy have joined UE and FAT in a unique, North-South labor organizing coalition —an effort designed to improve conditions on both sides of the border by countering employer efforts to pit workers in the U.S. and Mexico against each other.

FAT is a federation of Mexican labor unions, worker-owned cooperatives, farmworker and community organizations. Founded in 1960, it now represents workers in over half the states of Mexico in a wide range of manufacturing industries, including textiles, garment, shoemaking, rubber, and auto parts, as well as in agriculture and construction. FAT has an influence which greatly exceeds its size due to its principled determination to create independent, democratic unions under extremely adverse conditions. For example, FAT was a key founder and active participant in RMALC (the Mexican Action Network Against Free Trade), a coalition of more than 100 Mexican organizations which opposed NAFTA and works to develop alternative development strategies.

UE and FAT launched the Strategic Organizing Alliance with ambitious goals: organizing, educating, promoting contact, and building cross-border solidarity between rank-and-file workers employed by the same transnational corporations in the U.S. and Mexico; promoting the organization of independent unions; protecting the human and labor rights of Mexican and U.S. workers; and building the foundation for trade unionists to work together to improve wages, benefits, and working conditions on both sides of the border.

The work of the UE-FAT Strategic Organizing Alliance can really be viewed as occurring in two phases. During the initial stage we chose the Juarez/Chihuahua area as the focus for our organizing activity, selected target plants, evaluated them and initiated two organizing campaigns. When workers in both plants were fired, we were joined by the Teamsters in filing the first complaints under the labor side agreement of NAFTA. Although this phase was invaluable in terms of developing the relationship between our organizations and evaluating the conditions on the border from an organizing perspective, the lack of a union culture and the fierce opposition by the companies and the "Panista" (PAN) state government led us to conclude that an alternative to a plant-by-plant organizing approach was needed.

During the current phase we have shifted the focus of the organizing work, expanded both the organizational and educational components, and worked on building infrastructure to support our work financially and in terms of solidarity. There is also a strong emphasis on leadership development to ensure full, meaningful participation by women. A brief outline of some of our work follows.

1993-1994

As a result of the FAT's organizing campaign at the General Electric plant in Juarez and the international pressure exerted by the UE and others, the FAT won the right to the first secret ballot election in Mexican labor history. We also focused extensive attention on the serious deficiencies in both the substance and administration of the labor side agreement of NAFTA by filing the first complaints under that agreement on behalf of Mexican workers who were fired by the U.S. based companies they were seeking to organize. The complaints focused attention both on the egregious company violations and the deficiencies in the labor side agreement. They also paved the way for subsequent cases which focused attention on the problem of interference by the Mexican government in the union registration process.

FAT, in turn, provided critical support for a successful UE organizing campaign at AceCo, a Milwaukee foundry with a predominantly Mexican workforce. At the UE's request, a rank-and-file activist from the FAT traveled to Milwaukee in December of 1994 for two weeks to accompany UE organizers. In meetings with the workers he was able to speak from his own experience in telling them that the UE is a democratic union, unlike the "official" unions they knew in Mexico. His presence had a dramatic impact on the immigrant workforce and substantially boosted support for the union. UE's NLRB victory in early 1995 made AceCo the biggest Milwaukee plant to go union in years. This effort is definitely a two way street!

1995-1997

In the Fall of 1995 the FAT hired and trained a core group of six organizers based in Mexico City. They have since won a series of election victories.

In November of 1995 and 1996, the Maquiladora Health and Safety Network conducted training for FAT activists and leadership in Mexico City. The first training was designed to provide a basic introduction, the second to develop local leaders as trainers.

Our biggest accomplishment of 1996 was the establishment of a workers' center —Centro de Estudios y Taller Laboral (CETLAC)— in the Mexican border city of Juarez. The Center provides education to workers and counseling about labor-related legal problems, and is hard at work projecting a different vision of how unions should operate. Most recently it co-hosted a seminar on labor law reform with the University of Juarez. Speakers included some of the most distinguished labor experts in Mexico, among them Nestor de Buen, Graciela Bensusan, and Arturo Alcalde. In connection with the inauguration of the workers' center, Professor Dale Hathaway wrote a short history of the FAT. A more polished version was published by the UE in April of 1997.

Also on the organizing front, in March of 1997 we joined with representatives from other unions from the U.S. and Canada in a tri-national meeting in Chicago to focus on Echlin, an auto-parts transnational which has plants in all three countries. At the conference there was a detailed review of information about the company and reports about the situation of participating locals. Participants pledged to coordinate support in collective bargaining, promote new organizing, and create a communications network.

In 1996 both organizations made great strides in their internal work with women. The FAT organized its first national women's conference, and for the first time the UE and FAT exchanged delegations of rank-and-file women. The discussions generated by these trips will have a marked impact on both of our organizations.

We organized five worker-to-worker delegations, including two women's delegations, and have done extensive educational and media work. Our worker-to-worker exchanges have been a valuable and exciting part of our relationship with the FAT, permitting rank-and-file members of both organizations to learn about each other and take the information back to their locals and communities. We have learned that the most effective way to educate workers in the United States and in Mexico and to motivate them to educate others is through direct contact. In 1997, we decided that instead of large delegations, we would have smaller exchanges so that workers could stay in particular cities for longer periods of time. These turned out to be invaluable experiences for the workers involved. In the most recent trip two women from the UE spent three days with their sisters at the women's center in Leon, accompanied them during the FAT's second national women's meeting, and remained for the FAT's National Congress. Marianne Hart, one of the UE participants, described her impressions of the trip:

> The experience was overwhelming ... in terms of what I learned, the breadth of the work the FAT does, and their commitment to organizing. On a personal level, I was able to share very personal experiences and feelings with women from the FAT because they were so open and generous. There were no walls between us. This experience actually made solidarity without borders real for me.

In connection with our 1996 exchange of delegations, we conducted a two-day "dismantling racism" workshop for the U.S. participants. The UE also hosted its first international panel at its 1996 national convention, and the presentation by women from the delegation to Mexico was considered one of the high points of the entire convention.

More recently, Benedicto Martinez, one of the FAT's national coordinators, attended the 1997 UE convention. While at the convention, he joined striking workers in Chicago during the first day of their walkout and met with workers at another plant who had an election scheduled for the week following the convention. I am happy to report that we won that election.

Art is also an important part of our joint work. Labor muralist Mike Alewitz from New Jersey and community muralist Daniel Manrique from Mexico City completed truly magnificent murals in Mexico City and Chicago with a common theme of cross-border labor solidarity. The artists were so inspired that instead of one mural they painted two, together with a banner which was used for the first time on May Day. Mike was the principal artist on a mural entitled "Sindicalismo Sin Fronteras" (Trade Unionism Without Borders) in the FAT's auditorium, and Manrique on a mural entitled "Marcha Por la Autogestion" (March for Self-Management —a concept very close to our idea of rank-and-file trade unionism) in the area used for celebrations. The Chicago mural, which is painted on the outside of the UE District 11 Hall, is entitled "Hands of Solidarity, Hands of Freedom — Manos Solidarios, Manos Libres." Three young muralists from the Chicago Public Art Group assisted Manrique in painting the Chicago mural; meanwhile, Mike Alewitz painted a mural a few blocks away at Teamster City commemorating the 1997 UPS strike victory. The inaugurations in both cities brought together a wide variety of organizations and individuals to focus on some of the problems facing workers and immigrants. The celebrations included poetry, music, and inspiring words from the artists and from labor and community activists expressing their common aspiration for economic and social justice in the U.S. and Mexico.

Through these kinds of events, we have developed an extensive solidarity network in the United States. This network is composed of local unions and other organizations, and of activists who support our cross-border work through small financial contributions, through targeted letter writing, petition campaigns, hosting of delegations, and other initiatives. Beginning in 1996, updates have been sent out every two or three months to activists and supporters.

The UE has established an international web page which can be viewed at HTTP://www.igc.apc.org/unitedelect/. Since January of 1996, author Dan LaBotz has edited the *Mexican Labor News and Analysis,* which is published electronically every two weeks. It focuses on labor and related events in Mexico, and is the best source of Mexican labor news available in English. In January of this year we were named "Labor web site of the week"!

Perhaps most significant, the UE and FAT have developed an excellent relationship based on mutual respect and trust and an innovative organizing model which serves as an example to others in the labor movement.

MAKING THE ROAD AS WE WALK

The heart of our relationship with the FAT is organizing, and this will remain true in the years ahead. This work now includes the organizing work of the Mexico City team, the Echlin organizing project, and the workers' center (CETLAC) in Juarez. We have also developed exciting educational work, including worker-to-worker delegations and murals devoted to labor solidarity.

I believe our relationship has worked for a number of reasons. First, we share a similar organizational approach: a common commitment to building democratic unions which are controlled by our members. In this sense, the UE principle of rank-and-file unionism is strikingly similar to the broader concept of "autogestion" or self-management that the FAT applies throughout their organization. Second, both organizations are pragmatic, accustomed to working with limited resources, and neither is bureaucratic. This has allowed us to move forward rapidly, evaluate the work as we proceed, and make changes where warranted. Third, our work involves real, important projects with tangible results. Fourth, we have come to know and really like each other as people, trade unionists, and as part of a movement for workers' rights. Last, and perhaps most important, our relationship has from the beginning been based on mutual respect and over time has become firmly based on mutual trust —a product of working closely together over time.

There can be no doubt that this has benefited our organizations, and has inspired many other locals and activists to participate with us or through their own initiatives. We welcome that participation, as we believe that the future of our labor movement depends on it. Together we are creating the road upon which we are walking. Adelante!

EL SINDICATO EN LA REESTRUCTURACIÓN INDUSTRIAL Y LABORAL EN DIESEL NACIONAL S.A. HOY GRUPO DINA (UNA SEMBLANZA PARA LA MEMORIA)

Lázaro Osorio[*]

"La indiferencia es nuestra cadena y somos
nosotros nuestros propios tiranos porque
no ponemos nada de nuestra parte para
destruirla ... cuando reflexionemos todos
los que sufrimos idénticos males, los que tenemos
un mismo interés, un interés común de todos
los oprimidos y hagamos el propósito de
ser solidarios, entonces seremos capaces
de transformar las circunstancias que nos hacen
desgraciados por otras que sean favorables
a la libertad y al bienestar"
Ricardo Flores Magón

INTRODUCCIÓN

Como parte de los obreros mexicanos y de la industria automotriz vivimos grandes problemas: desaparición de puestos de trabajo, paros laborales aplicados por los patrones con pérdida en un cuarenta por ciento de salario y prestaciones, ataque a la materia de trabajo bajo la forma de trasladarla a empresas subcontratistas y la falta sistemática de respeto a la Ley Federal del Trabajo y a los Contratos Colectivos de Trabajo.

Lo anterior lo observamos como una consecuencia estrechamente vinculada a las crisis económicas y sociales de 1982-1983, y 1994-1995, y también a los efectos de las políticas y estrategias institucionales que han propiciado la ausencia de un proyecto de desarrollo nacional, al ser en muchos sentidos dependientes de los procesos de globalización y reestructuración industrial a nivel internacional.

En este panorama, el Sindicato Nacional Independiente de Trabajadores de la Industria Automotriz, Similares y Conexos, DINA, al igual que todas los organismos representativos de los trabajadores de la industria automotriz, ha tenido que enfrentar muchos retos para conservar su condición de interlo-

---

[*] Sindicalista, miembro de la Comisión Revisora del Sindicato DINA.

cutor colectivo de sus agremiados y al mismo tiempo desarrollar su capacidad de negociación y lucha.

Si se observa el panorama sindical automotriz encontraremos que las ofensivas patronales han buscado limitar o anular esas dos condiciones de los sindicatos. En nuestro caso podemos decir que en el fragor de los cambios productivos hemos identificado que conservar nuestra organización es la única alternativa que nos puede garantizar la defensa de nuestras conquistas o la búsqueda de nuevas que compensen las pérdidas contractuales que en este difícil proceso han aparecido.

En este lugar queremos plantear un semblanza de nuestra condición de trabajadores sindicalizados, de las condiciones que nos han llevado a luchar y pensar que dentro de nuestras diversas posturas, buscaremos siempre la unidad sindical y al mismo tiempo que pretendemos mostrar los rasgos más distintivos del proceso de reestructuración de las empresas del hoy corporativo DINA y del papel que en este proceso han tenido las autoridades del trabajo.

Nuestra intención es que nuestra experiencia sirva a otros compañeros para avanzar juntos en la búsqueda de puentes de solidaridad sindical tan importantes en estos tiempos cuando vemos que las empresas se mueven libremente de una frontera a otra.

Nuestro trabajo está dividido en cuatro partes:

-Reestructuración en DINA

-Flexibilidad en los Contratos

-Falta de respeto a la Ley

-El consorcio DINA

REESTRUCTURACIÓN DE DIESEL NACIONAL, S.A.

A partir de 1977 Diesel Nacional estaba integrado en cinco plantas en donde se producían: automóviles Renault, motores, transmisiones, bielas, autobuses, camiones, autopartes de plásticos reforzados, termoformados por inyección y prensados al vacío y tractocamiones.

El 23 de marzo de 1979 se vende el cuarenta por ciento de las acciones de la planta automóviles al capital francés, separándose así de Diesel Nacional para constituirse como empresa con representatividad jurídica propia: "Renault de México". El sindicato tramita y acuerda con la empresa y autoridades del trabajo la sustitución de patrón de 2,300 trabajadores de conformidad al Artículo 41 de la Ley Federal del Trabajo, el salario que percibían por hora era de $ 112.50, con doce niveles salariales y 246 categorías.

En junio de ese mismo año se inicia el proceso de grandes modificaciones cuando la administración de DINA propone al sindicato la *descentralización* de la misma y la constitución de cinco nuevas empresas *con razones sociales diferentes*:

-DINA Autobuses

-DINA Camiones

-DINA Motores

-Plásticos Automotrices, DINA

-Servicios Alimenticios DINA

En la medida que la propuesta involucra de golpe la suerte de las condiciones de vida y trabajo de diez mil trabajadores la respuesta se dio en el sentido de rechazar la propuesta empresarial.

Midiendo la magnitud del rechazo, la empresa pospone el conflicto, pero se acuerda como salida negociada reducir la jornada de trabajo de 9 a 6 horas con pago de 7 y media, dejando los trabajadores de percibir por una sola vez las prestaciones de:

-Aguinaldo

-Juguetes

-Premios de Asistencia

Para el 7 de febrero de 1982, nuevamente la empresa plantea la división de DINA pero ahora acompaña a su petición nada menos que el reajuste de 2,552 trabajadores.

Estalla la huelga y treinta y cuatro días después se nos declara inexistente, conseguimos el amparo provisional y seguimos en huelga y cuando se llega a la fecha para concedernos el amparo definitivo del acto reclamado, las autoridad nos impone una cantidad de 36 millones de pesos como fianza. Una cantidad fuera de cualquier posibilidad y pensada justamente como una barrera infranqueable. El sindicato al no conseguir esa cantidad de dinero, acuerda el regreso a las labores para evitar ser despedidos.

Bajo estas maniobras y presiones es como el *23 de marzo se acuerda la constitución de las cinco empresas y la sustitución de patrón de 10 mil trabajadores* para que se integren a las empresas que les corresponden.

Como derivados importantes de esta nueva situación tenemos que mencionar lo siguiente:

- Se obtuvo un aumento salarial de 40% para todas las categorías.

- En la revisión salarial de 1983, se ajustaron las prestaciones en los Contratos Colectivos de las Cláusulas de 22, 66, 71, 82, 83, 84, 86, 89, 100, 102,103,107 y 112 del sustituido Contrato Colectivo de la empresa DINA y este ajuste fue prorrateado en función a los cinco nuevos Contratos Colectivos.
- Para la revisión salarial en la empresa Renault de México, la empresa gana el arbitraje al sindicato con relación a la calificación de los puestos que se establecían en la Cláusula 9 del Contrato Colectivo de Trabajo (CCT) como sindicalizados, incorporándolos ahora a la cláusula como empleados "de confianza": jefe de departamento, jefe de sección, jefe de taller, supervisor, ingenieros, técnicos, secretaria, operadores y vigilantes (en total este arbitraje afecto a 300 trabajadores).

En 1985 continuaban los conflictos en la empresa Renault, la empresa impone un Paro Técnico[1] y el sindicato logra defender las prestaciones y los salarios obteniendo un pago al 70%.

Para septiembre de ese mismo año la empresa promueve ante la Junta Federal un Conflicto de Naturaleza Económica[2]. En el juicio laboral el Sindicato demuestra su improcedencia y la Junta lo archiva, sin embargo, se reserva el derecho de imponer a la empresa la reapertura de los trabajos.

De nueva cuenta, con la presión de la autoridad laboral, en mayo de 1986 la situación se hace insostenible para los trabajadores y en una asamblea deciden aceptar su indemnización. Concluye así una lucha de más de cinco años cuyo saldo es la pérdida de 2,000 puestos de trabajo.

Los trabajadores de las demás secciones de la empresa DINA, para defender el CCT (a quienes se unieron trece trabajadores de Renault que no aceptaron su indemnización) emplazan y se estalla la huelga, cuyo efecto desafortunadamente es muy limitado porque sólo sirve para mejorar la indemnización de nueve trabajadores y el pago de prestaciones que adeudaba la empresa al sindicato.

Llegamos a 1987. Por decreto se liquida a la empresa "Servicios Alimenticios DINA" sumándose 47 trabajadores más al desempleo, de esto se logró la reubicación de 78 compañeros al crearse un nuevo departamento de alimentos en la empresa DINA Motores.

---

[1] Los Paros Técnicos fueron empleados con nosotros en esa fecha tan temprana, después en los años noventa se volverían en toda la industria automotriz, parte de una estrategia patronal para "racionalizar" los volúmenes de la producción.

[2] Otro recurso que años después se usaría contra los sindicalistas de VW y de Ford.

A mediados de ese mismo año las áreas de transmisiones y maquinado con 182 trabajadores pasan a la empresa DINA Motores.

Ese año, la empresa DINA Autobuses en forma violenta, apoyándose en los actuarios de la Junta Federal "dan fe" del reajuste de 256 trabajadores. El sindicato demanda el cubrimiento de 102 puestos y su respectivo corrimiento escalafornario, ganándose la demanda otorgándose categorías planta y la reinstalación de 16 trabajadores que no firmaron su indemnización.

Para el 10 de marzo de 1988 el Corporativo DINA anuncia la desincorporación de la empresa del sector paraestatal.

Dos semanas después, el 24 de marzo, el Sindicato firma un Convenio con las empresas privatizadas en el que se incluyen dos Cláusulas de suma importancia para el caso de operaciones de venta de las nuevas empresas, esta Cláusulas son:

"Tercera, por el caso de su venta que se anuncia las empresas se comprometen a respetar y cumplir los derechos colectivos e individuales vigentes y el futuro de cada uno de los trabajadores; antigüedades, categorías, prestaciones contractuales, contratos individuales y salario ... y

"Novena, las empresa y el sindicato están de acuerdo en impulsar esas empresas para desarrollo socioeconómico y cultural de las poblaciones aledañas a Ciudad Sahagún".

El primero de noviembre de ese año, se anuncia la venta de las empresas en $144 mil millones de viejos pesos al Grupo Guadalajara.

Con esto se inicia nuestra historia más reciente, trabajadores que sobrevivieron con su organización sindical y ahora al servicio del capital privado. Los aspectos más relevantes de esta fase la podemos describir como sigue:

Año de 1990.- Huelga de 92 días, a partir del 7 de febrero, en la empresa Plásticos Automotrices, la decisión sindical para estallar esta huelga se fundamentó en la petición de obtener una nivelación salarial de 8.5% y el conjunto de los trabajadores obtuvieran niveles similares a los salarios de las empresas camiones y autobuses.

Al final d este movimiento, 237 trabajadores levantan la huelga aceptando el pago del 50% de salarios y prestaciones por el tiempo que duró el conflicto. Como parte de este resultado, se destituye al Secretario General por firmar el Convenio de Terminación del Conflicto en el que se aceptó la obligación de establecer tiempos estándar en todas las áreas de trabajo en un término de 15 días situación que provocó una semana de paros hasta el punto que se negoció los cronometrajes a cambio de bonos por productividad ($60.00 semanales).

Enero de 1992, se liquída la empresa DINA motores, las prestaciones superiores de ese CCT se integran al CCT de la empresa DINA Autobuses, liquidándose 147 trabajadores con una compensación por aparte de su indemnización de $ 3 mil más.

Los 237 trabajadores de las áreas de transmisiones y maquinado se reubican a DINA Autobuses y 33 trabajadores sindicalizados restantes, pasan a régimen de confianza obteniendo también una retabulación del 12% a sus salarios.

7 de enero de 1994. La empresa Plásticos Automotrices plantea al sindicato su cierre por no ser rentable. Se llama a asamblea a los 236 trabajadores decidiéndose por negociar formándose una comisión especial para la comisión del conflicto.

Para fines de febrero se firma un Convenio con los siguientes acuerdos:

a. Liquidación hasta cien trabajadores indemnizados (cláusula 19 del CCT) más una compensación de $3,000.00.
b. Respetar el CCT de la empresa Plásticos automotrices DINA con 60 puestos de trabajo.
c. Crear una nueva empresa denominada COMPOSITES con un nuevo CCT, para contratar de planta hasta 25 trabajadores que fueran reajustados.
d. Reubicación de los 50 trabajadores restantes; 25 a la empresa DINA Autobuses y 25 a la empresa DINA Camiones.
e. Además se pacta un nuevo Convenio de Productividad en donde se establece como aspectos importantes: formar una Comisión Mixta de seis integrantes por cada parte; hacer un nuevo reglamento de escalafones para definir ascensos y movilidad tomando en cuenta la antigüedad; capacitación permanente dentro de las horas de trabajo; una escala de incentivos a la productividad a partir del 5% hasta el 25% del salario que esté percibiendo el trabajador; los bonos de productividad que ya estaban acordados se integran a las prestaciones de la canasta básica ($240.00 semanales) indexadas al salario.

Obtuvimos además, una prestación por cada trabajador adicional de $ 8,200.00 por una sola vez por aceptar los procesos de Mejora Continua, un aumento del 17% al compactarse los niveles salariales de 12 a 5 y las categorías de 240 a 27.

Febrero de 1995. Se reajusta a 275 trabajadores a DINA Autobuses, primero 100, después de dos meses a los restantes.

9 de octubre de 1995. Cierre ilegal de DINA Camiones, despedidos 864 trabajadores, demandamos su apertura y reinstalación de los despedidos.

Octubre 11: llegamos a un acuerdo en el cual se reconstituye la empresa DINA Camiones: se mantiene CCT vigente pero se acepta el reajuste de 150 trabajadores de los 375 que solicitaba la empresa antes del conflicto.

Marzo de 1997. El Sindicato emplaza a huelga a todas las empresas del grupo DINA por defender la materia de trabajo y los CCT de las empresas: Camiones, Autobuses y Plásticos Automotrices. 12. El sindicato presenta un emplazamiento a huelga el 14 de marzo para todas las empresas, misma que estalla el 22 de marzo a las 14 horas, si la empresa no retira la pretensión de crear dos nuevas empresas con la materia de trabajo de las empresas DINA Camiones y DINA Autobuses, así como regresar a 37 trabajadores a sus puestos de trabajo, cumplir con la capacitación del Convenio de Productividad.

FLEXIBILIDAD DE LOS CONTRATOS COLECTIVO DE TRABAJO

Un saldo de estas confrontaciones con la patronal ha sido la introducción de los criterios de la flexibilidad en las relaciones laborales. El cuadro siguiente busca presentar los aspectos más sobresalientes de las nuevas flexibilidades en las cláusulas más representativas del CCT, así como los períodos en las que fueron introducidas.

Flexibildades, Cláusulas afectadas y años de cambio

Cláusula	1982	1986	1989	1997
15 Porcentaje de Eventuales	14%	25%	abierto	abierto
44 Intensidad y Calidad de Trabajo	De acuerdo a la costumbre establecida	igual	igual	abierto
23 movimientos de personal	hasta por tres días	hasta por 15 días	hasta por 30 días	abierto
9 Personal de Confianza*	*1983 pasan a "de confianza" 300 trabajadores y 8 puestos a régimen de confianza			abierto

Fuente: Contratos Colectivos de Trabajo, 1980-1998.

FALTA DE RESPETO A LA LEY FEDERAL DEL TRABAJO

En las luchas del Sindicato DINA hemos acumulado una memoria en la que identificamos como parte de los problemas y las complicaciones, una constante falta de respeto a las regulaciones contenidas en la Ley Federal del Trabajo (LFT).

En un recuento sumario de este aspecto, podemos plantear que ha existido la aplicación de una política de "mano dura" y sucia de las autoridades laborales en complicidad con los patrones en los movimientos sindicales correspondientes a los años: 1983, 1986, 1989, 1995 y 1996, cuando, utilizando diversos tonos y pretextos, buscaron anular o derrotar nuestra capacidad de resistencia. Dentro del recuento de lo más sobresaliente en esta política antisindical podemos relatar lo siguiente:

1. Declaración de inexistencia de la huelga por "no haber sustituido el CCT que se revisaba por los nuevos contratos sustitutos".
2. Declaración de inexistencia porque "Diesel Nacional no tenía ningún trabajador sindicalizado".
3. Declaración de Inexistencia de la huelga después de 34 días de estallada, a pesar de que el Artículo 929 de la LFT, establece 72 horas para su calificación
4. Paro patronal ilegal porque se violó el procedimiento del artículo 429 de la LFT, la autoridad laboral lo validó fuera del marco de la disposición expresa de los conflictos de la naturaleza económica.
5. En el caso anterior, las autoridades resuelven al final la improcedencia del conflicto de orden económico presentado por Renault de México, pero no dan la orden expresa para reabrir la fuente de trabajo, liquidando a todos lo trabajadores sin fundamento jurídico.
6. Segunda declaración de inexistencia de la huelga, después de 20 días de estallada con el argumento de "no haber integrado en el emplazamiento las actas de la asamblea", por demás, requisito que no establece la ley.
7. Aunque en revisión salarial, no se pueden modificar los CCT, ni se puede plantear algún otro conflicto al estar emplazada a huelga, la Junta Federal dio entrada a la propuesta patronal para modificar 13 cláusulas del CCT .
8. Por segunda ocasión, las autoridades del trabajo dan entrada a un procedimiento ordinario de naturaleza jurídica, Artículo 870, solicitando la patronal la modificación de las cláusulas 9, 23 y 44 de los CCT estando en proceso de prehuelga.

9. Los patrones se amparan para no dar cumplimiento a los artículos 221, 224, 935 y 449 de la Ley Federal del Trabajo en los años: 1995 y 1996. Al final sus amparos son declarados improcedentes.
10. Las autoridades dan entrada a la terminación colectiva de las relaciones de trabajo para los trabajadores de DINA Camiones, violando el capítulo XIX en sus artículos 900 al 919.
11. Nuevamente la empresa DINA Camiones promueve ante las autoridades del trabajo un procedimiento especial (Artículo 892) para dar por terminado el CCT presentando en ese juicio los convenios de paros técnicos acordados para legitimar el problema de mercado y financiero, sin embargo, el sindicato probó que dichos convenios no pasaban como "cosa juzgada" y que por lo tanto los patrones de DINA tenía que ajustarse al procedimiento de conflictos de naturaleza económica.

DATOS GENERALES SOBRE EL CONSORCIO DINA

Tiene una capacidad instalada para producir 60,000 unidades al año.

Su plataforma de exportación descansa en el proyecto del sistema tecnológico industrial avanzado, involucrando a todas las empresas DINA; la empresa Packard y Navistar, éste última, en su condición de socio-tecnólogo en tractocamiones hasta 1998.

Producción en 1996: 2,600 camiones y 220 autobuses.

Producción proyectada en 1997: tractocamiones, camiones y autobuses 5 mil unidades, 70% para exportación y 30% para mercado interno.

Inversión en MCI de Estados Unidos de 30 millones de Dólares, para desarrollar un nuevo autobús de pasajeros que saldrá al mercado a finales de 1997.

Se constituye arrendadora Financiera DINA con capital de 240 millones de Dólares, y servicios financieros MCI con 250 millones de Dólares para dar financiamiento y así aumentar sus ventas.

Está funcionando DINAMEX en Chile y Argentina; se invirtieron 5 millones de Dólares para la compra en el municipio de Mercedes Argentina; una nave industrial para ensamblar el camión con cabina S-600 con proyección de producir 500 unidades con integración local. Todo esto indica que Argentina DINAMEX está en marcha con la posibilidad de ampliar la inversión en los próximos cinco años a 50 millones de Dólares.

El grupo DINA potencialmente busca diversificar sus exportaciones hacia diversos mercados, por ejemplo se tiene proyectado para India, África, Egipto y Arabia Saudita.

DINA esta en la búsqueda de su independencia tecnológica ya que el convenio con Navistar se acaba en marzo de 1998, es por esto que pretende invertir 30 millones de dólares para desarrollar una nueva cabina para camiones.

LA AUTÉNTICA CONTRATACIÓN COLECTIVA Y LOS SINDICATOS DE PROTECCIÓN

Luis Fonte Zenteno[*]
Evaristo Alvarez Alonso[**]
Guillermo Rivera Ramírez[***]

PRESENTACIÓN

La unidad y la solidaridad de los trabajadores es uno de los temas más actuales y urgentes en la agenda de lucha del movimiento obrero mexicano. En este sentido, buena parte de los avances existentes en los últimos años, se explican por el desarrollo de un proceso que ha podido concretar las iniciativas del movimiento sindical de avanzada. Por ejemplo, la fundación de la Unión Nacional de Trabajadores (UNT) organización en la que nuestro sindicato es miembro fundador- es una muestra vehemente de que los trabajadores buscamos formas reales para lograr nuestra unidad y mecanismos efectivos de solidaridad.

De manera particular, los trabajadores de la industria automotriz tenemos espacios de trabajo que incluyen la búsqueda de puentes de solidaridad entre los trabajadores del país y con los trabajadores que la industria tiene en otros confines. En este caso, partimos de la idea de que si la industria automotriz ha desarrollado estrategias mundiales y continentales para obtener beneficios del trabajo y de los mercados en diversas regiones y países, entonces nosotros tenemos que buscar estrategias de lucha y resistencia que busquen asimilar la experiencia acumulada de los trabajadores en diversos escenarios y culturas.

Pero en México la solución del problema no es fácil porque tenemos que pensar y resolver un conjunto de asuntos domésticos que impiden nuestra

---

[*] Secretario General del Sindicato Independiente de Trabajadores de la Industria Automotriz, Similares y Conexos, "Volkswagen de México" (SITIASCVWM).

[**] Miembro del Comité Ejecutivo, Secretario del Interior. SITIASCVWM

[***] Miembro del Comité Ejecutivo. Secretario de Educación y Prensa. SITIASCVWM

propia unidad. Para empezar, es bastante conocido que ahora tenemos un movimiento obrero automotriz que especialmente desde los años ochenta se ha estado fragmentando. Y si a lo anterior tenemos que agregar que en los años noventa, la modernización productiva de esta industria, está incorporado como sistema de producción el subcontratismo y la proveeduría en gran escala, y esto significa la proliferación de los mas variados "sindicatos" y "contratos colectivos" a donde están asignándose las materias de trabajo que han salido de las fábricas de ensamble o a donde están ubicándose las nuevas que están llegando con las empresas de autopartes. Con todo esto, encontramos que las barreras entre trabajadores mexicanos parece que se hacen más grandes. Se ha llegado al grado de que pareciera que los intereses de los obreros de las fábricas ensambladoras son distintos a los intereses de los trabajadores de las empresas de autopartes.

Dentro de esta problemática vamos a referirnos a uno de los temas más candentes dentro de los sindicatos automotrices: la existencia de "*sindicatos y contratos de protección*" que significan uno de los obstáculos mayores para la unidad y solidaridad entre trabajadores de nuestra región y de nuestro país.

INTRODUCCIÓN

El reconocimiento de los derechos instrumentales de sindicalización y huelga, que costó la vida a más de un millón de mexicanos en la Revolución, que los imprimió en el artículo 123 de su Ley Constitucional, fueron pensados para realizar las garantías de salario suficiente, igual por trabajo igual, profesionalización, permanencia y seguridad en el trabajo, con otra mínimas condiciones para la superación de un proletariado miserable.

La primera ley reglamentaria, la Ley Federal del Trabajo (LFT), creó la institución legal de la contratación colectiva como medio para lograrlas, sistematizarlas y superarlas para generar progreso compartido de trabajadores y empresas, como factor de justicia y paz social sustentada con la interlocusión legítima de sindicatos auténticos.

Sin embargo, a partir de la promulgación de la primera LFT, se generó una grave desviación de sus principales instituciones-sindicatos, contratación colectiva y huelga **provocada por la práctica casi generalizada de afiliación forzosa de los trabajadores sindicalizados al partido político creado para controlar a las diversas facciones revolucionarias, sujetándolos al control corporativo del voto y de los sindicatos.**

Desde entonces se estableció como política de cooptación, compensar a los líderes con puestos públicos y, por ejemplo, con la creación del INFONAVIT, se sumó la premiación como un medio por el cual los líderes charros del sindicalismo corporativo pudieron incluirse con gran éxito financiero en el negocio de la construcción de casas para los trabajadores[1].

Pero lo más grave de este proceso de "institucionalización" fue que con la contratación colectiva se inventó la trampa para falsificar la institución central que norma las relaciones de trabajo en los centros fabriles. Fue así como se gestan los *Contratos Colectivos de Protección*, negocio sucio que se cuenta entre las principales fuentes ilícitas de enriquecimiento y que ahora, para desgracia de los trabajadores, se constituyen ya en **el principal soporte de los sindicatos corporativos del país** al tomar cuerpo en los sindicatos "charros" y en los sindicatos "blancos".

Los *Contratos de Protección* son simulaciones "legales", firmadas entre sindicatos "fantasmas" (no tienen trabajadores por su voluntad) y empresas que buscan abaratar al máximo los costos laborales. A partir de los escenarios crónicos de desempleo y empobrecimiento de la población se ha creado uno de los mercados más ignominiosos en México, donde hay "dueños" de *Sindicatos* y de *Contratos* que están en condiciones de negociar y vender. Por otra parte, el negocio florece porque existen empresas que los compran y también porque ese "mercado" está auspiciado por juntas de conciliación y arbitraje venales que justifican y validan el procedimiento de compraventa.

Su finalidad -que explica su éxito en este espurio mercado- es contar con la mano de obra my barata e impedir a los trabajadores el ejercicio de sus derechos a la auténtica sindicalización, a la contratación colectiva y a la huelga para obtenerla.

Establecen salarios mínimos y aún salario por hora, no reconocen el derecho a la permanencia en el trabajo, porque ahí todo es eventual, temporal e inseguro; la bilateralidad -que es la representación y la intervención real de los trabajadores en las condiciones de trabajo por medio del sindicato- está eliminada, no cumplen con la capacitación, y con el pretexto de la productividad se sobreexplota a los trabajadores sin compensación económica alguna.

Por norma general los trabajadores son afiliados a esos sindicatos sin ser consultados y aún contra su voluntad. Es muy común encontrar que estos

---

[1] Como aconteció en nuestro sindicato con el negocio paralelo de construcción de viviendas que tenía Juan Ortega Arenas, que fuera nefasto asesor del mismo.

contratos suelen firmarse, sin que aún existan trabajadores, en las fases preliminares de negociación de las inversiones, y por supuesto, cuando los trabajadores llegan a la fuente de trabajo, generalmente se da el caso de que no conocen el clausulado, ni los estatutos del sindicato y a veces ni el nombre del mismo, la evidencia de que existe "algún" sindicato, llega cuando aparece el descuento por concepto de "cuota sindical".

Como proceso de simulación de una legalidad los "titulares" sindicales los trafican y como no pueden cederse, cuando es el caso, los dan por terminados y firman otros iguales o peores. Para todo ello se operan infinidad de trucos, todos a espaldas de los trabajadores y si se oponen, tratando de sindicalizarse acudiendo a la intervención de sindicatos auténticos o plantearse el derecho de hacer la huelga, los obreros se encuentran conque no pueden, porque "ya existe depositado un Contrato Colectivo". Si partiendo de lo anterior los afectados reclaman -como establece la ley- la titularidad y hay recuento, entonces entran en acción los grupos gansteriles de choque para violentar a los trabajadores e impedir que voten libremente. Y ante esto, las juntas competentes, pues como decimos en este país, "se hacen que la virgen les habla".

Para desgracia de los trabajadores mexicanos, la gran mayoría de los Contratos Colectivos de Trabajo (CCT) existentes son "de protección", es decir, que los sindicatos que afilian a los aproximadamente cinco millones de trabajadores sujetos a la Ley Federal del Trabajo, por lo menos dos terceras partes son simulaciones "charras" o "blancas", dependiendo del tipo de sindicato y central y de la región donde se encuentren.

Con estos procedimientos es como se crean las principales fuentes de reclutamiento de "militantes sindicales" a partir de la cual se abultan los registros "oficiales" del sindicalismo corporativo y de donde salen las cuentas alegres de afiliación, por ejemplo: la CTM dice tener 6 millones de afiliados, la CROC 4 y medio millones y la CROM 2 millones. Cifras que no soportan el cuestionamiento o la prueba de demostración de sus padrones de trabajadores debidamente legalizadas.

Así están las cosas respecto de los tristemente célebres *contratos de protección.*

LOS CONTRATOS COLECTIVOS AUTÉNTICOS

En cuanto a los contratos auténticos, debemos empezar por plantear que en su concepción legal son organizaciones que tienen como el procedimiento más eficaz para lograr su representatividad real, aplicar de entrada lo establecido en artículos de la Ley Federal del Trabajo, que como el 386 establece: "Contrato Colectivo de Trabajo es el convenio celebrado entre uno o varios sindicatos de trabajadores y uno o varios patrones, o uno o varios sindicatos de patrones, con objeto de establecer las condiciones según las cuales debe prestarse el trabajo en una o más empresas o establecimientos"; o el 387 que dice, "El patrón que emplee trabajadores miembros de un sindicato tendrá obligación de celebrar con éste, cuando lo solicite, un Contrato Colectivo. Si el patrón se niega a firmar el Contrato, podrán los trabajadores ejercitar el derecho de huelga consignado en el artículo 450".

El CCT auténtico, además de su función social y desde su concepto legal y su práctica, es un eficaz instrumento de lucha y de resistencia y, en el ámbito productivo, es un interlocutor con posibilidades de participar creativamente en la organización del trabajo. que puede proponer o participar en el diseño de sistemas de desarrollo de la productividad y de la capacitación donde los trabajadores tengan un papel relevante.[2]

En las condiciones que la reestructuración de la industria se ha hecho, el sindicalismo auténtico tiene que mostrar —ante las autoridades del trabajo y ante las patronales- que el camino aparentemente corto y barato de introducir relaciones laborales al margen de la ley o simulaciones de sus normas, en el mediano y largo plazo ese camino será el más costoso.

Es cierto que actualmente no son muchos los sindicatos que han logrado buenas contrataciones colectivas —dentro del promedio nacional—, pero los que hemos podido, estamos demostrando que la defensa de los derechos constituidos de los trabajadores no niega de ninguna manera la idea de desarrollo y progreso.

Dentro de esta perspectiva, estamos convencidos de que es falso que los *contratos de protección* sean la mejor alternativa para las empresas, porque está demostrado que quienes los tienen, quedan a merced del hampa sindical, que le obstaculiza su modernización al obtruirle el desarrollo de la productividad y de buenos niveles de competitividad. La experiencia muestra que las ventajas son aparentes y en el mejor de los casos de corto plazo para lo cual necesitan de proteccionismo gubernamental y, finalmente se extinguen por inoperantes, sumando desempleo y deterioro económico general.

---

[2] En otro sentido, podemos decir que incluso permite el desarrollo sano de las empresas en la medida que ésta posibilite compartir objetivos con sus trabajadores para que puedan mejorar profesionalmente y desarrollar en mejores condiciones su capacidad productiva.

Por todas esas razones, en nuestro sindicato,[3] nos hemos pronunciado contra eso que denominamos el "contratotráfico" o sea la compraventa de contratos de protección, porque el sistema de registro de sindicatos y CCT que es ahora es una práctica arbitraria, selectiva y secreta, puede y debe desde la ley ser saneada, estableciendo delitos penales por la simulación de contrato colectivo.

UNA PROPUESTA

Pensamos que se deben crear **registros públicos nacionales** de los sindicatos y de los contratos colectivos para que los trabajadores interesados podamos saber, por una parte, cuántos sindicatos hay, quiénes los constituyen y dirigen y cómo son sus estatutos; y por otra, quiénes han firmado los contratos colectivos y cuáles son los salarios y las condiciones laborales pactadas.

Una iniciativa de este tipo permitiría en principio descubrir la realidad de la corrupción imperante y se podría combatir desde la ley y estaríamos sentando las bases para el ejercicio transparente de relaciones laborales donde los organismos sindicales pueden asumir con toda su responsabilidad su función social y dentro de esto, practicar el principio de unidad y solidaridad.

Propugnar en torno a estrategias propositivas es una tarea del nuevo sindicalismo democrático independiente, incluyente y participativo (tal y como lo vemos en la UNT), y es lo que puede garantizar que en nuestros tiempos se constituya en alternativa de organización real para la gran mayoría de trabajadores, que ahora están encadenados por las simulaciones sindicales de viejos y nuevos cuños.

---

[3] Y dentro de la FESEBES de la que somos miembros.

Enfrentando el cambio, obreros del automóvil y producción esbelta en América del Norte (Confronting Change, Auto Labor and Lean Producction in North América), segunda edición, se terminó de imprimir en el mes de febrero de 1999 en los talleres de editorial Ducere S.A. de C.V., (cuyos trabajadores pertenecen a la Industria Nacional de las Artes Gráficas) con domicilio en Rosa Esmeralda 3 bis, colonia Molino de Rosas y con número de teléfono y fax 6 80 22 35.

La composición tipográfica es de José Luis Olazo García y el cuidado de edición estuvo a cargo de Ricardo Escárcega Méndez, Huberto Juárez Núñez y Steve Babson.

El tiraje consta de 1000 ejemplares.